C0-AQX-531

MENTAL RETARDATION

READINGS AND RESOURCES
Second Edition

JEROME H. ROTHSTEIN
San Francisco State College

HOLT, RINEHART AND WINSTON, INC.
New York Chicago San Francisco Atlanta
Dallas Montreal Toronto London Sydney

FOR SABRINA LYNN WILSON

Library of Congress Card Catalog Number: 70-143317
SBN: 03-084408-8
Printed in the United States of America
1 2 3 4 038 9 8 7 6 5 4 3 2 1

PREFACE

The decade following publication of the first edition of this book saw vast expansion of services for the mentally retarded and a sincere recognition of their "human rights." The chief motivating force was the interest of the late President John F. Kennedy. During the early days of his administration, he persuaded Congress to enact broad-scale legislation in all phases of mental retardation. This decade literally could be known as the era of federal involvement in mental retardation. Since mental retardation is a national problem, national interest was required to resolve some of the issues. Despite a decade of social crisis and war, new and expanded programs were conceived and implemented. The second edition of *Mental Retardation: Readings and Resources* is a total revision, reflecting this expanded activity. Of the 56 readings in the first edition, only 17 were retained in the second edition. Most of the new selections were published between 1965 and 1970.

Using a multidisciplinary approach, *Mental Retardation* attempts to balance readings and references so that they will be of interest to educators, psychologists, nurses, rehabilitation counselors, physicians, and social scientists. It is also designed to provide many sources of information for parents and parent groups concerned with mental retardation. Three major criteria were used to select the readings: (1) the overall importance of the subject, (2) the clarity and form of the article, and (3) the technical accuracy of the data. The vocabulary and concepts have been geared to both upper-division and graduate levels of instruction.

The organization of the book is a result of the editor's many years of experience in preparing personnel for work with the retarded. The book can serve as a college text in such courses as "Introduction to Mental Retardation," "Psychology of Mental Retardation," and "Nature and Needs of the Retarded." A chart in the back of the book correlates the readings of this volume with a number of basic texts. The left-hand column lists the chapters of the general textbooks; the other columns list numerically the readings in this book that are appropriate to specific chapters. Used in conjunction with curriculum guides and texts on curriculum and methodology, *Mental Retardation* will provide a satisfactory combination of resources for a course in "Curriculum and Methods for Teaching the Retarded."

Section introductions are intentionally structured to provide historical background, to present related problems, and, in lieu of adding lengthy suggested supplementary reading materials, to discuss related articles.

To complement and amplify the readings, the editor has provided a number of supplementary resource tables and charts interwoven into many readings. The appendix contains a wealth of resource materials. These include: (1) organizations interested in mental retardation; (2) survey of the literature on mental retardation; (3) journals in mental retardation; (4) bibliography of textbooks on mental retardation, including books for parents and about mentally retarded individuals; (5) specialized bibliographical listings; (6) U.S. government agency publications; and (7) an annotated listing of over 150 films on mental retardation, including sources of procurement.

I would like to extend my thanks to the authors, editors, and publishers who granted permission for their work to be reprinted here. I am especially appreciative of the efforts of my two secretaries, past and present, Sandi Zicke and Ann Salvi Juarez, who did much of the basic research. Gratitude is expressed to my wife, Dorothy, for her critical evaluation and editorial assistance, and finally, to Jacqueline, Harriet, Bob, and Fred who have enriched my life.

San Bruno, California
January 1971

J.H.R.

CONTENTS

SECTION ONE

General Considerations

This volume might easily be called the "new look" or modern trends and issues in mental retardation. Actually, it is a blending of ideas, both old and new, and, hopefully, a forecast for a brighter future for all retarded individuals.

Why was the terminology "mental retardation" used in lieu of many other descriptive terms? The best answer to this lies in a quote made by Edgar A. Doll, one of the most respected contributors to the field:

> changes are reflected in new modes of expression which indicate the alteration in thinking and values. As the term "feebleminded" gave place to "mental deficient," so this in turn has changed to "mental retardation." These changes in terminology show a drift away from precise clinical diagnosis toward more general appraisal of the child as a person in "softer" words and with more generally descriptive evaluation of total aptitudes.[1]

How great is the social and economic problem of mental retardation? It is conservatively estimated that there are five million mentally retarded individuals of all ages in the United States. Directly concerned with them are the parents and close relatives, which would indicate that a large percentage of the population has direct contact with mentally retarded individuals every day. Almost 70 percent of the permanently disabled population falls into the category of mental retardates. Table I provides comparative data concerning permanent afflictions.

Table II is an estimated distribution of retardates in the United States by age and degree of retardation.

Mental retardation is impervious to economic status, race, color, or religion. Simply stated, three to four children out of every 100 born are destined to be mentally retarded. It might be optimistically forecasted that current

[1] Edgar A. Doll, "The Second Decade," *The Training School Bulletin, 52*:2 (April 1955), 19.

studies on the prevention of mental retardation may ultimately change this picture.

TABLE I

Affliction	*Of Each 100,000 Population*
Mental retardation	3,000
Rheumatic heart	700
Cerebral palsy	350
Polio (permanent)	300
Blindness	200

Source: National Association for Retarded Children, *The Child Nobody Knows* (New York: The Association, 1955).

In summary, it must be reiterated that mental retardation is an unbelievably complex social and economic problem, the ramifications of which even the best trained professional worker cannot fully comprehend. The concept of mental retardation includes such a varying combination of factors and such a lack of uniformity in definition, terminology, classification, treatment, and training that its challenge may be considered of equal importance with any known to man.

The first reading covers in great detail a variety of definitions, systems of classification, and prevalency rates of mental retardation. Dr. R. C. Scheerenberger, who prepared this reading, carefully documents his report and provides us with a wide array of tables, figures, and charts. The second report, by Dr. Maurice G. Kott, is a comprehensive history of mental retardation starting with the earliest period of time. It brings historical data up to date. In addition, it shows how the State of New Jersey developed its program in a historical light. Recently, there has been a renewed

TABLE II Estimated Distribution of Retardates in the United States by Age and Degree of Retardation

Degree of Retardation	*All Ages* NUMBER	PERCENT	*Age by Years* UNDER 20	20 AND OVER
Total	6,000,000	100.0	2,454,000	3,546,000
Mild (IQ 52–67)	5,340,000	89.0	2,136,000	3,204,000
Moderate (IQ 36–51)	360,000	6.0	154,000	206,000
Severe (IQ 20–35)	210,000	3.5	105,000	105,000
Profound (IQ 0–20)	90,000	1.5	52,900	37,100

Source: Adapted from data in *Facts on Mental Retardation*, National Association for Retarded Children, Inc. (Arlington, Tex.: 1963), p. 15.

interest in historical aspects of mental retardation. Books by Mabel E. Talbot[1] and Leo Kanner[2] were published covering aspects in the long history of mental retardation.

The third report in this section is by Dr. Burton Blatt, who reexamines the characteristics of the mentally retarded in the light of findings culled from recent investigations. The final article is an in-depth study of poverty, intelligence, and life in the inner city by Whitney M. Young, Jr., Executive Director of the National Urban League. Nothing could be more poignant than the position that Young takes in bringing to our attention the desperate problems of ghetto families. A final touch to this section and a lead to other portions of this book is the Declaration of General and Special Rights of the Mentally Retarded, as proclaimed by the membership of the International League of Societies for the Mentally Handicapped at its 1968 meeting held at Hebrew University, Jerusalem, Israel.

[1] Mabel E. Talbot, *Edouard Seguin: A Study of an Educational Approach to the Treatment of Mentally Defective Children* (New York: Teachers College Press, Columbia University, 1964).

[2] Leo Kanner, *A History of the Care and Study of the Mentally Retarded* (Springfield, Ill.: Charles C Thomas, Publisher, 1964).

1 MENTAL RETARDATION: DEFINITION, CLASSIFICATION, AND PREVALENCE

Richard C. Scheerenberger

From *Mental Retardation Abstracts,* Vol. 1, No. 4, October–December 1964, pp. 432–441. Reprinted with the permission of the U.S. Department of Health, Education, and Welfare and the author. Dr. Scheerenberger is Superintendent of the Central (Wisconsin) Colony, Madison. He is also on the faculty of the University of Wisconsin.

The gift of verbal communication is unique to man and places him at the apex of the phylogenetic scale. Unfortunately, the versatility with which he can manipulate his linguistic symbols frequently results in ambiguity and general confusion. This is certainly true with respect to the concept of mental retardation.

Although mental retardation has been acknowledged in the writings of man for a period of 2500 years, no single, universally recognized definition has been developed.[1] The absence of such a definition reflects upon the highly relative and complex nature of this human phenomena. Mental retardation, regardless of its cause or form, is determined primarily on the basis of the socio-cultural standards of a given society. Kanner (1949, p. 8) aptly illustrates the relativity of mental retardation:

> In less complex, less intellectually centered societies, they [mentally retarded] would have no trouble in obtaining and retaining a quality of realizable ambitions. Some might even be capable of gaining superiority by virtue of assets other than those measured by the intelligence test. They could make successful peasants, hunters, fishermen, tribal dancers. They can, in our own society, achieve proficiency as farmhands, factory workers, miners, waitresses. . . . Their principal shortcoming is a greater or lesser degree of inability to comply with the intellectual requirements of their society. In other respects, they may be as mature or immature, stable or unstable, secure or insecure, placid or moody, aggressive or submissive as any other member of the human species. Their "deficiency" is an *ethnologically determined phenomenon* relative to the local standards and even within those standards, relative to the educational postulates, vocational ambitions, and family expectancies. They are "subcultural" in our society but may not be even that in a different, less sophisticated setting.

It is only natural, therefore, that definitions frequently emphasize the sociological aspects of mental retardation:

[1] Hippocrates (460?–357 B.C.) described several forms of mental retardation involving cranial anomalies; Confucius (551–478 B.C.) wrote about man's responsibility for the "weak-minded."

> The mentally retarded are children and adults who, as a result of inadequately developed intelligence, are significantly impaired in their ability to learn and to adapt to the demands of society. . . . The term "mental retardation" is a simple designation for a group of complex phenomena stemming from many different causes, but one key common characteristic found in all cases is inadequately developed intelligence.—President's Panel on Mental Retardation (1962, p. 1, 4).

> Mental retardation [refers] to a condition of intellectual inadequacy which renders an individual incapable of performing at the level required for acceptable adjustment within his cultural environment.—Masland (1963, p. 286).

> Mental deficiency is a state of incomplete mental development of such a kind and degree that the individual is incapable of adapting himself to the normal environment of his fellows in such a way as to maintain existence independently of supervision, control, or external support.—Tredgold (1937, p. 4).

Other definitions, in addition to acknowledging social implications, have attempted to identify the nature and characteristics of mental retardation:

> Psychologically, mental defectiveness represents a condition of mental nondevelopment (ageneses), arrest, deficiency, or deterioration which is very grave and permanent, which dates from early life, and which always affects the intelligence, judgment, or understanding and the capacity for social and economic adjustment. . . . The intelligence defect is a basic and constant feature; without a radical defect in the sphere of intelligence, the child could not be considered mentally defective no matter how ignorant or illiterate he may be, or how abnormal in his emotional, instinctive, volitional or moral reactions.—Wallin (1949, p. 13).

> Mental deficiency is a state of social incompetence obtaining at maturity, or likely to obtain at maturity, resulting from developed mental arrest of constitutional (hereditary or acquired) origin; the condition is essentially incurable through treatment and unremediable through training except as treatment and training instills habits which superficially or temporarily compensates for the limitations of the person so affected while under favorable circumstances and for more or less limited periods of time.—Doll (1941, p. 217).

Doll's definition, which has been quoted frequently, included six criteria which he considered essential to an acceptable concept of retardation: (1) social incompetence, (2) due to mental subnormality, (3) which has been developmentally arrested, (4) which obtains at maturity, (5) is of constitutional origin, and (6) is essentially incurable. These six criteria, in essence, summarize the various components or characteristics which, in the past, were incorporated into a generic concept of mental retardation. Their significance with respect to present-day thinking will be discussed in a later section.

In Russia, mental retardation is defined not only in terms of characteristics but also of cause: "Mentally retarded children . . . have suffered from a severe brain disease while in the uterus or in early childhood and this has disturbed the normal development of the brain and produced serious anomalies in mental development . . . its consequence is an anomalous development of brain function. The mentally retarded child is sharply distinguished from the normal by the range of ideas he can comprehend and by the character of his perception of reality."—Luria (1963, p. 5, 10). Thus, mental retardation is dependent upon the occurrence, or suspected occurrence, of brain injury. It also might be noted that this concept of mental retardation is not independent of socio-political implications. Luria described the approach to retardation in such countries as the United States and England in the following words:

> In order to separate this group of children (mentally retarded) in the Capitalist countries, all children between 10 and 11 years of age undergo short psychological tests—tests of intellectual ability. These consist of a series of tests requiring shrewdness and general knowledge. Those children who do well in these tests are placed in class "A" where pupils pursue an advanced programme and later transfer to an advanced type of school. The second group, placed in the middle by the test, are put in class "B" and the third group which has the lowest marks, are treated as having inferior ability and put in class "C."
>
> Pupils in this last group are considered incapable of receiving a complete education; they are sent to a lower type of school and when they are finished they cannot progress further and have to remain unqualified workers. It is quite clear that such a system of selecting children—as though they were of "low intellectual level"—openly carries a social class bias.

In addition to the relativeness and complexity of mental retardation, another factor has played an important role in impeding the development of an acceptable definition. There is no known technique for *directly* assessing intelligence or intellectual potential. For example, we cannot count an individual's neurons and conclude that he is retarded, normal, or gifted. Instead, we must rely on evaluative devices which sample behavior considered indicative of intellectual functioning. Subsequently, an individual's capacity is *inferred* on the basis of his performance on such tests as the Stanford–Binet Intelligence Scale or the Wechsler Intelligence Scale for Children.

Following the introduction and standardization of intelligence tests in the United States (approximately 1910 to 1920), there was a period during which an unwarranted emphasis was placed on the statistical indices of measured intelligence, i.e., the intelligence quotient (IQ) and mental age (MA). Definitions of mental retardation began to incorporate the IQ or MA. In 1910, Goddard considered a child feebleminded if he were more than "two years backward" on an intelligence test; Doll extended Goddard's concept by indicating that "feeblemindedness is defined psychologically as intellectual retardation of two years at an age below nine or three years at an age above nine" (Wallin, 1949, p. 17). In terms of IQ, the upper limits were set at 60 (Pintner, 1933), 65 (Wechsler, 1941), and 70 (Merrill, 1938).

The widespread acceptance of such definitions was predicated by the belief that an individual's IQ remained constant throughout life. Research, however, quickly dispelled this notion showing that the IQ varied with the type of test administered, maturation and experience, emotional stability, and education. Today there are numerous authorities in the field of mental retardation who desire to abandon completely the use of standardized intelligence tests. They believe that such tests, which place a great emphasis on verbal skills (vocabulary, arithmetic, reading and the similar), are too influenced by cultural factors. They are concerned also with the potential continuation of the unjustifiable practice of classifying children as mentally retarded simply on the basis of an obtained IQ or MA. The complete elimination of intelligence tests, however, would be equivalent to "tossing the baby out with the bath." When such tests are applied judiciously by qualified personnel, they may be of great assistance in diagnosis and general planning. As implied, they should never be used as the sole criterion for determining mental retardation.

In 1959, the American Association on Mental Deficiency adopted and proposed a new definition of mental retardation. This definition, which was prepared by Heber and revised in 1961, is as follows:

> Mental retardation refers to subaverage general intellectual functioning which originates in the developmental period and is associated with impairment in adaptive behavior.

In order to comprehend the implications of this definition, it will be necessary to consider its three prime components: (1) subaverage general intellectual functioning, (2) which originates during the developmental period, and (3) is associated with impairment in adaptive behavior.

Subaverage general intellectual functioning "refers to performance which is greater than one standard deviation below the population mean of the age group involved on measures of general intellectual functioning [such as] the various objective tests which have been developed for that purpose" (AAMD, 1961, p. 3). In other words, the connotation of subaverage general intellectual functioning with respect to the commonly employed statistical indices of measured intelligence is applied to those individuals whose assessed ability on a standardized individual test of intelligence falls below the point of minus one standard deviation (− 1.01 to >−5.01). The concomitant range of intelligence quotients, as exemplified by scores obtainable on the Stanford–Binet Intelligence Scale, is <20 to 83.

The developmental period extends from birth to approximately sixteen years of age. Thus mental retardation must have its onset prior to adulthood, a dimension consistent with the earlier definition offered by Doll.

The necessity for impairment in adaptive behavior constitutes the unique and essential feature of this definition. Heber (1962, p. 71) stated that "the critical factor in this concept of mental retardation is inclusion of the dual criteria of reduced intellectual functioning and of impaired social adaptation." According to the AAMD manual (1961), impaired adaptive behavior may be reflected in: (1) maturation, or the rate at which an individual develops his basic motor and self-care skills; (2) learning, or the ability with which an individual gains knowledge from his experiences; and/or (3) social adjustment, or the ability with which the individual is capable of independently sustaining himself in a manner consistent with the standards and requirements of his society. The need to consider both measured intelligence and adaptive behavior cannot be overemphasized. A person with an IQ of 75 or 80 who reveals no significant impairment in adaptive behavior is not labeled mentally retarded.

A comparison between the components of the AAMD definition and Doll's six criteria reveals several significant differences. The AAMD terminology does not include the necessity that mental retardation be of constitutional (physical) origin nor does it assume the pessimistic view that mental retardation is essentially incurable.

Two other types of definitions appear in the literature. First, since mental retardation is a total phenomenon involving the physiological, psychological, and sociological aspects of behavior, it naturally requires and elicits the interest and services of numerous disciplines, including education, psychology, sociology, and the medical sciences. In order to provide adequately for the retarded, it has been necessary for various disciplines to interpret retardation within the scope of their professional responsibilities and qualifications. For example, a mentally retarded child has been defined educationally as "one who is diagnosed as having low intelligence, who is unable to profit sufficiently from the curricula of the public schools, but who can be educated to become socially adequate and occupationally competent, provided special educational facilities are furnished" (Kirk and Johnson, 1951, p. 13).

Secondly, definitions may be based on theories appropriate to mental retardation. To illustrate, Benoit (1959, p. 551) proposed the following definition based on Hebb's theory:

> Mental retardation may be viewed as a deficit of intellectual function resulting from the varied intrapersonal and/or extrapersonal determinants, but having as a common proximate cause a diminished deficiency of the

nervous system (beginning with an impaired irritability and further involving a lowered capacity for impulse transmission and for developing primitive and integrating cell change through interfacilitating interneuronal connections), thus entailing a lessened general capacity for growth and conceptual integration and consequently in environmental adjustment.

Hebb's theory (1949), stated in terms of rank oversimplification, postulates that the mature development of the neurons and the interchanging pathways is dependent upon original endowment plus environmental experiences, especially perceptual. A paucity of perceptual and learning activities in early childhood may affect adversely the neurological capacity to the extent of resulting in mental retardation.

To this point, no term other than mental retardation has been introduced; however, the condition of retardation also is identified as mental deficiency, feeblemindedness, oligophrenia, subnormality, and amentia. Since these are common labels, their similarities and differences should be examined.

Mental deficiency generally is used in a manner synonymous with the AAMD concept of mental retardation, i.e., inclusive of all levels and forms of retardation. The World Health Organization (1954, p. 3), however, recommended the use of the generic term subnormality and distinguished between mental retardation and mental deficiency. Retardation is reserved for those individuals whose "educational and social performance is markedly lower than would be expected from what is known of the intellectual abilities." Deficiency describes those conditions in which "the mental capacities themselves are diminished as a result of pathological causes, as opposed to environmental causes which may lead to mental retardation." This type of definition, which differentiates retardation from deficiency, frequently appears in psychological and medical literature.

Feeblemindedness was common to American literature until approximately 1945 and constituted a general term for retardation. Today, it is rarely used in the United States because of its acquired undesirable connotations. In England, however, feeblemindedness is an accepted term and denotes the least affected mentally retarded, i.e., the moderately or educable retarded, or those whose intelligence falls within an IQ range of 50 to 80 (Penrose, 1963).

Oligophrenia, which occasionally appears in American medical reports, is the primary term applied to mental retardation in Russia, France, and the Scandinavian countries.

Subnormality is a relative newcomer to the literature on mental retardation. In addition to the recommendations of WHO, previously cited, the term subnormality was sanctioned officially in England by the Mental Health Act of 1959. Again, subnormality is used as a general descriptor which includes reference to all levels of retardation.

Amentia, which appears in the psychiatric and medical literature, is also a generic term for retardation. It frequently is used in a dichotomous relation to the term *dementia,* which is limited to the identification of the emotionally disturbed or mentally ill. The difference between mental retardation and mental illness is significant. Theoretically, in mental retardation the observed deficiencies in learning and social adaptability are a function of subnormal intelligence; in mental illness, the identical characteristics of performance are attributed to emotional and motivational disturbances (assuming normal intelligence). In practice, however, it is often difficult, if not impossible, to single out the prime factor *underlying* the inadequate behavior. When, over an extended period of time, an individual consistently reveals behavior indicative of both retardation and illness, it requires extreme diagnostic skill to determine whether that person is an emotionally disturbed retardate or whether the affective disorder has resulted in reducing the effectiveness of normal intelligence. The situation is compounded, furthermore, by the fact that certain forms of brain injury may result in both emotional disturbance and mental retardation (Kennedy and Ramirez, 1964). The AAMD definition of mental retardation does not preclude subaverage general intellectual functioning as a consequence of mental illness.

From the foregoing discussion, it readily can be observed that definitions of mental retardation are developed along numerous lines of interest and inquiry, and may include reference to cause, levels of functioning, social adaptability, intelligence test scores, and the characteristics of various disciplines. Even the concept of mental retardation promulgated by the AAMD, which constitutes the most comprehensive, flexible definition presently available, is not entirely satisfactory since many of the essential aspects of adaptive behavior have yet to be identified and measured. However, concepts, and the words by which they are expressed, are neither static nor absolute. It is expected that definitions of mental retardation will become more precise as our knowledge of this problem increases.

CLASSIFICATION OF MENTAL RETARDATION

Mental retardation is subject to an interminable number of classifications, formal and informal, which satisfy the needs of a given discipline, service, or area of investigation. The following discussion will be restricted to a description of three, interrelated systems of classification based on (1) degree of retardation, (2) educability, and (3) adaptive behavior. These systems, singularly or in combination, are utilized in the study and reporting of mental retardation.

The degree or severity of retardation nomenclature assumes that general intelligence can be plotted quantitatively along a continuum of lowest (severely retarded) to highest (gifted) measurable performance. This continuum usually is divided into various categories on the basis of standard deviation or a specified number of IQ points. Terman (1916) categorized the entire range of intelligence by arbitrarily selecting units of 10, 20, and 30 IQ points:

140+	Genius
120–139	Very superior
110–119	Superior
90–109	Normal
80–89	Dullness
70–79	Borderline retardation
50–69	Moron
25–49	Imbecile
<25	Idiot

The AAMD classification of measured intelligence, designed to augment the combined subaverage general intellectual functioning-impaired adaptive behavior definition, is divided into five categories: borderline, mild, moderate, severe, and profound. As shown in Table I, the boundaries for each division, which are based on standard deviations, will vary from test to test.

Although the AAMD quintuple classificatory structure is being widely accepted throughout the United States and numerous foreign countries, it has yet to replace traditional nomenclatures which include reference to only three degrees of retardation: mild, moderate and severe. Like definitions, there are authoritative and national differences with respect to the limits and terminology used to delineate between the levels of retardation. For the purposes of comparison, several nomenclatures are presented in Table II. It will be observed that the range in IQs associated with each subcategory will vary approximately five points; however, an IQ of 70 or 75, in contrast to 83 for the AAMD classification, usually is considered as the upper limit. These differences are primarily a matter of arbitrary preference. The elevated limit for the AAMD nomenclature, as previously discussed, is to provide for greater flexibility in diagnosis and treatment. It does not mean that an individual with an IQ of 81 or 82 is, of necessity, mentally retarded.

A second, common nomenclature divides mental retardation into three broad educational categories: educable mentally retarded (EMR), trainable mentally retarded (TMR), and the uneducable (SMR). Kirk (1962) defined the educable mentally retarded child "as one who has potentialities for development in (1) minimum educability in the academic subjects of the school, (2) social adjustment to such a point that he can get along independently in the community, and (3) minimum occupational adequacy to such a degree that he can later support himself partially or totally at the adult level." The trainable mentally retarded child was defined "as one who, because of subnormal intelligence, is not capable of learning in classes for educable mentally retarded but who does have potentialities for learning (1)

TABLE I AAMD Classification of Measured Intelligence

Level of Deviation in Standard Deviation Units	*Descriptive Terminology*	*Corresponding Range in IQ Scores*	
		REVISED STANFORD–BINET TESTS OF INTELLIGENCE	WECHSLER–BELLEVUE INTELLIGENCE SCALE CHILDREN & ADULT FORMS
−1.01 to −2.00	Borderline	83–68	84–70
−2.01 to −3.00	Mild	67–52	69–55
−3.01 to −4.00	Moderate	51–36	54–40
−4.01 to −5.00	Severe	35–20	<40
< −5.00	Profound	<20	

Adapted from the AAMD *Manual on Terminology and Classification in Mental Retardation* (2d ed.), 1961.

self-care, (2) adjustment to the home and neighborhood, and (3) economic usefulness in the home, a sheltered workshop, or an institution." The uneducable are those whose severe intellectual limitations preclude formal training. The associated ranges in IQ scores are: EMR–50 to 80; TMR–20 to 49; SMR–< 20.

In Britain, the term *educationally subnormal* (ESN) is applied to the educable mentally retarded and includes all school-age children who, because of limited ability or other conditions resulting in educational retardation, require special education. Thus, the educationally subnormal include both the mildly or educable mentally retarded and other students who, for various reasons, are educationally retarded. In the United States, the term educationally retarded usually is restricted to the identification of those students whose academic performance is significantly below their expectancy, regardless of intelligence.

While the degree-of-retardation nomenclatures based on intelligence scores are of value, especially with respect to demography and generic discussions or programming, they are extremely limited when applied for the purposes of identifying and planning for the individual retardate. The IQ, or the equivalent MA, is of minimal value in understanding the child's interests, cultural experiences, motivation, motor skills, personality characteristics, and potentialities for social and vocational adequacy. Furthermore, individuals with identical CAs and IQs do not possess identical potentials for learning or adjustment.

In order to compensate for the deficiencies associated with the statistically oriented nomenclatures, there has been a growing interest in developing a classification based on adaptive behavior—those abilities, skills, and responses essential to an individual's adjustment to his environment. According to Heber (1962, p. 76), adaptive behavior "is a composite of many aspects of behavior and a function of wide range of specific abilities and disabilities. Intellectual, affective, motivational, social, sensory, and motor factors all contribute to, and are a part of total adaptation."

Although administrators, educators, and therapists from various disciplines have long grouped children according to specific abilities and disabilities for the purpose of maximizing the benefits of available services, no standardized nomenclature on the behavioral characteristics has been developed. However, the scheme prepared by Sloan and Birch (1955) does illustrate the nature of a classification utilizing functional behavior. This system, which is presented in Table III, includes reference to both degree of debility and chronological age. As will be observed from examination of the various cells, the emphasis has been placed on sensory-motor skills, language and communication, learning (especially with respect to formal training), degree of self-sufficiency and vocational potential.

Though this classification is divided into levels, the behavior of many

TABLE II Nomenclatures of Mental Retardation

Degree of Retardation	*United States*	*Britain*	*France Russia Scandinavia*	*World Health Organization (WHO)*		*Comparison with the AAMD Classification*	*Approximate IQ Ranges (Stanford–Binet Scores)*
Mild (high grade; moron)	Mild	Feebleminded or Subnormal	Debile	Mild sub-normality	Mental retardation	Overlapping of mild and borderline	50 to 70 or 75
Moderate (medium grade; imbecile)	Moderate	Imbecile	Imbecile	Moderate sub-normality	Mental deficiency	Overlapping of moderate and mild	20 or 25 to 49
Severe (low grade; idiot)	Severe	Idiot	Idiot	Severe sub-normality		Overlapping of severe and profound	20 or 25
All levels; generic identification	Mental retardation Mental deficiency Mentally handicapped	Subnormal Mental deficiency Mentally handicapped Mental retardation	Oligophrenia	Subnormal		Mental retardation	20 to 70 or 75

Source: Based on the following references: AAMD (1961); Penrose (1964); *Report of the Mission to Denmark and Sweden* (1962); WHO (1954).

TABLE III Levels of Adaptive Behavior

	Preschool Age 0–5 Maturation and Development	*School-Age 6–21 Training and Education*	*Adult 21 Social and Vocational Adequacy*
LEVEL—IV (PROFOUND)	Gross retardation; minimal capacity for functioning in sensori-motor areas; needs nursing care.	Some motor development present; cannot profit from training in self-help; needs total care.	Some motor and speech development; totally incapable of self-maintenance; needs complete care and supervision.
LEVEL—III (SEVERE)	Poor motor development; speech is minimal; generally unable to profit from training in self-help; little or no communication skills.	Can talk or learn to communicate; can be trained in elemental health habits; cannot learn functional academic skills; profits from systematic habit training. ("Trainable")	Can contribute partially to self-support under complete supervision; can develop self-protection skills to a minimal useful level in controlled environment.
LEVEL—II (MODERATE)	Can talk or learn to communicate; poor social awareness; fair motor development; may profit from self-help; can be managed with moderate supervision.	Can learn functional academic skills to approximately 4th grade level by late teens if given special education. ("Educable")	Capable of self-maintenance in unskilled or semi-skilled occupations; needs supervision and guidance when under mild social or economic stress.
LEVEL—I (MILD)	Can develop social and communication skills; minimal retardation in sensori-motor areas; rarely distinguished from normal until later age.	Can learn academic skills to approximately 6th grade level by late teens. Cannot learn general high school subjects. Needs special education particularly at secondary school age levels. ("Educable")	Capable of social and vocational adequacy with proper education and training. Frequently needs supervision and guidance under serious social or economic stress.

Source: Sloan and Birch (1955, p. 262).

retardates will vacillate across boundaries depending upon the particular area or ability being considered. To illustrate, an adult retardate may function at Level I with respect to social adequacy, but an accompanying physical handicap may reduce his vocational effectiveness to the level of partial self-support.

While adaptive behavior is dependent on such variables as physical abilities, emotional stability, and social experiences, intelligence does retain an important role with respect to both general level of behavior and degree of variation. The profoundly and severely retarded will require maximum care and supervision and usually will not demonstrate behavior associated with the higher levels. In contrast, the mildly retarded will reveal highly variable behavioral patterns. In other words, both the level and variability of adaptive behavior will increase with increased intelligence. Some estimate of intelligence, furthermore, is necessary to the interpretation of adaptive behavior, e.g., there is a significant difference between a mildly and severely retarded adolescent who cannot read.

At present, our lack of knowledge concerning the essential components of adaptive behavior and the sequence of their development prevents the formulation of behavioral classifications capable of rendering reliable, sophisticated information. Behavioral scientists, however, have begun to investigate this problem, and it is anticipated that within five to ten years appropriate developmental norms will be available. A combination of these norms with relevant systems of classification and objective tests for assigning levels of functioning will constitute a major step in providing for accurate diagnosis and planning.

INCIDENCE OF MENTAL RETARDATION

Mental retardation is a common condition. In the United States, alone, it has been estimated that approximately 5.4 million individuals are mentally retarded. The prevalence of this condition is exceeded by only four other health problems: mental illness, cardiac diseases, arthritis, and cancer (President's Panel on Mental Retardation, 1962).

Unfortunately, it is impossible to posit absolute, comparative statistics on the incidence of mental retardation. Definition, tests used, size of sample, sampling technique, and geographic distribution are just a few of the variables which influence demographical estimates. A comparison of the Onondaga census (New York Technical Report, 1955) with the study conducted by Weiner (1964) will demonstrate clearly how definitional differences will affect the final results.

Mental retardation, according to the Onondaga census, included "all children under 18 years of age, and residents of Onondaga County on March 1, 1953, identified as definitely mentally retarded, or suspected of mental retardation on the basis of developmental history, poor academic performance, IQ score, or social adaptation when contrasted with their age peers" (New York Technical Report, 1955, p. 87). This broad definition readily encompassed problems involving subaverage intellectual functioning, educational retardation, and socio-personal inadequacy. Weiner (1958) in estimating the incidence of mental retardation in Hawaii, employed more specific criteria: when group test data were available, students with an IQ less than 65 were considered mentally retarded; if group test data were not available, retardation was estimated on the basis of academic performance.

For example, students in Grade 3 and above were considered mentally retarded only if they were three or more years below grade in reading and arithmetic; in Grades 1 and 2, the retarded were considered as those who could not read a preprimer nor do arithmetic computation with sums below ten. The results of these surveys, which have been plotted in Figure 1, show that the relatively indiscriminating concept of mental retardation employed in the Onondaga study consistently produced a much higher incidence of retardation. The discrepancies between the two studies are especially pronounced within the chronological age range of ten to sixteen years. The reported percentages were as follows:

Chronological Age	*Onondaga Census*	*Hawaii Study*
10		3.1
11	7.6	2.7
12		2.3
13		2.7
14	8.2	2.5
15	7.6	2.3

It is interesting to note that in spite of the statistical differences between these two studies, there is a similar pattern with respect to the distribution of incidence as related to chronological age. The lowest incidence of retardation occurred at the extreme ends of the distribution, i.e., CA 5 and

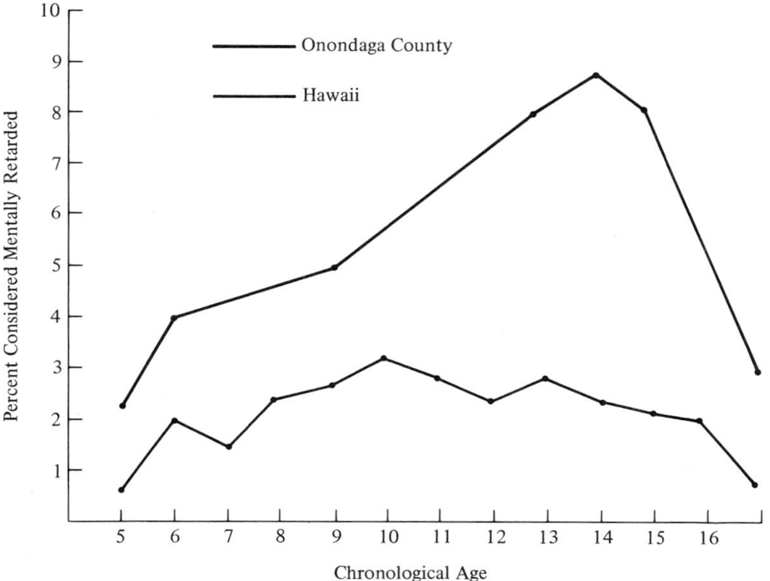

Figure 1 Incidence of Mental Retardation: Comparison of Onondaga County and Hawaii Study.

16–17; the highest incidence was encountered between the ages of eight through fifteen. This same pattern is apparent in the Lewis (1929) study conducted in England. As shown in Figure 2, the greatest incidence of retardation again occurred during late childhood and early adolescence: age group 5–9 (15.5 per thousand or 1.6 percent); 10–14 (25.6 per thousand or 2.6 percent); and 15–19 (10.8 per thousand or 1.1 percent).

Since these studies were based primarily on referrals, there are several possible explanations for their results:

1. During infancy and early childhood, mild retardation usually is not apparent. The demands of preschool life apparently are within the adaptive capabilities of nearly all children. Subsequently, the incidence of retardation among children between birth and six years of age reflects primarily on the occurrence of moderate and severe degrees of subaverage general intellectual functioning. The combination of behavioral inadequacies with the frequent accompaniment of observable physical stigmata tend to isolate the more seriously retarded.

2. As consistently reported in the literature, the highest incidence of retardation occurs during the years of formal educational training. This is natural in view of the heavy emphasis placed on the acquisition of abstract

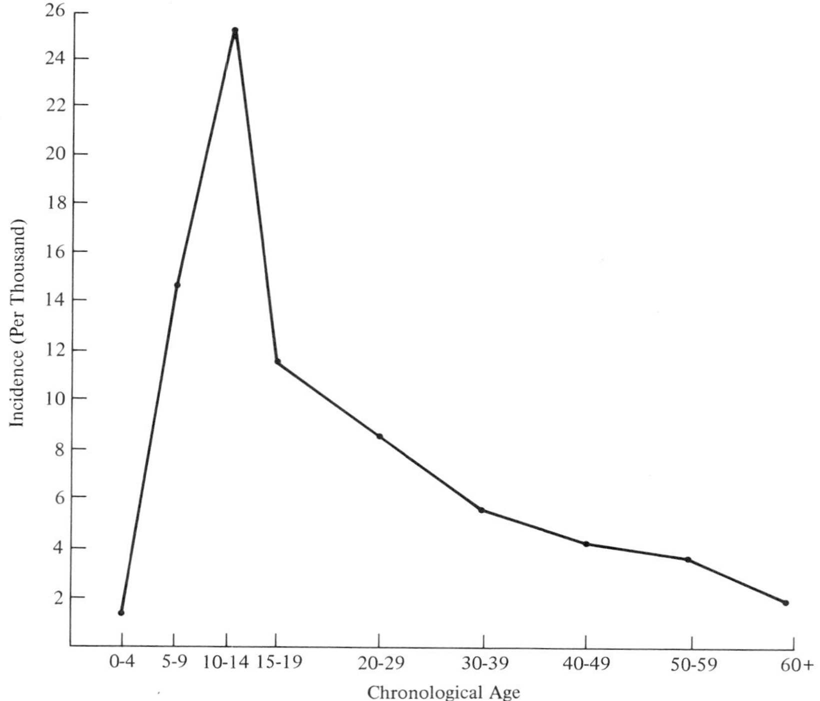

Figure 2 Incidence of Mental Retardation by Chronological Age (Adapted from Lewis, 1929).

academic skills. At no time is mental retardation quite as obvious as when a retardate is attempting to comprehend a complex verbal concept.

3. Following the termination of formal education, the incidence of retardation tends to subside. Once again the mildly retarded are capable of unobtrusively satisfying the less-verbal demands of adult society. The incidence of retardation during adulthood is reduced further by the relatively high pre-adult mortality rate among the severely and profoundly retarded.

When discussing the incidence of mental retardation, frequent reference is made to the theoretical expectancies associated with the normal distribution of intelligence. In 1869, Galton utilized the mathematical interpretations of Ouetelet in predicting that the intelligence of a population would be distributed along a continuous Gaussian, or bell-shaped curve.

According to this distribution, when mental retardation is defined as being greater than two standard deviations below the mean—or within an approximate IQ range of 20 to 70—2.15 percent of the general population would be retarded. Although the AAMD classification of measured intelligence set the upper limits of mental retardation at one standard deviation below the mean—or within an approximate IQ range of 20 to 85—15.74 percent of the population are not considered to be mentally retarded (Heber, 1958). Since the AAMD concept of mental retardation also requires evidence of marked impairment in adaptive behavior, only 3 percent of the general population are estimated to be retarded.

Galton assumed that the incidence of retardation would be equal to that of giftedness. Subsequent research (e.g., Pearson, 1931) has shown that retardation is more prevalent than superior intelligence. Miles (1963) estimated, on the basis of reported research, that only 1 percent of school-age children possess an IQ of 130 or higher. In contrast, the prevalence of mental retardation in a school population has been found to be 3.1 percent (Marbach, 1963) and 2.36 percent (Weiner, 1958).

It generally is estimated that 3 percent of the population in the United States are retarded (Masland, *et al.,* 1958; President's Panel, 1962). As shown in Table IV, this incidence is considerably higher than that reported

TABLE IV Incidence of Mental Retardation among Various Countries

Country	*Total Incidence (Percent)*	*Estimated Number of Retardates (1962 Census)*
Canada (Shaw, 1962)	3.4*	540,000
Denmark (Mission to Denmark, 1962)	1.0*	45,000
England (Lewis, 1929)	.9	420,395
Germany (Mutter, 1963)	3.0*	2,222,130
Sweden (Akesson, 1961)	1.8	135,000
USSR (Dunn and Kirk, 1963)	1.0*	2,214,650
United States	3.0*	5,400,000

* Approximations (not based on any specific census survey).

for Denmark, England, Sweden, and the U.S.S.R. While these differences undoubtedly reflect definitional discrepancies, the reduced incidence of retardation in the socialist countries is attributed partially to the greater availability—and use—of maternal and child care services. In Sweden, for example, it has been reported that during 1959, 82 percent of expectant mothers received health supervision (*Mission to Denmark and Sweden,* 1962, p. 15). In comparison, it is estimated that 35 percent of expectant mothers in the United States residing in cities with over 100,000 population are medically indigent (President's Panel, 1962, p. 52).

Of the total retarded population, the vast majority, 86.7 percent, are mildly handicapped; only 13.3 percent are moderately or severely retarded (Table V). These estimates, advanced by Masland and others (1958), are

TABLE V Incidence of Mental Retardation According to Degree of Retardation (Total Population, 180 million)

Degree	*Total Incidence (Percent)*	*Percentage of Mental Retardation*	*Estimated Population in the U.S.*
Mild	2.6	86.7	4,680,000
Moderate	.3	10.0	540,000
Severe	.1	3.3	180,000
Total	3.0	100.00	5,400,000

Based on estimates cited in the report of the President's Panel, 1962.

reasonably well supported by various independent surveys. Of the 2604 retardates in the Lewis (1929) study, 2091 (80 percent) were mildly retarded. The remaining 20 percent were moderately or severely retarded. Marbach (1963) found that approximately 2.9 percent of school-age children were educable mental retardates.

The recent interest in providing formal educational experiences for the trainable mentally retarded (TMR) has resulted in several studies on the incidence of moderate retardation. Wirtz and Guenther (1957), for example, surveyed communities in Illinois and Michigan and found an average incidence of 2.98 TMR per 1000 population. These results were consistent with the 2.34 TMR per 1000 school-age children reported in an earlier Illinois study (Superintendent of Public Instruction, 1954).

Although there are no known studies concerned with the incidence of the severely and profoundly retarded, it is assumed that the estimated 1 per 1000 population is reasonably accurate. Since these children and adults require constant attention, they comprise the majority of the 200,000 individuals receiving residential (institutional) care.

If the current estimated incidence of mental retardation—3 percent—remains constant, 126,000 babies born each year in this country may be considered mentally retarded (President's Panel, 1962). By 1970, there will be approximately 6.5 million retardates in the United States.

SUMMARY

Mental retardation is one of society's most complex, common problems. The totality of its psycho–socio–medical implications has precluded the development of a universally acceptable definition. Concepts of retardation have included reference to such variables as causation, curability, age of onset, intelligence quotient, mental age, educability, and social adequacy. The recent definition proposed by the American Association on Mental Deficiency is considered to be of particular merit since it places an emphasis on the broad aspects of functional behavior as well as measured intelligence: "Mental retardation refers to subaverage general intellectual functioning which originates during the developmental period and is associated with impairment in adaptive behavior."

The three major systems of classification based on degree-of-retardation, educability, and adaptive behavior were presented. It was concluded that the latter nomenclature, which remains to be developed and standardized, offers the greatest potential for both diagnosis and planning.

While the exact incidence of mental retardation has not been determined, it is estimated that 3 percent of the population, or 5.4 million individuals, in the United States are mentally retarded. According to the literature reviewed, there were significant differences with respect to the prevalence of mental retardation as reported among various countries; however, each nation considered mental retardation to be one of its prime social problems.

REFERENCES

Akesson, H. O. *Epidemiology and Genetics of Mental Deficiency in a Southern Swedish Population.* University of Uppsala, Sweden. The Institute for Medical Genetics, 1961.

American Association on Mental Deficiency. *A Manual on Terminology and Classification in Mental Retardation* (2nd Edition). Prepared by R. Heber, Monograph Supplement to the *American Journal of Mental Deficiency,* 1961.

Benoit, E. Towards a new definition of mental retardation. *American Journal of Mental Deficiency,* 1959, *63,* 550–565.

Doll, E. A. The essentials of an inclusive concept of mental deficiency. *American Journal of Mental Deficiency,* 1941, *46,* 214–219.

Dunn, L., and Kirk, S. Impressions of Soviet psycho-educational service and research in mental retardation. *Exceptional Children,* 1963, *29,* 299–311.

Galton, F. *Hereditary Genius.* New York: The Macmillan Company, 1869.

Guilford, J. *Fundamental Statistics in Psychology and Function.* New York: McGraw-Hill, Inc., 1956.

Hebb, D. *Organization of Behavior.* New York: John Wiley & Sons, Inc., 1940.

Heber, R. Mental retardation: Concept and Classification. In: Trapp, E. R., and Himelstein, P., *Readings on the Exceptional Child.* New York: Appleton-Century-Crofts, 1962, 69–81.

Kanner, L. A. *Miniature Textbook of Feeblemindedness.* Child Care Monographs, No. 1. New York: Child Care Publications, 1949.

Kennedy, C., and Ramirez, L. Brain damage as a cause of behavior disturbance in children. In: Birch, H. (Ed.) *Brain Damage in Children, The Biological and Social Aspects.* Baltimore: Williams & Wilkins Company, 1964.

Kirk, *S. Public School Provisions for Severely Retarded Children.* Albany, New York: Interdepartmental Health Resources Board, 1957.

Kirk, S. *Educating Exceptional Children.* Boston: Houghton Mifflin Company, 1962.

Kirk, S., and Johnson, O. *Educating the Retarded Child.* Cambridge, Massachusetts: Riverside Press, 1951.

Kirk, S. and Weiner, B. B. The Onondaga Census—fact or artifact. *Exceptional Children,* 1959, *25,* 226–231.

Lewis, E. O. *Report on an Investigation into the Incidence of Mental Defects in Six Areas.* Report of the Mental Deficiency Committee, Part IV. London: H.M.SO., 1929.

Luria, A. *The Mentally Retarded Child.* (English translation by W. P. Robinson and Dr. Brian Kirman.) New York: The Macmillan Company, 1963.

Marbach, S. Special education in Israel. *Digest of the Mentally Retarded,* 1963, *1,* 4–11.

Masland, R. Mental retardation. In: Fishbein, M., *Birth Defects.* Philadelphia: J. P. Lippincott Company, 1963.

Masland, R., Sarason, S., and Gladwin, T. *Mental Subnormality.* New York: Basic Books, Inc., 1958.

Mentally Retarded Subnormal Child: Report of the Joint Expert Committee Convened by WHO with Participation of the United Nations, ILO and GENESCO. Technical Report World Health Organization, 1954, *75,* 3–46.

Merrill, M. A. Significance of the IQs on the Revised Stanford–Binet Scales. *Journal of Educational Psychology,* 1938, 641–651.

Miles, C. Gifted children. In: Carmichael, L. (Ed.), *Manual on Child Psychology* (2nd Edition). New York: John Wiley & Sons, Inc., 1963, 984–1063.

Mutter, Tom (Ed.) Das geistig behinderte kind in der heutigen gesellschalt. (The mentally handicapped child in today's society.) Supplement 15, *Lebenshilfe,* 1963.

New York State Department of Mental Hygiene. *Technical Report of the Mental Health Unit.* Syracuse, New York: Syracuse University Press, 1955.

Pearson, K. On the inheritance of mental deficiency. *Annals of Eugenics,* 1931, *4,* 362–369.

Penrose, L. *The Biology of Mental Defect* (2nd Edition). New York: Grune & Stratton, Inc., 1963.

Pintner, R. The feebleminded child. In: Murchison, C. (Ed.), *Handbook of Child Psychology* (2nd Edition). Worcester, Mass.: Clark University Press, 1933.

President's Panel on Mental Retardation. *A Proposed Program for National Action to Combat Mental Retardation.* Washington, D.C.: U.S. Government Printing Office, 1962.

Report of the Mission to Denmark and Sweden. Published for the President's Panel on Mental Retardation by the U.S. Department of Health, Education, and Welfare. Washington, D.C.: U.S. Government Printing Office, 1962.

Report of the Mission to the Netherlands. Published for the President's Panel on Mental Retardation by the U.S. Department of Health, Education, and Welfare. Washington, D.C.: U.S. Government Printing Office, 1962.

Shaw, R. Every 25 minutes . . . *Canada's Mental Health,* 1962, *10,* ii.

Sloan, W., and Birch, J. A rationale for degrees of retardation. *American Journal of Mental Deficiency,* 1955, *60,* 258–259.

Superintendent of Public Instruction. *Report of Study Projects for Trainable Mentally Handicapped Children.* Springfield, Ill.: Superintendent of Public Instruction, 1954.

Terman, L. *The Measurement of Intelligence.* Boston: Houghton Mifflin Company, 1916.

Tredgold, A. F. *A Textbook of Mental Deficiency* (6th Edition). Baltimore: William Wood & Company, 1937.

Wallin, J. *Children with Mental and Physical Handicaps.* Englewood Cliffs, N.J.: Prentice-Hall, Inc., 1949.

Wechsler, D. *Measurement of Adult Intelligence* (2nd Edition). Baltimore: William Wood & Company, 1941.

Weiner, B. B. Hawaii's public school program for mentally retarded children. Unpublished doctoral dissertation, University of Illinois, 1958. Summarized in: Kirk, S., and Bateman, B. *10 Years of Research at the Institute for Research on Exceptional Children.* Urbana, Ill.: University of Illinois, 1964.

Wirtz, M., and Guenther, R. The incidence of trainable mentally handicapped children. *Exceptional Children,* 1957, *4,* 171–172, 175.

2 THE HISTORY OF MENTAL RETARDATION

Maurice G. Kott

From *The New Jersey Comprehensive Plan to Combat Mental Retardation,* 1966, pp. 153–165. Reprinted with the permission of the New Jersey State Department of Institutions and Agencies and the author. Dr. Kott is Director, Division of Mental Retardation, New Jersey State Department of Institutions and Agencies, Trenton. Associated with Dr. Kott were Michael J. DiBella, Carl R. Price, Research Associates and Robert W. Brumquell, Project Director.

EARLY PERIOD

Mental retardation is as old as man. The record of concern and care for the less fortunate prior to 1800, however, represents one of the most pathetic chapters in the history of man. Living in societies where the majority of people were unschooled and untrained, the "feebleminded" did not appear significantly different from their neighbors.

The severely retarded, however, have been recognized since ancient times. The Spartans exposed their handicapped offspring to the elements to die. The retarded were left to perish in the mountains or drown in the rivers. By the Middle Ages the plight of the retarded had not improved. At the pleasure of the lords and their ladies, the retarded were exploited as "fools" and "jesters." During the Protestant Reformation, the mentally ill and retarded were thought to be "possessed with the devil." The unusual behavior of the retarded, the convulsive, and the mentally ill was interpreted with mystical, religious overtones. For the most part such "strange" individuals were considered human aberrations possessed with unusual demoniacal powers. As such, they were tortured, tormented, punished, and ostracized. Even Luther and Calvin regarded them as "filled with Satan."

The Church provided the only hope for the less fortunate prior to 1800. From the thirteenth century on, the churches of Europe began rather systematically to provide asylums for the less fortunate members of society, including the intellectually handicapped. These "asylums" were intended solely to provide a sanctuary for those unable to survive in a cruel, competitive society. No attempt was made at treatment or education. In the sixteenth century, St. Vincent de Paul and his "Sisters of Charity" established the Bicetre of Paris for the care and protection of those with behavior disorders.

The unfortunate status of the retarded was further complicated by the prevailing philosophy which influenced the thinking of most professionals of that day. The relative effects of heredity and environment on the growth and development of the individual were being considered. The "nature–nurture controversy," which is still with us today, was dominated primarily by the "naturalists" school of thought. They believed that heredity was the primary cause of mental retardation. As such, they thought that the condition was incurable. This pessimistic and defeatist point of view precluded treatment and education. The prevailing belief was "Once retarded, always retarded; nothing can be done."

In retrospect, the mentally subnormal were punished or largely ignored prior to 1800. At any rate, they did not come within the social arena of human concern.

AFTER 1800

Around the turn of the 19th century, experimental psychology, which had not influenced professional thinking to any discernible degree, received a forward thrust with discoveries in neurology, physics, mathematics, and physiology. A discovery of another sort, however, influenced the course of mental retardation. In 1798 hunters chanced upon a twelve-year-old boy, naked, untrained, and inarticulate, who had been living in the forest of Aveyron, France. Jean Itard took charge of Victor, "The Wild Boy of Aveyron." Itard had been influenced by the teachings of John Locke of England and Jean Rousseau of France who believed that learning came only through the senses and that all persons could develop the ability to learn if given adequate stimulation. The Golden Rule that "practice makes perfect" was in direct opposition to the pessimistic teachings advanced by the "hereditarians" and "naturalists." The effects of environment on learning were coming into play. From this perspective, Itard proceeded to teach Victor intensively, emphasizing sensory and motor training. With courage, enthusiasm, and vigor, Itard struggled valiantly to produce changes in the behavior of this boy. While his efforts resulted in marked behavioral changes in Victor, Itard was unable to teach him to talk or to live independently in Parisian society. Even though some progress was made, he considered his experiment a failure. Nevertheless, it represents the first scientific attempt at training a retarded child. It marked a radical change of emphasis from incurability and isolation to treatment and education. It stimulated a new movement in which professionals began to assume responsibility from the Church for the retarded.

The residential school program in the United States can be traced directly to Itard's work, through his student Edward Seguin. He expanded and formalized his teacher's techniques into a complex, systematic, sequence of training which he called the "physiological method." To test his procedures, Seguin established the first residential school for the retarded in Paris in 1837 as part of the famous Bicetre Hospital. With the success of this training school, in addition to his classical contributions, *The Moral Treatment, Hygiene and Education of Idiots and Other Backward Children* (1846), Seguin was recognized as an international figure in the field prior to his arrival in America. He was the guiding force in establishing the first American residential institution at South Boston in 1848. He became the first president of the organization which is known today as the American Association on Mental Deficiency.

Inspired by Seguin's method and his "model" school in Massachusetts, other states followed rapidly. New York opened a school at Albany in 1851, Pennsylvania in 1852, Ohio in 1857. By 1890, 14 states had separate facilities for the retarded. By 1900, residential schools were established in most of the states of New England, the Great Lakes Area, and in California, with a total number of patients approximating 14,000. The twentieth century has witnessed a rapid spread of public and private residential institutions throughout the country. According to the *President's Panel Report* (1962), there are more than 300 public and private institutions for the mentally retarded in the country. It states, "Based on 1960 data, approximately 160,000 are in 108 public residential institutions specifically designed for the mentally retarded, 10,000 are in 200 private institutions."

With the exception of the small beginning of the special class movement in the public schools, mental retardation appeared almost entirely as an institutional problem in 1900. The outstanding accomplishments and success which Seguin demonstrated in particular cases of retardation resulted in a philosophy of unrestrained optimism. The first schools emphasized education and training. They were begun as "experimental laboratories" to test Seguin's methods and the effects of environment on retardation. Intended as training schools and not asylums, state institutions were developed with the motivating belief that most all the mentally deficient could be "cured" through education and training and returned to the community as average citizens. Seguin (1866, pp. 249–250) emphasized this approach by stating: "We are aware that the appellation of asylum has been attached to several of the most important schools. But this term conveys exclusively the idea of a custodian, lifelong place of retreat, whereas the institution or school is only temporarily open for educational and physiological treatment. In it, idiots and their congeners are expected to remain during the period assigned by nature for progress in young persons, unless it sooner becomes manifest that they cannot be improved at all or any more, in which case their parents should take them out to make room for new pupils."

State institutions were created for the trainable pupils of school age who through training could assume a normal place in society. The untrainable were relegated to the asylum. New Jersey substantiated this view when the 1873 Commission recommended that "the counties should be required to protect and care for the unimprovable defective especially of the feeble-minded class while the state gathers into these institutions by a gradual process all those who are susceptible to the influences of education and capable of being so improved by its agency as to be elevated in the scale of intelligence, raised from a condition of hopeless dependence and fitted to become useful to society and measurably or wholly self-supporting."

With increasing numbers of the less trainable being admitted to institutions and the unsuccessful adjustments of those released from state schools, residents were being retained beyond school age and the philosophy of "curing through training" or "restoring to a normal life" was gradually substituted by the concept of permanent custody. A number of factors effecting this major change of emphasis by state residential schools has been suggested.

> First, experience soon taught professional persons in the field that the extreme claims of the environmentalists were ill-founded. Second, society was seldom prepared to provide needed funds for professional persons in the quality and quantity needed to provide intensive training programs. Too often, states, considering their responsibilities terminated with the construction of elaborate physical plants, were content to see the retarded removed from society and placed in a setting where only custodial care could be provided. Third, professional persons themselves must accept part of the responsibility for the neglect of retardates; until recently, few have been prepared to devote their lives to the study or treatment of this group of citizens. Fourth, a new development began in this country about 1900, aimed at educating a larger and larger percentage of moderately retarded boys and girls through public day schools and classes (Dunn, 1961, p. 16).

Such was the thinking during the first quarter of this century. As new institutions sprang rapidly into being, with them came new ideas. The belief that all the retarded must be forever institutionalized was rejected in part. By the third decade it was generally agreed that many would not require the specialized services of an institution; that of those who had been institutionalized, a selected group could be returned to the community under controlled conditions; and that all social anomalies were not solely or directly traceable to retardation. Three major developments followed. First was the Colony Plan whereby competent individuals were employed extra-institutionally during the day and were supervised by school personnel. In New Jersey an example of this was the Red Bank Colony established in 1925 for girls from Vineland. Second, a parole system was evolved. Previously, the community failure of many retardates upon leaving the institution was due in great measure to the fact that there was little post-institutional supervision and guidance. Third, local school systems accelerated the establishment of special classes for the slow learner in accordance with statutes enacted in 1911.

In the more recent past, the day-school movement has played an ever-increasing role. The first class for "backward children" was started in Providence, Rhode Island, in 1896. Since individual intelligence tests had not been devised at that time, it is likely that this class and others established before 1915 enrolled pupils who were "problem children" because of educational, social, and/or intellectual difficulties. With the advent of efficient psychometric devices, especially the original Stanford–Binet Test of Intelligence in 1916, all retardation was translated into numbers. With the introduction of intelligence tests, the IQ became an idol. The number of retarded appeared to increase markedly for it was believed there was definite, incontestable proof in the intelligence test. In any event, educators became more aware that various levels of intellectual functioning among children warranted the development of special classes to deal with individual differences. As a result, special day schools and classes have increased fairly rapidly. In 1922, 23,000 retarded pupils were enrolled in such facilities; by 1940 the number had increased to 99,000; in 1953 it was up to 114,000. The 1953 U.S. Office of Education survey revealed a new trend. Almost 5000 of the 114,000 retarded pupils in day classes were "trainable" children. Very few facilities for this group existed in day school before 1953. Day-school facilities are restricted largely to urban communities. Children in rural areas, by and large, continue to be neglected.

The impetus which the "mental retardation movement" received in the early years of the twentieth century was hampered by the pressures of the depression followed by World War II. Immediately after the war, interest spread rapidly. There was a resurgence of effort and purpose. The phenomenal growth and development of interest in mental retardation after World War II can probably be attributed to four events: (1) a thorough revulsion toward the Nazi mass slaughter of retarded persons; (2) a reawakening of interest on the part of biological and social scientists; (3) renewed public awareness of how little had been done for these "forgotten people"; and (4) an adamant, unashamed, and well-organized parent movement.

In 1950, the National Association for Retarded Children was formed. Composed chiefly of parents of mentally retarded children, this organization has done much to develop and stimulate public awareness of the problems of mental retardation. Initially, NARC conducted educational programs on a demonstration basis. Responsibility for many of these pilot enterprises was subsequently assumed by the public schools. As concern developed for those who did not meet the requirements of the public school program, parents expanded their efforts to include groups beyond school age, the preschoolers, and the more severely retarded. With a membership of more than 95,000 persons, NARC has grown from a few isolated individual groups scattered over the country to more than 1000 units in 50 states. It has been most effective in urging state legislatures to enact laws fostering new improved programs and services for the mentally retarded. It has been instrumental in creating several state commissions to delineate total, comprehensive, and statewide plans of service for the mentally retarded. Increased interest on the part of the Federal Government is due partly to their efforts.

Other organizations have played an important role in the field. The American Association on Mental Deficiency, organized in 1876, draws its members from the professional disciplines of medicine, education, psychology, social work, and administration. In recent years, through its committee for "technical planning in mental retardation," it has developed and conducted numerous conferences and studies in the broad areas of (1) research, (2) training of personnel, and (3) programming. Also, the Council for Exceptional Children of the National Education Association has stimulated the development of teacher-training programs, assisted in delineating the qualifications of teachers of the mentally retarded, and encouraged the dissemination of scientific information in the broad field of special education through state, regional, and national conferences and publications. Also, numerous private organizations conduct a variety of programs and services for the retarded. Efforts of these groups have contributed to a better understanding of mental retardation and to the growing philosophy that the mentally retarded person should be served with as little dislocation from his normal environment as is consistent with the special character of his needs.

Based on this philosophy, the development of day-care centers represents an identifiable trend in the history of mental retardation. The operation of day-care centers as a function of the units of NARC began as early as 1953, but the majority of the programs were started within the past four years. The developing pattern of this embryonic program appears similar to that of the early day classes for trainable retarded children. In 1957, Delaware passed legislation establishing daytime care centers for severely retarded children; the first of several state-supported, state-operated programs of care for severely retarded children was opened in 1958. In 1957, Massachusetts started a program of preschool classes for mentally retarded children. Several other states have enacted legislation providing financial support for day-care services for the mentally retarded since 1957.

A recent survey of day-care centers operated by NARC units indicated that there were 3948 children attending 100 of these centers. This number did not include any state operated or supported programs. Of concern are the 750 children reported to be on waiting lists and the additional undeclared number in the 12 centers reporting only the presence of waiting lists. The services offered in these programs varied from supervision of a small number of children for two hours twice a week to complete clinical, educational, and social welfare programs. Some centers reported group therapy for parents, diversified programs for children, and complete health services. Other centers indicated that they have none of these services. The need to secure inspection and licensing procedures of the barest minimal standards is evident. In any event, it is still too early to determine the relative impact of the "day-care movement" on the history of mental retardation.

MENTAL RETARDATION IN NEW JERSEY

In 1846 Stephen A. Garrison, assemblyman from Cumberland County and father of the Reverend Stephen O. Garrison who was to found the Vineland Training School, introduced a bill in the legislature to create a state school for the feebleminded.[1] This failed to pass, but in 1860 New Jersey consented to support a limited number of its retarded at the Elwyn Training School in Pennsylvania. In 1873 a commission was appointed "On the Deaf and Dumb, Blind and Feebleminded in the State of New Jersey." The commission's report of 1874 estimated that there were 1000 retarded persons in the state and concluded that one or more institutions for defective classes were needed. Not until 1888, however, did New Jersey open its first State School at Vineland, simultaneously with the Vineland Training School, private but closely entwined with New Jersey history.

A second state commission on the care of the feebleminded was appointed in 1913. Meanwhile, the Vineland Training School was investigating social delinquencies in the rural areas of Burlington County and set up a county colony at New Lisbon in 1914. In 1916 New Jersey inherited this as its second state institution. Recommendations of the commission of 1913, together with those of the Prison Inquiry Commission, caused the legislature to enact laws in 1918 which created a Board of Control and the Department of Charities and Corrections, renamed the following year the Department of Institutions and Agencies. Charged with the operation and responsibilities of a new welfare and correctional system, the department proceeded to integrate the then existing institutions and agencies and to expand services and facilities. At that time there were two state schools for the retarded, the State School at Vineland and the State Colony at New Lisbon. A number of wards, however, were maintained by the state at the Vineland Training School.

New Jersey approached the problem of residential care for the feebleminded rather uniquely. Small in size, it apparently saw no need for a geographical division in which institutions served certain areas. Rather, sex was the determinant, males being sent to New Lisbon and females to the Vineland State School. With the State Colony at Woodbine, established in 1921, a more refined and then radical criterion was added, namely, degree of retardation. Woodbine was planned as an institution for males who, for the most part, were severely retarded. This was an innovation and the sys-

[1] A partial reprint of "Institutions—a Brief Summary through the Mid-Twentieth Century," by VonBulow, *Welfare Reporter,* October 1959, pp. 151–153.

tem of classifying institutional population by sex and degree of retardation has remained peculiar to New Jersey as schools in other states are for both sexes of all grades. One result of the New Jersey plan has been more aggressive training for, and a greater emphasis upon, the severely retarded.

New Jersey now had two state schools for males—Woodbine for the seriously retarded, and New Lisbon for the educable and the defective delinquent. Classification at the central office level became a more significant task. The laws of 1918, however, had adequately included methods and authority for the interchange of residents, so that if an individual had been improperly classified or had progressed or regressed as to demand different programming, he could be readily transferred between these two schools or the Vineland Training School.

The Vineland State School was the only institution for female retardates of all grades (excluding the relatively small number at the Training School) until 1928, when the North Jersey Training School at Totowa was opened for girls ranging in age from six to twenty years who could profit from comparatively advanced training and be returned to the community. Thus, the younger, more competent girls were classified for Totowa and the situation at Vineland changed over the years in that the percentage of higher grade females diminished while those of middle and lower grades increased. As the Vineland State School was gradually outgrowing its physical resources, in 1925 the Almond Road Colony about four miles west of the main school was started. Today this adjunct cares for about one third of Vineland's population, primarily the more seriously retarded.

For 28 years these four residential schools served but did not meet all of the demands. There was little expansion either in facilities or program during the depression and World War II. One pressing need, however, was eased. None of the four schools accepted children below five and there were many tragic situations where families required assistance before the child reached that age. In 1948 a nursery for 100 children of both sexes below five was established in Totowa, one of the first such units in the country.

Since the turn of the century, New Jersey has been a leader in the field of mental retardation. Garrison, Goddard, E. R. Johnstone, Earle, Ellis, Doll, and Yepsen are some of the names engraved in the state's history. Their contributions have been recognized far beyond the boundaries of New Jersey. As the midcentury mark approached, however, a new force began to exert itself. This was the Association for Retarded Children. In this organization parents banded together to arouse public concern and to foster greater understanding and awareness of public responsibility. A vital, determined, inspired organization, it stimulated efforts on the local, state, and national level on behalf of the retarded. As 1950 approached, there was a revival of interest in this field.

Special education in New Jersey received its greatest impetus with the passage of the Beadleston Bills in 1954. This legislation came as a result of the many unmet educational needs of handicapped children and youth. For the first time in the history of New Jersey, the classification and special education of mentally retarded and physically handicapped children were made mandatory. The law specifies that each board of education must ascertain which children between the ages of five and twenty in the public schools of the district cannot be properly accommodated through the school facilities usually provided because of the extent of their mental retardation or physical handicaps. Mentally retarded children must be classified as educable or trainable. Suspected cases of mental retardation must be classified by psychological examiners approved by the State Department of Education. Mentally retarded children are placed in special classes with limited enrollments. *The Education of Handicapped Children in New Jersey 1954–1964* indicates the progress that has been made in providing educational services to the mentally retarded during the past decade:

> New Jersey was one of the first states to pass mandatory legislation providing educational services and school attendance for the mentally retarded. The 1954 legislation has served as a guide for other states. In spite of the fact that many administrators were not fully prepared to undertake such a program at its inception, a good job has been done. Over the ten-year span there has been an increase of 647 classes for educable children. The present number of such classes is 934. The classes for the trainable increased in number during the same period from five to 217. A study of the growth pattern shows that special education programs are no longer confined to large cities as they were in 1954. Indeed it is now the large cities which report the most serious shortage of classes for the mentally retarded. Geographic expansion now makes the special education program more accessible to trainable and educable children any place in New Jersey. . . . Despite these gains, as of June 1963, there were 1380 educable pupils reported as classified but not attending educable classes. Thirty-one were reported as not attending school. One hundred and seventy-two trainable children were excluded pending placement and twenty-eight were in regular classes.

Although the establishment and acceleration of institutional and educational programs represented substantial advances in meeting the needs of the retarded, obvious gaps still remained. In an attempt to bridge these gaps a number of new programs were initiated. First, in 1955, the Field Services Program of the Division of Mental Retardation was begun. Its initial responsibility was to provide postinstitutional supervision. The decision to locate its offices in the community rather than at institutions reflects the trend toward integrating the retarded in the community as opposed to a life of isolation apart from society. Over the years, the scope of this agency has expanded. It now provides a host of social services for the retarded and their families. Second, in 1963, the Public Day Care Program was established to meet the needs of those retarded children who, classified as neither "trainable" nor "educable," are excluded from public school. As a community-centered program designed specifically to provide for the social-developmental adjustment of these children, it enables the severely and profoundly retarded to remain at home and in the community. It affords real relief several hours a day to mothers who face the tremendous burdens of daily care of these children. Although 15 Day Care Programs are now in operation, they are housed in unsuitable physical structures. To meet this need, the construction of physically suitable Day Care Centers has been designated as the first priority in the *New Jersey State Plan for the Construction of Mental Retardation Facilities 1964–1965*. Third, in January 1965, the Woodbridge State School for severely retarded boys and girls was opened. This brings the total number of institutions for the retarded to six. Plans for the development of a seventh institution, the Hunterdon State School, are underway.

On June 26, 1963, Governor Richard J. Hughes created an Interdepartmental Committee on Lifetime Disability composed of the Commissioners of Education, Health, Institutions and Agencies, Labor and Industry, the Secretary of State and a representative of the Governor's office. Also, a "Governor's Advisory Council" to this Committee, with broad representation of lay and professional citizens, was formed. As a reflection of governmental and private concern at all levels, the Committee's first stated objective was the development of a comprehensive plan to combat mental retardation. Toward this end, a Working Party on Mental Retardation was established. From various state agencies representatives having a particular competence in this area were designated by appropriate Commissioners. The charge of the Working Party was to "review" the present available State Services to the retarded, identify the Executive Department which is or should be discharging responsibilities and report to the Interdepartmental Committee the extent and manner in which each function should be strengthened. This Working Party will, as well, develop a comprehensive plan involving public and private, statewide and local activities to combat mental retardation.

THE PRESENT

Three distinct periods of development in the history of mental retardation care in the United States have been noted: (1) 1850–1900 saw the growth of institutions; (2) 1900–1950 witnessed the development of public school classes for retardates and the development of intelligence and personality tests; and (3) 1950 to the present has seen an emphasis on research and the rise of community resources.

The role of the Federal Government represents the beginning of a new chapter in the history of mental retardation. In 1961, President Kennedy appointed a panel of experts to prepare a national plan to combat mental retardation. In 1962 the panel presented its report. In 1963, Congress responded with new major legislation. Also the White House Conference on Mental Retardation was held. In 1964, comprehensive planning by every state in the union was underway. In its report, "National Action to Combat Mental Retardation," the panel summarizes its almost 200 recommendations in the following eight broad areas:

1. *Research* in the causes of retardation and in methods of care, rehabilitation, and learnings.
2. *Preventative health measures* including (a) a greatly strengthened program of maternal and infant care directed first at the centers of population where prematurity and the rate of "damaged" children are high; (b) protection against such known hazards to pregnancy as radiation and harmful drugs; and (c) expanded diagnostic and screening services.
3. *Strengthened educational programs generally and extended and enriched programs of special education* in public and private schools closely coordinated with vocational guidance, vocational rehabilitation, and specific training and preparation for employment; education for adult mentally retarded and workshops geared to their needs.
4. *More comprehensive and improved clinical and social services.*
5. *Improved methods and facilities for care,* with emphasis on the home and the development of a wide range of local community facilities.
6. *A new legal, as well as social, concept of the retarded,* including protection of their civil rights; life guardianship provisions when needed; an enlightened attitude on the part of the law and the courts; and clarification of the theory of responsibility in criminal acts.
7. *Helping overcome the serious problems of manpower* as they affect the entire field of science and every type of service through extended programs of recruiting with fellowships and increased opportunities for graduate students and those preparing for the professions to observe and learn at first hand about the phenomenon of retardation. Because there will never be a fully adequate supply of personnel in this field and for other cogent reasons, the panel has emphasized the need for more volunteers in health, recreation, and welfare activities and for a domestic Peace Corps to stimulate voluntary service.
8. *Programs of education and information to increase public awareness* of the problem of mental retardation.

In addition to a strong emphasis on *research* and *prevention,* the report recommends the following:

1. That programs for the retarded, including modern day care, recrea-

tion, residential services, and ample educational and vocational opportunities, be *comprehensive.*

2. That they operate in or close to the communities where the retarded live—that is, that they be *community-centered.*
3. That services be so organized as (a) to provide a central or fixed point for the guidance, assistance, and protection of retarded persons if and when needed, and (b) to assure a sufficient array or *continuum* of services to meet different types of need.
4. That private agencies as well as public agencies at the local, state, and federal levels continue to provide resources and to increase them for this worthy purpose. While the Federal Government can assist, the principal responsibility for financing and improving services for the mentally retarded must continue to be borne by the states and local communities.

There is no doubt that through the active and immediate implementation of the panel's recommendations, one will witness increased coordinated efforts on behalf of the Federal Government, all directed toward "a search for solutions to the problems of mental retardation."

The attack on mental retardation has gained tremendous momentum. President Johnson has stated, "Today we can say objectively that more has been done by the government in the past two years than in the previous 200 years to meet the challenge of mental retardation." Significant advancements have been made in many areas, ranging from genetics and biochemistry to special education and vocational rehabilitation. Dr. Stafford Warren, who served as the President's Special Assistant on Mental Retardation said that "The toll of mental retardation could be reduced by fully one half if all we know today could be applied successfully everywhere." Much, however, remains to be accomplished. This is where we stand today. The future belongs to those who, through coordinated effort and planned action, will bring to the mentally retarded a brighter tomorrow.

3 SOME PERSISTENTLY RECURRING ASSUMPTIONS CONCERNING EDUCATION OF THE MENTALLY RETARDED

Burton Blatt

This chapter is a revision of an article originally published in *The Training School Bulletin,* Vol. 57, No. 2, August 1960, pp. 48–59 and in *Mental Retardation: Readings and Resouces,* 1st edition (Jerome H. Rothstein, Editor). New York: Holt, Rinehart and Winston, Inc., 1961, pp. 113–125. Because of the absence of a consistent and universal nomenclature, it should be pointed out that, for the purposes of this text, the term "mentally retarded" is used as an all-inclusive classification embracing all individuals who, on clinical and standardized evaluations, function intellectually one and one-half standard deviations below average. Reprinted with the permission of The Training School, Vineland, N.J., and the author. Dr. Blatt is Chairman, Special Education Department, Syracuse University, Syracuse, New York.

In 1948, I. Goldstein published a penetrating paper dealing with causes, characteristics, and implications of mental deficiency. This work received a great deal of attention, partly, it is supposed, because of its clear and readable style and, more importantly, because it purported to separate fact from fiction, ". . . cite the fact, nail the lie; construe the implication; act" (p. 149).

Goldstein's paper originally deserved its place of prominence as a recapitulation of existent practices and assumptions from which were derived a series of definitive statements concerning mental retardation. However, evidence brought forth during the 15 years since the publication of his work, and the disconcerting questions raised by research completed and suggestive of research yet to be done, limit the usefulness of his article to its gross impact in upgrading the understanding of the unsophisticated and the uncritical and raises the possibility of its effect in confusing rather than clarifying one's perceptions of mental retardation. Today, the student examines "Implications of Mental Deficiency" and is not sure what is fact and what is fiction, what is myth and what is reality.

Because of the continuing tendency of many special educators to base decisions and actions on unwarranted or unclear assumptions, and considering the diligent research of those who have provided answers during the past years, it is desirable to reexamine some of Goldstein's facts, determine their right to this label, and offer other possibilities for consideration. Unfortunately, much of Goldstein's position of 15 years ago is, today, accorded wide acceptance by teachers and other professionals. Therefore, the purposes of this chapter seem clear: to focus upon the rigidities of a profession that encumber change; to outline questions that require study; and to instill a healthy unrest in all who work with the mentally retarded. In a sense, the chapter provides the reader with an overview of the major areas to be attended to in this book.

FACT OR FICTION?

> Mental deficiency is basically a physical or constitutional defect. Abnormal, incomplete, or arrested growth of certain cells results in the crippled arm, the crippled leg. Similarly, although not always as outwardly apparent as in the instance of the crippled leg, deficiencies in brain structure or defects of somatic organization result in mental deficiency. Mental retardation is thus a symptom of some constitutional disturbance or defect (Goldstein, p. 150).

ANALYSIS

A review of pertinent literature leads one to the unmistakable conclusion that children, variously called mentally retarded, subcultural, familial, non-organic, aclinical or garden-variety, do not, as a group, upon the most thorough neurological and psychological examinations, exhibit ". . . deficiencies in brain structure or defects of somatic organization." Sarason and Gladwin sum up the neurological consensus by stating that the mentally retarded (as defined by these authors), who constitute the bulk of those in public-school special classes and the majority of "high grade" institutionalized children, presumably do not exhibit any central nervous system pathology (1958, p. 11). They call attention to the need to differentiate this group, called mentally retarded, from the mentally deficient, who have demonstrable central nervous system disorders and who probably will never achieve a normal social and intellectual status.

Therefore, in the absence of any evidence to the contrary and until such evidence is forthcoming, mentally retarded children who exhibit no central nervous system pathology should be assumed free of constitutional disturbances that in some way act to produce inferior intellectual development. It appears, from the standpoints of educational programming and research, that an uncritical adherence to a traditionally all-inclusive concept of mental retardation, which rules out the possibility that many of these children have intact central nervous systems and have capacities for at least typical development, is a dubious practice for the following reasons:

1. Such a viewpoint is unduly restrictive to the researcher in that its emphasis on the apparent irremediability and constitutionality of this condition detracts from potentially promising investigations into the role of cultural and psychological variables in mental retardation.
2. It establishes unwarranted limitations on what might be attempted and accomplished educationally with mentally retarded individuals to improve their intellectual, social, and psychological functioning.
3. It relegates to public-school special classes for the mentally retarded thousands of children for whom such "educational" placement may not be indicated in the light of our professional understanding and knowledge, or justified on the basis of a "diagnosis" of mental retarda-

tion. This "diagnosis" and placement largely determine the course of the lives of these children.

4. It engenders in the teacher a predeterministic mental set which discourages experimentation and hope in the classroom.
5. A positive position does not assume that, in the absence of demonstrable central nervous system disorder, the possibility of organicity is ruled out. Rather, it recognizes that neurological procedures and criteria are not now completely valid or reliable and this positive position is taken in the interests of research and experimentation.

Implication

If the large group of children described above does not exhibit central nervous systems that are different from the typical group, the question to be asked is, "Why are these children mentally retarded?" It must be determined whether these children are retarded as a result of functional rather than constitutional causes. It should be noted that the evidence available, albeit scanty, points to the conclusion that a great number of children presently classified as mentally retarded cannot be so classified using Goldstein's definition.

FACT OR FICTION?

"Mental deficiency exists from birth or early age. . . ." (Goldstein, p. 151) ". . . is incurable and irremediable" (p. 150).

Analysis

As long ago as 1952, Kirk cautiously generalized that nurture may be an important underestimated factor in the causation of mental retardation—not all mental retardation exists from birth or an early age. In trying to locate preschool children with IQs between 45 and 80 for an experimental study, Kirk contacted schools for the names of siblings of known school-age retardates, social agencies, clinics, pediatricians, and public health department officials. His search was relatively unsuccessful. He found a few children ". . . referred by doctors were grossly deficient, with retardation usually of organic nature, but a large percentage of children from all of these sources was found to be of average intelligence . . ." (p. 699). Since it is generally agreed that high-grade mental retardates are frequently found in subcultural environments and, as a result of Kirk's lack of success in finding such children at preschool ages, there is a suggestion:

> . . . that many children later placed in special classes or institutions are not mentally retarded in terms of intelligence test scores at the ages of three, four, or five. Some children whose older brothers and

> sisters were in special classes tested approximately normal at the pre-school ages. This raises the question as to whether children from low cultural levels who are approximately normal at an early age may later become mentally retarded because of their cultural environment or other unknown variables (p. 698).

IMPLICATION

Kirk's experiments with the early education of the mentally retarded once again raises the controversy of nature versus nurture in the development of intelligence. In a recent (1958) publication, describing the results of a five-year experiment analyzing the effects of preschool education on 81 young mentally retarded children, Kirk outlines both the nativist and environmentalist points of view. The nativist's position is clear: intelligence is mainly a factor of central nervous system maturation from conception on; children grow evenly at their own rates; early stimulation will not increase potential; mentally retarded children cannot be made "normal," regardless of any kind of training or education now known; when such changes in intelligence do occur, they are more likely due to errors of original diagnosis; mental retardation is incurable and irremediable.

The position of the environmentalists is less clear-cut, but from this viewpoint, more promising: within broad limitations, the development of children is significantly affected by the kinds of early rearing they have experienced; to explain all changes in intelligence as being due to erroneous original diagnosis is only to beg these intriguing questions. Why are researchers unable to locate preschool educable mentally retarded children? What are the conditions that promote increments in intelligence among certain children?

A review of Kirk's findings raises the following questions in the mind of the serious student:

1. What is the significance of the acceleration in rates of growth of 30 (in a total sample of 43) children who received preschool education?
2. Why did the study disclose that it was much more difficult to displace the rates of growth of organic children than non-organic children? (However, one may argue that the apparent irreversible defect or the organic child may be due to the educator's inability to adequately compensate for this defect. A dramatic example of the use of compensatory educational techniques can be found in a study of the education of Helen Keller.)
3. Why was it generally found that the greater the changes made in the environment, the greater were the changes in the rates of growth?

It is interesting to note that: familial educable children do not usually exhibit mental retardation during the preschool years; familial educable adults marry, find jobs, solve problems on a typical level, and maintain themselves independently and indistinguishably in the community (Sarason and Gladwin, pp. 13–50). It appears that only when this individual is of school age is he diagnosed and does he function as mentally retarded; it appears almost as if the schools predestine the child to mental retardation. Therefore, it would seem logical to designate the nature–nurture issue an open one and to find answers to the following problems:

1. What is the relationship of cultural and psychological variables to early rearing practices and their effects on intellectual growth and development?
2. What are the factors comprising this general ability we call intelligence and how can they be more adequately measured?
3. What is the relationship, if any, between test problem-solving behavior and nontest problem-solving behavior? Do different racial, religious, and cultural groups score differently on conventional tests of intelligence because of actual differences in innate intelligence or because of the ways children are brought up to solve problems?
4. What is the relationship between motivation and status goals? Is academic achievement a status goal of all who go to school?

FACT OR FICTION?

Mental retardation ". . . results in the inability of the individual to profit from ordinary schooling . . ." (Goldstein, p. 151) and ". . . by providing him with a different educational program suited to his needs, we can make him more capable of facing the world which lies ahead of him" (p. 165).

No one who has worked with mentally retarded children in school would question the validity of Goldstein's remarks. However, one may question the implication that there is substantial evidence as to what the proper program should be. From his article, one can conclude that retarded children in special classes are receiving a great deal more purposeful education than retarded children in regular classes.

In a rare moment of candor, a distinguished special educator recently remarked that special education isn't special nor can it, in many instances, be considered education. Early studies found that, insofar as measurable abilities are concerned, mentally retarded children in special classes are very similar in development to those in regular grades (Bennett, 1932; Pertsch, 1936). In fact, the reports of Bennett and Pertsch found that retarded children in special classes did poorly in physical, personality, and academic areas as compared with retarded children in regular classes. Notwithstanding the obvious and valid criticisms of these prototype studies comparing special versus regular-class membership (Cowen, 1938), it has yet to be demonstrated that the special class offers a better school experience for retarded children than does regular-class placement, as revealed in more recent research explorations, and discussed in the first three chapters of this book.

Certainly, there is little evidence to support the belief that special-class provisions, even the best available today, are the millennium, nor can we even say that the best of our special classes are "good enough."

IMPLICATION

Disturbing as it may be to those who have conscientiously developed curricula for the mentally retarded, and while providing convenient rationalizations for the "do-nothings" who reject responsibility by saying either we do not know enough to plan or each teacher should plan according to the individuals in her class, there is little evidence to support the widespread notion that, by placing mentally retarded children in conventional special classes, society is meeting their educational needs. There is no doubt that this group of children, regardless of etiology or permanence of condition, requires special provisions in school. There is doubt, at least among some educators and psychologists, as to what should constitute the program of special education and who can benefit from it. In this regard, some intriguing questions to be asked are:

1. How many children are placed in special classes after careful differential diagnosis? How many are placed after the simple administration of Binet and WISC Tests? Does the administration of these tests constitute a differential diagnosis?
2. Using more than the limited evaluations to be derived from the IQ, how many children in special classes do not belong there? Do we have a moral obligation to these children regarding diagnosis, placement, and the ultimate effects of these on their lives?
3. What are the best ways to teach mentally retarded children to read, to understand numbers, to understand themselves? What is different about the methods, materials, and content in special classes commonly found today?
4. What is really meant by the statements:
   a. "She is not a good student but she may make a good teacher."
   b. "This person isn't a skilled teacher but she has a good attitude. She will not do any harm to children."
   c. "We can't measure the differences, but these children in the special class are receiving a finer education than if they were to remain in the regular grades."

Do these statements indicate that we don't know how to evaluate special education because we, as yet, do not know what special education should be?

The implication here is evident. What is needed is an infusion of bold, creative thinking into the field. Experimentation with new and unorthodox methods and materials must be encouraged. A more discerning study of the mountain of research in education, special education, psychology, anthropology, and sociology must be made in order to separate the valuable from the nonessential. We must reject many of our present curriculum practices because they have been so eminently unsuccessful. When Goldstein describes the retarded as ". . . incapable of logical thought, unable to make generalizations or work with abstractions," and therefore, ". . . response must be habituated. He must be taught specific responses to specific situations," is he merely perpetuating the retardation with the supposed educational treatment (p. 152)? Is there the possibility that, for some children, the retardation is due to an early rearing emphasizing habituation? Can some retarded children profit from programs involving creative thought processes rather than from the continuation of "strait-jacketed" stereotyped curricula which reflect the same kind of thinking?

FACT OR FICTION?

"The general consensus at the present time seems to be that 40 to 50% of mental deficiency are (sic) of an hereditary nature . . ." (Goldstein, p. 152).

Analysis

The recent work of Sarason and Gladwin has pointed up the meagerness of the evidence offered by adherents of hereditarian theories of mental retardation (pp. 63–78). Their investigations have convinced them:

> . . . that an hereditary determinant of mental capacity must not be assumed to exist unless proven. Furthermore, proof should be sought in terms of our present knowledge of human genetics and of the nature of human intellect, rather than, as is commonly done, through the administration of routine intelligence tests to a variety of "racial" and other groups. We do not propose to deny that heredity is a factor, particularly in mental deficiency, but rather that we should leave it out of our accounting until it is supported by more than speculation and bias (p. 63).

Every day, recommendations are being made in regard to sterilization, prohibition of marriage, court placement of children, and counselling of adults—all based on the assumption that mental retardation has a genetic basis. Should such crucial decisions be made without more evidence? What are the genetic factors in the causation of mental retardation?

FACT OR FICTION?

"He (the mentally retarded) is more liable to illness and physical defects and generally lacks the physical stamina of the normal child" (Goldstein, p. 152).

ANALYSIS

Our analysis of the literature does not lead to the above conclusion. The mentally retarded are not necessarily "limited in physical prowess" (Goldstein, p. 155). Especially among the group called "familial," there are many who far surpass the norm in every aspect of physical ability.[1] Mentally retarded children do not have to be malnourished. They do not have to be poor athletes. They are weak for the same reasons that typical children are weak; they are strong for the same reasons. Because a significant percentage of these children reside in substandard environments and because a significant percentage have central nervous system impairment, some retarded children are physically limited. The bulk of those in the "higher grade" category are not.

IMPLICATION

Mentally retarded children do not necessarily have to be physically limited. To assume that these children are so limited because of mental inability is to use a handy but poor excuse to remain inactive when rehabilitation may be indicated. We do not explain malnourishment in a gifted child by quoting his high IQ; evidence dictates that we do no less for the retarded. Although, as a group, mentally retarded children both in special and regular classes surpass their academic expectancy as measured against their mental age, it is ironic that special-class teachers continue to feel their greatest anxiety in reconciling actual reading and arithmetic achievement of children with what teachers expect and hope for (Blatt, 1956, pp. 45–50, 98). Fewer teachers have anxious moments rationalizing physical-education and health programs for these children regardless of what is being accomplished.

FACT OR FICTION?

"Early studies (circa 1900), purporting to show that as high as 85% of delinquents and criminals in the studies were mentally deficient, have been

[1] Studies of characteristics of the mentally retarded, using this term generically, often become meaningless because of differences in abilities among the various subgroups considered retarded. Particularly in the area of physical status, it should be emphasized that there are very significant differences between organic and nonorganic children and between higher grade and lower grade children.

challenged. Today the figure is believed to be closer to 50%" (Goldstein, p. 154).

Analysis

In a recent review of the literature, Blatt found numerous studies, with few exceptions written at least 15 years ago, reporting high relationships between delinquency and intelligence (1956, pp. 39–45). More recent research reports low relationships, "j" shaped in character, and suggests the following factors that influence these relationships and affect their validities:

1. There appears to be a multiplicity of causes of criminality and delinquency. Lower IQ, per se, does not play an important role in the causation of such behavior unless this factor combines with other causes (as Goldstein points out) such as: poor homes, mental disease, alcoholism, and marital strife among adults and community rejection toward children.
2. Some delinquents receive low IQ scores on tests because of their subcultural environment rather than as a result of constitutional defect.[2]
3. There are selective factors operating with respect to the intelligence level of delinquents in institutions. One institution may not admit the retarded while another may care for this type of child exclusively.
4. Brighter delinquents may escape detection and apprehension.
5. On the basis of a more promising prognosis, the mentally able delinquent may receive a suspended sentence while the retarded child, committing the same act, may be placed in an institution.

In summary, ". . . it appears that the retarded are more frequently represented among delinquent populations than typical groups but this representation may not be as significant as once was believed. It is probable that the relationship between intelligence and delinquency is "j" shaped in character. The group known as 'borderline normal' may comprise the most significant population among delinquents" (Blatt, 1958, p. 811 of *A.J.M.D.* article).

Implication

Mentally retarded children do not have to become delinquents; nor can we explain delinquency as a manifestation of the retardation. It is not surprising that some of these children become delinquents; it is amazing that more do not. Society must recognize the need for psychiatric and social services,

[2] The term "subcultural" may be an unfortunate selection of the author as it does, among some, imply a judgment that one particular culture is in some way superior to another. No such implication is intended and we, in fact, prefer the term "multicultural" (alluding to a different type rather than quality). However, for the purpose of less cumbersome communication we will use the more familiar term.

realistic education, and vocational counseling for all its citizens. More importantly, we must cease looking with derision at those in a different cultural milieu.

SUMMARIZING CONCLUSIONS

1. The large group of mentally retarded children presently classified "familial" should be assumed free of constitutional deficiencies or genetic aberrations that may result in inferior intellectual development.
2. A great many children presently classified as mentally retarded cannot be so classified using the conventional definition that requires constitutional defect.
3. There is impressive evidence that numerous children presently classified mentally retarded acquire this retardation some time after birth or early age.
4. There is impressive evidence that numerous children and adults originally classified as mentally retarded cannot be so classified on later evaluations.
5. There is impressive evidence that the role of cultural and psychological variables in the causation of mental retardation has been greatly underestimated.
6. There is little evidence to support the widespread practice of placing educable mentally retarded children in conventional special classes rather than in the regular grades or in some other, as yet unknown, more suitable classes.
7. There is a dearth of evidence supporting hereditary theories of mental retardation.
8. As a group, educable mentally retarded children are not significantly different in physical attributes from typical children.
9. There are low relationships, "j" shaped in character, between delinquency and intelligence.
10. Many present assumptions concerning the mentally retarded are unsubstantiated, are reinforced with prejudice, and flourish in an atmosphere of rigid and stereotyped thinking.

REFERENCES

Bennett, A., *A Comparative Study of Sub-normal Children in the Elementary Grades.* New York: Teachers College Press, Columbia University, Contributions to Education, 1932, 81 pp.

Blatt, B., *The Physical, Personality, and Academic Status of Children Who Are Mentally Retarded Attending Special Classes as Compared with Children*

Who Are Mentally Retarded Attending Regular Classes. Unpublished doctoral thesis, The Pennsylvania State University, University Park, Pennsylvania, 1956, 134 pp. (Also published as an article in the March 1958 issue of the *American Journal of Mental Deficiency.*)

Cowen, P. A., "Special Class vs. Grade Groups for Subnormal Pupils," *School and Society,* 1938, *48*:27–28.

Goldstein, I., "Implications of Mental Deficiency," *Occupational Education,* 1948, *5*: 149–172. (Also published in October 1948 issue of the *American Journal of Mental Deficiency.*)

Kirk, S. A., *Early Education of the Mentally Retarded.* Urbana: University of Illinois Press, 1958, 216 pp.

Kirk, S. A., "Experiments in the Early Training of the Mentally Retarded," *American Journal of Mental Deficiency,* 1952, *56*:692–700.

Pertsch, C. F., *A Comparative Study of the Progress of Subnormal Pupils in the Grades and in Special Classes.* New York: Teachers College Press, Columbia University, Contributions to Education, 1936, 101 pp.

Sarason, S. B., and Gladwin, T., "Psychological and Cultural Problems in Mental Subnormality: A Review of Research," *Genetic Psychology Monographs,* 1958, *57,* 289 pp. (Also published in monograph form in the May 1958 issue of the *American Journal of Mental Deficiency* and in the Basic Books edition of 1958, titled, *Mental Subnormality.* In addition, it is included in the 1959 edition of Sarason's *Psychological Problems in Mental Deficiency.*)

4 POVERTY, INTELLIGENCE, AND LIFE IN THE INNER CITY

Whitney M. Young, Jr.

Reprinted by permission from *Mental Retardation,* Vol. 7, No. 2, April 1969, pp. 24–29, a publication of the American Association on Mental Deficiency, and the author. Mr. Young is Executive Director, National Urban League, Chicago.

There is now ample documentary evidence to show that poverty—and the physical, intellectual, and emotional deprivations that go with it—can be a direct cause of mental retardation.

The poor of all races are affected and—in *absolute* numbers—there are more whites than Negroes who suffer from it. I am, however, particularly interested in this subject because the Negro poor are victimized by this alarming situation more than others, since, in *relative* numbers, there are far more poor Negroes than poor whites. Too many children, and all too frequently, Negro children, thus pay a heavy price for the injustices of our society.

We know today that only a few among all those who are mentally retarded suffer from an obvious organic defect with genetic cause. Genetic defects affect all levels of society in the same way, whether those afflicted are rich or poor, white or Negro. But it is quite different when damage to the brain is due *not* to a genetic cause but to disease before or after birth, or else to accident, infection, or poisoning. The *poor,* whether they are white or Negro, are more often its victims. And the mentally retarded who do *not* show any organic brain damage—those who are only *functionally* retarded—come predominantly from the poorer sections of our society. Functional retardation is very rare among those with high incomes and among well educated segments of the community. But it is very common—it can be detected in as many as 15 percent of all children—in deprived rural areas and in the chaos of the inner cities. This is now so well accepted that we have given the name of "socio-environmental retardation" to this kind of functional retardation prevalent among the deprived. More than half of all mentally retarded people fall into this last category.

What in fact are the environmental factors in the life of the poor that stunt their intellectual development?

To begin with, we are now convinced that intelligence itself is largely controlled by the kind of diet a child receives. Evidence was presented at a recent international conference that malnutrition in the first three years of life may permanently impair intelligence and it has been estimated that more than half of the 90 million babies born each year may run a risk of permanent retardation resulting from malnutrition. Moreover, experiments with several kinds of laboratory animals suggest that malnutrition at certain critical times during development of the brain—for the human species this would be about the time of birth—can cause long-term damage to brain structure and to the bodily functions it controls.

So, malnutrition among pregnant women as well as newborn children can be an important cause of mental retardation and is its *major* cause, on a worldwide basis.

In our own country, the Department of Agriculture found that in two Mississippi Delta counties 60 percent of children receive less than two-thirds of the minimum dietary allowance recommended by the National Research Council. Among the underprivileged children of our society in general, still other factors are at work, probably more often than simple malnutrition. There is a whole catalog of them—ranging from all those circumstances that threaten physical development to insidious but powerful psychological factors.

The children of poverty—those who inherit the circumstances rather than the genes that predispose to mental retardation—have to fight against heavy odds from the very moment they are conceived.

Their mothers—often undernourished themselves—are still victims of toxemia of pregnancy, as well as of infections and physical hardships that the more affluent do not encounter. Thirty percent of the women who live in poverty, either in rural areas or else in towns of over 100,000 people, never get medical supervision during their pregnancies. Among the 500,000 indigent women giving birth each year, 100,000 need special medical help for complications. Most of them never get it. For one thing they give birth to premature children three times more often than middle-class mothers, and it is well known that three-quarters of all premature children, weighing less than three pounds at birth, develop physical and mental defects.

Knowledge of family planning, as well as realization of the importance of medical attention during pregnancy, is still widely lacking among the poor. Moreover, they don't know how to use, or else, for many reasons, cannot avail themselves of the resources that provide such knowledge and services. So illegitimate births, as well as families which are too large, not only for the parents' income, but also for their emotional and physical resources, occur all too frequently.

Brain damage resulting from continuous low-level exposure to lead, to which the children of the poor are commonly exposed because of the cheap, lead-containing paints frequently used in the slums, occurs almost exclusively among the deprived. One study showed that as many as 5 percent of the children in slum areas had dangerous levels of lead in their bloodstreams.

In addition, infectious diseases are far more common among the poor: tuberculosis, for example, is three to five times more prevalent among them than among middle income or affluent groups. Crowded living conditions increase the incidence of several chronic and latent infections that have been suspected as a direct cause of mental defects in unborn babies when their mothers are exposed to such conditions during pregnancy. Childhood infections, some of which—such as measles—can cause brain damage, are more widely spread because too many children remain unvaccinated.

It has been reported, for example, that in New York, in 1961, 21 percent of children from families whose incomes were 3,000 dollars or less, have not received smallpox vaccinations; only 4 percent of children from families with incomes of nine thousand dollars and over remained unvaccinated. The corresponding figures for diphtheria–tetanus vaccination are 19 percent and 2 percent. "The situation is even worse in the small, minor income groups. In one of these groups (the second-lowest income) 31 percent of all students did not receive smallpox vaccinations, and 2.8 percent had no diptheria–tetanus shots."

So there are still children who have suffered brain damage, after catching whooping cough, although vaccination has been available for this disease for several decades!

Even accidents are more likely to happen to poor children, usually because they are inadequately supervised: in this country, one million children each year suffer head injuries—about eight out of each 1000 children between the ages of four to eighteen every year. Such injuries alone account for 10 percent of the institutionalized population.

All these physical and environmental causes of mental retardation—most of them *preventable*—account for more cases of brain damage in the total population than all the genetic causes lumped together.

And I have mentioned so far only grossly obvious, physically injurious factors.

Let us now consider some others, social and psychological factors that are themselves byproducts of the misery of the few and the prejudice of the many.

In poor households, many children are badly cared for and so are deprived of intellectual, sensorial and emotional stimulation.

There are many "unavailable mothers"—not only working mothers, but also those who are unable to supply the needs of their children because of difficulties of their own: they are *emotionally* unavailable. Among them are those who cannot arouse themselves sufficiently from their passivity or lethargy to show affection for their children. Others are deeply depressed or mentally ill and reject their children for any of a multitude of reasons.

As a result of this there is often no proper family structure; the home becomes disrupted and damaging to the child's character. Parents do not seek help and very often distrust the social institutions that can provide it.

Under such conditions, every individual has to use all his meager energies just to keep body and soul together. He has to fight all the time just to survive. Parents have neither the means nor the ability to provide their children with stimulating conversation, with books, music, travel, or the other intellectual and cultural advantages bestowed almost automatically on most children of the middle and upper income groups.

When a lack of motivation and opportunity for learning in early years are added to other adverse conditions such as poor diet, bad health habits and inadequate sanitation, lack of prenatal and postnatal care, emotional disorders, and crowded living conditions—it should come as no surprise that the result is often stunted intellectual development.

Children from families like these come to school for the first time without either the experience or the skills necessary for learning. They are backward in language and have no ability for the abstract thought necessary for reading, writing, and arithmetic. Their failure to learn becomes complicated by emotional disorders like frustration and anxiety.

And then, too, just being poor is a frightful stigma in this country—where accomplishment is largely measured by economic success.

Anyone who has watched poor children and their families in countries where poverty is the usual condition of humanity—in Africa, South America, and Asia—is aware that poverty by itself does not necessarily preclude warmth and communication within the family. But in countries where poverty is found side by side with affluence, a new condition exists. It has been aptly described by Oscar Lewis as the "culture of poverty," that appears in all large, poor communities isolated in the midst of general prosperity. It involves an attitude of lethargy and indifference, or sometimes strange forms of escapism and rebellion, that represent both a reaction to the stigma imposed by the affluent world and a defense against the poor opinion the underprivileged have of themselves. In Lewis' words, "the individual who grows up in this slum culture has a strong feeling of fatalism, helplessness, dependence and inferiority."

In the competitive and puritanical white society that prevails in this country, social and economic success have often become equated with goodness and, as a result, the unsuccessful and the economically weak have been regarded as inferior and bad. This belief was frankly and brutally expressed by a New Jersey farmer, who referred to the migrant workers on his land as "nothing . . . they never were nothing, they never will be nothing and you and me and God almighty ain't going to change them."

The tragedy is that the American dream, the myth of equal opportunity for all in this country, is so deeply ingrained, that even the unsuccessful often believe in it, and have therefore a painfully poor opinion of themselves.

So the world of the "culture of poverty" is a world that rejects our targets of success and social status, ethics, and social values not for intellectual reasons, but out of despair. Nevertheless, it is a world with its own rules, taboos, pride, and scale of values. This is a world we have to learn to understand with intelligence and compassion, with which we have to learn to communicate, and which we must convince, despite its skepticism and its suspicion, that our goals are worthwhile. We have to prevent its spread, because it breaks the human spirit and so becomes the breeding ground of retardation.

We, the Negroes, have suffered discrimination, abuse, and neglect for generations and we still live, by and large, a life isolated from the mainstream of society. Crowded into urban slums, pressured from all sides, poorly educated, and poorly equipped to compete, we are further demoralized by the indifference of the affluent society around us. So the poorer among us acquire the psychological characteristics of the slum culture. A chronically impoverished and humiliated population cannot respond to opportunity—the better opportunity recently offered by new legislation—as if poverty was a temporary accidental setback. The harm already done is too deep. It has long ago penetrated to the very souls of its victims.

By the time they reach school, poor Negro children already often possess built-in physical and psychological handicaps and in school, they are likely to face new obstacles which, although less obvious, may be just as harmful. What these obstacles are is best illustrated by an experiment of fundamental importance, recently carried out in California by Robert Rosenthal and Lenore Jacobson. To study the effect of teachers' attitudes on the performance of their pupils they chose a school with mixed Caucasian and Mexican children, picked out 20 percent of the children at random, and then told the teachers casually that these children were expected as a result of psychological tests to be "spurters"—that is, to make considerable progress during the next school year. Although these particular children did not receive special tutorial attention, and the curriculum of the school remained unchanged, their IQ—when tested a year later—had gone up remarkably. Those children whose IQ was the lowest to start with, made relatively the most progress. The children not designated originally as "spurters," on the other hand, showed much less progress. This was observed for many teachers, over several grades, as well as in classes designed specially for bright, average, and slow learners. Even more interesting, when the teachers were asked to evaluate their pupils' progress, they described the progress of "bright" children in very positive terms, like "outgoing, curious, sociable, interested, etc." But when they described progress made by an undesignated child, particularly one originally labeled "slow-learner," their evaluation had negative connotations.

What are the implications of this? Mainly that when a child is expected by his teacher to be slow, he conforms to expectations. When the teacher expects the child to be bright—even when he never tells him so and does not change his method of teaching—the child feels it and blooms. The California teachers were busily and, quite unconsciously engaged in fulfilling their own prophecies, communicating to the children, in quite subtle and unintended ways, expectations which, in fact, did influence the child's performance. Moreover, their evaluations expressed resentment towards pupils who made unexpected progress.

It cannot be doubted that similar insidious—even unconscious—prejudice is widespread. In a society where the poor are generally considered inferior beings, where the Negro's potential for intellectual development is still largely doubted, what expectations a middle-class teacher may have for her deprived Negro pupils can be easily guessed and—maybe—their effect can be measured by the thousands of dropouts, misfits and little rebels that our present school systems produce every year.

Considering all the injurious factors that oppress the poor and particularly poor Negroes, I submit that when we come across a disproportionate number of poor Negro children dropping out of school or sitting in classes for slow-learners or the retarded, there is no need to look for anything *intrinsically* wrong with the Negro people or "the Negro family."

The Negro has been studied, inspected, analyzed, and dissected ad infinitum. Thank you for so much attention. I am not against approaching the problem scientifically, nor do I want to discourage a substantial number of white scholars from an interesting academic exercise. But, in view of the conclusions reached by the President's Commission on Civil Disorders on the amount of white racism in this country, may I suggest that instead of more studies of the riots of black people, the anatomy of Watts, or the pathology of the Negro family, we should maybe start investigating the anatomy of Cicero, a city that can welcome Al Capone and reject Ralph Bunche; or the pathology of a Congress that widely applauds the President for saving the redwood trees, but sits on its hands when he talks of saving the lives of black people. Such new subjects of research could also provide some employment for Negroes, for who is better qualified than a former domestic to study white folks? I have always been told by white ladies how much they liked their Negro maids and how much they confide in them. Also who would know better the character of Congress than a former bellhop?

That much maligned Negro family has shown remarkable endurance. After being systematically broken during centuries of slavery, the mere number of Negroes in this country after 300 years of oppression, deprivation, and discrimination, testifies to a remarkable talent for survival.

As one further instance of strength within the Negro family, let me point out that Negro families tend to react far more sympathetically to the presence of a retarded child than do white families. A Michigan State University study shows that "in middle-class white families the consequences of having a child labeled retarded usually results in social isolation for the child, whereas, lower class Negro families seem to treat retarded children very much as they do other youngsters."

May I also point out that the higher rates of illegitimate births occurring among deprived Negroes is not evidence of the higher virtues of the white middle-class woman. It is due to the high cost of illegal, and the unavailability of, legal abortion; a 12-year study of therapeutic abortion in New York City from 1951 to 1962, reported that only 79 Puerto Ricans and 263 nonwhites had obtained legal hospital abortions. By comparison, legal, therapeutic abortions were performed on 4361 white women. On the other hand, it has been estimated that of all the maternal deaths caused by abortions performed by quacks and criminal abortionists in New York County, 50 percent were Negroes, 44 percent Puerto Ricans, and only 6 percent women from other groups. When Negro women find themselves bearing an unwanted child, not only are they more likely to carry their pregnancies to term, but they are also much more likely to keep their babies. They know that adoption for Negro babies is almost impossible, and abandoning the child would mean, for him, childhood in an institution or an orphanage. We need go no further than this to understand the greater proportion of unmarried mothers among Negro women.

Despite the realities of existence in the slums of our cities and in the dilapidated shacks of rural poor, many a "deprived" child is remarkably healthy and well equipped to cope with life. It may not be a reality we would wish on him, but it is *his reality*, and in relation to it, he often functions with an intelligence and a ready exercise of native wit that would leave the child of the white middle class, temporarily put in similar circumstances, hopelessly outclassed.

Insofar as the slum child is adapted to cope with a brutal world and has learned to survive in it, he is well adapted socially and is capable of intelligent behavior.

It is revealing that most of the deprived people who are labeled as retarded at some time in their lives, are usually recognized as such in the school situation. They are not "retarded" either before or after their school years, since they do not then fit the definition of retardation, which includes *both* a low intelligence quotient *and* a failure to adapt to social environment. *School* is the social environment they fail to adapt to. We are at last beginning to recognize that this is so because the attitudes and behavior required by the school, as well as the methods used for measuring what we call intelligence, are charged with cultural concepts foreign to the world of the deprived. Conventional aptitude and achievement tests, largely based on middle-class standards, concepts and experience, can be expected to, and we now know *do,* fail to measure accurately the potential aptitudes of slum children.

In simple terms, it is stupid to give a question on cable cars to a New York child (who will fail to understand it) and to one from San Francisco (who obviously knows the answer) and then conclude that the child from San Francisco is more intelligent. One researcher working with the children of the Negro poor found they usually gave an incorrect answer to the question "What is wrong?" when shown a picture of a house with broken windows. In the experience of these children broken windows are normal and it would have been unintelligent of them to have answered otherwise. In the course of testing a group of Negro children at the University of Pittsburgh, researchers asked them to color a picture of a banana. Every one of them colored it brown. None of them had ever seen a fresh banana, but they all knew the color of the bananas they had seen.

Testing materials based on a white middle-class environment, complete with trees, flowers, pets, parks, toys, and comfortable surroundings, are simply incomprehensible to deprived youngsters; yet the same children may be able to operate anything that moves and fix anything that breaks. That which a child has not touched, tasted, seen, heard, learned, or experienced, he simply does not know, whatever his intellectual potential.

It is important to bear in mind that the elusive quality *we* call intelligence is intimately related to the amount and quality of verbal ability and schooling. The slum child has little preschool exposure to informed talk, and the schooling he gets has little relevance to his world.

Extensive informal channels of learning, however, exist within the slums, and new tests could be devised that would reveal the truth about the intelligence and aptitudes of the slum child.

I wish you could have, as I often do, the experience of visiting a barber's shop in Harlem on a Saturday afternoon. There the barber shop is a real social institution; few people are interested only in having a haircut. In one corner a group debates philosophical questions, in another international affairs, a few play checkers; when I come in they all start telling me how to solve the race problem. One feels proud of the great natural wit and the intelligence of these men, and at the same time saddened and depressed by all this human potential that society has obviously failed to utilize. Because if you read the thoughts and the intentions behind the rustic vocabulary and the faulty grammar, you recognize the richness of the substance in their minds and of the feelings in their hearts. As an acquaintance of mine said about the importance of speaking correctly, "It is better to say 'I's rich' than 'I am poor!' "

The alarming thought that a large number of Negro children might be labeled as mentally retarded because of inappropriate intelligence testing methods is supported by a finding of a Michigan State University study; it showed that employability among Negro mentally retarded youngsters was much higher than among white mentally retarded youths. More than 70 percent of the Negroes were in the top employability group as compared to only 36 percent of white youngsters. It was calmly pointed out that the difference might be due to standardized intelligence tests which were acknowledged to be less accurate for Negro children than they were for middle-class white children. "Due to such inaccuracy" the study reported, "some of the Negroes in the study should not have been classified as mentally retarded."

I suppose one could take refuge in the position that "our mentally retarded are better than your mentally retarded" but, there being little merit in this kind of comfort, I would rather say that poor Negro children have enough handicaps already without being falsely labeled as retarded. Employability, and the fact that such individuals disappear into society—into *their* society—after they leave the school system, is the real proof, that they were—even if deficient in the school system—functionally adaptable to the society they came from and to which they returned as adults.

Let us now consider the condition of Negroes who are so retarded that their deficiencies require special care beyond the slow-learner classes.

Among the severely retarded, Negroes are underrepresented in institutions because all institutions have long waiting lists, and getting to the top of the list requires a spokesman—which the Negro seldom has. On the other hand, among the mildly retarded, who may be institutionalized because of mild delinquent behavior, the Negro is overrepresented. A white middle-class child, equally retarded and having committed the same offense, often remains with his family; while the Negro child, not having the same social protections, is apt to end up in an institution. Again the system works against him.

And does the proportion of Negroes in relation to whites in such community programs as day-care centers, sheltered workshops, etc., reflect the proportion of Negroes in need of them in the community? Possibly it does in some places, but in most places it does not. Negroes remain largely unreached by those offering the services they most urgently need. And those needs are desperate because the Negro's ability to cope economically with a retarded child at home is usually less than that of his white counterpart.

That Negroes are isolated from the services they need is not only—as often thought—due to their lack of awareness, or to their timidity and reluctance in asking for such services. A survey conducted by the President's Committee on Mental Retardation revealed that—essentially because local communities are required to provide matching funds in order to receive federal funds—95 percent of all institutions for the mentally retarded are built in middle or high income areas, often a long way from the inner cities that need them most. This geographic separation of services from the people who need them is of course basic to the problem of retardation among all the rural poor.

What can be done to prevent a tragic and costly waste of human potential?

In the order of their efficacy per cost, I will mention a number of preventive programs, either already in existence or else in the planning stage, that should be greatly expanded or established promptly so as to reach all of the poor:

1. Easily accessible community-centered *birth control clinics* whose staffs should not only be highly trained in the technicalities of birth control

but who should have respect for human dignity, privacy and freedom of conscience, are an important—maybe the most important—element in the prevention of mental retardation.

2. There is a crying need for *maternal and infant care centers* in the heart of areas inhabited by "high risk mothers." President Johnson's proposed Child Health Act of 1968 would assure medical supervision during pregnancy and delivery for indigent mothers and pediatric care for their children during their first year of life. Such centers could prevent most of the complications of pregnancy and delivery, and make it easier to treat those abnormalities that can be diagnosed early. Such centers would also improve the child rearing practices of indigent or ignorant mothers.
3. A *Head Start-type program* is needed to be combined with a comprehensive health care program, begun at an earlier age than at present, and sustained throughout the elementary school years; this would compensate for cultural deprivation in the home. It would also prevent the unjust classing of thousands of deprived youngsters as mentally retarded. Remedial education and health care, geared specifically to the needs of deprived children, is the only real way to break the vicious cycle of the culture of poverty.

   Whether IQ tests measure intelligence or not, it remains true that they do measure the capacity to operate within the present culture of most people in this country, where a certain capacity for abstract thought, communication through verbal expression with a certain accent, and writing using a certain vocabulary are necessary. It is therefore imperative for all children to learn such skills equally well and early in life, to make sure that they will be able first to cope with the demands of school and later to compete in the search for employment.

These three programs are measures that can save the next generation.

Since so much retardation is due to preventable disease or accident, health care for all must also have a high priority in any program for the prevention of retardation.

Although the Negroes' bad health is largely due to poverty, increasing the number of Negro doctors, psychiatrists, and health workers is probably the best way to correct its many deficiencies.

This is so because in most cities, the amount of health care available for Negroes is directly related to the number of Negro physicians. Every white doctor has 779 potential patients. In the Negro community, there is only one doctor for each 3745. At the time of the Watts riot in 1965, there were an overwhelming 4200 persons for every physician in the Watts area. In Boston, the new Columbia Point Housing Project area, serving over 5000 people, was not able, to start with, to attract a single doctor or dentist, Negro or white.

Largely owing to the lack of physicians in Negro communities, one third of all nonwhites' visits to physicians were to hospital clinics rather than to private doctors. Clinics in low income areas operate under overcrowded conditions and therefore on very impersonal terms. Many Negroes are suspicious of "charity medicine," which they feel quite correctly, as being operated less to serve the poor than the academic interest of medical practitioners. The result is that a disproportionate number of Negroes are suffering, even dying, from diseases the rest of the country conquered as long ago as the 1940s. By comparative standards, the relative health of the Negro continues to deteriorate all the time. Nonwhite maternal mortality, for example, was twice the white rate before World War II. Since then, it has grown to over four times the white rate, the latter having decreased in the interval.

Negro technicians, nurses, but above all physicians of all specialties, are needed. They will be the most effective, speedy, and willing messengers of modern medical service, to the Negro population. The American Association on Mental Deficiency, concerned as it must be with the alarming and shocking existence in this country of retardation due to socio-economic factors, should act on the pressing necessity of increasing the participation of Negroes in all phases and aspects of its activities for the retarded.

But don't forget that we can never eliminate the threat of retardation due to environmental deprivation unless the whole fabric that produces the "culture of poverty" is destroyed. Woven into it are overt and insidious discrimination, inferior education, poor nutrition and health care, substandard housing, unemployment, and underemployment. You are in a position to know how these can break the spirit of millions of human beings and make them feel faceless and nameless. Your responsibility therefore is also to work at changing that destructive environment.

Since the death of Martin Luther King, I have received thousands of telegrams, letters, and calls from white people expressing their sympathy, grief, embarrassment, and sorrow. Unless this grief and sympathy can be changed into tangible action, Martin Luther King will have died in vain. But you can do something tangible now, and need not miss your chance to show your humanity. This meeting will have been worthwhile only if it ends with strong resolutions followed by action on the part of each of you and of your organization. Your agencies and institutions should be looked at in terms of the composition of their board membership, their staffs, and their services. The best teaching is by example, not by exhortation alone. Moreover, for too long, your profession, like mine, has been more interested in methodology and technique than in its social impact. If the poor and the families of the mentally deficient are really going to believe the sincerity of our concern for them, we shall have to see that organizations like this one are on their side. The leaders in the movement to eradicate chronic injustice and poverty in this country, should be those people who have benefited the most from the American system. White Americans should stop riding on the moral coattails of the Negro; no longer should the burden of purifying America fall upon the victim; no longer should the patient be expected to be his own surgeon. I therefore insist that the most urgent need of America, in the striving for civil and economic justice for all, is for a tangible, visible commitment on the part of decent, responsible, white people. The responsibility of taking an outspoken, visible leadership in such a movement rests with the "elite" of our citizenry and of our institutions. Only this can justify their claim to high moral standing.

A Greek philosopher was once asked: "When shall we achieve justice in Athens?" To which he replied: "We shall achieve justice in Athens when those who are not wronged are more indignant than those who are." And so it must be in America.

DECLARATION OF GENERAL AND SPECIAL RIGHTS OF THE MENTALLY RETARDED

WHEREAS *the universal declaration of human rights, adopted by the United Nations, proclaims that all of the human family, without distinction of any kind, have equal and inalienable rights of human dignity and freedom;*

WHEREAS *the declaration of the rights of the child, adopted by the United Nations, proclaims the rights of the physically, mentally or socially handicapped child to special treatment, education, and care required by his particular condition.*

NOW THEREFORE

The International League of Societies for the Mentally Handicapped expresses the general and special rights of the mentally retarded as follows:

ARTICLE I. The mentally retarded person has the same basic rights as other citizens of the same country and same age.

ARTICLE II. The mentally retarded person has a right to proper medical care and physical restoration and to such education, training, habilitation, and guidance as will enable him to develop his ability and potential to the fullest possible extent, no matter how severe his degree of disability. No mentally handicapped person should be deprived of such services by reason of the costs involved.

ARTICLE III. The mentally retarded person has a right to economic security and to a decent standard of living. He has a right to productive work or to other meaningful occupation.

ARTICLE IV. The mentally retarded person has a right to live with his own family or with foster parents; to participate in all aspects of community life, and to be provided with appropriate leisure-time activities. If care in an institution becomes necessary it should be in surroundings and under circumstances as close to normal living as possible.

ARTICLE V. The mentally retarded person has a right to a qualified guardian when this is required to protect his personal well-being and interest. No person rendering direct services to the mentally retarded should also serve as his guardian.

ARTICLE VI. The mentally retarded person has a right to protection from exploitation, abuse and degrading treatment. If accused, he has a right to a fair trial with full recognition being given to his degree of responsibility.

ARTICLE VII. Some mentally retarded persons may be unable, due to the severity of their handicap, to exercise for themselves all of their rights in a meaningful way. For others, modification of some or all of these rights is appropriate. The procedure used for modification or denial of rights must contain proper legal safeguards against every form of abuse, must be based on an evaluation of the social capability of the mentally retarded person by qualified experts and must be subject to periodic reviews and to the right of appeal to higher authorities.

ABOVE ALL THE MENTALLY RETARDED PERSON HAS THE RIGHT TO RESPECT.

The International League of Societies for the Mentally Handicapped, October 24, 1968.

SECTION TWO

Assessment and Diagnosis of Mental Retardat

The need for efficient and reliable methods for assessing and diagnosing mental retardation is basic. This need can be met only if the purposes of these procedures are understood by all professional workers. Assessment and diagnosis lead to classification and hence make up the triad that will provide the foundation for: (1) prevention; (2) treatment, training, and education; and (3) research. Since assessment and diagnosis involve procuring information from all available sources, analyzing and interpreting these data, and determining the prognosis, a large variety of specialists are required to perform these tasks.

New information and techniques are improving both diagnostic and prognostic procedures. Assessment devices of every kind are being developed. New approaches in sociology, education, and psychology make the future look exceedingly bright. During this period of transition, there will obviously be many conflicting theoretical concepts, methods, and techniques. Time and patience are needed until there can be a crystallization of ideas.

A major improvement in the assessment process has been the development of comprehensive mental retardation and child development centers. These clinics were rare in the 1950s, but by 1970, more than 150 of these clinics had been opened.[1] The diagnostic clinic serves more than one purpose. It provides parental guidance, short-term treatment service, referral, and a central fixed point of reference for the retardate and his family.

Important developments have taken place in the field of psychological testing in the last few years. The ITPA (Illinois Test of Psycholinguistic

[1] Rudolf P. Hormuth, *Clinical Programs for Mentally Retarded Children: A Listing* (Washington, D.C.: Children's Bureau, 1966).

…bilities), the WPPSI (Wechsler Pre-School and Primary Scale of Intelligence Test), the Cain–Levine Social Competency Scale, and the Adaptive Behavior Scale [2] have all helped in refining the assessment process. There still has been little research done, nor are there any reliable projective techniques that have been found applicable for the mentally retarded. Sue Warren [3] has listed the "danger signs" that should be observed in determining when serious consideration should be given to psychological consultation and overall assessment. Warren's "danger signs" are:

Delayed Speech: No words by eighteen months; less than 100 words by thirty months; no phrases or simple sentences by thirty-six months. Speech which does not approximate adult distribution of parts of speech by age six.

Delayed Motor Development: Sits alone later than twelve months. Walks later than twenty-four months. Cannot hop by age four.

Delayed Psychomotor Development: Cannot pile five or six small blocks into a tower by age three. Cannot hold a pencil and "scribble" by age two, draw a circle spontaneously by age four, or a square by age six. Cannot write his name by age eight.

Delayed Development of "Common Sense": Does not "come in out of the rain," literally or figuratively, or show caution toward strangers by age five or six. Does not know enough to avoid common home dangers, such as matches or knives, by age four. Cannot get about immediate home neighborhood by age six. Cannot handle small amounts of money accurately by age eight. Is easily "conned" by others his own age or younger.

Delayed Academic Development: Cannot recognize most single letters of the alphabet by age seven. Cannot recognize single simple words by age eight. Does not understand concept of two objects by age four; ten objects by age seven.

The above bits of behavior are suggestive; they do not necessarily indicate *general* intellectual retardation. They do suggest that something is amiss and further professional investigation is needed.

The first reading in this section has been prepared by Stanley W. Wright and George Tarjan. They cover in great detail the whole gamut of medical and pediatric factors relating to mental retardation. This report is written very clearly but may require a medical dictionary at times. Do psychologists really assess or do they merely test children? Harold A. Delp discusses some of the problems encountered in psychological evaluation and makes a number of valuable suggestions. His article is supplemented by a table, devised by G. Orville Johnson and Rudolph J.

[2] Editor's note: For further information regarding test booklets and manual of instruction for the Adaptive Behavior Scale, contact the American Association on Mental Deficiency, 5201 Connecticut Avenue, N.W., Washington, D.C.

[3] Sue A. Warren, "Psychological Evaluation of the Mentally Retarded: A Review of Techniques," *Pediatric Clinics of North America, 15*:4 (November 1968), 953–954.

Capobianco, showing the applicability of various psychological tests for assessing the severely retarded. No evaluation of mentally retarded individuals would be complete without a determination of their social maturity. Such a measure is the Vineland Social Maturity Scale, developed by the late Edgar A. Doll and, along with the Binet and Wechsler tests of intelligence, a major contribution to psychometric and evaluative techniques. The scale is a developmental schedule for determining personal independence and responsibility. Through the kindness of Dr. Doll, a copy of the scale and information concerning its use are included here. In the fourth reading, Henry Leland describes the use of adaptive behavior as one of the diagnostic dimensions of mental retardation. It is suggested that the concept of adaptive behavior would be more useful if it could be tied more tightly to rehabilitation goals. A method of further separating the concept of measured intelligence is also proposed.

Diagnostic and assessment data are valuable only if they are reported and interpreted in a form which has real meaning for the practitioner who is in constant contact with the subject. In his second contribution to this volume, Harold A. Delp makes a fervent plea for the type of case reporting that will be meaningful to the personnel using it.

Not all retarded children are examined in special diagnostic clinics. The largest percentage of these youngsters fall into the educable retarded group and are identified and diagnosed by public school personnel. The Illinois State Department of Public Instruction has devised precise methods for the use of school psychologists in selecting and placing retarded children in special classes. This article, which can serve as a guide for all school systems, carefully outlines the step-by-step procedures in case evaluation. The article by George Tarjan, which discusses the role of the interdisciplinary team in case evaluation, ties together the other readings in this section.

5 MENTAL RETARDATION: A REVIEW FOR PEDIATRICIANS

Stanley W. Wright
George Tarjan

From *American Journal of Diseases of Children,* Vol. 105, May 1963, pp. 511–526. Dr. Wright is Professor of Pediatrics and Psychiatry, University of California Medical School, Los Angeles. Dr. Tarjan is Professor of Psychiatry, School of Medicine and School of Public Health at UCLA. He is also Program Director, Mental Retardation, Neuropsychiatric Institute at UCLA.

When mental retardation is suspected early during a child's life, it is the pediatrician who is usually confronted with the problems of diagnosis and the difficulties of parental counseling. Pediatricians are also assuming increasing responsibilities in community programs for retarded children. It is, therefore, timely to review current concepts in this field. In sequence, we will discuss definition and epidemiology, diagnosis, somatic problems, behavior and intelligence, management, community resources, family crises, and implications for prevention. Throughout we will focus attention on the practical, clinical issues.

DEFINITION AND EPIDEMIOLOGY

Mental retardation is a syndrome which can have a number of causes, producing a variety of symptoms and degrees of impairment. The most commonly used definition describes it as "subaverage general intellectual functioning which originates during the developmental period and is associated with impairment in adaptive behavior."[1] Impaired intelligence, delayed maturation, slowness in learning, and failure in social adjustment are the most common symptoms. The mentally retarded child falls in the lowest third percentile, both in his intelligence and in his ability to adapt to the daily demands of his environment.

The incidence rate for mental retardation, i.e., the number of new cases occurring per year per 100,000 population, is not available due primarily to difficulties in definition of the disorder. Such rates are available for some specific conditions, e.g., phenylketonuria, mongolism, Tay–Sachs disease, etc. The prevalence rate for mental retardation, i.e., number of patients present in a given population at a specific time per 100,000 individuals, is about 3 percent for children.[2]

[1] Second Edition of the Manual on Terminology and Classification in Mental Retardation, American Association on Mental Deficiency (A.A.M.D.), Monograph Supplement. *Amer. J. Ment. Defic.,* April 1961

[2] *New York State Department of Mental Hygiene: Technical Report of the Mental Health Research Unit,* New York, Syracuse University Press, 1955

The retarded population can be divided into two overlapping groups.[3] Group 1 constitutes about 85 percent–90 percent of the retarded population. The degree of retardation is mild, i.e., the IQ is usually above 50. The handicap is often suspected in the schools because of academic failure, or acting out behavior. The pediatrician, particularly the school physician, usually sees them through referral from teachers. Specific diagnoses in this group include "cultural–familial" and "psychogenic" mental retardation.[1] After testing, they are often placed in classes for the "educable retarded." On examination their appearance is usually normal; physical handicaps and congenital malformations are uncommon. Often they come from economically and socially depressed families; their parents' educational background is limited. Other members of the family may have subnormal intelligence or evidence of social inadequacy. Some minority groups are overrepresented. Few are ever institutionalized, and the majority remain within the community. After the school years, they form part of the semiskilled and unskilled occupational groups. Many achieve a relatively good adjustment, and their identity as a retarded individual is lost.[2]

The second group of patients represents about 10 percent–15 percent of the retarded population. The pediatrician is more familiar with these children. Specific diagnoses include mongolism, cranial anomalies, genetic defects, tumors, cerebral palsy, as well as the sequelae of traumata, infections, and neurotropic poisons. The intellectual deficit is moderate, severe, or profound. [The following classification of the degree of mental defect and corresponding IQs will be used: mild, IQ 50–70; moderate, IQ 35–49; severe, IQ 20–34; profound, IQ 1–19.[1]] The IQ is usually below 50. Organic components, malformations, physical handicaps of ambulation, arm and hand use, and sensory impairments are common.[4] Developmental milestones and habit training are grossly delayed. Behavior is consistent with the degree of mental defect. A trainable segment of this group, i.e., the moderately retarded, can benefit from special education programs, and some school systems provide classes for them. The family background is similar to that of the general population in terms of economic status, education, religion, etc.

In this review, the first group will be discussed as the mildly retarded and will be covered in more detail in later sections; the second as the moderately, severely, and profoundly retarded. Differences between these two groups in diagnosis, IQ, physical signs, family constellation, prognosis, and natural history have implications for daily practice. The mildly retarded outnumber the moderate, severe, and profound group by a factor of 10. How-

[3] G. Tarjan, et al.: Natural History of Mental Deficiency in a State Hospital: III. Selected Characteristics of First Admissions and Their Environment, *Amer. J. Dis. Child. 101*:195, 1961.

[4] G. Tarjan, et al.: The Natural History of Mental Deficiency in a State Hospital: II. Mentally Deficient Children Admitted to a State Hospital Prior to Their Sixth Birthday, *A.M.A. J. Dis. Child. 98*:370, 1959.

ever, the pediatrician will more often encounter children in the latter group because they are identified early, and they usually belong to the social classes that seek private pediatric care.

DIAGNOSIS

The diagnosis of mental retardation is established at different age levels depending upon the severity of the condition. Retardation which is apparent in the first two years of life is often of a severe or profound type, i.e., an IQ less than 35. In infancy, somatic signs of mongolism, hydrocephalus, microcephalus, grossly delayed motor development, or the presence of seizures will focus attention upon the infant's problems. When highly specific symptoms are not present, a diagnosis is often difficult to make on one examination, e.g., in infants with suspected birth anoxia or trauma, emotional deprivation, etc. On repeated studies increasing deviation from developmental norms will be found. A hasty diagnosis should be avoided. For example, Illingworth has described a small group of children who exhibited considerable delay in general maturation during the first years of life, but who were later found to be normal.[5]

During the preschool years, delay in walking, speech, and habit training and poor coordination will call attention to another group who may lack specific neurological findings. Such signs as simplicity of play, inability to use sentences, lack of imagination, and choice of younger playmates may be among the presenting complaints. The intellectual deficit is apt to be of moderate degree in this group, i.e., IQ 35–50.

During the school years, the mildly retarded, i.e., IQ 50–70, will come to attention. Their problems are academic incompetence, often combined with behavioral patterns of aggressiveness, withdrawal, or negativism. The child may succeed at a marginal level through the first several years. This group of patients is often referred to the pediatrician to determine the role of organic versus emotional factors.

SOMATIC ASPECTS

Selected somatic aspects, recently highlighted by research findings, will be briefly summarized, particularly as they relate to diagnosis, prognosis, treatment, and prevention.

CHROMOSOMAL DISORDERS [6]

Technical advances suggest that chromosomal studies on patients may be-

[5] R. S. Illingworth: Delayed Maturation in Development, *J. Pediat. 58*:761, 1961.

[6] K. Hirschhorn and H. L. Cooper: Chromosomal Aberrations in Human Disease: A Review of the Status of Cytogenetics in Medicine, *Amer. J. Med. 31*:442, 1961.

come a procedure available to the clinician within the next decade. The practical aspects as well as limitations of these techniques should be stressed. The procedure still demands considerable technical skill and is time-consuming. The number of diseases studied in which no chromosomal abnormalities have been found is imposing, and it is not recommended as a routine diagnostic measure. In certain situations, e.g., familial and doubtful instances of mongolism, it may prove of value.[7] The chromosomal disorders may be conveniently divided into those involving (1) autosomes, (2) sex chromosomes, or (3) both. The first two groups may be subdivided according to the presence of a numerical or structural abnormality, e.g., translocation, deletion, inversion, duplication, etc.

The most common clinical condition associated with a chromosomal anomaly is mongolism.[8] All patients are trisomic for chromosome No. 21, and the majority have 47 chromosomes. Less than 5 percent do not; these may have (1) double trisomy, i.e., both mongolism and Klinefelter's syndrome, chromosome count 48, 45A-XXY; (2) mosaicism, i.e., cell lines containing different chromosome numbers, e.g., 46 and 47; (3) 46 chromosomes with translocation, i.e., an exchange of chromosome segments between two nonhomologous chromosomes. The third subtype, i.e., translocation, has implications for genetic counseling. This form of mongolism, though clinically similar to the others, is unrelated to maternal age and shows a strong familial trend. The translocation is passed from a clinically normal parent with 45 chromosomes to the offspring and results in a "genetically unbalanced" individual with mongolism. The risk figure, estimated at one in three, may be modified by (1) the specific chromosomes involved in the translocation, and (2) the parent who carries the translocation.[9] Mongolism with typical trisomy, i.e., 47 chromosomes, can also recur, though here the risk appears to be dependent on maternal age. For mongolism in general, a recurrence rate of 1 to 2 percent has been suggested.[10]

Two other autosomal trisomic syndromes have been described and confirmed. These are the D (Nos. 13–15) and the 18 trisomy (Group E) syndromes, both associated with multiple congenital malformations and with increasing maternal age.[11,12] The number of trisomic conditions may be limited, since the presence of an additional larger autosome may prove

[7] C. H. Lee; W. Schmid, and P. M. Smith: Definitive Diagnosis of Mongolism in Newborn Infants by Chromosome Studies, *J.A.M.A. 178*:1030, 1961

[8] L. S. Penrose: Mongolism, *Brit. Med. Bull. 17*:184, 1961.

[9] J. L. Hamerton and A. G. Steinberg: Progeny of D/G Translocation Heterozygotes in Familial Down's Syndrome, *Lancet 1*:1408, 1962.

[10] C. O. Carter and K. A. Evans: Risk of Parents Who Have Had One Child with Down's Syndrome (Mongolism) Having Another Child Similarly Affected, *Lancet 2*:785, 1961.

[11] D. W. Smith; K. Patau, and E. Therman: Autosomal Trisomy Syndrome, *Lancet 2*:211, 1961.

[12] D. W. Smith, et al.: The No. 18 Trisomy Syndrome, *J. Pediat. 60*:513, 1962.

lethal. It is also unlikely that monosomy, involving an autosome, will be found, since the loss of genetic material, as well as the presence of lethal recessive genes on the one remaining autosome, would prove fatal.

Numerical abnormalities and mosaicism, as well as structural alterations of the X and Y chromosomes, have been described.[6] As will be seen in Table I, mental retardation is more frequently found with additional "X"

TABLE I Estimated Frequency of Sex Chromosome Abnormalities as Determined by Buccal Chromatin Pattern

			Frequency per 1000	
Sex	*Disorder*	*Sex Chromosome Complement*	AT BIRTH	IN INSTITUTIONS FOR MENTALLY RETARDED
Male	Klinefelter's syndrome	XXY	2.65	8.1*
Female	"Triple X" syndrome	XXX	0.8	4.5
Female	Turner's syndrome	XO	0.3	0.4

* If patients with XXXY, XXXXY are included with these, the frequency per 1000 in institutions is raised to 9.5/1000. Figures adapted from MacLean (Reference 13).

chromosomes and less so with deficiencies.[13] There is a significantly higher frequency of Klinefelter's syndrome among institutionalized patients. The "triple X" syndrome, identified by the presence of two chromatin bodies, is also more frequent among retarded females. These women show normal genital development, no malformations, may have normal menstrual histories, and several have had pregnancies resulting in normal children.[14] Females with gonadal dysgenesis, i.e., Turner's syndrome, chromosome count 45, 44A-XO, do not appear to have an increased incidence of mental handicap.

The frequency with which these abnormalities are found among retarded patients suggests that a buccal chromatin smear should be done routinely in any child with mental defect, particularly if combined with an anomaly of the genital system. Determination of the sex chromatin mass leads to an indirect assessment of the number of "X" chromosomes. The chromatin body is presumed to represent a heteropyknotic "X" chromosome. The total number of "X" chromosomes is equal to the number of chromatin bodies plus one.[15]

This brief summary has focused on practical aspects of the chromosome abnormalities. Academically, additional knowledge may be expected

[13] N. MacLean, et al.: A Survey of Sex-Chromosome Abnormalities among 4,514 Mental Defectives, *Lancet 1*:293, 1962.

[14] A. W. Johnston, et al.: The Triple-X Syndrome: Clinical, Pathological, and Chromosomal Studies in Three Mentally Retarded Cases, *Brit. Med. J. 2*:1046, 1961.

[15] B. Lennox: Indirect Assessment of Number of X Chromosomes in Man, Using Nuclear Sexing and Colour Vision, *Brit. Med. Bull. 17*:196, 1961.

on genetic linkages, control of biochemical reactions, and mechanisms of chromosome nondisjunction. In addition, studies on sex chromosome abnormalities may shed more light on the role of the X and Y chromosome in embryogenesis, sexual differentiation, and significance of the chromatin mass.

Biochemical Diseases

There are 25–30 rare, genetically determined biochemical disorders presently identified that are associated with mental defect.[16] They account for less than 3 percent of all instances of mental defect among institutionalized patients. For a few of these inborn errors, e.g., phenylketonuria, galactosemia, and "maple syrup" urine disease (one patient),[17] dietary therapy instituted at an early age is effective in the prevention of brain damage. Recently, hyperglycinemia,[18] histidinemia,[19] citrullinuria,[20] imidazolaciduria,[21] pyridoxine dependency,[22] and hyperprolinemia [23] have been added to the list. A possible disorder of fatty acid metabolism, the "sweaty feet" syndrome, is now under investigation.[24] Biochemical investigations of these "inborn errors of metabolism" have yielded considerable information on normal and abnormal metabolic pathways. For each, genetic counseling is of importance to the family.

The majority of these disorders are associated with autosomal recessive genes. Consanguineous marriages are frequent. About 25 percent of the siblings of an index patient are also affected. It is rare to find the disease in parents, aunts, uncles, or cousins. Sex-linked recessive genes are responsible for a few of these diseases, e.g., cerebro–ocular–renal disease, subtypes of vasopressin (Pitressin)-resistant diabetes insipidus, and gargoylism.

[16] S. W. Wright, et al.: Etiologic Factors in Mental Deficiency: Errors of Metabolism That May Lead to Mental Deficiency, *A.M.A. J. Dis. Child 95*:541, 1958.

[17] L. E. Holt, et al.: The Treatment of a Case of Maple Syrup Urine Disease, Abstract, *Fed. Proc. 19*:10, 1960.

[18] B. Childs, et al.: Idiopathic Hyperglycinemia and Hyperglycinuria: A New Disorder of Amino Acid Metabolism; I, *Pediatrics 27*:522, 1961.

[19] V. H. Auerbach, et al.: Histidinemia, *J. Pediat. 60*:487, 1962.

[20] W. C. McMurray, et al.: Citrullinuria—A New Amino Acid Associated with Mental Retardation, *Lancet 1*:138, 1962.

[21] S. P. Bessman and R. Baldwin: Imidazole Aminoaciduria in Cerebro-Macular Degeneration, *Science 135*:789, 1962.

[22] C. R. Scriver: Vitamin B_6-Dependency and Infantile Convulsions, *Pediatrics 26*:62, 1960.

[23] I. A. Schafer; C. R. Scriver, and M. L. Efron: Familial Hyperprolinemia, Cerebral Dysfunction and Renal Anomalies Occurring in a Family with Hereditary Nephropathy and Deafness, *New Engl. J. Med. 267*:51, 1962.

[24] J. B. Sidbury, Jr.; Harlan, W. R., and B. Wittels: Description of an Apparent Inborn Error of Short-Chain Fatty Acid Metabolism, presented at the Society of Pediatrics Research Meetings, Atlantic City, N.J., May, 1962.

Three of these disorders will be commented on briefly: phenylketonuria, galactosemia, and nonendemic familial cretinism. Once suspicion has been raised, there is urgency in diagnosis, since early recognition and treatment in these disorders may do much to prevent further brain damage.

Diagnosis of phenylketonuria is important in the newborn, the "well" infant, and the infant or child with a neurological disorder. In the newborn, suspicion of phenylketonuria is raised when there is already an affected sibling. The serum phenylalanine increases rapidly after milk feedings in the phenylketonuric infant. It is recommended that a serum phenylalanine be obtained after the fifth or sixth day of life. Phenylpyruvic acid may not be detected in the newborn's urine until as late as five weeks; hence, "diaper testing" is of very limited value in detection during the first month of life.[25]

The routine use of the ferric chloride "diaper test" or ferric-chloride-impregnated paper strips, "Phenistix," has been widely recommended for the general detection of phenylketonuria during early infancy and before the suspicion of mental retardation is raised. The few reports of "diaper" surveys among well infants indicate considerable difficulty in attaining complete coverage; more personnel time is involved than was anticipated, especially in follow-up studies on infants with false positive reactions.[26] As would be expected with a disease which has a frequency of one in 25,000, only rarely has a new patient been found. In known patients with phenylketonuria, it is not unusual to obtain a negative test on an occasional urine specimen. For this and other reasons it is our opinion that there is reason for caution in relying on the results of routine mass "diaper testing."

The pediatrician should test any infant or child in whom there is suspicion of a neurological disorder. Vomiting, irritability, eczema, seizures, and a peculiar odor to the urine are frequent early signs of phenylketonuria.[27] Final diagnosis is based on the elevated serum phenylalanine. The pediatrician should encourage detection of phenylketonuria in "high-risk" populations, i.e., institutions for the retarded, special education classes, cerebral palsy clinics and schools, etc. Identification of these families can result in intelligent genetic counseling and early detection of the disease in future infants.[28]

Guthrie has recently introduced an agar inhibition assay method for rapidly screening large numbers of patients for elevated serum phenyl-

[25] M. D. Armstrong, et al.: The Development of Biochemical Abnormalities in Phenylketonuric Infants, in *Chemical Pathology of the Nervous System,* New York, Pergamon Press, Inc., 1961.

[26] W. G. Harding and C. W. Shaddick: Phenylketonuria: A Pilot Screening Survey in London, *Med. Off. 106*:51, 1961.

[27] M. W. Partington: The Early Symptoms of Phenylketonuria, *Pediatrics 27*:465, 1961.

[28] R. W. Deisher, et al.: Phenylketonuric Families in Washington State, *Amer. J. Dis. Child. 103*:818, 1962.

alanine levels.[29] The method has been successful in detecting phenylketonuria among institutional populations. Its use in the newborn nursery for early detection remains to be evaluated.

The value of the low-phenylalanine diet in the treatment of phenylketonuria is well established. Knox reviewed 87 patients treated with the diet and found a significant correlation between age at onset of treatment and mental ability.[30] Beyond two to three years, little effect on mental ability can be anticipated. Although no final decision can be made as to length of treatment, Horner has reported three children who were taken off the diet at four to five years of age and in whom no deterioration in mental level has taken place.[31]

Galactosemia should be suspected in any infant with failure to thrive.[32] Cataracts, hepatomegaly, and jaundice may be present. Large amounts of reducing substances are found in the urine if the child is on a milk diet. The urine must be tested with an agent which will detect reducing substances, e.g., Clinitest tablets or Benedict's reagent. Glucose oxidase strips should be used only as a secondary test. Absolute diagnosis is based on the absence of the transferase enzyme in the red blood cells. Galactose tolerance tests may produce hypoglucosemia and should be avoided. Early treatment with the galactose-free diet has been very successful; minor degrees of retardation were only found when the affected children were compared to their normal siblings.

The nonendemic familial goitrous cretins represent a group of patients with genetically determined defects in thyroid synthesis. They comprise 5 percent to 10 percent of all patients with cretinism. Recognition is important because of the need for early treatment and because there is a one-quarter probability of the disorder occurring in future siblings. They can be distinguished from athyreotic cretinism by the finding of a normal or increased thyroidal I uptake.[33]

For the majority of the inborn errors, a clinical approach will be sufficient to suspect the presence of a biochemical abnormality. Further investigations may then be necessary to establish the diagnosis. Somatic signs may be present, e.g., the odor of the urine in phenylketonuria and "maple syrup" urine disease; seizures in hypoglycemia; the facial features of gargoylism, cretinism, and idiopathic hypercalcemia; the cherry red macula

[29] R. Guthrie: Blood Screening for Phenylketonuria, *J.A.M.A. 178*:863, 1961.

[30] W. E. Knox: Evaluation of Treatment of Phenylketonuria with Diets Low in Phenylalanine, *Pediatrics 26*:1, 1960.

[31] F. A. Horner, et al.: Termination of Dietary Treatment of Phenylketonuria, *New Engl. J. Med. 266*:79, 1962.

[32] G. N. Donnell; W. R. Bergren, and R. S. Cleland: Galactosemia, *Pediat. Clin. N. Amer. 7*:315, 1960.

[33] J. B. Stanbury; J. B. Wyngaarden, and D. S. Frederickson: *The Metabolic Basis of Inherited Disease,* New York, McGraw-Hill Book Co., Inc., 1960

in Tay–Sachs disease; the short stature, round faces, and stubby hands of pseudohypoparathyroidism; the cataracts in cerebro–ocular–renal disease. Examination of the urine is very important. The specific gravity is continually low in diabetes insipidus; proteinuria is present in cerebro–ocular–renal disease; a positive ferric chloride test is found in phenylketonuria, "maple syrup" urine disease, and histidinemia; large amounts of urinary reducing substances are present in galactosemia.

A few disorders are characterized by mental defect with a specific amino-aciduria, e.g., cystathioninuria,[33] argininosuccinic aciduria,[33] hyperglycinemia,[18] hyperprolinemia,[23] and citrullinuria.[20] In these, diagnosis would have to be established by paper chromatography of the urine for the specific substance.

Prematurity

Among premature infants, weighing less than 1500 gm. at birth, follow-up studies indicate a high percentage, 70 percent, with various physical and mental disorders, e.g., spastic diplegia, mental retardation, speech and hearing difficulties, visual disorders, and behavioral problems.[34,35] The specific role of socioeconomic class, prenatal and perinatal complications, and parental characteristics remains to be clarified.[36]

Three principles should be kept in mind: (1) Prematures may be more sensitive to the actions of medications, e.g., O_2, sulfa compounds, chloramphenicol, etc.; (2) because of the high frequency of physical and mental handicaps, the pediatrician should perform careful follow-up developmental examinations; (3) developmental age should be calculated, allowing for the shorter gestational period until the differences between birth age and developmental age become insignificant in calculation of the IQ. Excessive lag or failure to achieve a normal level suggests neurological damage.

Immunological Disorders

Erythroblastosis Fetalis: Early diagnosis and exchange transfusions will reduce to less than 1 percent frequency of kernicterus among infants with Rh or ABO incompatibility. The pediatrician should be present at the birth of every infant with potential erythroblastosis. He should be familiar with the prognostic value of serial hemoglobin and bilirubin determinations and have available the facilities for exchange transfusion. Jaundice within

[34] C. M. Drillien: A Longitudinal Study of the Growth and Development of Prematurely and Maturely Born Children: III. Mental Development, *Arch. Dis. Child.* *34*:37, 1959.

[35] H. Knobloch and B. Pasamanick: Mental Subnormality, *New Engl. J. Med.* *266*: 1045, 1092, 1155, 1962.

[36] G. Weiner: Psychologic Correlates of Premature Birth: A Review, *J. Nerv. Ment. Dis.* *134*:129, 1962.

the first 24 hours should be regarded as due to erythroblastosis until proved otherwise.

Erythroblastosis may serve as a model for diseases in which transfer of antibody from the mother to the fetus may lead to fetal damage. Maternal antithyroid antibodies have been identified in the serum of newborns with athyrotic cretinism.[37] Although their significance and the mechanisms by which they are formed are not known, further studies of these cellular immune reactions may have important implications in the field of mental defect.[38]

Intrauterine Growth Retardation

The Postmaturity and Dysmaturity Syndromes: Studies are not available on the ultimate prognoses in these ill-defined syndromes, and the pediatrician should be aware of the need for careful follow-up studies. Infants with intrauterine growth retardation have birth weights less than 2000 gm. (4 lb. 7 oz.) and a gestation of at least 36 weeks.[39] Clinically, these patients range from "extreme microcephaly with dwarfism and mental defect," to "mild growth deficiencies with eventual favorable mental and physical development." Cardiovascular, skeletal, ocular, and renal defects were frequent. No common etiologic factor could be determined.

The postmature infant has a gestation of 42 weeks or longer. His appearance and development are more mature than a term infant. The weight and length may be increased.[40] The dysmature infant usually has an increased gestation time; he shows evidence of wasting, respiratory distress, neurological signs, and an increased neonatal mortality.[41]

Cardiac Arrest

Pediatricians are seeing an increasing number of children with severe neurological sequelae following cardiac arrest. Some have occurred during minor and elective surgical procedures, e.g., tonsillectomy, umbilical hernia, dental surgery, etc. Such catastrophic events should make the pediatrician cautious when evaluating the indications for surgical procedures.

Pharmacology of the Newborn

The pediatrician should be acutely aware that the fetus, premature, and full-term infant react differently to drugs as compared to the reactions of chil-

[37] R. M. Blizzard, et al.: Maternal Autoimmunization to Thyroid as a Probable Cause of Athyrotic Cretinism, *New Engl. J. Med. 263*:327, 1960.

[38] R. J. Blattner: Homologous Disease: Autoimmunization, *J. Pediat. 60*:154, 1962.

[39] J. Warkany; B. B. Monroe, and B. S. Sutherland: Intrauterine Growth Retardation, *Amer. J. Dis. Child 102*:249, 1961

[40] S. H. Clifford: Postmaturity, *Advance. Pediat. 9*:13, 1957.

[41] S. Sjöstedt; G. Engleson, and G. Rooth: Dysmaturity, *Arch. Dis. Child. 33*:123, 1958.

dren.[42,43] A summary of relevant and frequently used drugs and their more important effects on the fetus, premature, and newborn is given in Table II.

As can be seen in Table II, metabolic, hematological, hormonal, or neurological disturbances are common. Overdosage is the most frequent cause of toxicity. Little is known of the processes of biochemical maturation in the brain of the fetus and the newborn. The vulnerability of this system to the actions of certain drugs is established, e.g., kernicterus related to sulfa compounds. Less obvious neurological sequelae may follow exposure to drugs causing respiratory depression and cyanosis, or drugs which may interfere with normal enzyme activity through competitive inhibition, or alter the permeability of the blood-brain barrier.

INFECTIONS

Rubella, herpes simplex, and toxoplasmosis, acting during fetal life, will cause severe mental defects.[44] Syphilis is no longer a major cause. Weller and Hanshaw have recently reported on 17 patients with cytomegalic inclusion disease. Thirteen were mentally defective: Microcephaly, chorioretinitis, and cerebral calcifications were frequent.[45] Possibly any severe viral

TABLE II Summary of Commonly Used Drugs Which May Affect the Fetus and Newborn

Drug	*Abnormality*
A. Fetus	
Aminopterin (4-aminopterolyglutamic acid)	Multiple congenital malformations
Progestins	Masculinization
Testosterone	Masculinization
Thalidomide	Amelia, phocomelia, other malformations
Thiouracil, iodides, I^{131}	Goiter
B. Newborn (full-term and prematures)	
Oxygen (prematures only)	Retrolental fibroplasia
Chloramphenicol	Gray cyanosis, flaccidity, cardiovascular collapse
Sulfisoxazole diethanolamine* (Gantrisin)	Kernicterus
Vitamin K (synthetic)†	Hemolysis, hyperbilirubinemia
Reserpine (Serpasil)†	Severe nasal congestion
Opiates**	Respiratory depression
Novobiocin	Hepatic toxicity: hyperbilirubinemia

* It is postulated that other long-acting sulfa drugs, e.g., sulfamethoxypyridazine (Kynex), sulfadimethoxine (Madribon), may also cause toxicity.

† Vitamin K, reserpine, and opiates cause damage to the fetus when given to the mother.

[42] M. G. Wilson: The Effect of Maternal Medications upon the Fetus and the Newborn Infant, *Amer. J. Obstet. Gynec. 83*:818, 1962.

[43] W. L. Nyhan: Toxicity of Drugs in the Neonatal Period, *J. Pediat. 59*:1, 1961.

[44] H. F. Eichenwald and H. R. Shinefield: Viral Infections of the Fetus and of the Premature and Newborn Infant, *Advance. Pediat. 12*:249, 1962.

[45] T. H. Weller and J. B. Hanshaw: Virologic and Clinical Observations on Cytomegalic Inclusion Disease, *New Engl. J. Med. 266*:1233, 1962.

infection occurring in the first eight weeks of pregnancy may seriously injure the fetus. It is speculative to suggest that viral infections occurring later in pregnancy may have more subtle effects and produce varying degrees of mental impairment.

Postnatally, the bacterial meningitides, e.g., Escherichia coli, Hemophilus influenzae with chronic subdural effusion, Mycobacterium tuberculosis, may be followed by permanent neurological sequelae. Chronic encephalopathies which follow routine immunizations, viral encephalitides, prolonged seizures during acute infections, e.g., roseola, continue to be reported.

For the pediatrician there are the implications here for prevention: The need for a vaccine against rubella; the use of measles vaccine; early recognition and prompt treatment of the bacterial meningitides; tuberculosis control.

Perinatal Traumata

Knobloch and Pasamanick, in a series of retrospective studies, found a higher incidence of complications of pregnancy among mentally defective children as compared to a control series.[35] "Chronic prenatal anoxia-producing complications, primarily bleeding and toxemia" together with premature birth resulted in a significant number of children with cerebral palsy, epilepsy, and mental retardation. In the absence of prematurity, minor degrees of cerebral damage including "behavioral and specific learning disabilities" were present. Mechanical injuries at birth, e.g., cord prolapse, malpresentations, mid and high forceps, etc., were of little or no significance. These studies, as well as those of others, suggest that pre- and perinatal factors which produce anoxia and fetal distress are of more importance than mechanical birth injury in relation to postnatal neurological sequelae. Prospective studies now being carried out in the Child Development Study, sponsored by the National Institutes of Health, may give valuable information on these problems.

BEHAVIOR AND INTELLIGENCE

Behavior has many components. In the mentally retarded, intelligence is the most important aspect of this complex phenomenon. It is age-related and has different prognostic values in the newborn, the infant, child, adolescent, and adult. Intelligence is difficult to measure because of the numerous factors which contribute to it. In general it is the power to conceptualize, to take past experiences and use them to solve a new problem. At the highest levels, intelligence is the measure of one's ability to grasp the symbolic meaning of science, language, and arts and to use these in a constructive manner.

Judgments about children are made by comparing them with their

TABLE III Psychological Tests Commonly Used with Mentally Retarded Children

Measures of Intelligence

TEST	USEFUL MENTAL AGE (MA) RANGE	COMMENT
Ammons Picture Vocabulary Test	2 yr.–adulthood	Nonverbal
Columbia Mental Maturity Scale	3–12 yr.	Nonverbal; suitable for cerebral palsied
Draw-a-Man (Goodenough)	3–13 yr.	Nonverbal, requires motor coordination
Gesell Developmental Schedules	4 wk.–6 yr.	Motor, language, adaptive, social behavior
Cattell Infant Intelligence Scale	3 mo.–30 mo.	Extension of Stanford–Binet to infancy
Kuhlmann–Binet Infant Scale	Birth–2 yr.	Extension of Binet Scale to birth
Kuhlmann Tests of Mental Development	4 mo.–adulthood	Scaled test with few items at each age group
Leiter International Performance Scale	2 yr.–adulthood	Nonverbal; suitable for deaf, speech handicapped
Merrill–Palmer Scale of Mental Tests	18 mo.–6 yr.	Performance test
Minnesota Preschool Scale	18 mo.–6 yr.	Verbal and nonverbal test
Peabody Picture Vocabulary Test	2½ yr.–adulthood	Nonverbal test
Point Scale of Performance Test (Arthur)	5–15 yr.	Nonverbal; requires motor coordination
Porteus Maze Test	3 yr.–adulthood	Nonverbal; requires motor coordination
Stanford–Binet Intelligence Scale	2 yr.–adulthood	Verbal and nonverbal skills (IQ)
Wechsler Intelligence Scale for Children	5–15 yr.	Verbal and performance quotients (VQ, PQ)
Van Alstyne Picture Vocabulary Test	2–7 yr.	Nonverbal test

Measures of Emotional and Social Behavior

TEST	COMMENT
Blacky Pictures	Personality
Children's Apperception Test	Personality
Draw-a-Person (Machover)	Personality
MAPS Test	Personality
Rorschach	Personality
Vineland Social Maturity Scale	Social competence (SQ)
Visual-Motor Gestalt Test (Bender)	Perceptual-motor organization

peers. Tests of intelligence, development, and social maturity are based on this approach. The intelligence quotient (IQ) is a numerical expression of this comparison. This quotient can only be a measure of performance present at a specific age. In infants, neuromuscular development, verbal, social, and adaptive abilities can be measured; later, competence in symbolic communication and abstractions can be evaluated.

There are many tests of intelligence depending on the age of the child, estimated mental age, and information desired. The pediatrician is advised to familiarize himself with the type of tests that are given to children and to understand their implications. A list of commonly employed tests is given in Table III. It should be apparent that, before testing, the pediatrician should inform the psychologist of the child's neurological and sensory handicaps, e.g., speech, vision, hearing, etc.

The pediatrician must fit the results of the tests to his observations and to the age of the child. In normal children less than two years of age, the prognostic value of developmental tests is limited. Predictive value may be better for mentally retarded infants.[46] The tests have maximal value during childhood years in predicting academic competence. Nevertheless, the physician must be aware that intellectual ability does not always correlate accurately with social competence, memory, learning abilities, and other aspects of human behavior upon which society places definite values. A retarded child may show social competence, or incompetence, out of proportion to his IQ. Many retarded children have relatively good memories, but perform poorly on other tests. Moderately and severely retarded individuals can learn many activities by rote memory, particularly those which have a well defined goal, are repetitive in character, and require little in the way of individual decision. Studies in England indicate that the moderately retarded have greater potential for learning than previously realized.[47]

In the severely retarded child, behavior is usually consistent with the mental age. There is uniform depression in motor development, speech patterns, and adaptive and social behavior. In the child with severe neuromuscular handicaps, e.g., cerebral palsy, careful attention must be paid to the physical handicaps which may interfere with test performance. Special tests may be needed, e.g., the Leiter Non-Verbal Scale, the Columbia Mental Maturity Scale (Table III).

The mildly retarded child is identified at a later age, and behavioral problems are frequently the presenting complaint. Failure to learn is often associated with various forms of acting out behavior, e.g., laziness, indolence, hyperactivity, aggressiveness, etc. In the adolescent, delinquent behavior may occur, e.g., infractions against persons, morals, and property. Their behavior is related to a need for self-identification and represents an expression of hostility and frustration towards a society that is making increasing demands upon their limited abilities. Academic, social, and, in boys, athletic failures are common.

In this group, careful psychological tests are often necessary to define a degree of retardation that may not be evident on clinical examination. The diagnosis of organic versus emotional problems may be raised. It is precisely in these patients that such tests will often give the physician clues

[46] A. H. Parmelee, Jr.: Personal communication to the authors.

[47] A. D. B. Clarke: Constructing Assets in the Severely Retarded, *Lancet 1*:40, 1962.

which may be helpful towards diagnosis, counseling the family, and establishing treatment programs. Unfortunately, few communities have facilities and personnel for handling this large group of patients.

The prognosis for the mildly retarded individual is not necessarily a pessimistic one.[48] Many achieve a more satisfactory adjustment after the school years when their need for academic competence is greatly lessened. With maturity they develop more socially acceptable behavior. Their prognosis is considerably improved if they can find a job in the semiskilled and unskilled labor market and demonstrate their ability to earn an income. Such traits as dependability, honesty, and willingness are valuable assets in holding a job. Girls frequently marry; domestic tasks, a family, and a limited sphere of social activity act to mask safely their retardation.

MANAGEMENT

In the overall management, the pediatrician should be guided by the following two points: (1) the maintenance of close interpersonal relationships between the family and the child, and (2) the recognition of the child's responsiveness to sensory stimuli. Vision, hearing, and tactile sensation may be remarkably acute in many retarded children, and stimulation in these areas may be used to advantage for training. A survey of the child's hearing and vision may be desirable in order to improve prognostic estimates.

Systematic habit training has much to offer the child with multiple handicaps. Repetition is important. Each step must be very slow, and the parents should be apprised of this before training is started. The child learns much by mimicry and practice, e.g., dressing, buttoning, feeding, brushing his teeth, etc. Specific problems should be handled in a direct manner and management scaled to the child's ability. Walker, bars, etc., can be used to teach ambulation. Toilet training is best accomplished by taking the child at specific intervals. The pediatrician, however, should also be alert to situations in which the parents, through their oversolicitousness and concern for the child, inadvertently impede natural progress.

The retarded child and his family have many problems. A few that pertain specifically to the child will be presented here; others are discussed later under "Family Crises."

Multiple Handicaps

Multiple physical handicaps are frequent in the severely retarded, e.g., in speech, gait, arm–hand use, vision, and hearing. Other common problems are slowness in habit training, sleeping difficulties, feeding problems, con-

[48] C. D. Windle: Prognosis of Mental Subnormals, Monograph Supplement, *Amer. J. Ment. Defic. 66*:1, 1962.

stipation, seizures, etc. The earlier the handicaps are noted, the less likely is there expectation for spontaneous improvement. The retarded child who by four years of age cannot walk, shows no arm and hand use, is not toilet-trained, and does not speak has a less than 50 percent likelihood to show improvement in these areas with increasing age. If these handicaps have not been overcome by eight years, there is very little chance for further improvement.[49] The development of more intensive treatment methods may alter these figures.[47]

In addition to age, intelligence quotients can also be helpful in evaluating prognosis in the multiple-handicapped group.[49] Children with quotients above 20 can usually be expected to show improvement in ambulation, arm–hand use, speech, and toilet-training. Specific defects such as cataracts, deafness, or spasticity may interfere selectively with progress in these areas. Children with true microcephaly and quotients below 20 frequently learn to ambulate, feed themselves, and can be toilet-trained. Patients with hydrocephalus and a myelomeningocele will develop speech and arm–hand use, but ambulation and toileting will remain as serious handicaps.

Speech Problems

The most common handicap of the retarded child is speech and communication.[3,49] This leads to serious difficulties in the child's relationships with his parents, teachers, and peers. It impedes his ability to be taught, to learn, and to communicate. Speech defects are usually better tolerated in young children than in adolescents. The pediatrician should be alerted to the need for trial speech therapy when the level of speech development lags behind mental age. Treatment should be initiated early, as the child will become increasingly isolated from society. The physician should indicate to the therapist the child's intelligence and neurological and behavioral handicaps. Together with his own findings, this will enable the therapist to develop definite programs. In general, the outcome of therapy will depend on the child's handicaps. It may range from learning to use simple signs, or pronunciation of a few words, to speech commensurate with IQ.

Sexual Behavior

A frequent problem is concern about sexual misbehavior. The following brief summary may help the pediatrician in counseling parents. In the moderately and severely defective patient, sexual drive is quite limited; interest is minimal and few problems develop. There is frequently failure in this group to understand the complexities of sex, i.e., what society considers to be "public" versus "private." These difficulties are best prevented by measures started at earlier ages, e.g., proper discipline, the setting of limits,

[49] G. Tarjan; H. F. Dingman, and C. R. Miller: Statistical Expectations of Selected Handicaps in the Mentally Retarded, *Amer. J. Ment. Defic.* 65:335, 1960.

and avoidance of sexually stimulating situations. "Yes" or "no" has a clearer meaning than complex explanations. Once stimulated, their lack of judgment may lead them to assume a more active role.

Parental concern over masturbation in the severely retarded poses a major problem in counseling. Structured activities and mild sedatives may offer some help. In the mildly retarded, parents may express fear about its occurrence. Again, reassurance and provision for structured activities are reasonable suggestions.

In the mildly retarded, there is normal sexual drive. Problems are created by lack of judgment and inability to control their sexual feelings. Parents more often express towards daughters a fear of sexual delinquency, though often there is no specific information of such behavior. The avoidance of situations which are sexually stimulating, the use of simple explanations, parental supervision commensurate with the child's mental abilities, structured activities, and a healthy home environment will do much to prevent these problems from developing.

Sterilization [50]

Sterilization has no relevance to the severely retarded child. Their activities are limited, and they are almost always under close surveillance. In the mildly retarded, the issue is more complicated. Eugenic implications apply to a few specific disorders, e.g., dominantly inherited conditions such as tuberous sclerosis, neurofibromatosis, etc. Generally the issue is concern over illegitimacy or competency for parenthood. In these instances, the pediatrician's judgment must be guided by the specific statutes of his state and by his own and the family's religious and philosophical convictions. Even when sterilization appears indicated, the procedure may be difficult to obtain in private practice. Studies carried out in institutions indicate that sterilized patients have strong and lasting feelings regarding this procedure and that, when these were in a negative direction, they seriously hindered their adjustment following discharge.[51]

Medical Management

Despite extravagant claims, drug therapy in the retarded has been of limited value, unless given for a specific symptom, e.g., seizures. Tranquilizers and energizers may occasionally be useful for relief of tension, anxiety, and hyperactivity, but are of no value for general use. Drugs have not been useful in improving IQ, speech, and learning patterns.

[50] Reappraisal of Eugenic Sterilization Laws, Medicine and the Law, *J.A.M.A. 173*: 1245, 1960.

[51] G. Sabagh and R. B. Edgerton: *Sterilized Mental Defectives Look at Eugenic Sterilization, Eugenics Quart.*, to be published.

COMMUNITY RESOURCES

The pediatrician should be aware of his community facilities for the care, training, and education of the retarded. Knowledge of their functions is essential to a proper referral.

Schools

Normal education has as its purpose the teaching of an individual to live independently in a manner consistent with his maturity. Training and education are an important part in the maturation of the retarded child. For many moderately and severely retarded children, the school can only prepare him for a semi-independent or dependent life within a sheltered environment. Programs for these children are oriented towards training, e.g., personal care, craft work, play activities, simple reading and writing skills. Little emphasis is placed on educational materials. These programs should begin in the preschool years. Some nursery schools will accept retarded children, and parent groups have also established cooperative programs. Between five and eight years, the pediatrician will be concerned with the problem of admission to a public school. He must be familiar with local classes for special education. Many communities provide classes for the educable (IQ 50–70) and trainable children (IQ 25–50); others only for the educable; some for none.

The pediatrician must help the parents to estimate their child's abilities and what may be anticipated from schooling. Children graduating from programs for the educable may achieve a substantial degree of independence. This outcome is unlikely with the trainable child, and long-term goals should be set. Parents often have unrealistic expectations about their child, and the pediatrician can assist them in understanding that the child will be best in a program designed to fit his capabilities.

Placement

Foster homes or private boarding homes are often necessary as an initial step in placement. Even for minimally adequate care the expense is considerable. In many states, these homes are not licensed and are poorly supervised. Many operate on a custodial basis and offer either limited or no training programs. The pediatrician who refers a child to a private boarding home should know something of the type of care, attitude of personnel, school programs, etc., so that he can discuss these with the parents. He should inform the caretaker of the child's problems as well as the attitudes of the parents toward placement. Close cooperation between the pediatrician and the caretaker can do much to reduce the family crisis that occurs when a child is placed.

State hospital facilities vary considerably from those with good medical, training, rehabilitation, educational, and recreational programs to those that are primarily custodial. Changing attitudes of the public, assistance from parent groups, and acquisition of trained professional personnel have done much to improve and develop both service and research programs in the state hospitals. Again the pediatrician is advised to acquire some knowledge of his state's hospital system and its facilities, so that he can discuss these with the parents. Information is available which indicates the relationship of such variables as age, diagnosis, and IQ at time of admission to the probabilities for release, retention, or death following admission.[3,4,52,53]

Work Programs

Productive work during adulthood is a significant aspect in the life of the retarded individual. In some states there are programs available through vocational rehabilitation. The mildly retarded person can obtain help through these agencies in preparing himself for competitive employment. Unfortunately, there are few such programs for the moderately and severely retarded, i.e., sheltered workshops, in which these persons may be semigainfully employed over many years.

Parent Organizations

The parent organizations have played an important role in improving the relationship between the community, the family, and the pediatrician. Depending upon their size, initiative, and financial support, they have established schools, diagnostic facilities, counseling and guidance services, day-care centers, baby-sitting arrangements, sheltered workshops, recreational projects, summer camps, and placement programs. They are serving a useful purpose in educating the community to the problems of retardation. Some have cooperated with educational facilities, in training programs for teachers, social workers, and nurses.

The pediatrician should encourage families to participate in these organizations. The parents can obtain much help, particularly from other families with similar problems. The counseling and guidance programs may give the parents considerable support and assist them in coping with practical everyday problems.

The pediatrician should participate in and support these organizations. He can play a valuable role in helping them to develop community projects, advising on health programs, assisting in diagnostic clinics, etc. Unfortunately, few pediatricians have seen the importance of their role in these programs.

[52] G. Tarjan, et al.: The Natural History of Mental Deficiency in a State Hospital: I. Probabilities of Release and Death by Age, Intelligence Quotient, and Diagnosis, *Amer. J. Dis. Child. 96*:64, 1958.

[53] S. W. Wright; M. Valente, and G. Tarjan: Medical Problems on a Ward of a Hospital for the Mentally Retarded, *Amer. J. Dis. Child. 104*:142, 1962.

FAMILY CRISES

Crises occur frequently in the families of retarded individuals. The pediatrician should know how to cope with these and how, when possible, to prevent them. The causes of parental dissatisfactions, tensions, and anxieties have recently been reviewed in this journal by Bryant and Hirschberg.[54] A few such situations are as follows: (1) suspicion of diagnosis, (2) actual diagnosis, (3) resultant guilt and hostility, (4) hopelessness, (5) acute illnesses, (6) general family crises, e.g., succeeding pregnancies, moving, etc., (7) schooling, (8) neighborhood rejection, (9) sibling relationship, (10) sexual problems with puberty, (11) vocational adjustments, (12) marriage, (13) placement, and (14) separation following placement.

Before discussing several of these, it is well to point out that the physician often faces crises within himself. These may develop in him because of his past experiences with retarded children, his attitudes toward social incompetency, his difficulties in making value judgments, the parents' questions, etc. Frequently he may resort to defensive mechanisms such as avoiding the diagnosis, reassuring the parents, making dogmatic statements, e.g., a "mongoloid child should not be seen by the mother," etc. Most crises on the part of the parents and the physician can be resolved with time and proper understanding.

A common crisis occurs immediately after the birth of a mongoloid infant. Two decisions confront the pediatrician: what to tell the parents, and should he recommend home care or placement. In answer to the first question, the diagnosis should be confirmed by at least one consultant. After confirmation, both parents should be told at the same time. The diagnosis and prognosis should be presented first. The discussion of placement versus home care can be postponed for a day or so. These may have to be discussed several times before the parents can objectively participate in future planning. Recent articles have suggested that the mongoloid infant shows greater improvement in motor and mental development when reared at home as compared to similar infants who are placed out of the home shortly after birth.[55,56] Several difficulties in these studies have been pointed out, e.g., sample selection, small differences between groups, etc.

The actual decision will depend on the pediatrician's own personal feelings, as well as on the parents' being financially able to make the choice of placement or home care. Professional people, and those with moderate

[54] K. N. Bryant and J. C. Hirschberg: Helping the Parents of a Retarded Child, *Amer. J. Dis. Child. 102*:52, 1961.

[55] S. A. Centerwall and W. R. Centerwall: A Study of Children with Mongolism Reared in the Home Compared to Those Reared Away from Home, *Pediatrics 25*: 678, 1960.

[56] R. B. Kugel and D. Reque: A Comparison of Mongoloid Children, *J.A.M.A. 175*: 959, 1961.

to large incomes, usually make the choice of placement in spite of recommendations to the contrary. Families with less means and different value judgments about intellectual inadequacy will keep the child at home. The oriental, Mexican-American, and Negro families rarely place at birth.

Another crisis which may occasionally confront the pediatrician arises in the preschool child with a mental defect that is not recognized by the parent. In this instance the physician should be cautious in directing questions toward the retardation; several visits may be necessary to determine how much the parents really understand. The reasons for diagnostic studies should be made clear. Consultation may be necessary; the consultant, as well as the family, should know why he is seeing the child. The diagnosis and discussion with the parents is the responsibility of the pediatrician and should not be delegated to the consultant.

In spite of all these measures, many families cannot accept the diagnosis and will seek advice from other persons in the medical and paramedical fields. Each new visit may result in a different opinion, a trial with another medication, a new diagnostic test, etc. Each visit only heightens the anxiety within the family. Often this is expressed as a marked hostility toward physicians. This type of parental crisis is very difficult to cope with; it can only be handled through patience, understanding, thoroughness, and tact on the part of the physician. He may seek the advice of a psychiatrist for suggestions in counseling the parents; in some instances direct psychiatric help for the parents is advisable.

In explaining the diagnosis, the pediatrician should be aware of the parents' need for a total diagnosis with reference to themselves and the child.[54] Each family represents a unique unit, and the physician must plan his approach according to his knowledge of why the family is seeking help, what effect the child is having on the family, what the parents know of the situation, what community resources are available. Planning and recommendations should be made in terms that the parent can understand. Several interviews may be necessary, and action may have to be delayed on some recommendations. Answers to questions should be truthful and objective, yet sympathetic and understanding.

The most severe and prolonged crisis occurs when the parents face the sudden realism of placement. The crisis may develop insidiously or acutely. The reasons for placement may be multiple, and these in turn are related to such variables as age, IQ, sex, diagnosis, and family constellation.[3] In general they may be summarized as: (1) somatic and behavioral problems relating directly to the patient, e.g., multiple physical handicaps, sleep disturbances, seizures, hyperactivity, self-destructiveness, etc.—these are more common in the younger age groups, with quotients below 50, and in diagnoses which include birth injuries, genetic defects, cranial anomalies, fetal malformations, etc.; (2) problems within the family, e.g., parental tension, anxiety, divorce, separation, or death of the parents; (3) problems in social interactions, e.g., acting out behavior, adverse effect on siblings, rejection by the community, sexual delinquency, infractions of the law, etc. These are more frequently found among adolescents and teen-agers from the minority groups, with quotients over 50, and in diagnoses which include "cultural–familial" and "psychogenic" mental retardation. By tactful questioning, the physician can determine how the family feels about this problem, e.g., inquiry about long-range planning for the child, interactions with other siblings, physical problems in caring for the child, etc. Rarely should the physician take a direct lead in suggesting placement to the family. To the parent, placement may represent defeat and inadequacy. Their hope of caring for their child, the possibility that he might recover, the chance that he would learn to support himself have now vanished. The pediatrician can do much to support the family during this critical period and to relieve their guilt and anxiety.

Placement involves considerable administrative problems; application must often be made through agencies which are not directly concerned with retarded children, e.g., probation departments. The parents may be contacted by professional persons whose training is not in this area. Some hospitals have long waiting lists; others have age limits; a few provide care for only certain types of patients, e.g., training schools. Institutional personnel are well acquainted with the problems that parents face during placement. The pediatrician should acquaint himself with these people and work closely with them. He should know his state's facilities for the care of the retarded. Armed with this knowledge, he is in an excellent position to discuss placement with the parents. No matter what decision is reached, the pediatrician should help the parents to act in a reasonable and objective manner and should support them in their decision.

MENTAL ILLNESS AND MENTAL RETARDATION

The pediatrician is often confronted with evaluating the role of emotional factors either as a causation or complication of retardation. In the young child, emotional disturbances of a neurotic or milder nature rarely cause mental impairment. Long-standing and severe psychoses, however, e.g., autism, may cause the child to function at a defective level. At times, organic damage will account for both severe retardation and deviant behavioral patterns.

The differential diagnosis between infantile autism and mental deficiency requires careful, detailed observation, as well as psychological testing and psychiatric consultation. Reexaminations are necessary; the autistic child will show no progress, the retarded child will demonstrate slow, continuing growth. The autistic child shows withdrawal, negativism, disparity in motor and social behavior, heightened sensory responses, repetitive body movements, absence of affect, failure to relate to individuals, functional deafness, and lack of speech. The child with organic mental retardation will have general retardation in all areas, e.g., habit training, speech development, motor coordination, social behavior, and learning ability. In contrast to the autistic child, he is friendly with people, shows awareness of his surroundings, and responds to stimulation, e.g., speech, affection, etc.

Diagnosis is difficult when, because of a long-standing severe psychosis, the child has come to function at a defective level. Schain and Yannet have recently reviewed 50 patients with autism in a hospital for the mentally defective.[57] All have severe mental defect despite an absence of serious motor retardation. Although physical examinations were for the most part normal, 40 percent had a history of seizures and 20 percent were diagnosed as epileptics on admission. This problem of organic versus emotional components in the etiology of childhood autism remains unanswered.[58]

The retarded child with emotional problems may present difficulties in diagnosis as well as in parental guidance. It may appear that such problems are primary; however, he is "psychologically vulnerable" to superimposed emotional disturbances. The child's delay in maturation, e.g., toilet-training, thumb sucking, failure to feed or dress himself, short attention span, disorganized play activities, etc., may lead to disturbances in the parent–child relationships. When no neurological signs are present, the distinction between emotional and organic causation in this group may be difficult to make; oftentimes careful study together with frequent reexaminations will clarify the etiology.[59]

A psychiatrist's help may occasionally be necessary, not only in the diagnosis, but in the treatment of the child whose emotional problems are secondary to his mental handicap. There are also occasions when the pediatrician should consult with the psychiatrist to obtain help in the handling of the parents and child.

IMPLICATIONS FOR PREVENTION

Although further research is needed on the etiology of mental disorders in childhood, significant preventive measures can be instituted on the basis of current information.[60] In preparation for parenthood and during pregnancy,

[57] R. J. Schain and H. Yannet: Infantile Autism, *J. Pediat. 57*:560, 1960.

[58] L. Bender: Autism in Children with Mental Deficiency, *Amer. J. Ment. Defic. 64*: 81, 1959.

[59] S. L. Garfield; J. B. Wilcott, and N. A. Milgram: Emotional Disturbance and Suspected Mental Deficiency, *Amer. J. Ment. Defic. 66*:23, 1961.

[60] G. Tarjan: Somatic Etiologic Factors in the Prevention of Childhood Mental Disorders, presented at the 5th International Congress of Child Psychiatry and Allied Professions, Scheveningen, Holland, 1962.

these measures include such things as: (1) early diagnosis of pregnancy and prompt prenatal care; (2) identification of carriers of genetically transmissible diseases; (3) protection of the fetus against infections; (4) avoidance of unnecessary maternal medications or known teratogenic agents, e.g., high-energy radiation.

During the perinatal period, the following measures are important: (1) prevention of prematurity; (2) the avoidance of unnecessary medications, anesthetics, and instrumentations; (3) prenatal diagnosis of those conditions which require specific therapy during labor or shortly after birth, e.g., replacement transfusions; (4) careful use of medications for the mother and the newborn and avoidance of those drugs which are known to be harmful.

During the postnatal period, the pediatrician should be particularly aware of the following: (1) careful examination for congenital anomalies, e.g., craniostenosis, hydrocephalus; (2) testing for detectable inborn errors of metabolism and prompt initiation of dietary treatment or other specific therapy when necessary; (3) prevention by immunization procedures; (4) parent education concerning the prevention of accidents and poisonings.

A clear relationship between somatic factors and psychosocial forces has not been established and requires future research. Although no complete program is as yet available which can assure every child of a healthy central nervous system, there is, however, a substantial body of knowledge which if applied could produce a major impact.

6 PSYCHOLOGICAL EVALUATION: SOME PROBLEMS AND SUGGESTIONS

Harold A. Delp

From *The Training School Bulletin,* Vol. 56, No. 3, November 1959, pp. 79–84. Reprinted with the permission of The Training School, Vineland, N.J., and the author. Dr. Delp is Professor of Education, Temple University, Philadelphia.

All too many psychologists still believe and practice with conflicting ideas involved. Consequently, this has an effect on their reports and interpretations. Educators, social workers, medical personnel, and others need a basis for using reports with understanding. Persons using reports should have some idea of what they can expect from the data obtained in psychological evaluations. The comments and suggestions contained here will seem trite to some psychologists—but the problems appear frequently enough in practice and in reports to be worthy of comment.

In the area of psychological testing, especially in terms of the mentally retarded, there are several conflicting ideas. First, there are those who believe that no test is really useful in terms of obtaining valid estimates of the mental level (IQ) of an individual. Second, there are those who believe they can get everything from one test. We have heard discussion from people that administering a Stanford-Binet will allow them to obtain mental level, personality characteristics, and the like. In the same vein there are those who believe the Rorschach will give them everything. Third, there are those people who admit that *the* test administered in a particular case is not satisfactory for any number of reasons, such as hearing loss, reading difficulty, physical handicap, and the like. However, many of these same people proceed to interpret the score from the test as though it were completely reliable and valid. It should be pointed out that in general all three of these attitudes provoke difficulties in terms of the actual results of psychological measures for individual persons.

The standards or norms on any psychological tests pose problems for most people in their uses. Either the standards are not accepted in general for such testing or the persons placed too much arbitrary confidence in the results. It should be pointed out that psychological evaluation does not produce an "all or none" result. To be at all consistent the score itself is necessary to any kind of adequate evaluation of psychological material. Next, there must be a study of the accuracy (validity, reliability, objectivity) of the score for the particular individual being evaluated. Finally, there is the interpretation of the evaluation procedures which, of necessity, must go into all of the factors relating to the use of the scores in various areas as well as describing how this applies to the particular individual being tested.

Psychological tests (particularly mental tests) are specific samples of the behavior and abilities of the individual. For some tests, these samples are less limited than for other tests but nevertheless all such tests produce only samples. Almost any basic battery of test items might be best for a particular psychologist to use. Its primary value is in the general information which is obtained concerning the individual as well as defining the areas needing added evaluation. After the basic test battery is administered the psychologist in most cases will need to use other evaluation devices to supplement and complement the material obtained on the first. There is a tendency for some psychologists to overinterpret the information in the direction of the individual being evaluated. Perhaps an example of this might be given.

Suppose a particular psychologist feels that the Binet or the Wechsler test allows him to obtain the best general estimate of the person being tested. This test would then be administered in most cases initially. However, the person being tested might pose a problem concerning the extent to which his malcoordination has affected performance items on the test administered. In this case the psychologist should always make use of another test battery which for the most part eliminates the need for coordination in terms of the estimate to be obtained. Similar situations often exist for individuals with problems of speech, hearing, reading, and other handicaps. If this multiple testing is done, the situation would not occur where the examiner makes a comment in his report that the subject's reading difficulty may have produced errors resulting from inability to read and blocks to reading situations which may make the scores inadequate—and then proceed to interpret the results as though he had never made a comment concerning limitations from the reading problem.

All textbooks concerning measurements have used the words "validity, reliability, objectivity, and standardization." In most cases these terms have been defined in their relationship to the construction of the tests. Perhaps they should be redefined in terms of the value of the results obtained in an actual testing situation. From this point of view one could label the results of a particular test administration for a definite individual in terms of *validity*. This would mean the feeling of the psychologist as to any factors existing in this individual which might cause constant error in the results for the individual. These would be factors which, for the particular test administered, would produce a constant deflecting influence in the score. This might be the situation with the hearing handicapped person taking the Binet. Reliability in terms of the test results would involve the degree to which the psychologist feels that there have been accidental errors and inaccuracies resulting in obtaining the score. This factor should in most cases be able to be kept to a minimum. However, in some cases the individual being tested may be constantly looking out the window or being disturbed by other factors existing in the situation, such as noises, persons passing by, and the like. It may be that occasionally an item will be spoiled because of an accident in terms of the administration. Nevertheless, in these terms reliability has to do with variable and unpredictable errors which may occasionally crop up in an administration at a particular time. The degree to which these factors may have occurred, however, should always be pointed out by the psychologist.

Objectivity in terms of test results might involve the personal error in terms of the opinions of the psychologist together with other factors which restrict the objective point of view—objectivity, of course, should exist in all testing situations to the largest possible degree. The degree to which the psychologist involves subjective points of view to too great a degree would influence this characteristic of objectivity but would be less recognized by the examiner in many cases. *Standardization* as related to test results has to do with the interpretation of those scores. If the psychologist misunderstands some of the data he has obtained, if he gives incorrect meanings to data existing, or if assumptions are made which are not valid in terms of the particular case being evaluated, the results, and hence all interpretations based on those results, will not conform to standardized information and procedures.

It has been pointed out that, especially with clinic cases, we have definite difficulty. These individuals tend to be like the ones who caused the measurement errors in the original standardization of the test materials. If there were not the handicapped and disturbed individuals who need special consideration and if these persons had not been included in the original standardization of the test battery, the error of measurement of a particular test would in most cases be much smaller. Each type of handicap which persons might have requires specific consideration in psychological evaluation. In any sample of a thousand cases picked at random for standardizing a test there will be those who have at least mild hearing problems, visual problems, crippling problems, emotional problems, as well as many others. Each of these handicaps should be evaluated in terms of a test which in general eliminates that factor as a requirement. We have tests which have been developed and standardized for use with deaf children. We have tests which eliminate the use of oral language on the part of the subject. We have tests which fit the blind, the cerebral palsied, and the like better than the most used test batteries. It should be obvious that, when multiple handicaps come into the picture, there are limits beyond which the psychologist cannot go in obtaining a test battery ideally suited to the particular individual. Nevertheless, it is possible in a great majority of cases, even in the clinic to use a test battery or at least selected test items which do a much better job in the field of psychological measurement for the particular kind of person involved.

In projective testing there are like problems which occur. Too often the psychologist feels that the Rorschach, the TAT, or some other device will work in all cases. This obviously is not true. The problem of age of the individual being examined, as well as the particular types of emotional problems anticipated, will in a great measure determine which of the projective devices will best elicit the kind of responses necessary for an evaluation of the personality of the individual.

Many other factors are involved in good practice in terms of psychological evaluation. One of the biggest handicaps to good evaluation is the limited repertoire of evaluation devices which most psychologists have. At one time while sitting on a state board evaluating state psychologists, the author incidentally asked the candidate to "name all of the individual intelligence tests or mental tests which you know." It was surprising the number of persons who could only name at most two or three such test batteries. It is not at all unusual to find psychologists who feel that, if they are experienced in the administration of three or four test batteries, they can accomplish adequate results with any types of case. This, of course, would seem to be beyond any amount of reason. There are at least 30 to 40 different mental measurement devices which at times should be called upon to assist in the evaluation of particular individual cases. When one considers the breadth of evaluation from the young to the old, from the retarded to the gifted, the emotionally disturbed to the nondisturbed, and including all types of physical handicapping problems, the background of the competent clinical psychologist must be quite enormous. And even with the broad background, evaluation devices used should be fitted to the individual being evaluated and his particular problems. (See the table on pp. 92–93 of age ranges and specialty uses for a number of mental tests.)

An adequate psychological evaluation must go beyond the mere reporting of test scores, and even the statement of problems. In numerous cases the psychologist in the past has simply stated problems or made recommendations which were only restatements of the reasons for referral. To be useful the report must include descriptions, interpretations, and recommendations which are useful to others in actually improving or solving the basic issues.[1]

In any reporting the final summary must go beyond that which many psychologists use. It must include a global description of the indivdual as a person rather than merely being a set of isolated statements about mental level, personality status, or even specific problems. This summary must lead into a set of recommendations which are pointed to the person as an individual, to his limiting problems, and to what the using personnel might be able to do to assist this child whether it be in school, in an institution, or whether it is related to his mental, emotional, or physical status.

Briefly, then, it is anticipated that the psychologists will develop a large

[1] H. A. Delp, "Interpretation and Report to Using Personnel," *Training School Bulletin, 52* (1956), 231–236. See Reading No. 10.

TABLE I Age–Ranges for Selected Individual Mental Tests

(Solid lines indicate probable most usable range)

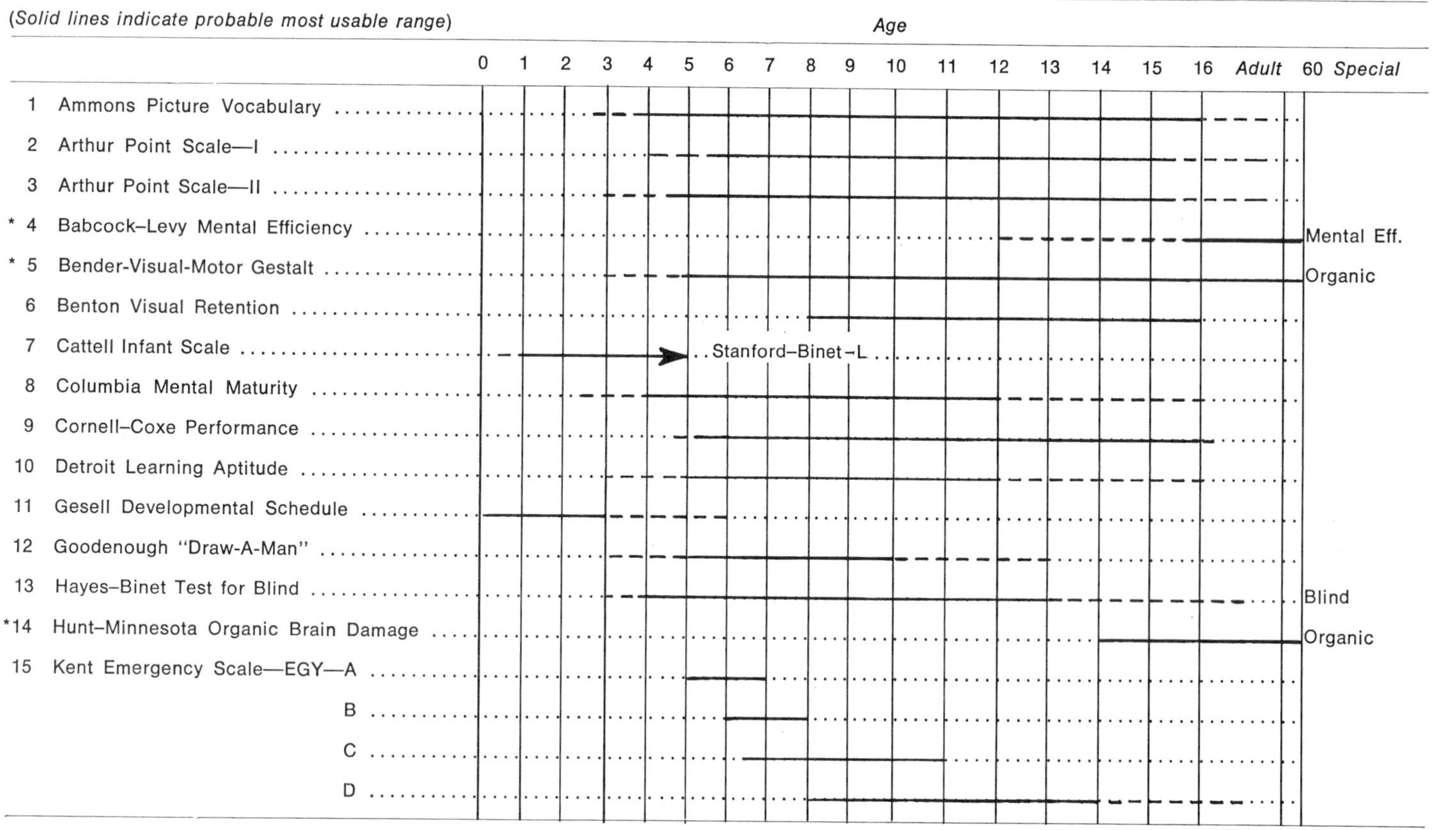

Age: 0 1 2 3 4 5 6 7 8 9 10 11 12 13 14 15 16 *Adult* 60 *Special*

No.	Test	Special
1	Ammons Picture Vocabulary	
2	Arthur Point Scale—I	
3	Arthur Point Scale—II	
* 4	Babcock–Levy Mental Efficiency	Mental Eff.
* 5	Bender-Visual-Motor Gestalt	Organic
6	Benton Visual Retention	
7	Cattell Infant Scale (→ Stanford–Binet–L)	
8	Columbia Mental Maturity	
9	Cornell–Coxe Performance	
10	Detroit Learning Aptitude	
11	Gesell Developmental Schedule	
12	Goodenough "Draw-A-Man"	
13	Hayes–Binet Test for Blind	Blind
*14	Hunt–Minnesota Organic Brain Damage	Organic
15	Kent Emergency Scale—EGY—A	
	B	
	C	
	D	

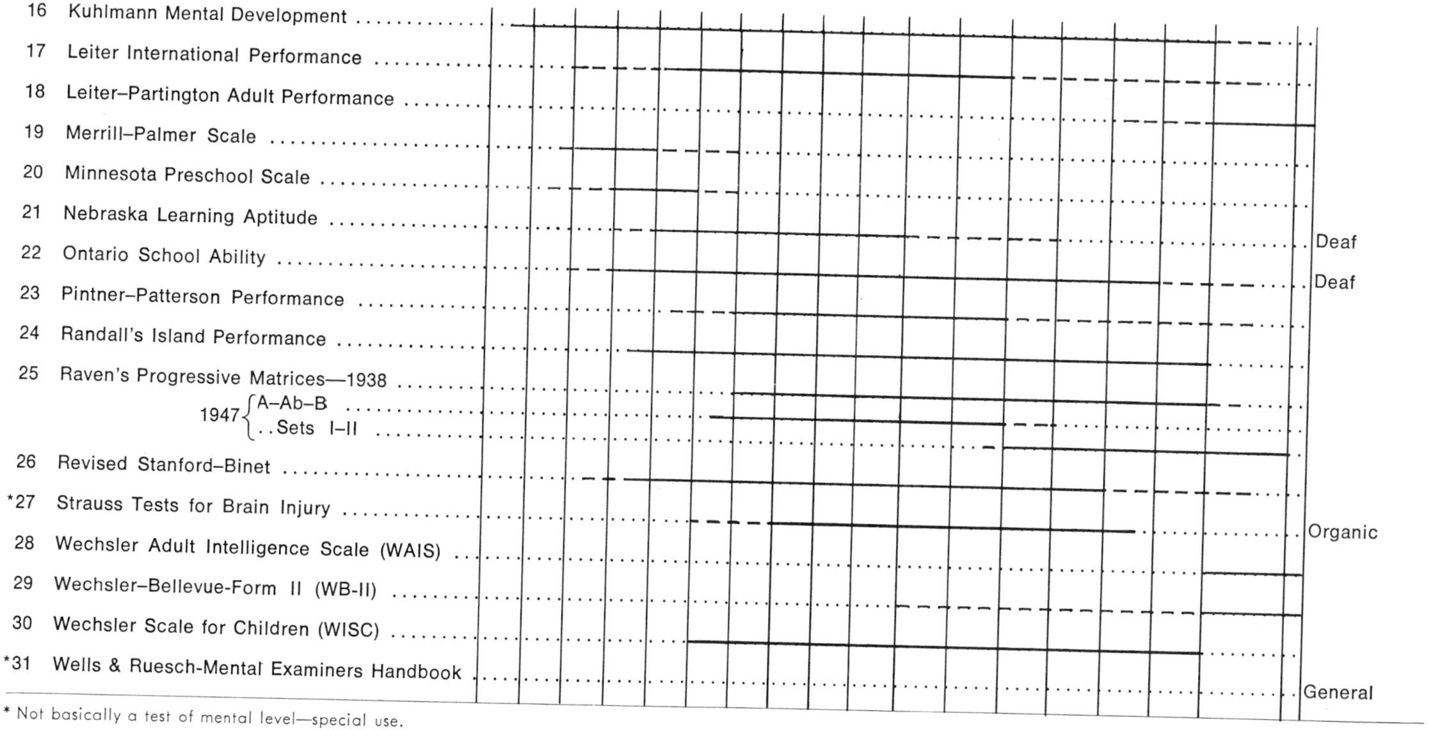

16 Kuhlmann Mental Development

17 Leiter International Performance

18 Leiter–Partington Adult Performance

19 Merrill–Palmer Scale

20 Minnesota Preschool Scale

21 Nebraska Learning Aptitude — Deaf

22 Ontario School Ability — Deaf

23 Pintner–Patterson Performance

24 Randall's Island Performance

25 Raven's Progressive Matrices—1938

1947 { A–Ab–B
 ..Sets I–II

26 Revised Stanford–Binet

*27 Strauss Tests for Brain Injury — Organic

28 Wechsler Adult Intelligence Scale (WAIS)

29 Wechsler–Bellevue-Form II (WB-II)

30 Wechsler Scale for Children (WISC)

*31 Wells & Ruesch-Mental Examiners Handbook — General

* Not basically a test of mental level—special use.

Applicability of a Variety of Psychological Tests for the Severely Mentally Retarded

Test	*Applicability*	*Comments*
Raven's Progressive Matrices	Not applicable in present form	Too difficult. No range of scores. Scoring system not appropriate to population.
Columbia Mental Maturity Scale	Limited value with older or relatively more intelligent children	Many children guessed. Test colorful, relatively short, and held interest of children. Suitable for children with speech and motor deficiencies.
Arthur Point Scale of Performance Tests—II	Not applicable except for Seguin Form Board	Too difficult; Seguin satisfactory; clinically useful.
Wechsler Intelligence Scale for Children	Three subtests applicable	Too difficult—does not go down far enough. Information, Digit Span, and Picture Completion applicable.
Ontario School Ability Examination	Three subtests applicable	Short and varied in nature. Subtests I, II, and V suitable. Subtests III, IV, and VI not suitable.
Nebraska Test of Learning Aptitude	Nine subtests applicable	Useful—only three of twelve subtests too difficult (Completion of Drawings, Puzzle Blocks, and Pictorial Analogies). However, these had clinical usefulness. Sufficient number and variety of subtests adequate for motor handicapped. Too long—administer in two sessions.
Merrill–Palmer, Minnesota Preschool Scale, and Kuhlmann Tests of Mental Development	Applicable—can be substituted for Stanford–Binet, or provide a downward extension of the Stanford–Binet	Useful—though slightly weighted in verbal tasks. Very similar to Stanford–Binet and redundant if latter is administered.
Stanford–Binet	Best single test	Most useful, though subjects with speech and motor coordination difficulties were handicapped. Enough variation to compensate for this major lack.
Draw-a-Man	Clinical evaluation only	Useful in most cases to add some information as to intellectual level, concept of self, and "organization" or integration (personality).

Source: G. Orville Johnson and Rudolph J. Capobianco, *Research Project on Severely Retarded Children*, Special Report to the New York State Interdepartmental Health Resources Board (Albany, N.Y.: 1957), pp. 14–15.

body of background devices in both mental testing and personality testing which would be usable on demand to more completely satisfy the needs in evaluation of particular indivduals. It is also assumed that evaluation devices will be used, both in a sense of administration and for the persons involved, in such a way that they obtain the maximum information with the fewest limiting conditions. Tests must be used for the purposes for which they were intended. It is rather absurd for one to assume that a mental test should also be used to evaluate the personality characteristics of the individual, or that a projective test would also be used for the measurement or prognosis of mental level, when we have many adequate evaluation devices in each of these areas which do a better job when they are used for their intended purposes. If tests are used for their intended purposes, and with the added understanding that we gain all available clues as to the additional specialty evaluation devices which might best be used to complete the situation, then it is felt that an adequate complete evaluation of the person would result.

7 THE VINELAND SOCIAL MATURITY SCALE

Edgar A. Doll

From the *Manual of Directions of the Vineland Social Maturity Scale,* Educational Test Bureau, Minneapolis, 1947. Reprinted with the permission of The Training School at Vineland, N.J., Educational Publishers, Inc., and the author. The late Dr. Doll was consulting psychologist of the Bellingham Public Schools, Bellingham, Washington. Since the original publication of the *Manual of Directions* for the scale, Dr. Doll has published the complete text relating to the scale, providing expanded content and statistical data. See Edgar A. Doll, *Measurement of Social Competence,* Educational Publishers, Minneapolis, 1953.

A first formulation of the Vineland Social Maturity Scale was published in April 1935.[1] The scale provides a definite outline of detailed performances in respect to which children show a progressive capacity for looking after themselves and for participating in those activities which lead toward ultimate independence as adults. The items of the Scale are arranged in order of increasing average difficulty, and represent progressive maturation in self-help, self-direction, locomotion, occupation, communication, and social relations. This maturation in social independence may be taken as a measure of progressive development in social competence.

The underlying principles involved in the construction of this scale are much the same as those employed by Binet and Simon for their scale for measuring intelligence. Each item is conceived as representing a general growth in social responsibility which is expressed in some detailed performance as an overt expression of that responsibility. Consequently, the value of the detailed items is to be determined principally by the extent to which they reflect this personal independence in personal activities, in respect to which the detailed performances are otherwise relatively unimportant.

The usefulness of the Scale for practical purposes and as a technique for research in the social sciences will immediately be evident to those interested in social problems. The Scale affords: (a) a standard schedule of normal development which can be used repeatedly for the measurement of growth or change; (b) a measure of individual differences and, consequently, of extreme deviation which may be significant in such problems as mental deficiency, juvenile delinquency, child placement, or adoption; (c) a qualitative index of variation in development in abnormal subjects such as the maladjusted, the unstable, the psychopathic, the epileptic; (d) a measure of improvement following special treatment, therapy, and training; (e) a schedule for reviewing developmental histories in the clinical study of retardation, deterioration, and rates or stages of growth and decline.

The Scale is also useful in distinguishing between mental retardation

[1] Edgar A. Doll, "A Genetic Scale of Social Maturity," *The American Journal of Orthopsychiatry, 5* (April 1935), 180–188.

with social incompetence (feeblemindedness) and mental retardation without social incompetence (which is often confused with feeblemindedness). It also affords assistance in child guidance and child training, by indicating the relative aspects of social competence. It provides another means of evaluating the influence of environment, of cultural status, and the effects of such handicaps as blindness, deafness, or crippling. In short, the social status of the individual is a basic consideration in many scientific studies where human adjustment is a consideration.

THE SCALE

The revised Scale is printed herewith. Each item of the Scale has been given a categorical designation which is indicated by the following letters:

S H G—self-help general	O—occupation
S H E—self-help eating	C—communication
S H D—self-help dressing	L—locomotion
S D—self-direction	S—socialization

The items of the Scale are arranged in order of average age norms and are numbered in arithmetical succession from 1 to 117. They have also been separated in year groups according to the average age scores obtained for the Scale as a whole. The method combines both the year-scale and point-scale principles. The arrangement facilitates the interpretation of total scores in terms of year values from the blank itself without the use of conversion tables as employed in the earlier manual for the original Scale.

VINELAND SOCIAL MATURITY SCALE

EDGAR A. DOLL, *Director of Research, The Training School at Vineland, New Jersey*

Name________________ Sex______ Grade______ Date__________
Year Month Day

Residence________________ Descent______ Born__________
Year Month Day

M.A. or IQ or
M.G.U.______ P.A.______ Test Used______ When______ Age__________
Years Months Days

Occupation	Class	Yrs. Exp.	Schooling
Father's Occupation	Class	Yrs. Exp.	Schooling
Mother's Occupation	Class	Yrs. Exp.	Schooling

Informant Relationship Recorder
Informant's est. Basal Score*
Remarks: Additional Pts.
Total Score
Age Equivalent
Social Quotient

---

* For method of scoring see *Manual of Directions*.
Reprinted with the permission of Edgar A. Doll, the Vineland Training School, and Educational Publishers, Inc.

VINELAND SOCIAL MATURITY SCALE *(cont.)*

CATEGORIES	Age Levels 0–I
C	1. "Crows"; laughs
S H G	2. Balances head
S H G	3. Grasps object within reach
S	4. Reaches for familiar persons
S H G	5. Rolls over
S H G	6. Reaches for nearby objects
O	7. Occupies self unattended
S H G	8. Sits unsupported
S H G	9. Pulls self upright
C	10. "Talks"; imitates sounds
S H E	11. Drinks from cup or glass assisted
L	12. Moves about on floor
S H G	13. Grasps with thumb and finger
S	14. Demands personal attention
S H G	15. Stands alone
S H E	16. Does not drool
C	17. Follows simple instructions
	I–II
L	18. Walks about room unattended
O	19. Marks with pencil or crayon
S H E	20. Masticates food
S H D	21. Pulls off socks
O	22. Transfers objects
S H G	23. Overcomes simple obstacles
O	24. Fetches or carries familiar objects
S H E	25. Drinks from cup or glass unassisted
S H G	26. Gives up baby carriage
S	27. Plays with other children
S H E	28. Eats with spoon
L	29. Goes about house or yard
S H E	30. Discriminates edible substances
C	31. Uses names of familiar objects
L	32. Walks upstairs unassisted
S H E	33. Unwraps candy
C	34. Talks in short sentences
	II–III
S H G	35. Asks to go to toilet
O	36. Initiates own play activities
S H D	37. Removes coat or dress
S H E	38. Eats with fork
S H E	39. Gets drink unassisted
S H E	40. Dries own hands
S H G	41. Avoids simple hazards
S H D	42. Puts on coat or dress unassisted
O	43. Cuts with scissors
C	44. Relates experiences
	III–IV
L	45. Walks downstairs one step per tread
S	46. Plays cooperatively at kindergarten level
S H D	47. Buttons coat or dress

VINELAND SOCIAL MATURITY SCALE *(cont.)*

CATEGORIES		*Age Levels III–IV*
O	48.	Helps at little household tasks
S	49.	"Performs" for others
S H D	50.	Washes hands unaided
		IV–V
S H G	51.	Cares for self at toilet
S H D	52.	Washes face unassisted
L	53.	Goes about neighborhood unattended
S H D	54.	Dresses self except for tying
O	55.	Uses pencil or crayon for drawing
S	56.	Plays competitive exercise games
		V–VI
O	57.	Uses skates, sled, wagon
C	58.	Prints simple words
S	59.	Plays simple table games
S D	60.	Is trusted with money
L	61.	Goes to school unattended
		VI–VII
S H E	62.	Uses table knife for spreading
C	63.	Uses pencil for writing
S H D	64.	Bathes self assisted
S H D	65.	Goes to bed unassisted
		VII–VIII
S H G	66.	Tells time to quarter hour
S H E	67.	Uses table knife for cutting
S	68.	Disavows literal Santa Claus
S	69.	Participates in pre-adolescent play
S H D	70.	Combs or brushes hair
		VIII–IX
O	71.	Uses tools or utensils
O	72.	Does routine household tasks
C	73.	Reads on own initiative
S H D	74.	Bathes self unaided
		IX–X
S H E	75.	Cares for self at table
S D	76.	Makes minor purchases
L	77.	Goes about home town freely
		X–XI
C	78.	Writes occasional short letters
C	79.	Makes telephone calls
O	80.	Does small remunerative work
C	81.	Answers ads; purchases by mail
		XI–XII
O	82.	Does simple creative work
S D	83.	Is left to care for self or others
C	84.	Enjoys books, newspapers, magazines

VINELAND SOCIAL MATURITY SCALE *(cont.)*

CATE-GORIES		
		Age Levels XII–XV
S	85.	Plays difficult games
S H D	86.	Exercises complete care of dress
S D	87.	Buys own clothing accessories
S	88.	Engages in adolescent group activities
O	89.	Performs responsible routine chores
		XV–XVIII
C	90.	Communicates by letter
C	91.	Follows current events
L	92.	Goes to nearby places alone
S D	93.	Goes out unsupervised daytime
S D	94.	Has own spending money
S D	95.	Buys all own clothing
		XVIII–XX
L	96.	Goes to distant points alone
S D	97.	Looks after own health
O	98.	Has a job or continues schooling
S D	99.	Goes out nights unrestricted
S D	100.	Controls own major expenditures
S D	101.	Assumes personal responsibility
		XX–XXV
S D	102.	Uses money providently
S	103.	Assumes responsibility beyond own needs
S	104.	Contributes to social welfare
S D	105.	Provides for future
		XXV+
O	106.	Performs skilled work
O	107.	Engages in beneficial recreation
O	108.	Systematizes own work
S	109.	Inspires confidence
S	110.	Promotes civic progress
O	111.	Supervises occupational pursuits
S D	112.	Purchases for others
O	113.	Directs or manages affairs of others
O	114.	Performs expert or professional work
S	115.	Shares community responsibility
O	116.	Creates own opportunities
S	117.	Advances general welfare

GENERAL INSTRUCTIONS

The central purpose of each item of the Scale is to represent some particular aspect of the ability to look after one's own practical needs. The specific items aim to sample such various aspects of social ability as self-sufficiency, occupational activities, communication, self-direction, and social participation, and to reflect progressive freedom from need of assistance, direction, or supervision on the part of others. The items aim to avoid measuring intelligence, skill achievement, personality, emotionality, and the specific results of environmental opportunity, training, incentive, habit, and so on, as such. The influence of such factors is expressed in terms of their composite capitalization for socially independent behavior.

To facilitate administration of the Scale, the detailed items are roughly grouped according to general similarity of content. However, each item is to be understood as a measure of general social maturation. By grouping similar items in categorical hierarchies the examiner is able to apply the Scale with more facility, thus quickly appraising the position of the subject examined in respect to each of these major aspects of social competence. This grouping is for purposes of convenience only, and the examiner should not hesitate to employ such an order as may seem to him most practicable in examining a given individual. The examiner is also expected to exercise discretion as to the order to be followed for the major groups themselves, since this also will be influenced by the particular circumstances surrounding each examination as well as by the range of the Scale that will apply to a given subject.

Each item of the Scale has a growth span of several years from which an average age may be derived as a standard for purposes of scaling, the curve as a whole reflecting individual differences in development. The results from the sum of items passed by a given subject are then reduced to age scores according to the average performance of normative life-age groups. These average scores are indicated by separating the items into year groups at total scores. Age scores may be calculated from total scores by interpolation as indicated below. Sex differences in item difficulty and in average age scores are so small as to be negligible for practical purposes.

It has proved impracticable to present here the detailed instructions with sufficient completeness to provide for all contingencies. The item definitions serve to indicate the central idea of each item, which is elaborated in detail by interview. This places on the examiner a definite responsibility for sensing the central theme of each item so that he may decide whether or not the particular manner in which that item is performed should or should not receive credit, or which type of credit.

The Scale is not a rating scale and scores are not to be based on mere opinions. The informant does not make the scoring judgment. This is done by the examiner after obtaining from the informant as much detail as practicable regarding the behavioristic facts which reveal the manner and extent of the subject's actual performance on each item. This is particularly important where lack of opportunity or other limiting circumstances seriously affect such performance. If opinions are submitted by the informant in lieu of factual information, the factual basis for such opinions should be reported. These requirements make it clear that the Scale cannot be used with precision except by duly qualified examiners who will devote at least as much care to mastering the technique as that required for administering the Binet Scale. Examiners should not be misled by the apparent simplicity or homeliness of the method. All details presented herewith have been carefully considered and these details may not be ignored if the Scale is to be used effectively.

The items of the Scale are to be scored on the basis of information obtained from someone intimately familiar with the person scored, such as the mother, the father, a close relative, guardian, attendant, or supervisor. The subject examined (the S) need not be present or observed, since the informant acts as proxy for the S. As will be noted later, the S may be used under certain conditions as his own informant.

In proceeding with the examination, information is first sought regarding the S's life age, schooling, general ability, occupation, special handicaps, and other orienting data. Other general information should also be sought bearing on the general social status of the S as indicated by father's usual occupation, general environment, and the like, to facilitate examining, avoid embarrassment, and allow for limiting circumstances in evaluating the information obtained.

The recorder, retaining the scoring sheet himself and not supplying one to the informant, begins by questioning the informant well below the anticipated final score in each serial group of items, as assumed from age and general presumption of the subject's ability. The recorder completes one item at a time, but notes incidental information relative to other items. Kindred items of progressive difficulty as provided in the grouping of items are to be followed through as in serial Binet testing, thus "raking" the Scale throughout the effective range rather than following all items in the numerical sequence of the scoring sheet. The examiner will use his own judgment in adapting the order of items within groups and the groups as wholes according to circumstances.

In obtaining this information the recorder is expected to quiz the informant in a sympathetic rather than a belligerent manner, avoiding naive credulity as well as open skepticism, encouraging spontaneous description, and eliciting detailed facts as to the specific limits of the S's actual performance by supplementary questions appropriate to the issues involved. It is difficult in this condensed guide to elaborate the technique of interview. This will be done in the more complete manual to be published later. It is important to avoid asking whether the S can do so-and-so, but rather does he usually or habitually do so. These answers are then checked by detailed questioning until the examiner is able to score the item as a whole. It is also important to avoid leading questions and to follow up all general answers with detailed questions. Thus the examiner asks to what extent does the S feed himself, or how much does the S do for himself in dressing, or in what ways does the S help around the house, or what kind of work does the S perform. In this way the examiner may score several items at once in the same category on the basis of the degree of accomplishment in a series of related items. There is no substitute for finding out just what the S actually and habitually does in respect to each item.

Under favorable conditions the Scale may be administered with the subject of the examination acting as his own informant. This has been found practicable with normal children as young as five years of age, and with subnormal subjects with Binet mental age as low as five years. Results obtained in this way tend to be slightly higher on the average, but are in some cases lower, than those obtained from independent informants. Such results should be scrutinized carefully in relation to the S's rapport as indicated by cooperation, honesty, candor, and insight. Often the subject is a better informant than someone else. However, modesty, self-depreciation, undue optimism, lack of auto-criticism, and the like may render self-informing somewhat misleading. Some check on this may be had by reviewing a few items through an independent informant for accuracy, or by checking a few items by observation or actual performance. (In the latter case the examiner would have to infer whether such performance is likely to be usual or habitual.)

In general we have found that actual misrepresentation of fact, either intentional or unintentional, by the S or independent informants does not present a genuine difficulty. A more serious hazard is the failure of the examiner to establish with sufficient detail the actual basis for passing judgment on each item. The interview method, the emphasis on actual and habitual performance, and the internal consistency and progression of items all serve as controls. The chief advantage of the use of independent informants is the assumed freedom from overstatement or understatement of fact. The reliability of the method under these conditions has been examined experimentally and statistically, and found satisfactory.

8 SOME THOUGHTS ON THE CURRENT STATUS OF ADAPTIVE BEHAVIOR

Henry Leland

Reprinted by permisison from *Mental Retardation*, Vol. 2, No. 3, June 1964, pp. 171–176, a publication of the American Association on Mental Deficiency, and the author. Dr. Leland is Associate Professor, Mental Retardation Training Program, Ohio State University, Columbus.

The dimension of adaptive behavior as described by Heber (AAMD, 1961) was said to refer "primarily to the effectiveness with which the individual copes with the natural and social demands of his environment." This concept seems to be important and useful to psychologists. However, as it is presently described, adaptive behavior is too closely related to the concept of measured intelligence and has not been able to take its place as a separate and distinct quality.

We at Parsons (Kansas) State Hospital and Training School (PSHTS) have long felt that there was a separate and distinct dimension present in the functioning of the retarded child. This is noted, for example, in many of the mongoloid children who may measure between 25 and 40 in IQs, but who are able to do many things for themselves in terms of self-help and self-care. They are often able to develop good interpersonal relationships and can be trained at certain occupational tasks so that they can often fit into a sheltered workshop.

Thus, in terms of measured intelligence, these children would be designated as severely retarded, but we would certainly want to describe them as only moderately retarded in terms of adaptive behavior. We are all familiar with other children who, because of severe orthopedic handicap or severe physical damage, as in the case of some hydrocephalic children, are bedridden, and generally nonfunctional, but who, nonetheless, may have a measured intelligence with IQs in the 70s and 80s or even higher. These would be the children whom we would describe as being borderline in measured intelligence; however, they would appear to be profoundly retarded in terms of their adaptive behavior if, for example, the Vineland Social Maturity Scale was used as the criterion. These and other differences between the way the child functions and his psychometric score illustrate, we feel, a definite need for the consideration of the two dimensions as suggested in the *Manual on Terminology and Classification in Mental Retardation*, published by the American Association on Mental Deficiency in 1961.

While we are convinced that the two separate dimensions exist, and while we are in accord with the idea of describing the retarded in terms of the two concepts of measured intelligence and adaptive behavior, we believe that, as presently defined, the dimension of adaptive behavior has three major failings: First, it does not take into consideration the child who is either grossly physically handicapped or who functions in that manner; second, it seems to be tuned toward measurement of absolute capacity rather than rehabilitation and growth concepts (Leland and Goldberg, 1957); and third, it has not been established clearly as a dimension independent of measured intelligence.

PROBLEMS OF THE NONAMBULATORY

Taking these one by one, the problem relating to the patient who demonstrates motoric as well as social maladaptation is an important one for all persons dealing with the mentally retarded. Patients who are either totally nonambulatory or could not be considered effectively ambulatory function at various intellectual levels. They present special medical-nursing problems and often require hospitalization in order to receive the continuous care necessary for their survival. This does not mean that a well-organized training center should not have rehabilitation objectives for these patients. However, the treatment and training programs devised must take into consideration their lack of ambulation or lack of *effective* ambulation to a far greater degree than other aspects of their training needs.

The rehabilitation objectives for the nonambulatory, while quite minimal, are equally as important as the rehabilitation objectives for patients whom we hope will become full and self-sustaining members of the noninstitutional community. Thus, for example, a child at this level may be taught to sit up, to open his mouth at feeding time, to turn himself over in bed, or to perform other activities which will make his nursing needs less severe. If he could be returned to a facility in the home community equipped to care for persons at this level of functioning, the institution will have accomplished a great deal for him. Our temporary suggestion here, as will be noted on Table I, is that the concept of adaptive behavior should encompass five separate levels, and that Level V be conceived in terms of the retarded patient who is not ambulatory, or not effectively ambulatory. We realize that this will have to be further modified in terms of age differences, but even in the face of that major objection, this still seems to be an effective starting point.

REHABILITATION

As to the second and third questions relative to a rehabilitation approach and the development of a separate dimension, this is the heart of our objection to the present procedure. We have always regarded rehabilitation to be a constant, ongoing process, as reflected in the following definition: "Re-

TABLE I Proposed Definitions of General Adaptive Behavior Levels

Level I

DESCRIPTION

Children of this level are capable of effective social and economic functioning in a low-demand competitive environment, but will need some support and supervision in the management of their personal affairs.

TREATMENT AND TRAINING OBJECTIVES

The objectives are to ensure that each child acquires, to the limit of his ability, those understandings, attitudes and behaviors which will enable him to develop adequate self-concept, self-help and self-care skills, interpersonal relationships, personal responsibility, economic functioning, and social and civic responsibility.

Level II

DESCRIPTION

Children of this level are capable of effective social and economic functioning in a partially competitive environment, but will need some continuing support and supervision in the management of their personal affairs.

TREATMENT AND TRAINING OBJECTIVES

The objectives are to ensure that each child acquires, to the limit of his ability, those understandings, attitudes, and behaviors which will enable him to develop adequate self-concept, self-help, and self-care skills, interpersonal relationships, personal responsibility, economic functioning and limited social responsibility.

Level III

DESCRIPTION

Children of this level are capable of limited social and economic functioning in a noncompetitive or sheltered environment, but will be dependent upon some general control and support.

TREATMENT AND TRAINING OBJECTIVES

The objectives are to ensure that each child acquires, to the limit of his ability, those understandings, attitudes, and behaviors, which will enable him to develop adequate self-concept, self-help and self-care skills, interpersonal relationships, personal responsibility and limited economic functioning.

Level IV

DESCRIPTION

Children of this level are capable of responding to the simplest of environmental stimuli and interpersonal relationships, but will be dependent upon nursing supervision for their maintenance and help in following the routines of daily living.

TREATMENT AND TRAINING OBJECTIVES

The objectives are to ensure that each child develops, to the limit of his ability, those attitudes and behaviors which will enable him to develop adequate self-concept, self-help and self-care skills, and limited interpersonal relationships.

Level V

DESCRIPTION

Children of this level are the grossly physically handicapped, or those who function in that manner, and require continuous medical-nursing care for their survival.

TREATMENT AND TRAINING OBJECTIVES

The objectives are to ensure that each child acquires, to the limit of his ability, those behaviors which will enable him to develop such self-concept and self-help and self-care skills as he is capable of developing.

habilitation is a continuous process which utilizes all services working as a team to help an individual with physical, mental, and social disabilities and handicaps to raise the level of his physical, mental, and social efficiency" (Leland and Goldberg, 1957).

Therefore, this new dimension of adaptive behavior should be utilized for the definition of rather precise rehabilitation objectives. That is, the major reason for introducing a new dimension should be that we are motivated to more clearly define the patients' functioning and this should, in some way, reflect our objectives for them. In a sense, this makes the diagnostic efforts of the psychologist more meaningful. Thus, under present procedures, when we diagnose a patient as functioning at a severe level of measured intelligence, this does not always have treatment implications. It more often has negative implications in the sense of saying that this is a patient whom we do not train or treat.

We hope that the new diagnostic tool, adaptive behavior, will be used to indicate what particular form of treatment or training might be feasible for the child in terms of his functioning ability. This, in many respects, seems to go back to some of the original thinking of Sloan and Birch (1955) when they first set up their scale. Though the term "adaptive behavior" was not used by them, they were attempting a "quantification of degree of retardation . . . indicating the subject's level in each of a number of different areas of functions." The basis of their original thinking, however, seems to be a scale which was a substitute for the IQ, rather than a second dimension.

The idea of a second dimension is more palatable because the IQ does have value in evaluating and comparing retardates in academic areas, but the measurement of adaptive behavior, using the procedure suggested in the *AAMD Manual,* is sitting on the middle of the fence between the IQ and a new dimension based on function. We feel that it can best get off this fence by becoming clearly a method of defining, in a generalized sense, rehabilitation objectives so that it can be useful not only to the psychologist in labeling his patient, but more important, to rehabilitation and training personnel, such as teachers, occupational therapists, music therapists, recreational therapists, and others, in their attempts to develop programs. Thus, those aspects of mental retardation which are measured by the dimension of adaptive behavior can be considered as the more reversible aspects of the problem.

In this regard, we feel that the change in the definition of levels reflected by Table I represents a clearer basis for assigning an adaptive level to the child, and that the series of objectives outlined in Table II become the basis for this assignment. Thus, this approach, indicating that the patient can be trained, changes the frame of reference in regard to the measure and, at the same time, gives a training objective.

One further point on the question of an independent dimension is that

TABLE II Rehabilitation Objectives

Level of Adaptive Behavior	*Objective*
LEVEL I	A level of functioning at which the patient may become a full-fledged member of a noninstitutional community, with ability to assume personal, civic and economic responsibility.
LEVEL II	A level of functioning at which the patient may become a full-fledged member of the noninstitutional community, but still lacking in total ability to assume social and civic responsibility and, therefore, in need of a continuing quasi-dependent relationship.
LEVEL III	A level of functioning at which the patient can develop proper interpersonal relationships and relative personal responsibility with supervision, and may thus be able to leave the institution for a sheltered workshop or some other form of highly supervised activity.
LEVEL IV	A level of functioning at which the patient can develop self-help and self-care skills, with particular emphasis on development of communication abilities, socialization, etc., leading to eventual placement in the community, in either an individual or group care program where he can be part of the outside community but, nonetheless, still in a quasi-institutional setting.
LEVEL V	A level of functioning at which the patient can develop a sufficient level of self-help that he can relieve the constant need for total medical-nursing care necessary for his survival.

the suggestion in the Manual (AAMD, 1961, p. 63) that the psychologist use the Vineland Social Maturity Scale, the Gesell Development Schedules, the Cattell Infant Intelligence Scale, and the Kuhlmann Tests of Mental Development for assigning adaptive levels, needs further consideration, both for the reasons mentioned above and because it is important that this be separated from the concept of measured intelligence. This leaves the examining psychologist without a specific scale against which to refer his patient for the assignment of a level. However, this need not be as threatening as it seems to be. If the proposed modification introduced here is used, the psychologist has a guidepost against which to compare his own personal observations, the material found in case histories, the reports of other services, and other sources to determine the proper level. *However, there is a clear-cut need for research to establish the parameters of this new dimension and to develop more objective scaling.*

SOCIAL DEMANDS

There is an additional factor related to the social implications of this new dimension which should be introduced here. Adaptive behavior by its very terminology implies the behavior the child uses to adapt himself to social demands. Since social demands differ from one community to another, it would seem to follow that a universal scale for measuring adaptive behavior would be definitely counter-indicated and that possibly a group of scales would be more fitting. Each psychologist must utilize the demands of the social–psychological factors present in his own setting and in the surrounding areas from which he draws his patients before he can properly discuss adaptive behavior in terms of any one item.

Thus, this is as much a test of the psychologist's knowledge of the social-cultural background of the patient as it is any one other thing. This is an important area which has been discussed for years among professionals who have felt that a major factor has been overlooked. We gain, thus, a way of judging whether or not the patient could be returned to his own community or whether he should rather be returned to some other community where the needs are different and more in keeping with his actual functional level. The value of this to vocational rehabilitation counselors, social workers, people operating halfway houses, and sheltered workshops, and others should be obvious.

Within the institution it becomes a much clearer indicator of whether or not the patient's needs are primarily training or whether the extent of his emotional disturbance is such that he would also require treatment. While the measure of the IQ in no way indicates whether or not the child is primarily emotionally disturbed, the use of adaptive behavior as a measure with which to compare the IQ will give valuable information in this area. Thus, we have a basis for assigning the patient to the institution program that is most tuned to his specific needs, as well as a way of knowing which children are ready to leave the institution and to what community area they should be returned.

SUMMARY

In summary, we feel that the dimension of adaptive behavior is valuable and is an important new dimension to be added to our thinking in regard to the diagnosis and evaluation of the retarded patient. However, we feel that to be of real value it must be stated more positively in rehabilitation terms and must exist as an independent dimension, separate from measured intelligence. Further, we feel that a major category of patients has been omitted in the original thinking. We have offered a set of definitions which we feel takes these factors into consideration.

We have also offered rehabilitation objectives which we feel should be incorporated into the thinking in this area so that evaluations and diagnoses will gain value in terms of establishing programs for treatment and training. Further, we have suggested that an intensive research program be instituted to more clearly define the concept.

REFERENCES

American Association on Mental Deficiency. A Manual on Terminology and Classification in Mental Retardation (2nd Edition). Prepared by Rick Heber. Monograph Supplement to the *American Journal of American Deficiency,* 1961.

Leland, H. and Goldberg, I. Rehabilitation of the Institutionalized Mentally Retarded. *American Psychologist,* 1957, *12,* 528–530.

Sloan, W. and Birch, J. W. A Rationale for Degrees of Retardation. *American Journal of Mental Deficiency,* 1955, *60,* 258–264.

9 INTERPRETATION AND REPORT TO USING PERSONNEL

Harold A. Delp

From *The Training School Bulletin,* Vol. 52, No. 9, January 1956, pp. 231–236. Reprinted with the permission of The Training School, Vineland, N.J., and the author. Dr. Delp is Professor of Education, Temple University, Philadelphia.

The purpose of all interpretations and reports of diagnosis is to enable the user to understand the child and to help solve his problems. To do this, the interpretation must first be in terms that are comprehensible to the user. For mentally retarded children, the interpretation must make it possible for the user to understand the general and specific levels for school placement and to further the education to the maximum for each individual child. No report is satisfying its purpose if the interpretation involved does not add to the knowledge of the child and give material and specific suggestions for working with the child as contrasted with a simple description of the child and its problems.

CONTENT

The content as well as the style of the interpretation makes for a major problem in psychological diagnosis. This is particularly true when working in the area of mentally retarded and attempting to satisfy the need of teachers, physicians, parents, and others who are required to produce results in the training and improvement of the child's everyday behavior. Several specific problems are pertinent to this content.

1. The analysis of the findings must be developed into an integrated picture of the total child as he actually functions and in terms of his potential. It is not sufficient simply to state that a child has taken a particular test and what the specific findings might have been without analyzing these into a coordinated description of the whole child. In addition to the description of the whole child as he is functioning at present the interpretation must make an attempt to describe the potential of the child and what appears to be the paramount description of the child for the future.
2. The interpretation must *not* extend beyond the established implication of the particular procedures used. Some examiners in their description will indicate limitations of the test in the particular case, and then will proceed to interpret the individual as though those limitations did not exist. Reports have been given in which it was stated

that the child made a low score on a Binet because of a reading difficulty and a verbal handicap, but the examiner then proceeded to interpret the rest of the material assuming that the IQ was satisfactory.

3. The interpretation must explain the extent to which adaptation *had* to be made in the standardized test administration and, hence, the degree to which the results can be given in any statistical terms or for which comparisons can be made. This is a particularly critical point in interpretation. There are those examiners who will make exceptions because of handicaps or maladjustment on the part of the child and then proceed to catalogue the child in the statistical term given in the manual. On the other hand there are those individuals who will insist that the statistical evidence has no value and will proceed to make arbitrary variations in test administration without any particular need for doing so. It is assumed by most psychologists that tests should be administered in as nearly the normal described procedure as possible and that then the test has both its objective and subjective values in interpretation.
4. The emphasis on the mere use of IQ and/or MA in the diagnosis of the mentally retarded is seriously questioned, especially because of the wide variation among such individuals and within each individual. Again, it is the extreme point of view in either direction which is a disadvantage. Scores can be of great value if they are properly obtained and used. Some users, with all that has been written, are inclined to make use of the IQ as some miraculous score which gives all the answers merely by knowing the numerical value.
5. In the interpretation there is need to separate mental retardation as the primary problem from those common overlapping problems such as loss of hearing, aphasia, motor handicaps (cerebral palsy), emotional disturbances, and so forth. Adequate tests must have been used when these other handicaps are suspected, if the score of the mental level is to have maximum value. It is rather absurd to administer a test to a child and to conclude with the interpretation that the score does not tell the whole information because the child was not able to hear or for other reasons to do the required material. In almost every case we do have available tests which delimit other handicaps and so allow the qualified examiner to produce a score more nearly descriptive of the mental level of each particular individual.
6. To report simply that the child is mentally retarded and even needs special placement is absurd in many cases. Teachers and others referring the child need to know the degree of retardation in total and in as many different specifics as possible. The examiner must determine and indicate the advantages and disadvantages of certain methods and techniques of training, whenever possible. So often the interpretation of such a diagnosis stops with the simple statement of the facts of the child's limitations.

7. In some cases the examiner may anticipate that the test score has been reduced because of other factors (such as physical, emotional, and so forth). It is *not* possible to know, and so it is very poor practice to predict in the interpretation a "true level." This is especially so for brain-injured children. High test points may be related to areas not as much damaged as other areas, rather than being predictions of a higher possible total as is assumed in some cases by some examiners. The critical point in the interpretation is the statement by the examiner in words that can describe his own feelings of doubt, or belief, without making the assumption that some other direction is necessarily the correct one.
8. Care should be taken *not* to make an issue of the numerical rating. While statistical comparison is extremely important in its proper place, many users such as physicians, social workers, teachers, and even some psychologists seek only the score and base all of their work with the child on a prior conception of a meaning of that score, regardless of other information given about the test. The interpretation must include the content which seeks to avoid this possible result.
9. Often the average score obtained on a battery is not adequate for the brain-injured. Peaks and valleys of performance may be of differential value in interpretation as to the special strengths and weaknesses of the individual and to the learning possibilities and methods. The average score may actually be very misleading in these areas of discussion. It is not infrequent on a test with a wide variety of items that the individual who has an organic problem will score some items at almost normal or even above, while certain specific items will be failed almost completely. A simple fact that the average comes out with an IQ of 55 may be entirely meaningless in terms of any help given to the teacher or to other persons who are to work with the particular child. There are, however, those occasions when the score becomes extremely important in itself.
10. The interpretation must include explanation of all other patterns shown to occur and to have meaning for the child. As the various results of tests are laid out in front of the examiner he usually can see certain generalities, certain patterns of strengths and weaknesses, and the like which would have an advantage to the user if properly explained. References should be made to everyday tasks which might be involved with the behavior pattern shown, either to the advantage or disadvantage of the child and his learning.
11. The examiner must include in the interpretation those situations where he himself feels that the score is unreliable. At times the examiner may decide the test has been so poor that it is "no test" but merely a set of qualitative observations. Observations are always of definite value but they are not subject to the usual test quantifications or comparisons.

RECOMMENDATIONS

The only value of examinations and interpretations is to give basis for recommendations to be used to benefit the child. This is definitely true for the school psychologist in the diagnosis of mental retardation.

1. Recommendations *must* be practical and workable. They must be given in terms of the actual situation—the actual child, the school (its personnel and facilities), the family (its members and their feelings), and the community as well as its level of understanding and acceptance. If the recommendations are too idealistic or impossible to put into action in the real case, often nothing is accomplished for the child. If certain recommendations are highly desirable but doubtful of achievement, alternatives of these "best solutions" should be developed and recommended. The better the examiner can be acquainted with the actual situation in total, the more chance there is for giving maximum help to the child through the users of the report.
2. The need for and the type of placement appropriate for the particular case should be stated. This is a particular problem in school systems where two levels of special classes are operated.
3. A necessary recommendation includes present and potential levels of ability. This must be in specific as well as in general terms.
4. Recommendation should indicate methods and techniques which should be found most effective in the total education of the particular individual child. These must be given in line with findings of organic, personality, or other particular problems.
5. School adjustment of the curriculum should be recommended. Areas included are academic learning, social development, vocational-occupational training, and personality. This is in line with the fact that all retarded children will not profit from the identical curriculum regardless of whether their so-called mental levels are the same or not. Adjustments in the actual curriculum must be made for the particular child in terms of his own strengths and weaknesses and peculiar needs.

REPORTS

There is great confusion as to whether psychological reports and particularly the report of diagnosis of mental deficiency should be made written or oral to parents, schools, school personnel, and others. All of these considerations are possible and the particular situation, public school or private school, and the like, will determine which combination is actually put into force. The form and content of the report obviously differs for different users and under different circumstances.

Language of Report

In the past few years several articles have been written in professional journals concerning the problems of professional writing and reporting. Several particularly valuable articles appeared in *Science,* which is a journal of the American Association for the Advancement of Science. A coined word has been used to express such poor writings ("gobbledygook"). Menninger, in his book *A Manual for Psychiatric Case Study,* criticizes psychiatrists for their reports. The same criticism applies to many psychologists. Much of the style of writing or talking is mainly for the purpose of impressing others, or because of the inability of the writer to make a simple explanation. Excessive and undiscriminating use of technical terms and excessive and inappropriate use of qualifying expressions in reports lead to confusion rather than erudition from the user's point of view.

Too many psychologists attempt to use abstract language rather than to be specific in terms of the actual child under study. Most professional persons today agree that simple language seldom needs to reduce a report's effectiveness.

The report should distinguish between observation and inference. Too frequently statements are given as facts which are only opinions deduced from minor facts not stated. Statements should be made as facts only when they are actually known to be facts. The report has the primary function of coordinating *all* the data about the child from *all* sources—history, social data, educational, medical, and psychological—for the most complete integrated picture of the individual as a whole.

Form

There are many organizations of reports of such psychological examinations. The particular form of a report will depend upon local needs and desires. However, a possible outline of a report on diagnosis, usable in most cases, is given below.

1. Reason for referral. In many cases the child will have been referred as a behavior problem, a reading problem, or some other problem, rather than accepted in advance as a case of probable retardation. On the other hand, some students are referred as problems of retardation and are later found not to have been so.

2. Child's behavior during examination. Cooperation, attitude toward a situation, level of comprehension, productivity, emotional status, special handicaps, and appreciation of his own problem are noted. Leave out spurious, colorful, and nonessential description.

3. Test findings. These should be discussed first in terms of each test and its meaning for the individual. Each area should then be discussed as to intelligence, personality, and so forth which should be summarized in terms of all evidence in these major areas. Statistical terms and quantities should be given where advantageous to users but should not be allowed to

make up the major part of the findings for those individuals who are not confident of this type of data.

4. OTHER FINDINGS. These include informal tests and observations used by the examiner as well as the information accumulated from all other sources such as medical, social, and others. Findings from auxiliary agents referred to during examinations are given here.

5. COORDINATED ESTIMATE. Disregarding individual tests and sources of information, this part should describe from the total diagnosis the whole child as a personality together with his problems and needs. This is the primary place where the child, and not the tests or procedures, is important. It is here where the major areas of difficulties, strengths, and weaknesses are described and discussed with their meanings for the child.

6. RECOMMENDATIONS. Again this is the most important part of any report as it tells the user where the child is, what is necessary to help the child to the maximum, and just where the user fits into the total situation of getting the best results for the child.

10 THE CASE CONFERENCE

Ray Graham

From *The Illinois Plan for Special Education of Exceptional Children: Handbook and Manual for Qualified Psychological Examiners,* edited by Ray Graham, Department of Public Instruction, Springfield, Ill., June 1949, pp. 24–27. Reprinted with the permission of the Department and the editor. The late Mr. Graham was director of the Division of Special Education, Office of the Superintendent of Public Instruction (Illinois).

One of the most important features of the psychological examination in the Illinois Program for the Mentally Handicapped is the case conference. This is an attempt to get all of the people who know a child to see that child from each other's point of view so that all aspects of the educable mentally handicapped individual's personality will be understood by those who have to work with him. At the same time, this conference provides the psychologist with case history material which is often very important in the making of a final diagnosis. This is also an important procedure from the standpoint of making recommendations to the school. As a result of the conference, both the school and the psychologist are assured that no impractical recommendations are made. Quite often the public schools have become dissatisfied with psychological service in general because of impractical recommendations.

The case conference serves still another purpose than just that of understanding the child and planning a program for him. It provides the school personnel with a type of in-service training which is very important to special education in general. It is at such conferences as these that some school teachers may learn to recognize that there is much more to a child than they see in their classrooms. Also, many of their stereotyped notions concerning the mental defective or other types of handicapped children are eliminated as a result of the better understanding which they obtain through the case conference. Most of the progressive superintendents in the State of Illinois have come to recognize the significance of the case conference in the handling of the educable mentally handicapped. Consequently, they now expect the psychologist to conduct such a conference following his examination. The case-conference procedure has become so important in the program for the mentally handicapped in Illinois that the State Department of Public Instruction insists that such conferences be held for every child certified for placement in this special class. It is also advisable for the psychologist to hold conferences on the children whom he finds to be ineligible for the special class. In this way the school personnel gets an opportunity to see the differences in the children who are approved from those who are not approved for the special class.

There is no definite time for the scheduling of these conferences. This is a matter to be worked out between the psychologist and the school personnel. Furthermore, the procedure for holding the case conference differs in various school systems. For example, arrangements for conferences might be made one way when the psychologist is not employed full time by the schools and in another way when he is a regular part of a school staff. In those instances in which the psychologist is employed full time by the public schools, the director of special education or someone else who has the equivalent authority arranges the case conference. Sometimes it might be the psychologist who is the most logical person to arrange for the conferences. On the other hand, the psychologist who is employed by the school merely to certify children for the program for the mentally handicapped never arranges the conferences himself. These conferences are usually arranged by the superintendent of schools, his assistant, or the director of special education. Occasionally it is the principal of the building in which the examinations are made who arranges the case conferences. The normal amount of time required for a case conference is approximately 30 minutes per child. Of course, there are times when as much as an hour or an hour and a half may be spent in discussing one case.

The people who attend these conferences are:

1. THE SUPERINTENDENT OF SCHOOLS, ASSISTANT SUPERINTENDENT OF SCHOOLS, OR THE DIRECTOR OF SPECIAL EDUCATION. It is important for someone with administrative authority to be present because very often a plan is worked out which requires approval by some member of the school administration.

2. THE TEACHER OF THE CHILD. This person usually can give the psychologist and the other people at the conference the most complete information concerning the educational progress of the pupil.

3. THE PRINCIPAL OF THE BUILDING IN WHICH THE CHILD IS ATTENDING SCHOOL. Often the principal has observed the child in situations that are completely strange to the teacher. Also, the principal frequently has had contacts with the parents of the child, or with other people who are working with him.

4. THE SPECIAL-CLASS TEACHER TO WHOM THE CHILD IS LIKELY TO GO IF FOUND ELIGIBLE. Certainly, it is important that this person be present at the conference because the special class teacher is the one who will have to work with the child and will need all the information that she can get in order that she may better understand the psychologist's report and at the same time be better prepared to handle the child the moment that he enters her room. Also, she is in the best position to determine how a given child will fit into her particular group.

5. THE PRINCIPAL OF THE BUILDING IN WHICH THE SPECIAL CLASS IS LOCATED. As mentioned in a previous section, special education in Illinois is a part of and not apart from the regular school program; therefore, it is important for the principal of the building in which the special class is located to be in on the case conference of a child who is to enter

the special class. The principal will be very instrumental in helping to integrate the child's special class program with the normal program in the school building. For example, it is the principal who can give the authority for placing a child from the special class in the art class, or the manual training class, with regular pupils.

6. THE SCHOOL NURSE. The school nurse is the most important person in the school as far as being the connecting link between school and home is concerned. Very frequently she has visited the homes of the mentally handicapped children in an effort to care for their physical needs. Thus, she becomes intimately acquainted with the background from which the child comes. Furthermore, the school nurse is usually the one who will see to it that necessary physical examinations are made so that the psychologist can make a more accurate diagnosis. Finally, the school nurse provides such information as the health history of the child and the results of vision and hearing tests.

7. THE VISITING TEACHER, OR SCHOOL SOCIAL WORKER. This person is not found on the staffs of many schools in Illinois. However, when a visiting teacher is employed by the schools, she is a very important person to have at the conference because of the work that she can do in the home and the information about the child which she can provide.

A great many schools in Illinois that have programs for the mentally handicapped also have programs for the socially maladjusted. Frequently it is necessary to coordinate these two programs because the mentally handicapped child is also a socially maladjusted child, except in rare instances. Thus, the visiting counselor for the socially maladjusted may make a valuable contribution toward the working out of the psychologist's recommendations. Also, occasionally he is able to provide a great deal of information regarding the child's background.

8. OTHER SPECIAL SCHOOL PERSONNEL. Sometimes a child who is a candidate for placement in a special class for the mentally handicapped has been worked with by a speech correctionist. The speech correctionist should be present at the conference in order to round out the total picture of the child. In the case of a high school pupil, the dean of boys or the dean of girls may be able to make a valuable contribution and, therefore, should be present. The truant officer is another school staff member who may be able to assist the psychologist and the other school personnel in reaching a complete understanding about a child and his background.

9. OUTSIDE SOCIAL AGENCIES. It is not infrequent that a child who is a candidate for the class for the mentally handicapped is known to some local social agencies, such as the Juvenile Court, Aid for Dependent Children, or Family Welfare Association. In such instances, it is important to invite a worker from such an agency to the case conference. Such a worker can usually contribute valuable information about the child and his family, and at the same time the worker might be quite instrumental in carrying

out a treatment program for the child, especially where work with the family and community resources are involved. Furthermore, such a procedure helps to make a closer connection between the school and other social agencies in the community.

It is good policy to permit teachers, principals, and other school personnel who may not necessarily be concerned with the case to be present at the case conference. They can learn a great deal about the general philosophy of the Illinois Plan and the program for the mentally handicapped. Thus, a better understanding of special education throughout the school system may be effected by such a procedure.

The experience of the state psychologists with the case conference in public schools throughout Illinois has demonstrated that it is most important for the psychologist to enter the case conference without having made a definite decision concerning the eligibility of a child. Of course, the exception to this is the child who as a result of the psychological examination is obviously a child of normal intelligence. The psychologist calls upon various people at the conference to make their contribution to the understanding of the child. No particular order for calling upon these people has been established. The psychologist may call upon them to suit the particular case involved. After all who know the child have had an opportunity to make their individual contributions, the psychologist then summarizes and interprets his own findings, makes his diagnosis and his recommendations. These recommendations are discussed by the entire group so that all may have a part in planning for the child. In borderline cases in which it is difficult to decide whether a child should be considered eligible or ineligible for the special class program, the psychologist would be very wise to leave the decision up to the entire group. This helps to give them a feeling that they are definitely a part of this program and that their opinions are respected.

Some psychologists have entered a case conference with their report on the examination already written. This has proved to be very ineffective. Oftentimes the psychologist learns things at the case conference that had completely escaped him in his previous contacts with school personnel and the child. Consequently, it is necessary for him to rewrite his report. It is important to note that this is the rule rather than the exception.

The psychologist should bear in mind at all times that this case conference should be a democratic procedure. At no time should the conferences be completely dominated by the psychologist. If anyone is to dominate the conference, it should be the school personnel. Last, but not least, the conference should not be scheduled at a time when it is necessary to hurry through the cases. This makes for a very ineffective conference, and the result is that everyone has wasted his time.

11 INTERDISCIPLINARY TEAMWORK

George Tarjan

From *Diagnostic Problems in Mental Retardation,* compiled and edited by Eli M. Bower and J. H. Rothstein, Vol. 27, No. 7, California Department of Education, Sacramento, August 1958, pp. 61–64. Reprinted with the permission of the California Department of Education and the author. Dr. Tarjan is Professor of Psychiatry, School of Medicine and School of Public Health at UCLA. He is also Program Director, Mental Retardation, Neuropsychiatric Institute at UCLA.

One of the clichés of our time pertaining to professional work advocates praise for the team in lieu of the individual. We often hear the cheer, "Rah, Rah, Team." I thought it worthwhile to look at the dictionary definition of "team." The first definition was, "two or more animals harnessed together; also animals with their harness and the vehicle they draw." Obviously this is not the team we are here to discuss in relationship to our work in mental retardation. The next definition of a team was, "a number of persons working or playing together as a unit, especially one side of a competitive game." The final definition, "a litter or brood of young, especially of ducks."

Though in principle all of us will agree that there are certain advantages in teamwork, we hear so many terms bandied about in connection with it that it would seem worthwhile to examine this concept as it relates to our endeavors. We hear that in a team there must be cooperation, coordination, equality, and hierarchy—all at the same time. Occasionally, we even hear that anything which can be done by more than one person ought not to be done by one individual alone; that nothing can be properly done without the use of a team; that everything is better accomplished if five people do the same thing. It takes a little longer, it is true; it is perhaps a little wasteful, but then "more egos are satisfied."

Even the inner sanctum for the lone wolf or for the person who wants to work by himself has disappeared. This inner sanctum used to be a refuge in the world of research; a place for the seclusive, the introspective, or the lonely individual. In the past, people wrote papers alone. Nowadays a scientific paper, to be looked upon with favor, must have at least four, preferably six or eight, authors and a long list of acknowledgments and appreciations.

For the purpose of this presentation I would like to use the following definition of team: "A group of workers organized to act in a coordinated fashion toward the achievement of a specific goal." The first essential requirement is the existence of a specific, well-defined goal which is known to all members of the team. Only in this way can they work toward a common aim. They all should know what it is that they are expected to produce, whether it be a diagnosis, a program of treatment, an educational program, or a specific discovery.

A good team should also have a clear-cut leading philosophy which is compatible with its goal. It is essential that members recognize and accept this leading philosophy, particularly if the team is to operate on a routine, day-to-day basis. In a medical agency it seems desirable that the basic philosophy be that of medicine; in a school setting it should be that of education, and so on. Members of the team may well maintain the philosophies of their particular professions, and still have an understanding of, and belief in, the leading philosophy of the team as a whole.

It is necessary that a common language exist as a method of communication between team members. Though this seems to be a minor point, quite often it takes a substantial length of time before interdisciplinary teams, with individuals of varied backgrounds, begin to call the same things by identical names. The closer the individual philosophies of the team members, the less obtrusive the language barrier, though even among psychiatrists of different schools of thought communication difficulties may become a serious problem.

Each team must have an organizational structure which delineates roles, and defines as clearly as possible the independence of, and relationship of, team members. A goal-directed team can hardly exist without hierarchy. As in every organization with a defined hierarchy, it is desirable that the practical lines of communication coincide as much as possible with those which were originally set down on a theoretical basis.

Since a team will arrive at its goal through the various contributions of its members, it is important that the specific skills of the members not be lost. It is, therefore, important that each member conceptualize himself for what he is, for what he knows, and for what he has to contribute. Even if team members have a very broad knowledge, values would be lost if pediatricians on a team were to think of themselves as psychiatrists; social workers as psychologists, and so on. When roles become indistinct, the team may encounter absurdities in its operation. Undemocratic as it may seem, it is illogical to expect equal "voting rights" or contributions from all members, as, for example, on a strictly medical or educational question.

Accomplishments are the reason for a team's existence. It exists primarily to produce, not to satisfy the needs of its members. Still, it is a group subject to the intricacies of the personalities of each member, and to the forces of group interaction. All that applies to individual personality adjustment and is applicable to a group has its influence upon the team. As a group it has its unifying, cohesive forces and its negative, destructive forces.

Members of a good team must have a concern for each other's problems and for mutual problems. A positive step forward occurs in the function of the team when each of its members begins to measure his own success in terms of the group; when he begins to view the team's problems as his own. Positive forces increase as members begin to respect each other, first as individuals and later for the contributions which their respective professions can make.

Each team, as any group, develops its own leader. The team will be most successful when its assigned leader and its actual leader is one and the same person, when he represents the primary philosophy of the team, and when he and his philosophy are liked and respected by the members.

Were I asked to list in rank order the essentials necessary for a good team I would enumerate them as follows:

1. Mutual respect by the team members for each other as persons
2. Mutual respect for one another's profession
3. The presence of good leadership
4. A clear and accepted common primary philosophy
5. A clearly defined goal compatible with the team philosophy
6. Defined roles of the members, with identifiable contributions of their particular professions
7. Clear organizational structure in which the channels of theory and practice are not far apart
8. A system and a language of communication which is known and understood by all.

It is likely that even the best team will have its problems. Most of these come from difficulties within the individuals constituting the team; others, from the interaction of the individual. The smooth performance of any group can be seriously interrupted by an emotionally disturbed member whose constant concern is not with the success of the organization but what he considers to be his "constitutional rights." Always feeling hurt or insulted, always griping (at times with logic), he hampers progress and emphasizes extraneous issues. The person who conceives himself to be something other than what he is constitutes another problem. He may have wanted to become a teacher, though he is a physician. Now he feels that he knows more about education than the educators; he contributes little as a physician and hampers the work of the teacher by imagining himself an expert in that field.

Usually good teams survive these disturbances and they sequester hampering members. In a large organization where many teams operate, there is constant danger that all the good people will tend to gather on the good teams and all the others to join the rather ineffectual teams.

The most appropriate sphere of operation for a team is where a problem must be solved which, because of its complexity, requires the contributions of various professional disciplines. Mental retardation, in my opinion, is such a complex problem. We should, however, not forget that certain aspects of mental retardation can be better solved by individuals with specific professional competencies than by a team. For example, it is hard to conceive how, in the daily classroom setting, a teacher could be replaced by a team. Though other professionals have much to contribute to the totality of an educational program for the mentally retarded, a classroom environment may not be improved by the introduction of other disciplines into its routine operation.

As teamwork assumes an increasing role, we must be on the lookout not to let it become a substitute for the line of responsibility in the management of a large operational unit like a major hospital or a total school system. There is a tendency toward such development and I have often spoken of the socalled "newer concepts of management" which unfortunately often replace methods of administration, which operate through leadership and know-how. Time does not permit going into detail, but some of the pseudoteams one can identify in certain management hierarchies merely further management by committees, by walking delegates, by edicts, by analysis or by catalysis.

Let me return now to the role of the interdisciplinary team in the field of mental retardation. This team can make valuable contributions in the field of diagnosis, but it is important for it to know what purpose the diagnosis is to serve. Is it one of medical importance, or is it to be for educational classification, or for vocational placement? Under each of these conditions a different team with a different structure would serve best. The planning of a life-program for any retarded person can best be accomplished through the interdisciplinary team approach. The same is true in the field of treatment, including such areas as educational planning, community programing, prevention, and research.

Though I may at times have sounded critical, I have seen in my daily work significant contributions made by several teams and I would not forego this method of operation. I would plead, however, that we never view the team as an aggregation of people who are alike, but rather as a structure through which each individual can best make his unique contribution.

Systems of Classification of Mental Retardation

Name	*System*
Ireland	Congenital
	Acquired
Tredgold	Primary amentia (hereditary)
	Secondary amentia (environmental)
Doll	Grade (idiot–imbecile–moron)
	Form (hereditary–acquired)
	Type (clinical typology)
Kanner	Absolute feeble-mindedness (idiot–imbecile)
	Relative feeble-mindedness (moron)
	Apparent feeble-mindedness (pseudo-feeble-mindedness)
Binet	Idiot
	Imbecile
	Moron
Strauss	Endogenous (genetic dysfunction)
	Exogenous (minor neurological symptoms)
Lewis	Subcultural (hereditary–environmental)
	Pathological (organic lesion or abnormality)
Kugelmass	Developmental (skull, facial, or body deviation)
	Metabolic (endocrine disorders)
	Neuromotor (convulsive disorders)
	Psychological (behavioral, sensory, and psychic defects)
Ackerman and Menninger	Functional (minor physical stigma)
	Structural (extreme physical stigma)

REFERENCES

Ackerman, N. W., and C. F. Menninger, "Treatment Techniques for Mental Retardation in a School for Personality Disorders in Children," in C. L. Stacey and M. DeMartino (eds.), *Counseling and Psychotherapy with the Mentally Retarded* (Glencoe, Ill.: Free Press, 1957).

Binet, Alfred, and T. H. Simon, *The Development of Intelligence in Children* (Baltimore: Williams and Wilkins, 1916).

Doll, Edgar A., "The Feebleminded Child," in L. Carmichael (ed.), *Manual of Child Psychology* (New York: Wiley, 1946).

Ireland, W. W., *Idiocy and Imbecility* (London: Churchill, 1877).

Kanner, Leo, *A Miniature Textbook of Feeblemindedness* (New York: Child Care, 1949).

Kugelmass, I. N., *The Management of Mental Deficiency in Children* (New York: Grune and Stratton, 1954).

Lewis, E. D., "Types of Mental Deficiency and Their Social Significance," *Journal of Mental Science, 79* (1933), 298–304.

Strauss, A. S., and L. E. Lehtinen, *Psychopathology and Education of the Brain-injured Child* (New York: Grune and Stratton, 1947).

Tredgold, Alfred F., *Mental Deficiency,* 7th ed. (Baltimore: Williams and Wilkins, 1947).

SECTION THREE

Learning Theory and Mental Retardation

The intriguing question of "how mentally retarded individuals learn" has been in the minds of all teachers since the moment that Itard first tried to educate the Wild Boy of Aveyron in 1799.[1] Educators, psychologists, and parents have searched for an answer. The special class teacher is often rocked back on his heels when a retarded child apparently "learns" something that the teacher did not think he was capable of. Or did the teacher reach this child by applying a theoretical concept of learning which was successful without the teacher's being aware of it? The psychologist, in a clinic or experimental situation, often observes such changes in learning behavior. Yet why learning occurs and how this information can be abstracted into a theoretical concept still eludes us.

Definitions of learning are as numerous and controversial as those of mental retardation. A. W. Melton[2] simply states that "learning is a change in behavior which is correlated with experience or training" and that, further, "learning occurs when a person must react to a situation for which his previously acquired modes of response are inadequate, and it is therefore essentially a process of adjustment to satisfy a need or a motive." Learning involves a great many factors such as motivation, adaptive and organizational ability, and practice.

The influence of experimental psychology is being felt very strongly as the development of a rather unique approach to learning theory is evolved. Operant conditioning and behavior modification theorists have been elaborating on the descriptive behaviorism of B. F. Skinner and his associates. Techniques have been developed that

[1] J. M. Itard, *The Wild Boy of Aveyron* (New York: Appleton-Century-Crofts, Inc., 1932).

[2] A. W. Melton, "Learning" in W. S. Monroe (ed.), *Encyclopedia of Educational Research* (New York: The Macmillan Company, 1941).

can be directly applied to the development of adaptive behavior in mentally retarded individuals.[3]

What is meant by "operant conditioning"? Kenneth Mazik and Roger MacNamara [4] provide us with this explanation: "A very simple and cursory explanation of operant conditioning principles necessitates some defining. Perhaps the most primary is the principle of reinforcement which basically dictates that a reward be given for a certain response so that the probability of the same response recurring will be increased. A likely example would be the giving of praise when a child has effectively washed his face and hands. Immediacy of reward is considered part of reinforcement especially since it may affect intermittent behavior between response and reward." A variety of experimental learning approaches has been studied in the last few years. They include: (1) attention theory; (2) stimulus trace theory; (3) discrimination learning; (4) paired associate learning, and (5) learning set. The reader is referred to the reading in this volume by John H. Hollis and Chester E. Gorton (Reading 30) for a description of the utilization of many of these theories with profoundly retarded individuals. Further discussion and a review of many similar studies will be found in the section on research (Reading 52). The most productive workers in this field of learning theory have been Ogden Lindsley, Sidney Bijou, Norris Haring, Alfred Baumeister, and Norman Ellis. The reader will find fascinating studies developed by these researchers which hold great promise as teaching techniques with the retarded. A major word of caution: operant conditioning techniques and other experimental devices are not playthings. They hold great promise as breakthroughs in teaching the retarded but only when utilized by trained personnel and carefully supervised by knowledgeable staff.

The two articles in this section specifically refer to the application of learning theory to the mentally retarded. An intriguing subject for both educators and psychologists is the relationship between sensory stimulation and specific responses. From the early work of Itard to contemporary studies by Samuel A. Kirk, there has been frequent reference to this subject. In his article, Oliver P. Kolstoe carefully analyzes this concept of learning as it relates to specific teaching situations. Hebb's theories of learning seriously question the concept of dividing mentally retarded individuals into separate etiological groups, such as organic and familial. E. Paul Benoit has long advocated the application of Hebb's theory, based on a neuropsychological concept, to the study of the learning process as it relates to mental retardation.

[3] Alfred A. Baumeister, *Mental Retardation: Appraisal, Education and Rehabilitation* (Chicago: Aldine Publishing Co., 1967), p. 191.

[4] Kenneth Mazik and Roger MacNamara, "Operant Conditioning at the Training School Unit," *The Training School Bulletin, 63*:4 (February 1967), 153–154.

12 SENSORY STIMULATION VERSUS SPECIFIC RESPONSES

Oliver P. Kolstoe

From *Exceptional Children,* Vol. 23, No. 1, October 1956, pp. 2–4. Reprinted with the permission of the Council for Exceptional Children and the author. Dr. Kolstoe is Professor of Special Education at Colorado State College, Greeley.

Many modern writers credit Itard with developing the first systematic approach to the teaching of mentally handicapped children some time around the year 1799 with Victor, the wild boy of Aveyron. Itard himself described his work in great detail, and let the world know that he embraced a philosophy of sensationalism upon which he based his methods of instruction. There seems to be little doubt as to the effectiveness of his methods in trying to teach Victor to be less "animal-like" in his behavior and more "human." And while Itard viewed his own effort as a dismal failure, later writers, notably Seguin, have hailed him as a pioneer, a great teacher, and have pointed to the inadequacy of the raw material with which he was presented as a reason for his feelings of failure.

If we accept that Itard embraced the general philosophical position he says he did, it would be reasonable to suppose that Itard perhaps agreed with the notion that the final intellectual level at which any individual might function was largely a product of the environmental influences which shaped those functions during the development of the person. One could speculate that Itard believed geniuses were made, not born, and that the difference between a child becoming mentally handicapped, a normal person, or a genius depended not on his hereditary endowments but rather on the kind of environmental stimuli to which he was exposed during his lifetime. To carry this a step further, one could sensibly arrive at the position that Itard believed Victor to be "animal-like" in his behavior because the environmental stimuli to which Victor had been exposed during his early growth period had been "animal-like." From the methods used, Itard must have believed it possible to "cure" feeble-mindedness or mental handicap by the simple expediency of replacing the animal associations with "human" experiences as Itard was able to discern these in the culture in which he lived. This logical supposition can be given added strength on the evidence that his sense training methods were essentially those which aimed at providing "civilized" stimuli for Victor. For example, Itard attempted to teach the sense discrimination of hot and cold to Victor, presumably not to make him aware of hotness and coldness as such, but rather to make him sufficiently aware of temperature changes that he might dress in an appropriate manner and thus appear more human and less like an animal. It would be appropriate to surmise that Itard felt he had failed with Victor because he believed idiocy to be curable, and Victor was not cured. Improvement was not enough to satisfy Itard. Presumably, he could be happy with little less than complete cure.

THE METHODOLOGY—SENSORY STIMULATION

Seguin, publishing his book, *Idiocy: Its Treatment by the Physiological Method,* in 1866, gives credit to Itard for interesting him in the treatment of idiots. A sensationist, as Itard was, Seguin better identified his position by postulating a theory of mental deficiency which was related to the defects in the central or peripheral nervous system of an individual. He explained idiocy on the basis of neurophysiological defects which would not allow the sensations to reach the brain. In either case, his method of treatment was the same. That is, he first tried to make as efficient a machine as possible, by physical education and muscle training presumably to increase the efficiency of sensation transmission. Secondly, he seemed to believe that if the sense receptors were bombarded with strong enough stimuli, that these would somehow get through the defective parts of either the peripheral or the central nervous system and reach the brain. If these sensations were repeated often enough, enough of them would get through to the brain to form more adequate associations, in this manner ultimately the idiocy condition would be "cured." For this he used a system of sense training not unlike Itard had employed.

This well written work of Seguin is a clear recognition of an organic basis for mental handicap. To be sure, it is not precise, and the emphasis is on inadequate receptor–connector chains, still the condition is considered organically caused.

THE RESULT—IMPROVEMENT

Maria Deteressa Montessori's activities would lead one to believe she must have embraced somewhat the same philosophical precept as Itard and Seguin when she developed her auto-education techniques to train each sense separately. One cannot deny the effectiveness and efficiency of the Montessori system, but it would be difficult to see how such a system could spring from other than a fairly optimistic philosophy that the human organism achieves a level of intellectual functioning closely related to the stimuli provided in the environment of the child during his development. The difference, then, between the mentally handicapped, the normal, and the genius would have to have been thought of in terms of the quantity and intensity of the stimuli provided in the environment of the child in his developing period.

It is quite well assumed that Itard worked with what today would be considered a rather low grade of mental deficient. Yet he made "some" progress with Victor. Seguin used "idiocy" as a generic term. That is, in the frame of reference within which he lived in the France of the later 1800s, Seguin seemed to use the term idiocy as meaning almost any degree of mental handicap. It is possible that his better results may have been because he worked more with what present-day specialists recognize as mentally retarded than with the mental deficient. This guess is supported by the evidence that Montessori found her methods to be quite useful with bright and gifted children as well as with the mentally retarded. Thus all three of these creative people demonstrated that progress in the intellectual functioning of mentally handicapped children could be made. Seguin and Montessori showed rather well that the higher grade the children, the better the progress. The goal was cure, the methodology, sensory stimulation, and the result was improvement. This is reasonable evidence that a highly stimulating environment appeared to result in generally improved intellectual functioning.

The work of Skeels and Dye on the effects of early environmental stimulation of infants gives added evidence of the possibility of improving intellectual functioning through early stimulation. In 1950 Kirk started a training experiment with young (ages three–five) mentally retarded (IQ 50–80) children. In a forthcoming publication, Kirk is reporting finding spurts in mental growth, seemingly as a result of the stimulation surrounding the youngsters. The work of Nancy Bayley serves to reinforce these suggestions with the effect that two conclusions seem warranted:

1. Systematic environmental stimulation seems to have "some" effect in improving intellectual functioning.
2. The effect seems to be greater with young, high grade mentally retarded. It would seem that the expectation of "cure" attributed to Itard and Seguin is unrealistic, but that improvement as a result of systematic stimulation is a distinct possibility.

THE DEVELOPMENT OF SPECIFIC RESPONSES

As early as 1896, John Dewey began to make his genius known in educational philosophies. His emphasis on the necessity of the learner taking an active part in the education process led many followers to develop methods of instruction which allowed the child to "learn by doing." The later work of Duncan in England placed emphasis on teaching the skills of housewifery and handiwork. Ingram's program presented in her 1935 edition of *Education of the Slow Learning Child* placed major emphasis on engaging the learner in activities. The occupational education curriculum developed by

Hungerford in New York likewise emphasized the activity of the learner. Thus the philosophy of Dewey seems to be reflected in the curricula for mentally handicapped children of Duncan, Ingram, and Hungerford.

This activity approach certainly has resulted in improving the effectiveness of these youngsters. Yet the emphasis is just the opposite of that of Itard and Seguin. While Itard and Seguin were concerned with the systematic presentation of stimuli, present-day workers like Ingram and Hungerford seem to be concentrating on the systematic development of specific responses. This appears to be a radical switch from stimuli to response.

Both approaches seem to produce more effective behavior. Yet certain limitations seem inherent in either the stimuli or response emphasis when used exclusively. It would appear, for example, that those who advocate the intensifying of instructional procedures in order to try to teach mentally handicapped children enough to enable them to keep up with their age peers are acting as though the method is based on an optimistic faith in the possibility of cure.

It would seem that a school system in which educable mentally handicapped children follow the regular class routines of the other children for most of the day, but are pulled out for specialized instruction during part of the school day is operating "as if" this extra stimulation given to the children will do something to increase the associations in the "mind" and increase the level of mental functioning. One could well wonder to what extent this type of reasoning enters into the operation of a remedial program consciously, yet it seems inescapable that some such philosophical position would lead, by one logical extension, to a remediation program.

On the other hand, in view of the fact that trauma, cultural deprivation, and emotional disturbance have a generally depressant effect on intellectual functions, the positive results of Itard, Seguin, and Montessori give a clue for action. That is to say, if there is a lesson to be learned from past workers in this area, it is that since we do not know all the effects environment has on changing intellectual functioning, then in all fairness to each child maximum stimulating must be systematically pursued in the special class curriculum. On the other hand, most of the graduates of the special classes probably will not become "normal" under this treatment. Indeed, some will scarcely profit.

SENSE TRAINING AND BEHAVIOR PRACTICE

It would seem, then, that the emphasizing of specific response skills is also necessary. Unfortunately, some limitations are inherent in this type of programming also. For example, in a program which deals primarily with unit work, often children who are quite limited in ability seldom do much more than what they can do. A child who can do little more than paint may find himself painting in every unit. Thus no systematic attempt is made to improve his performance in other areas. Reading, likewise, is apt to suffer. Although a very exceptional teacher may be able to weave a systematic reading program into a unit plan, it is difficult. Since reading is a necessary tool as well as a method of instruction, it would follow that both systematic instruction in "learning to read" per se and practice in "reading to learn" need emphasis. This combined sense training and behavior practice approach would indicate a curriculum which maintains a careful balance between general education and specific training for occupation.

In the area of general education a systematic approach to the academic subjects would need to be planned for and carried out. This would be aimed at careful attention to the basic skills including sense training, formal instruction in reading, writing, arithmetic, and spelling, and would recognize that this training could result in an increase in the child's level of general intellectual functioning as well as insure maximum skill in his use of the basic tool subjects. It would include teaching the child to think, to solve problems, to manage his own affairs, to write, read, and function efficiently in the quantitative areas. It would call for a systematic, step-by-step, developmental approach.

The unit method of instruction provides excellent opportunities for the practice of transferring basic skills to behavior areas. Problems in social behavior, occupational information, applying for jobs, conduct on the job, demands of specific jobs, and employee–employer and employee–employee relationships demand the learning of specific response behaviors.

This balance between the two approaches gives one the assurance that everything possible is being done to upgrade the mental efficiency of the youngsters, and everything is being done to give them the behavior skills required of them in the work-a-day world. Neither approach seems to be able to do both these tasks alone. Nor are the approaches equally effective at the same time. It would appear that up until the age of about 10 or so, the major curricular emphasis should be on the systematic presentation of stimuli in a sense-training program. This emphasis should gradually change until youngsters at a junior high school level are involved in a response emphasis program. In this program general education provides the child the opportunity of increasing his intellectual efficiency up to the limits imposed by nature, and specific behavior training insures the development of patterns of behavior of a socially acceptable nature. Although the stimuli approach is aimed at vertical development and the response approach at horizontal, the combination seems to be necessary for the total development of mentally handicapped youngsters in special classes.

13 APPLICATION OF HEBB'S THEORY TO UNDERSTANDING THE LEARNING DISABILITY OF CHILDREN WITH MENTAL RETARDATION

E. Paul Benoit

From *The Training School Bulletin,* Vol. 57, No. 1, May 1960, pp. 18–23. Reprinted with the permission of The Training School, Vineland, N.J., and the author. Dr. Benoit is Director, Comprehensive Rehabilitation Planning Project for the District of Columbia.

In December 1958, the author joined in a meeting of the American Association for the Advancement of Science at Washington, D.C. The aim of participants was to present data in support of specific hypotheses or theories. However, it was the frank purpose of this paper merely to define Hebb's [1] neuropsychological theory of behavior and its implications for understanding learning in mentally retarded children.

Current theorizing in the field of learning supposes that learning is effected essentially in the nervous system, and that it is furthered or impeded as a function of qualitative and quantitative changes in the neural apparatus. While basic research in neurology has come up with many discoveries about the structural and functional characteristics of neural tissue, psychologists have tended to deal with learning without availing themselves of this information. Among others, Hull [2] has explicitly been content to regard the central nervous system pretty much as a mere little black box in which stimulus-response connections are built up.

Hebb's view of learning is distinguishable from that of his predecessor's in a number of major ways, but perhaps the most outstanding point of difference in the eyes of the behavioral engineer is that he takes into account the nature of the central nervous system. Since human beings learn with a mechanism that has a number of known features, he assumes that a more meticulous respect of these is likely to facilitate learning, in much the same way as pen manufacturers produce more efficient pens by considering the contours of the hand.

Still another point of difference is Hebb's broader view of the phenomenon of learning. Hull was concerned with the formation of associations between stimuli and responses. Hebb's formulation goes back formally to the initial processes of perception and attention, and the derived process of memory; and he visualizes these phases as points where learning can be promoted.

These two areas of emphasis are decidedly not treated as crucial in

[1] D. O. Hebb, *The Organization of Behavior* (New York: Wiley, 1949).

[2] C. L. Hull, *Principles of Behavior* (New York: Appleton, 1943).

speculations on learning as such. Today, Osgood [3] and Jenkins,[4] among others, do not go much beyond describing learning in terms of the development of a mediational process which represents and accounts for observable responses. Staying on this plane, they are able to bring out a large number of useful operational laws of associative learning.

However, these two peculiarities of Hebb's behavioral theory—concern for neurology and perceptual foundation—are of marked relevance to learning in the mentally retarded. For this group, it is imperative that we explore every possible way of maximizing functionality.

BRIEF OUTLINE OF HEBB'S THEORY

Hebb begins with the concept of cell-assembly, which he sets forth as the basic mechanism of sensory and motoric response, and the neurological counterpart of psychological experience. He assumes that the impinging of a stimulus on a sense organ activates a chain of cells, distributed mostly in the upper portions of the central nervous system; he reasons similarly regarding motoric impulses. Repetition is viewed as strengthening intercellular bonds through the enlargement and multiplication of synaptic knobs by some kind of neurobiotaxis, very likely at a rate and to a limit that jointly suggest a typical biological exponential curve. This type of growth derives some support from the evidence that postulates a structural change to account for the facts of memory.

The cell-assembly concept leads one to infer that its formation requires an optimal extension and intensity of stimulation on the receptor surface and also optimal excitation in the correlated structures in the neural centers. Already both the nature and the origin of cell assemblies recommend adaptations that are likely to enhance perceptual efficiency and stabilize attention.

Once constituted, cell assemblies become the essential building blocks in associative learning of progressive degrees of complexity. At this point, the primitive perceptual structures cooperate to generate integrators. Such an organizational structure develops when two or more stimulations repeatedly occur in close temporal proximity; the firing of the perceptual structures tends to foster the development of a higher-order structure, so that the occurrence of one perceptual act may cause the transmission of excitation through synaptic bridges into the associative structure, and through it deliver facilitation to the other subordinate perceptions, even in the absence of the appropriate stimuli.

[3] C. E. Osgood, *Theory and Method in Experimental Psychology* (New York: Oxford, 1953).

[4] J. J. Jenkins, "Associative Clustering during Recall," *Journal of Abnormal Social Psychology, 47* (1952), 818–821.

The superordinate structure is postulated as consisting of the interconnecting neuronal elements and new cells recruited along the way; it may also include neural elements common to the subordinate structures, as the basis for the perception of partial identities.

The formation of organizational structures is assumed to proceed progressively, as new percepts or more involved perceptual complexes are acquired.

At this point, one may suppose that gradual rise in integration is not independent of the condition of the central nervous system, but that an upper limit is set by the total mass of healthy neural tissue.

It may further be noted that both subordinate and superordinate structures extend into both the sensory and motor segments of the central nervous system, so that motoric elements lend facilitation to related sensory structures, and vice versa.

Hebb's formulation, presented in rough summary, is hopefully intended to account for all the facts of learning. Hebb himself has attempted to show its fertility by applying it to various departments of behavior. More recently, it was extended by Bousfield [5] to explain many facts pertaining to clustering in verbal behavior.

APPLICATION TO LEARNING IN THE MENTALLY RETARDED

Hebb's theory is highly pertinent to the mentally retarded, because of its concern for making the most of impaired neurology. Crowbars vary in strength, but efficiency can be increased by adjusting the fulcrum point to best advantage. Hebb's thought is significant because it subsumes established rules of thumb, and calls attention to further manipulations in the learning situation.

Anyone familiar with the original work of the two great pioneers in the teaching of retarded children, Seguin [6] and Itard,[7] knows that they furthered their success with the children by using larger materials, e.g., alphabet, pencils, tools. As was noted above, Hebb's theory assumes that spread of stimulation at the sensory surface is associated with a more abundant excitation in the higher centers of the nervous system, and that perceptual structures arise more readily; superordinate structures emerge

[5] W. A. Bousfield, "The Occurrence of Clustering in the Recall of Randomly Arranged Associates," *Journal of General Psychology, 49* (1953), 229–240.

[6] E. Seguin, *Traitement moral, hygiene, et education des idiots* (Paris, 1866).

[7] J. M. Itard, *The Wild Boy of Aveyron,* trans. by G. and M. Humphrey (New York: Appleton, 1932).

more easily because there is then a greater number of points at which interfacilitation can take place. Optimal maxima have yet to be determined experimentally.

This general principle suggests several adjustments regarding teaching content. Initial training obviously should be thing-oriented, because of the opportunity thereby provided for fuller cortical participation. If thing-percepts are well established, it is then easier to link them with words; these are clearly more difficult to recognize than things, because of their more constricted configurations as stimuli. The matter of optimal mobilization of the cortex in this area presents a problem of prohibitive proportions. One can, for example, helpfully enlarge the stimulus field in a few ways, e.g., by exaggerating slowness and distinctiveness in the adult's speech, by sharp inter-word contrasts (negatively, by avoidance of confusing homonyms). Finally, the theory cautions against the careless inclusion of reading in the children's curriculum. After they have managed to succeed in the difficult task of extending their knowledge by associating a large number of auditory symbols with familiar objects, it may not be wise to launch into the deeper waters of symbolism by trying to teach too many associations between written and oral symbols. The written word is two steps away from the object; learning here operates on the level of markedly circumscribed stimulus patterns, and involves the association of auditory and visual percepts, with the latter group having far less opportunity for reinforcement than the former.

Closely related to the above principle regarding spread of stimulation is the frequently underscored advantage deriving from the multiplication of sensory modalities or dimensions in a given perception. Thus, emphasizing distinctiveness of both design and color has been shown to aid the learning of the alphabet. The use of audio-visual aids is recommended on the same basis at every level of learning. Further propping can be provided by enlisting the autonomic nervous system, viz., by arousing desires in line with the teaching aims.

Several decades ago, Grace Fernald [8] demonstrated that the slow learners picked up speed in learning to recognize words by tracing the letters with finger or stylus. Hebb's system leads one to infer as much: by engaging more cortex, viz., by including the motoric portion of the brain, more opportunity is provided for interfacilitation. The same logic applies to do-it-yourself practices, the follow-through of projects, the carrying out of instructions, even the vocal recitation of thought sequences.

The need of motoric support makes one wonder to what extent the children's handicap might be accentuated by the curtailment of opportuni-

[8] Grace M. Fernald, *Remedial Techniques in Basic School Subjects* (New York: McGraw-Hill, 1943).

ties for self-help in cases of overservice on the part of protective adults. Many experimental studies have shown that stimulation privation diminishes response capacity even into adulthood in animals.

Some 20 years ago, Alfred Strauss [9] dealt with the problem of distraction in organically impaired children by insisting on the artificial simplification of the stimulus situation. According to Hebb, attention is controlled through the delivery of facilitation from one organizational structure to another. Accordingly, the successful induction of new learning may require the eliminating or minimizing of irrelevant stimuli, until interstructure facilitation has been developed enough to permit the easy channeling of in-coming stimulation to the appropriate organizational structures. Hence, the need of simplicity in the learning situation is a function of the level of habit strength and the integration level. Without regard for adaptation of this sort, there is likely to be mass activation of structures and diffuse thinking.

The theory strongly emphasizes the importance of progression in the teaching of new material. Each task must be broken down in terms of acquired elements in the child's frame of reference; else a double task is faced, and progress must be all the slower. Much efficiency is lost in teaching because of lack of sensitivity to units that are appropriate for the individual. Steps must presumably be short, if they are to get the learner anywhere. Undoubtedly much research is needed into the nature of sequentiality in the evolution of behavioral patterns, and into modes of meaningful analysis.

This consideration regarding rate of growth raises two further questions about developmental ceiling and also about early learning. The difficulty of establishing perceptual structures obviously applies throughout the lifetime of the individual; there is reason to stress the early learning, because there is a tendency to underestimate its significance. Every effort must be made to expose the children to all such experiences as may be likely to be within the scope of their readiness, so as to reinforce as many perceptual and organizational structures as possible. Otherwise behavior becomes permanently constrained within the limits of primitive habits. Slow learning necessarily entails the reinforcement of a scanty set of perceptual structures, both subordinate and superordinate. This condition is presumably behind such characteristics as rigidity and stimulus bound behavior. These psychological manacles must be directly counteracted by the proper organization of the learning situation. Perception must be guided with relatively more explicitness.

Drill is recognized as inherently more necessary for the retarded than for the normal by and large. It may well be that a given degree of response strength in organizational structures may call for a high degree of total

[9] A. A. Strauss and L. E. Lehtinen, *Psychopathology and Education of the Brain-injured Child* (New York: Grune & Stratton, 1947).

reinforcement. This deduction leads to the corollary that the limit of complexity in integration is perforce not high in the retarded. It is therefore imperative to stress learning that is within the limits of possibility rather than to try at all costs to rise to higher levels. He who saws boards with many strokes and hammers nails with many blows had better not attempt to build a castle.

Since the level of integration rises so slowly because of the great need of practice, it stands to reason that proper selection be made of materials. There is no point to building a base broader than the height of a tower calls for.

This principle applies to the motoric sphere no less than to the sensory. The retarded are likely to fail in precision activities, in complex sequences; they do better on tasks involving large objects, molar muscle systems, and hence lower level integrations. They should be oriented to such areas of social service in which interpersonal interaction is primary, and the degree of refinement in perception and muscular function is relatively low.

Finally, to cite one more of many points of application, Hebb observes that new associations are built up independently of awareness. The essential condition is the relatively synchronous perception of related elements. Accordingly, incidental learning has a real place for retarded children, especially in situations in which there are problems of distractibility and disinhibition. After a certain amount of repetition at this phase, attention is likely to operate at the conscious level.

SUMMARY OF IMPLICATIONS

There is much curiosity regarding the relevance of Hebb's concepts of cell assembly and organizational structures. While they do not appear to contradict known neurological facts, they do involve an embarrassingly large number of postulates that cannot readily be verified. Hence one cannot but wonder about justification for utilizing them. We are entitled to say that the proof of the pudding is in the eating. If Hebb's system of assumptions leads to a useful set of organized hypotheses, we should pursue the line of thought and not be inhibited by excessive concern for operational neatness. The theory has the advantage of taking many procedures, many of which might even be in common use, and of subsuming them under a single set of postulates. Should the hypotheses derived from the theoretical framework be supported by experimental evidence, the likelihood is great that insights would gain in depth. Besides, if one may be allowed a morbid analogy, it is better to look at a skeleton than at a clumsy sack of odd bones—which is pretty much the status of currently educational thinking on the mentally retarded.

The research ideas proposed above suggest an important deviation from current practice. As a rule, basic research in learning is done on highly molecular phases and by means of exceedingly primitive tasks. This approach has not startled the world with its fruitfulness. Perhaps controlled observation in everyday life can enlighten us more than the artificial problem boxes, mazes, and other apparatus of the psychological laboratory.

SECTION FOUR

Early Childhood Education

Fifteen years ago, Samuel A. Kirk [1] devised a research project to determine the effects of preschool education on the social and mental development of young educable mentally retarded children. The results of this experiment were positive and, generally speaking, children in the experimental group showed significant development. Why then has it taken all this time for communities and the public schools to accept the concept of preschool programs for the mentally retarded? The answer probably lies in the fact that public school programs for the retarded are mandated by law only for those of legal school age. Secondly, public educational funds were not made available even on a permissive basis for early childhood education of the retarded. Precedent has been established for many years to show the value of preschool programs for deaf, blind, and physically handicapped youngsters.

The earliest preschool programs for the retarded were established on a cooperative basis by parents. These programs were in the main for trainable mentally retarded children with a few severely disturbed educable children also being enrolled. Most of these programs were poorly financed, housed, and staffed. However, NARC developed guidelines for these programs, and they became the forerunners of new and emerging programs.

There is a great deal of evidence that the preschool years are most critical for a child's development. The lack of attention to a child's handicapped condition during the early childhood developmental period can lead to irreversible deterioration of his potential for leading a normal and useful life. Research conducted recently indicates that at age four, a child has already developed 50 percent of his intellectual capacity. The best time to attack a child's mental and

[1] Samuel A. Kirk, *The Early Education of Mentally Retarded Children* (Champaign, Ill.: The University of Illinois Press, 1958).

emotional handicaps appears to be the period from birth through early childhood years.

In addition to the lack of funding, early childhood programs for the retarded have been inhibited by the absence of model or prototype programs. Because of the absence of viable models for preschool retarded children, state and local educational agencies overlook the fact that it may be less expensive to channel resources toward infancy and early childhood development, thus reducing the need for more expensive services later on in the retardate's life.

It is interesting to note that in practically every professional conference and report of priorities, the need for suitable preschool programs for the retarded has been emphasized.

Some development of this program arose under Title VI-A of the Elementary and Secondary Education Act. However, it was not until the passage of Public Law 90-248, the Social Security Amendments of 1967, that progress was made. These amendments have had a far-reaching effect by providing for vastly increased maternal and child health services. This act provides for early case-finding and treatment programs which naturally led to educational programs.

Recognizing the important need for preschool programs, Congress, in late 1968, passed the Handicapped Children's Early Education Act (Public Law 90-538), which provided for the establishment of 75 to 100 model programs designed to develop successful approaches in assisting preschool aged handicapped children. The salient features in this law are: (1) projects will be established in both rural and urban areas; (2) preschool and early childhood education present unique problems to various areas and should therefore transcend geographic boundaries; and (3) it is intended that there be as great a diversity among projects as possible, so that models will be developed that are applicable to many different handicapping areas and particular environmental areas. The model preschool program should stimulate all areas of the handicapped child's development, including emotional, physical, intellectual, and social needs. Finally, a portion of the act encourages the establishment of: (1) programs of counseling and guidance for parents of the handicapped preschool child, and (2) supportive supplementary programs which will aid parents in coping better with problems as they arise.

By late 1969, the Bureau for the Education of the Handicapped of the U.S. Office of Education had funded several operational grants and planning grants and provided for an ongoing evaluation service and training of needed personnel. At least a start has been made in the development of much needed help.

In the initial reading in this section, Will Beth Stephens suggests priorities in preschool provisions for the mentally retarded. Consideration is addressed to assessment of early cognitive development and to intervention programs for infants as well as preschool children. She recommends extended observation of the child's ability to learn in a structured situation in order to determine the level and tempo of development prior to class assignment. Richard C. Scheerenberger, while serving as Assistant Director of the Mental Retardation Division of the Illinois State Department of Mental Hygiene, pioneered the development of preschool community programs for the trainable mentally retarded. In the second reading of this section, he provides us with a rationale for preschool programs and includes a discussion of educational goals in the nursery school program for the trainable mentally retarded. The report describes curricular content, methodology, and program implementation.

14 PROVISIONS FOR THE YOUNG MENTALLY RETARDED

Will Beth Stephens

From *Education and Training of the Mentally Retarded,* Vol. 3, No. 4, December 1968, pp. 180–188. Reprinted with the permission of the Council for Exceptional Children and the author. Dr. Stephens is Associate Professor of Education, Department of Educational Psychology, Temple University, Philadelphia.

Although early remediation is an accepted fact it is not an established service. Currently many schools provide retarded pupils with individual assessment and assistance only after the pupils have shown a year or more of failure to learn from a first grade curriculum that has a predetermined level and tempo. If this neglect is to seem incredible a decade hence, priorities must be established which utilize findings in the area of infant and early childhood assessment and which formulate approaches that will make individually planned instruction available to preschool retarded children.

Present interest in early development stems in part from advances in technology, from new methods in psychophysiology, and from advances in evaluation, which emphasize levels of development, as boundaries between these levels afford a basis for experimental comparison. These methods of early appraisal generally do not involve questioning or complex directions. Instead, reliance is placed upon naturalistic observation of behavior as planned intervention offers an opportunity to observe the child's reactions.

The major event that seems to have stimulated the current intense empirical effort with infants is Fantz' demonstration that with simple methods one can tell what a baby is looking at; to the investigator's amazement the young human has not been found to be perceptually innocent. The neonate does attend to patterned visual targets. For several decades psychology has tabulated the crawling, standing, and walking sequence; now the Zeitgeist points to work in the area of cognitive development (Kagan, 1967). An example of this analytical interest in early cognition is found in Bruner's (1967) current work with infants which seeks to:

1. Study the initial development of human skills which are used in adapting to the environment.
2. Assess the component for voluntary activity and the role of will.
3. Analyze what leads a person from one tract activity to complex adult mental processes.
4. Follow the development of the ability to attend and to hold attention across invariants in the environment.

A large portion of Bruner's ongoing research centered on sucking. By age ten weeks the infant's sucking usually has developed a suck, pause, suck, pause pattern. In order to observe this action, a mechanical apparatus was utilized which had a fixed interval in which milk was delivered; the infant's sucking was found to change to meet the contingencies of the environment. Negative sucking dropped out if there was a two-second delay in milk, and the fixed sucking pattern was abandoned as the infant regressed to a prior routine. To extend these findings, Bruner has been seeking to determine the stage at which the child is capable of more than sucking. He found that if a hungry infant looks at a visual target he stops sucking—but only if he looks toward the object with convergence. At a latter stage it becomes possible for him to look as he sucks, but the processing of the visual information appears to occur between, rather than during, sucks. In a subsequent stage of development, sucking continues when an object appears, but stops if the object disappears suddenly. As a variation of the above experiment, the mechanical nipple was organized so that the child's sucking brought a picture into focus. Findings indicated that children do adopt the sucking pattern that brings the visual reward. Bruner believed that this series of early learning mechanisms was valuable; the way the child deals with these situations may give him basic competencies. The necessary study, perhaps, is not in stimulation, but in what stimulation makes possible.

COGNITIVE ASSESSMENT OF INFANTS

Both observational studies and longitudinal investigations have served to delineate the thought processes of young children. It is now established that cognitive development occurs from birth onward as a person interacts with his environment (Piaget, 1952). With this continuous interaction between a person and his surroundings, the early sensory motor thought processes evolve into more complex mental operations. To accomplish this, the person passes through sequential stages of cognitive development. Knowledge of these stages and activities that are common to them has made it possible to devise methods of assessment which serve to indicate intellectual gaps and deficits as well as possible arrestations at various levels of cognitive development. In turn, information concerning these deficits provides a basis for early remediation.

In a review of instruments designed to measure early intellectual development, Stott and Ball (1965) emphasized the need for an infant test which registers sequential qualitative changes in intelligence and suggested consideration of Piaget's theory of cognitive development as a model. The recent Instrument for Assessing Infant's Psychological Development was developed by Uzgiris and Hunt (1966) in answer to these needs. In this instrument is a scale which is derived from Piaget's developmental sequence of qualitatively different levels of cognitive functioning and which registers the developmental changes as they occur or fail to occur in infants during early stages of life (birth to two years). When knowledge of early deficits has been derived, it should become possible to approach issues involving higher levels of cognition with confidence (Uzgiris and Hunt, 1966).

The Uzgiris–Hunt instrument consists of six series of behavioral schemata with directions for presenting the situations to elicit them, as well as a listing of the most commonly observed behavioral reactions to these situations. The areas included are:

Series I: Visual Pursuit and Permanence of Objects

The assessment begins with the ready made schema of looking. The first accommodations of this schema are manifest in the pursuit of slowly moving objects held at a constant distance from the infant's eye. This is followed by "lingers with glance on the point where a slowly moving object disappeared." Later the infant "obtains a partially hidden object"; still later he may "obtain an object hidden under one or two screens" (or layers of material or paper).

Series II: Development of Means for Achieving Desired Environmental Events

The second series begins with commonly observed handwatching behavior. Piaget described the development of handwatching as an assimilation of the manual schema by the visual schema. With coordination comes the ability to grasp. The development of intention comes out of the feelings of effort in reaching for desired objects. From this development, the series proceeds to clearer evidence of intention in the differentiation of means and ends. The series starts with observed "handwatching behavior" and proceeds to "grasps object when both hand and object are in view," on through a series of accomplishments to such actions as "uses string as means to obtain object (pull toy) after demonstration," and later "without demonstration."

Series III: Development of Schema in Relation to Objects

The series begins with the appearance of coordinations between schemata already present at birth such as sucking, continues to coordination between the manual schema and sucking (hand mouth coordination or thumbsucking), and then to the schema of bringing objects in front of the eyes in order to look at them. Later such schemata as hitting and shaking develop. Examination of objects which provoke interest in the novel, then provoke social interaction, is observed as the schema of showing becomes evident. Later there is recognition of objects as their names are verbalized.

Series IV: The Development of Causality

The series begins when the infant attempts to hold on to desired inputs and may be viewed as branching from Series II, development of means for achieving desired environmental events. Initially "handwatching behavior is observed"; later the infant keeps an object active by means of "secondary circular reactions"; several steps later he seeks to continue an interesting performance by touching the performing agent (touches a top that has stopped spinning to see if the touch will cause spinning to be resumed). Still later he "recognizes another person as an independent causal agent by giving back an object to have it activated again" (hands his father the top to be rewound), and at an even later stage he "activates a mechanically operated object after demonstration" (winds the top himself).

Series V: The Construction of the Object in Space

As the infant coordinates the schema of looking and listening, he begins to localize sounds and their sources; things heard become things to find and view. Later there is interest in the trajectory of objects. Items on the scale include, "localizes the source of sound," "follows the trajectory of a rapidly moving object" (looks at spoon as it drops to the floor), acquires an "understanding of gravity shown by permitting an object to roll down an incline," and "makes detours in order to retrieve objects from behind obstacles" (when a ball is in back of a table he goes around the table to retrieve it).

Series VI: Development of Imitation

This series consists of two sections, one pertaining to vocal and the other to gestural imitation. The vocal series begins with the already present schema of vocalizing. As interest in novelty develops the infant starts to imitate unfamiliar sound patterns, at first by gradual approximation and later by direct imitation. The infant progresses to imitate words which are within his vocabulary.

The gestural series follows a similar progression. Initially the infant imitates simple gestures (handwaving); he later progresses to the imitation of unfamiliar gestures which he can watch himself perform (stretching leg out straight) to gestures which he cannot watch himself perform (facial gestures such as winking the eye).

Although it would have been feasible to describe an infant's development in terms of Piaget's stages, a finer grading of steps along these developmental sequences was desired, especially for diagnostic work (Uzgiris and Hunt, 1966). Research indicates that normal infants do progress through the hierarchical sequence of situations listed in each of the six series outlined in the Uzgiris–Hunt scale. Early remediation is indicated when infants do not make this progress.

Use of the measure in a project concerned with the intellectual stimulation of culturally disadvantaged infants, ages eight months to two years (Stephens, Kirk, and Painter, 1966) revealed information on the cognitive development of motor impaired infants that was not revealed by performance on the Cattell Infant Intelligence Scale.

As a supplement to purely cognitive measures, Frankenburg and Dodd (1968) have devised and standardized a scale for infants and small children, which serves to detect developmental lags in four functional areas: gross motor, fine motor adaptation, language, and personal social. Through application of the scale the examiner may become alerted to irregularities in development. The value of the Denver Development Screening Test lies in the fact that it was designed to note, and implement detection of, irregularities —not to present an observed sequence of development.

EARLY INTELLECTUAL STIMULATION

The value of determining the infant's level of performance and providing remediation derived from activities basic to that level has been confirmed by numerous research efforts. Included in these efforts is a study involving infants with Down's Syndrome (Coriat, Theslenco, and Waksman, 1967). Here, the experimental group which was afforded early psychomotor stimulation had a mean IQ of 67 upon entrance into kindergarten, whereas the mean IQ of the control group was 49. Remediation, which started during the neonatal period, concentrated on three of the connected elements that constitute the chain of oral reflexes—searching, sucking, and swallowing. In addition, tonic neck reflexes were stimulated so that movement necessary for ocular fixation on objects in the environment was provided. Bright, appealing objects were displayed in an effort to promote and strengthen the palmar grasp. Exercises also included adduction and flexion of the legs. During the second quarter of the first year sensorial organs and development of the body schemata were stimulated, and there was guided use of hands. Continued remediation was provided until it was possible for these subjects at age four or five years to attend a kindergarten with normal children.

In a recent tutorial program for culturally deprived children between eight months and two years of age (Stephens, Kirk, and Painter, 1966), it was found that some subjects had difficulty in making the transition from concrete objects—a shoe and comb—to symbolic representation—pictures of a shoe and comb. Initially, perhaps because the environment had been barren of pictorial symbols, pictures had no interest or meaning for the majority of these subjects. Attention centered on the manipulative value of the paper and scant heed was paid to the picture. In an effort to promote interest and recognition, realistically colored life size pictures which represented objects found in the child's daily environment were selected. However, when these were presented the young children continued to evidence no sign of recognition. Therefore, decision was made to present realistic, colored photographs of an orange while the tutor and subject were engaged in peeling and eating an orange. The task required the child to put half of an orange in an envelope to which a picture of half an orange was attached. On successive days a whole orange was put in an envelope to which a picture of a whole orange was attached. Later an apple and an envelope with an attached picture of an apple replaced the orange. Still later, envelopes for both the apple and the orange were placed in front of the child and he was requested to "put the orange in the bag," or "put the apple in the bag." Correct placement was made using the pictured orange or apple as the cue. As bananas, peaches, and other fruits were introduced it became necessary for the child to discriminate between four pictured objects to achieve correct placement. Following this, the task was expanded to include such everyday objects (and their envelope picture) as a bottle, shoe, sock, and comb. After success was achieved in this activity the child identified these same items in picture books. In this manner the transition from concrete object to pictorial representation was made, and nursery books which contained these pictured items began to have interest and meaning for these culturally disadvantaged subjects. Later the printed name of the object was inserted as a preparatory step for transition from pictorial to symbolic representation. Thus, the tutorial approach consisted in: (a) locating the child developmentally in a particular area, (b) devising methods which would aid transition from one developmental level to the next, and (c) dividing the training task into a sequence of activities.

PRESCHOOL COGNITIVE ASSESSMENT

Although there have been many efforts to achieve early childhood assessment, as yet no one has furnished a standardized scale based on Piaget's theory of cognition which measures development from two through six years. The lack of research in this area has been noted by Woodward (1963), and her current effort centers on this period. Unfortunately, children's needs cannot be held in abeyance. There is need for preschool diagnostic instruments now. Although not based on Piaget's developmental stages, per se, there is an instrument available which reflects 25 years of careful research on the part of the developer, Elsa Haeussermann; it is designed as an inventory of developmental levels in the child from two to six years old (Haeussermann, 1958). The instrument determines the stage the subject has reached in various areas of learning, and affords a description of the level and pattern of functioning. Haeussermann's objective has been to determine the potential for development by circumventing certain assessment obstacles—visual, auditory, or motor—which are present. In testing a child with visual impairment, effort is made to determine if he has learned to use auditory clues and to determine if his memory has served to compensate for the unreliability or insufficiency of his perception or vision. The goal is to sample the child's intactness as the nature and extent of the impairment is explained. Areas included in the assessment are:

1. Recognition of concrete familiar life-size objects
2. Recall of missing picture from memory
3. Orientation in time
4. Recognition of symbols and forms
5. Color discrimination
6. Form discrimination
7. Multiple choice color form sorting
8. Manipulative ability
9. Amount recognition
10. Eye motion and gross vision.

Because Haeussermann's evaluation was based on tasks which were sequential in development, the instrument itself is suggestive of remedial techniques. Review of the sequence indicates what is to be accomplished next; remedial effort centers on how to provide the necessary experiences.

As the emphasis on early diagnosis has increased, efforts have been made to develop measures (a) which are capable of identifying children who have motor, perceptual, or cognitive deficits and (b) which can be administered easily and quickly, preferably by the classroom teacher and usually through systematic observational procedures in natural or normal settings. An instrument designed to meet these demands is the Valett Developmental Survey of Basic Learning Abilities (Valett, 1966) for use with children two to seven years old. The survey, which is concerned with the developmental tasks prerequisite to more formal learning, was compiled through the selection or adaptation of items formerly used by Baker and Leland, Bender, Binet, Doll, Frostig, Gesell, Haeussermann, Hiskey, Jastak, Wechsler, and Valett. Areas which are measured include: motor integration and physical development, tactile discrimination, auditory discrimination, visual discrimination, visual motor coordination, language development and verbal fluency, and conceptual development. Users of the test should remember, however, that when the number of items measuring a specific area is decreased the reliability of the test is lowered. Studies of the reliability of the Valett Developmental Survey are needed. Until these are furnished its adequacy for individual assessment is problematic.

PRESCHOOL TRAINING

After early identification of deviant development is accomplished, attention turns to training of preschool groups. One of the major contributions of the current plethora of programs, materials, and methods for this age group is the finding that to provide curriculum based on a developmental sequence requires a reeducation of teachers and demands creative contributions to content and methodology. Piaget's statement that a child knows an object only to the extent he has acted upon it (Piaget, 1964) indicates a need to provide experiences involving concrete manipulation of objects. Guided by these requirements, Connor and Talbot (1966) designed a curriculum for preschool retardates based upon seven broad categories: (a) intellectual development, (b) imaginative and creative expression, (c) social development, (d) emotional development, (e) manipulative development, (f) gross motor development, and (g) self help skills. Because language was viewed as cross sectional it had inherent emphasis in all activities. Growth in these areas was directed through 190 curriculum items. Analysis of the task and observation of pupil behavior indicated that there were five definable levels of functioning for each task. The first was the lowest observed level of functioning and the fifth was the highest achievement expected. At each level activities were indicated which should aid progression to the next higher one. Although designed for kindergarten age retardates, the method warrants careful analysis as a curriculum development technique useful with all children.

PRIORITIES IN PROGRAMS FOR THE YOUNG MENTALLY RETARDED

Because early identification of deficits in cognitive development can be achieved and because early remediation is possible, it becomes necessary to determine priorities in their accomplishment. When faced with this task, the *Philadelphia Collaborative Study of Educational Programs for Handicapped Children* (Philadelphia Public Schools, 1968), firm in its belief that educational programs must be integrated with medical and social programs for children at very early ages, proposed the following plan:

1. Establishment of an Early Childhood Center which would serve as a central information agency to keep records on children with handicapping or potentially handicapping conditions. Hospitals, clinics, and other health agencies would notify this central agency of potential handicaps appearing in children from their first day of life onward. Clues to handicaps in preschool children would be lags in physical, social, or intellectual development. Inservice training would be required to sensitize health agencies to the educational significance of handicapping conditions. Information thus provided by public and private agencies would be kept on file at a central information agency, with dossiers maintained on individual children.
2. Provision of a school-based service for parents of preschool handicapped children which would be responsible for notifying parents of the facilities available to them at the moment their child is diagnosed as handicapped. The service would also develop early educational programs (from infancy onward) to help parents prepare their children for school. These programs might, in some instances, be operated by

the parents themselves. With training, mothers and grandmothers could help develop language skills in children beginning at the age of one year.

3. Preregistration of all children prior to their entrance into preschool classes. At this point, the central information agency would supply schools enrolling these children with all available information on their diagnosis, condition, and treatment.
4. Home visitations during the six-month period between preregistration and school entrance. A public health nurse and/or an agent of the school board's services to parents of handicapped children would be required to make three visits to the home of each handicapped child. Reports on these visits would include observation of physical conditions, parent child relations, and child behavior. If necessary, additional data would be obtained on the child's social, motor, language, and cognitive development.
5. Establishment of preschool classes of reduced size with a teacher supervisor supplied for each seven classes. The supervisor would observe, over a period of time, the level and tempo of each child's development as well as his ability to profit from school programs.
6. Provision for intensive remediation for children with visual, auditory, speech, motor, emotional, or cognitive impairment. Reassignment of pupils would occur at various times during the observation period in order to permit homogeneous grouping for remedial work.
7. Nutritional needs to be met by supplementary diets. During this early education period, provision would be made for correct nutrition where inadequacies were demonstrated.
8. Transitional classes to be available during the early elementary grades to afford students further individual development and learning opportunities before final placement decision is made.

In summary, more intensive study of all children during preschool years is urged. Such study should provide a developmental diagnosis followed by an observation period in which learning opportunities are furnished the child. During this extended observation period, assessment can be made of the child's tempo of development as well as his basic level of functioning in deficit areas. No child should have to fail before he is provided an individually appropriate chance to succeed.

REFERENCES

Bruner, J. S. Cognition and learning. In *Issues in Human Development.* Symposium presented at St. Christopher's Hospital, Temple University, Philadelphia, November, 1967.

Connor, F. P., and Talbot, M. E. *An Experimental Curriculum for Young Mentally Retarded Children.* New York: Teachers College Press, Columbia University, 1966.

Coriat, L., Theslenco, L., and Waksman, J. *The Effects of Psychomotor Stimulation on the IQ of Young Children with Trisomic 21.* Buenos Aires, Argentina: Neurological Center Hospital de Ninos, Gallo, 1330, 1967.

Frankenburg, W. K., and Dodds, J. B. *Denver Developmental Screening Test.* Bethesda: National Institutes of Health, Division of Research Facilities, 1968.

Haeussermann, E. *The Development Potential of Preschool Children.* New York: Grune and Stratton, 1958.

Kagan, J. Earliest influences. In *Issues in Human Development.* Symposium presented at St. Christopher's Hospital, Temple University, Philadelphia, November, 1967.

Philadelphia Public Schools. *Collaborative Study of Educational Programs for Handicapped Children.* Philadelphia: School District for Philadelphia, 1968.

Piaget, J. *The Origins of Intelligence in Children.* New York: International University Press, 1952.

Piaget, J. Cognitive development in children: The Piaget papers. In R. E. Ripple and V. E. Rockcastle (Eds.), *Piaget Rediscovered: A Report of the Conference on Cognitive Studies and Curriculum Development.* Ithaca, N.Y.: School of Education, Cornell University, 1964. Pp. 6–48.

Stephens, W. B., Kirk, S. A., and Painter, G. *Intellectual Stimulation of Culturally Disadvantaged Children Ages Eight Months to Two Years.* Progress Report. U.S. Office of Education Project 5-1181, Department of Health, Education, and Welfare, 1966.

Stott, L. H., and Ball, R. S. Infant and Preschool mental tests. *Monograph of the Society for Research in Child Development, 1965,* 30 (No. 3).

Uzgiris, I., and Hunt, J. McV. *Instrument for Assessing Infant Psychological Development.* Urbana, Ill.: The University of Illinois, 1966.

Valett, R. E. *Valett Developmental Survey.* Palo Alto, Calif.: Consulting Psychologists Press, 1966.

Woodward, M. The application of Piaget's theory to research in mental retardation. In N. R. Ellis (Ed.), *Handbook of Mental Deficiency.* New York: McGraw-Hill, Inc., 1963. Pp. 297–324.

15 NURSERY SCHOOL EXPERIENCES FOR THE MENTALLY RETARDED

R. C. Scheerenberger

From *Mental Retardation: Selected Conference Papers,* Illinois State Department of Mental Hygiene, Springfield, Ill., 1969, pp. 47–60. Reprinted with the permission of the Illinois State Department of Mental Hygiene and the author. Dr. Scheerenberger is Superintendent, Central (Wisconsin) Colony, Madison, and on the faculty of University of Wisconsin.

A well-conceived, effectively implemented nursery school program can play a significant role in a child's development and formal education. This is true for most children, regardless of their level of intelligence. In fact, research has indicated that such training may be of greatest value to the retarded, especially when they come from emotionally or intellectually impoverished environments.

A brief review of the literature finds a number of studies which have reported that nursery school experiences can result in increased measured intelligence among children in general, e.g., Wooley (1925), Barrett and Koch (1930), Ripin (1933), and Wellman (1940). Other studies, especially those conducted by Skeels and his associates at Iowa (e.g., Skeels and Dye, 1939) and Spitz (e.g., 1945, 1946), demonstrated that changing a young child's environment from one of deprivation to one of wholesome mothering and enrichment could produce marked increments in measured intelligence, even to the extent of ameliorating previously assumed retardation. This does not mean to imply that every nursery school program, or even the best, will effect such drastic changes in behavior. The subjects included in the Iowa studies, for example, came from abnormally sterile environments. In addition, methodological weaknesses tended to vitiate the significance of the obtained results.

Perhaps a study of greater value in terms of the present concern was reported by Kirk in 1958. In this research project, 81 mentally retarded children between the ages of three and six were studied for a period of three to five years. Of these 81 children, 28 participated in a community preschool program, and 15 participated in an institutional preschool program. The remaining 38 subjects served in appropriate contrast groups.

An overall conclusion to this study was that the proffered training experiences did result in improved functioning among the majority of subjects. Of the 43 retardates participating in the preschool program, 30 (70 percent) made and maintained significant gains with respect to both measured intelligence and social performance.

Of equal importance was the fact that the greatest gains were enjoyed by those children residing in inadequate psycho-social environments. As shown in the table below, institutionalized retardates enrolled in the preschool program had an average IQ gain of 10.2; in contrast, the nonparticipating institutionalized retardates had an average IQ loss of 6.5. Other findings indicated that retardates with organic involvement and those from adequate homes received minimal benefit from preschool training.

Preschool Study: Changes in Measured Intelligence

	Experimental Subjects			*Contrast Subjects*		
	FIRST PRE-SCHOOL TEST (MEAN IQ)	FIRST FOLLOW-UP* (MEAN IQ)	OVERALL CHANGE	INITIAL TEST (MEAN IQ)	FIRST FOLLOW-UP (MEAN IQ)	OVERALL CHANGE
Community Program	72.5	84.2	+11.8	75.8	82.7	+6.9
Institution Program	61.0	71.2	+10.2	57.1	50.6	−6.5

* One year following termination of classroom participation.
Adapted from Kirk (1958).

On the basis of the cited literature, it can be concluded that, though it is impossible to predict precisely the net value of formal preschool training, it is highly probable that such experience can increase the retardate's functioning and, perhaps, his potential capabilities.

GENERIC GOALS OF EDUCATION

In order to discuss and interpret the objectives underlying the activities of a nursery school program for the trainable retarded, it is of prime import to recognize that all education has certain basic commitments. When, as educators, we accept the responsibility for the formal instruction of any child, we also accept those obligations inherent to an education in a democratic society. Education in this country is the expressed and defined right of all children capable of benefiting from such experience; *but* education is also the prime means by which society preserves its status, transmits its heritage, and provides the foundation for further development. In light of this, all education, regardless of the characteristics of the child or the level of his functioning, is obligated towards the realization of several fundamental objectives.

These objectives have been formulated by various professional organizations and societies. For the purpose of this paper, the seven cardinal objectives defined by the Commission on the Reorganization of Secondary

Education (1918) will be cited. Accordingly, it is desired that each child gain knowledge and understanding, skill and confidence, appropriate attitudes and interests, and effective strategies of action relative to: (1) good mental and physical health; (2) a command of the fundamental processes, which includes communication skills, reading, writing, and arithmetic; (3) worthy home membership; (4) vocational preparation; (5) citizenship; (6) wise use of leisure time; and (7) character or ethical development.

While these goals serve as a broad foundation for all education, it becomes necessary to interpret their significance in terms of the characteristics of the child being served, his ultimate expectancies, and his present level of adaptive behavior. In other words, one needs to establish a set of meaningful, attainable objectives which will provide a realistic basis for planning and evaluating nursery school training.

EDUCATIONAL GOALS OF NURSERY SCHOOL PROGRAMS FOR THE TRAINABLE MENTALLY RETARDED

The nursery school program will be considered as one which is concerned with extending appropriate educational experiences to those retardates between the chronological ages of four and eight years and whose measured intelligence falls within an approximate IQ range of 35 to 50. The corresponding mental age range, taking into consideration both chronological age and IQ, is one and one-half to four years.

The objectives underlying nursery school training for the trainable retarded, discussed in terms of the seven cardinal principles, are as follows:

Mental and Physical Health

With respect to mental health, one of the primary objectives of a nursery school program is the development of personally, emotionally, and socially secure individuals. It is generally recognized by psychologists and educators alike that all children possess basic needs for emotional stability. In brief, each individual needs to acquire a sense of (a) self-respect, (b) belonging, (c) success, (d) accomplishment, (e) achievement, (f) recognition, (g) responsibility, and (h) that personal security which can emanate only from a self-understanding and the development of realistic goals. The classroom environment, the teacher's attitudes and capabilities, and the training experiences are all of consequence in satisfying this global goal for emotional security.

With respect to physical health, it is essential that the nursery school extend to the TMR numerous opportunities to develop the basic habits, attitudes, and skills associated with self-care, grooming, safety, and proper nutrition. Psychomotor development is also of significance to both physical and mental development.

Fundamental Processes

Experience to date would indicate that the trainable child rarely attains a functional level of reading, writing, and arithmetic beyond the first grade. It is necessary, however, that the nursery school program begin to lay a foundation for the child to recognize and print his own name and address and become familiar with basic numerical concepts. The major concern of this objective as it relates to the nursery school situation is to provide the child with innumerable opportunities and experiences to develop oral language and related communicative skills.

Worthy Home Membership

The trainable child needs to acquire those attitudes, skills, and habits essential to being a desirable, pleasant, and contributing member of his family. This objective is closely related to that of mental health.

Vocational Preparation

While the nursery school program for the TMR will not be concerned specifically with formal vocational training, it is necessary to recognize that the basic attitudes and habits involving inter-personal relationships, the ability to attend to the task at hand, the development of a sense of responsibility, and the similar are all important aspects of vocational preparation.

Citizenship

Though this goal is interpreted primarily in terms of the child's functioning within his home and school, the nursery school program should begin to provide some exposure of the child to his community and emphasize such important social responsibilities as respecting the rights and property of others.

Wise Use of Leisure Time

This goal has limited implications for the nursery school training program; however, many of the play, art, and musical experiences offered within the classroom are transferred to the home and become good leisure-time activities.

Character or Ethical Development

The nursery school can play an important role in assisting the trainable child develop desirable standards of behavior. Like all young children, the TMR need to acquire appropriate attitudes and habits relative to honesty, truthfulness, and dependability.

To summarize, the objectives underlying the nursery school program for the trainable child emphasize the development of (1) emotionally secure, socially adaptable children; (2) oral language; (3) basic skills and habits associated with health, self-care, and personal grooming; and (4) a foundation for continual growth in the areas of social and vocational adequacy. These goals provide the basis for the designation of curricular activities.

CURRICULAR PROVISIONS

Several pages have been included in this report which illustrate the major types of activities usually included in a curriculum for the nursery school, trainable child. It should be observed that these activities are based on a combination of teacher experience and tradition, rather than representing the results of controlled, long-term, experimental studies. This does not, in any manner, depreciate the significance of intelligent classroom experience. It does point out, however, that neither the educator nor the psychologist has seriously attempted to develop and perpetuate scientifically constructed curricula. We still do not know, with any appreciable degree of knowledge, what activities, introduced at what age, will impede or accelerate learning. This, of course, is closely allied with our lack of understanding concerning child development and those variables which positively or adversely affect intellectual functioning.

Prior to proceeding to the actual outline of curricular activities, it should be recognized that both the curriculum and its schedule of presentation should be flexible and readily modifiable to meet the needs of the individual student and his environment. Structure in programming is desirable; rigidity is not.

It is also of consequence to realize that much of the knowledge gained by a child in a nursery school is incidental to the actual classroom program. Swift (1964, page 263), in her review of the research related to nursery school programs, stated that "much learning takes place in a non-specific way as the child explores his environment, is exposed to different types of experience, and has the opportunity to experiment at first hand with many kinds of materials. Behavior that often seems purposeless to the observer supplies the child with basic experiences from which he draws the data to solve problem situations which may arise later."

A second reason for encouraging the nursery school to extend a variety of experiences to the young retardates is theoretical in orientation. According to Piaget, who has been long concerned with the development of intellectual function and logic in children, there are two fundamental processes of learning: *assimilation* and *accommodation*. Assimilation involves the individual's intake of environmental stimuli and experiences; in other words, mental assimilation is the incorporation of sensory data into existing response patterns. Every mental act involves the individual's interpretation of his encountered experiences. In contrast, accommodation refers to the individual's reactions or adaptation to the realities of his environment.

Mental accommodation involves the adjustment of the individual's response pattern to the sensory input and to the realities of his world.

Piaget also indicates that the child between the ages of one and one-half and four, or who is within the "pre-operational" period, begins to internalize and symbolize his experiences and concepts of reality. Of great significance at this particular level in the child's development is Piaget's notion of *signifiers* and *significates.* A signifier is an internal representation, such as an image or a word that symbolizes some phase of reality which may be present or absent, real or imagined. The significate is the thing, object, or experience which the child has symbolized. There are two kinds of signifiers: the *symbol* and the *sign*. Symbols are private, highly individualized signifiers. In contrast, signs are those verbal signifiers which have acquired a social meaning and can be communicated to others. Of significance to the nursery school teacher is Piaget's contention that it is the private, personalized symbols which emerge first. The social sign, or the commonly accepted label for an object, is acquired secondly. Thus, it is not the incorporation of verbal signs which initially produces representational thought. According to this interpretation, while the acquisition of language is of utmost importance in the development of conceptual thinking, it does not provide the first or sole basis for such reasoning.

The combination of this concept concerning the role of symbols with the entire process of assimilation emphasizes the need for the nursery school to provide a wide range of experiences and numerous opportunities for the child to experiment and develop a sense of curiosity. Perhaps this is the greatest value of the nursery school.

ILLUSTRATIVE CURRICULAR ACTIVITIES

The following outline of activities, stated in terms of what the child is expected to do, is designed merely to give the educator an overview of typical curricular content. The listing is by no means exhaustive.

Social Training

1. Participate in group activities.
2. Acquire and use basic manners.
3. Learn to share, take turns, and respect the rights of others.
4. Share in the responsibilities of maintaining the classroom.
5. Orally identify members of the family (e.g., mother, father, and brother).
6. Become acquainted with the respective roles of mother and father.
7. Become familiar with common community services (e.g., store and church) and related personnel (e.g., policemen and postmen).

Oral Language Development

1. General Vocabulary Development.
   a. Acquire and use words pertaining to making needs known (e.g., eat, hungry, tired, cold, bathroom, and help).
   b. Acquire and use words pertaining to parts of the body (e.g., head, eyes, ears, nose, mouth, legs, and feet).
   c. Acquire and use words pertaining to common courtesies (e.g., please, thank you, hello, goodbye, Mr. and Mrs.).
   d. Acquire and use words pertaining to the home (e.g., kitchen, living room, stove, refrigerator).
   e. Acquire and use words pertaining to the community (e.g., store, church, street).
   f. Acquire and use words basic to common transportation (e.g., bus and cars).
   g. Name objects common to the school room (e.g., table, chair, door,. toys).
   h. Name objects and animals common to the child's experiences (e.g., flowers, water, trees, common domestic pets).
2. Follow simple oral direction.
3. Describe pictures, including the identification of the objects, scenes, or actions, simple counting, and basic colors.
4. Identify by name the primary colors: red, yellow, and blue.
5. Listen to and retell stories.
6. Participate, whenever possible, in group or individual discussions concerning home or school activities.

Self-Care and Personal Grooming Skills

1. Acquire desirable attitudes toward cleanliness and grooming.
2. Learn to wash hands and face properly.
3. Develop appropriate habits relative to the brushing of teeth—when, how, and care of implements.
4. Keep pointed and foreign objects out of the ears.
5. Dress neatly, change clothes before playing, hang up coats and caps, etc.

Health

1. Acquire desirable attitudes towards personal cleanliness.
2. Acquire proper attitudes of skills related to basic eating habits (e.g., do not eat rapidly, do not eat too much, do not gulp food, and avoid eating too much candy).
3. Identify and use properly basic implements of eating, including cup, plate, spoon, fork, and napkin.

4. Acquire basic food vocabulary of such items as cereal, milk, meat, bread, butter, and water.
5. Develop basic lavatory skills, including when to go to the bathroom, use tissue correctly, take proper care of clothing, wash hands.
6. Acquire basic habits and skills related to safety (e.g., do not run on stairs, avoid hot radiators, recognition of stop sign, how to cross the street, avoid playing in the street, and basic safety associated with playground equipment).

Development of Psycho-Motor Coordination

1. Develop general muscular coordination through such activities as running, skipping, throwing, and playing with such vehicles as tricyle and wagon.
2. Develop finer coordination through pounding activities, puzzles, pegboard, and cutting and coloring.
3. Develop both general and finer coordination through rhythmic activities, such as walking, skipping, hopping, in accordance with a defined rhythmic pattern and/or imitating birds, musical animals.

Academic Activities

With the exception of oral language development, the academic area receives only minimal attention.

1. Develop retentive ability:
   a. Improve visual retention through games, such as hide and seek, puzzles, missing parts, recalling visualized objects.
   b. Improve auditory memory through listening activities, stories, poems, rhymes, music, finger plays, and rhythms.
2. Participate in group discussions concerning movies, film strips, daily activities, television programs.
3. Describe action and objects in pictures related to personal experiences.
4. Enjoy looking at and discussing picture books and magazines.
5. Develop discrimination ability:
   a. Visual: match objects by color, form, family, and size; match objects by associated meaning (e.g., head and cap, cup and plate, etc.); find objects and animals and people in pictures; basic psycho-motor activities, such as coloring, pasting, drawing, and tracing; develop some concept of space relationships, including top, middle, and bottom, near and far, up and down, front and back, inside and outside; develop some notion of quantity (e.g., big and little, tall and short, more or less).
   b. Auditory: identify and discriminate between common sounds

(e.g., high- and low-pitched voices, loud and soft, the differences between the cat and the dog, the voice of adult and a child).

   c. Tactual: identify and discriminate between such phenomena as soft and hard, hot and cold, and sharp and dull.
   d. Reading: recognize one's own name.

6. Numerical concepts:
   a. Count by rote 1 through 12.
   b. Recognize basic groupings of two to five.

Vocational Training

1. Begin to develop those attitudes which are essential to success in any job (e.g., follow directions and take criticism pleasantly; get along well with fellow classmates; desire to do well).
2. Develop habits, such as finishing what is started, practicing good safety habits, and being neat and clean.
3. Accept simple assignments in the room, such as dusting, washing desks, assisting with washing and drying of dishes.

Creative Expression

1. Music
   a. Learn simple eight-measure songs, learn simple finger plays, and enjoy singing simple songs.
   b. Experience free rhythmic expression, playing rhythmic instruments, imitating a musical animal, moods and tempos, and participating in such activities as marching, skipping, walking, and running to music.
   c. Enjoy listening to a wide variety of musical selections developed especially for the young child.
2. Arts and Crafts
   a. Gain experience with the following materials: crayons, temper paint and brushes, plasticine, chalk, construction paper, paste, and scissors.
   b. Freely express ideas and feelings through various media.
   c. Participate in such general art activities as scribbling on large paper; drawing to music; drawing on the blackboard; painting various lines, forms and free patterns; manipulating clay-coils, balls, pinching and squeezing; cut, fold, tear, paste, and color, using a variety of materials and paper.

Play Activities

Engage in a variety of basic play activities, including (a) housekeeping play (e.g., setting table, sweeping, putting clothes on dolly, and dressing up in various adult clothes); (b) sand play; (c) water play; (d) block play; and (e) play with toy animals, dolls, etc., in meaningful situations.

Principles Governing Methodology and Implementation

As is generally recognized, an educator cannot posit within a child any form of knowledge, or even a single bit of information. In fact, the best he can do is: (1) create a motivation for learning; (2) establish an emotionally secure, stimulating atmosphere; (3) provide the child with hopefully meaningful experiences; and (4) introduce the educational program in such a manner that the child, *through his own self-activity,* can increase his knowledge, insight, skills, appreciation, and attitudes. In order to maximize the probability of developing appropriate educational procedures for the nursery school TMR, it is necessary to consider some of the basic learning and developmental characteristics of children within a mental age range of approximately one and one-half to four years.

For this purpose, let us again draw upon the experiences and theory of Jean Piaget. On the basis of his intensive observations of the behavior of his own children and the students enrolled at the Rousseau Institute in Geneva, Switzerland, Piaget postulated that there are four general periods in the development of intellectual thought:

1. The Sensorimotor Period, which extends from birth to approximately two years of age;
2. The Preoperational Period (two to seven years);
3. The Period of Concrete Operations (seven to eleven years);
4. The Period of Propositional or Formal Operations (eleven to fourteen years).[1]

Though the nursery school teacher of the TMR is concerned with the level of preoperational thought, which most closely parallels the mental functioning of the preschool trainable child, it is necessary to first review the basic features of the sensorimotor period. During this period, the child progresses from responding on the basis of inborn reflexes to the point of beginning to manipulate and combine images and symbols internally. In essence, by the age of eighteen months, the normal child begins to show the first signs of forethought and planning; however, he tends to deal only with the very concrete aspects of reality and is interested primarily in determining the effectiveness of his responses (i.e., Do they produce the desired effect?).

As previously stated, it is during the preoperational period that the

[1] It is recommended that the uninitiated reader interested in pursuing Piaget's thinking initially consult secondary sources. Piaget's own writings are rather abstract, involving the highly complex language of mathematical logic. Short overviews of Piaget's developmental theory are provided by Wolinsky (1962) and Robinson and Robinson (1965). The most frequently consulted text is by Flavell (1963).

child begins to internalize and symbolize his experiences and reality. He is beginning to establish a cognitive system capable of transcending concrete reality; in other words, the child can think in terms of the past, the present, and, in a limited sense, the future. He is capable of distinguishing between the real and the hypothetical. Of equal importance, the child now begins to communicate with others, testing the adequacy of his social responses, as well as his feelings, attitudes, and emotions.

There are still, however, a number of restrictions and limitations with respect to the child's thinking:

1. The preoperational child is basically egocentric, i.e., he thinks and acts primarily in terms of himself and his needs.
2. He remains unable to adopt various points of view concerning a particular problem. He is neither concerned with the consistency of his thought processes nor whether his ideas adhere to any particular social or logical norms. Subsequently, he feels no great need to defend his opinions or to justify his thinking.
3. Though the child is beginning to think in terms of signifiers and significates, his internal representation still remains at the level where everything is exactly as he perceives it.
4. Of significance to the educator is the fact that the preoperational child tends to focus his attention, or "center," on the most interesting aspect of any stimuli or stimulus situation. His lack of ability to "decenter" means simply that he cannot see or understand the integral parts of which a situation or task may be composed.
5. A further limitation involves the inability of the child to reverse his thinking without producing some major distortion. In other words, the child thinks and proceeds from one instance, or particular, to another in an irreversible sequence. Piaget believes that this phenomenon of "irreversibility" is the most important characteristic associated with the preoperational period.
6. The child's thinking is very rigid; he has yet to see the "grays" of a situation. This is exemplified by his rigid concepts of justice and morality, his difficulty in discriminating between fantasy and reality, and his naive and inadequate notions concerning time, space, number, and quantity.

From these observations and notations of Piaget, a number of principles can be inferred concerning appropriate methodology. For example, the teacher should:

1. Be specific, direct, and concrete.
2. Introduce only one activity at a time.
3. Minimize verbalization when giving directions.

4. Be sure that the child is attending to the exact desired characteristic of the stimulus being presented.
5. Program the instructional material into specific, identifiable substeps and be certain that the child can progress in a definite sequential manner. Do not expect him to be able to review his thinking or analyze his errors.
6. Minimize the need for transfer of training. To illustrate, if you wish a child to gain some experience in tying his shoes, do not use the typical shoe-tying teaching aid. Rather, get the child some oversized boots so that he can put them on and learn to lace and tie his shoes in the correct perceptual field. Further, do not expect the child to generalize his learning.

Piaget, like many psychologists and educators, both recognizes and emphasizes the tremendous value of play activities with the preoperational child. It is through play that the child has an opportunity to express and test newly acquired ideas and concepts. This, in turn, enables him to consolidate his thinking. In addition, play can assist the child in developing his imagination and creativity; it serves as an excellent outlet for emotional expression; and it provides an effective means for the acquisition of social skills and habits. An astute educator can learn much about her students by observing their play behavior.

Another technique, which has proven to be quite successful in working with the young moderately and severely retarded, is based on the principles of operant conditioning. In essence, this technique requires that a task be sequestrated into very small, sequential steps and that the child be rewarded when he makes a correct response. Naturally, the child will tend to retain and repeat those responses that are reinforced and eliminate those which are not. In this manner, the child's behavior is "shaped" into that which is desired.

A number of studies have shown that this technique is particularly useful in teaching social and self-care skills (e.g., Bensberg, *et al.,* 1965; Gorton and Hollis, 1965; and Roos, 1965). An excellent, illustrated description of operant conditioning procedures as applied to the retarded is provided by Stuckey, Breland, and Colwell (Bensberg, 1965) in an instructional manual designed for ward personnel.

SUMMARY

This paper has attempted to provide a broad overview of the various aspects associated with a nursery school program for the TMR, including its underlying objectives, appropriate curricular provisions, and suggestions relative to methodology. The emphasis was placed on developing emotionally and socially secure, competent children and with providing a wide variety of experiences essential to learning and language development. The discussion of methodology included reference to both the theory of Piaget and the utilization of techniques based on the principles of operant conditioning.

Though the nursery school for the TMR is a relatively recent innovation, its place in the total educational picture is not challenged. Many educators and psychologists, both as practitioners and researchers, are interested in nursery school training with the TMR and suspect that the combination of continued research and practical experience will result in producing a better foundation for the total education of all retarded children.

REFERENCES

Barrett, H. E., and Koch, H. L. The effect of nursery school training upon the mental test performance of a group of orphanage children. *Journal of Genetic Psychology, 37*:102–122, 1930.

Bensberg, G. J. (ed.). *Teaching the Mentally Retarded.* Atlanta, Georgia: Southern Regional Education Board, 1965.

Bensberg, G. J., Colwell, C. N., and Cassel, R. H. Teaching the profoundly retarded self-help activities by behavior shaping techniques. *American Journal of Mental Deficiency, 69*:674–679, 1965.

Commission on the Reorganization of Secondary Education. *Cardinal Principles of Secondary Education,* Washington, D.C.: Superintendent of Documents, Government Printing Office, 1918.

Educational Policies Commission. *The Purpose of Education in American Democracy,* Washington, D.C.: National Education Association, 1938.

Flavell, J. *The Developmental Psychology of Jean Piaget.* New York: D. Van Nostrand Company, Inc., 1963.

Girardeau, F. L., and Spradlin, J. E. Token rewards in a cottage program. *Mental Retardation, 2*:345–351, 1964.

Kearney, N. C. *Elementary School Objectives,* New York: Russell Sage Foundation, 1953.

Kirk, S. *Early Education of the Mentally Retarded,* Urbana: University of Illinois Press, 1958.

Molloy, J. S. *Trainable Children: Curriculum and Procedures.* New York: The John Day Company, Inc., 1963.

Ripin, R. A comparative study of the development of infants in an institution with those in homes of low socio-economic status. *Psychological Bulletin, 30*:680–681, 1933.

Robinson, H. B., and Robinson, N. M. *The Mentally Retarded Child: A Psychological Approach.* New York: McGraw-Hill, Inc., 1965.

Roos, P. Development of an intensive habit-training until at Austin State School. *Mental Retardation, 3*:12–15, 1965.

Rosenzweig, L. E., and Long, T. *Understanding and Teaching the Dependent Retarded Child,* Darien, Conn.: Education Publishing Corporation, 1960.

Skeels, H. M., and Dye, H. D. A study of the effects of differential stimulation on mentally retarded children. *American Journal of Mental Deficiency, 44*:114–136, 1939.

Spitz, R. A. Hospitalism: An inquiry into the genesis of psychiatric conditions in early childhood. *The Psycho-Analytic Study of Children, 1*:53–74, 1947.

Spitz, R. A. Hospitalism: A follow-up report. *Psycho-Analytic Study of the Child, 2*:113–117, 1946.

Swift, Joan W. Effects of early group experience: The nursery school and day nursery. In: Hoffman, M. D., and Hoffman, L. W. (eds.). *Review of Child Development Research.* New York: Russell Sage Foundation, 1964, 249–288.

Wellman, B. Iowa studies on the effects of schooling. *Yearbook of the National Study of Education, 39*:377–399, 1940.

Wolinsky, G. F. Piaget and the Psychology of thought: Some implications for teaching the retarded. *American Journal of Mental Deficiency, 67*:250–256, 1962.

Wooley, H. T. The validity of standards of mental measurement in young childhood. *School and Society, 21*:476–482, 1925.

SECTION FIVE

School Programs for the Educable Mentally Retarded

The whole concept of school programs for the educable mentally retarded is currently under serious review. Leonard S. Blackman states:

> In view of the increasing numbers of educable mentally retarded children being placed in special classes, the mushrooming of teacher training programs, and the ever growing financial support by both federal, state and local governments, a review of studies comparing the efficiency of regular classes versus special classes for educable mentally retarded children becomes important. The findings reveal that children remaining in regular classes almost invariably demonstrate academic achievement superior to that of special classes. Gains, if any, from special class placement, seem to accrue in the areas of personal and social adjustment.[1]

What is the typical composition of a special class for educable mentally retarded children in the elementary grades? A composite pupil would probably be a youngster who: (1) was of a minority group, that is, in many classes, black children or Spanish-speaking children; (2) lived in a ghetto or lower socioeconomic class home; (3) came of parents who, in many cases, placed very little value on education; (4) in early childhood was impoverished in terms of enrichment or adequate overall health; (5) was tested briefly on a psychological device that did not take into serious consideration social class experiences and background of the child; (6) exhibited mild behavior disorders; and (7) on an individual intelligence test had an IQ ranging between 65 and 78, and was two to three years retarded in actual achievement or grade placement. This child has known defeat and frustration from the day he entered

[1] Leonard S. Blackman and Howard L. Sparks, "What is Special about Special Education Revisited: The Mentally Retarded," *Exceptional Children, 31*:5 (January 1965), 242.

kindergarten or the first grade. While he has language skills, his vocabulary tends to be restricted.

Population studies tend to show that the greatest number of classes for the educable retarded group are located in ghetto schools or lower socioeconomic neighborhoods. Recently, many cases have been pointed out in which minority class children are severely penalized by the psychological test that is used and the fact that the examiner is not familiar with the vernacular of the subculture, or for that matter, administers a test in English to a Spanish-speaking child. Examples have been given where the IQ jumped as much as 25 to 30 points when the examiner gave the test in the native language of the pupil or attempted to compensate for an impoverished background by utilizing family case history data in the diagnostic process rather than the coldly objective test data.

Unclear curriculum goals and lack of suitable methodology have often hampered the academic growth of a special class child. The typical curriculum has been a watered-down version of a normal curriculum guide with some effort spent on developing social and physical maturity skills. L. Wayne Campbell has provided us with a chart that outlines curriculum goals at various school levels. Currently, Goldstein and his associates at Yeshiva University, in New York City, have underway a nationwide curriculum project entitled, *A Research and Demonstration Project in Curriculum and Methods of Instruction for Elementary Level Mentally Retarded Children.* The proposed curriculum by Goldstein is primarily social-skills oriented and may provide us with a wealth of knowledge as a result of its carefully designed field trials. Of recent vintage is a completed curriculum study by Dr. Marguerite Thorsell, State of Kansas Department of Education, entitled, *Conceptual Models for Development and Implementation of Curricular Content Structures* (September 1969). This study provides a totally new, simplified, model structure developed for establishing relationships (horizontal and vertical) throughout the administrative structure of any specialized subject or content area of the curriculum for the educable retarded. This structure begins with the components of the instruction and learning process and is directly related to multiple concepts from the work of Piaget, Bruner, Bloom, and Krathwhol. The Thorsell study is one of the most creative approaches to curriculum development seen in a long time.

The last few years have seen the development of new clinical teaching methodological approaches. The works of Robert M. Smith [2] and Laurence J. Peter,[3] which emphasize the clinical teaching approach based on the utilization and interpretation of psychological data in the remediation of specific learning disorders associated with mental retardation, hold much promise but require a greater degree of school organization in special education than now exists. It also demands an updating and retreading of teacher knowledge and skills.

[2] Robert M. Smith, *Clinical Teaching: Methods of Instruction for the Retarded* (New York: McGraw-Hill, Inc., 1968).

[3] Laurence J. Peter, *Prescriptive Teaching* (New York: McGraw-Hill, Inc., 1965).

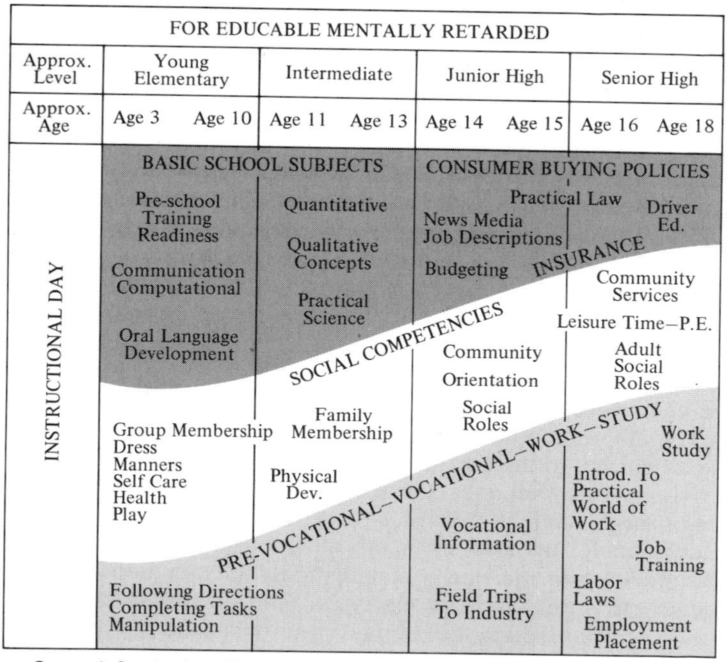

FOR EDUCABLE MENTALLY RETARDED				
Approx. Level	Young Elementary	Intermediate	Junior High	Senior High
Approx. Age	Age 3 Age 10	Age 11 Age 13	Age 14 Age 15	Age 16 Age 18
INSTRUCTIONAL DAY	BASIC SCHOOL SUBJECTS Pre-school Training Readiness Communication Computational Oral Language Development	Quantitative Qualitative Concepts Practical Science	CONSUMER BUYING POLICIES News Media Job Descriptions Budgeting INSURANCE	Practical Law Driver Ed.
	SOCIAL COMPETENCIES Group Membership Dress Manners Self Care Health Play	Family Membership Physical Dev.	Community Orientation Social Roles	Community Services Leisure Time–P.E. Adult Social Roles
	PRE-VOCATIONAL–VOCATIONAL–WORK–STUDY Following Directions Completing Tasks Manipulation		Vocational Information Field Trips To Industry	Work Study Introd. To Practical World of Work Job Training Labor Laws Employment Placement

General Curriculum Emphasis. Source: "Study of Curriculum Planning," L. Wayne Campbell, Curriculum Consultant, California State Department of Education, 1968.

This section is eclectic in approach, and the various authors state their points with great clarity. To attempt to go into greater detail on the subject of the educable mentally retarded would be duplicative. One final word: the need for flexibility and alternative educational opportunities is an obvious fact. The student should find the chart by Gallagher of value in noting a variety of alternative educational possibilities for retarded children.

In the first reading, philosophies of homogeneous and heterogeneous groupings are discussed in an excerpt from a report prepared by J. Wayne Wrightstone and his associates for the New York City Board of Education. In Reading 17, Herbert Goldstein and Dorothy M. Seigle discuss, with considerable perception, the characteristics of retarded children in relationship to school programs—the influence and use of intelligence quotient scores and mental-age estimates, and the importance of such learning disabilities as short attention span, oversimplification, and retarded language development. In Reading 18, Godfrey D. Stevens examines statements of the goals of educating the mentally retarded found in the literature. He finds that many such goals are vaguely or ambiguously phrased and need to be restated in terms of life situations. Lloyd M. Dunn, in one of the classic articles written on the subject, indicates that we have been living at the mercy of general educators who have referred their problem children to us. Further, we have been generally ill-prepared and ineffective in educating the mildly retarded. He warns that we must stop being pressured into continuing and expanding a program for the educable retarded that we know now to be undesirable for many of the children we are dedicated to serve.

Robert L. Erdman and James L. Olson in Reading 20 have prepared a review of the literature covering relationships between educational programs for the mentally retarded and the culturally deprived. In the Reading 21, Norman J. Niesen discusses the expansion and extension of special education programs for the mentally retarded. This paper discusses how to organize for the development of effective curricula, and treats some of the basic principles, factors, and techniques to be considered in the organization and the development of curriculum projects. In Reading 22, Robert Fuchigami reviews and summarizes changes currently taking place in curriculum development for the elementary-level educable mentally retarded. The author suggests that the new directions in curricula will reflect changes occurring in the curricula of regular education, compensatory education, prescriptive education, and special education. Leroy Aserlind presents reviews of services offered through the Instructional Materials Center Network. It is followed by a directory of the Instructional Materials Center Network and the newly established regional resource centers. In the final article in this section, Marvin J. Fine discusses counseling services needed by the educable mentally retarded child in the schools, and indicates that a number of unresolved issues exist regarding counseling with the retarded. The article reviews related studies, issues and considerations, and also reports critically on a pilot study that utilized a group client-centered approach.

Supplementary tables prepared by the editor are placed at the end of this section. These tables summarize (1) concepts of curriculum and methods for teaching the retarded, and (2) special class organizational programs in the public school system.

16 SOME PHILOSOPHIES OF EDUCATION FOR THE MENTALLY RETARDED

J. Wayne Wrightstone
George Forlano
J. Richard Lepkowski
Marvin Sontag
J. David Edelstein

From *A Comparison of Educational Outcomes under Single-Track and Two-Track Plans for Educable Mentally Retarded Children,* mimeographed, Board of Education of the City of New York, Brooklyn, 1960, pp. 5–9. Reprinted with the permission of the Board of Education and the authors. Dr. Wrightstone is director of the Bureau of Educational Research of the Board.

Educators of the mentally retarded generally favor a different developmental program rather than a remedial adaptation of a normal program for these pupils. Social and vocational competence, broadly conceived, are the major goals for such a program. It is generally accepted that these goals can be furthered only in special classes for the mentally handicapped, rather than within the regular grades. Kirk and Johnson, for example, include in their definition of the mentally handicapped child the qualification that he be one who is "unable to profit sufficiently from the curriculum of the public schools, but who can be educated to become socially adequate and occupationally competent, provided special educational facilities are furnished." By special educational facilities Kirk and Johnson mean special classes for the mentally handicapped.[1]

Some educators have gone further and advocated narrower ranges of individual differences, where possible, for special classes for the mentally retarded. The reasons advanced are in many respects similar to those advanced for special developmental programs and special classes. For example, Ingram points out the desirability of limiting the overlap in learning ability, physical maturity and social maturity within classes of mentally handicapped.[2] One important advantage in reducing the range of age and social development within a class, Ingram believes, is the narrowing of the range of pupil interests and of probable responses to any given appeal.[3]

However, the idea that the 50–75 IQ group of retardates belong in special classes has been questioned by some educators. As is usually the case for the arguments advanced in favor of special or more homogeneous classes, the reasons for questioning or opposing such classes are also often quite general, and might very well be applied in some fashion to excessive homogeneity at any level of ability. Featherstone, in questioning the value

[1] Samuel A. Kirk and G. Orville Johnson, *Educating the Retarded Child* (Boston: Houghton Mifflin, 1951), p. 13.

[2] Christine P. Ingram, *Education of the Slow-Learning Child* (New York: Ronald, 1953), p. 81.

[3] *Ibid.,* p. 85.

of special, segregated groupings for slow learners of 70–85 IQ, makes the following points: [4]

1. Many or most of the difficulties in instructing slow-learners in mixed groups derive from the attempt to apply an overly fixed curriculum.
2. All classes are heterogeneous. "Segregated slow groups are about as heterogeneous in ability and in every other way, and as hard to teach effectively as are mixed groups."
3. ". . . what kind of group offers the best possibilities for a particular individual is extremely difficult to say. Some children achieve good belongingness, security and status in families made up of very diverse ages and backgrounds; others do not."
4. The cohesiveness of a group is a function of its purpose—whether there exists "a problem, plan, activity or project in which all are involved in some measure, and to which all can make a contribution."
5. ". . . many teachers do not have as much skill as is needed to teach heterogeneous groups. . . ." This may be the fault of the teacher educating institutions, or of the school systems.
6. Individuals of diverse backgrounds and talents should learn to live together. The schools should not "persist in emphasizing the difficulties that divide people rather than the likenesses that unite them."

Clearly some of Featherstone's cautions have application to the issue of homogeneous versus heterogeneous classes within the 50–75 IQ group in the public schools, as well as to special versus regular grade classes for the sections of mentally retarded pupils.

Even the value of relatively narrow ranges of chronological age within classes has been questioned by educators. This point of view is relevant to the present experiment, since the reorganization of classes in the two-track plan provides for narrower ranges of age, as well as of educability, as advocated by Ingram and others. Jeannette Veatch of New York University Elementary Education Department has suggested the following possible advantages for a general policy of including broader age levels within regular classes by foregoing yearly promotions: [5]

1. The children would be more cooperative and less segregative in character;
2. The richness of individual differences would stimulate the children's interests; and

[4] The quotes in these points are taken from W. B. Featherstone, "Grouping in Relation to the Education of Slow-Learners," *Journal of Exceptional Children,* XIX (1948), 172–175.

[5] Jeannette Veatch, "Grouping in the Whole School," *Childhood Education,* V; XXX (1943), 2.

3. The teacher would be released, by virtue of the circumstances, from the confines of a strict body of subject matter.

While the latter point would hardly apply to classes of mentally handicapped organized around broad core units of instruction, it is conceivable that overly homogeneous groups of retardates might decrease tolerance of individual differences and provide inadequate stimulation for pupil interests.

RESEARCH STUDIES

Apparently there has been little research in recent years on homogeneity of class grouping within the mentally handicapped range. Even the value of special classes for the mentally handicapped is still a matter for investigation, and it is in this area that research most relevant to the present experiment has been conducted. Previous research on the value of special classes is relevant to the present study partly because special classes for the mentally handicapped are themselves relatively homogeneous groupings, and partly because the research methods were related in some respects to those of the present study. Two recent studies, concluded in 1956, are described below.

Ellenbogen conducted a study of mentally handicapped children in regular and special classes of the Chicago elementary public schools.[6] The special classes had smaller memberships, a specially designed curriculum, and teachers trained to work with the mentally handicapped. The pupils had been in the special classes for the previous two years. The pupils in regular classes followed a regular academic program. The two groups of pupils were matched on age, sex, IQ, and school district. The mean age was 13.46 for both groups, and the mean IQs were approximately 70.5. The IQs were the most recent obtained on the Revised Stanford–Binet Scales administered by qualified psychologists. Academic achievement in reading and arithmetic were measured by the Stanford Achievement Tests, with no more than five children tested at a time. The classroom teachers evaluated the pupils on school adjustment by means of ratings given during personal interviews. Pupils were interviewed on vocational aspirations, social adjustment, and attitude toward school.

The children in the regular classes were found to have significantly higher mean scores over children in the special classes in paragraph meaning, word meaning, arithmetic computation, and arithmetic reasoning. On the other hand, the children in special classes had significantly higher mean

[6] Morton L. Ellenbogen, *A Comparative Study of Some Aspects of Academic and Social Adjustment of Two Groups of Mentally Retarded Children in Special Classes and in Regular Grades,* doctoral dissertation, Northwestern University, 1957 (Publication No. 23,562).

teacher ratings of school adjustment, more realistic vocational aspirations, and more after-school jobs. The attitudes toward school were similar in both groups. The significant differences were attributed to the effects of the different class placement. Ellenbogen's finding of higher teacher ratings of school adjustment for the pupils in special classes seems related to previous findings of Johnson,[7] and Johnson and Kirk,[8] that mentally retarded children are isolated and rejected by other children in the regular grades.

A study by Blatt [9] on mentally handicapped elementary school children in Blair and Clearfield counties, Pennsylvania, compared 75 special-class pupils with 50 pupils in regular elementary classes. The groups were equated on age, sex, and IQ. The total of 125 children came from 19 different schools and 45 classrooms.

Although the heights and weights of the two groups did not differ significantly, 25 percent of the special-class children as compared to 10 percent of the children in regular classes were found to be more than 10 percent underweight. The special-class children had significantly more uncorrected or permanent physical defects. Thus, the two groups were not precisely matched on physical characteristics at the time of the investigation.

No significant differences were found between the two groups on days absent from school, strength of grip, vertical jump, motor ability (as measured by the Brace Scale of Motor Ability), scores on the California Test of Personality for personal and social adjustment, delinquencies and behavior records, numbers of hobbies and interests, or scores on the California Achievement Tests for reading, arithmetic, and language achievement.

INSTANCES OF HOMOGENEOUS CLASS GROUPINGS

At the time of writing, the public school system of Kansas City, Missouri, had special classes for upper and lower classification of retardates.[10] Children were placed in classes for the deficient group, IQ approximately 50–65 (performance and other factors in agreement), or in classes for the ungraded group, IQ 65–80. Class sizes were limited to approximately 15 and 20 for the deficient and ungraded groups, respectively.

[7] Johnson, G. O., "A Study of the Social Position of Mentally Handicapped Children in the Regular Grades," *American Journal of Mental Deficiency, 55* (July 1950), 60–89.

[8] Johnson, G. O. and Kirk, S. A., "Are Mentally Handicapped Children Segregated in the Regular Grades?" *Journal of Exceptional Children* (December 1950), 65–68, 87–88.

[9] Burton Blatt, *The Physical Personality, and Academic Status of Children Who Are Mentally Retarded Attending Special Classes as Compared with Children Who Are Mentally Retarded Attending Regular Classes,* doctoral dissertation, Pennsylvania State University, 1956 (Publication No. 19,333).

[10] Based upon a personal communication from Nelle Dabney, director of Special Education, Public Schools, Kansas City, Mo.

In addition to the new program of homogeneous classes which was evaluated by the study, New York City had for some time been selecting its more capable retardates from special-education classes in the junior high schools and sending them to special classes in the high schools.

Elizabeth M. Kelly, director of Special Education of the Newark, New Jersey, public schools, has advocated a three-way division of older retardates in special classes. After a close observation of retardates in special classes for those between the ages of 12–6 and 14–5, a division is suggested into classes for high and low educable up to the age of 17–5. With the understanding that IQs are not to be used rigidly for classification purposes, and that intellectual and social functional ability should be given first consideration, IQ groupings of 50–64 and 65–79 are recommended. Kelly expresses the view that "it is just as important for those in this classification of the mentally retarded (IQ 65–79) to be unhampered educationally and emotionally as it is for normal and above normal boys and girls of the same chronological age group to be unimpeded scholastically by the dull normal and the mentally retarded."[11]

In addition to the division into groups corresponding roughly to the two IQ groups mentioned above, Kelly believes that perhaps the 50–64 group should be further divided into retardates of the endogenous and exogenous types, with different kinds of school organization and planning for these two groups. The outlook for the endogenous type is considered by Kelly to be better, since these retardates tend to be more stable emotionally. The exogenous type is "inclined to have narrow interests and in general adjustment to be rigid and conforming. This type of mentally retarded person is usually verbal and derives his greatest satisfaction from academic achievement. . . . A program with emphasis on the occupational approach is not only unsatisfactory for persons in this group, but it is frustrating."[12]

[11] Elizabeth Kelly, "Are We Providing Opportunities for the Older Mentally Retarded?" *Journal of Exceptional Children* (May 1955), 297–299, 309.

[12] *Ibid.*, 298.

17 CHARACTERISTICS OF EDUCABLE MENTALLY HANDICAPPED CHILDREN

Herbert Goldstein
Dorothy M. Seigle

From *A Curriculum Guide for Teachers of the Educable Mentally Handicapped*, Illinois Department of Public Instruction, Springfield, 1958, pp. 4–18. Reprinted with the permission of the Division of Special Education of the Office of Public Instruction of the State of Illinois, the Institute for Research on Exceptional Children, University of Illinois, and the authors. Dr. Goldstein is Director, Curriculum Research and Development Center in Mental Retardation, Yeshiva University, New York City. Miss Seigle is Consultant in Mental Retardation, Clark County Public Schools, Las Vegas, Nev.

Over the years workers in the various disciplines concerned with the mentally handicapped have developed a body of descriptive terms certain of which have crystallized into what is commonly known as the characteristics of the educable mentally handicapped. While the characteristics of the educable mentally handicapped are stated, for the most part, in psychological language, they receive common usage in all interested disciplines. It is, therefore, very important that a discussion of characteristics take place within a clearly defined frame of reference to minimize semantic problems. For the purpose of the Curriculum Guide,* the characteristics of educable mentally handicapped children will be discussed within the framework of education.

Before setting forth the characteristics of the educable mentally handicapped, certain assumptions must be reviewed. First, all characteristics associated with the educable mentally handicapped are typical of the characteristics of the population as a whole. Differences in characteristics are a matter of degree and not of kind. Thus, any person regardless of intellectual status may, under certain conditions, show evidence of frustration and, to some degree, an inability to handle abstractions in problem solving. Second, while the term "characteristics of the educable mentally handicapped" implies a group behavior, individuals in the group may exhibit any one or combination of characteristics and, in some cases, none worthy of mention. Third, despite the fact that the behavioral characteristics are more frequently noted in the educational setting, the primary characteristics such as rate of mental development and physical status are continuously exerting a critical influence on the total performance of the child.

In order to indicate the interrelationship between the characteristics of the educable mentally handicapped, it might be convenient to consider the characteristics in two categories: (1) the primary characteristics which precipitate and influence certain types of behavior in the educable men-

* To avoid a break in continuity, the term "curriculum guide" has not been edited from this reading. It refers to the complete report from which this article was taken. —ED. NOTE.

tally handicapped, and (2) the secondary characteristics which are manifested by the interaction of the child's inherent characteristics with his physical and social environment.

PRIMARY CHARACTERISTICS

The primary characteristics might best be viewed as those which are literally built into the child. These characteristics are representative of intellectual and physical growth and development. As such, they have their roots in the anatomy and physiology of the child from the moment of conception. For many years, it was held that these characteristics were constant and incapable of being modified. In recent years, however, research and experience have shown that modifications introduced into the child's environment in the form of cultural, dietetic, and educational measures can have a marked effect on the rate and nature of the child's intellectual and physical growth.

Physical Characteristics

For the purposes of the Curriculum Guide, the physical characteristics of the educable mentally handicapped will be treated comparatively briefly because of their limited influence on educational procedures. There is no intention to minimize the importance of these characteristics since it is generally recognized that there is often a relationship between physical condition and intellectual ability. Nevertheless, when one considers the role of the educator in this area, it can be seen that it is one of regulation and accommodation; the administration and the teacher most frequently follow the rules or see that the children follow the prescription of the diagnostician and therapist. Rarely, if ever, does the educator initiate direct procedures designed to correct or ameliorate a specific condition. Certainly, administrators and educators make provisions for children with specific physical handicaps such as brain injury. These provisions, however, are designed to accommodate the learning and behavior problems arising out of the physical handicap and not to correct or ameliorate the basic physical condition itself.

In terms of their general physical growth and maturation, educable mentally handicapped children follow the same sequence as their normal peers. It has been contended that, as a group, they are somewhat inferior in size and weight as compared with children of the same age, that they are more prone to illness and that the prevalence of physical handicaps is greater. Of the first two, inferiority in physical development and proneness to illness, it is difficult to determine whether these characteristics are directly associated with mental handicap or with environmental conditions or both. Environmental conditions should merit considerable attention since studies have shown that, at least in large metropolitan districts, a sizable proportion of educable mentally handicapped children come from substandard homes. In some instances, the existence of a physical handicap and mental handicap may have a direct relationship as in the case of some brain-injured children. In other cases, the mental handicap may be independent of the source of the physical handicap.

For the educator, the nature of the physical handicap and its effect on the learning and behavior of the educable mentally handicapped child transcends its etiology. While it is important for the administrator and the teacher to obtain knowledge about the basic nature of the physical handicap, this is but a preliminary step toward modifying or adapting the classroom and classroom techniques in order to reduce the negative effects of the handicap on learning and behavior. It is here that the educator assumes a leadership role in the development of methodology for instruction and evaluation. Experience has shown that a variety of physical handicaps may be effectively subsumed under one system of instruction and classroom modification regardless of the diversity of etiology.

It is therefore very important that administrators and teachers be alert to the existence of physical handicaps in terms of relevant techniques and services. In all cases, educational treatment should be focused on the educable mentally handicapped child as a total organism and not on unique conditions.

Intellectual Characteristics

Basically, the intellectual characteristics of educable mentally handicapped children are similar to those of their normal peers in that they follow the same developmental sequence. The differences that exist are not so much in the kind of characteristics as they are in the rate and degree with which they develop. Educable mentally handicapped children learn in the same way as do normal children, through experience. In contrast, their rate of learning is slower and they rarely learn as much, particularly in academic areas. In the course of learning, they apply, like other children, the processes of imitation, reasoning, and generalization. To the degree that they can, they acquire concepts and develop value systems consistent with social living.

Psychologically, educable mentally handicapped children, like all children, require and seek love, security, recognition, and a sense of belonging. It is important that the administrator and teacher recognize the relationships between the educable mentally handicapped child's basic psychological needs, certain aspects of our culture, and the child's intellectual subnormality. Our culture generally smiles upon the bright, successful, creative individual and frequently rewards him with gestures of affection and recognition. Conversely, it frowns upon the incompetent and the laggard and confers on him the very antithesis of his basic needs, rejection. It is obvious that the educable mentally handicapped child's intellectual subnormality must, in all too many cases, operate to prevent the fulfillment of his needs for affection, acceptance, and security, if not in the home, at least in the more competitive and depersonalized activities in the school setting.

The administrator and teacher can play an active and positive role in helping some educable mentally handicapped children meet their basic needs within the limits imposed by their relationship with the children and with other children within the public school. Knowledge of the child, his assets and liabilities, plus an understanding of his social and emotional environment outside of school will help the teacher develop a method for working with the child to the extent that she can. It is important to recognize, however, than an effective teacher–child relationship is not always possible in every case and that this avenue toward need fulfillment for the child may be partially if not entirely closed. This is a reflection of many uncontrollable factors in the child's psychosocial environment and does not imply that the teacher or administrator has failed. In any case, to the extent that it is possible, the classroom should be a desirable locale for the child and acceptance and recognition should not be something he has to earn.

Most frequently, the intellectual characteristics of educable mentally handicapped children are stated in terms of their intelligence quotient (IQ) and then mental age (MA). For the purposes of the Curriculum Guide, the IQ and MA will be discussed in functional terms as they relate to the administrative and pedagogic aspects of special class provisions for educable mentally handicapped children.

The Intelligence Quotient

In and of itself the IQ represents the position of the individual and his rate of mental development with respect to the total distribution of intelligence of the population as measured by a specific instrument. In a sense, then, the test of intelligence implicitly defines intelligence and this may vary in nature from test to test. It is, therefore, mandatory that the IQ be considered within a dynamic context, in relationship with a definable and describable activity or situation, if it is to acquire meaning. As a point of reference, the teacher has the test situation wherein the IQ is derived.

Essentially, the administration of the intelligence test is a sampling of the child's behavior under specified conditions. The psychologist's report will contain his evaluation of this situation and his impressions. Ideally, for the teacher, the examiner's evaluation and his impressions will extend beyond the testing situation and project into the classroom. Realistically, however, the administrator and teacher should recognize that certain limitations in the testing situation restrict the extent to which the psychologist can project his evaluation and impressions of the child's behavior and performance. For one, the nature of the test situation does not reveal to the psychologist how the child will behave in a group setting with other children such as in a classroom or on the playground. Second, while the psychologist can form some judgments as to how the child relates to an adult, he has no evidence upon which he can base an estimate of how the child will relate to an adult in the presence of other children. For these reasons, it is always profitable for all concerned if the school personnel will discuss psychological test results with the psychologist and clear up questions first-hand rather than rely on inferences from the data.

Administrative Use of the IQ

The IQ and all that it implies serves as one of the major criteria in the definition of educable mentally handicapped children for purposes of special class placement. In determining the eligibility of the child for admission to a special class, the child's rate of mental development is drawn into perspective with all other data available to the examiner. In many states, the IQ limits for admission to special classes are set down as a range from 50–75 or 80. In the Illinois Plan, however, no definitive range is stated, thus permitting the examining psychologist to take the rate of mental development into consideration as part of the total evaluation of the child.

In cooperation with public school functions, many community agencies consider the IQ along with other characteristics as ascertaining eligibility and feasibility for rendering service. This is most frequently the case with vocational rehabilitative agencies.

Pedagogic Use of the IQ

As a single measure of intellectual status, the IQ is of very limited service to the teacher. Mainly, the IQ is used as a basis for preliminary classification and for estimating the child's rate of mental development.

Teachers frequently ask: How much reliance can I place on the IQ? The answer to this question is drawn, in great part, from the test used to determine the IQ. Of prime importance is the fact that no test of intelligence is completely infallible particularly at the educable mentally handicapped level or above. The answer to the question then becomes one involving degree of reliance.

Of the two types of tests most common in school use, the individual tests of intelligence and the group tests, more reliance can be placed on the individual tests. Comparatively, the individual test is a much more controlled instrument both situationally and administratively and it is administered by an individual well versed in its characteristics and interpretation. On the other hand, group test situations are not so easily controlled; many difficult-to-detect conditions can enter the test situation and affect the results. Even in those cases where the test administrator can account for unusual factors in the situation, he has a difficult time effecting a comprehensive relationship between the factors and the test results. In most cases he can only make an intelligent guess in retrospect. For these reasons, the IQ derived from a well standardized individual test such as the Binet or

Wechsler Intelligence Scale for Children is a more reliable measure. Possibly, it would be more profitable if the teacher looked upon the group test as one type of screening device for detecting children who deviate from the norm. An IQ derived from a group test may then be looked upon as an initial estimate of level of intelligence which is to be more clearly ascertained by an individual test.

While it has been generally accepted that the IQ may be employed as an index of rate of learning, experienced teachers have found that this use of the IQ has extremely limited application with educable mentally handicapped children because of the great variety of learning patterns in children of comparable IQs. Also, resorting to the IQ as an estimate of rate of learning implies the use of regular classroom texts and materials as a frame of reference. Since special class teachers of educable mentally handicapped children do not apply regular class materials in the form or frequency for which they have been designed, there is no long range basis for making an estimate of their rate of work in the special class.

The IQ as an index of rate of learning has most relevance in the primary-level educable mentally handicapped class with those children emerging from the reading- and arithmetic-readiness stage. The teacher may employ the IQ as an index of rate of learning as one criterion in her early attempts at forming reading and arithmetic groups. The assumption in this case is that children of comparable IQ who are also of comparable ability will make progress at a comparable rate and thereby maintain the homogeneity of the group. The teacher will undoubtedly find that the actual reading and arithmetic performance of the children will take precedence over the IQ as a criterion for grouping as the children become more mature. In areas of classroom work other than academic, the teacher will find experiences of the child and his academic ability better judgment criteria than IQ alone.

In keeping with the notion of the IQ as an index of rate of learning, the teacher may resort to the IQ as a basis for estimating the amount of repetition and practice the child will require to master a given learning task. Again, the IQ serves here as a rough preliminary criterion to guide the teacher in her first experiences with the child. As the teacher becomes more familiar with the child's learning behavior, she will invoke other criteria in making judgments.

Occasionally it is found that the IQ is used as a basis for predicting the school achievement of educable mentally handicapped children. This is an unwarranted use of this measure because of the many factors in the child's environment and/or personality that can affect the rate and nature of learning. There have been many instances of educable mentally handicapped children from culturally deprived environments making remarkable gains following their introduction to an enriched environment. Educable mentally handicapped children with serious personality problems have also made marked changes for the better as their problems were ameliorated. These are but two familiar examples that indicate that the arbitrary establishment of a ceiling of learning based on the IQ is a hazardous undertaking.

Mental Age

The child's mental age is a measure of his present intellectual status as determined by a standardized test of intelligence. The use of the mental age to designate intellectual status invokes the notion of abilities as they are related to age. Tests of intelligence such as the Binet express test results in terms of age norms and say, in effect, that the abilities of any given child correspond with the average abilities of children of a certain age. Thus, regardless of his CA, a child is assigned a mental age of eight years when his total performance on the test is on a par with the average for eight-year-old children. It should be kept in mind that the abilities sampled by the test are specific to the test and that no test actually samples all of the abilities of any one child. Thus, the Binet mental age has considerable implication in judging the academic ability of a child but tells little if anything about his artistic or athletic ability, among others.

Since intelligence tests sample limited segments of the child's abilities, it is very important that the concept of mental age not be oversimplified by indiscriminately comparing educable mentally handicapped children with other educable mentally handicapped children or with normal or gifted children of the same mental age. Very often the life experiences of the educable mentally handicapped child alter the qualitative nature of his mental age simply because he has lived longer and has had experiences not yet available to the normal and gifted child of the same mental age. Among educable mentally handicapped children of comparable mental ages, differences may be due not only to experience but also to biological factors. Not only are the effects of these experiences evident to the practiced administrator and teacher, but they also show up in the success and failure pattern of the educable mentally handicapped child in items in the intelligence test.

The performance and behavior of the educable mentally handicapped child may very well vacillate between his mental age and his chronological age depending upon the nature of the task and/or of the situation in which he is involved. Within this range, certain factors are most frequently in the vicinity of the educable mentally handicapped child's mental age and have considerable connotation for both administrative and pedagogic functions in the schools. For example, it is most frequently found that the educable mentally handicapped child's academic ability will most nearly approximate his mental age while his physical status reflects his chronological age. Emotionally, the educable mentally handicapped child will frequently react to many situations in terms of his mental age. At the same time, his social maturity will, in some areas, approach his chronological age. This becomes more obvious as the child matures and is evidenced in clothing styles, leisure-time activities, and the like. These and other phenomena will be discussed more specifically under relevant headings.

Administrative Use of the Mental Age

The mental age has considerable implication in the admission and placement of educable mentally handicapped children in special classes. In considering the advisability of admitting a very young educable mentally handicapped child to a special class, it is well to weigh the child's intellectual status in terms of the general status of the class as a whole. If his mental age indicates that he may be far below the lower academic and social level of the class, it might be advisable to forestall admission until the child becomes more socially amenable to a classroom setting and to suggest provisions that will enhance the child's maturity.

The mental age should also be carefully considered in the admission of more mature children to the special class as well as when moving children to special classes on a higher level. Even though the child may conform physically to the more advanced class, he may not have the academic and emotional maturity to achieve acceptance by his classmates or to operate at an acceptable academic level.

Discrepancies between mental age and chronological age become more critical as the demands on the child for independent behavior increase. This becomes most obvious in junior and senior high school special classes where the student must assume a variety of responsibilities for self-direction. Planning to move a child to a secondary-level class should include a thorough evaluation of the child wherein his mental age may well help to decide on immediate promotion or postponement pending further preparation.

Pedagogic Use of the Mental Age

The child's mental age is the best single criterion for estimating his academic status. Thus, the teacher may resort to the mental age in determining the reading and arithmetic aptitude of the educable mentally handicapped children in her class. Since, in the majority of cases, a mental age of six years must be reached before meaningful reading can take place, reading readiness activities might be indicated for educable mentally handicapped children with mental ages below six regardless of their chronological age. This should be a precautionary rule rather than a hard and fast one and subject to test with the individual child.

The teacher has two sources for a more specific determination of the child's academic status. Once she has established a general expectancy for the child's ability as indicated by his mental age, she can resort to either a formal or informal diagnostic procedure. Formally she can, if conditions permit, administer an achievement test. Informally, she can develop her own procedure. For example, if the child has a mental age of seven years, the teacher might be justified in estimating that he might be reading somewhere in the vicinity of a primer level. She can then more nearly ascertain his reading level by selecting a primer, asking the child to read to her, and then observing to what extent he is successful in recognizing words and in comprehending. If necessary, she can continue to give him more simple or difficult reading, as dictated by his initial attempt, in order to establish more clearly his reading status. The child's arithmetic and social studies skills can be tested informally in an analogous manner.

It occasionally happens that educable mentally handicapped children who have had two or three years in regular classes acquire a mechanical reading and arithmetic ability that appears almost commensurate with their chronological age. A child exposed to considerable drill and rote learning can sometimes acquire work- and number-recognition skills without acquiring much comprehension. To develop an understanding of reading and arithmetic it might be necessary to backtrack to a lower level in one or both areas. This calls for the introduction of new instructional material to assure maintenance of the child's interest. Again, the child's mental age is a good indicator for determining the level of materials. Since the child has a sizable sight vocabulary and some computational skills, it might be expected that he will progress at a slightly faster rate than younger children of the same mental age who are experiencing the materials for the first time.

The mental age will also help the teacher in the assignment of children to group activities such as committees in social studies. The readiness of the child to make realistic decisions, to work with others in a group, and to comprehend group goals is often revealed by his mental age. A child with a mental age below six years may be "too young" to perceive the totality of the rationale for a class mural or the need for sharing in a group game, even though his chronological age suggests otherwise.

The allocation of time in the daily program of instruction and activities should more nearly conform to the children's mental ages than their chronological ages. The ability to attend to and work at a lesson or task is, in part, a function of the child's mental maturity. Even interesting materials and tasks will become tiresome to the child if he is held to them for too long a period. It may be taken as a rule of thumb that lessons and activities should be comparatively short for the younger children and increased as the child becomes more mature mentally. In any case, time allocations should not be rigid. At times, the teacher's estimate may be in excess of the child's ability to attend. Observation of the child initially and during the course of the activity will often indicate that the lesson has ended as far as he is concerned. Glassy or wandering eyes, seat polishing, and shifting feet are the common early signs. Forcing the lesson beyond the time most appropriate to the mental ages of the children tends to create an aversion in them for the subject matter at hand and develops problems in management.

At times, the teacher is called upon to designate the equipment and materials she will require in the classroom. While a graded list of materials and equipment will be found in another part of this Curriculum Guide, it might be well to mention here the relationship between mental age and level of interest as they are related to classroom equipment. This relationship has most impact at the primary and intermediate levels. Interests related to games, puzzles, crafts, "free-time" reading, recordings, and others are most frequently on a level with the child's mental age. An eight-year-old child with a mental age of five will probably be more successful and receive more pleasure from materials graded near the five-year level than from those designed for eight-year-old children.

Adults who work with children frequently develop expectations related to the behavior of the children. Some expectations tend to become developmentally and situationally stereotyped. That is, experience and training tell the teacher that six-year-old children will display certain mannerisms when faced with denial of a pleasurable situation, while ten-year-old children will display a different set. From these experiences comes the frequently heard admonition, "act your age." This is, in effect, an order to the child to behave in a manner that is consistent with those behaviors historically associated with children of his life age in analogous situations.

Contrary to all of the evidence suggested by their overt behavior, educable mentally handicapped children are not nearly so inconsistent as might appear. It must be remembered that these children have two distinct ages as referrents for behavior: their mental ages and their chronological or life ages. It should not be unexpected then, to find that the behaviors of educable mentally handicapped children vacillate somewhere between their mental and chronological ages. It is not unusual to see an adolescent girl sulk or even dissolve in tears over what appears to be a very insignificant incident such as playful teasing by a classmate. Such an immature reaction can be quite puzzling to the uninitiated. But to the teacher of educable mentally handicapped children who has a good understanding of behaviors in their developmental strata, the rapid shift of behaviors is not unexpected. A good understanding of the relationship between mental age and associated behaviors is therefore necessary.

Understanding the implications of the mental age for the behavior of educable mentally handicapped children in the classroom setting is a major point of departure in the development of acceptable social habits in the children. The teacher's aim is to help each child develop a habit system that most nearly approaches expectations for his chronological age. The development of acceptable behaviors rank in importance with the acquisition of academic and occupational skills in the eventual adjustment of the educable mentally handicapped person in society.

Finally, a more realistic appraisal of the child's status can be obtained if the mental age is viewed as a maturing phenomenon rather than as a static characteristic. A good rule of thumb to be used in estimating the child's mental age between testing sessions is to multiply the child's age in months by his last IQ of record and divide by 100. Thus a child who was tested at the age of ten years (120 months) and who had an IQ of 70 would have a mental age of seven years (84) months. One year later he would be eleven years (132 months) of age. Multiplying 132 months by 70 and then dividing by 100 shows that this child's estimated mental age is now 92.4 months or seven years and eight months. In other words, while he gained one year in chronological age, he gained roughly eight months in mental age.

The assumption, in this procedure, is that the IQ remains relatively stable. From a functional point of view, a few points change of IQ in either direction will not affect the mental age too drastically. If, for any reason, the child's IQ undergoes a radical change, it will undoubtedly be evident to the teacher and she can make adjustments in her estimate of mental age accordingly.

It is of paramount importance that children in special classes be examined by a qualified psychological examiner at designated periods. The procedure advocated by the State Department of Public Instruction provides for testing at least every three years. Since very dramatic things can occur with respect to a child's rate and level of mental development, the notion of "testing as required" should prevail with teachers; three-year lapses between intelligence tests may actually work to the detriment of those children whose rate of progress requires confirmation and whose mental age needs redefinition.

SECONDARY CHARACTERISTICS

Unlike the primary characteristics, the secondary characteristics of educable mentally handicapped children are not an integral part of their physical or intellectual make-up. Rather, they are the outcome or expression of conflict or imbalance between the child's primary characteristics and his physical and social environment. As such, the secondary characteristics most frequently take the form of behavior and attitudes.

Behaviors and attitudes most frequently attributed to educable mentally handicapped children include overaggressiveness, self-devaluation, short attention span, poor memory, delayed language development, low tolerance for frustration, and others. These behaviors will be discussed later in greater detail.

Since the secondary characteristics vary in intensity and frequency with the degree and nature of interaction between the primary characteristics and the child's environment, they are amenable to change. In many cases, it is possible to control or alter the interaction between the child's primary characteristics and conditions in his environment and thereby effect changes in his secondary characteristics. Most frequently such control or alteration is directed at conditions in the child's environment since they are far more subject to change than his primary characteristics. For example, when a teacher sees that an educable child is about to select a task that is far beyond his intellectual ability and directs his attention to a challenging task more within his capabilities, she has manipulated his environment so as to reduce the potential for such behaviors as hostility, withdrawal, tantrums, and others.

The teacher often finds that she must work backwards from an overt behavior or attitude to determine the source of conflict. In some cases, the source of conflict is outside of the school; home and neighborhood conditions can and do stimulate unacceptable behaviors long after the child has entered the classroom. Even so, it is often possible for the teacher to minimize or ameliorate the secondary characteristics of educable mentally handicapped children. For this reason, these characteristics will be discussed from a corrective point of view.

Frustration-Proneness

The notion that educable mentally handicapped children have a low tolerance for frustration is one that is generally held by workers in this field. From the educator's point of view, there is some question as to the serviceability of this concept both in terms of classroom function and for purposes of communication. One might be justified in asking, "Low frustration tolerance as compared with whom and under what conditions?"

Accepting this concept without qualification may make for blind spots within the totality of the teacher's function. For example, a child may get up in the morning and have difficulty in dressing. At the same time, he sees a younger brother breeze through this task with ease. He may well find this annoying. After breakfast he may have to run an errand for his mother wherein he is to get a variety of items at the grocery store. His mother, not understanding or accepting his handicap, gives him verbal orders as she does his younger brother, rather than a written list. The child, unable to retain the verbal list, either omits or substitutes items. He may have a feeling that all is not well and this is certainly reinforced when he returns home with the garbled results of his errand. This is a second annoying experience. Later, on the school bus, the children quiz him about his school work and deride his obvious lack of ability to read and write. This is a third difficult experience. Shortly after arriving at school, one of his classmates snatches a pencil from him and playfully teases him. This seemingly minor event may well be the last straw for him and he erupts in any one of a number of unacceptable behaviors. He may strike out blindly, he may dissolve in tears or simply give up. The teacher, seeing only this last incident in the chain of events, may conclude that the child simply "can't take it" and that he has low tolerance for frustration. If this is her conclusion, she may very well enforce a no-teasing rule or she may conclude that she must stay alert to intercede for this child in all possible incidents in the classroom. What she may not realize is that this child may actually have the patience of Job and that he is consistently tolerating far more frustration than might his normal peers under similar conditions.

It might therefore be more profitable to take into account the persisting conflict engendered by the child's intellectual characteristics and the nature of the conditions around him and to consider the educable mentally handicapped child as being frustration-prone rather than a child with low frustration tolerance.

The concept of frustration-proneness draws into realization the fact that the educable mentally handicapped child is operating in a "normal" world—a world for which he is inadequately equipped, particularly in those duties and activities that call for intellectual adequacy. Purely on the basis of probability, then, chances are that the educable mentally handicapped child will be faced with difficult or impossible situations more frequently than might be expected for his normal peers. He is therefore more liable to find himself obviously inadequate while others around him succeed. The increased frequency of such situations for the educable mentally handicapped child renders him comparatively more prone to frustration than his normal peers.

The concept of frustration-proneness encourages the teacher to look far behind the precipitating incident in order to explain existing behaviors. It suggests procedures that may lead to amelioration of unhappy conditions outside of school. Parent counseling referrals by the teacher may help to develop increased understanding in the home. The attention of a school social worker may provide the child with an outlet for feelings hitherto stored and accumulating. Consultation with the bus driver and other teachers may lead to greater understanding and acceptance.

The concept of frustration-proneness has meaning in classroom-learning situations. Knowing that the educable mentally handicapped child is frustration-prone sensitizes the teacher to the conditions surrounding the child in the classroom as well as to the events occurring outside of the school. Planning activities and tasks will be based on more inclusive considerations than the immediate goals of the task.

Certainly the educable mentally handicapped child should and will experience some frustrating situations in the classroom and school; this is consistent with the realities of life. Careful planning, however, may effectively reduce the number of frustrating situations by eliminating those that have no obvious benefit for the child. This reduction of frustrating situations may enhance the child's ability to withstand hitherto intolerable situations outside of school and make him more acceptable socially and emotionally.

Self-Devaluation

A characteristic of educable mentally handicapped children closely related to frustration-proneness is that of self-devaluation. This characteristic is a result of imbalance between the child's competencies, intellectual and physical, and the demands of his environment. Self-devaluation most frequently manifests itself in behaviors and attitudes signifying that the child has strong feelings of general unworthiness and that he holds his abilities in low esteem.

A tendency toward self-devaluation is an almost inevitable outcome of two related major factors in the child's interaction with persons and things in his physical and social environment. First, there is the persisting condition of the generally inadequate child searching for his place in a world that stresses adequacy. Second, there is the child's frequent misjudgment of his abilities and limitations.

The educable mentally handicapped child, in a majority of cases, operates under preestablished standards for behavior and performance. There are both antecedent and current performances against which the educable mentally handicapped child's activities can be evaluated by anyone interested in so doing. For example, older siblings may serve as historical models as seen in such statements directed at the educable mentally handicapped child as, "When Henry was your age, he could travel to any part of town alone. You can't even find your way to the corner store and back."

In the ordinary course of events, he suffers from a comparison with children of his own age as well as with younger children who are more adept, swift, and efficient in performing tasks and accomplishments seemingly at his level of achievement.

A tendency toward self-devaluation is aided by the educable mentally handicapped child's limited ability to assess his capabilities and limitations realistically. Studies have shown that educable mentally handicapped children, when confronted with a task, will more frequently over- or underestimate their abilities than will their normal peers. It might therefore be expected that those children who overestimate their abilities with some degree of consistency will be loading the deck against themselves and in favor of failure. A chain of failing experiences may very well reinforce the child's feelings of unworthiness and establish strong anticipations of failure. The child who underestimates his ability will often find that his finished work is substandard when compared with that of his peers. He may accept this as evidence of inferiority.

The educable mentally handicapped child, like all children, sets up defenses against failure and against further reinforcement of self-devaluation. One of the more obvious is a kind of suspended animation wherein the child manages to stay apart from as many activities or tasks as possible. Great urgings and even coercion are often required to move the child into a new activity. He becomes engrossed in very low-level tasks. He may cut, paste, color, and paint for interminable periods.

Another child may seem to persevere at an academic task and be very happy at it. If the teacher will look back at the child's experiences, she will often find that it was in this academic area that the child was most successful. Quite often, this may be the only area of endeavor in which the child will forge ahead; even so, the teacher can expect considerable anxiety in the child if he is pushed too fast or feels that he is being pushed.

Much can and must be done to help the educable mentally handicapped child acquire a realistic basis for self-appraisal. As he matures, he will be called upon to exercise his judgment independently of the shelter and guidance of teachers and parents. The extent to which he can correctly estimate his abilities and limitations will frequently determine the quality of his adjustment in society. It is therefore necessary that the teacher institute measures to counteract tendencies toward self-devaluation as early as possible.

Again, here is where manipulation of the child's environment may help to ameliorate a secondary characteristic. By arranging conditions and assignments, the teacher can make certain that the child will experience success in almost every undertaking. The child needs a concentration of successful experiences to help him dissipate his feelings of unworthiness. The teacher should make certain that the child's successes are real and that her recognition of his successes are sincere, since the entire plan can be destroyed should the child sense that the teacher is merely making gestures. Knowledge of the child and his needs will guide the teacher in her selection of the tasks and activities and their levels of performance.

As the child begins to show increasing signs of self-confidence, the realities of failure should be permitted to enter the plan. Just as consistent failure is detrimental to the child's self-concept so is consistent success; neither is true to life. Occasional experiences of failure plus an understanding of why failure occurred provide a basis for the child's evaluation of the situation as well as his role in the task. By discussing what happened and why, the child may begin to see the factors of failure as they apply specifically to him. It is hoped that he will come to realize that failure in some degree comes to all persons and that the factors precipitating failure can sometimes, but not always, be controlled. Learning to take failure in his stride and to evaluate the cause may help the child to acquire the skill of studying a situation as best he can in order that he might anticipate those factors of failure highlighted by previous experiences.

The educable mentally handicapped child who is prone to forge blindly ahead into tasks and situations because of a poor assessment of his assets and liabilities can also be helped in a teacher-controlled environment. Such help is predicated upon the teacher's knowledge of what the child can do and how well he can do it. First, the teacher will have to work closely with the child helping him to develop some ability to see the commonalities in the nature of past and present tasks. This may help him to see that in many cases past occurrences can be used as a reference point in evaluating current tasks. Next, the child should be helped to acquire some skill in looking back on his past experiences to recall how well he did under the conditions that existed. This can be done by exploiting immediate situations. For example, before the child is permitted to embark on a task, the teacher and child should discuss the demands of the task. The teacher should draw from the child his estimate of how well he will do and help him to refer back to similar experiences as a basis for his estimate.

As the child proceeds with the task, it might be advisable for the teacher to observe the child's progress and note the relationship between his stated and actual abilities. In some cases, it might be necessary for the teacher to rescue the child from an impossible situation. In other situations it might be advisable to permit the child to complete the task as best he can. A criterion for judging the relevance of teacher intervention is the child's emotional status. If the task renders him so overwrought that evaluation seems about to be precluded, the teacher should subtly intervene. Evaluation immediately upon completion of the task is of primary importance since this gives the child an opportunity to relate his abilities and limitations to an immediate, concrete experience.

It is important to keep in mind the fact that self-devaluation as a characteristic has two implications for the adjustment of the educable mentally handicapped child. First, there is its effect on classroom performance and adjustment. This is an immediate problem wherein the child's feelings tend to intervene between himself and both academic and social learning to the extent that he works far below his potential. Second, there is the effect of self-devaluation on the child's self-concept. This is a long-term problem and one that may well have its most deleterious effects when the child reaches maturity. The often quoted phrase, "The child is father to the man," is most dramatically true of the phenomenon of self-concept. Authorities generally agree that a self-concept formed and reinforced during childhood will persist throughout adulthood. If the educable mentally handicapped child is permitted to nurture and develop his feelings of unworthiness during the school years, he will approach many situations in adulthood with anticipations of failure. Thus he will virtually assure failure where success might have been. By possibly guiding the child in his solution of problems, the teacher may help him shape his self-concept to one more nearly consistent with reality.

LEARNING DISABILITIES

Conflicts between the educable mentally handicapped child's intellectual ability and the demands of academic and social situations often manifest themselves as disabilities in learning. These disabilities may be identified as a tendency to oversimplify ideas and concepts, reduced ability in generalization, short memory and attention spans, and limitations in incidental learning.

Oversimplification of Concepts

One of the intellectual characteristics attributed to the educable mentally handicapped child is his tendency to do comparatively better with concrete or functional ideas and concepts than he can with abstractions. For example, when asked to define or describe an object, the educable mentally handicapped child will most frequently do so in terms of its utility. Thus, an orange is for eating, a chair for sitting, a book for reading, and so on.

In the early years of the child's academic education this is, at least superficially, no serious problem since most of his reading texts and arithmetic learnings are at a concrete level. As the child makes progress, however, it becomes obvious that his ability to comprehend and to conceptualize lag behind his technical skills in academic areas such as word recognition and computation.

Similarly, the educable mentally handicapped child functionalizes or oversimplifies the ideas, concepts, and abstractions typical of social learnings. Rules for classroom living may be learned to the extent that the child can recite them verbatim. The child may be able to live up to some rules and not to others. This is not unlike being able to understand the meanings of individual words in a sentence without being able to grasp the central idea of the total sentence.

Limited Ability in Generalization

Closely related to the educable mentally handicapped child's tendency to concretize or functionalize concepts is his difficulty in developing generalizations. The more abstract the related concepts in situations embodying a common principle the more difficulty the educable mentally handicapped child has in seeing the commonalities in the situations. Thus, a child may quickly recognize the addition sign in a problem in computation without seeing its relationship to the word "and" in the verbal problem: Tom has five pencils and Mary has three pencils. How many do they have together? This is often true despite the fact that in describing the purely computational problem the child states: five and two are seven.

In social learnings the educable mentally handicapped child may have considerable difficulty in seeing the common features of two similar situations separated in time and space. He may quickly learn the rules governing behavior in the school cafeteria line and quietly await his turn at the hot tables. Three hours later, however, in boarding the school bus he may storm through the line of waiting children in his eagerness to get to his favorite seat.

Such contradictions in the child's academic and social behaviors are the bane of the teacher's existence, not to mention others with an investment in the child's adjustment and progress. Yet, in this area of intangibles, concept formation and generalization, the teacher may effectively manipulate the environment to the advantage of the educable mentally handicapped child by (1) teaching in such a way that both mechanical and conceptual skills are integral with each lesson and activity, and (2) by helping the child to see how a principle with academic or social connotation applies in a variety of situations.

It is not sufficient for the educable mentally handicapped child to know how to add. He must also acquire the concept of addition so that he may independently differentiate *when* to add from any one of a number of arithmetic behaviors available to him. Likewise, in reading, he must learn to recognize words on sight, but he must also learn the concepts they represent if his reading is to have any meaning to him. Devoid of concepts, arithmetic becomes nothing more than exercises with numbers and reading becomes word calling. In social learnings, the acquisition of concepts underlying many rules for group living is basic to the educable mentally handicapped child's ultimate social adjustment. Without concepts for social behavior the educable mentally handicapped child may well become obedient to rules—but only to those rules for which he can foresee immediate enforcement.

Once the teacher has helped the educable mentally handicapped child to acquire a conceptual repertoire, the process of generalization becomes more nearly possible. It seems reasonable to assume that the child must have some understanding of a situation before he can effect even a minimal relationship between the given situation and others requiring analogous behavior or action. Thus, it is not only important for the child to learn that he must wait his turn quietly while standing in the cafeteria line but he must also learn *why* if he is to be expected to generalize this behavior to the school bus line, the line at the local theater, and the line at the drinking fountain.

It is not too difficult to see the relationship between the many academic and social behaviors expected of the adult in our society and the behavior expected of the school child. The major difference between the two may be found in the degree of independence with which the individual anticipates the need for and fulfills behavioral expectations. Just as obvious, the ability to foresee the results of one's behavior is basic to differentiating between the appropriate and inappropriate. The extent, then, to which the educable mentally handicapped child in the special class is able to acquire and develop a conceptual base for his academic and social learnings may very well determine the extent to which he will generalize desirably both in his youth and in his adulthood.

Short Memory and Attention Span

With the phenomena of conceptual learning and generalization still fresh, it might be well to consider two other learning disabilities characteristic of the educable mentally handicapped. These are short memory and short attention span. As in the case of other secondary characteristics, these are relative to the memory and attention span of so-called normal children of the same age or, more accurately, to the teacher's conception of the memory and attention span of normal children.

The extent to which these characteristics exist will vary with the child. Some children in a reading group will recall many of the new words learned in a previous session while others will stare at them as though seeing them for the first time. In the same reading lesson, some will begin to fidget or show signs of wavering attention before others.

In the case of the child's characteristically short memory or poor retention of learning, the teacher may be guided by the results of research. Studies show that learnings which have meaning to the student will be remembered longer than those that have relatively little or no meaning. These findings have considerable implication for planning of instruction, provision of learning materials, and the teacher's selection of language in communicating with the children.

The instructional or lesson plans should incorporate and stress the learnings most relevant to the child in accordance with his needs. The principle of conceptual distance should receive prime consideration in the plans. To discuss the implications of city elections with primary-level children is conceptually far more remote for them than a discussion of behavior in the school halls.

Learning materials such as texts and seat work should be within the child's limits of comprehension. The teacher must continuously be alert for the factor of comprehension because of the facility some educable mentally handicapped children have for "word calling." All too often these children learn to recognize words without learning or understanding their meaning. Through rote learning, they can "read" entire pages without error. In arithmetic, they may learn the mechanics of computation without learning the principles underlying the operation. The teacher can test for comprehension in reading by asking the child to relate in his own words what he had read. In arithmetic, she can base a verbal problem on an algorism with which he has demonstrated facility.

The level of the teacher's language will often determine how long, if at all, the children will remember rules, directions, and other information to be retained. If the teacher employs language beyond the comprehension of her class, she will probably hold their attention while her voice dominates the scene but not for long after. Lack of comprehension rather than short memory span may be the reason some of those supposed to be doing seat work start the parade to the teacher's side for a repetition of directions.

Another pertinent result of research indicates that materials that are overlearned are retained longer than those learned only to familiarity. For example, in teaching a child a new word, the child may identify it correctly after the fifth presentation. The teacher may stop there and go on to a new word or she may go right on working with the same word with a number of presentations beyond the fifth. The probability that the child will remember the new word longer is enhanced by the few additional presentations of the word. This will undoubtedly hold for other learnings as well.

Duration of attention span may also be related to the extent to which the child comprehends or is interested in what is going on around him. Even as adults, most of us have become involved in situations that are beyond our comprehension or of little interest. This may have been a lecture, concert, or movie. The tendency of most, under these conditions, is to leave the scene in the most acceptable manner. If we cannot get up and depart, we may doodle, read the ads on the program, or doze. Educable mentally handicapped children will also leave the scene in their own way once they lose understanding or interest in proceedings. They cannot get up and leave the circle or their desk without attracting censure so they fidget, poke, hum, daydream, and invent activities with greater appeal to them.

Again, manipulating the classroom environment may help the teacher ameliorate the secondary characteristics of limited memory and short attention span. By ascertaining that classroom work is within the comprehension of the children and by organizing activities and materials so that they stimulate the interest of the children, the teacher may effectively reduce learning loss and disciplinary problems.

Limitations in Incidental Learning

The typical classroom learning situation has both a central theme and information peripheral to the theme. Some peripheral information might be contributory to the central theme while some might be quite irrelevant. Both types of information comprise the learnings which are termed incidental. For example, in a lesson in simple grouping the central theme might be the discrimination of groups of three from groups of two. As learning aids, the teacher might use blue irregular counters for the groups of two and yellow blocks for the groups of three. The identification of the contrasting colors and shapes of the learning aids might be considered information contributing to the central theme. The material relationship between the blocks and the table top, the teacher's costume, number of children in the group, and the lighting in the room might be considered irrelevant to the lesson.

As compared with normal children, the educable mentally handicapped child will frequently learn something about the central theme but very little, if anything, incidental to it. He may learn to differentiate the group of three from group of two in the lesson cited above. It is likely, however, that he will not learn very much about the materials with which he worked. He might not see that the yellow in the blocks and the blue in the counters are not only a part of the learning materials but that they also have intrinsic value as colors. This may be so despite the fact that the teacher used the colors as cues stating, "Hand me three yellow blocks."

The educable mentally handicapped child's limited ability to learn incidental information indicates that the teacher cannot take for granted that the child will acquire information simply because it is immediately in his presence. Further, it means that the teacher will have to plan in considerable detail not only how she is going to present the central theme but also which of the peripheral learnings she wants the child to acquire.

It is possible, with some educable mentally handicapped children, to increase the amount of incidental learning by helping them to increase their skills of observation. This must be a calculated plan wherein the teacher helps the children to identify the central theme and then to look beyond the central theme to the other factors in the setting. In the lesson on the fireman as a community helper, the class may be discussing a picture of a fireman from the viewpoint of his contribution toward protection. Once it appears that the children have a good grasp of this theme, the teachers can begin to draw the children's attention to the uniform and equipment. Occasionally, the teacher should draw the children back to the central theme so that the prior learning will not become overwhelmed by the incidental learning.

Most important, the teacher must study each area of learning to ascertain the facts and skills to be acquired by the child. Rarely can the teacher take for granted that educable mentally handicapped children will learn simply because they are in the immediate vicinity of information. After ascertaining the facts and abilities to be learned, the teacher must studiously incorporate them in the totality of the lesson.

Retarded Language Development

When one considers the role of conceptualization, generalization, and rote learning in the development of language, it is not too surprising to find that many educable mentally handicapped children are markedly retarded in this respect. In language ability, the educable mentally handicapped child most nearly approximates a level consistent with his mental age. This is often true of both his ability to produce language and the quality of the language itself.

At the primary level, some educable mentally handicapped children exhibit speech defects typical of the preschool child. Baby talk and imperfect articulation are not only evident but also persist for some time. Immediate and concerted action by both a qualified speech correctionist and the classroom teacher is necessary if the child is to make progress at an effective rate. It would be very unrealistic to assume that the special-class teacher has the time or critical skills necessary to effect a change in the child's speech production. It is just as unrealistic to assume that time will "cure" the speech defect.

The fact is, the educable mentally handicapped child pays a considerable penalty if his speech defect is permitted to go unremedied by a speech correctionist. The time that the teacher might devote to helping him develop an expanded, effective vocabulary is necessarily spent in helping him learn to produce words clearly. Thus, the acquisition of higher skills in communication are delayed. Further, an obvious speech defect has a psychological impact on the child in that it draws undesirable attention to him. If this is permitted to persist, the child may develop an aversion to speaking and minimize his efforts in this skill as a protective measure.

One of the more prevalent language characteristics of some educable mentally handicapped children is their tendency to limit their communication to single words or fragments of sentences. While this mannerism in normal or gifted children might be attributed to laziness or sloppy habits of communication, in the educable mentally handicapped child it may be due to impoverished ideas or concepts as well as a limited vocabulary.

The development of a functional vocabulary is a major goal in the education of educable mentally handicapped children. Learning to identify new words is but a preliminary stage in this development. The child must also be helped to learn, to the best of his ability, the meanings of words as well as the multiplicity of concepts associated with them. Once the child shows evidence of expanding his vocabulary, he should undergo considerable practice in using the new words within the context of sentences. This may take considerable urging and encouraging but it is only through long and constant practice that acceptable language habits will be developed.

The teacher has many language situations to exploit in helping the child make progress in language development. These range from conversational situations to more complex dramatizations of life situations and role playing.

Educability

The most important and constructive characteristic of the educable mentally handicapped child is the fact that he is educable. All too often the phrase "educable mentally handicapped" rolls off the speaker's tongue as a verbal label without any recognition of the fact that the very use of the label signifies that the child can learn—that he is in some degree amenable to education as it is defined in the public school frame of reference.

The fact that the child is educable means that he has the potential to profit from a learning situation that takes into account all of the characteristics discussed earlier according to the frequency and intensity that they exist in the individual child. Fortunately, while educable mentally handicapped children, like others, exhibit individual differences, they also generally have commonalities in ability, performance, and behavior that permit for both individual and group programing and instruction.

The crucial factors in dealing with the educable mentally handicapped child's characteristic of educability are the extent to which the teacher is trained and able to work constructively with them, the extent to which teachers and administrators plan and develop a consistent educational program for them and the ability of teachers and administrators to carry out a comprehensive program of education for them that will fulfill the long-range goals of public school education.

18 AN ANALYSIS OF THE OBJECTIVES FOR THE EDUCATION OF CHILDREN WITH RETARDED MENTAL DEVELOPMENT

Godfrey D. Stevens

From the *American Journal of Mental Deficiency*, Vol. 63, No. 2, September 1958, pp. 225–235. Reprinted with the permission of the American Association on Mental Deficiency and the author. Dr. Stevens is professor of education, Department of Special Education and Rehabilitation, University of Pittsburgh.

The problems of curriculum design and development have been coming into focus in recent years with the increased activity on the part of special educators to develop curriculum guides and courses of study for the mentally handicapped. Several large city school systems have either recently completed, or have underway, a study of the problems of curriculum development. Some states have started or are giving consideration to state-wide curriculum development projects and the production of study guides for teachers of the mentally retarded. This new interest in curriculum development should cause the educator to take a look at the purposes of education.

There are several reasons why it is necessary and desirable to examine the goals of education for the retarded. As stated above, the rapid growth of programs of education for the mentally retarded has been one source of pressure to restate the purposes of education and training. The increase in the quality and quantity of research in the various aspects of mental retardation has thrown new light on the problems and given them new dimension. Educators are becoming aware of a need for a more clearly defined goal-centered approach to learning as a basis for the development of clearly stated objectives.[1]

A cursory examination of the history of education for the retarded suggests that there have been limited and isolated attempts at developing goals which could serve as a basis for the design and development of a curriculum. Moreover, we may need to question the validity of the organization of concepts that have been set forth. This is not to say that the early workers concerned with this problem were superficial in their thinking. One gets the impression that they were preoccupied with program development and had little time for the development of the theoretical aspects of education for the mentally retarded.

For nearly fifty years educators have been preoccupied with problems of educational methodology and organization rather than with the content

[1] Ralph W. Tyler, *Translating Youth Needs into Teaching Goals,* National Society for Study of Education Fifty-second Yearbook, Part I, ed. by Nelson B. Henry (Chicago: University of Chicago, 1953), pp. 215–229.

of the curriculum. In spite of this, educational programs have developed reasonably well since those responsible for the emerging programs had insight into the needs of children. By systematically focusing on the problems of curriculum with equal vigor and preoccupation it is likely that we can come to an early resolution of the problems by attacking them on a sound and fundamental theoretical basis. It is therefore timely that some attention be directed to a reappraisal of the purposes of education for the mentally retarded.

Another basis for reexamining statements of goals have their origins in the findings of follow-up studies. As evidence accumulates from such follow-up studies, modifications in educational programs need to be made to provide for the constantly shifting needs of children and youth. As these needs change, goals for education must be modified accordingly.

STATEMENT OF THE PROBLEM

It is the purpose of this discussion to examine numerous statements of goals in the education for the mentally retarded. These statements are frequently referred to as purposes, or objectives. An analysis of these statements may serve as a basis for modifications and restatement of existing objectives which may serve as effective guidelines in the future development of educational programs for the mentally handicapped. In addition, such an analysis may provide the basis for the reduction of the inevitable semantic problems that inevitably attend the descriptions of abstractions of this sort.

A number of pertinent questions might be raised.

1. Are there inconsistencies in statements of objectives as set forth by competent workers concerned with the education of the retarded?
2. Are statements of goals consistent with recognized needs of the mentally retarded as presently delineated in the professional literature?
3. Are goals stated in terminology free of ambiguity; and do they permit ease of interpretation by other workers interested in the problems of educating the retarded?
4. Are the general goals sufficiently universal in that they will fit a wide variety of social conditions?
5. Are the goals consistent with existing social philosophies of American democracy?
6. Are the goals stated in terms of "specifics" rather than in broad generalities?
7. Are goals stated in terms of a curricular theory in singular frame of reference or do they appear as different aspects of the problem?

THE SOURCES OF OBJECTIVES

There are a number of sources from which goals for the education of the mentally handicapped can be developed.

1. *Students of education of the mentally handicapped who have considerable maturity and sophistication can develop statements of goals on the basis of their impressions and observations.* This procedure is likely to be attended with some risk since the biases of a single person may set into motion certain kinds of educational activities that ultimately prove to be undesirable. In recent years, however, this introspective approach has become a group process so that thinking of any individual can be checked against the experiences of others.
2. *Educational tradition is another source of data in the development of goals.* It has been a common practice in the past 25 years to restate the objectives as found in current literature. There are obvious risks inherent in this practice since no one can be certain that the earlier statements have any sound validity growing out of careful study of the nature and needs of the learner. It was not until 1938 when the Educational Policies Commission organized the goals for all education which have come to influence the course of education for the mentally retarded.
3. *The nature of the learner is a source of data that will help the educator in the formulation of statements of goals.* It is in this that we have invested rather heavily in recent years, and a great deal is now known about the phenomenon of mental retardation and its implications for learning and ultimate total adjustment. It is obvious that there is much yet to be learned but certainly there is much knowledge available that can serve effectively as a basis for the design and development of educational experiences for the retarded.
4. *The study of contemporary social organization is a primary source of objectives.* The sociologist can throw much light on the needs of the individual in terms of the problems of group living that can well serve as the basis for the development of sound and desirable statements of goals. The research in this area in more recent years has been increased in tempo and the educator can look with some promise to the sociologist who will continue to focus on the social problems of the mentally defective.
5. *Contemporary school curriculum guides and programs.* The evaluation of contemporary school curricula may shed some light on the problems of goals. It is likely that teachers are carrying out many educational activities that may need to be stated as a specific goal. These flashes of insight that have been put into practice should be accumu-

lated and evaluated and subsequently measured against existing philosophic positions set forth as statements of the purposes of education for the retarded. It is certain that many meaningful, purposeful experiences have long been a part of good curriculum practices that have not had their origins in the retrospection of the educational philosopher.

In summary, there are several sources from which the goals of education for the mentally retarded can be drawn. In reality, all of the above-mentioned sources will serve as a basis for the organization of goals.

CRITERIA FOR THE DEVELOPMENT OF STATEMENTS OF GOALS

In view of the many problems associated with the development of goals for the mentally retarded it would seem that there is a need for suggesting certain criteria which would aid in the development of these statements. Some of them are as follows:

1. *Statements of goals or objectives should remain within a single contextual framework.* If statements tend to vacillate from one frame of reference to another, it is difficult to analyze them in such a way as to check their validity and to convert them to educational practice.
2. *Statements of needs should be fortified with evidence from scientific literature.* While there is a place for the sophisticated observer who has the capacity for philosophic retrospection, it is only by checking goals in terms of needs against studies of the mentally handicapped that we will be able to provide statements of goals that are realistically derived and consequently will stand the test of objectivity.
3. *Goals should be stated with accepted educational terminology to avoid difficulties in semantics and the communication of concepts to others concerned with the problem.* There is little doubt that much of the difficulty in the area of the theoretical aspects of education have their origins in the breakdown in communications growing out of semantic difficulties. Thus, the student of educational theory must make every effort to develop statements of educational goals in a language that permits ease of understanding and thereby enhancing communication of these very complex abstractions.
4. *Goals should be stated in terms of the interaction of the individual and his environment* since these are no longer abstractions but real problems. It is generally agreed that the kind of educational experience that is most likely to be satisfying to the learner is that which tends to give him skills in solving his every day problems of adjusting to a vacillating, kaleidoscopic world. Thus, if some device could be de-

veloped by which this interaction could be dealt with as a facet of multidimensional construct this would facilitate the development of goals and the conversion to educational activity. Such a device or model can be developed.

5. *Objectives can probably be best stated in terms of persistent life situations of the mentally retarded* rather than in terms of subject matter, or the study of social phenomena. The persistent life situations concept as set forth by Stratemeyer, Forkner, and McKim is a somewhat unique approach to curriculum design.[2] It is based on the notion that the interaction in the dynamic relationship between the individual and every aspect of his environment is the basis for identifiable problems which exist in varying dimension at various times. The assumption is made that educational experiences can be developed which relate to these real problems to the end that the child is able to resolve them and develop skills that enhance later adjustment.
6. *Goals should be stated in terms of the limits imposed upon the school by our traditional and legal structure.* The school is only one of many powerful educating agencies that influence the behavior of the child. Moreover, the school has had certain limits imposed upon it by virtue of certain moral, traditional, and legal restrictions. The legal structure alone will impose definite limitations which serve as a basis for the delineation of goals and objectives.

   There is little point in the development of statements of goal for educational purposes if it is not within the province of the school to convert such goals to action. This, in one sense, tends to simplify the problem of curriculum design and development and should be constantly kept in focus. If goals are too comprehensive and extend beyond the scope of the traditional and legal role of the school, it is difficult or impossible to develop educational programs.
7. *The statement of the goals or outcomes of educational experience ought to be an expression of a basic curricular theory for the mentally retarded.* It is unfortunate that there has not emerged during the past half century a fundamental curricular theory which would serve as a point of departure for the design and development of a curriculum for children, and insufficient and frequently unrelated body of research knowledge.
8. *Goals should be stated in terms that coincide with the maturational aspects of development* so that the so-called developmental tasks give sequence to the curriculum.[3]

[2] Florence B. Stratemeyer, Hamden L. Forkner, and Margaret G. McKim, *Developing a Curriculum for Modern Living* (New York: Teachers College Press, Columbia University, 1947).

[3] Robert J. Havighurst, *Human Development and Education* (New York: Longmans Green, 1953).

SOME ASSUMPTIONS WITH WHICH TO EVALUATE GOALS OF EDUCATION

There are a number of assumptions that can serve as a basis for the critical evaluation of objectives and for the reformulation of goals for the mentally retarded. Some of them are as follows:

1. The nature of the learner and the nature of the society in which he lives is an effective basis for the development of specific goals.
2. The interaction between the learner and his culture is the basis for an infinite variety of complex problems of adjustment that can serve as a basis for the development of statements of goals.
3. The interaction between the learner and his physical environment with its associated constellations of problems can be stated in terms of certain persistent life situations.
4. The persisting life situations of the mentally retarded child can be stated in such a way as to serve as a basis for the development of educational experiences that will tend to provide for effective personal–social interaction reflected in ultimate adjustment.
5. The persisting life situation can be converted to educational experiences that are as dynamic as the environment from which they arise.
6. Persisting life situations tend to focus on the real and specific needs of the learner, thus permitting the investment of maximum instructional energies directed toward the solution of specific problems which grow out of these needs.
7. The persisting life situations provide a single frame of reference which permits a systematic appraisal of the problem of curriculum, and a systematic development of curriculum content with scope and sequence.
8. The task of selecting goals from the wide variety of sources is a primary responsibility of the professional educator. This responsibility is one in which he must provide intelligent and responsible leadership, and the ability to utilize every available resource.

A REVIEW OF THE LITERATURE

We shall attempt to examine the statements of recognized students of special education who have attempted to set forth a philosophic position in the past quarter century. The statements are excerpts from the literature that have become recognized as the standard work in the field.

The materials which were selected are thought to be typical illustrations of statements of educational objectives and it is not suggested that this is an exhaustive review of all statements that have been developed.

Inskeep[4] set forth certain goals. Her specific goals were based on the general purpose of education, i.e., the training of self-controlled, self-supporting citizens. She places an emphasis on "a trained hand, guided by a thinking head, and controlled by disciplined emotions."

She proposed several specific goals as follows:

1. Health
2. Social living
3. Getting and holding a job
4. Thrift
5. Efficient use of leisure time

Descoeudres [5] itemizes the objectives for the education of the mentally retarded in terms of a child-centered approach as follows:

1. The child
    a. His physical and mental constitution
    b. His needs—food, clothing, housing, instruction, vocational training, moral and esthetic needs, their existence and their inevitableness.
2. His environment
    The child and his family
    The child and the school
    The child and society
    The child and the animal world
    The child and the vegetable world
    The child and the mineral world
    The child and the sun
3. Training and the senses and the attention
4. Physical training
5. Handwork
6. Drawing
7. Speech
8. Reading
9. Spelling
10. Arithmetic
11. Moral training

The Educational Policies Commission developed a report [6] in which

[4] Annie D. Inskeep, *Teaching Dull and Retarded Children* (New York: Macmillan, 1926).

[5] Alice Descoeudres, *The Education of Mentally Defective Children,* trans. by E. F. Trow (Boston: Heath, 1928).

[6] National Education Association, Educational Policies Commission, *The Purposes of Education in American Democracy* (Washington, D.C., 1938).

four broad objectives were stated. While these goals were developed with the general needs of all children in mind, we need to examine them inasmuch as these statements have tended to influence the objectives developed by many communities in the development of a curriculum for the mentally handicapped. They are as follows:

I. The Objectives of Self-Realization

1. *The inquiring mind.* The educated person has an appetite for learning.
2. *Speech.* The educated person can speak the mother tongue clearly.
3. *Reading.* The educated person reads the mother tongue efficiently.
4. *Writing.* The educated person writes the mother tongue effectively.
5. *Number.* The educated person solves his problems of counting and calculating.
6. *Sight and hearing.* The educated person is skilled in listening and observing.
7. *Health knowledge.* The educated person understands the basic facts concerning health and disease.
8. *Health habits.* The educated person protects his own health and that of his dependents.
9. *Public health.* The educated person works to improve the health of the community.
10. *Recreation.* The educated person is participant and spectator in many sports and other pastimes.
11. *Intellectual interests.* The educated person has mental resources for the use of leisure.
12. *Esthetic interests.* The educated person appreciates beauty.
13. *Character.* The educated person gives responsible direction to his own life.

II. The Objectives of Human Relationship

14. *Respect for humanity.* The educated person puts human relations first.
15. *Friendships.* The educated person enjoys a rich, sincere, and varied social life.
16. *Cooperation.* The educated person can work and play with others.
17. *Courtesy.* The educated person observes the amenities of social behavior.
18. *Appreciation of the home.* The educated person appreciates the family as a social institution.
19. *Conservation of the home.* The educated person conserves family ideals.
20. *Homemaking.* The educated person is skilled in homemaking.
21. *Democracy in the home.* The educated person maintains democratic family relationships.

III. The Objectives of Economic Efficiency

22. *Work.* The educated producer knows the satisfaction of good workmanship.
23. *Occupational information.* The educated producer understands the requirements and opportunities for various jobs.
24. *Occupational choice.* The educated producer has selected his occupation.
25. *Occupational efficiency.* The educated producer succeeds in his chosen vocation.
26. *Occupational adjustment.* The educated producer maintains and improves his efficiency.
27. *Occupational appreciation.* The educated producer appreciates the social value of his work.
28. *Personal economics.* The educated consumer plans the economics of his own life.
29. *Consumer judgment.* The educated consumer develops standards for guiding his expenditures.
30. *Efficiency in buying.* The educated consumer is an informed and skillful buyer.
31. *Consumer protection.* The educated consumer takes appropriate measures to safeguard his interests.

IV. The Objectives of Civic Responsibilities

32. *Social justice.* The educated citizen is sensitive to the disparities of human circumstance.
33. *Social activity.* The educated citizen acts to correct unsatisfactory conditions.
34. *Social understanding.* The educated citizen seeks to understand social structures and social processes.
35. *Critical judgment.* The educated citizen has defenses against propaganda.
36. *Tolerance.* The educated citizen respects honest differences of opinion.
37. *Conservation.* The educated citizen has regard for the nation's resources.
38. *Social applications of science.* The educated citizen measures scientific advance by its contribution to the general welfare.
39. *World citizenship.* The educated citizen is a cooperating member of the world community.
40. *Law observance.* The educated citizen respects the law.
41. *Economic literacy.* The educated citizen is economically literate.
42. *Political citizenship.* The educated citizen accepts his civic duties.
43. *Devotion to democracy.* The educated citizen acts upon an unswerving loyalty to democratic ideals.

It is not uncommon for local school systems to develop statements of goals as a point of departure in curriculum planning at the local level. One such statement, "The Fundamental Purposes of Education," which is included is fairly typical of this kind of statement.[7]

1. To develop and maintain physical and mental health.
2. To develop competency in the fundamental tools traditionally called the three R's.
3. To think critically and act responsibly.
4. To develop and strengthen home and family life.
5. To respect, understand, and live well with others.
6. To develop moral and spiritual values.
7. To understand and to cope with the physical world.
8. To grow in appreciation of the arts and in desire and ability to express oneself creatively through various media.
9. To develop interest and skill in worthwhile leisure-time activities.
10. To develop understanding of and respect for the cultural heritage.
11. To develop the knowledge, skills, attitudes, and understanding essential for earning a living.
12. To develop consumer effectiveness.
13. To appreciate the duties, responsibilities, and privileges of citizenship.

Martens [8] has stated some objectives as follows:

General Objectives

1. Education for achievement in the world of knowledge.
2. Education for achievement in occupational life.
3. Education for achievement in social relations.
4. Education for achievement in worthwhile use of leisure time.

Specific Goals

I. The knowledge and disposition to keep physically well in order to enjoy life to its maximum.
II. An ease and a joy in social relationships that help him to make friends and to participate in social and civic experiences.
III. An ability to plan and to choose his leisure activities wisely.
IV. An ability to live as a contributing member of a family and a neigh-

[7] Claude V. Courter, *Schools and the Means of Education: A Statement of the Policies, Principles and Procedures of Cincinnati's Program of Public Education,* a Special Report to the Board of Education (Cincinnati: Board of Education, 1954).

[8] Elise H. Martens, *Curriculum Adjustment for the Mentally Retarded: A Guide for Elementary and Secondary Schools,* rev. ed. 2, no. 2 (Washington, D.C.: Government Printing Office, 1950).

borhood group, and later to maintain his own home as head of a family.

V. The ability to earn as much of the necessities of life as possible.

VI. The knowledge and ability to spend his salary wisely.

Featherstone,[9] in discussing the "slow learner," lists several goals, and suggests the Educational Policies Commission formulations would be suitable as a guide to developing specific goals. He further suggests that "the goals must be immediate and tangible." He lists the following:

1. Health
2. Vocation
3. Home and family
4. Personal development
5. Social competence
6. Foundational skills and abilities

Graham and Engel [10] state very generally that "All children are entitled to the best training to promote their growth and welfare." They suggest that "it is not, however, to be conceived of as a modified plan of regular education, but as a unique program planned in terms of the needs of a particular group or an individual child." They do not isolate the specific instructional areas with statements or descriptive terms, but tend to draw on the Educational Policies concept.

Delp [11] listed certain "goals" for the mentally retarded. In his list he probably extended his concept to include some things other than the purposes of education. His list is as follows:

1. Correct diagnosis
2. Understanding
3. Acceptance
4. Maturation
5. Physical defects and well-being
6. Habits of living
7. Social adjustment
8. Personality
9. Academic fundamentals
10. Information

[9] William B. Featherstone, *Teaching the Slow Learner* (New York: Teachers College Press, Columbia University, 1951).

[10] Ray Graham and Anna Engel, "Administering Special Services," in National Society for the Study of Education Forty-ninth Yearbook, Part Two, *The Education of Exceptional Children,* ed. by Nelson B. Henry (Chicago: University of Chicago, 1950).

[11] Harold A. Delp, "Goals for the Mentally Retarded," *American Journal of Mental Deficiency, 55* (April 1951), 472–478.

11. Day-to-day standards
12. Self-care and self-support
13. Adequate leisure time activities
14. Supervision and guidance
15. Adequate placement

It is evident from the headings used that this statement of goals includes content beyond the purview of educational experience. One might guess he is really thinking in terms of "a total program for the retarded."

A state group interested in the education of the retarded adolescent developed the following statements: [12]

1. Mastering the tools of communication.
2. Developing a strong body and a sound attitude toward it and toward good health practices.
3. Developing satisfactory social relationships with other adolescents and adults.
4. Understanding and appreciating the values of family life together with a desire for the ability to improve family living.
5. Acquiring knowledge of, practice in, and zeal for democratic processes.
6. Becoming sensitive to the importance of group action in the attainment of social goals and proficient in the skills involved in such action.
7. Becoming an effective consumer.
8. Becoming occupationally adjusted.
9. Developing meaning for life.

Kirk and Johnson [13] state that "Objectives can be stated in a number of ways and in different terms. In general, however, all specialists agree that the more specific aims for the mentally handicapped include the following:

1. They should be educated to get along with their fellow men; i.e., they should develop social competency through numerous social experiences.
2. They should learn to participate in work for the purpose of earning their own living; i.e., they should develop occupational competence through efficient vocational guidance and training as a part of their school experience.
3. They should develop emotional security and independence in the school and in the home through a good mental hygiene program.
4. They should develop habits of health and sanitation through a good program of health education.

[12] Vernon Nickell, *Educating the Mentally Handicapped in the Secondary Schools*, Illinois Secondary School Curriculum Program, Bulletin No. 12 (Springfield: Department of Public Instruction, 1951).

[13] Samuel A. Kirk and G. Orville Johnson, *Educating the Retarded Child* (Boston: Houghton Mifflin, 1951).

5. They should learn the minimum essentials of tool subjects, even though their academic limits are third to fifth grade.
6. They should learn to occupy themselves in wholesome leisure-time activities through an educational program that teaches them to enjoy recreational and leisure-time activities.
7. They should learn to become adequate members of a family and a home through an educational program that emphasizes home membership as a function of the curriculum.
8. They should learn to become adequate members of a community through a school program that emphasizes community participation.

"The program for the mentally handicapped stresses (1) occupational adequacy, (2) social competence, and (3) personal adequacy."

A recent reexamination of goals for adolescents has become a recognized statement described as "Imperative Educational Needs of Youth."[14]

1. All youth need to develop salable skills and those understandings and attitudes that make the worker an intelligent and productive participant in economic life. To this end most youth need supervised work experiences as well as education in the skills and knowledge of their occupations.
2. All youth need to develop and maintain good health and physical fitness.
3. All youth need to understand the rights and duties of the citizen of a democratic society, and to be diligent and competent in the performance of their obligations as members of the community and citizens of the state and community.
4. All youth need to understand the significance of the family for the individual and society and the conditions conducive to successful family living.
5. All youth need to know how to purchase and use goods and services intelligently, understanding both the values received by the consumer and the economic consequences of their acts.
6. All youth need to understand the methods of science, the influence of science on human life and the main scientific facts concerning the nature of the world and of man.
7. All youth need opportunities to develop capacities to appreciate beauty in literature, art, music, and nature.
8. All youth need to be able to use their leisure time well and to budget it wisely, balancing activities that yield satisfaction to the individual and with those who are socially useful.
9. All youth need to develop respect for other persons, to grow in their

[14] National Education Association, Educational Policies Commission, *Education for All American Youth: A Further Look* (Washington, D.C., 1952).

insights into ethical values and principles, and to be able to live and work cooperatively with others.

10. All youth need to grow in their ability to think rationally, to express their thoughts clearly, and to read and listen with understanding.

Ingram[15] has stated the objectives in five topical categories.

1. Mental and physical health
2. A practical working knowledge of the tool subjects
3. Worthy home and community life
4. Worthy use of leisure time
5. Adjustment in industry

Wallin[16] has developed a rather elaborate statement of the goals of special classes. He states them as follows:

> The specific functions or goals of the life adjustment program of the special class should include:
>
> 1. Continuous systematic study of each child by clinically minded teachers to discover individual aptitudes, potentials, proclivities, and needs and to devise more effective methods of remediation and therapy.
> 2. The formation of likeable personalities free from crippling distortions and injurious compensations by providing an atmosphere of contentment and acceptance, together with opportunities for joyous, successful achievement which will tend to dissipate feelings of insecurity, frustration, and disheartenment and will engender feelings of hope, confidence, and determination; by applying sound mental-hygiene principles to all the learning situations; and by using individual and group psychology.
> 3. The development of maximal motor, occupational, and economic efficiency.
> 4. The development of practical social understandings and skills, desirable civic qualities, and ethical character.
> 5. The development of practical literary tool skills as far as the child's limitations permit.
> 6. The provision from the time the child enters school of personal, educational, and vocational guidance based on all the data available and on intimate personal contacts.
> 7. The provision of job information and job placement.
> 8. Follow-up investigations to determine the value of the training provided and to further job and social adjustment.

[15] Christine P. Ingram, *Education of the Slow Learning Child* (New York: Ronald, 1953).

[16] J. E. Wallace Wallin, *Education of Mentally Handicapped Children* (New York: Harper, 1955).

9. Preparation for wholesome leisure-time diversions in both home and community.
10. The development of physical and mental efficiency and health.

DeProspo [17] in discussing curriculum says the goals might be variously termed:

1. Occupational and social adjustment
2. Human relationships
3. Better living
4. Personal development
5. Personal growth
6. Total adjustment

He makes the following observation: "In one sense, all of these are the same thing, yet each is too general a term to serve as an objective."

SUMMARY

In an attempt to develop a basic statement of goals for the education of the mentally retarded the writer has attempted to analyze by statements that have been set forth by students of the problem for the last quarter century.

An examination of the statements suggests a number of generalizations.

1. There is a tendency to agree on many items in a listing of educational objectives; for example, "tool subjects," "making a living," "using one's leisure time wisely," and others.
2. Most students of the problem tend to agree that objectives need to be "specific." This is presumed to mean that they need to be stated in terms of the nature and needs of the mentally retarded learner.
3. There seems to be agreement that the general goals for the retardate are the same as for all learners since the mentally retarded child is more similar than different from his normal peers.
4. Statements of objectives tend to be set forth in too broad a category such as "learn to be an effective member of a family," "an effective member of a community," and others.
5. Statements tend to be handed down from one student of the problem to another with minor variations.
6. There was a marked shift away from the specific training of certain "functions" which represented the influences of European physiologically oriented workers.
7. Statements do not tend to be parallel and are frequently restated.

[17] Chris DeProspo, "A Suggested Curriculum for the Mentally Retarded," in Merle E. Frampton and Elena Gall (eds.), *Special Education for the Exceptional* (Boston: Porter Sargent, 1955), Vol. 3, pp. 472–478.

8. Statements sometimes tend to intermix the problem of the content of the curriculum with educational methodology and organization. This tends to produce some confusion.
9. There are some gaps in statements as set forth in the past 25 years. For example, there is no mention of "learning to travel about."
10. Certain statements tend to be included in combination by virtue of tradition. For example, safety education is usually included under health education. Mental and physical health are usually spoken of in the same breath.
11. Certain statements of objectives as described by some authorities did not remain within the confines of the problem and tended to include many irrelevant items having little bearing on the problem of curriculum, usually focusing on educational methodology.
12. Statements tend to be ambiguous, or tend to use rather "high-flown" language that produce problems of interpretation of meaning.

CONCLUSIONS

In the opinion of the writer, there is a need to restate the objectives or goals in terms of persisting life situations which are a function of the needs of the individual as dictated by his unique growth and the kind of society in which he lives. These problems have their foundation in the fundamental problems of daily existence of the mentally retarded. It is intended that they meet the criteria pointed out earlier and are contained within a single contextual framework. They are stated in terms of what the learner needs rather than in terms of what the teacher should teach.

1. Learning to maintain a state of physical well-being.
2. Learning to live safely.
3. Learning to understand one's self.
4. Learning to get along with others.
5. Learning to communicate ideas.
6. Learning to use leisure time.
7. Learning to travel and move about.
8. Learning to earn a living.
9. Learning to be a home-maker.
10. Learning to enjoy life through the appreciation of art, dance, and music.
11. Learning to adjust to the forces of nature.
12. Learning to manage one's money.

It is obvious that many problems of ambiguity and definition are inherent in such simply constructed statements, and it is the intention of the writer to develop each of the concepts in forthcoming publications.

19 SPECIAL EDUCATION FOR THE MILDLY RETARDED—IS MUCH OF IT JUSTIFIABLE?

Lloyd M. Dunn

From *Exceptional Children,* Vol. 35, No. 1, September 1968, pp. 5–22. Reprinted with the permission of the Council for Exceptional Children and the author. Dr. Dunn is Professor of Educational Psychology, University of Hawaii, Honolulu.

A better education than special class placement is needed for socioculturally deprived children with mild learning problems who have been labeled educable mentally retarded. Over the years, the status of these pupils who come from poverty, broken and inadequate homes, and low status ethnic groups has been a checkered one. In the early days, these children were simply excluded from school. Then, as Hollingworth (1923) pointed out, with the advent of compulsory attendance laws, the schools and these children "were forced into a reluctant mutual recognition of each other." This resulted in the establishment of self-contained special schools and classes as a method of transferring these "misfits" out of the regular grades. This practice continues to this day and, unless counterforces are set in motion now, it will probably become even more prevalent in the immediate future due in large measure to increased racial integration and militant teacher organizations. For example, a local affiliate of the National Education Association demanded of a local school board recently that more special classes be provided for disruptive and slow learning children (Nashville *Tennessean,* December 18, 1967).

The number of special day classes for the retarded has been increasing by leaps and bounds. The most recent 1967–1968 statistics compiled by the US Office of Education now indicate that there are approximately 32,000 teachers of the retarded employed by local school systems—over one-third of all special educators in the nation. In my best judgment, about 60 to 80 percent of the pupils taught by these teachers are children from low status backgrounds—including Afro-Americans, American Indians, Mexicans, and Puerto Rican Americans; those from nonstandard English speaking, broken, disorganized, and inadequate homes; and children from other nonmiddle class environments. This expensive proliferation of self-contained special schools and classes raises serious educational and civil rights issues which must be squarely faced. It is my thesis that we must stop labeling these deprived children as mentally retarded. Furthermore we must stop segregating them by placing them into our allegedly special programs.

The purpose of this article is twofold: first, to provide reasons for taking the position that a large proportion of this so-called special education in its present form is obsolete and unjustifiable from the point of view of the pupils so placed; and second, to outline a blueprint for changing this major segment of education for exceptional children to make it more acceptable. We are not arguing that we do away with our special education programs for the moderately and severely retarded, for other types of more handicapped children, or for the multiply handicapped. The emphasis is on doing something better for slow learning children who live in slum conditions, although much of what is said should also have relevance for those children we are labeling emotionally disturbed, perceptually impaired, brain injured, and learning disordered. Furthermore, the emphasis of the article is on children, in that no attempt is made to suggest an adequate high school environment for adolescents still functioning as slow learners.

REASONS FOR CHANGE

Regular teachers and administrators have sincerely felt they were doing these pupils a favor by removing them from the pressures of an unrealistic and inappropriate program of studies. Special educators have also fully believed that the children involved would make greater progress in special schools and classes. However, the overwhelming evidence is that our present and past practices have their major justification in removing pressures on regular teachers and pupils, at the expense of the socioculturally deprived slow learning pupils themselves. Some major arguments for this position are outlined below.

Homogeneous Groupings

Homogeneous groupings tend to work to the disadvantage of the slow learners and underprivileged. Apparently such pupils learn much from being in the same class with children from white middle-class homes. Also, teachers seem to concentrate on the slower children to bring them up to standard. This principle was dramatically applied in the Judge J. Skelly Wright decision in the District of Columbia concerning the track system. Judge Wright ordered that tracks be abolished, contending they discriminated against the racially and/or economically disadvantaged and therefore were in violation of the Fifth Amendment of the Constitution of the United States. One may object to the Judge's making educational decisions based on legal considerations. However, Passow (1967), upon the completion of a study of the same school system, reached the same conclusion concerning tracking. The recent national study by Coleman, *et al.* (1966), provides supporting evidence in finding that academically disadvantaged Negro children in racially segregated schools made less progress than those of comparable ability in integrated schools. Furthermore, racial integration appeared to deter school progress very little for Caucasian and more academically able students

What are the implications of Judge Wright's rulings for special education? Clearly special schools and classes are a form of homogeneous grouping and tracking. This fact was demonstrated in September 1967, when the District of Columbia (as a result of the Wright decision) abolished Track 5, into which had been routed the slowest learning pupils in the District of Columbia schools. These pupils and their teachers were returned to the regular classrooms. Complaints followed from the regular teachers that these children were taking an inordinate amount of their time. A few parents observed that their slow learning children were frustrated by the more academic program and were rejected by the other students. Thus, there are efforts afoot to develop a special education program in D.C. which cannot be labeled a track. Self-contained special classes will probably not be tolerated under the present court ruling but perhaps itinerant and resource room programs would be. What if the Supreme Court ruled against tracks, and all self-contained special classes across the nation which serve primarily ethnically and/or economically disadvantaged children were forced to close down? Make no mistake—this could happen! If I were a Negro from the slums or a disadvantaged parent who had heard of the Judge Wright decision and knew what I know now about special classes for the educable mentally retarded, other things being equal, I would then go to court before allowing the schools to label my child as "mentally retarded" and place him in a "self-contained special school or class." Thus there is the real possibility that additional court actions will be forthcoming.[1]

Efficacy Studies

The findings of studies on the efficacy of special classes for the educable mentally retarded constitute another argument for change. These results are well known (Kirk, 1964) and suggest consistently that retarded pupils make as much or more progress in the regular grades as they do in special education. Recent studies such as those by Hoelke (1966) and Smith and Kennedy (1967) continue to provide similar evidence. Johnson (1962) has summarized the situation well:

> It is indeed paradoxical that mentally handicapped children having teachers especially trained, having more money (per capita) spent on their education, and being designed to provide for their unique needs,

[1] Litigation has now occurred. According to an item in a June 8, 1968, issue of the *Los Angeles Times* received after this article was sent to the printer, the attorneys in the national office for the rights of the indigent filed a suit in behalf of the Mexican-American parents of the Santa Ana Unified School District asking for an injunction against the District's classes for the educable mentally retarded because the psychological examinations required prior to placement are unconstitutional since they have failed to use adequate evaluation techniques for children from different language and cultural backgrounds, and because parents have been denied the right of hearing to refute evidence for placement. Furthermore, the suit seeks to force the District to grant hearings on all children currently in such special classes to allow for the chance to remove the stigma of the label "mentally retarded" from school records of such pupils.

should be accomplishing the objectives of their education at the same or at a lower level than similar mentally handicapped children who have not had these advantages and have been forced to remain in the regular grades [p. 66].

Efficacy studies on special day classes for other mildly handicapped children, including the emotionally handicapped, reveal the same results. For example, Rubin, Senison, and Betwee (1966) found that disturbed children did as well in the regular grades as in special classes, concluding that there is little or no evidence that special class programing is generally beneficial to emotionally disturbed children as a specific method of intervention and correction. Evidence such as this is another reason to find better ways of serving children with mild learning disorders than placing them in self-contained special schools and classes.

Labeling Processes

Our past and present diagnostic procedures comprise another reason for change. These procedures have probably been doing more harm than good in that they have resulted in disability labels and in that they have grouped children homogeneously in school on the basis of these labels. Generally, these diagnostic practices have been conducted by one of two procedures. In rare cases, the workup has been provided by a multidisciplinary team, usually consisting of physicians, social workers, psychologists, speech and hearing specialists, and occasionally educators. The avowed goal of this approach has been to look at the complete child, but the outcome has been merely to label him mentally retarded, perceptually impaired, emotionally disturbed, minimally brain-injured, or some other such term depending on the predispositions, idiosyncrasies, and backgrounds of the team members. Too, the team usually has looked for causation, and diagnosis tends to stop when something has been found wrong with the child, when the why has either been found or conjectured, and when some justification has been found for recommending placement in a special education class.

In the second and more common case, the assessment of educational potential has been left to the school psychologist who generally administers —in an hour or so—a psychometric battery, at best consisting of individual tests of intelligence, achievement, and social and personal adjustment. Again the purpose has been to find out what is wrong with the child in order to label him and thus make him eligible for special education services. In large measure this has resulted in digging the educational graves of many racially and/or economically disadvantaged children by using a WISC or Binet IQ score to justify the label "mentally retarded." This term then becomes a distructive, self-fulfilling prophecy.

What is the evidence against the continued use of these diagnostic practices and disability labels?

First, we must examine the effects of these disability labels on the attitudes and expectancies of teachers. Here we can extrapolate from studies by Rosenthal and Jacobson (1966) who set out to determine whether or not the expectancies of teachers influenced pupil progress. Working with elementary school teachers across the first six grades, they obtained pretest measures on pupils by using intelligence and achievement tests. A sample of pupils was randomly drawn and labeled "rapid learners" with hidden potential. Teachers were told that these children would show unusual intellectual gains and school progress during the year. All pupils were retested late in the school year. Not all differences were statistically significant, but the gains of the children who had been arbitrarily labeled rapid learners were generally significantly greater than those of the other pupls, with especially dramatic changes in the first and second grades. To extrapolate from this study, we must expect that labeling a child "handicapped" reduces the teacher's expectancy for him to succeed.

Second, we must examine the effects of these disability labels on the pupils themselves. Certainly none of these labels are badges of distinction. Separating a child from other children in his neighborhood—or removing him from the regular classroom for therapy or special class placement—probably has a serious debilitating effect upon his self-image. Here again our research is limited but supportive of this contention. Goffman (1961) has described the stripping and mortification process that takes place when an individual is placed in a residential facility. Meyerowitz (1965) demonstrated that a group of educable mentally retarded pupils increased in feelings of self-derogation after one year in special classes. More recent results indicate that special class placement, instead of helping such a pupil adjust to his neighborhood peers, actually hinders him (Meyerowitz, 1967). While much more research is needed, we cannot ignore the evidence that removing a handicapped child from the regular grades for special education probably contributes significantly to his feelings of inferiority and problems of acceptance.

Improvements in General Education

Another reason self-contained special classes are less justifiable today than in the past is that regular school programs are now better able to deal with individual differences in pupils. No longer is the choice just between a self-contained special class and a self-contained regular elementary classroom. Although the impact of the American Revolution in Education is just beginning to be felt and is still more an ideal than a reality, special education should begin moving now to fit into a changing general education program and to assist in achieving the program's goals. Because of increased support at the local, state, and federal levels, four powerful forces are at work:

CHANGES IN SCHOOL ORGANIZATION. In place of self-contained regular classrooms, there is increasingly more team teaching, ungraded primary departments, and flexible groupings. Radical departures in school organization are projected—educational parks in place of neighborhood schools, metropolitan school districts cutting across our inner cities and wealthy suburbs, and, perhaps most revolutionary of all, competing public school systems. Furthermore, and of great significance to those of us who have focused our careers on slow learning children, public kindergartens and nurseries are becoming more available for children of the poor.

CURRICULAR CHANGES. Instead of the standard diet of Look and Say readers, many new and exciting options for teaching reading are evolving. Contemporary mathematics programs teach in the primary grades concepts formerly reserved for high school. More programed textbooks and other materials are finding their way into the classroom. Ingenious procedures, such as those by Bereiter and Engelmann (1966), are being developed to teach oral language and reasoning to preschool disadvantaged children.

CHANGES IN PROFESSIONAL PUBLIC SCHOOL PERSONNEL. More ancillary personnel are now employed by the schools, i.e., psychologists, guidance workers, physical educators, remedial educators, teacher aides, and technicians. Furthermore, some teachers are functioning in different ways, serving as teacher coordinators, or cluster teachers who provide released time for other teachers to prepare lessons, etc. Too, regular classroom teachers are increasingly better trained to deal with individual differences—although much still remains to be done.

HARDWARE CHANGES. Computerized teaching, teaching machines, feedback typewriters, ETV, videotapes, and other materials are making autoinstruction possible, as never before.

We must ask what the implications of this American Revolution in Education are for special educators. Mackie (1967), formerly of the US Office of Education, addressed herself to the question: "Is the modern school changing sufficiently to provide [adequate services in general education] for large numbers of pupils who have functional mental retardation due to environmental factors [p. 5]?" In her view, hundreds—perhaps even thousands—of so-called retarded pupils may make satisfactory progress in schools with diversified programs of instruction and thus will never need placement in self-contained special classes. With earlier, better, and more flexible regular school programs many of the children should not need to be relegated to the type of special education we have so often provided.

In my view, the above four reasons for change are cogent ones. Much of special education for the mildly retarded is becoming obsolete. Never in our history has there been a greater urgency to take stock and to search out new roles for a large number of today's special educators.

A BLUEPRINT FOR CHANGE

Two major suggestions which constitute my attempt at a blueprint for change are developed below. First, a fairly radical departure from conventional methods will be proposed in procedures for diagnosing, placing, and teaching children with mild learning difficulties. Second, a proposal for curriculum revision will be sketched out. These are intended as proposals which should be examined, studied, and tested. What is needed are programs based on scientific evidence of worth and not more of those founded on philosophy, tradition, and expediency.

A Thought

There is an important difference between regular educators talking us into trying to remediate or live with the learning difficulties of pupils with which they haven't been able to deal; versus *striving to evolve a special education program that is either developmental in nature, wherein we assume responsibility for the total education of more severely handicapped children from an early age,* or *is supportive in nature, wherein general education would continue to have central responsibility for the vast majority of the children with mild learning disabilities—with us serving as resource teachers in devising effective prescriptions and in tutoring such pupils.*

A Clinical Approach

Existing diagnostic procedures should be replaced by expecting special educators, in large measure, to be responsible for their own diagnostic teaching and their clinical teaching. In this regard, it is suggested that we do away with many existing disability labels and the present practice of grouping children homogeneously by these labels into special classes. Instead, we should try keeping slow learning children more in the mainstream of education, with special educators serving as diagnostic, clinical, remedial, resource room, itinerant and/or team teachers, consultants, and developers of instructional materials and prescriptions for effective teaching.

The accomplishment of the above *modus operandi* will require a revolution in much of special education. A moratorium needs to be placed on the proliferation (if not continuance) of self-contained special classes which enroll primarily the ethnically and/or economically disadvantaged children we have been labeling educable mentally retarded. Such pupils should be left in (or returned to) the regular elementary grades until we are "tooled up" to do something better for them.

PRESCRIPTIVE TEACHING. In diagnosis one needs to know how much a child can learn, under what circumstances, and with what materials. To accomplish this, there are three administrative procedures possible. One would be for each large school system—or two or more small districts—to establish a "Special Education Diagnostic and Prescription Generating Center." Pupils with school learning problems would be enrolled in this center on a day and/or boarding school basis for a period of time—probably up to a month and hopefully until a successful prescription for effective teaching had been evolved. The core of the staff would be a variety of master teachers with different specialties—such as in motor development, perceptual training, language development, social and personality development, remedial education, and so forth. Noneducators such as physicians, psychologists, and social workers would be retained in a consultative role, or pupils would be referred out to such paraeducational professionals, as needed. A second procedure, in lieu of such centers with their cadres of educational specialists, would be for one generalist in diagnostic teaching to perform the diagnostic and prescription devising functions on her own. A third and even less desirable procedure would be for one person to combine the roles of prescriptive and clinical teacher which will be presented next. It is suggested that 15 to 20 percent of the most insightful special educators be prepared for and/or assigned to prescriptive teaching. One clear virtue of the center is that a skilled director could coordinate an in-service training program and the staff could learn through, and be stimulated by, one another. In fact, many special educators could rotate through this program.

Under any of these procedures, educators would be responsible for the administration and interpretation of individual and group psychoeducational tests on cognitive development (such as the WISC and Binet), on language development (such as the ITPA), and on social maturity (such as the Vineland Social Maturity Scale). However, these instruments—with the exception of the ITPA which yields a profile of abilities and disabilities —will be of little use except in providing baseline data on the level at which a child is functioning. In place of these psychometric tests which usually yield only global scores, diagnostic educators would need to rely heavily on a combination of the various tools of behavior shapers and clinical teachers. The first step would be to make a study of the child to find what behaviors he has acquired along the dimension being considered. Next, samples of a sequential program would be designed to move him forward from that point. In presenting the program, the utility of different reinforcers, administered under various conditions, would be investigated. Also, the method by which he can best be taught the material should be determined. Different modalities for reaching the child would also be tried. Thus, since the instructional program itself becomes the diagnostic device, this procedure can be called diagnostic teaching. Failures are program and instructor failures, not pupil failures. In large measure, we would be guided by Bruner's dictum (1967) that almost any child can be taught almost anything if it is programed correctly.[2]

[2] By ignoring genetic influences on the behavioral characteristics of children with learning difficulties, we place responsibility on an inadequate society, inadequate parents, unmotivated pupils, and/or in this case inadequate teachers. Taking this extreme environmental approach could result in placing too much blame for failure on the teacher and too much pressure on the child. While we could set our level of aspiration too high, this has hardly been the direction of our error to date in special

This diagnostic procedure is viewed as the best available since it enables us to assess continuously the problem points of the instructional program against the assets of the child. After a successful and appropriate prescription has been devised, it would be communicated to the teachers in the pupil's home school and they would continue the procedure as long as it is necessary and brings results. From time to time, the child may need to return to the center for reappraisal and redirection.

Clearly the above approach to special education diagnosis and treatment is highly clinical and intuitive. In fact, it is analogous to the rural doctor of the past who depended on his insights and a few diagnostic and treatment devices carried in his small, black bag. It may remain with us for some time to come. However, it will be improved upon by more standardized procedures. Perhaps the two most outstanding, pioneering efforts in this regard are now being made by Feuerstein (1968) in Israel, and by Kirk (1966) in the United States. Feuerstein has devised a *Learning Potential Assessment Device* for determining the degree of modifiability of the behavior of an individual pupil, the level at which he is functioning, the strategies by which he can best learn, and the areas in which he needs to be taught. Also, he is developing a variety of exercises for teaching children with specific learning difficulties. Kirk and his associates have not only given us the ITPA which yields a profile of abilities and disabilities in the psycholinguistic area, but they have also devised exercises for remediating specific psycholinguistic disabilities reflected by particular types of profiles (Kirk, 1966). Both of these scientists are structuring the assessment and remediation procedures to reduce clinical judgment, although it would be undesirable to formalize to too great a degree. Like the country doctor versus modern medicine, special education in the next fifty years will move from clinical intuition to a more precise science of clinical instruction based on diagnostic instruments which yield a profile of abilities and disabilities about a specfic facet of behavior and which have incorporated within them measures of a child's ability to learn samples or units of materials at each of the points on the profile. If psychoeducational tests had these two characteristics, they would accomplish essentially the same thing as does the diagnostic approach described above—only under more standardized conditions.

ITINERANT AND RESOURCE ROOM TEACHING. It is proposed that a second echelon of special educators be itinerant or resource teachers. One or more resource teachers might be available to each sizable school, while an itinerant teacher would serve two or more smaller schools. General educators would refer their children with learning difficulties to these teachers.

---

education of the handicapped. Perhaps the sustained push proposed in this paper may not succeed, but we will not know until we try it. Insightful teachers should be able to determine when the pressures on the pupil and system are too great.

If possible, the clinical teacher would evolve an effective prescription for remediating the problem. If this is not possible, she would refer the child to the Special Education Diagnostic and Prescription Generating Center or to the more specialized prescriptive teacher who would study the child and work out an appropriate regimen of instruction for him. In either event, the key role of the resource room and itinerant clinical educators would be to develop instructional materials and lessons for implemening the prescription found effective for the child, and to consult and work with the other educators who serve the child. Thus, the job of special educators would be to work as members of the schools' instructional teams and to focus on children with mild to moderate school learning problems. Special educators would be available to all children in trouble (except the severely handicapped) regardless of whether they had, in the past, been labeled educable mentally retarded, minimally brain injured, educationally handicapped, or emotionally disturbed. Children would be regrouped continually throughout the school day. For specific help these children who had a learning problem might need to work with the itinerant or resource room special educator. But, for the remainder of the day, the special educator would probably be more effective in developing specific exercises which could be taught by others in consultation with her. Thus, the special educator would begin to function as a part of, and not apart from, general education. Clearly this proposed approach recognizes that all children have assets and deficits, not all of which are permanent. When a child was having trouble in one or more areas of learning, special educators would be available to devise a successful teaching approach for him and to tutor him when necessary. Perhaps as many as 20 to 35 percent of our present special educators are or could be prepared for this vital role.

TWO OTHER OBSERVATIONS. First, it is recognized that some of today's special educators—especially of the educable mentally retarded—are not prepared to serve the functions discussed. These teachers would need to either withdraw from special education or develop the needed competencies. Assuming an open door policy and playing the role of the expert educational diagnostician and the prescriptive and clinical educator would place us in the limelight. Only the best will succeed. But surely this is a responsibility we will not shirk. Our avowed *raison d'etre* has been to provide special education for children unable to make adequate progress in the regular grades. More would be lost than gained by assigning less than master teachers from self-contained classes to the diagnostic and clinical educator roles. Ainsworth (1959) has already compared the relative effectiveness of the special class versus itinerant special educators of the retarded and found that neither group accomplished much in pupil progress. A virtue of these new roles for special education is that they are high status positions which should appeal to the best and therefore enhance the recruitment of master regular teachers who should be outstanding in these positions after having obtained specialized graduate training in behavior shaping, psychoeducational diagnostics, remedial education, and so forth.

Second, if one accepts these procedures for special education, the need for disability labels is reduced. In their stead we may need to substitute labels which describe the educational intervention needed. We would thus talk of pupils who need special instruction in language or cognitive development, in sensory training, in personality development, in vocational training, and other areas. However, some labels may be needed for administrative reasons. If so, we need to find broad generic terms such as "school learning disorders."

New Curricular Approaches

Master teachers are at the heart of an effective school program for children with mild to moderate learning difficulties—master teachers skilled at educational diagnosis and creative in designing and carrying out interventions to remediate the problems that exist. But what should they teach? In my view, there has been too great an emphasis in special classes on practical arts and practical academics, to the exclusion of other ingredients. Let us be honest with ourselves. Our courses of study have tended to be watered down regular curriculum. If we are to move from the clinical stage to a science of instruction, we will need a rich array of validated prescriptive programs of instruction at our disposal. To assemble these programs will take time, talent, and money; teams of specialists including creative teachers, curriculum specialists, programers, and theoreticians will be needed to do the job.

What is proposed is a chain of Special Education Curriculum Development Centers across the nation. Perhaps these could best be affiliated with colleges and universities, but could also be attached to state and local school systems. For these centers to be successful, creative educators must be found. Only a few teachers are remarkably able to develop new materials. An analogy is that some people can play music adequately, if not brilliantly, but only a few people can compose it. Therefore, to move special education forward, some 15 to 20 percent of our most creative special educators need to be identified, freed from routine classroom instruction, and placed in a stimulating setting where they can be maximally productive in curriculum development. These creative teachers and their associates would concentrate on developing, field testing, and modifying programs of systematic sequences of exercises for developing specific facets of human endeavor. As never before, funds are now available from the U.S. Office of Education under Titles III and VI of PL 89-10 to embark upon at least one such venture in each state. In fact, Title III was designed to support innovations in education and 15 percent of the funds were earmarked for special education. Furthermore, most of the money is now to be administered through state departments of education which could build these curriculum centers into their state plans.

The first step in establishing specialized programs of study would be to evolve conceptual models upon which to build our treatments. In this regard the creative teachers would need to join with the theoreticians, curriculum specialists, and other behavioral scientists. Even the identification of the broad areas will take time, effort, and thought. Each would require many subdivisions and extensive internal model building. A beginning taxonomy might include the following eight broad areas: (a) environmental modifications, (b) motor development, (c) sensory and perceptual training, (d) cognitive and language development including academic instruction, (e) speech and communication training, (f) connative (or personality) development, (g) social interaction training, and (h) vocational training. (Of course, under cognitive development alone we might evolve a model of intellect with some 90 plus facets such as that of Guilford [1967], and as many training programs.)

In the area of motor development we might, for example, involve creative special and physical educators, occupational and physical therapists, and experts in recreation and physical medicine, while in the area of language development a team of speech and hearing specialists, special educators, psychologists, linguists, and others would need to come together to evolve a conceptual model, to identify the parameters, and to develop the specialized programs of exercises. No attempt is made in this article to do more than provide an overview of the problem and the approach. Conceptualizing the specific working models would be the responsibility of cadres of experts in the various specialties.

ENVIRONMENTAL MODIFICATIONS. It would seem futile and rather unrealistic to believe we will be able to remediate the learning difficulties of children from ethnically and/or economically disadvantaged backgrounds when the schools are operating in a vacuum even though topflight special education instructional programs are used. Perhaps, if intensive around the clock and full calendar year instruction were provided beginning at the nursery school level, we might be able to counter appreciably the physiological weaknesses and inadequate home and community conditions of the child. However, the field of education would be enhanced in its chances of success if it became a part of a total ecological approach to improve the environments of these children. Thus special educators need to collaborate with others—social workers, public health officials, and other community specialists. Interventions in this category might include (a) foster home placement, (b) improved community conditions and out of school activities, (c) parent education, (d) public education, and (e) improved cultural exposures. For optimal pupil development, we should see that children are placed in a setting that is both supportive and stimulating.

Therefore, we must participate in environmental manipulations and test their efficacy. We have made a slight beginning in measuring the effects of foster home placement and there is evidence that working with parents of the disadvantaged has paid off. The model cities programs would also seem to have promise. But much more human and financial effort must be invested in this area.

MOTOR DEVELOPMENT. Initial work has been done with psychomotor training programs by a number of persons including Delacato (1966), Oliver (1958), Cratty (1967), Lillie (1967), and others. But we still need sets of sequential daily activities built around an inclusive model. Under this category, we need to move from the early stages of psychomotor development to the development of fine and large movements required as vocational skills. Programs to develop improved motor skills are important for a variety of children with learning problems. In fact, one could argue that adequate psychomotor skills constitute the first link in the chain of learning.

SENSORY AND PERCEPTUAL TRAINING. Much of our early efforts in special education consisted of sensory and perceptual training applied to severe handicapping conditions such as blindness, deafness, and mental deficiency. Consequently, we have made a good beginning in outlining programs of instruction in the areas of auditory, visual, and tactual training. Now we must apply our emerging technology to work out the step by step sequence of activities needed for children with mild to moderate learning difficulties. In this regard, visual perceptual training has received growing emphasis, pioneered by Frostig (1964), but auditory perceptual training has been neglected. The latter is more important for school instruction than the visual channel. Much attention needs to be given to this second link in the chain of learning. Children with learning problems need to be systematically taught the perceptual processes: they need to be able to organize and convert bits of input from the various sense modalities into units of awareness which have meaning.

COGNITIVE AND LANGUAGE DEVELOPMENT INCLUDING ACADEMIC INSTRUCTION. This is the heart of special education for slow learning children. Our business is to facilitate their thinking processes. We should help them not only to acquire and store knowledge, but also to generate and evaluate it. Language development could largely be included under this caption—especially the integrative components—since there is much overlap between the development of oral language and verbal intelligence. However, much of receptive language training might be considered under sensory and perceptual training, while expressive language will be considered in the next topic.

A major fault of our present courses of study is failure to focus on the third link in the chain of learning—that of teaching our children systematically in the areas of cognitive development and concept formation. A major goal of our school program should be to increase the intellectual functioning of children we are now classifying as socioculturally retarded. For such children, perhaps as much as 25 percent of the school day in the early years should be devoted to this topic. Yet the author has not seen one curriculum guide for these children with a major emphasis on cognitive development—which is a sad state of affairs indeed!

Basic psychological research by Guilford (1959) has provided us with a useful model of intellect. However, little is yet known about the trainability of the various cognitive processes. Actually, Thurstone (1948) has contributed the one established set of materials for training primary mental abilities. Thus, much work lies ahead in developing programs of instruction for the training of intellect.

We are seeing more and more sets of programed materials in the academic areas, most of which have been designed for average children. The most exciting examples today are in the computer assisted instruction studies. Our major problem is to determine how these programed exercises need to be modified to be maximally effective for children with specific learning problems. Work will be especially needed in the classical areas of instruction including written language and mathematics. Hopefully, however, regular teachers will handle much of the instruction in science and social studies, while specialists would instruct in such areas as music and the fine arts. This will free special educators to focus on better ways of teaching the basic three R's, especially written language.

SPEECH AND COMMUNICATION TRAINING. This area has received much attention, particularly from speech correctionists and teachers of the deaf. Corrective techniques for specific speech problems are probably more advanced than for any other area, yet essentially no carefully controlled research has been done on the efficacy of these programs. Speech correctionists have tended to be clinicians, not applied behavioral scientists. They often create the details of their corrective exercises while working with their clients in a one to one relationship. Thus, the programs have often been intuitive. Furthermore, public school speech therapists have been spread very thin, usually working with 75 to 100 children. Many have been convinced that only *they* could be effective in this work. But remarkable changes have recently occurred in the thinking of speech therapists; they are recognizing that total programs of oral language development go far beyond correcting articulation defects. Furthermore, some speech therapists believe they could be more productive in working with only the more severe speech handicaps and devoting much attention to the development and field testing of systematic exercises to stimulate overall language and to improve articulation, pitch, loudness, quality, duration, and other speech disorders of a mild to moderate nature. These exercises need to be programed to the point at which teachers, technicians, and perhaps teacher aides can use them. Goldman (1968) is now developing such a program of exercises to correct articulation defects. This seems to be a pioneering and heartening first step.

CONNATIVE (OR PERSONALITY) DEVELOPMENT. This emerging area requires careful attention. We must accept the position that much of a person's behavior is shaped by his environment. This applies to all aspects of human thought, including attitudes, beliefs, and mores. Research oriented clinical psychologists are providing useful information on motivation and personality development and before long we will see reports of research in shaping insights into self, the effects of others on self, and one's effects on others. It is not too early for teams of clinical psychologists, psychiatric social workers, creative special educators (especially for the so-called emotionally disturbed), and others to begin developing programs of instruction in this complex field.

SOCIAL INTERACTION TRAINING. Again we have an emerging area which overlaps considerably with some of those already presented, particularly connative development. Special educators have long recognized that the ability of a handicapped individual to succeed in society depends, in large measure, on his skill to get along with his fellow man. Yet we have done little to develop his social living skills, a complex area of paramount importance. Training programs should be developed to facilitate development in this area of human behavior.

VOCATIONAL TRAINING. Closely tied to social interaction training is vocational training. Success on the job for persons that we have labeled educable mentally retarded has depended on good independent work habits, reliability, and social skills, rather than on academic skills. Consequently, early and continuing emphasis on developing these traits is necessary. In fact, it is likely to be even more important in the years ahead with fewer job opportunities and increasing family disintegration providing less shelter and support for the so-called retarded. Therefore sophisticated programs of instruction are especially needed in this area. Even with our best efforts in this regard, it is likely that our pupils, upon reaching adolescence, will continue to need a variety of vocational services, including trade and technical schools, work study programs, and vocational training.

ANOTHER OBSERVATION. It seems to me to be a red herring to predict that special educators will use these hundreds of specialized instructional programs indiscriminately as cookbooks. Perhaps a few of the poor teachers will. But, the clinical teachers proposed in this article would be too sophisticated and competent to do this. They would use them as points of departure, modifying the lessons so that each child would make optimal progress. Therefore, it seems to me that this library of curriculum materials is necessary to move us from a clinical and intuitive approach to a more scientific basis for special education.

AN EPILOGUE

The conscience of special educators needs to rub up against morality. In large measure we have been at the mercy of the general education establishment in that we accept problem pupils who have been referred out of the regular grades. In this way, we contribute to the delinquency of the general educations since we remove the pupils that are problems for them and thus reduce their need to deal with individual differences. The *entente* of mutual delusion between general and special education that special class placement will be advantageous to slow learning children of poor parents can no longer be tolerated. We must face the reality—we are asked to take children others cannot teach, and a large percentage of these are from ethnically and/or economically disadvantaged backgrounds. Thus much of special education will continue to be a sham of dreams unless we immerse ourselves into the total environment of our children from inadequate homes and backgrounds and insist on a comprehensive ecological push—with a quality educational program as part of it. This is hardly compatible with our prevalent practice of expediency in which we employ many untrained and less than master teachers to increase the number of special day classes in response to the pressures of waiting lists. Because of these pressures from the school system, we have been guilty of fostering quantity with little regard for quality of special education instruction. Our first responsibility is to have an abiding commitment to the less fortunate children we aim to serve. Our honor, integrity, and honesty should no longer be subverted and rationalized by what we hope and may believe we are doing for these children—hopes and beliefs which have little basis in reality.

Embarking on an American Revolution in Special Education will require strength of purpose. It is recognized that the structure of most, if not all, school programs becomes self-perpetuating. Teachers and state and local directors and supervisors of special education have much at stake in terms of their jobs, their security, and their programs which they have built up over the years. But can we keep our self-respect and continue to increase the numbers of these self-contained special classes for the educable mentally retarded which are of questionable value for many of the children they are intended to serve? As Ray Graham said in his last article in 1960: [p. 4.]

> We can look at our accomplishments and be proud of the progress we have made; but satisfaction with the past does not assure progress in the future. New developments, ideas, and facts may show us that our past practices have become out-moded. A growing child cannot remain static —he either grows or dies. We cannot become satisfied with a job one-third done. We have a long way to go before we can rest assured that the desires of the parents and the educational needs of handicapped children are being fulfilled [p. 4].

REFERENCES

Ainsworth, S. H. *An Exploratory Study of Educational, Social and Emotional Factors in the Education of Mentally Retarded Children in Georgia Public Schools.* US Office of Education Cooperative Research Project Report No. 171(6470). Athens, Ga.: University of Georgia, 1959.

Bereiter, C., and Engelmann, S. *Teaching Disadvantaged Children in the Preschool.* Englewood Cliffs, N.J.: Prentice-Hall, 1966.

Bruner, J. S., Olver, R. R., and Greenfield, P. M. *Studies in Cognitive Growth.* New York: Wiley, 1967.

Coleman, J. S., *et al. Equality of Educational Opportunity.* Washington, D.C.: USGPO, 1966.

Cratty, P. J. *Developmental Sequences of Perceptual Motor Tasks.* Freeport, Long Island, N.Y.: Educational Activities, 1967.

Delacato, C. H. (Ed.) *Neurological Organization and Reading Problems.* Springfield, Ill.: Charles C Thomas, 1966.

Feuerstein, R. *The Learning Potential Assessment Device.* Jerusalem, Israel: Haddassa Wizo Canada Child Guidance Clinic and Research Unit, 1968.

Frostig, M., and Horne, D. *The Frostig Program for the Development of Visual Perception.* Chicago: Follett, 1964.

Graham, R. Special education for the sixties. *Illinois Educational Association Study Unit,* 1960, *23,* 1–4.

Goffman, E. *Asylums: Essays on the Social Situation of Mental Patients and Other Inmates.* Garden City, N.Y.: Anchor, 1961.

Goldman, R. *The Phonemic–Visual–Oral Association Technique for Modifying Articulation Disorders in Young Children.* Nashville, Tenn.: Bill Wilkerson Hearing and Speech Center, 1968.

Guilford, J. P. *The Nature of Human Intelligence.* New York: McGraw-Hill, 1967.

Hoelke, G. M. *Effectiveness of Special Class Placement for Educable Mentally Retarded Children.* Lincoln, Neb.: University of Nebraska, 1966.

Hollingworth, L. S. *The Psychology of Subnormal Children.* New York: Macmillan, 1923.

Johnson, G. O. Special education for mentally handicapped—a paradox. *Exceptional Children,* 1962, *19,* 62–69.

Kirk, S. A. Research in education. In H. A. Stevens and R. Heber (Eds.) *Mental Retardation.* Chicago: University of Chicago Press, 1964.

Kirk, S. A. *The Diagnosis and Remediation of Psycholinguistic Disabilities.* Urbana, Ill.: University of Illinois Press, 1966.

Lillie, D. L. The development of motor proficiency of educable mentally retarded children. *Education and Training of the Mentally Retarded,* 1967, *2,* 29–32.

Mackie, R. P. *Functional Handicaps Among School Children due to Cultural or Economic Deprivation.* Paper presented at the First Congress of the International Association for the Scientific Study of Mental Deficiency, Montpellier, France, September, 1967.

Meyerowitz, J. H. Family background of educable mentally retarded children. In H. Goldstein, J. W. Moss and L. J. Jordan. *The Efficacy of Special Educa-*

tion Training on the Development of Mentally Retarded Children. Urbana, Ill.: University of Illinois Institute for Research on Exceptional Children, 1965. Pp. 152–182.

Meyerowitz, J. H. Peer groups and special classes. *Mental Retardation,* 1967, *5,* 23–26.

Oliver, J. N. The effects of physical conditioning exercises and activities on the mental characteristics of educationally sub-normal boys. *British Journal of Educational Psychology,* 1958, *28,* 155–165.

Passow, A. H. *A Summary of Findings and Recommendations of a Study of the Washington, D.C. Schools.* New York: Teachers College, Columbia University, 1967.

Rosenthal, R., and Jacobson, L. Teachers' expectancies: Determinants of pupils' IQ gains. *Psychological Reports,* 1966, *19,* 115–118.

Rubin, E. Z., Senison, C. B., and Betwee, M. C. *Emotionally Handicapped Children in the Elementary School.* Detroit: Wayne State University Press, 1966.

Smith, H. W., and Kennedy, W. A. Effects of three educational programs on mentally retarded children. *Perceptual and Motor Skills,* 1967, *24,* 174.

Thurstone, T. G. *Learning to Think Series.* Chicago, Ill.: Science Research Associates, 1948.

Wright, Judge J. S. *Hobson vs. Hansen: U.S. Court of Appeals decision on the District of Columbia's track system. Civil Action No. 82–66.* Washington, D.C.: U.S. Court of Appeals, 1967.

20 RELATIONSHIPS BETWEEN EDUCATIONAL PROGRAMS FOR THE MENTALLY RETARDED AND THE CULTURALLY DEPRIVED [1]

Robert L. Erdman
James L. Olson

From *Mental Retardation Abstracts,* Vol. 3, No. 3, July–September 1966, pp. 311–318. Reprinted with the permission of the U.S. Department of Health, Education, and Welfare and the authors. Dr. Erdman is Chairman, Special Education Department, University of Utah, Salt Lake City. Dr. Olson is Professor of Special Education, University of Wisconsin, Milwaukee Branch.

The United States is currently witnessing an era of major concern for the problems of the culturally disadvantaged. Federal monies and legislation are being used to implement ideas and programs within most of our social institutions. Of the many institutions involved, the school has been charged with a major role in helping youth from disadvantaged environments achieve life styles commensurate with their ability.

For several decades, the schools have been seeking ways to provide adequate educational experiences for children with a wide variety of individual differences. Many patterns for educational programs have emerged to provide for these differences. One pattern involves special education programs which provide opportunities for children needing help above and beyond that found in regular classrooms. Included in this program are provisions for the educable and trainable mentally retarded.

As the schools have worked with retarded children, particularly the educable, there has been a growing awareness of the relationship between the incidence of educable retarded children and their concentration in culturally disadvantaged environments. Similarly, this awareness has had some influence on programs designed for the educable retarded. Formal research evidence to support this relationship is still somewhat fragmentary, although through observation and experience professional workers have testified to the interrelatedness of the two variables. Some illustrative examples of the evidence available to support the relationship between mental retardation and cultural deprivation are given in the following paragraphs.

Havighurst (1964), in a comprehensive study of the Chicago Public Schools, observed a relationship between areas in which classes for the educable mentally retarded were concentrated and districts characterized by low incomes and low educational levels. The need for additional special classes and the length of waiting lists for special class placement were proportionately much greater in the socially and culturally deprived areas of Chicago than in other areas of the city.

[1] The assistance of Miss Anita Hermann in the preparation of this paper is gratefully acknowledged.

Data[2] reported by the Milwaukee Public Schools indicate that 91 out of 129 classes for the educable retarded are located within the central city. More specifically, 80 percent of the educable retarded children enrolled in elementary school special classes come from this geographical area. Secondary classes for the educable retarded have 60 percent of their enrollment coming from the central city. That portion of Milwaukee referred to as the central city is characterized by a high population density, high mobility of the residents, an annual family income of less than $3,000 a year, a proportionately higher unemployment rate, a heavy concentration of nonwhite individuals, a relatively low educational level of parents, and a high percentage of public assistance payments.[3]

The Onondaga Census (1955) revealed that a group of four census tracts in the city of Syracuse, New York, produced a large variety of health and welfare problems. These tracts were characterized by low economic status and a large Negro and Jewish population. Data indicated that approximately twice as many white referrals for suspected mental retardation came from these four census tracts as from all other areas in the city of Syracuse. If figures for nonwhite children were included, the ratio of referred cases of suspected mental retardation would increase dramatically.

Although the methods used to identify retardation in the Onondaga study have been questioned by Kirk and Weiner (1959), use of the results to support a relationship between retardation and deprivation does appear to have some validity in light of other available data.

While the data cited refer to urban areas, cultural deprivation as a socially disintegrating force knows no boundaries or limits. There is substantial evidence in the literature which describes the impact of a wide variety of impoverished environments on human behavior. However, the task confronting society today is how cultural deprivation and its negative ramifications can best be greatly reduced or eradicated.

As educational programs for the culturally disadvantaged and the retarded continue to develop, the evidence to date suggests the need for closer articulation between the two areas. The purpose of this paper, therefore, is to review the educational concerns of both groups in an effort to more clearly delineate differences and similarities of approach.

The paper is organized into three major sections. Section I describes the different philosophies and goals which have been associated with educational programs for the educable retarded. Section II summarizes some of the relevant research findings and program suggestions for the culturally deprived. Section III derives educational implications from relationships existing between the fields.

[2] Personal communication with Dr. E. Blodgett, Executive Director of Special Education, Milwaukee Public Schools.

[3] As defined by the Social Development Commission of Milwaukee, Wisconsin.

THE EDUCABLE RETARDED

Historical records reveal a variety of curricular objectives for the educable retarded. Some programs were developed on the premise that intellectual development was irreversible. Consequently, school activities were designed primarily to effect behavior changes which would enable children with very slow intellectual development to live more effective lives as retarded individuals. Other programs took a more dynamic quality by assuming that intellectual development could be modified for some retarded children through the process of education. Both approaches were greatly influenced by the controversies concerning the nature and nurture of intelligence.

Beginning about 1800, the efforts of European pioneers (Itard, Sequin, Montessori) in educating the retarded reflected the concept that intelligence could be modified through stimulation of the senses. Therefore, the activities they proposed encompassed a variety of sensory and muscle training techniques which were designed to stimulate intellectual development. It is interesting to note that many of the individuals they chose to "educate" came from extremely impoverished environments.

Best (1965) suggested that the early provisions for educating retarded children in the United States were created through the establishment of institutions. These institutions were conceived as a logical extension of the public schools and were designed to educate retarded children so that they could be returned to society. Great enthusiasm was engendered not only for this goal but also for the idea that it was possible to "cure" the mental defects of some children, or at least improve them considerably. Since these early efforts in the United States were influenced by European thought, it is not surprising to note the concern with the possibility of modifying intellectual development in some children.

Public school provisions for retarded children came into existence at about the turn of the nineteenth century. Compulsory school attendance laws and the movement from a rural to an urban society were factors which contributed to the placement of retarded children in a school setting. Public school educators found themselves in the position of having to provide special curricula for these children because they could not achieve the prescribed academic work Hungerford, DeProspo, and Rosenzweig (1948) suggest that the first special classes were created around a "relief philosophy." The major objective was to get the retarded out of the regular classroom. Consequently, the curriculum was non-structured and the programs were often characterized by meaningless activity. During the next several decades the philosophies associated with the purposes of public school special classes for the retarded centered around a variety of themes such as "happiness," and "handwork." There is little or no evidence to suggest that during this period school programs reflected the early efforts of the

European pioneers. Quite the contrary, the schools may have been reflecting the strong convictions prevalent in American society concerning the inherited aspects of retardation and the irreversibility of mental growth.

During the early 1900s when special classes for the retarded were being established in the United States, Binet was proposing his scale for the measurement of intelligence. Associated with his well-known contribution was a proposal for the educability of intelligence. He advocated that the retarded child's measured rate of mental development was not constant and proposed a training method to educate intellectual functioning.

Kirk (1964) indicated that educators and psychologists reacted enthusiastically to Binet's contribution to the testing movement, but few followed his proposal for the remediability of intelligence. Once again, prevailing beliefs about inherited retardation and the irreversibility of mental growth may have served as inhibiting influences on the acceptance of Binet's concept.

School programs for the retarded, up until the past decade, have given little attention to the modifications of intellectual development. In certain respects this is difficult to understand because of the many studies which had been published by psychologists and sociologists on the influence of environment on intellectual functioning of the retarded. McCandless (1964) summarized the many different types of research completed in this area.

The period from 1930 to the present has been marked by the concern of educators with development of curricula which contribute to the social and vocational competence of the educable retarded. Of more recent origin is the emphasis on content for the trainable retarded, the concern for special methodological approaches in educational programs, and the research concerned with modification of intellectual development through education.

Efforts to develop curricula have reflected a cognizance of the limited environmental backgrounds of many of the students. In a sense, these educational efforts could be described as compensatory in nature for they are seeking to provide learning experiences for children coming from backgrounds of environmental deficits. Most of these programs were developed through a trial and error approach with little research evidence to suggest one approach being superior to another. Selected examples of such curricula follow.

Ingram (1935) proposed an approach which enabled the teacher to correlate many instructional activities around central themes which were meaningful to the retarded. These units were to evolve from life experiences of the children and were to be so designed that they provided them with opportunities to utilize their reading, writing, and arithmetic skills. This activity or unit approach to educational programming, even though it was a direct application of the then prevailing general education thought, sought to identify and facilitate meaningful learning experiences for the retarded.

Duncan (1943) developed an educational program which emphasized concrete as opposed to verbal activities. His program placed special emphasis on exercises with things that could be handled, seen, touched, or heard. All of these activities were to be utilized in helping children observe relationships and in stimulating thinking in series and sequences. Duncan's emphasis upon nonverbal experiences may be compared to the sensory training activities propounded by the European pioneers. These special exercises seem to be designed for children functioning at a higher intellectual level than those children with whom Itard, *et al.* were concerned.

Hungerford, *et al.* (1948), proposed a program of occupational education for the retarded in the New York City schools. The goal of the curriculum was to help retarded youth become contributing members of society. Curricular content and activities centered around five major areas: (1) occupational information, (2) vocational guidance, (3) vocational training, (4) vocational placement, and (5) social placement. This curriculum represented one of the earliest efforts in the United States to utilize a theoretical model for the selection and organization of curricular content.

Two curriculum proposals of a more recent nature are the Illinois Curriculum—*A Curriculum Guide for Teachers of the Educable Mentally Handicapped* (1958), and the Cincinnati Curriculum—*The Slow Learning Program in the Elementary and Secondary Schools* (1964). Both plans have as a curricular model the concept of persisting life situations, i.e., learning to keep healthy, learning to live safely, learning to earn a living, learning to manage money. These situations are central to the existence of all human beings. Content selection, according to Goldstein and Seigle (1958), was based on such characteristics of educable retarded children as: frustration-proneness, self-devaluation, limited ability to deal with abstractions, and retarded language development.

Frustration-proneness simply means that educable mentally retarded children because of their overt similarity to intellectually normal children, are often placed in situations where they are consistently expected to acquire skills and perform tasks of which they are incapable. This constant failure and its attendant frustrations thus provide a picture of children with a low frustration tolerance, when actually they are reacting normally to a failure-loaded environment.

Self-devaluation refers to a personality aberration to be expected when generally inadequate children search for a place in a society which stresses adequacy. Thus, EMR children learn from "important others" (parents, teachers, peers, etc.) that they are often unable to perform at the expected level and, in time, the internalization of these reflected images results in a poor self-concept.

A limited ability to deal with abstractions and retarded language development are directly related to the primary characteristics of subnormal intellectual development. Limited ability to conceptualize and the necessity for operation at a more concrete level handicap EMR children as proficient learners of the symbol system we call language.

The selected curricular approaches described thus far have been concerned primarily with the organization and selection of content. Their goals and objectives provide limited evidence for a concern with the displacement of the rate of intellectual development.

A somewhat different approach to curriculum is currently being proposed by individuals concerned with specific learning disabilities in children. Illustrative of this approach are the two following examples.

Kephart (1960) proposed that a rather substantial number of retarded and normal children have learning problems because of inadequate motor development. He has developed a series of activities which are designed to improve motor functioning with the intent that many of the learning problems will be alleviated or their magnitude reduced considerably.

Smith (1962), Olson, Hahn, and Hermann (1965), and Wiseman (1965) have proposed suggestions for language curricula based on the Illinois Test of Psycholinguistic Abilities (ITPA) developed by Kirk and McCarthy (1961). The ITPA identifies specific components of language and assesses a child's strengths and weaknesses in each area, e.g., auditory decoding, visual-motor association, and auditory-vocal sequential. Curricular experiences are designed to strengthen global language and specific functioning in the components of language as identified by the ITPA.

These approaches, plus those of Gallagher (1960), Cruickshank, *et al.* (1961), and Frostig and Horne (1964) are suggestive of the trend to develop curricula based on specific behaviors of children in contrast to the previous concern with teaching of content *per se*.

In addition to approaches which emphasize specific areas such as motor and language development, educational programs are again being developed to modify total intellectual behavior in retarded children.

Although the validity of the data and results were challenged by Kirk (1948), the work of Schmidt (1946) brought renewed attention to the possibilities of intellectual displacement through a total educational program for the educable retarded. She studied 245 children in special classes in Chicago in an eight-year study. The initial average IQ was reported as being 52.1 and the average IQ at the completion of five years of postschool experience was 89.3. Twenty-seven percent of the group graduated from high school and 5.1 percent continued beyond high school training. Schmidt attributed this dramatic rise in IQ to the training received in the special class.

Kirk (1958) studied the effects of preschool training on the social and mental development of 81 retarded children between the ages of three and six residing in communities and in institutions. Their IQs generally ranged between 45 and 80. Results of the study suggested that retarded children from culturally disadvantaged homes who did not attend preschool tended to retain their rate of development or drop as they become older. The preschool experience did not appear to be as beneficial for those children with a definitive diagnosis of "organicity" as it was for the culturally disadvantaged. Further results suggested that children coming from relatively adequate homes tended to increase in mental development during their first year in school without the benefit of preschool experiences.

Goldstein, Moss, and Jordan (1964) in a longitudinal study, compared the mental, social, and academic progress of 129 mentally retarded children randomly assigned to special classes with that of children remaining in the regular grades. The IQs generally ranged between 56 and 85. Both the experimental and the control group had significant IQ gains (seven and eight IQ points respectively). This significant increase occurred primarily during the first year of school experience for six-year-old children. Some children in both groups made such significant gains in IQ that they could no longer be classified as mentally retarded. The authors hypothesized that the observed gains might be accounted for by variables not related to school experiences. No significant differences were observed between the two groups in three areas of academic achievement (reading and language, arithmetic, and basic social information). The results also supported the idea that the special class contributed to the social adjustment and personality development of the retarded.

In summary, a variety of educational programs have been developed for the retarded. Some of these programs have been concerned with the development of social and vocational competence while others have focused more on the remediation of learning disabilities or the modification of the rate of intellectual development.

THE CULTURALLY DEPRIVED

This section will be concerned with a review of recent research and curricular concerns in the area of cultural deprivation. As contrasted to the field of mental retardation, the relatively recent interest in the educational problems of the deprived negates the need for a historical review.

A conclusion generally supported by research findings is that culturally deprived children develop linguistic patterns which are significantly different from the language patterns of the dominant middle class culture. These differences are apparent early in the child's life. Sampson (1956) reported that by the age of two years, upper and middle class children have surpassed their lower class peers in speech development. Irwin (1948) found that infants from high income families learned speech sounds faster than infants from low income families. Deutsch (1963) hypothesized that the noise level of lower class life combines with the absence of adult–child language interplay to retard the child's verbal development.

Studies by Rheingold and Bailey (1959) suggest that the rather typical slum home condition characterized by a large family with a number of mother-surrogates tends to retard the language development of the children. Bernstein (1961) described the speech characteristics of the lower class child: rigid formation and syntax, a limited variety in the structure of sentences, high use of idiomatic expressions, limited use of adverbs and adjectives, and inability to stay with the subject. The speech of lower income groups which Bernstein calls a "public language," is highly predictable, descriptive, and not sufficiently flexible to cover the nuances and subtleties of abstract thought and ideas. The opposite, a "formal language," has high variance in structure, in flexibility, in the increased use of adjectives and adverbs, and in application to the problems of analysis and abstraction. According to Bernstein, the middle class child can use either the public language, as with peers on the playground, or the formal language which develops at home through conversation with parents. The lower class child has mastered only the public language; it is this factor which handicaps his school success.

Bernstein's findings and hypotheses may partially explain the findings of Milner (1951). Milner found a .86 correlation of reading readiness to a social class index with Negro subjects. Deutsch (1964) found statistically significant correlations in a group of first grade children between socio-economic status, race, language development, and cognition. Deutsch hypothesized that these deficiencies are cumulative, and determine in part the degree of academic achievement in later school experiences. The relation between cognition and language development is further described by Mitchell (1957), who reported that low income groups have a verbal skill which is diffused through general intelligence and not sharply focused in any specific areas of ability.

Listening is commonly accepted to be a critical classroom skill, as the majority of the school demands upon children's time rely on that single language factor. Collins (1964) compared the linguistic skills of culturally advantaged and disadvantaged kindergarten children and reported that the ability to garner meaning from auditory stimuli was the least developed of all linguistic skills among the disadvantaged, while the advantaged group achieved its higher scores in this all important skill.

The meaning of much of this research is clear if Ausubel's (1963) hypothesis proves to be correct. He stated that retarded language development limits deprived children in their ability to move from concrete to abstract thought.

In addition to differences in language development, personality differences are also reported in a number of studies dealing with social and economic deprivation. Bronfenbrenner (1961) summarized the literature by stating that lower class homes have greater possibilities for providing inadequate discipline for boys and overprotection for girls than do middle class homes.

Mitchell, reported in Goff (1954), found that lower class students reflected the presence of far less emotional satisfaction than subjects from the highest socio-economic levels. They expressed feelings of inadequacy, friendlessness, unfair treatment, hostility, mistreatment by teachers, discouragement, and physical ailment two to five times more frequently. Feelings of inadequacy among lower income children were reported to increase with age among boys, while girls felt least secure about future success.

Sears (1940) hypothesized that the lower class child's unrealistically high expressed levels of academic and vocational aspirations probably reflect impairment of realistic judgment caused by the impact of chronic failure. When this characteristic is coupled with Record's (1957) observation that lower class Negroes tend to withdraw from the competition of the wider American culture, a rather unhealthy and frustration-prone personality stereotype begins to emerge.

Ausubel and Ausubel (1963) indicated that lower class children, because of their early childhood experiences, tend to develop ambivalent attitudes toward authority figures. They felt that this attitude causes children to make an overt show of exaggerated compliance to authority figures on the basis of formalized role attributes rather than as persons. This behavior covers an underlying hostility toward all authority figures.

Srole, *et al.* (1962) summarized the consequences of a lower class childhood with indisputable evidence of a much higher incidence of severe behavior disorders among the disadvantaged than is found in the middle classes.

Much has been written suggesting the kind of curriculum necessary if the culturally deprived are to achieve their full academic potential. The following are selected as representative of current thinking in the area.

Early education is essential to successful school programs: Deutsch (1964) supported this point of view citing data indicating that preschool or kindergarten experience is associated with higher group intelligence test scores; the scores are higher in the first grade and the differential tends to be accentuated as the children grow older. Bloom (1964) presented data which indicate quite clearly that the best time to attempt to change human characteristics is in the first years of life.

The use of concrete props is essential in teaching the disadvantaged: Ausubel (1963) stated that concrete teaching aids are necessary if the teacher hopes to facilitate transfer to the abstract. Riessman (1962) supported this contention and adds that the deprived child must be carefully taught formal language skills, deductive reasoning powers, and flexibility in approach to problem solving.

Deprived children must be taught the skills which allow them to develop their intelligence: Davis (1962) felt that the curriculum should stress oral English and emphasize activities which teach conceptualization, generalization, and other cognitive abilities. Smilansky (1961) suggested that there is a need to teach activities which increase perceptual powers, vocabulary development, conceptual powers, and numerical concepts.

Deprived children need help in developing a positive but somewhat realistic self-concept: Deutsch (1963) discussed the effect on self-concept of continual failure and frustration in the typical school the deprived child attends. Implied in this discussion is a need for the schools to develop curricula which take note of the necessity for positive self-image. Olson and Larson (1965) utilized self-concept as one of four major curriculum concepts in their attempt to develop a theoretical structure for the development of curriculum for deprived children.

Thus, it would seem that an ideal school program for culturally deprived children would include an emphasis on language development, a planned movement from the concrete to the abstract, an organized approach to the development of cognitive abilities, and an arrangement of activities designed to develop a positive but somewhat realistic self-concept. This program should begin at an early age and be carried through beyond the traditional secondary school years.

IMPLICATIONS

The samples of research findings and curriculum development presented in this paper would seem to indicate four important points.

1. Demographic studies indicate that a disproportionately large number of children from economically depressed areas are presently attending special classes for the educable mentally retarded.
2. A strong interest in early educational programs and curricula designed to remediate special learning disabilities may mean that those who develop curriculum for the retarded are again assuming that school experiences can make significant changes in a child's rate of intellectual growth.
3. Among many variables, a shared emphasis on the importance of self-concept and language development indicates that a common structure may exist between curriculum designed for the retarded and curriculum proposed for the deprived.
4. Psychological characteristics commonly used to describe the educable mentally retarded are, in many respects, similar to the characteristics attributed to the culturally deprived. For example: "A limited ability to deal with abstractions," "a poor self-concept," and "retarded lan-

guage development" are phrases commonly used to describe both groups.

These four points were basic to the development of the following educational implications.

We will use a model of cognitive growth presented by Bruner (1964) in describing educational programs for retarded and culturally deprived children.

Bruner stated that human beings construct models of their world by utilizing three information processing systems: action, imagery, and language. These three modes of representation are respectively labeled enactive representation, iconic representation, and symbolic representation. They appear in that order in the life of the child, each depending on the previous one for its development, yet all remaining intact throughout normal life.

Enactive representation is a mode of representing past events through appropriate motor response. For example, knowledge of familiar sidewalks, floors, tying knots, bicycle riding, and certain aspects of driving are represented in our muscles. We cannot describe these skills, nor do we have an image of what they are like, yet we do have an intimate knowledge of them.

Iconic representation summarizes events through the organization of percepts and images so that they "stand for" experiences similar to the way that a picture stands for the object pictured.

Symbolic representation is a method of representing things by design features that include remoteness and arbitrariness. The word "democracy" neither points directly to an object, nor does it resemble a picture. Most important, symbolic representation allows an individual to combine thoughts far beyond what can be done with images or acts. The understandings communicated through poetry or a mathematical equation would not be possible if only action or imagery were utilized.

Thus, Bruner described the hierarchy of cognitive development as three evolving and continuing stages which can be likened to levels of sophistication of information processing. It is possible also to describe curriculum models utilized in special classes for the educable mentally retarded and in educational programs for the culturally deprived in a somewhat analogous fashion. Curriculum guides such as that issued by the Cincinnati Public Schools (1964) seem to be successful in pointing out and suggesting methods for teaching the minimal skills necessary for successful living in our society. These skills and the level of intellectual development necessary to their achievement may be likened to the enactive and iconic methods of representation described by Bruner. They are essential to the development of the child.

Perhaps skills at these two levels provide all that is necessary for the intellectual fulfillment of the educable mentally retarded child as he is described by the authors of the 1920s and 1930s; but do they ensure complete intellectual fulfillment for the culturally deprived child who happens to be placed in a class for the retarded simply because he scored in the high seventies on one intelligence test? Are the curriculum components which are analogous to Bruner's intellectual level of symbolic representation missing from the picture?

On the other hand, are the curriculum builders for the culturally deprived, with their continuing emphasis on language development (symbolic representation) ignoring curricular needs basic to the development of language? Are they slighting the less glamorous, but nonetheless essential enactive and iconic curricular counterparts? Could they profit from the work of those who have designed curriculum for the educable mentally retarded? Could these curricula form the groundwork, the first steps of a complete curriculum for the culturally deprived which would encompass all three stages of cognitive development?

Even though results of research in the area of cultural deprivation are far from complete, some studies (Kirk, 1958; Larson and Olson, 1965) are completed and may be interpreted to say that no matter what curricular strengths are built into developing nursery and elementary school programs for the deprived, it is probably safe to say that not all of the children who can be helped through special educational techniques will achieve their full intellectual potential in the early years of schooling. It is probable that a number of the deprived children will, in spite of improved school experiences, reach the secondary schools with a level of intellectual development which could be likened to reaching one or two steps on the continuum between the iconic and the symbolic representation levels. That is, their intellectual development would still be in process. As yet, environment of the schools may not have provided enough stimulation for the achievement of their full potential. This means that the secondary schools may find it necessary to revise their curricula beyond the ideas utilized in enrichment-type programs. It also may mean that secondary school programs for the culturally deprived should experiment with curricula developed for the educable retarded in order to bridge the gap between the concrete, enactive–iconic level and the symbolic representational level necessary for manipulating abstractions in a competent fashion. If the above hypotheses prove to be correct, the obvious implication is that secondary school programs, if they are to achieve their stated goals, probably will need to be lengthened beyond their traditional four years.

An additional implication suggests that the emphasis upon early educational programs for both the culturally deprived and the educable mentally retarded (Deutsch, 1964; Kirk, 1958) may lead to the development of a new type of preschool-primary educational organization. The commonalities found between characteristics for the deprived and the mildly retarded child indicate that differential diagnosis, especially at an early age, is extremely difficult if not impossible. Therefore, school systems, particularly urban school systems, may need to develop diagnostic type classes for their young children. Since it is probable that both the EMR and the deprived child of preschool age will be operating mainly at the enactive and the iconic levels of cognitive development, and since the major educational objective for these children will be to help them develop the symbolic mode of representation, the curriculum for both groups could be similar. Thus, programs of early education for the deprived or the retarded *per se* may be replaced by early educational programs designed to develop intelligence. These diagnostic teaching classes could take the form of the ungraded primary classes in the central city, thus reducing the stigma often associated with special classes for the retarded or the deprived.

This form of early education could be the beginning of programs designed to bridge the gap between special and regular education. Teachers could be trained cooperatively by special education and early childhood education facilities of universities. The teachers would need a typical background in early childhood education plus skills in differential diagnosis and a sensitivity to recognizing in young children the possibilities for displacing the apparent rate of intellectual growth.

The final and perhaps the most important implication to be derived from the hypothesized relationship between the culturally deprived and the educable mentally retarded is that within the relatively near future we may see a drastic reduction in the number of classes for the EMR in our urban centers. As adequate educational programs for the deprived are developed it does not seem logical that urban centers would continue to require the large number of special classes for the educable mentally retarded in the economically and socially deprived sections of the city. Further, this same phenomenon may lead to a reevaluation of the accepted incidence figures for mental retardation in the general population. The educable population constitutes approximately three-fourths of the oft-quoted three percent incidence figure. However, many of these children are also the culturally deprived who may have intellectual potential beyond that typically considered to be the limits of mental retardation, which may mean that the incidence of retardation is actually less than the generally accepted figure.

If these hypothesized changes in our educational planning and programming do develop, we may find a way of resolving the paradox created by the disappearance of large numbers of the mildly retarded into the general population after they leave our public schools.

In summary, this article has attempted to highlight some of the important relationships present among existing educational programs for the mentally retarded and emerging special educational procedures for culturally deprived children.

REFERENCES

Ausubel, D. P. How reversible are the cognitive and motivational effects of cultural deprivation? Implications for teaching the culturally deprived child. Paper read at the Conference on Teaching the Culturally Deprived Child. Buffalo, New York, March 28–30, 1963.

Ausubel, D. P., and Ausubel, Pearl. Ego development among segregated Negro children. In: Passow, A. H., ed. *Education in Depressed Areas*. New York, Teachers College, Columbia University, 1963.

Bernstein, Basil. Social class and linguistic development: A theory of social learning. In: Halsey, H. H., Floud, J., and Anderson, C., eds. *Education, Economy and Society*. New York, Free Press, 1961.

Best, H. *Public Provision for the Mentally Retarded in the United States.* Worcester, Massachusetts, Heffernan Press, 1965.

Bloom, B. S. *Stability and Change in Human Characteristics.* New York, Wiley, 1964.

Bronfenbrenner, V. The changing American child—a speculative analysis. *Merrill–Palmer Quarterly, 7*:73–84, 1961.

Bruner, J. S. The course of cognitive growth. *American Psychologist, 19*:1–15, 1964.

Cincinnati Public Schools. *The Slow Learning Program in the Elementary and Secondary Schools.* Curriculum Bulletin No. 119. Cincinnati, Ohio, Cincinnati Public Schools, 1964.

Collins, Susan. A comparison of the language development of advantaged and disadvantaged kindergarten children. Unpublished Master's thesis. Milwaukee, Wisconsin, University of Wisconsin, 1964.

Cruickshank, W. M., Bentzen, Frances A., Ratzeburg, F. E., and Tannhauser, Miriam T. *A Teaching Method for Brain-Injured and Hyperactive Children.* Syracuse, New York, Syracuse University, 1961.

Davis, Allison. *The Future of Children from Low Socio-Economic Groups.* Mimeographed speech. University of Chicago, 1962.

Deutsch, M. The disadvantaged child and the learning process. In: Passow, A. H., ed. *Education in Depressed Areas.* New York, Teachers College, Columbia University, 1963, pp. 163–180.

Deutsch, M. *The Role of Social Class in Language Development and Cognition.* New York, Institute for Developmental Studies, 1964, Mimeo.

Duncan, J. *The Education of the Ordinary Child.* New York, Ronald Press, 1943.

Frostig, Marianne, and Horne, D. *The Frostig Program for the Development of Visual Perception.* Chicago, Follett, 1964.

Gallagher, J. J. *Tutoring of Brain-Injured Mentally Retarded Children.* Springfield, Ill., Charles C Thomas, 1960.

Goff, R. M. Some educational implications of the influence of rejection on aspiration levels of minority group children. *Journal of Experimental Education, 23*:179–183, 1954.

Goldstein, H., and Seigle, Dorothy. *A Curriculum Guide for Teachers of the*

Educable Mentally Handicapped. Illinois Department of Public Instruction, Circular Series B-3, No. 12, 1958.

Goldstein, H., Moss, J., and Jordan, L. *The Efficacy of Special Class Training on the Development of Mentally Retarded Children.* (U.S. Office of Education, Cooperative Research Program, Project No. 619.) Urbana, Ill., University of Illinois, Institute for Research on Exceptional Children, 1964.

Havighurst, R. J. *The Public Schools of Chicago.* Chicago, The City Board of Education, 1964.

Hungerford, R., DeProspo, C., and Rosenzweig, L. *Philosophy of Occupational Education.* New York, The Association for the New York City Teachers of Special Education, 1948.

Ingram, Christine P. *Education of the Slow-Learning Child.* Yonkers, New York, World Book, 1935.

Irwin, O. C. Infant speech: Development of vowel sounds. *Journal of Speech and Hearing Disorders, 13*:31–34, 1948.

Kephart, N. C. *The Slow Learner in the Classroom.* Columbus, Ohio, Charles E. Merrill, 1960.

Kirk, S. A. Changes in personal, social, and intellectual behavior of children originally classified as feebleminded. (An evaluation of the study by Bernadine G. Schmidt.) *Psychological Monographs, 45*:321–333, 1948.

Kirk, S. A. *Early Education of the Mentally Retarded.* Urbana, Ill., University of Illinois, 1958.

Kirk, S. A. Education. In: Stevens, H. A., and Heber, R. F., eds. *Mental Retardation: A Review of Research.* Chicago, University of Chicago, 1964.

Kirk, S. A., and McCarthy, J. J. The Illinois Test of Psycholinguistic Abilities: An approach to differential diagnosis. *American Journal of Mental Deficiency, 66*:399–412, 1961.

Kirk, S. A., and Weiner, Bluma B. The Onondaga census—fact or artifact. *Exceptional Children, 22*:226–231, 1959.

Larson, R., and Olson, J. L. *A Pilot Project for Culturally Deprived Kindergarten Children.* Milwaukee, Wisconsin, University of Wisconsin, 1965, Mimeo.

Milner, E. A study of the relationship between reading readiness in grade one children and patterns of parent child interaction. *Child Development Monographs, 22*:95–112, 1951.

Mitchell, J. V., Jr. Identification of items in the California Test of Personality that differentiate between subjects of high and low socio-economic status at the fifth and seventh grade levels. *Journal of Educational Research, 51,* 1957.

McCandless, B. R. Relation of environmental factors to intellectual functioning. In: Stevens, H. A., and Heber, R. F., eds. *Mental Retardation: A Review of Research.* Chicago, University of Chicago, 1964.

New York State Department of Mental Hygiene, Mental Health Research Unit. A special census of suspected referred mental retardation, Onondaga County, New York. In: *Technical Report of the Mental Health Research Unit.* Syracuse, New York, Syracuse University, 1955.

Olson, J. L., Hahn, H. R., and Hermann, Anita. Psycholinguistic curriculum. *Mental Retardation, 3*:14–19, 1965.

Olson, J. L., and Larson, R. An experimental curriculum for culturally deprived kindergarten children. *Educational Leadership, 22*:553–558, 1965.

Record, W. Social stratification and intellectual roles in the Negro community. *British Journal of Sociology, 8*:235–255, 1957.

Rheingold, Harriet, and Bailey, Nancy. The later effects of an experimental modification of mothering. *Child Development, 30*:363–372, 1959.

Riessman, F. *The Culturally Deprived Child.* New York, Harper, 1962.

Sampson, O. C. A study of speech development in children 18–30 months. *British Journal of Educational Psychology, 26*:194–202, 1956.

Schmidt, Bernadine G. Changes in personal, social, and intellectual behavior of children originally classified as feebleminded. *Psychological Monographs, 60*:1–44, 1946.

Sears, Pauline S. Levels of aspiration in academically successful and unsuccessful children. *Journal of Abnormal and Social Psychology, 35*:498–536, 1940.

Smilansky, Sarah. Evaluation of early education. *Evaluating Educational Achievements,* UNESCO Educational Studies and Documents, No. 42, 1961.

Smith, J. O. *Effects of a Group Language Development Program Upon the Psycholinguistic Abilities of Educable Mental Retardates.* Peabody College Special Education Research Monograph Series. Nashville, Tenn., George Peabody College for Teachers, 1962.

Srole, L., Langner, T. S., Michael, S. T., Opler, M. K., and Rennie, T. A. C. *Mental Health in the Metropolis: The Midtown Manhattan Study.* New York, McGraw-Hill, 1962.

Wiseman, D. E. A classroom procedure for identifying and remediating language problems. *Mental Retardation, 3*:20–24, 1965.

21 ORGANIZING FOR THE DEVELOPMENT OF EFFECTIVE CURRICULA FOR THE EDUCABLE MENTALLY RETARDED

Norman J. Niesen

From *Education and Training of the Mentally Retarded,* Vol. 2, No. 2, April 1967, pp. 51–55. Reprinted with the permission of the Council for Exceptional Children and the author. Dr. Niesen is Chairman, Department on Mental Retardation, State University College, Buffalo, N.Y.

Today there is widespread public and professional acceptance of the belief that most of the mentally retarded can be helped to become self sufficient and contributing members of society if they receive adequate education and other necessary services. A recent publication has described the present climate surrounding the condition of mental retardation as a revolution in understanding, research, education, recreation, employment, and maternal and child care (Joseph P. Kennedy, Jr. Foundation, 1966). The impact of this revolution is being felt heavily by special education personnel everywhere. Expansion and extension of special education programs in the form of preschool, high school, work study, and postschool classes are progressing at a highly accelerated rate, often without the benefit of a sufficient supply of professional personnel. In addition, new knowledge and thinking regarding the relationship of learning, environment, and culture are making their effects felt in programs for the retarded. The net result of this present state of affairs is a growing awareness on the part of most special educators that the time has come to examine what is being taught to the mentally retarded in special education programs. Consequently, there is widespread interest concerning how to organize to facilitate the development of effective special class curricula for the mentally retarded.

The development of effective curricula for the retarded is influenced to a large degree by three categories of considerations. These are:

1. Basic principles which serve as a foundation for curriculum development.
2. Factors which influence the structure of curriculum content.
3. Organizational techniques which influence the operation of a curriculum project.

These three categories have been used by the Division of Special Education of the Cincinnati Public Schools to guide a ten year curriculum development project (Niesen *et al.,* 1964). The Division, through this project, recently developed a curriculum guide which has received wide acceptance and recognition.

SOME BASIC PRINCIPLES OF CURRICULUM DEVELOPMENT

Teachers, supervisors, and administrators must be involved in development of a curriculum project. Developing an effective curriculum takes the efforts of many people, not just a few. Gone are the days when a curriculum guide or a course of study was the sole responsibility of the specialist, supervisor, or administrative staff. Curriculum developed by the specialist, with little teacher involvement, usually is not fully understood, accepted, or implemented by teachers in their classrooms. Most specialists are too far removed from children, classroom practices, and school problems to do much more than bring an armchair approach to solving the problems which confront teacher and child in a learning situation. Better solutions to educational problems and a generally higher level product are developed when interested teachers are actively involved in determining the content and nature of the curriculum.

The first consideration, then, is to involve as many interested people as possible in the curriculum project—especially those who have had first-hand experience with children.

Curriculum development takes time, effort, interest, research, dedication, and hard work. Many curriculum projects fail because people who direct or participate in them do not realize the amounts of time and personal investment necessary for the development of a first rate product. In any curriculum project, the idea should emerge early that curriculum development is a continuous ongoing process which really has only a beginning and never an end.

Participants must have an understanding of what is meant by curriculum development. Unless the participants in the project have a clear understanding of what is implied by the term curriculum, a limited product is likely to result. First, an understanding must emerge that curriculum means the sum total of those experiences which pupils have under the guidance, supervision, and direction of the school. The second understanding of curriculum which must emerge is that curriculum development as a process is nothing more or less than determining the what, when, and how of teaching, modified by clear analysis of the why of these processes. The curriculum development process may be viewed as an equation:

$$\text{C. D.} = \frac{\text{What} + \text{When} + \text{How}}{\text{Why}}$$

A curriculum project must be guided by long-range goals. A curriculum project must be guided by an understanding of the end product it hopes to achieve.

Ragan (1961) states that educational objectives emerge from a combination of factors including a philosophy of education, a study of contemporary society, a knowledge of children and the learning process, and the thinking of specialists. Certainly all of these sources should be used in arriving at a statement concerning the long-range goals which a curriculum project sets forth to guide its activities.

A curriculum project must be based on an understanding of principles of human growth and development and upon the belief in the inherent worth of each child. Any curriculum project in the area of special education must be guided by a thorough understanding of the way handicapped children grow, develop, and learn. Equally important is an acceptance of the belief that each child has intrinsic worth and dignity, no matter how mentally limited. Curriculum development not guided by this kind of thinking usually sets expectancy levels of achievement which are not realistic for the majority of children and thus becomes worthless as an aid to the instructional process.

FACTORS RELATED TO CURRICULAR CONTENT

The development of an effective curriculum project must give attention to a second set of considerations which relate to and influence the content. Probably the first issue which must be resolved is related to selecting a format or organizational structure. Traditionally, special education classes for the mentally retarded have used such curricular organizational structures as subject matter, activity programs, experience units, cores of work, and life problems. Much has been written about the advantages and disadvantages of each of these organizational structures. Probably any of these structures can be adapted to do an adequate instructional job, providing attention is given to certain considerations which influence the selection of content. Following is a review of these considerations:

The nature and needs of the learner influence curricular content. Even though the retarded child is more like than different from ordinary children, he has special needs related to his handicap. The degree to which these needs are met will determine his adjustment in society. Essentially, the school program must equip him to survive in a highly competitive, symbol oriented society. The educable mentally retarded child is poorly equipped for active and full participation in this kind of society. Therefore, a major task confronting the developers of curricula is the selection of those essential elements which are necessary for the learner's survival at each stage of his development. These elements which are directly related to his needs become the basis of the curricular content for the special class program.

Society's demands should influence curricular content. A second dimension to the selection of curricular content is related to the demands that society makes on all its citizens. By and large, society will make few concessions for the condition of mental retardation. Therefore, those engaged in the development of curricula must be cognizant of society's expectations for its citizens at each level of their development. The school program must reflect societal expectations if it is to prepare the mentally retarded pupil for survival and participation in his community. The failure of special class programs is often related to the fact that expectancy levels have been unrealistically low and the learning environment so sheltered that pupils have not been prepared to meet even minimum standards set by society.

The content of the curriculum must have purpose, meaning, and utility for children at each stage of their development. The mentally retarded learn best through personal involvement with those things which have meaning and use to them. Effective learning requires reinforcement. Reinforcement can be accomplished by selecting activities which are useful in helping pupils meet the problems which confront them daily. Curriculum content therefore must be carefully selected so that it has purpose, meaning, and utility for the learner.

The curricular content should be guided by goals which are stated in terms of specific behavior. Curriculum goals which give direction to a classroom program should be stated specifically so that concrete help is provided for teachers. Ultimately, learning should be reflected in observable or measurable behavior. By stating curriculum goals in behavioral terms, teachers will be helped to identify needs and plans for meaningful learning experiences for pupils.

Curricular content should have scope and sequence. The content selected at each instructional level should provide for the sequential development of skills, understandings, habits, and attitudes. In addition, provision must be made for sequence of learning to become ever expanding in its application to solving problems of living.

SOME ORGANIZATIONAL TECHNIQUES FOR CURRICULUM DEVELOPMENT

A curriculum development project requires that people work together effectively and productively. Certain organizational techniques will facilitate effective production.

The experience of participants should be utilized fully. A curriculum project should be so structured that groups are organized around activities and problem solving in which the participants have considerable interest, experience, and skill. For example, the content of a developmental reading program for preadolescent retarded pupils should be decided by teachers working with this age group. The skills of the high school teacher of the retarded should be used to solve content problems related to the work-study program. In short, the "what" and the "how" should be determined by the teachers who are expected to implement the curriculum in a classroom setting.

A curriculum project must be structured so that leadership, direction, articulation, and coordination are provided. A curriculum development project usually does not emerge merely by bringing a group together to discuss instructional problems. The emergence and effectiveness of a curriculum project is directly related to the degree of structure provided. Structure implies that the project must have direction, and direction means that leadership must be present. While leadership may reside in a single individual, it is usually more effective if this responsibility is entrusted to a small group. This is essentially the concept of a steering committee, which permits a small group to decide on the structure and direction for the larger group. The function of this leadership committee is to:

1. Develop operational procedures
2. Set priorities for project concern
3. Provide for the necessary articulation and coordination among groups and their activities
4. Resolve issues and problems which grow out of small group activity which affect the course of the total project
5. Evaluate and edit the work of small groups
6. Put the guide into publishable form
7. Provide for continued revaluation and modification of the guide

An illustration of how the committee might function may be seen in this example:

> The steering committee decides that a meeting will be devoted to the delineation of curricular content related to health. Prior to a meeting of all interested teachers, the steering committee, with the help of resource people, and research, develops a skeletal outline of desired goals for each level of health program. The goals selected for development are based upon a predetermined rationale.
>
> At the meeting of the large group of participating teachers, the chairman of the steering committee presents the problem under consideration. Small groups of teachers, according to their instructional levels, meet to discuss, modify, and add to the skeletal goals. In addition, activities implementing the goals are devised by these small groups. The material developed by each small group is returned to the steering committee for revision and editing.

The steering committee should include representatives from each small group. These representatives will play leadership roles in the small group activities. This procedure provides for a built-in method of control, articulation, coordination, and direction of the total project.

This organizational technique may also provide for the employment of resource specialists when problems arise which require competencies beyond those found in the groups.

REFERENCES

Nebraska Community Education Project. *The Curriculum Experiment.* Lincoln: Nebraska University, 1959.

Niesen, N. J., *et al. The Slow Learning Program in the Elementary and Secondary Schools.* Cincinnati, Ohio: Cincinnati Public Schools, 1964.

Ragan, W. B. *Modern Elementary Curriculum.* New York: Holt, Rinehart and Winston, Inc., 1961.

The Joseph P. Kennedy, Jr. Foundation. *The Mentally Retarded . . . Their New Hope.* Washington, D.C.: U.S. Government Printing Office, 1966.

22 EMERGING CURRICULA FOR THE ELEMENTARY LEVEL EDUCABLE MENTALLY RETARDED

Robert Fuchigami

Reprinted by permission from *Mental Retardation,* Vol. 7, No. 5, October 1969, pp. 37–40, a publication of the American Association on Mental Deficiency. Dr. Fuchigami is Associate Professor of Education, Sonoma State College, Rohnert Park, Calif.

In recent years an increasing number of prominent special educators have directed criticism toward existing curricula and guides used with elementary level educable mentally retarded (EMR) children. The purpose of this article is to consider the nature of their criticism, discuss primary sources of influence for curriculum change, and attempt to identify possible trends in curriculum development for the elementary level retarded.

REVIEW OF CURRICULUM CRITICISM

After reviewing the usage of various guides by special classroom teachers, Thorsell (1961) made the following criticism of curriculum guides and teaching practices:

1. There is a haphazard selection of unit topics, most of which have been borrowed from regular elementary education.
2. There are worn-out or outdated unit topics which have been borrowed from published guides and worksheets for the mentally retarded.
3. There are short experience activities which are isolated and sandwiched between formal subject matter presentation.

She called for greater effort by special educators to combine their knowledge of the characteristics and needs of the mentally retarded with the knowledge and skill of curriculum specialists in developing a more uniform pattern of instruction for the retarded.

Rothstein (1962) surveyed available curriculum guides and reported that most of them were "watered down, conventional approaches. . . . with little meaning in the true sense of a developmental special education program."

Simches and Bohn (1963) examined over 250 curriculum guides for the educable mentally retarded and stated that existing guides lacked sequence and comprehensive development in subject matter areas. Furthermore, they concluded that the special curriculum is in reality "not distinctive, but a watered down version of the curriculum for normal children."

By 1963, some special educators were beginning to explore possibilities for curriculum change. Gorelick (1963) called for more specificity and precision in stating curriculum objectives. She suggested a "typology of curriculum objectives" based on a systems approach which would analyze complex skills, concepts, and attitudes into single and simple definable behavioral outcomes which could be objectively measured. By 1966, curriculum reform was clearly a major issue. Blackman and Heintz (1966) conducted a recent review of educational research in retardation and stated that "the next step in educational research with the mentally retarded would involve the development and evaluation of a taxonomy of the school relevant disabilities of retarded learners." In 1967 Blackman reiterated his interest in designing an instructional system which would move retarded learners toward more efficient mastery of appropriate educational content. In a recent issue of *Exceptional Children* Gallagher (1967) posed a provocative question, "Is curriculum development for exceptional children too important to be left to the classroom teacher or, for that matter, to the special educator?" He proceeded to point out the weaknesses of our present system in special education, in which local groups of teachers gather together to write a curriculum. The result of such group efforts is generally a modified, localized version of the *Illinois Curriculum Guide* (Goldstein and Seigle, 1958) or the *New York Core* developed by Hungerford. Gallagher suggested that consideration be given to the possibility of a massive curriculum project involving psychologists, sociologists, anthropologists, and special educators.

MAJOR SOURCES OF CURRICULUM CHANGE

The brief review of the critical literature on curriculum development reveals that we are in a period of transition—the old curricula are inappropriate or inadequate and new curricula are emerging. Some of the forces or sources of major influence which indicate possible directions in curriculum development include the following: Regular education; Compensatory education; Prescriptive education; and Special education.

Regular Education

The curricula in regular education has been changing dramatically in the past few years. The Woods Hole Conference in 1959, which was the basis for Bruner's widely read book *Process of Education* (1961) can probably be identified as one of the major pivotal points in modern education. This conference gave its distinguished participants encouragement to expand their initial explorations in developing curricula which focused primarily on the process of education rather than the product. Since that time, regular educators have seen a wide variety of new curricula in various subject matter areas, including mathematics, physics, biology, English and, most recently, health education.

The trend in regular education has been to organize curriculum experiences which will enable pupils to develop basic generalizations and understanding for themselves. Through a process of self motivation, individual inquiry, and discovery, regular class pupils are expected to eventually learn to conduct their own investigations and make their own interpretations, instead of remaining dependent on textbooks or instructors.

The curricula changes in regular education have considerable implications for special educators.

A reasonable question to ask is, "How much difference should exist between special class and regular class curricula at the elementary level?" More specific questions asked by special class teachers who are aware of recent changes in regular class curriculum include: (1) How much modern math should I teach? (2) Should I incorporate elements of Suchman's inquiry training in my program and, if so, to what degree? or (3) How much attention should I give to using the discovery method with my pupils to learn the larger generalizations advocated in most of the curriculum projects in regular education?

It is quite evident that special education and regular education are not mutually exclusive programs and cannot function independently of each other. The new curricula for special education will probably include basic elements of the trend in new curricula for regular education, which means that some consideration will be given to including the learning of large generalizations and utilizing elements of the discovery or inquiry training approach.

Compensatory Education

A second influence for possible change in special class curriculum is the knowledge gained from research and demonstration projects in compensatory education. Compensatory education is that education provided for economically disadvantaged children, youth, and adults. The majority of compensatory education projects such as Headstart, Parent Child Care, Follow-Through, and others are under the supervision of the Federal Office of Economic Opportunity. Some of the research projects have involved well-known special educators such as Blatt and Garfunkel (1967), and Bereiter and Englemann (1966), who included in their projects subjects who might have been placed in classes for the educable mentally retarded. The curricula used in these projects ranged from highly structured no-nonsense academic approaches to almost laissez faire curricula emerging from the children's needs.

Since the majority of the educable mentally retarded pupils at the elementary level come from economically disadvantaged homes and neighborhoods and have similar problems, the compensatory curricula which are successful should be carefully studied for their possible adaptation and application to programs for the retarded. The new curricula in special education will probably reflect elements of some of the more successful compensatory education programs. A project for psychosocially deprived preschool mentally retarded children by Spicker, Hodges and McCandless (1966) is a recent example of this influence.

Prescriptive Education [1]

A third influence is prescriptive education. The term prescriptive education refers to that education which is given to children with disability conditions which have some possibility for remediation, utilizing very specialized diagnostic and remedial techniques. In recent years, considerable attention has been given by many special educators to the problems of children with various types of learning disabilities (Kirk and Bateman, 1962; Frostig, 1963; Barsch, 1965; Getman, 1962). Although this form of education is relatively new on the public school scene, many school systems have established a wide variety of diagnostic and remedial type programs and services for children with perceptual, visual, auditory, motor, and other specific disabling conditions.

Responsibility for the education of children with learning disabilities has been placed in the hands of special educators, because of their previous experience and knowledge in working with children who have chronic handicapping conditions. However, as the information accumulates and sophistication in diagnosis and remediation increases, we are beginning to find that the diagnosis and remediation process involves far more than education. Optometrists, neurologists, occupational therapists, physical therapists, ophthalmologists, and personnel representing other diagnostic and habilitative disciplines, are expressing their considerable and varied opinions in increasing numbers. The term "education" is being considerably broadened to include visual and auditory exercises, trampoline bouncing, and in some instances, creeping and crawling (Delacato, 1963).

Of the four primary forces with possible influence on the special education curricula of the future, the research findings and practices from prescriptive education are most evident in the literature. A curriculum research project currently in progress at Illinois under the direction of Dr. Merle Karnes should reveal considerably more information about the appropriateness and effectiveness of curricula where an attempt is made to match educational remediation for children with learning deficits. Advocates of prescriptive education type programs have already shown a tendency to remind special educators that elements of their program should be a standard part of all special education programs based on the premise that the

[1] From L. J. Peters, *Perspective Teaching.*

objectives, methods and materials cannot "harm" the child and may "help" him to function more effectively. We can expect to hear considerably more from these advocates in the near future, although there are some indications (Mann and Phillips, 1967) that the fractional approach has its limitations.

Special Education

The fourth major source of influence is special education. As early as 1962, Mackinnon delineated at least four overlapping subgroups among those persons classified as educable mentally retarded: The brain injured, the familial retarded, the culturally deprived, and the multiply handicapped. He suggested that curricula be developed for the various subgroups based on what research had revealed about the general knowledge of the retarded, their learning abilities and disabilities, and changes in postschool needs. Rothstein (1962) made similar statements. Hirsch (1965) called for a re-examination of the homogeneity of retarded pupils and suggested more appropriate curricula to match groups of pupils with specific learning deficits.

CURRICULUM DEVELOPMENT FOR THE EMR SINCE 1963

A review of curriculum projects since 1963 reveals limited involvement by special educators in the area of curriculum development. One of the significant contributions made during this time period was a project completed at Teachers College, Columbia, by Connor and Talbot (1964). Their experimental curriculum for the retarded differed from more traditional guides in several ways: First, the content was organized in a way that led to objective evaluation; second, the behavioral outcomes were described very specifically; and third, the teaching procedures were considerably more explicit than other guides. Unfortunately, the limited emphasis on cognitive development made the guide more appropriate for trainable level retarded children.

More recently, a project in curriculum development for the educable mentally retarded at the elementary level was completed at Yeshiva University under the direction of Dr. Herbert Goldstein and George Mischio (1967). A preliminary report of the curriculum developed in this project reveals some exciting changes in organizational format. The Yeshiva project attempts to operationalize Coghill's three phases of learning. Coghill (1929) hypothesized that all learning takes place in three phases: Mass, differentiation, and integration. The Yeshiva curriculum incorporated the idea into three instructional stages: Primary, secondary, and tertiary. The primary stage in their curriculum consists of: (1) Teacher preparation, including knowledge of prerequisite skills and concepts, organization of children, and physical grouping; (2) Structure, and introduction of concepts which included knowledge and sequential presentation of the concept; and (3) The expansion and mastery of learning skills and concepts which included restatement and reteaching of various concepts. The secondary stage consists of the reinforcement of generalizations. The final or tertiary stage consists of application of the generalization to various problem solving situations. The inclusion of elements of teaching strategies in a curriculum is a major step forward in curriculum design.

THE NEXT DECADE

The next ten years will probably be the most exciting period in the history of curriculum development. Several recent events have made it possible to make the prediction more probable. First, a new research demonstration and training center has been established at Columbia under the direction of Dr. Leonard Blackman, a longtime advocate of curriculum reform.

Second, the Yeshiva University curriculum development team, under the direction of Dr. Herbert Goldstein, has received approval from the U.S. Office of Education to continue their investigations. They are currently testing their newly-developed curriculum on a regional 12-state basis.

Third, the Division for Handicapped Children and Youth has been elevated to a Bureau level with a broader and stronger fiscal base. Furthermore, the new head of the Bureau, Dr. James Gallagher, has specified curriculum review and reform as a primary focus of investigation that should be pursued by special educators.

Fourth, the establishment of a national network of regional instructional materials centers for handicapped children and youth makes it possible for curriculum innovations to be more easily implemented.

Fifth, a rapidly expanding practice in regular education has been the formation of partnerships between educational institutions and commercial–industrial firms in curriculum design, development, and dissemination. It is highly reasonable to expect that curriculum developers in special education will also team up with commercial–industrial firms in developing instructional systems.

Finally, the possibility of developing and testing regional special education curricula, based on the experience of the Yeshiva curriculum developers, may lead us to examine the feasibility of a national basic curriculum with regional and local supplements.

REFERENCES

Barsch, R. *Movigenic Curriculum,* Bulletin No. 25. Wisconsin State Department of Public Instruction, 1965.

Bereiter, C. and Englemann, S. *Preschool Education for Disadvantaged Children*. Englewood Cliffs, New Jersey: Prentice-Hall, 1966.

Blackman, L. S. "The Dimensions of a Science of Special Education." *Mental Retardation,* 1967, *5,* 7–11.

Blackman, L. S. and Heintz, P. "The Mentally Retarded" in *Review of Educational Research,* XXXVI (February 1966), 5–36.

Blatt, B. and Garfunkel, F. "Educating Intelligence: Determinants of School Behavior of Disadvantaged Children." *Exceptional Children,* 1967, *33,* 601–608.

Bruner, J. *The Process of Education*. Cambridge: Harvard University, 1961.

Coghill, G. E. *Anatomy and the Problem of Behavior*. Cambridge: Cambridge University Press; New York: Macmillan, 1929.

Connor, F. and Talbot, M. *An Experimental Curriculum for Young Mentally Retarded Children*. New York: Bureau of Publications, Teachers College, Columbia University, 1964.

Delacato, C. H. *The Diagnosis and Treatment of Speech and Reading Problems*. Springfield: Charles C Thomas, 1963.

Frostig, M. and Horne, D. *The Frostig Program for the Development of Visual Perception: Teacher's Guide*. Chicago, Follett, 1964.

Gallagher, J. J. "New Directions in Special Education." *Exceptional Children,* 1967, *33,* 441–447.

Getman, G. N. *How To Develop Your Child's Intelligence*. C. N. Getman, O. D. Luverne, Minnesota, 1962.

Goldstein, H. and Seigle, D. *A Curriculum Guide for Teachers of the Educable Mentally Handicapped*. Springfield, Illinois Department of Public Instruction, 1958.

Goldstein, H. and Mischio, G. *A Research and Demonstration Project in Curriculum and Methods of Instruction for Elementary Level Mentally Retarded Children*. Ferkauf Graduate School of Education, Yeshiva University. (Final report not ready for distribution.)

Gorelick, M. C. "Issues: A Typology of Curriculum Objectives for Mentally Retarded: From Ambiguity to Precision." *Mental Retardation,* 1963, *1,* 212–215.

Hirsch, E. "Another Approach to Homogeneity in the Mentally Retarded." In Selected Convention Papers, *New Frontiers in Special Education,* 43rd Annual C.E.C. Convention, 1965, 57–60.

Kirk, S. A. and Bateman, B. "Diagnosis and Remediation of Learning Disabilities." *Exceptional Children,* 1962, *29,* 73–78.

Mackinnon, F. "Curriculum Trends for the Educable Mentally Retarded at the Elementary School Level." *In Selected Convention Papers,* 40th Annual C.E.C. Convention, 1962, 114–117.

Mann, L. and Phillips, W. A. "Fractional Practices in Special Education: A Critique." *Exceptional Children,* 1967, *33,* 311–317.

Peters, L. J. *Prescriptive Teaching*. New York: McGraw-Hill, 1965.

Rothstein, J. H. "Curriculum Development for the Mentally Handicapped: Present and Emerging Phases of the Program for EMH" in Emerging Patterns for the Education of the Mentally Retarded, reference papers prepared for the Ella Sullivan Institute, Chicago, 1962.

Simches, G. and Bohn, R. J. "Issues in Curriculum: Research and Responsibility." *Mental Retardation,* 1963, *1,* 84–87.

Spicker, H. H., Hodges, W. L. and McCandless, B. R. "A Diagnostically Based Curriculum for Psychosocially Deprived Preschool, Mentally Retarded Children: Interim Report." *Exceptional Children,* 1966, 215–220.

Thorsell, M. "Organizing Experience Units for Educable Mentally Retarded," *Exceptional Children,* 1961, 177–185.

23 A REVIEW OF SERVICES OFFERED THROUGH THE INSTRUCTIONAL MATERIALS CENTER NETWORK

LeRoy Aserlind

From *Exceptional Children,* Vol. 35, No. 3, December 1968, pp. 267–272. Reprinted with the permission of the Council for Exceptional Children and the author. Dr. Aserlind is Associate Professor of Education and Director, Special Education Instructional Materials Center, Department of Studies in Behavioral Disability, University of Wisconsin, Madison.

The unavailability of adequate instructional materials for use by the teacher in the special classroom was cited by the President's Panel on Mental Retardation as being a "major barrier" to education of the handicapped. Subsequent legislation, PL 88-164, was passed in 1963 which provided funds for an innovative approach to the problem.

Heretofore instructional materials centers had been from a more or less traditional mold—libraries of instructional materials available for loan to teachers. The special class teacher often had to rely primarily on her own collection of materials, with this collection supplemented by that of a city, county, or district library. For the most part the materials that were more generally available to this teacher were those materials which had been developed for the child with no perceptual, learning, or behavioral handicaps. These materials often contained intrinsic elements incompatible with the learning characteristics of the handicapped child (Aserlind, 1968).

Under Title III, Section 302, of PL 88-164 two centers were funded—one at the University of Wisconsin and one at the University of Southern California. One of their express purposes was to enlarge the concept of a Special Education Instructional Materials Center (SEIMC). The SEIMC's were initially seen as being in a position to offer a number of services beyond that of housing a basic collection of materials. By 1964 both centers were in their first stages of operation. From these early operational experiences several general goals of Special Education Instructional Materials Centers were proposed, most of which were service oriented. These were:

> First, a center must have an operational radius. If only local clients are served, many teachers in small towns and rural areas will be deprived of services. . . .
>
> Second, a center should be in a position to remark to clients on the effectiveness and characteristics of materials. . . .
>
> Third, such centers must offer workshops, conferences, and ultimately, as accumulated information increases, credit courses. . . .
>
> Fourth, such a center should have a consultative staff. This would include a field man who could guarantee a constant and vital rapport within the center's operational radius, including consultation with field clients. . . .

> Fifth, such a center should issue, at regular intervals, a publication or newsletter containing at least two things: an acquisition list and an evaluation section. . . .
>
> Sixth, the center should have, ideally, a search and retrieval system so that among increasing masses of materials, certain items can be identified and located. . . .
>
> Seventh, and the final basic characteristic of such an ideal center, the center's staff should have the motivation and ability to engage in design and arrange for the production of educational materials [McCarthy, 1966, pp. 27–28].

On such a basis the two initial centers predicated much of their developmental activity over the first years. By 1965 it became evident that these centers were able to provide needed services to special education personnel within a relatively circumscribed area. Because of their apparent success and the approval of an ad hoc advisory committee on instructional materials centers, the U.S. Office of Education drew up a plan for expanding the program (Olshin, 1967). The expansion program called for establishing a number of regional centers in the United States; these centers then were formed into the Instructional Materials Center Network for Handicapped Children and Youth, funded through the demonstration phase primarily by the United States Office of Education.

Each basically operates as an independent center, offering direct services to special educators and to the satellite centers being established in its region. Each of the independent centers, however, coordinates its activities with those of the other centers and the network in general. Vital to this coordination is a continuing communication maintained through reports and meetings.

As previously stated, the principal goals of these centers are largely service-oriented at the present time. A number of the services were originally envisaged as having an empirically demonstrated need. Others have been developed through continual field operation and evaluation; still some services were designed to meet new needs which have been created by the existence of the centers themselves. The present article deals only with the general services offered within the network centers and will not discuss the more unique, specific aspects of individual center servicing, which are discussed in the articles by Rotberg and Ensminger elsewhere in this issue.

LENDING

Almost without exception, the service of lending is seen as the most important function of a center in its early stages, since it is of the most immediate benefit to special class teachers and answers one of the persisting needs in special class. All of the centers, with the exception of the Reference Center at the American Printing House for the Blind, maintain an acquisition, cataloging, and shelving operation for the purpose of providing a lending service. The general policy of the centers is to lend books and manipulative material for a short term period. IMCs do not supply materials for total school year classroom use, but give the teacher the opportunity to use materials in practice and to make judgments in terms of future purchase. Exception to the short term use of single copy material is found in the fact that several of the centers supply classroom materials for the blind (Illinois, Michigan, and American Printing House). The loan periods for materials in the centers generally range from two weeks to a month with both renewal and recall privileges available.

A variation of the lending services, necessitated by the size of the regions, is mail order lending, which centers now provide. Some, such as the Kentucky Center, allow a longer lending period for mail order loans. Similar special arrangements are made by centers servicing an extraordinarily wide geographic area—for example, the Oregon Center of over 840,000 square miles.

The lending service is important because it entails a direct and vital contact between the center and the teacher in the field and, conversely, between the teacher and the center.

SEARCH AND RETRIEVAL

Search and retrieval will undoubtedly gain in importance. Two factors leading to this are the increasing number of materials, methods, and pertinent research studies and an increasing attention to the concept of diagnostic, precision, or prescriptive teaching. From this will emerge materials and references with a high degree of specificity to individually diagnosed learning problems and with an attendant academic prescription.

At the present time the principal purposes of search and retrieval are to supply teachers, administrators, or classroom researchers with lists of shelved or cataloged materials relevant to a particular need or problem. This type of service is still in its relative infancy. Three centers—California, Texas, and Michigan—have independently developed computer programs and compatible cataloging systems which are specially designed to perform a search and retrieval operation. These systems have a number of possibilities. Some requests received by the computerized centers require searches and retrievals by author, title, grade level, subject matter, activity level, etc., and numerous combinations thereof. Traditionally, teachers browse through the shelves or look through the card catalogs. Computers now print "browser's catalogs," making available to the center user discrete listings directly applicable to his immediate interests.

Other centers such as Wisconsin maintain a search and retrieval system based on IBM machines such as the keypunch, sorter, and printer. At present a number of the centers are relying on manual searches, but it seems likely from existing trends that all centers will eventually have a direct tie to a computer center with a cataloged program which will be developed within the network. CEC–ERIC is presently compiling a library of computer retrievable abstracts provided by the regional centers. In the near future, printouts of these abstracts will be available to special education practitioners.

RESEARCH DESIGN

This is an available but little used service offered by a number of centers to special education teachers and administrators. One of the purposes of this type of service is based on the fact that the special education classroom and teacher are potential sources of a great amount of practical, *in situ* information. The "teacher as a researcher" is one of the concepts accepted by the network. To encourage the teacher to enter into some type of research activity or commitment, centers will offer consulting services to the classroom practitioner on basic elements of experimental design, measurement, statistics, and evaluation of results. As more satellite centers are developed through the regions it may be anticipated that the regional centers will be devoting more energies to the development of the special classroom as a prime research site.

MATERIAL DEVELOPMENT AND DESIGN

The original purpose of this category of service was to help and encourage the special class teacher to design and develop materials for her own special situation. Also, it was felt that the centers would be in excellent position to enter into experimental creation of special education instructional materials which, if successful, would become public domain. Again, attention to other immediate problems and to copyright problems has precluded a great deal of activity in this service area. Perhaps some of the existing materials developed by centers may well be considered as unique projects, although falling under the aegis of particular services (see Ensminger article in this issue).

As originally premised, the centers were to offer this service to help make up for the lack of special materials developed by commercial producers. Present indications are that within a comparatively short time more commercial producers will begin to market materials developed expressly for use in special classrooms.

EVALUATION

All centers in the network accept evaluation of instructional materials as one of its services to special educators. Several of the earlier established centers—Wisconsin, California, Colorado, and Michigan—have done preliminary work on establishing an effective evaluation model. A network committee is currently functioning toward this end. Independent efforts of several centers have suggested approaches to the critical but difficult evaluative process. To date most efforts, such as those at Oregon, involve the use of teacher evaluation groups which use and discuss materials to arrive at a consensus regarding the effectiveness of the materials. California also is concerned with developing methods of utilizing teachers' judgments and ratings and validating these procedures against the more typical pattern of professional evaluation by supervisory or curriculum specialists staff.

It is evident from initial approaches that the use of practicing teachers in field evaluation of materials will be increasing in all regions of the United States.

MOBILE VANS

Both empirical and research evidence suggests that use of lending facilities of an IMC decreases in direct proportion to the distance away from the center. Means of nullifying this distance effect which have proven to be effective are increased field consultant activity and the use of mobile vans.

The Colorado Center pioneered in the mobile van concept. The vans bring materials directly to schools and teachers in outlying, and in many instances, remote locations. The teacher is offered the opportunity to see, discuss, and select materials that may be of immediate interest or need. Other centers are adapting the mobile van idea to private or state automobiles or other means of first hand dissemination. Wisconsin, while not using the mobile materials van as a direct service, is supporting the use of these vehicles in subregions served by satellite centers.

CONSULTATION

Consultation services offered through the centers can take many forms ranging from consultation and participation in full year training programs under ESEA Title I (such as the California Center), to on the spot document specialists to consult with users who come to a center (such as Kentucky). Presently most of the consultation services offered through all the centers in the network consist of direct consultation with state and local administrative personnel on programing and consultation with teachers on the selection of methods and materials for use in the special class. Increasingly, the consultation expertise efforts of the centers have been instrumental in developing state plans for the establishment of satellite centers (New York, New England) and for consultative help in the preparation of satellite center grants (Texas, Kansas, Oregon, Wisconsin, etc.).

Eventually a point will be reached at which a number of the direct services in a region can be taken care of by proximally located satellite centers. The areas of programatic, research, educational, and developmental consultation will fall increasingly upon the specially prepared personnel at the regional centers.

MATERIALS DEMONSTRATION AND DISPLAYS

A significant portion of the direct services offered by all centers in the network relates to materials demonstration and display. Each center perceives this as an important service and develops its programs accordingly. Through direct display a larger number of teachers are acquainted with the purposes of a center as well as with a particular center's acquisitions. Demonstrations are most often conducted either by center field and specialist personnel or by master special education teachers enlisted for that purpose. Records kept at Wisconsin indicated a rise in usage of lending services from a subregion following a materials demonstration or display program in that area.

Oregon, Kentucky, New York, New England, and California centers have prepared, or are in the process of preparing, videotapes or other audiovisual presentations of materials demonstrations and displays. This is expected to further enhance the distribution of these services which is limited by the number of materials available for display and the amount of professional time for preparation and demonstration. Particularly effective videotapes will be reproduced and made available to all network centers for distribution throughout their regions.

CONFERENCES, INSTITUTES, AND INSERVICE PROGRAMS

All centers are involved in an active program of offering conferences, special institutes, and inservice programs. Many inservice programs are related to preparation and use of materials, as well as to learning theory, reinforcement, research findings, etc. Most of the programs are developed in cooperation with school administrators, supervisors, and universities. An increasing number of administrators are allowing and suggesting that a portion of the school allotted inservice training time be spent at one of the centers working with its staff on some previously determined topic or area of study.

Institutes and conferences, along with lending, display, and demonstration activities, are another means of offering services to current and potential users of the IMC's. Examples of recently offered programs are: Education Rhythmics and Motor Development for Exceptional Children (Oregon), Materials for Teaching Children With Learning Disabilities (Kentucky), Materials Used in Self Directive Study (New York), Teaching Mathematics to the Exceptional Child (Wisconsin), and Institute for Special Education Administrative Personnel (California). These topics represent only a portion of the offerings made through the centers as, for instance, Florida, Kansas, and Texas each conducted approximately 25 of these special programs.

In addition, all centers have supplied speakers for a significant number of programs sponsored by other professional, public, and private agencies on local, regional, and national levels.

CURRICULUM AND CREDIT COURSES

A number of the centers associated with colleges or universities are in the process of developing on-campus and extension courses relating more directly to instructional materials for the handicapped children than do many existing courses today. The centers realize that service should be offered to students in preparation for careers in special education. It is anticipated that within two years the majority of the university affiliated centers will be offering credit courses based extensively on knowledge gained through research and through Network accumulated findings on selection, utilization, and evaluation of these special materials.

PUBLICATIONS

All centers have developed or are in the process of developing some type of publication for the teacher readership within their particular region. Two examples are *The Winnower* (Wisconsin) and *The Torch* (Oregon). These publications contain articles on issues in the field of special education, informative and educative articles, and discussions of materials. *The Winnower* maintains an acquisition list for the purpose of bringing the readers up to date on the latest holdings in the center.

An essentially similar function but somewhat different format is seen in the *UKRS–EIMC Quarterly* (Kentucky), *IMSCE Communicator* (California), and *IMCing in New York* (New York). In two of the older centers (Wisconsin and California), circulation runs approximately 3,500 and 8,500, respectively. The advent of a national publication will preclude and eventually replace extensive publication services on the part of the centers; however, all of these centers will continue to offer a newsletter service containing primarily regional information.

ABSTRACTING

As mentioned earlier under search and retrieval, one of the functions of CEC–ERIC will be to maintain a constantly updated file of pertinent abstracts. These files will be accessible to the practitioner in special education. The centers will supply abstracts and evaluations to the central file using a Network thesaurus as the basis for selection of key descriptor terms.

OBTAINING SERVICES

In order to make use of the IMC Network, it is important that special educators contact the center servicing their region. If that center is not yet operational or does not have the desired material or service, the request will be referred to another center known to be able to answer the request.

It is important that requests be as specific as possible; for example, asking for "materials for teaching arithmetic to the retarded" will probably be met with a request for further details. Asking for "samples of workbooks for teaching arithmetic to the intermediate level educable retarded" will more likely bring the desired material or service.

As this article has described, the IMC Network provides numerous services to special educators. The centers lend out materials; supply listings of materials by area, level, and subject, etc.; send out field consultants and mobile vans to local areas; set up courses; provide consultative assistance for instructional materials use, evaluation, research, programing, and development; send out newsletters informing of available services and acquisitions; and set up inservice training programs and workshops.

REFERENCES

Aserlind, L. Research and instructional materials for the mentally retarded. In International Association for the Scientific Study of Mental Deficiency, Proceedings of the International Association for the Scientific Study of Mental Deficiency. Amsterdam: Excerpta Medica Foundation, 1968.

McCarthy, J. Educational materials for the mentally retarded: A quandry. *Education and Training of the Mentally Retarded,* 1966, *1,* 24–31.

Olshin, G. IMC Network report. *Exceptional Children,* 1967, *34,* 137–141.

Instructional Materials Center Network for Mentally Retarded Children and Youth *

Center	Region Served	Publication
CALIFORNIA Instructional Materials Center University of Southern California 2120 W. 8th St. Los Angeles, California 90057	Arizona California Nevada	*IMCSE Communicator*
COLORADO Rocky Mountain Instructional Materials Center Colorado State College Greeley, Colorado 80631	Colorado Montana New Mexico Wyoming	
ERIC (NATIONAL NETWORK OFFICE) Jefferson Plaza 1499 Jefferson Davis Highway Suite 928 Arlington, Virginia 22202	National	*Teaching Exceptional Children*
FLORIDA Southeastern Materials Center University of South Florida Tampa, Florida 33620	Alabama Florida Georgia Mississippi South Carolina Puerto Rico Virgin Islands	
ILLINOIS Instructional Materials Center 726 South College St. Springfield, Illinois 62706	Illinois	
KANSAS Instructional Materials Center University of Kansas 1115 Louisiana St. Lawrence, Kansas 66044	Iowa Kansas Missouri Nebraska North Dakota South Dakota	
KENTUCKY Instructional Materials Center University of Kentucky 641 S. Limestone St. Lexington, Kentucky 40506	Kentucky North Carolina Tennessee West Virginia	*UKR-SEIMC Quarterly*
MASSACHUSETTS New England Materials-Instruction Center Boston University 704 Commonwealth Ave. Boston, Massachusetts 02215	Connecticut Maine Massachusetts New Hampshire Rhode Island Vermont	

* Note: In addition to the major IMCs listed, the reader should contact the regional center that serves him to locate names and addresses of affiliate and associate IMC centers. It is expected that the new CEC publication "Teaching Exceptional Children" will eventually replace extensive publication services on the part of the centers.

Instructional Materials Center Network for Mentally Retarded Children and Youth (*cont.*)

Center	*Region Served*	*Publication*
MICHIGAN USOE/MSU Instructional Materials Center 343 B Erickson Hall Michigan State University East Lansing, Michigan 48823	Indiana Michigan Ohio	
NEW YORK Special Education Instructional Materials Center N.Y. State Dept. of Education 800 N. Pearl St. Albany, New York 12204	Central New York State	
Instructional Materials Center State University College 1300 Elmwood Ave. Buffalo, New York 14222	Western New York State	
Instructional Materials Center Hunter College Box 563x 695 Park Ave. New York, New York 10021	Eastern New York State	*IMCing in New York*
OREGON Instructional Materials Center Northwest Regional Special Education Clinical Services Building Eugene, Oregon 97403	Alaska Hawaii Idaho Oregon Washington	*The Torch*
TEXAS Instructional Materials Center University of Texas 304 W. 15th St. Austin, Texas 78701	Arkansas Louisiana Oklahoma Texas	
WASHINGTON, D.C. Instructional Materials Center George Washington University 820 20th St., N.W. Washington, D.C. 20006	Delaware D.C. Maryland New Jersey Pennsylvania Virginia	
WISCONSIN Instructional Materials Center University of Wisconsin 415 W. Gilman St. Madison, Wisconsin 53706	Minnesota Wisconsin	*The Winnower*
COORDINATOR Instructional Materials Center Network for Handicapped Children and Youth 1507 M St., N.W. Washington, D.C. 20005		

Instructional Materials Center Network for Mentally Retarded Children and Youth (*cont.*)

Center	*Region Served*	*Publication*
U.S. OFFICE OF EDUCATION Research Laboratories and Demonstration Branch Division of Research Bureau of Education for the Handicapped U.S. Office of Education 7th & D Sts., S.W., Room 2010 Washington, D.C. 20202		

REGIONAL RESOURCE CENTERS [1]

Regional Educational Resource Center
Department of Public Instruction, Iowa
The University of Iowa
County Systems of Cedar, Johnson, Linn, and Washington Counties
Regional Resource Center for Improvement of the Education of Handicapped Children
New Mexico State University
College of Education
Regional Resource Center for Handicapped Children
University of Oregon
College of Education
Department of Special Education
Regional Learning Center for Handicapped Children
The City University of New York
Division of Teacher Education

[1] Authorized by Title VI, Part B, of the Elementary and Secondary Education Act (Public Law 89-10 as amended by Public Law 90-247). These centers are established to develop and apply methods of appraising special needs of the handicapped.

24 COUNSELING WITH THE EDUCABLE MENTALLY RETARDED

Marvin J. Fine

From *The Training School Bulletin* of the American Institute for Mental Studies, Vineland, N.J., Vol. 66, No. 3, November 1969, pp. 105–110. Reprinted with the permission of The Training School, Vineland, N.J., and the author. Dr. Fine is Associate Professor of Educational Psychology, University of Kansas, Lawrence.

The establishment of special classes for retarded children in public schools seems to have ignored the implementation of certain necessary supportive services, such as counseling. Secondary and even elementary school guidance programs are geared primarily for the normal student and in many school systems the special class teacher has questionably assumed the role of counselor.

There are some general assumptions about educable mentally retarded children that support a need for counseling services. These are children with an IQ range between approximately 50 and 80 and it is likely that as a group they have experienced academic failure with related anxieties and frustrations. There is often a negative stigma attached to being in a segregated special class and the parental concern over the child's poor school achievement also may be disturbing to the child. In regard to emotional adjustment, Fine (1966) found a group of educable mentally retarded boys to be significantly less secure than age-matched normal boys and the retardates also demonstrated a greater preference for defensive and consequence-avoiding behavior.

The literature and theory related to counseling with retardates is rather sparse and most of the reported studies deal with moderately retarded, institutionalized children. The literature also reflects a bias against psychotherapy with the mentally retarded. The basic arguments are: (1) the client needs to have the capacity for insight or self-awareness, and the lower the IQ the less evident is this capacity, (2) the client needs to have a fairly high capacity for verbalization and the mentally retarded are frequently limited in verbal skills, and (3) after all of the time and effort one spends with a retardate he is still a retardate; hence time may be more productively spent with a nonretarded child who presumably has more potential as a human being.

A sizeable percentage of the educable mentally retarded reflect a lower socio-economic background and this social status raises some additional problems in relation to counseling. For example, Dewey (1965) discusses the need for empathy on the part of the counselor, but points out that in certain instances the client's need for spatiality may interfere or work counter to the therapist's attempts to empathize. Specifically, Dewey feels that in the culturally deprived population the child has a felt need to maintain a private territory that he must defend from others; this private territory being his inner feelings, motivations and beliefs. While this sense of spatiality may exist in many clients, Dewey suggests that it develops very quickly and strongly in the culturally disadvantaged.

Cotzin (1948) described a group psychotherapy project for problem, mentally defective, adolescent boys. The project took place in an institutional setting, and the nine boys in the group ranged from 11 to 14 years of age, and had IQ scores from 50 to 79. The project in total, included ten therapeutic sessions over a three-week period. Therapy was deemed a success in that after two months following therapy the behavior and personality of the students was considered improved according to therapist and teacher judgment, as well as by the reduction of referrals to the Psychology Department.

The report of the content of therapy suggests that the therapist "played it by ear," much of the time. He described the first session as being a chaotic and unmanageable affair. The overtly aggressive and destructive behavior of the boys precipitated the therapist into becoming less passive or neutral and more active. His role became one of initiating ideas and activities and structuring an activity-oriented program that included role-playing, boxing matches, and arts and crafts. Cotzin, also pointed out that the first several sessions were considered as warm-up sessions. He felt that it takes time for the mentally defective child to adjust to the demands and procedures of the therapy situation.

The main part of the project was in a sense, a therapy session within a therapy session. The role playing was expanded to encompass a court room scene where the group members would "try" a fellow, with the therapist being judge. This approach maintained the group's interest and allowed opportunity for the group to both express hostility and to share their insights regarding the boy on trial.

One additional study reported (Fisher and Wolfson, 1953) engaged in a more detailed analysis of the movement of the children in therapy. In this instance the subjects were institutionalized adolescent girls and Activity Group Therapy (Slavson, 1943) was the technique used. This approach to therapy revolves around play activity with the therapist also engaging in open discussion and offering interpretations either individually or to the group. Children are free within broad limits to express their feelings. In the Fisher and Wolfson project individual sessions were also held with the children selectively, based on the child's request or the therapist's judgment.

Thirty-six sessions were held with the two groups of the project, and when these sessions were analyzed, there seemed to be several distinct phases through which the group process moved. The process of interaction and the focus of attention shifted from being ego-centered, to in-group centered, to out-group interest. As with Cotzin's group, the first stage was a testing the limits situation which included both elaborate verbal and motor expression by the children. The behavior was individualistic rather than group-oriented and each member seemed to be attempting to discover for herself the limits of behavior. There seemed to be a point of transference whereby the group members perceived the therapist in a mother role. This point perceived the second, regressive stage where there was an increased amount of infantilized behavior. Subsequently the maturational level of behavior increased and the group members became more aware of each other. The last stage reached was depicted by a heightened interest and valuing in the attitudes of others.

PILOT PROJECT

The need for counseling services for the educable retarded, coupled with the sparsity of research in the area, are the bases of the project being reported. The client-centered orientation to counseling (Rogers, 1959) was selected, partly because of the writer's interest in this approach, and also because many school counselors are of this orientation. In a survey by Woody and Billy (1966) client-centered counseling was second in popularity only to an eclectic approach, as a frame of reference for counseling with the mentally retarded. It is doubtful if public schools are going to hire special personnel to counsel with retarded students. It is more likely that the existing counseling staff will in time come to view the educable mentally retarded child as also deserving this service.

An urban school system in Kansas that has special classes for the educable mentally retarded was contacted. The project was introduced as an attempt to explore client-centered therapy with adolescent educable retardates. Five boys between twelve and fourteen years of age were selected by a special class teacher who verbalized her feelings that they all had "problems." The subsequent eight sessions represented the counselor's total experience with the group.

The approach to counseling, as indicated, was client centered. This was viewed operationally as establishing a permissive setting, with broad though definite limits (e.g., not harming another child, not damaging school property, remaining in the room) and the counselor being nonevaluative and accepting of the participants. The counselor's verbal expression was calculated to be reflective rather than directive, and to indicate an understanding of the child's feelings, concerns and perceptions. It was hoped that an empathic relationship could develop between the counselor and the group members.

The meetings were held in a conference room located off the main counseling office. There was one large table, a few easy chairs and a stack of folding chairs.

The first session was introductory in terms of the counselor identifying himself, describing his interest in knowing about children, and attempting to communicate to the boys the permissive nature of the meetings. The boys were curious and asked a number of questions of the therapist. The inquiries were of an exploratory testing nature. For example, "You mean we can talk about our teacher?" After a while the boys began interacting with each other physically via Indian wrestling. Although they did not direct any questions or attention at this time to the therapist, they were probably sensitive to his presence, and their display and competing of physical strength was a way of presenting themselves.

During subsequent sessions, regressive behavior was noted in terms of the kind of physical play, mouthing of word sounds and diminishing of personal control over behavior. There appeared to be a reaching out by some members to the counselor. It seemed that some wanted to relate and communicate, but at these times the rest of the group was behaving noisily and this had an apparent distracting effect on the individual student–counselor contact.

Occasionally a boy would ask a question, and several times the counselor would attempt to engage a boy in discussion. However, there seemed to be almost a selective avoidance of prolonged communication or attention with the counselor. This ignoring of the counselor subsequently seemed to generalize to the point where stated limits, such as staying in the room, were more frequently challenged.

After a few sessions one boy, Gene, inquired if they could bring down different kinds of school work or hobby projects. For the following meetings the boys brought school work, and while there was still a great deal of yelling and chasing, each boy attended for a period of time to his own materials. Some cooperative interaction among the boys existed, especially in relation to a geography assignment where they had to fill in names of cities from an atlas. Two of the boys even brought down scrap books made in class to show the counselor.

The growing concern by school officials over the group's unruliness and the apparent lack of direction to the sessions, was communicated to the counselor by the teacher and other school personnel. The school's reaction precipitated the termination of counseling following the eighth session.

DISCUSSION

The eight sessions described, though constituting a highly limited experience, raise certain questions about counseling with educable mentally retarded boys.

One important factor in this project is the apparent lack of goals that the group members were experiencing. They remained confused on why they were meeting and there is some question as to whether they felt that they had a "problem" or whether they needed help from an adult. The feelings and perceptions of the five boys are reflected in a note the teacher sent to the counselor at his request. The note was received after the termination of counseling, and here is part of it.

> *Initially the five boys were curious about why they had been chosen and what they had been chosen for. They were quite satisfied with the explanation that you wanted to talk to five junior high boys about "teenage problems" and that, as Gene put it, this was something like an assignment for you. Their enthusiasm was high for the first meeting.*
>
> *The boys seemed to view it as a pleasant interlude from the classroom. They told me that it was fun. As time progressed they appeared to be somewhat incredulous at the freedom they were allowed during the sessions and to wonder just what kind of an adult you were. They would come back quite awed at having been allowed to sail paper airplanes and to turn off the lights. They were pleased with the power they had during the meetings.*
>
> *The Friday after you told them that they didn't have to go if they didn't want to, there was some talk (Gene not included) of not returning. However, when they considered the alternative of remaining in my room and working on their lessons, they went quite happily. I have noticed since then that Robert often announces to me that he will not go to one of his other classes but will, in the last minute before the bell rings, rush off with a laugh.*

Individual counseling via a client-centered approach might hold more potential for this kind of child than a group experience. At least an initial series of meetings with individuals could function to establish greater client–counselor rapport, as well as orienting the students to the structure of the sessions. Eventually a number of students, counseled individually, could be brought into a group. This approach might precipitate greater coherence and direction to the group and group-counselor behavior.

The sessions were actually geared for verbal interaction. This raises the question as to whether these boys in light of their cultural background and intellectual capacity are capable of dealing with their feelings at a verbal level. Activity therapy or play therapy techniques seem to afford a concrete vehicle, via the activity or play materials, for a verbally limited child to express and become aware of his feelings. The need for spatiality, earlier discussed, may also have been reduced if the group had access to games or other play materials. These activities could serve as a less threatening way for the child to reveal himself to the counselor and to begin to share experiences with the counselor.

Some of the research reviewed on therapy with the mentally retarded stressed permissiveness as a desirable phenomenon, but also depicted the therapist in a much more directive role. A permissive approach with acting-out kinds of children certainly demands a great tolerance for ambiguity and faith in the technique by the therapist. The movement from permissiveness to directness as reported in other studies, may be as much related to the therapist's anxiety as to any formulated notions about what might benefit the children on a long term basis. Is a highly permissive approach to counseling where regressive and acting-out behavior are likely to be precipitated, tolerable in most public schools?

While it is true that, in a sense, more questions have been raised than answered by this particular paper, it is felt that the issue of counseling with the retarded does merit additional discussion. The trend toward special classes is increasing and much more attention is going to have to be given to affective-adjustment factors if their educational experiences are to prepare these kinds of children for a productive adult life.

REFERENCES

Cotzin, Milton, "Group Psychotherapy with Mentally Defective Problem Boys." *American Journal of Mental Deficiency,* 1948, *53,* pp. 268–283.

Dewey, C. S. "Empathy vs. Spatiality in Counseling Encounter." *Chicago Schools Journal,* May, 1965, pp. 355–9.

Fine, M. J. "Security Patterns of Normal and Educable Mentally Retarded Boys." *The Bulletin of the Institute of Child Study* (University of Toronto), 1965, *27,* pp. 13–17.

Fisher, Louise, and Wolfson, I. N. "Group Therapy of Mental Defectives." *American Journal of Mental Deficiency,* 1953, *57,* pp. 463–476.

Rogers, C. R. *Client-Centered Therapy.* Boston, Houghton Mifflin, 1951.

Slavson, S. R. *An Introduction to Group Therapy.* New York: The Commonwealth Fund, 1943.

Woody, R. H. and Billy, J. J. "Counseling and Psychotherapy for the Mentally Retarded: A Survey of Opinions and Practices," *Mental Retardation,* 1966, *4,* pp. 20–23.

REVIEW OF CONCEPTS FOR TEACHING THE MENTALLY RETARDED [1]

JEAN ITARD (EARLY NINETEENTH CENTURY)

Itard emphasized sensory-motor exercises to provide competency in audition, vision, touch, and taste. Fundamental academic skills—vocabulary, comprehension, and the ability to generalize, for example—were taught from concrete examples.

[1] See the Bibliography on pp. 630–653 for specific references to the theories summarized here.

EDWARD SEGUIN (MID-NINETEENTH CENTURY)

"The physiological method" was a refinement of Itard's ideas, which emphasized the development of imperfect sense organs, supplemented by academic and occupational training.

MARIA MONTESSORI (EARLY TWENTIETH CENTURY)

The program was a refinement of the ideas of Froebel and Pestalozzi, using the natural setting as a background and providing sensory-motor training. An attitude of apparent permissiveness with regard to choice of activities was emphasized, although direction for self-help was provided. It closely resembles present programs for the trainable mentally retarded.

ALICE DESCOEUDRES (1920s)

Based on Dewey's concept of "learning by doing," the program correlated subject matter around a "theme." It emphasized perceptual defects and provided individual instruction for overcoming or compensating for such defects.

ANNIE D. INSKEEP (1920s)

The regular curriculum was modified by "watering it down." Retarded children were taught fewer skills, less material, and at a slower pace than normal children.

JOHN DUNCAN (1930s)

The "project method" utilized many manual activities and correlated academic subject matter with shop work, crafts, and home economics.

RICHARD HUNGERFORD AND MARCELLA DOUGLAS (LATE 1930s AND 1940s)

The emphasis here was on preparation for employment. Occupational information was correlated with academic materials and a formal program of guidance, vocational training, selective job placement, and on-the-job placement. The method utilized a series of core curricula beginning with the central theme of the home and developing through the role of the worker in the community. The program is more widely known as "Occupational Education."

CHRISTINE P. INGRAM (MID-1930s)

The classroom became a laboratory for living through the development of "units of work" based on real-life experiences. Units were based on the developmental characteristics of children. The correlation-of-materials concept, as described by J. E. W. Wallin several years earlier, was also emphasized.

ALFRED STRAUSS, LAURA LEHTINEN, AND NEWELL KEPHART (EARLY 1940s)

A distinctive methodology, based on the etiological classification of "endogenous or exogenous" retardation, was developed. Experimental psychological techniques, such as cues or crutches to deal with exaggerated tendencies of brain-injured children, were used. A considerable amount of individual instruction was provided to deal with such specific problems as perseveration, hyperactivity, distractability, and perceptual disturbances.

ELISE H. MARTENS, SAMUEL A. KIRK, AND G. O. JOHNSON (EARLY 1930s AND LATER)

(More recently elaborated by Herbert Goldstein and Dorothy Seigle.) This "eclectic method" utilized units of work based on persistent life situations and took into consideration the developmental needs and characteristics of retarded children. The program, articulated from early childhood through adolescence, emphasized personal-social adjustment and occupational competence. Retarded children were integrated with normal children in nonacademic activities.

FLORA DALY, LEO CAIN, AND IVAN GARRISON (EARLY 1950s AND LATER)

This is a secondary education program for the retarded—a recent development. The curriculum has as its nucleus experiences in the home and family living, societal relationships, and guidance, imposed upon the teaching of tool subjects with personal and occupational adjustment as the major goal. The subject matter is occupationally oriented and noncompartmentalized, and a maximum degree of integration in regular activity courses is encouraged. The complete program would include prevocational testing and exploration, in-school vocational training, and finally a supervised school-work period with job placement as the ultimate goal.

LOUIS ROSENZWEIG, JULIA LONG, AND BERNICE BAUMGARTNER (LATE 1950s AND LATER)

A program for the trainable retarded to develop self-help, social, motor, academic, vocational, and recreational skills. Centered in a sheltered school environment, the curriculum has as its guide the persistent demands of daily living as outlined by the Vineland Scale of Social Maturity. Academic work is based on the idea of "learning for survival purposes." Goals are training in sensory acuity, cooperative behavior, and future possible adjustment within a terminal sheltered workshop, employment under sheltered and highly supervised conditions, or possible institutionalization.

LAWRENCE J. PETER AND ROBERT M. SMITH (1960s)

Developed the concept of prescriptive and clinical teaching methods. This provides for a systematic approach to translate diagnostic information into usable remedial therapy to ameliorate any specific learning disabilities that retardates exhibit.

OGDEN LINDSLEY, GERARD BENSBERG, NORMAN ELLIS AND ALFRED BAUMEISTER (1960s)

The application of experimental psychological techniques, adapted from the work of B. F. Skinner, to modify behavior through operant conditioning techniques. This approach has been highly successful with profoundly retarded children.

SPECIAL PROGRAMS IN THE PUBLIC SCHOOL SYSTEM

EDUCABLE MENTALLY RETARDED: ELEMENTARY LEVEL (CA 6–14)

The Homogeneous Special Class

Effective with a narrow range of chronological and mental ages. Nondepartmentalized program with special-class teacher providing experiences in correlated educational materials and with some degree of integration with regular-class pupils in general school activities. Ordinarily organized in school systems with a large enough number of pupils to make up classes at the lower-primary, upper-primary, and junior high-school levels.

The Heterogeneous Special Class

Invariably encompassing a great range of chronological and mental ages and usually limited to fifteen children. Nondepartmentalized and usually highly segregated program. Dependent upon the skill of the special-class teacher to provide a great variety of activities. Typically organized in small school systems.

The "Two-track" Homogeneous Class [1]

Similar to the homogeneous special-class pattern, except that at each level special classes are organized for upper-level educables (IQ's 65–80) and lower-level educables (IQ's 50–65). The attempt here is to provide special opportunities for children with greater and lesser potential for social, educational, and vocational adjustment. Probably limited to large city school systems with heavy enrollments in special classes. Also useful at the junior-senior-high-school levels.

The Special School

A highly segregated scheme. Children are transported from various areas to a center for the mentally retarded. Ordinarily organized on several levels with some degree of departmentalization. At times, classes for the trainable retarded are also included in the special school. Usually operated in large cities or counties.

Other Types of Plans

1. Placement of one or a few educable pupils in regular classes where enrollment is small and the teacher is able to supervise individual work and to consult with a special-education supervisor.

[1] J. Wayne Wrightstone, *et al., A Comparison of Educational Outcomes under Single-Track and Two-Track Plans for Educable Mentally Retarded Children,* Cooperative Research Project No. 144, U. S. Office of Education, 1960. Conducted by the Board of Education of the City of New York through the University of the State of New York.

2. Placement in a special class for part of the school day and a regular class for the remainder of the day. The special-teacher would spend approximately half the school day providing individual instruction for educable and regular-class pupils requiring remedial instruction.

EDUCABLE MENTALLY RETARDED: SECONDARY LEVEL (CA 12½–18)

The Integrated Special Class

A modified plan. Approximately three periods per day are devoted to a special class with an adjusted core program of language arts, social sciences, arithmetic, and general science. An additional three or four periods per day may be spent in regular classes in industrial arts, home economics, physical education, music, arts and crafts, typing, and other activity courses, depending upon the pupil's ability, needs, and interests. Emphasis is placed on personal adjustment through guidance. The subject matter is often taught in relationship to occupational adjustment. Many secondary schools are experimenting with school-work and exploratory prevocational programs.

The "Two-track" Homogeneous Class

Similar to the elementary two-track program. The upper-educable group is given special occupational training for employment in competitive industry. The lower-educable group is guided toward low-level job placement or sheltered workshop training. The curriculum is similar to that taught in an integrated class.

The Special Occupational High School

An antique in some large cities. A "special" high school for mentally retarded pupils. The emphasis is on training for unskilled and certain types of apprenticeship jobs.

The Adjusted Regular-class Program

Pupils are placed in the "slow" sections of regular classes. They receive some individual attention in the form of personal guidance and remedial work.

TRAINABLE MENTALLY RETARDED

The Special Center or School

A segregated special school, providing training for all CA levels in homogeneous classes. Often includes a preschool and sheltered workshop plan to round out the total school program.

The Special Class

A class in a regular school, usually limited to one class for a heterogeneous group of trainable children.

The Community School

Similar to the special center, but operated and financed by a cooperative group, as in Ohio (operated by the State Department of Mental Hygiene, county welfare departments, and local public schools; financed by tuition charges). Another version of this plan is the parent-sponsored community school, which, in most cases, is eventually integrated into the local public school's special-education program. These schools often have preschool and postschool programs.

A FRAMEWORK FOR CONSIDERING SOME ISSUES IN SPECIAL EDUCATION

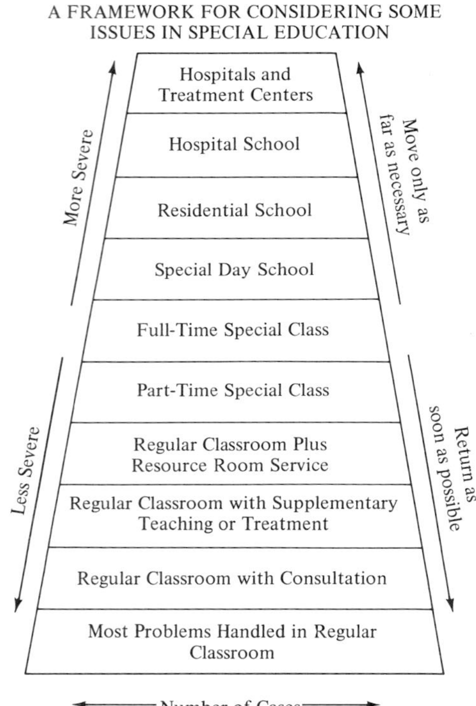

Source: James Gallagher in *PCMR Message*, July, 1969, p. 2.

SECTION SIX

Secondary School Programs for the Mentally Retarded

The development of secondary school programs for educable mentally retarded pupils was a direct result of the recognition of the need for additional training, especially in occupational areas. Prior to World War II, except for a few isolated instances, most retardates remained in elementary special classes until the age of sixteen. They invariably dropped out of school at that time, totally unprepared for economic and social independence. A few school districts have had high school programs for this group for many years, but frequently the retarded group was segregated or placed in purely vocational training schools.

The modern secondary school system, with its high degree of holding power, has, in many situations, accepted the challenge of developing suitable programs for mentally retarded adolescents. Oriented to the primary psychological characteristic of teen-agers—the desire for conformity and peer acceptance—the evolving program is highly integrated with regular classes and emphasizes personal and occupational adjustment.

American public schools follow three basic organizational patterns: (1) the 8–4 plan (elementary plus four-year high school); (2) the 6–3–3 plan (elementary, junior high, and senior high), and (3) the 6–6 plan (elementary plus a combined junior–senior high). Thus, one of the vexing problems facing program development is how to fit suitable special-class programs into these varying patterns. A high-level secondary school program for the educable mentally retarded should include a core of common learnings that is directly related to occupational adjustment. Services must include guidance, prevocational testing and try-out periods, in-school exploratory work projects, school work plans, selective job placement, and some degree of supervision in the early phase of employment. The latter two functions are carried out in many systems in cooperation with rehabilitation services, state employment agencies, and community service groups.

With the enactment of the Vocational Education Amendments (Public Law 90-576), a new force for providing human development resources for mentally retarded youth was created. Through this legislation, several previous vocational education acts (Smith–Hughes Act, George–Barden Act, and the Vocational Education Act of 1963) have been updated and their major provisions extended to the handicapped. Under the new amendments, federal funds are earmarked for disadvantaged persons and for persons who have completed or left high school and are available for school or specialized programs for the mentally retarded. This act provides that 10 percent of each state's allotment of federal funds appropriated for vocational education be earmarked for handicapped youth. Additionally, federal funds are provided for: (1) the training of vocational education teachers preparing to work with the mentally retarded, and (2) research or experimental, developmental, or pilot programs designed to meet the special needs of the retarded.

In the first reading, Charles J. Kokaska identifies the early beginnings of secondary programs for the educable mentally retarded, the major influences upon their growth, and the development of three aspects of work experience: the role of the employer; the expansion of school services, and the problem of general versus specific skill training. In addition, data are included related to the enrollments and vocational placement of urban secondary special education programs. This is followed by a unique article by Professor I. Gardner in which he reviews research data concerned with social and emotional adjustment characteristics of mildly retarded children and adolescents. Contrary to a number of statements appearing in various texts and review articles, little is known concerning the type and frequency of occurrence of behavior adjustment problems among the mildly retarded. In addition, there is no suitable evidence to indicate that the adjustment level of special class children and youth is superior to that of retarded children attending regular classes. In Reading 27, Rudolph J. Capobianco and Helen Jacoby provide a description and rationale for a suitable secondary education program for the mentally retarded. They indicate that there is a continuing increase in the number of mildly retarded youngsters who remain in public schools, thus making it necessary for educators to provide a more realistic educational program for the mentally retarded segment of the school population. The Fairfax Plan is a three-year structured program specifically designed to habilitate these students. The planned academic curriculum is a functional part of the program. Completion of specified courses, in addition to vocational work training, entitles the student to a Diploma in Vocational Special Education. The evaluation of this program includes difference measures between demonstration and control groups as well as an analysis of the salient characteristics of various subgroups with segregated male and female classes. This section is concluded by a report by Richard L. Shick in which he briefly reviews the concepts of a work experience program and provides the reader with a substantial annotated listing of various classroom instructional materials.

25 SECONDARY EDUCATION FOR THE RETARDED: A BRIEF HISTORICAL REVIEW

Charles J. Kokaska

From *Education and Training of the Mentally Retarded,* Vol. 3, No. 1, February 1968, pp. 17–26. Reprinted with the permission of The Council for Exceptional Children and the author. Dr. Kokaska is Assistant Professor, Department of Educational Psychology and Social Foundations, California State College, Long Beach.

The development of programs for the educable mentally retarded at the senior high school level has been a relatively recent phenomenon in the history of American education. One of the difficulties in locating the exact date of origin is due to the fact that educators spoke of special education programs as being located in a senior high school facility, but regarded the retarded's secondary education as complete at sixteen years old, which in most states was the compulsory school attendance age. A good example of this may be found in Lovell and Ingram's (1947) description of a two-year training program for mentally retarded females in Rochester, New York, which had its genesis in 1939. From its conception, students took part in regular high school activities, but the seventh and eighth year program "did not lead to graduation."

By 1939, and certainly in the early 1940s, high school programs existed in several larger cities, i.e., Cleveland, Los Angeles, Newark, and New York ("Educational Provisions for Mentally Deficient Adolescents," 1942; Hungerford, 1941; Hungerford and Rosenzweig, 1944; Mones, 1941, 1948). Hungerford (personal communication, 1966) described the organization of one of these early programs.

> In Detroit both the educable and certain borderlines had access to certain actual or equivalent senior high education. Some went to trade schools, roughly equivalent to the vocational high schools of New York City. However, in Detroit the special (educable) and special preparatory (borderline) in the trade schools had no special status; they became a part of the general school population.
>
> The special and special preparation pupils in Detroit also could go to special schools (for those CA 13 or over) where they completed their schooling. And there also was one special class in a senior, academic high school, where pupils had a special teacher for academic subjects but joined regular students for shop, gym, and "cultural" subjects. The above three-phase administrative program was in effect in Detroit in 1939 and was largely the creation of Anna Engel.

In reviewing the early development of high school programs during the late 1930s and early 1940s, one may discern an increased interest in the ability of the retarded to assume a productive role in society, primarily in the vocational sphere. Hungerford (1941) identified this concern in stating that the mentally retarded had become less able, in relation to workers as a whole, to meet employment demands. His subsequent formulation of the concept of "occupational education" was intended to shift the educator's allegiance from an emphasis on what he regarded as banal philosophies to one that placed a vigorous emphasis upon the retarded's ability to assume vocational responsibility if given the proper training.

At the same time, other educators felt that, although the retarded may not be able to profit from inclusion in regular high school classes, there was another value of social enjoyment and enrichment to be gained from their involvement in the school community. Due to their similarity in chronological age and size, it was consistent with an enlightened philosophy of education to place the retarded with their peers. It was obviously socially reprehensible and demeaning to place adolescents, and sometimes young adults, in educational units with elementary school aged children.

THE INFLUENCE OF THE SECOND WORLD WAR

One may note that the above changes took place during a period in our nation's history during which modifications and adjustments were occurring throughout the social structure. It is the investigator's opinion that the Second World War both assisted and delayed the growth of special programs in two ways.

The war created a deficit in labor supply, thereby allowing every employable individual, retarded or not, an opportunity to work. Those school programs which included provisions for occupational education were able to meet the labor market situation, since they centered their attention upon providing the student with the social and vocational skills necessary for successful employment. Later follow-up studies and program progress reports drew upon those students who left school and found employment during the war years to demonstrate the retarded's employability and their many capabilities.

However, the manpower shortage was such that students had only to wait until their sixteenth birthday to seek active employment. As a result, most school systems only provided education and training until that age.

It wasn't until 1945 that evidence began to appear in the literature to the effect that some of the larger city school systems were organizing programs which extended from the elementary years through senior high school (Femiami, 1945). These ventures were not without their problems of teacher resistance, program coordination, instructional quality, and student selection (Backal, 1947; Dosek, 1946; Hollingshead, 1949).

Gradually, educators began to think of the total expanse of the learning process in a context in which those who were given labels such as "mentally handicapped," "ungraded," "special," "Binet students," "slow learners," or "students with retarded mental development" could be assigned a position within the structure and community of the secondary school. There were three modifications in the conceptualization of secondary education which helped alter previous attitudes (Hegge, 1949; Levisohn, 1949; Mones, 1948):

1. The public high school could no longer be thought of as a selective institution in the sense that it would identify those intellectually unqualified to attend college. It had been transformed into an essential educational step for all of the nation's children, and therefore was required to develop the necessary curriculum to prepare all of those students.
2. Considering the increased numbers of students that would enter secondary education and the expanded role that the high schools would exercise, educators began to discuss the total amount of responsibility that they must accept and exercise for the benefit of society.
3. Educators began to understand the dynamics of social contact that exists within the secondary school community and its direct effect upon the students' social and civic nurturing.

The end of the war not only brought about new realizations concerning the goals, purposes, and functions of public education, but also prompted modifications in industrial organization. Mones (1949) identified the effects of industrial alterations upon the school's role with the retarded.

> As industry abolished its apprenticeship systems, as laws abolished street-trades and other work-opportunities for young people, we had to take them into our schools [p. 49].

These changes not only influenced the schools as far as their provisions for in-school programing were concerned, but also accentuated the fact that if these programs were going to lead to some form of postschool occupational success, special educators would have to rely upon other community agencies to assist them. One such agency was the United States Employment Service, which cooperated with school systems in such cities as Rochester, New York, and St. Louis, Missouri, to help counsel and place students in community jobs (Murray and DiMichael, 1950). The extent of the cooperation appeared to have been only in the direction of stimulating effective communication between the school and agency, and although this cooperation in itself was an important accomplishment, it signaled the beginnings of what would, in time, prove to be a powerful alliance between the public school systems and agencies of the federal government.

THE INFLUENCE OF THE FEDERAL GOVERNMENT

Although written primarily for vocational rehabilitation counselors, the publication in 1950 of *Vocational Rehabilitation of the Mentally Retarded*

(DiMichael, 1950) by the federal government marked another development in secondary programing on a level equal to that of the importance of the occupational education philosophy. The publication provided reviews of several functioning programs at the secondary level, as well as previous follow-up studies of the occupational accomplishments of the retarded. In other words, it served as the first major centralization of information relevant to the vocational training of the adolescent retarded.

Secondly, it introduced the next logical step in programing, namely, the necessity of the diploma and of supervised work experience or work study. Both ingredients represented a sophistication which would place special education in a new relationship to the rest of the educational structure of which, up until that time, it had only been an adopted sister.

Finally, it documented the organization of a cooperative relationship between the Minnesota Division of Vocational Rehabilitation and the Minneapolis Public High School System. The arrangement developed when rehabilitation counselors noted that the two year discrepancy between the compulsory school attendance age (16) and the minimum working age (18) resulted in high rates of unemployment for special class members who were not in school during those years. The discovery resulted in a program which would hold the student for a few more years while specifically preparing him for the working world. The joint effort included testing, counseling, curriculum development, and student selection, and may be considered a prototype of the several cooperative arrangements that began to appear in the late 1950s and, principally, the 1960s.

One must not be misled into thinking that the Minneapolis project initiated a golden age in special education. Kirk's (Kirk, Black, Duffin, Garrison, and Johnson, 1951) review of secondary provisions for the retarded illuminated the same problem that motivated the above arrangement. "No satisfactory program has evolved which has made possible the holding of most of these children beyond compulsory age limits [p. 8]." Kirk's recommendations for containing students were similar to Hungerford's in the sense that both men sought to change the educator's conceptualization of the special class curriculum. The former focused on areas of experience and personal guidance, but clearly identified the ultimate aim.

> The heart of the program for the mentally handicapped in the high school is one of general information, of development of skills needed in broad vocational areas, and of familiarization of the pupils with vocational possibilities [Kirk, *et al.,* 1951, p. 43].

Despite the initial beginnings of federal assistance, the development of other large cooperative projects did not occur again until the late 1950s. During the intervening years, additional organizational reports appeared in the literature which indicated that several school systems throughout the country were continuing their efforts to confront a growing problem (Allen and Retherford, 1955; Wickliffe, 1955). However, it was Keney's (1955) opinion that the development of special programs was lacking in too many states while the nation witnessed rising unemployment and delinquency rates among teenagers. It was during these years that educators, vocational rehabilitation personnel, parents, and others increased their attention and efforts to construct school experiences that prepared the retarded for vocational success.

THE EMPHASIS ON WORK EXPERIENCE

Special educators have been writing about preparing the retarded for work since their programs first began. After all, economic survival is one of the basic educational goals.

> There is probably no aspect of education of mentally retarded children which is more important than that which concerns itself with the social and occupational adjustments in adult life [Engel, 1952, p. 80].

The researcher avoided a purely progressive discussion of the historical development of this aspect of secondary education, due to the fact that the term work experience or work study refers to one of the more recent additions; rather, attention was focused upon three areas which concern program directors.

The Role of the Employer

One may state that, in reading the early literature on work experience, the emphasis in this area was on the careful selection and placement of students in employment situations. One may conceive of the placement procedure as a "buyer's market" in which educators or vocational rehabilitation counselors had to present convincing arguments to "sell" their clients. It is possible that the threat of failure hung heavy over placement programs, thereby emphasizing the divisions and delicate relations between the school and prospective employer.

The essential breakthrough in the area of employer relations developed when the entire community, including the industrial leaders of the geographic area, was organized to promote the retarded's vocational opportunity. One such effort was described in a report of the organization of a Citizens' Advisory Committee of a work experience program in Dayton, Ohio.

> A Citizens' Advisory Committee was organized when the project began. It consisted of 26 leading business men, labor representatives, and members of the Ohio State Employment Service.
>
> The committee was organized to communicate with business and industry and to gain their support for the program. Since many of the

> members represented large business and manufacturing concerns, their function was not designed to provide jobs for the program. Rather their public, personal, and organizational endorsement helped develop community acceptance. It was felt that acceptance by top labor and management was necessary for the initiation and continuation of the project [McPherson and Stephens, 1964, p. 9].

Secondly, new opportunities were opened when school systems or vocational rehabilitation agencies presented a different kind of proposal to the businessman. This plan was founded on the premise that the school was primarily limited in its training facilities and had to turn to other agencies, including private business, without requiring the financial sustainment of the trainee's salary by the training installation. At the same time, private business was offered an opportunity to directly prepare possible future employees (if they cared to entertain such ideas) without having to absorb the financial expense that normally accompanies the training period.

By the late 1950s, school systems had established several forms of cooperative relationships with business and industry to secure the training locations that the retarded so desperately needed (Garrison, 1956; Vocational Rehabilitation Administration, 1961). These arrangements extended from a relationship in which the business establishment functioned as a training site but not an employer, to one in which the establishment would both train and eventually absorb the student. Financial sustainment included situations in which the student received training and a small wage which was supported by the state vocational rehabilitation agency. In some instances, the state decreased its financial assistance to a training site as the student became more proficient at the job, thus requiring the installation to increase its financial investment (Richman and Spinelli, 1961). In other situations, the students would not only be trained at a particular establishment, but would also progress into future employment with the same firm (Shawn, 1964).

There was an additional effort in the 1960s to influence possible employers of the retarded. The researcher refers to the publications by agencies of the federal government (President's Committee on Employment of the Handicapped, 1964; Vocational Rehabilitation Administration, 1964a) which were aimed at informing employers of the problems and advantages of hiring the retarded. By providing information relative to the retarded's limitations and capabilities, they attempted to alter employer's social attitudes as well as their business sense.

Not all directors of secondary programs share the opinion that their students should be identified as mentally retarded when placement counselors approach prospective employers. Kalwara (personal communication, 1967) discussed the philosophy and approach of the Phoenix (Arizona) High School System in regards to placing their students, as follows:

> I think it is unfair to the student to take him to a new situation which would include the employer and possibly other workers and say: "Look, here's Charlie, he's mentally retarded, but we feel he can do such and such and will you hire him?" I don't think we used the term "mental retardation" once last year in taking our students out on initial job interviews. This is simply because we felt that these students had social competency, good work habits, the skill for the particular job, and I could see no earthly reason to identify them as retarded. When we used to identify our students, say some four or five years ago, we noticed that it absolutely crushed them. Why should they be regarded as any different if they can do the particular job we are taking them out to do?

It must be pointed out that Kalwara is discussing students who have been prepared for specific positions which also have been carefully screened by the placement people within the school system. However, his opinion is a strong caution to other teachers or counselors who may tend to emphasize the student's retardation more than his ability.

School Programs

The inclusion of cooperative arrangements between the school, public agencies, and private business required alterations in administering programs for the retarded. A great many of the discussions in the literature about work experience are concerned not only with the arrangements between the school and community, but also with the manner in which the objectives of the program can be accomplished while still maintaining some semblance of a school program. In other words, it is a problem of how to gain the best of two possible worlds—the social and educational environment of the school community, and the training and related experiential environment of the working world.

Although differences appear in the literature as to the amount of time that should be spent in work experience during the student's entire high school career, and its allotment over a three or four year program, there is complete agreement to the effect that the student is to participate in some form of evaluation, training, and work experience during his school career (Kolstoe and Frey, 1965).

One of the more recent additions to the work experience programs has been the prevocational evaluation units in the school or community agencies which are established to secure samples of the student's ability in various work tasks before actual skill training is introduced. This ingredient may be traced to the influence of vocational rehabilitation counselors, who have been instrumental in strengthening the school's vocational role with the retarded (Arizona Division of Vocational Rehabilitation, 1965; Deno, Henze, Krantz, and Barklind, 1965; Oklahoma Board for Vocational Education, 1964).

It must be noted that, insofar as the work experience program is concerned, there is evidence to indicate that the various cooperative arrangements have been beneficial to the parties concerned, primarily due to the crossfertilization of ideas which have fostered new attitudes and program innovations. For example, educators have begun to visualize the vocational preparation of the retired as a multidimensional process in which students advance through classroom instruction, in-school work experience, prevocational evaluation, on the job training, vocational placement, and postschool follow-up. Furthermore, each step in the progression contains additional alternatives in order to meet the needs and abilities of any particular individual. The increased sophistication in programing has led DiMichael (1964) to feel that special education students should be classified and receive instruction on the basis of their employment possibilities, i.e., competitively employable, marginal competitively employable, sheltered employable, and marginal sheltered employable. This would require the structuring of school and training programs on the basis of evaluated occupational skills rather than intelligence quotients.

The cooperative arrangements have also provided increased resources in the area of counseling, for both social and vocational purposes. The counseling of students has always received emphasis as educators aspired to prepare the retarded for the social demands they would encounter in the work setting, in addition to the skill demands (DiMichael, 1953; Goldstein and Heber, 1959). The additional resources have allowed educators to experiment with such clinical considerations as multidisciplinary staffings, counseling teams, and expanded assistance to parents (Capobianco and Jacoby, 1966; Oklahoma Board for Vocational Education, 1964).

General versus Specific Skill Training

One of the more urgent problems involved in a work experience program has to do with the type and quality of the training offered to the student. Since the early beginnings of work experience, educators were not only concerned with the vocational success of the retarded, but also with the school's training provisions which would help accomplish that success.

There appears to be a slight confusion in the literature concerning the meaning of the terms general and specific skill training. Some authors regard general skill training as including those activities in the school program designed to prepare the individual in the social and attitudinal elements of work responsibility. In this sense, the term general has nothing to do with the actual physical mastery of an occupational task. Thus, when Mallek (1964) called for an emphasis in work experience programs on specific skill training, he contrasted this with a philosophy which he identified as a generalized effort at training for attitudes and responsibilities.

A second point is that when various authors discuss the abandonment of specific job training, they often are referring to training offered in those jobs in the unskilled or service areas.

> Research has shown that many jobs into which retarded clients are placed require a minimum of specific occupational skills. The minimum skills that may be required can often be learned on the job in a short period of time. As a consequence, many public school programs which formerly stressed specific skill training have abandoned this program in favor of one which stresses development of attributes which may be generalized to any job situation . . . [Vocational Rehabilitation Administration, 1964b, p. 36.]

It is somewhat ironic that the previous quote represents the very thing that Mallek was against. Obviously, the issue hinges upon one's view of where the retarded are to be placed in the community. If they are going to be continually placed in the unskilled or entry level positions, then very little school training is needed since the skills can be learned on the job. However, Mallek raised a consideration of the type of skill training that special educators should be considering for the future.

It is this concern for the future which prompted Capobianco and Jacoby (1966) to express their warning. It was their opinion that since there is greater competition for the unskilled and semiskilled jobs, due to (a) a greater number of entrants into the labor market, and (b) the large high school dropout rate which forces these individuals to seek employment in lower skill areas, then what is needed is an educational program which will provide the retarded with general skills, making them more adaptable to fluctuations in labor force demand. They stressed "some form of competence in a number of work settings rather than developing a specialty [p. 17]."

Obviously, the two authors have moved from a narrow discussion of whether the retarded should be trained as bus boys or office girls to a consideration of the broad framework of the labor market, and the possibility of providing individuals with skills that can be transferred across specific jobs in order to allow the individual to adjust within a rapidly changing industrial technology. The danger of discussing training objectives along a dichotomy of general or specific skills is that in choosing one position, special educators may ignore the possibility that the vocational preparation program is a multidimensional continuum which must include both kinds of skills in order to meet the variety of needs and abilities of their students.

ESTIMATES OF ENROLLMENTS

As one part of this study, the investigator has estimated the total number of students who were enrolled in secondary urban special classes during the 1965–1966 school year and the number that took part in some form of vocational placement. Up until this study, no national statistics were available on secondary classes for the educable retarded. There are some data on vocational placements, but these originate in the statistics released by the Vocational Rehabilitation Administration and include retarded clients of all ages. In addition, not all secondary school systems cooperate in their vocational placements with the Vocational Rehabilitation Administration.

The data were obtained from a survey of a sample of 316 urban secondary school systems that conducted classes for the retarded. The total figure of the population of 1449 systems was obtained from a previous survey of state directors of special education. These systems were stratified according to region and urban population category so that projections could be made from a sample drawn from each subdivision of the population.

The estimated enrollments in secondary special education programs and vocational placements for the 1965–1966 school year were 66,373 and 11,368, respectively. Some difficulty was encountered in attempting to compare these figures with other indicators of enrollment for the retarded at the secondary level. The latest enrollments for the retarded were dated February, 1963 (Simon and Grant, 1966), and indicated that 393,430 students attended public schools. However, the statistics were not subdivided into academic levels.

In order to arrive at some comparative estimates, the investigator calculated that high school enrollments during 1963 constituted 27.1 percent (11,618,000) of the total population in the nation's public schools. Assuming that an equal percentage of the special class enrollments are at the secondary level, the total would be 106,619. However, this study's projections of high school enrollments were only for urban areas. If one considers that approximately 70 percent of the American population resides in urban areas, and this percentage is deducted from the previous total, the estimate is reduced to an enrollment of 74,634 students for 1963–1964.

A second method was also utilized. Enrollments in special education classes for 1963 constituted .96 percent of the total public school population. This percentage was applied to the high school enrollment, although it is hazardous to assume that special education classes at the elementary and secondary level are in the same ratio to the regular classes. A further reduction of the estimated enrollment by the 70 percent factor of urban population resulted in an estimate of 78,072 for the 1963–1964 school year.

In either case, the expected enrollments were in excess of the investigator's projections. In addition, the expected enrollments were computed for the 1963–1964 school year, while the projections were for the 1965–1966 year. An explanation of the apparent low enrollments may be related to the fact that only 4.6 percent of the total number of school districts in the United States (31,705) conduct secondary classes for the educable retarded (Simon and Grant, 1966). This percentage is based on the investigator's tabulation of replies from state directors of special education with lists of secondary programs. It is quite possible that the lack of programs, the relative infancy of those that are in operation, and the existence of other kinds of programs for slow learners and the educationally disadvantaged within urban areas all contribute to what appears to be a low enrollment rate at the secondary level for the educable retarded.

REFERENCES

Allen, Amy, and Retherford, Gwen. A place in high school for the mentally retarded. *Bulletin of the National Association of Secondary School Principals,* 1955, *39,* 25–33.

Arizona Division of Vocational Rehabilitation. *The Phoenix Plan for Special Education Students.* Phoenix, Ariz.: Arizona Division of Vocational Rehabilitation, 1965.

Backal, J. The mentally retarded child in the vocational high school. *High Points,* 1947, *29,* 23–28.

Capobianco, R., and Jacoby, Helen B. The Fairfax plan: a high school program for mildly retarded youth. *Mental Retardation,* 1966, *4,* 15–20.

Deno, Evelyn, Henze, R., Krantz, G., and Barklind, K. *Retarded Youth: Their School-Rehabilitation Needs.* Final report of project RD-681, Vocational Rehabilitation Administration. Minneapolis, Minn.: Minneapolis Public Schools, 1965.

DiMichael, S. G. (Editor) *Vocational Rehabilitation of the Mentally Retarded.* Washington: Government Printing Office, 1950.

DiMichael, S. G. Vocational rehabilitation for the mentally retarded. *Personnel and Guidance Journal,* 1953, *31,* 428–432.

DiMichael, S. G. Providing full vocational opportunities for retarded adolescents and adults. *Journal of Rehabilitation,* 1964, *30,* 10–12, 30–31.

Dosek, A. The CRMD goes to high school. *High Points,* 1946, *28,* 34–39.

Educational provisions for mentally deficient adolescents. *American Journal of Mental Deficiency,* 1942, *47,* 79–99.

Engel, Anna M. Employment of the mentally retarded. In S. G. DiMichael (Editor), *Vocational Rehabilitation of the Mentally Retarded.* Washington; Government Printing Office, 1950. Pp. 80–107.

Femiami, Winifred. The mentally retarded go to high school. *High Points,* 1945, *27,* 23–32.

Garrison, I. K. Special programs for the mentally retarded in secondary school. In P. M. Halverson (Editor), *Frontiers of Secondary Education.* Volume 1. Syracuse: Syracuse University, 1956. Pp. 85–95.

Goldstein, H., and Heber, R. F. Summary of the conference. In H. Goldstein and R. F. Heber (Editors), *Preparation of Mentally Retarded Youth for Gainful Employment.* Washington: Government Printing Office, 1959. Pp. 23–28.

Hegge, T. G. Education for mentally retarded pupils of senior high school age. *American Journal of Mental Deficiency,* 1949, *54,* 190–191.

Hollingshead, M. T. Selective techniques used in the placement of mentally retarded boys and girls in the secondary schools. *American Journal of Mental Deficiency,* 1949, *53,* 562–567.

Hungerford, R. H. The Detroit plan for the occupational education of the mentally retarded. *American Journal of Mental Deficiency,* 1941, *46,* 102–108.

Hungerford, R. H., and Rosenzweig, L. E. The mentally retarded. *Journal of Exceptional Children,* 1944, *10,* 210–213.

Kelley, Elizabeth M. Are we providing opportunities for the older mentally retarded? *Exceptional Children,* 1955, *21,* 297–309.

Kirk, S., et al. Educating the mentally handicapped in the secondary schools. *Curricular Series* A, No. 51, Illinois secondary school curriculum program bulletin No. 12. Springfield, Illinois: Office of the State Superintendent of Public Instruction, 1951.

Kolstoe, O. P., and Frey, R. M. *A High School Work–Study Program for Mentally Subnormal Students.* Carbondale, Ill.: Southern Illinois Press, 1965.

Levisohn, Hortense H. What program for the slow learner? *Bulletin of the National Association of Secondary School Principals,* 1949, *33,* 58–64.

Lovell, Catherine, and Ingram, Christine P. A high school program for mentally retarded adolescent girls. *Journal of Educational Research,* 1947, *40,* 574–582.

Mallek, N. S. Grossmount Union High School program. In F. E. Lord (Editor), *Work Education for Educable Retarded Youth: Report on Institutes.* Los Angeles: California State College Bookstore, 1964. P. 33.

McPherson, H., and Stephens, T. M. *Developing a Work–Experience Program for Slow Learning Youth: A Report of a Three-Year Extension and Improvement Project of the Ohio Bureau of Vocational Rehabilitation.* Columbus, Ohio: Ohio Bureau of Vocational Rehabilitation, 1964.

Mones, L. Experimenting with mentally retarded pupils in high school. *American Journal of Mental Deficiency,* 1941, *46,* 89–93.

Mones, L. The Binet pupils get a chance. *School and Society,* 1948, *67,* 281–283.

Mones, L. What programs for the slow learner? *Bulletin of the National Association of Secondary School Principals,* 1949, *33,* 47–58.

Murray, Evelyn, and DiMichael, S. G. Employment for the mentally retarded. *Employment Security Review,* 1950, *17,* 30–32.

Oklahoma Board for Vocational Education, Division of Rehabilitation Service. *A Cooperative Program of Special Education–Vocational Rehabilitation.* Final report of grant RD-771, Vocational Rehabilitation Administration. Oklahoma City: Oklahoma Vocational Rehabilitation Service, 1964.

President's Committee on Employment of the Handicapped. *Guide to Job Placement of the Mentally Retarded.* Washington: Government Printing Office, 1964.

Richman, S., and Spinelli, W. C. New York's work–study program. *Rehabilitation Record.* 1961, *2,* 20–22.

Shawn, B. Review of a work–experience program *Mental Retardation,* 1964, *2,* 360–364.

Simon, K. A., and Grant, W. V. *Digest of educational statistics, 1966.* Washington: Government Printing Office, 1966.

Vocational Rehabilitation Administration. *Preparation of Mentally Retarded Youth for Gainful Employment.* Washington: Government Printing Office, 1961.

Vocational Rehabilitation Administration. *So You Are Going to Supervise a Mentally Retarded Employee.* Washington: Government Printing Office, 1964. (a)

Vocational Rehabilitation Administration. *Special Problems in Vocational Rehabilitation of the Mentally Retarded.* Washington: Government Printing Office, 1964. (b)

Wickliffe, Letty M. Reports from the field-description of programs in action. *Bulletin of the National Association of Secondary School Principals,* 1955, *39,* 45–55.

26 SOCIAL AND EMOTIONAL ADJUSTMENT OF MILDLY RETARDED CHILDREN AND ADOLESCENTS: CRITICAL REVIEW

William I. Gardner

From *Exceptional Children,* Vol. 33, No. 2, October 1966, pp. 97–105. Reprinted with the permission of the Council for Exceptional Children and the author. Dr. Gardner is Professor and Chairman, Department on Behavioral Disabilities, University of Wisconsin, Madison.

Recent publications (Beier, 1964; Robinson and Robinson, 1965; Sarason and Gladwin, 1958) report that behavioral disturbances among the mentally retarded have a high rate of occurrence. In reviewing the evidence, however, it becomes apparent that little is available which bears directly on the question of the occurrence of such disorders among noninstitutionalized mildly retarded children and adolescents. While some data are available on the institutionalized retarded, these can hardly be viewed as characteristic of those residing in the community, since behavioral disturbance is one of the major factors determining institutionalization.

The present paper will review the available evidence which has relevance to the following questions: What types of behavior problems occur among the school age noninstitutionalized mildly retarded? What is the rate of occurrence of these types of problems, and how does this rate compare with that of the nonretarded? Are there sex and age differences in type and rate? Are there differences in type and prevalence of problems between those who attend special education programs and those who remain in the regular grades? This last question, as noted by Johnson (1963b), is of interest since one would expect the program of the special class to be more conducive to desirable emotional and social development.

In searching for data pertaining to these questions, the writer was impressed with various statements concerning behavior disorders among the mentally retarded which did not appear to be justified on the basis of the supporting data provided. Since such statements could lead the reader to draw inappropriate conclusions, brief discussion of a sample of these statements should be of value prior to a review of other pertinent data.

Garrison and Force (1965) report, "There is considerable evidence that maladjustment looms large among mentally retarded children" (p. 446). These authors summarize the first of two studies presented in support of this conclusion as follows: "An early study by Lurie (1935) dealt with the types of problems encountered by 1000 mentally retarded boys and girls referred to a child guidance clinic" (p. 447). Lurie's summary of the article, published in 1937, differs substantially from the previous statement: "In a series of 1000 children studied at the Child Guidance Home, 15.7 percent rated as definitely feebleminded; 18 percent rated as borderline cases of probable mental defect; and 22.5 percent rated as subnormal" (p. 1033).

The object of the study was to determine the nature of problems of children who were intellectually subnormal as defined by intelligence quotients in the 80 to 89 range. This study, while possibly suggestive of types of problems which may occur among the mentally retarded, offers nothing of a definitive nature to support the statement "that maladjustment looms large among mentally retarded children."

The second study presented in support of the maladjustment statement was one reported by Hinkelman (1951). In this study, scores on the California Test of Personality of subjects forming an upper intellectual group were compared with scores obtained from those forming a lower intellectual group. Subjects were attending seventh grade in public schools. Hinkelman reported significant differences in the sections of the test concerning self-adjustment and social and total adjustment.

These results, however, are of questionable applicability to the mentally retarded. The mean intelligence quotient reported for the subjects forming the lower intellectual group was 89.48. Although no index of variability was provided, it is evident from other data in the report that the lowest intelligence quotient for subjects of this group was 69. As the intermediate form of the personality test was used, one can assume that most of the subjects were well within the 80's and 90's in intellectual quotient level; otherwise, it would be highly unlikely that they would have been able to read or comprehend the questions of the test. Again, evidence presented by Garrison and Force in support of their "maladjustment looms large" statement may be relevant to the slow learner, but not to children who are typically viewed as mentally retarded.

A statement by Johnson (1963a) provides a second illustration of an error in appropriately representing reported data relative to the question of behavioral adjustment level of the mentally retarded. In considering personal adjustment differences between mentally retarded children attending regular classes with those in special classes, Johnson stated, "Blatt compared mentally retarded children in special classes with those in regular classes. He found the special class children are socially more mature and emotionally stable" (p. 471). Although Johnson's statement is taken almost verbatim from the Blatt reference, Johnson neglected to include Blatt's (1958) highly limiting qualification that "comparisons were based on Scales that have no established validity or reliability . . ." (p. 818).

The scales referred to were the New York Scales of Social Maturity and Emotional Stability. In addition, Blatt presented other evidence which does not support the Johnson statement. He indicated that neither California Test of Personality scores nor school records and teacher interviews revealed differences between regular and special class children.

Although one could readily question the adequacy of the California

Test of Personality as a measure of personal and social adjustment of mentally retarded children, it would appear that greater reliance could be placed on this test and the teacher interviews than on "Scales that have no established validity or reliability." Apparently, Johnson was not of this opinion, although in a later study (Johnson, 1961) he did use the California Test of Personality in evaluating personal adjustment of the retarded.

As another illustration, Heber (1964) commented in a review article, "A number of studies have reported a greatly increased incidence of behavioral disorders among retarded children attending special classes in public schools" and further, "The results [of studies of retarded children in schools] suggest that there is a strikingly high incidence of behavior disorders serious enough to warrant the attention . . . of the schools" (p. 306). Little support for these conclusions, however, is provided by the studies (Blatt, 1958; Trippe, McCaffrey, Dempsey, and Downing, 1959; Enos, 1961) reviewed by Heber.

In reference to the Blatt study, Heber concluded, "Blatt has reported a greater frequency of behavior disorders among retarded children remaining in regular classes as well as among those in special classes" (p. 306). Apparently this is a summary of Blatt's (1958) statement that "When compared with norms for typical children, the special class children and the regular class children have more problems in personal adjustment and social adjustment than typical children" (p. 816). This conclusion appears to be based on California Test of Personality data. As will be discussed later, the present writer takes the position that California Test of Personality results with the retarded should be viewed with caution.

The Trippe *et al.* (1959) study was concerned with identification of characteristics of children in a community who were not enrolled in a state or community institution or an accredited course of instruction. Although behavior and management problems were present among many of the 83 children studied, the findings of this study have little applicability to a consideration of problems among the mildly retarded, as most of the subjects were moderately or severely retarded. In addition, such a study can offer little concerning the rate of occurrence of problems among the retarded, since the representativeness of the sample is unknown. What percentage of the school population does the Trippe sample represent? How would the rate of occurrence of behavior problems compare with the rate in the nonretarded population? These questions cannot be answered on the basis of the data presented.

The Enos (1961) study reported that retarded boys made better adjustment than the normal male groups studied. Again, these studies offer little in support of Heber's "greatly increased incidence" statement.

As a final example, Hutt and Gibby (1965) state, "the mentally retarded child may show unusually severe behavioral reactions during puberty, even more so than those shown by the child of more average intelligence.

This is demonstrated by a study by Foale on the incidence of psychoneuroses in mentally retarded children. He pointed out that while only 6 percent of normal adolescents develop psychoneurotic reactions, 12 percent of mentally retarded adolescents show such personality involvements" (p. 223). An examination of the Foale (1956) reference reveals the statement "According to Burt six percent of normal adolescents are neurotic, but 12 percent of mental defective adolescents" (p. 868). As Foale did not include a reference list, the basis for the Burt statement could not be identified.

It is evident, contrary to the textbook and research review summary statements presented, that the studies reviewed up to this point provide little of a conclusive nature that would suggest that mildly retarded children are characterized by an unusual incidence of emotional or behavioral adjustment problems. Additional studies will be discussed in terms of the type of measurement approach used to evaluate the personal and social adjustment status of the mentally retarded.

PROJECTIVE CLINICAL EVALUATION STUDIES

A recent study reported by both Klausmeier and Check (1959) and by Enos (1961) provides some suggestion of satisfactory adjustment of the mentally retarded. Included among the numerous questions investigated by this study were those of the relationships between intelligence and the variables of emotional adjustment, integration of self-concept, expression of emotion, and behavior pattern among groups of public school children. Three groups of children (mentally retarded, average, superior) with an average CA of 112 months were formed on the basis of scores obtained on individual intelligence tests. Emotional adjustment level of each child was rated by psychologists on a ten-point scale. Enos (1961) reported:

> The psychologists based their opinions on (a) a "Draw-a-Person Test," (b) selected standardized questions about this test, (c) a complete Rorschach and an inquiry, (d) three selected cards of the Thematic Apperception Test, (e) a standardized questionnaire, and (f) a clinical interview. In many cases the psychologist had a chance to discuss the child with his classroom teacher (p. 607).

Each child was rated by his examiner and by a second psychologist, with the average of the two ratings being used. Concerning the interjudge reliability of these ratings, Klausmeier and Check reported, "A sample of 105 of the 120 subjects was drawn, and the ratings of emotional adjustment of the two psychologists were found to correlate .77, indicating high reliability of the independent ratings" (p. 1060). Enos was even more positive in his report of reliability findings. "As a reliability check, the ratings of the examiner and at least one independent rater were compared on 25 randomly selected subjects with a resulting Pearson Product Moment coefficient of correlation of .95 and a standard error of .02" (pp. 607–608). It is of interest to note that, as the sample size increased in the Klausmeier and Check analysis, the reliability decreased.

Enos reported that among the girls the low IQ girls were the most maladjusted, and among the boys the low IQ boys were judged as making the best overall adjustment. Although the low IQ girls were the most maladjusted among the girls, the average and high boys had a numerically lower mean score than did the retarded girls. In comparing the mean adjustment score of the low IQ children with that of the average and high IQ, no differences were evident. Only one group, the high IQ girls, received a mean adjustment score that was numerically larger than the 5.00 theoretical average of the scale. Enos also reported a significant negative correlation between IQ and emotional adjustment for the mentally retarded boys and a significant positive correlation for the bright girls. Since the individual group correlations were based on 20 cases, the question of the reliability of these findings should be considered in interpretation. The finding of a significant negative correlation between IQ and emotional adjustment level for retarded boys would certainly be in conflict with many opinions to the contrary.

Klausmeier and Check, in discussing their analysis of the same data, did not report these sex and IQ differences. These authors also reported no differences between normal and retarded groups in integration of self-concept (poorly integrated to well integrated), expression of emotion (highly introvert to highly extrovert), or behavior pattern (highly withdrawing to highly aggressive).

Since the specific test data signs used to rank a person from low to high on any of these dimensions were not presented in either of these articles, the reviewer is unable to address himself to the adequacy, theoretical or otherwise, of these criteria. Without question, the results are in contrast to the opinions of many who work with the retarded. The researchers did state, however, that they "recognize that had different assessments of personality . . . been secured, the results might possibly have been different" (Klausmeier and Check, 1959, p. 1060).

Mullen and Itkin (1961) reported on a rather extensive study of the characteristics of educable mentally handicapped children attending either special or regular classes. A large number of children matched on a number of variables were studied over a two-year period. Adjustment rating scales, a behavior checklist, and a projective personality test were used to gather personal adjustment data. In summarizing results of the projective personality test analysis, some support was offered for the hypothesis that the emotional climate in special classrooms has a salutary effect upon the emotional adjustment of mentally handicapped children. These authors also reported that educable mentally handicapped girls who were rated as poorly adjusted were more likely to be more acutely disturbed emotionally than the educable mentally handicapped boys.

Cassidy and Stanton (1959), in comparing special class children with regular class retardates, reported "superior social adjustment of the Special Class Group" (p. 72). This conclusion presumably was based on an evaluation of personal and social characteristics by means of items from the California Test of Personality and a clinical interpretation of the Goodenough Draw-a-Man Test. As no information concerning the theoretical or procedural basis for the clinical interpretation of the Goodenough was provided, no evaluation can be made concerning the meaningfulness of this finding. It was interesting to note, however, that the special class group also earned a statistically significant higher score on the Goodenough when the drawing was evaluated as a measure of the child's visual motor expression.

CHECKLIST AND RATING SCALE STUDIES

Chazan (1964) reported a study of the incidence and nature of maladjustment among special class and regular class children. One hundred sixty-nine educationally subnormal (ESN) pupils in the two age groups, 9+ to 10+ and 13+ to 14+, were matched with children in ordinary schools for age, sex, and socioeconomic background. ESN subjects were attending either day or residential special schools in South Wales. Approximately 18 percent of the ESN sample earned IQs below 60, 43 percent ranged from 60 to 69, and 39 percent ranged from 70 and over. The Bristol Social Adjustment Guide, completed by the subjects' teacher, was used to obtain the maladjustment data. On the basis of this inventory, over a third of the ESN children were maladjusted, with no significant sex differences found. This rate was significantly higher than that characteristic of the control group.

As to the types of maladjustment, Chazan reported, "the ESN children showed significantly more depression, hostility towards adults and inhibitions than the controls, as well as more symptoms of emotional tensions" (p. 298). In addition, in terms of sociometric data, the most accepted children tended to have good social adjustment and the least accepted children to have poor social adjustment. Finally, Chazan noted little difference in maladjustment between the senior boys and the junior boys, but the senior girls revealed a higher proportion of maladjustment than the junior girls. Since insufficient information was provided concerning the relationship between intellectual level and incidence and nature of the problems assessed (over 38 percent of the ESN sample earned IQs above 70), the degree of applicability of these findings to the mildly or educable mentally retarded is open to question.

Jordan (1959) constructed a teacher rating procedure to study the personal and social traits of mentally retarded children in special and regular classes. He concluded, "If these ratings are sound, mentally handicapped children in special classes are emotionally better adjusted, have a higher regard for their own mental ability, participate more widely in learning and social activities and possess more traits desired by their peers than do their counterparts in regular classes" (p. 170).

Ainsworth (1959) compared mentally retarded children who were enrolled in a regular class with no special service, in a regular class with an itinerant specialist, or in a special class. Two behavior checklists and a teacher rating scale were used to evaluate social and emotional status. In studying the groups over a one-year period, Ainsworth reported, "there were no differences among the three criterion groups with regard to observed behaviors and seriously deviant behaviors" (p. 135), and "It can be reasonably stated that the rating scales used did not indicate any changes in personality characteristics as considered by groups" (p. 137).

Ellenbogen (1957) reported that the special class group studied showed superior social adjustment when compared with retarded children attending regular classes. Subject characteristics were evaluated by teacher rating scales.

As mentioned earlier, Mullen and Itkin (1961) used checklists and rating scales in their study of regular and special class retardates. They reported that on the adjustment rating scales (Itkin, 1960) and the well adjusted scale of the behavior checklist (Itkin, Brauer, and Richards, 1960), initial ratings of special class pupils were significantly higher than ratings given to matched regular grade mentally handicapped children. In comparing the progress in adjustment of the two groups over a one-year and a two-year interval, no differences were noted on any measures of adjustment derived from teacher or examiner ratings or observations.

The results of these studies (Ellenbogen, 1957; Ainsworth, 1959; Jordan, 1959; Mullen and Itkin, 1961) which report differences between special and regular class retardates as measured by a teacher rating procedure should be viewed with some caution. Since there is no common, objectively based standard for the teacher ratings, differences in favor of the special class group may be a reflection of a different frame of reference for judging adjustment. The special class teacher, presumably more accepting of the retardate and having a different reference group on which to base his judgments, may well view the retardate as better adjusted, although the retardate may in fact exhibit the same behaviors or characteristics as those in the regular class. The regular class teacher, having as his reference group the normal children, would tend to confound the learning impairment with the personal and social adequacy of the retardate.

Itkin (1960), in reporting further on the adjustment rating scale used in the Chicago study, evaluated this possibility and concluded that his findings supported the hypothesis that adjustment rating scale scores were influenced by the frame of reference of teachers. Obviously, this does not disprove the hypothesis that educable mentally handicapped children may also make a better overt adjustment in special classrooms than in regular grades. However, as suggested, caution must be exercised in interpreting results of comparison studies based on teacher rating procedures.

SOCIOMETRIC STUDIES

A number of studies concerned with a comparison of the personal and social adjustment characteristics of the retarded attending special classes or schools and those retardates attending regular grades have utilized sociometric techniques. Johnson (1950), in a sociometric investigation of mentally handicapped children attending regular elementary classes, found that the peer acceptance and rejection scores of the retarded were significantly inferior to the scores of the normal children attending the same classes. In comparing IQ subgroups, he reported that the lower the mean IQ, the lower the acceptance score and the higher the mean rejection score.

In a later study in which an adaptation of the Syracuse Scales of Social Relations was used, Johnson (1961) found the social acceptance of special class retarded children to be superior to that of retardates in regular classes. Johnson and Kirk (1950), Miller (1956), Baldwin (1958), and Jordan (1959) reported similar results of low peer acceptance and, in some instances, active rejection, although some used different procedures in obtaining social status data. Lapp (1957), however, did not find the significant rejection scores reported by Johnson. This is similar to the Miller (1956) results. Although these findings in general would suggest that the regular class environment may not be conducive to adequate personal and social development, the studies do not provide specific information concerning the actual incidence or types of problems which may exist in a regular class environment.

It is of interest to note that Johnson (1950), Johnson and Kirk (1950), Lapp (1957), and Baldwin (1958) all gathered information from the nonretarded children concerning their reasons for not accepting the retarded. Bothersome or inappropriate behavior characteristics, rather than low intelligence, were generally reported to be the crucial factor resulting in low acceptance or active rejection. Although the inappropriate behavior variable may well be a factor resulting in peer rejection, none of these studies satisfactorily controlled the low intelligence variable. The pertinent variable could be that of inappropriate behaviors occurring in a person of low intelligence and not the inappropriate behaviors *per se*. In addition, Lapp suggested that the group he studied had no personality trait to make them disliked. They just had no special abilities to contribute to a group which would result in their acceptance.

PERSONALITY INVENTORY STUDIES

The California Test of Personality (CTP) has been used in four studies as a measure of the personal and social characteristics of educable mentally retarded children in different educational settings. The Blatt (1958) study mentioned earlier, while reporting differences between retarded children and test norms, found no differences between regular and special class children in CTP scores. Johnson (1961), in studying groups of special class and regular class children with the CTP, obtained similar results of no differences. In contrast, the Cassidy and Stanton (1959) study, in which items from the CTP were used, reported a difference in social adjustment in favor of the special class group. As the specific items were not identified, the significance of this finding is unknown. A study of the data presented reveals that the group differences were quite small, although they reached statistical significance. Meaningful implications of such differences would be quite difficult to enumerate.

Kern and Pfaeffle (1963) compared data obtained from the social adjustment section of the CTP for educable mentally retarded children attending either special classes in a regular school, special schools for retarded children, or regular classes. These writers concluded "that retarded children who are in special classes or special schools for retardates show much better school adjustment than do retardates who are in regular classess" (p. 412).

The reader should evaluate this "much better school adjustment" conclusion in light of the specific findings of the study. Although statistically significant differences were found on the school relations subtest, the meaningfulness of this difference is questionable. The statistical significance was derived from small numerical test score differences from subtests which have reliability coefficients in the .70s. Both Horrochs (1964) and Sims (1959) point to the danger of using subtest scores of the CTP and recommend that only the major category scores be used. Blatt (1958) and Johnson (1961) followed this advice, and neither found CTP differences between regular class and special class retardates.

In the three studies reviewed in which entire subtests or sections of the CTP were used (Blatt, 1958; Johnson, 1961; Kern and Pfaeffle, 1963), the retarded sample studied obtained mean raw scores which were substantially below the fiftieth percentile of the test norms. One could assume that, to the extent the CTP actually reflects significant and meaningful aspects of personal and social adjustment, the mentally retarded are inferior to the group represented by the test norms. As suggested earlier, an alternate interpretation is that the test is not an appropriate instrument for use with the mentally retarded.

It is apparent that the test items reflect a middle-class set of values (e.g., Would you rather stay away from most parties? Should children be nice to people they don't like? Is it necessary to thank those who have helped you?). Should the retardate be viewed as maladjusted if he does not respond in terms of these values? In addition, other items answered realistically in terms of the typical experience of retardates, especially those who attend regular classes, would be scored as deviant responses (e.g., Do your classmates think you cannot do well in school? Is school work so hard that you are afraid you will fail? Do most of your friends and classmates think you are bright?). Again, realistic answers to these questions would lower the adjustment score of the retardate. This type of procedure would appear to be an inappropriate approach to defining and evaluating adjustment and maladjustment with the mentally retarded, especially for those who are attending regular classes.

SUMMARY AND CONCLUSIONS

What types of behavior problems occur among the noninstitutionalized mildly retarded of school age? Blatt (1958), Johnson (1961), and Kern and Pfaeffle (1963) reported personal and/or social adjustment difficulties as evaluated by the California Test of Personality. Chazan (1964) reported depression, hostility toward adults, inhibitions, and symptoms of emotional tensions as evaluated by the Bristol Social Adjustment Guide. Enos (1961) reported emotional maladjustment of retarded girls as evaluated by a projective clinical procedure. Johnson (1950), Johnson and Kirk (1950), and Baldwin (1958) reported inappropriate or bothersome behaviors as identified by normal class peers. In view of the previously discussed limitations of these studies, however, it must be concluded that the question concerning the type of problem remains unanswered.

What is the rate of occurrence of various types of problems, and how does this rate compare with that of the nonretarded? Chazan (1964) reported that over a third of the educationally subnormal children studied were maladjusted and, further, that this rate was significantly higher than the 12 percent rate characteristic of the control group. No other study reviewed reported on rate of occurrence. Although the present writer agrees with the generally held opinion that personal and social adjustment problems are of sufficient prevalence and magnitude among the retarded to merit special consideration, if challenged to support this opinion with suitable evidence, he would have no other alternative than to conclude that such evidence is not available.

What sex and age differences are present? Enos (1961) reported poor adjustment among girls, but above average adjustment for boys. However, Klausmeier and Check (1959), in analyzing the same data, reported no sex differences. Mullen and Itkin (1961) reported that the retarded girls who were rated as poorly adjusted were likely to be more acutely disturbed emotionally than the boys. Chazan (1964), although finding no sex differences in maladjustment, did report a higher proportion of maladjusted pupils in the senior girl classes than in the junior girl classes. It is evident that there is no satisfactory evidence relative to this question of age and sex differences.

Are there differences between the retarded attending special class programs and those who remain in the regular grades? Ellenbogen (1957), Cassidy and Stanton (1959), Mullen and Itkin (1961), and Kern and Pfaeffle (1963) all reported some minor superiority of social and emotional adjustment of the special class students over those attending regular grades. On the other hand, Blatt (1958), Ainsworth (1959), and Johnson (1961) found no differences between the two groups. Although studies have reported that the retarded child is not accepted when attending the regular grades, the particular relationship between this observation and the personal and social adjustment of the retardate is unknown. In view of the deficiencies of the studies, the possible bias in selection and placement of subjects in special classes, and the conflicting results, it can only be concluded that the question of behavior adjustment differences between special and regular class students is presently unanswered.

REFERENCES

Ainsworth, S. H. *An Exploratory Study of Educational, Social and Emotional Factors in the Education of Mentally Retarded Children in Georgia Public Schools.* Athens: University of Georgia, 1959.

Baldwin, K. C. The social position of the educable mentally retarded child in the regular grades in the public schools. *Exceptional Children,* 1958, *25,* 106–108, 112.

Beier, D. C. Behavioral disturbances in the mentally retarded. In H. A. Stevens and R. Heber (Editors), *Mental Retardation: a Review of Research.* Chicago: University of Chicago, 1964. Pp. 453–487.

Blatt, B. The physical, personality, and academic status of children who are mentally retarded attending special classes as compared with children who are mentally retarded attending regular classes. *American Journal of Mental Deficiency,* 1958, *62,* 810–818.

Cassidy, Viola M., and Stanton, Jeanette E. *An Investigation of Factors Involved in the Educational Placement of Mentally Retarded Children.* Columbus: Ohio State University, 1959.

Chazan, M. The incidence and nature of maladjustment among children in schools for the educationally subnormal. *British Journal of Educational Psychology,* 1964, *34,* 292–304.

Ellenbogen, M. L. A comparative study of some aspects of academic and social adjustment of two groups of mentally retarded children in special classes and in regular grades. Unpublished doctoral dissertation, Northwestern University, 1957.

Enos, F. A. Emotional adjustment of mentally retarded children. *American Journal of Mental Deficiency,* 1961, *65,* 606–609.

Foale, M. The special difficulties of the high grade mental defective adolescent. *American Journal of Mental Deficiency,* 1956, *60,* 867–877.

Garrison, K. C., and Force, D. G., Jr. *The Psychology of Exceptional Children.* (Fourth edition) New York: Ronald Press, 1965.

Heber, R. Research on personality disorders and characteristics of the mentally retarded. *Mental Retardation Abstracts,* 1964, *1,* 304–325.

Hinkelman, E. A. Intellectual level and personality adjustment. *Elementary School Journal,* 1951, *52,* 31–35.

Horrochs, J. E. *Assessment of Behavior.* Columbus, Ohio: Charles E. Merrill Books, 1964.

Hutt, M. L., and Gibby, R. G. *The Mentally Retarded Child.* (Second edition) Boston: Allyn and Bacon, 1965.

Itkin, W. *The Chicago Adjustment Rating Scales.* Chicago: Chicago Board of Education, 1960.

Itkin, W., Brauer, L., and Richards, E. *A Behavior Checklist for the Personality Evaluation of Educable Mentally Handicapped Children.* Chicago: Chicago Board of Education, 1960.

Johnson, G. O. A study of the social position of mentally handicapped children in the regular grades. *American Journal of Mental Deficiency,* 1950, *55,* 60–89.

Johnson, G. O. *A Comparative Study of the Personal and Social Adjustment of Mentally Handicapped Children Placed in Special Classes with Mentally Handicapped Children Who Remain in Regular Classes.* Syracuse, New York: Syracuse University, 1961.

Johnson, G. O. Psychological characteristics of the mentally retarded. In W. M. Cruickshank (Editor), *Psychology of Exceptional Children and Youth.* (Second edition) Englewood Cliffs, New Jersey: Prentice-Hall, 1963. Pp. 448–483. (a)

Johnson, G. O. Special education for the mentally handicapped—a paradox. *Exceptional Children,* 1963, *29,* 62–69. (b)

Johnson, G. O., and Kirk, S. A. Are mentally handicapped children segregated in the regular grades? *Journal of Exceptional Children,* 1950, *17,* 65–68, 87–88.

Jordan, A. M. Personal-social traits of mentally handicapped children. In Thelma G. Thurstone, *An Evaluation of Educating Mentally Handicapped Children in Special Classes and in Regular Classes.* Chapel Hill: University of North Carolina, 1959. Pp. 149–179.

Kern, W. H., and Pfaeffle, H. A comparison of social adjustment of mentally retarded children in various educational settings. *American Journal of Mental Deficiency,* 1963, *67,* 407–413.

Klausmeier, H. J., and Check, J. Relationships among physical, mental, achievement, and personality measures in children of low, average, and high intelligence at 113 months of age. *American Journal of Mental Deficiency,* 1959, *63,* 1059–1068.

Lapp, Ester R. A study of the social adjustment of slow-learning children who were assigned part-time to regular classes. *American Journal of Mental Deficiency,* 1957, *62,* 254–262.

Lurie, L. A. Conduct disorders of intellectually subnormal children. *American Journal of Psychiatry,* 1937, *93,* 1025–1038.

Miller, R. V. Social status and socioempathic differences. *Exceptional Children,* 1956, *23,* 114–119.

Mullen, Frances A., and Itkin, W. *Achievement and Adjustment of Educable Mentally Handicapped Children in Special Classes and in Regular Grades.* Chicago: Chicago Board of Education, 1961.

Robinson, H. B., and Robinson, Nancy M. *The Mentally Retarded Child.* New York: McGraw-Hill, 1965.

Sarason, S. B., and Gladwin, T. Psychological and cultural problems in mental subnormality: a review of research. *American Journal of Mental Deficiency,* 1958, *62,* 1113–1307.

Sims, V. M. Review of California Test of Personality. In O. K. Buros (Editor), *The Fifth Mental Measurements Yearbook.* Highland Park, New Jersey: Gryphon Press, 1959. Pp. 102–103.

Trippe, M. J., McCaffrey, Isabel, Dempsey, P., and Downing, J. J. The school-excluded mentally retarded child. *American Journal of Mental Deficiency,* 1959, *63,* 1005–1009.

27 THE FAIRFAX PLAN: A HIGH SCHOOL PROGRAM FOR MILDLY RETARDED YOUTH

Rudolph J. Capobianco
Helen B. Jacoby

Reprinted by permission from *Mental Retardation,* Vol. 4, No. 3, June 1966, pp. 15–20, a publication of the American Association on Mental Deficiency and the authors. Dr. Capobianco is Professor of Education, University of Houston, Tex., and Mrs. Jacoby is an Educational Consultant, Charlottesville, Va.

The problem of employability of mildly mentally retarded youth is an enigma which has long plagued the independent and cooperative efforts of specialists representing the fields of education, psychology, vocational rehabilitation and others. The relative rise in the ratio of school dropouts and the unemployment upswing among workers who comprise the lower echelons of occupational titles has compounded the problem created by industry's rapid adaptation to automation. Relatively unaffected by recent strides toward automation, however, the service areas represent a new appeal to school dropouts and other unemployed normals.

One of the major criticisms of vocational programs for the mentally retarded, both in special education classes and rehabilitation centers, has been the tendency to overemphasize and elaborately train individual students for specific occupational placements. Underlying this approach is the traditional, but mistaken notion that the retardate is devoid of skills and aptitudes and must necessarily be overtrained in unique competencies to meet the requisites of a particular job—usually a low level one at that. This is, perhaps, the primary reason for the proportionately high percentage of retardates' placements in the service areas. Quite recently, mental retardates have demonstrated their efficiency in a wide diversity of job areas, many of them in the blue collar category. The training for these jobs, however, remains specific to the unique occupational goal for the individual student or trainee.

If "once a messenger boy, always a messenger boy" is the optimum goal for the mental retardate, then this system is succeeding in its purpose. However, a constantly changing society, together with a redefinition and evaluation of mental retardation itself, demands a radical departure from traditional educational and vocational training programs. The training of mental retardates needs a new emphasis—one demanding more competitive, more flexibly oriented occupational skills and a more highly developed spirit of initiative before these young adults may compete in a highly dynamic work world.

This is particularly true in the case of the Fairfax County, Virginia, school system which is one of the first in the country to implement the revised upper-level category in the new classification system developed by the American Association on Mental Deficiency. The upper limit of retardation, originally defined as 70 or 75 in the IQ points, has been extended to 84 IQ. This extension provides for special education services to many students who were originally classified as slow learners and left to their own devices within the regular class, which, no doubt, accounts for no small segment of the dropout population. The lower level of educability, according to the Fairfax Plan, excludes retardates sub-60 IQ from participation in this project. Hence, educational and vocational goals must be upgraded to be consistent with more diverse and complex vocational interests and aptitudes on the part of the project participants.

Various obstacles have impeded efforts to facilitate the placement of mental retardates in gainful occupations. An organized attack on the problem, generated by the U.S. Department of Health, Education, and Welfare, Office of Education (1964), isolates four criteria which are considered recurring pitfalls to the successful undertaking of adequate programming toward this goal:

Insufficient classroom space and inadequate diagnostic facilities;
Insufficient quantity of qualified teachers;
Limited training facilities and resources for the training of new professional personnel;
Incomplete training for those professionals already engaged in this work.

The Fairfax County system currently is not hampered by the bulk of these deficiencies. Adequate space and a high percentage of the technical equipment are readily available. Qualified teachers with proven sophistication are already employed. In addition, professional personnel are privileged to participate in periodic workshops which tend to upgrade their competencies and update their knowledge of new techniques and methodologies. The setting for the undertaking of the Fairfax Plan then is a relatively superior one—not only for the establishment of a productive program, but for its continuance as an impetus toward successful placement of retardates in the community, and as a model for other school systems and rehabilitation centers to follow.

The purpose of this project is to establish, evaluate, and maintain an intensive program of educational and vocational training geared specifically to the habilitation of mildly mentally retarded youth. The objectives are: (1) to establish an educational program which will incorporate the basic requirements of successful workership and productive citizenship, (2) to provide a series of occupational experiences which will train for flexibility of vocational sophistication rather than for specific job specialties, (3) to coordinate educational, social, and occupational training toward the establishment of responsible economic independence and citizenship, (4) to evaluate the total program in terms of its ultimate success, together with on-going analyses of specific phases of the program through periodic assessment.

In order to achieve these objectives, the program is designed to (1) provide realistic educational preparation for the world of work, (2) inculcate a positive attitude toward work and employment, (3) develop a feeling of self-worth and social responsibility, (4) encourage confidence and competence in associations with the world of work, and (5) evaluate techniques and methods used in the training of young retardates toward subsequent habilitation.

EMPLOYMENT PROBLEMS

Efforts to train, educate, and habilitate mentally retarded adolescents have been stimulated during the past and present presidential administrations. Cooperative demonstration and research projects jointly sponsored by federal, state, university, community, and/or private funds, have collectively reported, in various degrees, positive results utilizing both basic and applied research techniques. During the past decade there has been a noticeable increase in the successful placement of young mental retardates. Concurrently, there has been an increasing trend toward the establishment of a greater number and a more divergent collection of occupations which are considered within the ability structure of the mentally retarded. In fact, an extensive survey of the literature, including questionnaire returns, personal visits, etc. (Peterson and Jones, 1964) reflects a surge toward a wide range of occupations in which retardates are successfully placed outside sheltered workshops. Placement and follow-up programs (President's Committee, 1963) have revealed that the major occupational areas for rehabilitated mentally retarded individuals fall within the unskilled, semiskilled and skilled classifications with the majority falling in the service areas.

The recent impact of automation, however, has already dealt a severe blow to the laborer and unskilled workers. There exists today the greatest percentage of unemployed among those who constitute the semiskilled and unskilled groups. The service areas, however, are apparently unaffected by the recent increase in automation.

The U.S. Department of Labor (1963–1964) reports a stabilization of the percentage of job placements in the skilled category, but a gradual decrease in job opportunities for the semiskilled and unskilled. Given the high percentage of unemployment compounded with the prediction for fewer and fewer work opportunities in these areas, it must now be accepted as fact that the mentally retarded population must become more highly competitive applicants for jobs presently being held by normal semiskilled and unskilled workers. The higher level retardate incorporated in this plan justifies the assumption of competition for skilled occupations as well. Adding to this dilemma, the very large high school dropout rate composed of retarded and nonretarded students places many of these jobs at a premium. Hopefully, additional educational opportunities will discourage future high school dropouts, and better vocational facilities will enable the average worker to achieve a higher step on the occupational ladder.

The number of workers in the unskilled and semiskilled classification includes more than 35 percent of the total labor force. In view of the very high rate of unemployment within these groups, it is apparent that the untrained mentally retarded will have increasing difficulty competing in society. What is needed, then, is an extensive vocational educational program geared to the upgrading of mental retardates by providing them with general skills which would make them more adaptable to changing occupational demands; by stressing some form of competence in a number of work settings rather than developing a specialty; by undertaking new job analyses and job designs to make the most effective use of mental retardate manpower; by training them in the elements of good citizenship; and by developing within these individuals a feeling of self-worth and social responsibility.

THE PROCEDURE AT FAIRFAX

The Fairfax Plan, jointly sponsored by the Virginia Division of Vocational Rehabilitation and the Fairfax County School System, is concerned with educable retarded males and females who measure from 60–85 IQ and who are 15–17 in chronological age at enrollment. The first group of subjects was drawn from classes already in operation in the Fairfax County high schools. The sites for the demonstration and research phase of this investigation were selected to minimize the need for extended busing. Each class consists of 15 males or 15 females, segregated according to sex because of demonstrated differences in social and physical maturity at this age level. Almost universally, females have been found to excel in most maturity measurements including scholastic achievement, when compared to males of the same age level. In addition to these objective measures of performance differences between sexes, it is felt that an equally pertinent justification for separation of these subjects is the change in attitude toward learning when males and females attend separate classes—males feel it less necessary to display a cavalier attitude and females are less likely to demonstrate exhibitionistic behaviors.

Three male and three female classes (a total of 90 students) started their training simultaneously the first year. During the second year of the project, an additional group of 90 will begin their first year of training;

and the third year a new group of 90 will be enrolled. The total 270 subjects will serve as demonstration groups. An undetermined number of retardates who are not enrolled in special classes for a variety of reasons (parental refusal, travel prohibition, etc.) will serve as controls. The data collected during the progress of this project, together with subsequent information gleaned from the follow-up, may serve as excellent comparative data when viewed in the light of progress attained by earlier mentally retarded graduates from the Fairfax system.

The incorporation of these classes into the regular high schools of the Fairfax system rather than in an isolated and independent centrally located facility was done advisedly. The high-level retardates participating in this project are not typical mental retardates. Their social and emotional maturity approximates the normal; their interests and needs are also similar. Being enrolled in a high school program, attending classes as regular students, and enjoying the profits of their labor when they eventually receive high school diplomas (in cap and gown), all serve as strong motivating influences. To combat the potentially high number of dropouts, motivation must be maintained at its highest level. A separate facility would only serve to provide a feeling of "difference," remove these retardates further from the reality of the work world and lower their initiative and feelings of self-assurance.

PROGRAM SCHEDULE

The first year's program follows a specific schedule. Six classes of 15 subjects (three male and three female classes) are given an intensive academic program for two hours in the morning followed by one hour of physical education and a lunch hour. The physical education and lunch periods are integrated with the general high school students. In the afternoon, these subjects are given extensive prevocational training in shop and/or home economics for a two-hour period followed by a one-hour special reading course. The special reading course differs from the usual training offered during the language arts instruction. All of the teaching is individually oriented—providing special remedial instruction when needed and small group instruction when necessary. It is to be noted that no free period or elective is allowed to interfere with this highly structured program. Retarded subjects are assigned to regular 10th grade homerooms in accordance with the usual alphabetical placement system and participate in all regular homeroom activities.

The second-year program will follow a similar schedule, but the content of the educational and vocational training will be upgraded.

The schedule for the third year will vary throughout its course. Initially, the subjects will attend school on a half-day basis, and spend the remaining time on the job. Gradually, the school day will be shortened until the subjects are finally on a full-day work schedule. Periodic attendance at school will continue, however, for the full school year to facilitate testing, counseling, and assessment. Subjects will be exposed to four distinct work assignments—each approximately of two and one-half months duration. These assignments will be based upon the subjects' own preference and aptitude.

ACADEMIC PROGRAM

The academic program emphasizes productive citizenship through a core approach to English, social studies, and mathematics. The first year's educational aim is to familiarize the student with occupational prerequisites as they relate to his personal characteristics: interaction with others, decision-making, tolerance, sense of responsibility, and socially productive utilization of leisure time. Intensive developmental and remedial instruction in the language arts areas supplements work training.

The second year of the educational program will upgrade citizenship skills. Continuing the core approach, subjects will be given a basic understanding of the state and federal systems of government, voting procedures, and other responsibilities of community membership. Special emphasis will be placed upon techniques of job interviewing, filling out application forms, choosing, getting and holding a job, budgeting, and leisure-time activities. Extensive utilization of group counseling throughout the three-year program will stress the reality of reasonable and attainable vocational goals.

Because of the middle-class socioeconomic values held by the parents of a majority of the students to be included in the Fairfax Plan, it is necessary to reduce the discrepancy between their high expectations and realistic occupational goals for their progeny. Parents usually set occupational goals for their offspring at least one step higher than their own achievement. Therefore, continuous counseling from the onset of the project will be necessary. Although the primary responsibility for the parental counseling resides with the vocational rehabilitation counselors appointed by the State Division of Vocational Rehabilitation, all of the professional staff will be involved. Continuing parallel services will be supplied to the subjects.

The final year will relate academic skills directly to the job in which the subject is placed. Counseling and remedial techniques will be available according to the needs of the individual. Continued stress on "workership" skills will be maintained. Subjects will be allowed to select from various elective courses for additional study: females—art, ceramics, typing, etc.; males—selected phases of the home economics program.

VOCATIONAL PROGRAM

The vocational program follows a sequence of instruction progressively ordered to insure maximum development. Initially subjects are exposed to a general feel of the work situation—males with hand and power tools; females with simple homemaking experiences. Decision-making with regard to appropriate selection of particular job areas is encouraged early in training; however, a multiplicity of exposure to various kinds of work preparations and basic skills is emphasized. The Fairfax Plan is designed to lead to outside employment rather than terminal "sheltered workshop" type activities. It is for this reason that this rehabilitation program deemphasizes training for assembly work, material handling and other jobs melting away under automation and, instead, places new emphasis on training for service and blue-collar occupations (Russell, 1965).

The second year will continue to upgrade worker efficiency by utilizing the subjects' own preferences and aptitudes. Males may be encouraged to participate in auto body repairs, woodwork, welding, and various maintenance jobs, as well as bench work which requires fine motor coordination. Power equipment will become more readily accessible with less supervision and individual work projects will be expected. Females will make the transition from hand to machine sewing, initiate their own projects and be exposed to more complex, service-oriented tasks, such as cooking complete meals, following recipes, food servicing work, following patterns, etc.

Through the work experience provided during the last year of training, occupational skills will be upgraded until each individual arrives at his maximum level of employment potential. Personal preference, aptitude, and evaluation will determine the most fruitful placement area for each individual worker. Student–parent–counselor interviews will be structured to resolve apparent discrepancies between expressed and measured interests and serve as a foundation for actual job placement. The cooperation of the State Division of Vocational Rehabilitation, the State and Federal Employment Service, the State Association for Retarded Children, and other state and local agencies was established with the initiation of the project. In fact, the State Division of Vocational Rehabilitation assigned, at the onset of the project, a Rehabilitation Unit to serve the needs of clients in the Fairfax School System. The Unit consists of rehabilitation counselors, a psychologist, a social worker, and supporting nonprofessional personnel. In addition to providing counseling services to both parents and students, the Vocational Rehabilitation Agency will be responsible for the provision of general rehabilitation services, traditionally and legally a responsibility of the State Division of Vocational Rehabilitation as prescribed by state and federal rehabilitation Acts and the agency's state plan. This means the substantial supplementation by the agency through its regular service program, the rehabilitation services offered to project clients as individual situations require. Such service includes medical examinations, additional psychometrics, additional specific vocational training, special therapy, physical restoration, etc.

The Vocational Rehabilitation Agency has had a successful operating relationship with the Fairfax County school system for many years through its Alexandria District office. However, due to limitation of staff and resources, only a minimal number of retarded school youth could be served. With the initiation of the Fairfax Plan, the agency's level of service, as well as the knowledge of how to deal with the problem of retarded youth, has been tremendously increased. Close and frequent contacts between counselor and the new worker are especially important during the beginning stages of the work placement to ease employment shock. These contacts will diminish as the worker adjusts to the job. Evening sessions with parent participation will be arranged for the worker already on the job. Follow-up will continue in the form of employer interviews, additional employee counseling, and individual remediation when necessary. Ongoing evaluative measurements will be obtained at selected time intervals (approximately six-month periods).

It must be recognized that a certain proportion of the subjects will not complete the program. These dropouts will be provided with counseling, additional training, and on-the-job training by the State Vocational Rehabilitation Agency. The Vocational Rehabilitation counselors will be the liaison between the school system and the General Vocational Advisory Committee, whose function is to assist in planning and evaluating vocational curriculum content in order that the demands of the changing labor market may be coordinated with the school program. On this particular committee, because of the Right to Work Law in Virginia, the labor unions are not represented. However, every effort will be made to contact and cooperate with the representatives of the local labor unions.

AVAILABLE FACILITIES

General facilities for male students available at each high school location include industrial arts shops and maintenance and repair shops. These shops may be described as general shops. The industrial arts shop contains woodworking equipment, power and hand tools, work benches and classroom teaching areas. The maintenance and repair shops contain simple equipment in specific vocational areas such as automotive repair, plumbing, electrical, metalwork, and masonry.

General facilities for female students at each high school location include two general home economics laboratories. One may be best described as a foods and family living laboratory equipped with all types of cooking and laundry appliances, with living and dining room areas for socialization. The other laboratory is specifically equipped with sewing machines—two machines for every three persons. Additional facilities include classroom space for academic subjects and provisions for the personnel teaching these subjects.

PILOT STUDY

The first-year pilot program was established at a large high school in the county. The students were assigned to regular class homerooms at the 10th grade level. Four teachers were assigned to these groups. The males' program followed the first year projected part of the three-year program already described. The females' program followed the same projected program within their vocational areas. This program indicated both strengths and weaknesses. The continuation of the program in the school year 1965–1966 has further indicated the need for slight changes in the area of physical education. Since the physical education programs are taught by regular teachers and contain academic work at the ability level of the high school student, the special education student cannot compete in this portion of the program. Changes in future programs must be made to provide special education with physical education material geared to the retardate's level of achievement.

An outstanding strength of the program seems to be the holding power for continuing schooling. The average daily attendance of students increased in some cases as much as 85 percent to 90 percent.

PROGRAM OUTLINE

A brief description of the program contents follows. A diploma in Vocational Special Education will be awarded to each student upon completion of the following requirements:

Subject	*Units*
English	3
Math	2
Social Studies	2
Vocational Training	4
Placement Procedure	1
Principles and Practices for Successful Workership	1
Reading Skills	1
Physical Education	2
Elective (not required for diploma)	1
	17

First Year

English—Communication skills written and oral—emphasis on acceptable legible handwriting. Spelling and basic skills directly related to vocational training.

Math—Units related to vocational training or life situation. Example: measurement—liquid, solid, linear in relation to cooking, sewing, woodworking, etc.

Social Studies—American history with special emphasis on our heritage and our place as contributing citizens.

Reading Skills—Specific remedial and/or developmental reading on basis of individual diagnosis of each student's particular problem in relation to potential as determined by intelligence tests.

Vocational Training (Males)—Industrial Arts—Introduction to use of all hand and simple power tools through projects, wood and metal work, simple appliance repair.

Vocational Training (Females)—Family Living I—Introduction to homemaking skills through units such as cooking, sewing, home nursing, child care, nutrition and personal grooming.

Physical Education—Regular curriculum—intramural sports, health and physical fitness.

Second Year

English—Communication skills, written and oral—emphasis on letter writing, job interview, understanding the use of the newspaper. Continued emphasis on basic skills directly related to vocational training.

Math—Units related to vocational training and life situations. Budget (general and specific), banking, insurance, Social Security, income tax, time-payment plans.

Social Studies—American Government: local, state, and national—with special emphasis on the student's responsibility to his community.

Placement Procedure—Specific training in the mechanics of getting a job, job interviews, all types of applications, etc. Specific vocational information related to interests and attitudes investigated through group guidance.

Vocational Training (Males)—Maintenance and Repair Course—Welding, small gasoline engine repair; tool and saw sharpening, metal working, auto body repair, appliance repair.

Vocational Training (Female)—Family Living II—Sewing (hand and machine), cooking and serving, nurse's aide instruction, grooming, child care, nutrition.

Physical Education—Regular curriculum—intramural sports, physical fitness, and driver education.

THIRD YEAR

English—Communication, written and oral skills emphasized. Leisure-time reading, reading for information, writing letters (business and personal), additional reading activities connected with job training.

Principles and Practices for Successful Workership—Individual and group counseling for specific problems related to the student's daily life experiences, both on and off the job. Some attention given to directed leisure-time activities suitable to the student's interests and abilities.

Elective—May be art, music, typing, or homemaking for males, or other courses selected by students, with counselor's advice, to be adapted to meet student's needs. Course requirements will not be those required for students in regular curriculum. (Not required for diploma in Vocational Special Education.)

Work Experience—Each student will have four specific job experiences selected according to demonstrated interest and aptitude by the student with the counselors' help. Counselors will support students by frequent visits and individual counseling when requested or indicated.

INSTRUMENTATION

All subjects have been administered the Wechsler Adult Intelligence Scale (WAIS). The criterion for admission to special class is 60–85 IQ. Additional measurements administered to the demonstration and control groups include:

a. The Metropolitan Achievement Test (MAT)—to measure academic performance.

b. The Vocational Interest and Sophistication Assessment (VISA)—an interests and aptitudes test specifically devised for the retardate population.

c. Vocational Capacity Scale (VCA)—selected portions of an eight-factor vocational scale developed and standardized at the MacDonald Training Center Foundation, Tampa, Florida, a project of the Office of Vocational Rehabilitation (Vocational Rehabilitation Administration), 1963. The standardization population utilized in the above-mentioned investigation met criteria for selection almost identical to those of the Fairfax Plan subjects.

d. The MacQuarrie Test for Mechanical Aptitude (MTMA).
e. The Devereux Adolescent Behavior Scale (DABS)—a socioemotional, factor-analyzed measure.
f. Road-Map Test—a test of directionality.
g. Anecdotal records and significant information from cumulative folders will also be analyzed.

EVALUATION

Upon completion of the three-year course of training, the major part of the test battery (IQ, MAT, VISA, Achievement, VCA portions, DABS, and Personality tests) will be readministered. Particular attention will be given to changes on the interest tests, with special regard for the congruency of expressed interest and measured aptitude and the stability or improvement demonstrated on other tests. These difference scores will be analyzed according to subgroups (IQs and sex): interest and vocational preference subgroups and achievement subgroups. In addition to the comparison between demonstration and control groups (analysis of variance), a factor analysis will be applied to all of the separate measurements. Appropriate nonparametric tests will be utilized when the data prescribe them. Major focus of this activity will be aimed toward determining the variables which contribute to the relationship between curriculum content, response to training, and adequacy of job performance.

Follow-up information will be collected at six-month intervals to measure the stability of improvement in work settings. Hopefully, potential failures may be nipped-in-the-bud by ongoing assessment—recommending vocational counseling when needed and additional remediation when necessary.

SUMMARY

The true impact of automation on potential job opportunities for mental retardates may never be known. Its analyzed effects at present seem somewhat paradoxic. Admittedly eliminating many jobs comprising the semiskilled area of occupations (high resource potential for mental retardates), automation has effected little change in the service areas, where these workers enjoy a disproportionately high rate of employment success. Secondly, in spite of limiting the number of job opportunities in automated plants, the tasks remaining demand little or no decision-making responsibility on the part of the worker (Karsh, 1957)—a left-handed assist to mental retardates who are extremely limited in that capacity. Further, it has been demonstrated by some studies that automated plants decrease the need for any extended social interaction and teamwork (Faunce, 1958). These abilities are admittedly weak in retardates and are indeed cited by many investigators as disabilities which are often responsible for job failures (Michal-Smith, 1956).

Among other factors purported to influence success or failure on the job, IQ has been exhaustively analyzed. In spite of some contradictory results cited by the various investigators, a consensus seems to indicate that intellectual functioning (at least, as it is measured on standardized tests) does not differentiate between successful and nonsuccessful mentally retarded groups (Peterson and Jones, 1964).

Recent government legislation has stimulated efforts on the part of many professionals toward the establishment of "good" educational-vocational programs for mental retardates. While a number of projects have been initiated in various parts of the country under local, state and private sponsorship (often cooperatively with federal auspices), a "model" program has not been established. A major, exhaustive, joint effort (federal–city), recently started in New York City under Mobilization for Youth, Inc. (1963), underscores the concern for unemployment and its concomitant plights, such as delinquency, poverty, etc. The consequence of major unemployment among the normal workers in society place the burden of higher-level educational and vocational training for mental retardates squarely on the resources of the public school. A county-wide project, such as the one described in these pages, should serve as a "model" for the other counties and cities faced with a similar dilemma.

REFERENCES

Faunce, W. A. Automation in the Automobile Industry: Some Consequences for In-Plant Social Structure. *American Sociology Review,* 1958, *4,* 23.

Karsh, B. *The Meaning of Work in an Age of Automation.* Urbana: University of Illinois, Institute of Labor and Industrial Relations, 1957.

Michal-Smith, H. *The Mentally Retarded Patient.* Philadelphia: Lippincott, 1956.

Peterson, R. O., and Jones, E. M. *Guide to Jobs for the Mentally Retarded.* American Institute for Research, Pittsburgh, Pennsylvania. February 1964.

Russell, H. New Hope for the Retarded. *Public Personnel Review,* 1965, January, 29–32.

The President's Committee on Employment of the Handicapped in Cooperation with National Association for Retarded Children and The U.S. Employment Service, Bureau of Employment Security, U.S. Department of Labor. *Guide to Job Placements of the Mentally Retarded.* Washington, D.C.: U.S. Government Printing Office, 1963 0-677723 U.S. Dept. Labor 63-64.

U.S. Dept. of Health, Education, and Welfare, Office of Education. *The Organization and Implementation of Programs for Handicapped Children and Youth —1964*. Washington, D.C.: U.S. Government Printing Office, 1964. No. FS 5.235:35057. Peterson and Jones.

U.S. Department of Labor, Bureau of Labor Statistics. *Occupational Outlook Handbook. 1963–64 Edition*. Washington, D.C.: U.S. Government Printing Office, 1963. Bulletin No. 1375.

28 WORK EXPERIENCE PROGRAMS: EVOLVING CONCEPTS OF INSTRUCTIONAL MATERIALS WITH A SELECTED ANNOTATED LISTING

Richard L. Shick

From *Education and Training of the Mentally Retarded,* Vol. 2, No. 1, February 1967, pp. 21–28. Reprinted with permission of the Council for Exceptional Children and the author. Dr. Shick is Chairman, Department of Special Education, Mansfield (Pa.) State College.

Special education at all levels for the mentally retarded has experienced commendable growth in recent years. A significant aspect of this growth has been the development of secondary work experience programs for the retarded (Dunn, 1963; Peck, 1966). The general pattern of these work experience programs is two phased: (a) work experiences in school along with relevant classroom instruction at the junior high level; and (b) out of school or community work experience along with relevant classroom instruction at the senior high level (Dunn, 1963; Sengstock, 1964).

The goals and curricular experiences of work programs focus on the development of three essential skills for mentally retarded students: (a) satisfactory levels of vocational adequacy which will assist them in getting and maintaining employment as adults; (b) social competence which will enable the retarded to live effectively in the human group; and (c) personal adequacy which includes the development of a satisfactory self concept (Dunn, 1963; Peck, 1966).

EVOLVING CONCEPTS OF INSTRUCTIONAL MATERIALS

In implementing these goals and curricular experiences for retarded youth, the selection of appropriate instructional materials becomes an important consideration. Instructional materials in this context, then, are essential tools in the attainment of curricular goals (McCarthy, 1966a). To assist in meeting the need for an adequate supply of suitable instructional materials for the retarded in all curricular areas, including work experience, several model instructional materials centers are in the developmental stages (Mc-carthy, 1965; Reid and Rucker, 1966). On a smaller scale, but a still highly useful one, miniature materials centers are being developed in conjunction with some college and public school special education programs to serve regional areas.

In this evolving concept of instructional materials centers it is essential that appropriate centers periodically report the results of their efforts to the practitioner (McCarthy, 1966b). The final two sections of this article make up an annotated listing of selected instructional materials that appear particularly useful in accomplishing the goals of work experience programs for mentally retarded youth. The materials included make up but one category of instructional materials in a miniature materials center being developed at a college special education center (Shick, 1966). The various materials included have been received, examined, and in some cases, demonstrated in conjunction with the activities of a college special education program for preparing teachers of the mentally retarded.

ORGANIZATION OF ANNOTATED LISTING

The selected annotated listing is organized in a twofold fashion with overlap apparent in some cases: (a) selected materials for teacher use—these appear most useful for the teacher of the secondary work experience class as resources in planning and implementing an effective program; and (b) selected materials for student use, designed basically for special classes as texts or workbooks. Finally, the listing includes pertinent information on the title or name of the instructional material, a brief description of the nature and purpose of the material, and the source from which it can be obtained.

The following qualifying comments are relevant to the makeup of this listing: (a) inclusion of any instructional material does not necessarily constitute endorsement or evaluation; (b) the annotated comments are not conclusive nor entirely accurate as it is difficult to effectively describe a set of instructional materials in a few sentences; (c) the listing itself is not a complete one for work experience programs but rather includes only selected materials received at one center; and, (d) accurate and detailed information on purchasing may be obtained by writing directly to the source.

SELECTED MATERIALS FOR TEACHER USE

Altoona School District. *Occupational Education in the Altoona Senior High School,* 1965. 96 pp. $2.50. Department of Special Education, Altoona School District, Altoona, Pennsylvania. This curriculum guide, based on comprehensive curriculum studies, considers various aspects of work education and consumer education for older retardates. Included are such functional units as social education, social recreation, home repairs, child care, plus units on mathematics, English, and science for slower learners. Also included are suggestions for evaluation, discussions of work experience procedures, and occupational education programs. A highly recommended resource for the development of work experience programs.

Borreca, F. A., *et al. A Functional Core Vocabulary for Slow Learners,* 1953. 28 pp. $1.00. Robert Burger, P. O. Box 165, Rensselaer, New York. An extensive listing of functional basic vocabulary words necessary in preparing meaningful reading materials for mentally retarded youth. The words are classified into three lists: standard, core, and vocational (auto maintenance, building maintenance, food service, etc.).

Burchill, G. W. *Work–Study Programs for Alienated Youth,* 1962. 265 pp. $4.95. Science Research Associates, Inc., 259 East Erie Street, Chicago, Illinois 60611. A useful casebook describing in detail a project designed to identify and illustrate nine outstanding work–study programs aimed at the prevention of delinquent behavior and at the rehabilitation of alienated youth. Several of the programs are specifically for mentally retarded youth. Other useful materials included are selected forms and examples of instructional units used in work study programs.

Murphy, J. M. *Handbook of Job Facts* (Third edition), 1963. 98 pp. $3.95. Science Research Associates, Inc., 259 East Erie Street, Chicago, Illinois 60611. This handy book with an easy to use format provides the work experience curriculum planner with concise, accurate, up to date information about a wide range of occupations. Especially helpful in job analysis procedures.

Norris, W. *Occupational Information in the Elementary School,* 1963. 243 pp. $4.95. An excellent resource for teachers of occupations and work experience at any level. It approaches occupations at a simplified level which ties in well with special education programs. Part Two on resource materials is excellent and provides detailed information on occupational books and pamphlets, occupational pamphlets in series, occupational films and filmstrips, and occupational songs and recordings. Highly recommended source book for curriculum planners of work experience programs for retarded youth.

Junior Guidance Series. 40 pp. each. $.50 each. Science Research Associates, Inc., 259 East Erie Street, Chicago, Illinois 60611. Bailard, V., *Your Abilities,* 1957; Bauer, W. W., and Dukelow, D. A., *What You Should Know About Smoking and Drinking,* 1955; Beery, M., *Guide to Good Manners,* 1952; Clark, T. B., *Let's Talk About Honesty,* 1954; Dimond, S. E., *You and Your Problems,* 1952; Kirkendall, L. A., *Finding Out About Ourselves,* 1965; Kitch, D. E., *Exploring the World of Jobs,* 1952; Menninger, W. C., *All About You,* 1955; Neugarten, B. L., and Misner, P. J., *Getting Along In School,* 1951; Neugarten, B. L., *How to Get Along With Others,* 1953; Remmers, H. H., and Bauernfeind, R. H., *Your Prob-*

lems: How To Handle Them, 1953; Stevens, P., *Good Grooming for Boys and Girls,* 1957; Stoops, E., and Rosenheim, L., *Planning Your Job Future,* 1953; Taylor, K. W., *Getting Along With Parents,* 1952; Ullmann, F., *Life with Brothers and Sisters,* 1952.

These selections, although not written specifically for retardates, are good basic resources for secondary teachers of retarded youth, the titles indicating some of the important areas of personal, social, and occupational adjustment in which retarded youth need special instruction and guidance.

Fraenkel, W. A. *The Mentally Retarded and Their Vocational Rehabilitation—A Resource Handbook,* 1961. 87 pp. National Association for Retarded Children, Inc., 420 Lexington Avenue, New York, New York 10017. A basic resource handbook for the counselor working in vocational rehabilitation of the mentally retarded. Much of the information included is pertinent to the responsibility of planners of secondary work experience programs for the retarded, rehabilitation procedures, counselors' duties, resources in vocational rehabilitation for the retarded, and selective placement and follow-up.

Hutchinson, L. *Work Experience Education for the Educable Mentally Retarded,* 1963. 66 pp. $1.20. Office of the County Superintendent of Schools, 1104 West Eighth Street, Santa Ana, California. A collection of materials accumulated over a considerable period of time dealing with work experience education for the retarded. Included is information on objectives and need for this type program, role of key personnel, classroom and work experience activities, operational procedures, legal regulations, and insurance protection. A useful annotated bibliography plus a variety of sample work experience forms are also included.

Kolstoe, O. P., and Frey, R. M. *A High School Work–Study Program for Mentally Subnormal Students,* 1965. 179 pp. $5.00. Southern Illinois University Press, Carbondale, Illinois. This text presents a detailed discussion of the problems and procedures involved in developing a secondary work experience program for retarded youth. It deals specifically with historical considerations, curricular needs of the EMR, organization and administration of work experience, course of study, and sheltered workshops. Also included are a variety of helpful work experience and job analysis forms.

Lord, F. E. (Editor) *Work Education for Educable Retarded Youth,* Report on Institutes, 1964. 80 pp. $.50. California State College Bookstore, 5151 State College Drive, Los Angeles, California 90032. A useful report of two institutes covering all phases of work education for secondary retardates. The first institute covered guidelines for leadership personnel in education and rehabilitation and the second covered planning and instituting work education programs for retarded youth. Selected areas covered extensively in these reports on work education include: retardates in the work world; team role of special education and vocational rehabilitation; assessment and evaluation of students and programs; work experience programs; curriculum and materials; and supervision. Highly recommended as a basic reference for supervisors and teachers in this newly developing area.

Media Productions, P. O. Box 2005, Van Nuys, California. *Projections into the Future,* 1965. 34-minute tape. $7.00. Timely discussion of legal rights, vocational training, sheltered workshops, and work experience for retardates. Question and answer format. *The Education and Training of the Mental Retardate,* 1965. 37-minute tape. $7.00. Stimulating discussion of special education, training, and new and future developments for retardates.

These tapes are designed to inform, improve understanding, and stimulate discussion and action on newer programs in special education. May be used for in-service purposes with school administrators, supervisors, and teachers, and for general purposes with parents, the general public, and potential employers.

National Association for Retarded Children. *Selling One Guy Named Larry,* 1965. 17 minute film. $35.00. Also available on a rental basis. James J. McKenna, Business Manager, National Association for Retarded Children, 420 Lexington Avenue, New York, New York 10017. This 16-mm black and white film deals with the effective employment of mentally retarded youth and adults. Portrays retardates successfully at work in various jobs such as clerks, messengers, mechanics, waitresses, stockboys, and dishwashers. Highly recommended public information film for use with such groups as community service organizations, prospective employers, teachers, counselors, and parents.

Peterson, R. O., and Jones, E. M. *Guide to Jobs for the Mentally Retarded* (Revised edition), 1964. 50 pp. $5.00. American Institute for Research, Pittsburgh, Pennsylvania. This definitive publication presents a detailed overview of work for the mentally retarded. Contains much valuable information on school and community work training, workshops, job analysis, evaluation, and placement. Presents detailed job analysis information on a variety of job areas for the mentally retarded. Highly recommended as a basic reference for those involved in work experience at the junior and senior high school and postschool levels.

The High School Journal. Adapting the Secondary School Program to the Needs of the Mentally Retarded, 1964, *48,* 147–222. Single copies, $.50. University of North Carolina Press, Chapel Hill, North Carolina. A journal issue entirely concerned with meeting the needs of retardates at the secondary school level. Articles of particular relevance include: The Slow Learners—The Forgotten Student in Today's High School; Meaningful Mathematics for the High School Retarded; Planning an In-School Work Experience Program for Educable Mentally Retarded Boys and Girls; A Community Work Experience Program for the Mentally Retarded.

The President's Committee on Employment of the Handicapped. *Guide to Job Placement of the Mentally Retarded,* 1963. 16 pp. Superintendent of Documents, U.S. Government Printing Office, Washington, D.C. 20402. Brief but timely booklet overviewing the following aspects of work for the retarded: kinds of jobs for the retarded; getting the retarded ready for employment; role of the employer and worker; hiring the retardate; training and supervising the retarded worker; and follow-up needs. Useful booklet in preparing employers to receive retarded workers.

U.S. Department of Labor. *Job Guide for Young Workers,* 1964. 78 pp. $.45. Superintendent of Documents, US Government Printing Office, Washington, D.C. 20402. These booklets are published each year by the U.S. Employment Service. Written to youth, they present information on the importance of jobs, ways and means of getting a job, and kinds of jobs. Information on a variety of jobs is presented in table form and includes data on usual duties, characteristics of the job, qualifications, prospects, advancement, and where the job is found. These booklets have been found particularly useful by work experience teachers and guidance counselors.

SELECTED MATERIALS FOR STUDENT USE

Balinger, W. R. *You and Your World,* 1964. 118 pp. $2.00. Social studies worktext that helps the secondary student understand more about himself, his family, school, city, county, state, and country. Highly interesting and practical material written at a primary level. Includes perforated pages, teacher's manual. Kahn, C. H., and Hanna, J. B. *Money Makes Sense,* 1960. 140 pp. $2.00. Worktext to teach the principles of arithmetic through the use of money. Everyday functional problems built around the use of U.S. coins reproduced in actual size and paper money hold student's interest and provide motivation. Pages are perforated and a teacher's manual is included. For junior and senior high school. *Using Dollars and Sense,* 1963. 126 pp. $2.00. Fearon Publishers, Inc., 828 Valencia Street, San Francisco, California 94110. Worktext with same practical features as above but more advanced. Some functional areas covered are buying groceries, buying at sales, figuring salary, saving and checking accounts, and budgets.

Breed, A. E. *Building A Strong Body,* 1963. 83 pp. $1.95. Venture Media,

1061 Bonnie View Road, Hollister, California. Simplified worktext on some of the important basic concepts of physical and mental health. Covers such important areas as the bodily need for proper foods, building strong teeth; exercise, sleep, worry, and smoking. Illustrated. Could be used as a health text for secondary retardates.

Bright, E. L., and Mitchell, E. C. *Home and Family Life Series.* Croft Educational Services, 100 Garfield Avenue, New London, Connecticut. *A Day with the Brown Family,* Reader One, 1960. 34 pp. $.80. Provides mature reading about everyday experiences of adults in interpersonal relationships of home and family life. *Making a Good Living,* Reader Two, 1960. 28 pp. $.80. Provides mature reading about practical experiences of adults through working, spending, saving, and having fun. *The Browns at School,* Reader Three, 1961. 27 pp. $.80. Provides practical reading about the importance of education. *The Browns and Their Neighbors,* Reader Four, 1961. 14 pp. $.80. Provides mature reading about everyday experiences of adults in intergroup relations, religious, social, and civic life. *Workbook in Arithmetic,* 1959. 67 pp. $1.00. A practical guide for students in learning the meaning and application of numbers.

These illustrated books were originally designed for adult education under the literacy education project of the U.S. Office of Education. However, the readable format, lower level vocabulary, and high interest content make them appropriate for selected use with older retardates.

Carson, E. O., and Daly, F. M. *Teen-Agers Prepare for Work,* Book I, 1961. 84 pp. $1.95. Esther O. Carson, 18623 Lake Chabat Road, Castro Valley, California. Illustrated worktext covering employment in factories, messenger service, food trades, dishwashing machine operation, baby sitting, and service stations. For lower ability high school students; keyed to work experience.

Eye Gate House, Inc. *Occupational Education Filmstrips.* $35.00 per set. Eye Gate House, Inc., Jamaica 35, New York. Set of nine titles: *The Job Interview, Stocker in a Supermarket, The Waitress, Fixing a Flat Tire, How To Use Your Checkbook, The Variety Store, The School Cafeteria Worker, The Nurses Aid, The Gas Station Attendant.* Series of functional filmstrips dealing with various aspects of employment and some of the kinds of jobs that are included in contemporary work experience programs for the educable retarded. Generally the experiences and activities depicted are at a simplified, concrete level. Should prove a valuable resource to the secondary teacher. Teacher's manual is included.

Finney Company. *Finding Your Job,* 1961–1962. $20.50 per unit of five volumes. Finney Company, 3350 Gorham Avenue, Minneapolis, Minnesota.

These materials are published in units consisting of volumes, with 12 job briefs in each volume or 60 job briefs per unit. The practical content and coverage is thorough on the kinds of jobs for which the retarded would qualify. Recommended as basic text material in occupations for older retardates. The following are illustrated worktexts to accompany the unit materials: Dogin, Y. *Help Yourself to A Job*. Part I, 1965. 71 pp. $1.50; *Help Yourself to A Job*. Part II, 1965. 77 pp. $1.50; Granbeck, M. *Finding Your Job Workbook,* 1966. 72 pp. $1.50.

Gallagher, A. M., and Gallagher, J. J. *Keyboard Town Story,* 1965. 107 pp. Classroom kit. $5.95 Special program to teach the touch system of typewriting by association of story characters with the positions on the keyboard. Suggested for intermediate and secondary retardates and, possibly, remedial uses. Classroom kit includes both the manual and relevant charts. A reusable booklet entitled *Student's Typing Manual* is also available. $1.25.

Hartley, E. T. *Teacher's Manual, Snip, Clip, and Stitch,* 1965. 68 pp. Teacher's manual $2.00, student's workbook $2.95. R. W. Parkinson and Associates, 704 Mumford Drive, Urbana, Illinois. Complete clothing construction program designed for a homemaking course for mentally retarded girls. Includes detailed teacher's manual plus a student's workbook by the same title covering the most important concepts and skills in this area.

New Rochester Occupational Reading Series. 64 pp. each. Set of five, $2.00. Complete review set, $15.00. Science Research Associates, Inc., 259 East Erie Street, Chicago, Illinois 60611. Fraser, H. H., and Greenberger, B., *Starting Work,* 1963; Klee, R., *On the Job,* 1963; Kazmayer, C., and Osborne, E., *Keeping the Job,* 1964; Snyder, M. E., *Working for the City,* 1964; Beeler, E. L., *Time Out for Leisure,* 1964. These highly functional materials use a mature approach to actual life situations readily acceptable to older students who may be slow learners or remedial cases. Practical aspects of social adjustment are emphasized throughout. Differences in reading levels are provided by variation in story length, vocabulary, sentence, and paragraph complexity. A helpful teacher's guide available. Materials geared to work experience programs. Goldberg, H. R., and Brumber, W. T. *The Job Ahead,* 1963. 168 pp. $3.95 per volume. A hardbound multilevel textbook published in three companion volumes with three reading levels: Level I—second grade; Level II—third and fourth grade; Level III—fourth and fifth grade. Content emphasizes in story form the occupational attitudes and skills needed for success on the job and in society.

Federal Textbook on Citizenship Series. Superintendent of Documents, U.S. Government Printing Office, Washington, D.C. 20402. Immigration and

Naturalization Service. *English and Home and Community Life.* Book 1, 1963. 112 pp. $.50; *Our United States.* Book 2, 1964. 118 pp. $.75; *Teacher's Guide.* Book 1-2-3, 1964. 23 pp. $.25.

The primary purpose of these books is to prepare immigrants for citizenship. However, portions of Book 1 especially, and possibly Book 2 seem applicable as basic material for social skills areas for older retardates. Content is highly functional with relatively high interest level and somewhat lower level vocabulary. Illustrations, text, and related exercises are generally well presented. Illustrative units include a family, our homes, I work, good food, the city, and the employment office. The *Teacher's Guide* contains useful suggestions on techniques.

Laubach Literacy, Inc. *News for You,* 1965. 4 pp. $1.25 each semester for one issue. News for You, Box 131, Syracuse, New York 13210. This is a newspaper in easy English for youth and adults published weekly during the school year in two reading levels, B Edition and A Edition (easier). Highly recommended for use with secondary retardates.

Lawson, G. D. *Everyday Business,* 1958. 81 pp. $1.60. Gary D. Lawson, 9488 Sara Street, Elk Grove, California. Well illustrated functional workbook for secondary retardates covering the areas of banking, budgeting, buying, federal income tax, and insurance. *Newspaper Reading,* 1960. 77 pp. $1.60. Special workbook designed to train the student in the effective use of the daily newspaper. A series of practical exercises on newspaper use are provided. *Better Living,* 1964. 83 pp. $1.60. Useful personal and social skills worktext written for the secondary special education student. Practical units covered include: morals and virtues, marriage, parenthood. *Safe and Sound,* 1965. 83 pp. $1.60. This timely illustrated workbook written for the older retardate covers skills and learnings relevant to planned parenthood, prenatal care, body care, accident prevention, and first aid.

This series of four worktexts is written specifically for the older retardate. They could be used as basic texts in such course areas as health, social studies, English, business math.

Mafex Associates, Inc. *Employment Phase,* 1962. Classroom set for 20, $33.00. Mafex Associates, Inc., Box 114, Ebensburg, Pennsylvania. This set presents the important concepts basic to employment regardless of the type of job. Included are student texts, student activity books, teacher's guide, and eight classroom size posters. *Citizenship Phase,* 1963. Classroom set for 20, $33.00. This set presents basic concepts and experiences pertaining to citizenship adjustment in community, county, state, and nation. Includes student texts, student activity books, teacher's guide, group activity and display book. *Family Living, Family Business Phase,* 1963. Classroom set for 20, $33.00. Presents basic concepts related to family living, consumer practices, and budgeting for future homemakers. Includes student texts, student activity books, and teacher's guide.

Manning, A. *Magazines,* 1964. 46 pp. $1.95. Ardelle Manning Productions, P. O. Box 125, Palo Alto, California. Workbook designed to help remedial students and educable students learn how to use and enjoy magazines. Contains easier reading material with a variety of exercises for the student which require minimal supervision. Manning, A. S., and Wood, C. E. *A Modified History of the United States,* 1964. 176 pp. $3.25. Answer booklet $1.00. Illustrated modified text on U.S. history designed for high school students in either remedial or educable classes. Each chapter contains a pertinent vocabulary list and student exercises. Sentences are short and readable and only the most relevant historical facts are presented.

Pugh, T., and Bringhurst, N. *Preparing for Success in Life,* 1961. A prevocational arithmetic workbook prepared for junior high retardates. Highly functional math included. Teal, R. L. *Preparing for Job Success,* 1961. 157 pp. A prevocational reading workbook for junior high retardates covering health and grooming, courtesy, and handling money. *Teacher's Edition, Preparing for Job Success,* 1961. 157 pp. Teacher's manual to workbook. Houston Independent School District. Director of Special Education, Houston Independent School District, Houston, Texas. Write to source for price details. Heath, Z., and Cranim, M., *Building Maintenance,* 1958. 16 pp.; *Motor Vehicle Maintenance,* 1959. 14 pp. Houston Public Schools, *Building Trades,* 1956. 27 pp.; *Learning about Jobs,* 1955. 41 pp.; *Parking System,* 1954. 6 pp.; *Food Trades,* 1954. 32 pp.

This is a very practical selection of resource units for use in secondary work experience oriented programs for the retarded. These school-system prepared materials are excellent resources for prevocationally and vocationally oriented secondary programs. They may be considered exemplary in terms of showing what a special education department can do to prepare materials to meet their own program needs. Highly recommended on this basis.

Steck-Vaughn Company. P. O. Box 2028, Austin, Texas. Robertson, M. S. *Adult Reader,* 1964. 127 pp. $.96. This text is designed to teach adult beginners to read and features a vocabulary of words most used by adults.

Smith, E. H., and Lutz, F. R. *My Country* (Revised edition), 1964. 96 pp. $.72. Worktext in which basic reading skills are provided through easy stories about our country and government. Easy vocabulary, fourth and fifth grade reading levels, and a functional orientation are other features of this recommended text. Smith, H. A., and Wilbert, I. L. *I Want To Learn*

English (Revised edition), 1965. 112 pp. $.96. Worktext on the basic fundamentals of English, reading, and writing at the 4th to 5th grade level. *I Want To Read and Write* (Revised edition), 1965. 128 pp. $.96. Worktext for providing instruction in basic reading skills for beginners. Contains controlled vocabulary, exercises, reviews, and tests.

This highly practical series focuses on the adult's way of life and is built around adult interests, activities, and problems. The fact that the texts are well illustrated, have a high interest and mature format, and deal with opportunities in various kinds of work are other desirable features. Recommended for use as basic texts with older retardates and slow learners in work-oriented curricula.

Shawn, B. *Foundations of Citizenship.* Book 1 and Book 2, 1965. 92 and 99 pp. $3.75 each. Frank Richards, Publisher, 215 Church Street, Phoenix, New York 13135. Two functional special class texts for retardates at the secondary level. The content emphasizes social adjustment and occupational education. Corcoran, E. L. *Rights and Duties of Citizens.* Book 1 and Book 2, 1964 and 1965. 56 and 45 pp. $1.25 each. Two workbooks designed to supplement the above texts. Highly practical and functional exercises are included.

Tripp, M. F. *I Want a Driver's License,* 1962. 36 pp. $1.25. Fern Tripp, 2035 East Sierra Way, Dinuba, California 93618. This booklet is an adaptation of the California Motor Vehicle Code and is designed to help the non-academic secondary student prepare for the driver's license test. It contains the necessary materials for this, is written in easy to read form, and includes work–study exercises and sample tests. *Road Signs,* 1964. Packet. $1.25. This packet of 120 authentic road signs in a suitable size for individual use is designed for use with the above booklet.

REFERENCES

Dunn, L. M. (Editor) *Exceptional Children in the Schools.* New York: Holt, Rinehart and Winston, 1963.

McCarthy, J. J. A special education instructional materials center. *Mental Retardation,* 1965, *3,* 26–28.

McCarthy, J. J. Educational materials: educational materials for the mentally retarded—a quandary. *Education and Training of the Mentally Retarded,* 1966a, *1,* 24–31.

McCarthy, J. J. Educational materials: instructional materials for use with the mentally retarded. *Education and Training of the Mentally Retarded,* 1966b, *1,* 87–91.

Peck, J. R. The work-study program—a critical phase of preparation. *Education and Training of the Mentally Retarded,* 1966, *1,* 68–74.

Reid, W. R., and Rucker, D. P. A special education instructional materials center project. *Education and Training of the Mentally Retarded,* 966, *1,* 59–62.

Sengstock, W. L. Planning an in-school work experience program for educable mentally retarded boys and girls. *The High School Journal,* 1964, *48,* 179–184.

Shick, R. L. *Annotated Listing of Selected Resource Materials for Newer Programs in Special Education.* Mansfield, Pennsylvania: Mansfield State College, 1966.

SECTION SEVEN

School Programs for the Trainable Mentally Retarded

The phenomenal growth of public school programs for trainable mentally retarded [1] children is the outgrowth of three factors: (1) an awareness on the part of the parents of these children that psychologically it is better for the child and the family unit to avoid or delay institutionalization; (2) the questionable programs and the crowded conditions of many institutions; and (3) financial data that tend to show that it is more economical for society to keep retarded children in the community. There is no question that institutional care is a necessity in some cases, but current thinking leans toward giving the trainable retarded child every possible opportunity prior to institutionalization.

Initially, school programs for the trainable child were parent-sponsored. As permissive and mandatory educational legislation was developed in many states, the public schools gradually assumed the responsibility for these classes. By 1960 it was estimated that 12,000 children were enrolled in classes for the trainable retarded. An estimate of enrollments in 1970 is 20,000.

As programs for the trainable retarded child have developed, there has been serious controversy over which state agency should have primary responsibility for them. Public school personnel tend to feel that assistance in some form should come from other state agencies, such as departments of mental hygiene and social welfare. On the other hand, these agencies feel that mental retardation is primarily a community problem and should be supported through educational funds. The controversy can best be resolved by a

[1] In this section "trainable" and "severely retarded" are used interchangeably to indicate a pupil with an approximate IQ range of 25–50 with some potential for acquiring social maturity skills.

state coordinating committee [2] that theoretically should be able to develop a rationale for support.

The criteria for determining the eligibility of children for placement in classes for the trainable retarded have been subject to much discussion. Drawing a fine line between lower grades of educable retarded and upper grades of totally dependent children is an extremely difficult assessment problem. Goldstein [3] has suggested the possible use of the Kuhlmann Intelligence Test scores. He maintains that children with IQs below 25 on this test will usually be ineligible; that children with IQs between 25 and 35 are questionable cases and other criteria must be considered; and finally, that children with IQs above 35 stand a very good chance of making a suitable adjustment. No single criterion in itself is adequate. Complete assessment and a trial period is warranted in most cases.

The continued popularity of the community educational program for the trainable mentally retarded is attested to by the change in public attitude towards community living rather than institutional placement for the trainable retarded group. Many successes in the development of socially maturing skills and eye-catching achievements in these activities have been the result of the utilization of operant conditioning and behavior modification techniques. See Sections 3 and 15 of this volume for a lengthy discussion and the research findings. Coupled with preschool programs and programs for the adult retarded, a continuum of educational and training opportunities is available in many communities throughout the country.

The first reading by Wayne D. Lance reports on public school programs for trainable mentally retarded children, which are increasing in number and will continue to expand under state and federal funding. He recommends that special educators evaluate programs beginning with an emphasis on curriculum development. Studies on teacher selection provide tentative criteria for entrance into teacher preparation programs; an approach to the preparation of teachers of the trainable retarded is outlined. Instruments for evaluation of pupils by teachers are suggested, and trends in curriculum, methods, and school organization are discussed. In the second article, John Hollis and Chester E. Gorton present an overview of recent research applicable to the training of severely and profoundly developmentally retarded children. They briefly cover the following topics: prosthetic training; operant-imitation; social reinforcement; aversive stimulation; feeding training; toilet training; and behavioral engineering. After this survey of the literature, it became clearly evident that we now have operational procedures applicable to building training programs that are realistic for these children. In essence, the educator, psychologist, and therapist can no longer in good conscience hide behind the Binet kit and the time-worn excuses of yesteryear. This section also includes a chart by Campbell, an overview of curriculum needs of the trainable mentally retarded. The second tabular data is on the Criteria for Placing Trainable

[2] See Section 13 on national, state, and local programs.

[3] Herbert Goldstein (ed.), *Report Number Two on Study Project for Trainable Mentally Handicapped Children* (Springfield, Ill.: State Department of Public Instruction, 1955).

Retarded Children in Special Classes. The final article in this section, by Fred M. Hanson, covers the utilization and training of aides for classes for the trainable mentally retarded and delineates the role of the aide and his proposed training.

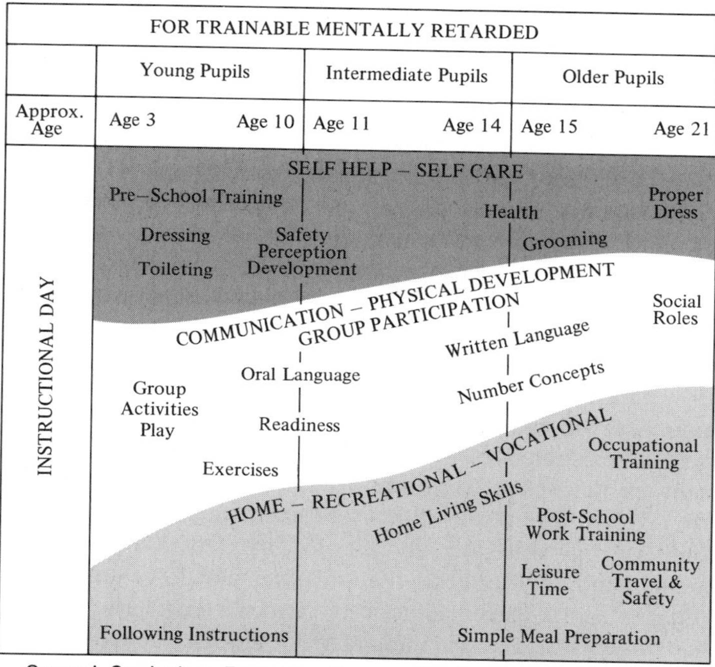

General Curriculum Emphasis. Source: "Study of Curriculum Planning," L. Wayne Campbell, Curriculum Consultant, California State Department of Education.

29 SCHOOL PROGRAMS FOR THE TRAINABLE MENTALLY RETARDED

Wayne D. Lance

From *Education and Training of the Mentally Retarded,* Vol. 3, No. 1, February 1968, pp. 3–9. Reprinted with the permission of the Council for Exceptional Children and the author. Dr. Lance is Associate Professor of Education, Special Education Department, University of Oregon, Eugene.

Ten years ago it would have been appropriate to begin this article with a rationale to support the operation of classes for trainable mentally retarded (TMR) children by the public schools. At that time a debate did exist among special educators as to where responsibility should be placed (Goldberg and Cruickshank, 1958). This appears to be a dead issue in 1967: legislation not only exists, making the operation of such classes permissive in many states, but it also has become a mandatory provision in some states. Without a doubt, funds from Title VI of the Elementary and Secondary Education Act will be used to initiate new programs for TMR children and to expand existing ones. Special educators must not shirk their responsibility to insure that school programs are effective and that federal and state funds are invested in ventures with a solid footing and realistic expectations.

The term trainable mentally retarded, as used in this paper, refers to children and youth falling within the moderate and upper level of the severe retardation category of the American Association of Mental Deficiency *measured intelligence* classification. TMR children function within Level III of the *adaptive behavior* classification, i.e., severe negative deviation from norms and standards of adaptive behavior (Heber, 1961a; Heber, 1961b).

Four areas of concern for programs for the TMR will be developed in this paper: (a) curriculum, (b) selection and preparation of teachers, (c) methodology and evaluation, and (d) school organization.

CURRICULUM

Curriculum development, including goals and objectives, should be given top priority when discussing school programs for the mentally retarded. Only after this important task has been completed can we begin to discuss personnel, methods, and organization.

Daly (1966) listed three major problems relating to curriculum for the TMR: (a) ". . . the lack of a clear guiding purpose . . ."; (b) ". . . the lack of agreement between parents and educators regarding worthy educational objectives . . ."; and (c) ". . . lack of a systematized instructional program . . . [pp. 117–118]." With evidence available to suggest the inappropriateness of an academically oriented program (Bach, 1965; Warren, 1963), it appears to the writer that our "clear guiding purpose" is somewhat fuzzy, and that parents and educators have not reached agreement on objectives. It is disturbing to note that in some instances special educators have conveyed the impression that academic achievement, especially formal reading skills, are a part and parcel of the curriculum for TMR pupils. This may result from (a) a belief that objectives other than pure academic ones are les than respectable or (b) a facade of academism which seems to placate parents and administrators who fail to understand the program. An encouraging note is that attempts are being made on statewide bases to formulate guidelines and courses of study that will in effect say, "This is what we shall teach!" The Division on Mental Retardation of The Council for Exceptional Children has a responsibility to take the lead in exploring ways to formulate and communicate the "clear guiding purpose."

The development of objectives for a course of study usually begins with an understanding of the characteristics of the population to be served. Intellectual characteristics may best be understood within a framework of a cognitive model such as the Structure of Intellect (Guilford, 1959), or the developmental approach of Piaget (Garrison, 1966; Wolinsky, 1966). Social characteristics seem to be more subject to classroom implementation when viewed within a framework of adaptive behavior (Leland, 1966). Physical and motor characteristics have been derived from an empirical approach and it is possible to make rather specific suggestions for objectives in this area (Cratty, 1966). No review of characteristics is complete without a study of the functioning of the moderately and severely retarded adult. Coupled with this is the need for some prediction regarding how TMR adults will perform in an adult world in 10, 15, or 20 years hence.

Specifically concerning the development of objectives, the author feels that we have been especially weak in stating operational objectives for perceptual-motor development of our TMR children. The Hudson study (Hudson, 1960), for example, lists many motor activities undertaken by teachers in the sample, but gives little evidence of prescriptive teaching that is developmentally planned. By applying a typology of curriculum objectives, e.g., Gorelick (1963), it is possible for the teacher to break the task to be learned into small sequential steps and to implement the appropriate methodology to help the child climb to the next higher level of performance.

An example of one approach to the operationalizing of objectives for the TMR is that developed in Santa Barbara, California (Cameron, 1966). The Individualized Diagnostic Course of Study enables the teacher to maintain a checklist of the pupil's development in each of the objectives set forth in the guide and to follow the child's progress over a period of years.

SELECTION AND PREPARATION OF TEACHERS

Some data presently exist to aid the teacher educator in the selection of candidates for preparation as teachers of the TMR. The Minnesota Teacher Attitude Inventory is an instrument providing useful data in the screening process (Condell and Tonn, 1965; Meisgeier, 1965). Johnson (1964) has developed a questionnaire that may expedite procedures for determining some of the important variables of past experience with the handicapped as related to current interest and possible success. Meisgeier (1965) used a battery of seven instruments in a study designed to identify successful teachers of mentally and physically handicapped children. This study should be replicated with students and teachers of the TMR. Hudson's (1960) tentative checklist of teaching competencies for teachers of TMR children offers promise as a screening or evaluative device. Jones (1966) reviewed research on the special education teacher and teaching, suggesting a rationale for a systematic research program. Teacher educators could profit by implementing the recommendations made by Jones, particularly the development of a model combining several variables pertinent to the teaching of TMR children. One of these variables to investigate is that of ordinary class teaching as a prerequisite to teaching TMR children. In the opinion of some, experience as a regular class teacher and even as an EMR class teacher is more of a detriment than a positive attribute. In the opinion of the author, greater efforts should be expended in recruiting young college students to prepare for the TMR program, even prior to their entrance into regular elementary or secondary programs.

A number of sources have listed the components of a TMR teacher preparation program (Cain and Levine, 1963; Connor and Goldberg, 1960; Council for Exceptional Children, 1966; Heber, 1963; Wolinsky, 1959). Of particular interest is the preliminary report to the Professional Standards Committee of The Council for Exceptional Children, in which preparation of teachers of the TMR was considered separately from teachers of the EMR. Areas requiring intensive attention for teachers of the TMR were as follows:

1. Cognitive growth, perception, and sensorimotor development.
2. Development of research and evaluative skills.
3. Language development.
4. Concepts of leisure time.
5. Occupational education.
6. Parent counseling.
7. The role of the teacher as an eliciting stimulus.

A recent informal survey of school districts in California revealed a concern that teachers of the TMR receive training in language development, behavior shaping, and perceptual-motor development in additional amounts to that provided for teachers of the EMR.

Procedures for the preparation of teachers of the TMR might parallel the clinical approach suggested by Lance (1966). "Clinical teaching" denotes adequate diagnosis of individual needs and abilities; prescription with specific, differential approaches to meet these specific needs; and the implementation of the program in the school setting. To achieve this end, students must be involved in programs rich in practicum experiences with ample opportunity for observation and individual instruction. As suggested by Blatt (1962), such a program requires rather intensive interaction between students and faculty, both being involved in the observation experience.

A pilot program currently being developed at California State College at Fullerton to prepare teachers of the TMR includes a one-semester seminar and practicum course to precede student teaching. During this seminar and practicum, the student will spend three hours per week in seminar and nine hours in practicum, all under the supervision of a college faculty member. The seminar and practicum will replace a separate course in curriculum and methods and will attempt to cover the same material in a more integrated and meaningful fashion.

METHODOLOGY AND EVALUATION

With the increasing emphasis upon a clinical teaching approach, methodology and evaluation depend upon the effective use of scales and instruments. Among those most useful to the teacher of TMR children and youth are the Cain–Levine Social Competency Scale (Cain, Levine, and Elzey, 1963) and the TMR Performance Profile for the Severely and Moderately Retarded (DiNola, Kaminsky, and Sternfeld, 1965). The Parsons Language Sample (Spradlin, 1963) and the Developmental Evaluation Scale for Mentally Retarded Children (Harvey, Yep, and Sellin, 1966) are two others worthy of note for classroom use. The Individualized Diagnostic Course of Study for Trainable Mentally Retarded (Cameron, 1966) should not be overlooked. Teachers also find the Purdue Perceptual-Motor Survey to be a valuable tool (Roach and Kephart, 1966).

The Illinois Test of Psycholinguistic Abilities (ITPA), although difficult for most classroom teachers to administer, is an instrument which has a number of implications for training TMR pupils (Bateman, 1966). Bateman lists six implications for teaching language to retardates and suggests how the ITPA may be used in individual language remediation. Bradley, Maurer, and Hundziak (1966) utilized the ITPA profile with TMR pupils in developing individual lessons over a period of several months and found that this form of language training produced significant gains in language and mental development.

National attention has turned to physical education, recreation, and perceptual motor training for the retarded. Hayden (1964) stressed the importance of physical fitness activities as an integral part of the curriculum. Cratty (1966) established a test battery for use with retarded children and, following the administration of these tests, arrived at some tentative conclusions for perceptual motor training of the TMR. Of particular interest were his findings regarding basic locomotor tasks and more complex motor tasks. He recommends a program including ". . . activities designed to enhance balance, body-part perception, body-to-object perception, agility, as well as ball skills, hopscotch, etc., designed to lead into socially approved playground activities [p. 69]." Also of interest is the finding that exercise combined with music is effective in promoting the development of self-help skills (Harrison, Lecrone, Temerlin, and Trousdale, 1966).

Social perceptual training is an area in which methodology needs to improve. Older TMR youth are capable of responding to social cues, yet need specific training. The use of slides and seat work materials such as those used by Edmondson, Leland, and Leach (1966) with EMR youngsters may be appropriate, and 8mm film loops certainly have an advantage for this type of training (Bitter and Bolanovich, 1966b).

The training of self-help skills is enhanced by both the methods and materials of Montessori. Teachers of the TMR would do well to study thoroughly the handbook (Montessori, 1965) and to become adept in acting as a mediator between the child and the environment (Gitter, 1965).

Among other TMR youth, it becomes important to be able to assess the potential for vocational adjustment and to determine those pupils suited for sheltered workshop placement or semiindependent work. Patterson (1964) lists many instruments appropriate for this purpose. The recently developed Personal–Social and Vocational Scale for the Mentally Retarded is ideally suited for this purpose (Levine and Elzey, 1966). The best means of assessment, no doubt, is the teacher's observations and anecdotal notes made in actual work or simulated work situations. Some form of a work program and prevocational experiences have a significant contribution to make to the curriculum. A review of Huddle's (1967) recent study involving TMR's in a television assembly task indicates that these individuals can perform some industrial type tasks.

In every aspect of the curriculum, methodology is being influenced by the increased application of behavior shaping techniques and conditioning procedures. No longer is this a procedure relegated to the laboratory or to institutional settings. Materials are available to a greater degree than ever before. Not only are sources available to aid the teacher in developing materials (Frankel, Happ, and Smith, 1966; Happ, 1967), but the network of Instructional Materials Centers is literally bringing materials to the teacher's door.

SCHOOL ORGANIZATION

Several changes in organization of programs for TMR children and youth must be made if progress is to continue in this rapidly growing area of special education.

1. Programs must begin early, preferably by the time the child is four years of age. A followup examination of 200 retarded children indicated that the TMR children who benefited most from training were between the ages of four and six (Lanyi, 1964).
2. Programs must be extended throughout the year. Summer programs, including camp experiences, have been described by Daly (1966); Harvey, Yep, and Sellin (1966); and Kokaska (1966). Harvey's study lends support to the concept of an all year school.
3. Work experience programs should be provided for older TMR youth. The St. Louis program (Bitter and Bolanovich, 1966a) is an example of an effective arrangement to bridge the gap between school and adulthood.
4. Whenever possible, the public school program should prepare the young adult for semiindependent living in the community. An example of this type of program is the San Francisco program (Katz, 1964).
5. Schools for the TMR should be organized so as to permit the teachers to develop curriculum, diagnose pupil needs, and work with various sized groups. This may involve forms of team teaching, use of teacher assistants and teacher aides, and a closer involvement of the speech and hearing specialist and school nurse. The school psychologist should be available for continual testing and evaluation and should be able to provide the teacher with such data within one week of request.

Programs for TMR children and youth are an integral part of the public school programs of education for all of America's children. Special educators must meet the challenge to make these programs among the best we have to offer.

REFERENCES

Bach, H. Die stellung der kulturtechniken in der sonderschule für praktisch bildbare. (The position of the basic skills in the special school for the trainable.) *Lebenshilfe,* 1965, *4,* 132–138. (*Mental Retardation Abstracts,* 1966, *3,* 892.)

Bateman, Barbara. The application of language and communication models in programs for the trainable retarded. In *Special Education: Strategies for Educational Progress. Selected Convention Papers.* Washington: Council for Exceptional Children, 1966. Pp. 45–49.

Bitter, J. A., and Bolanovich, D. J. Development of vocational competence in the moderately retarded. *Mental Retardation,* 1966, *4*(6), 9–12. (a)

Bitter, J. A., and Bolanovich, D. J. Job training of retardates using 8mm film loops. *Audiovisual Instruction,* 1966, *11,* 731–732. (b)

Blatt, B. Some observations and questions concerning an unstudied problem in special education. *Training School Bulletin,* 1962, *59,* 121–131.

Bradley, Betty H., Maurer, Ruth, and Hundziak, M. A study of the effectiveness of milieu therapy and language training for the mentally retarded. *Exceptional Children,* 1966, *33,* 143–150.

Cain, L. F., and Levine, S. Effects of community and institutional school programs on trainable mentally retarded children. *CEC Research Monograph,* 1963, No. B-1.

Cain, L. F., Levine, S., and Elzey, F. F. *Manual for the Cain-Levine Social Competencies Scale.* Palo Alto, Calif.: Consulting Psychologists Press, 1963.

Cameron, E. C. Individualized diagnostic course of study for trainable mentally retarded (Working copy). Santa Barbara, Calif.: Santa Barbara City Schools, 1966.

Condell, J. F., and Tonn, M. H. A comparison of MTAI scores. *Mental Retardation,* 1965, *3,* 23–24.

Connor, Frances P., and Goldberg, I. Opinions of some teachers regarding their work with trainable children: implications for teacher education. *American Journal of Mental Deficiency,* 1960, *64,* 658–670.

Council for Exceptional Children. *Professional Standards for Personnel in the Education of Exceptional Children.* Washington: CEC, 1966.

Cratty, B. J. The perceptual-motor attributes of mentally retarded children and youth. Unpublished manuscript, Mental Retardation Services Board of Los Angeles County, 1966.

Daly, Flora M. The program for trainable mentally retarded pupils in the public schools of California. *Education and Training of the Mentally Retarded,* 1966, *1,* 109–118.

DiNola, A. J., Kaminsky, B. P., and Sternfeld, A. E. *TMR Performance Profile for the Severely and Moderately Retarded.* Ridgefield, New Jersey: Reporting Service for Exceptional Children, 1965.

Edmondson, Barbara, Leland H., and Leach, Ethel M. Social-perceptual training of retarded adolescents. *Parsons State Hospital and Training Center Project News,* 1966, *2*(5), 6–11.

Frankel, M. G., Happ, F. W., and Smith, M. D. *Functional teaching of the mentally retarded.* Springfield, Ill. Charles C Thomas, 1966.

Garrison, M. (Editor) Cognitive models and development in mental retardation. *American Journal of Mental Deficiency,* 1966 (Monograph Supplement).

Gitter, Lena L. Montessori and the compulsive cleanliness of severely retarded children. *Bulletin of Art Therapy,* 1965, *4,* 139–148.

Goldberg, I. I., and Cruickshank, W. M. The trainable but non-educable; whose responsibility? *NEA Journal,* 1958, *47,* 622–623.

Gorelick, Molly C. A typology of curriculum objectives for mentally retarded: from ambiguity to precision. *Mental Retardation,* 1963, *1,* 212–215.

Guilford, J. P. Three faces of intellect. *American Psychologist,* 1959, *14,* 469–479.

Happ, F. W. Teaching aid for the mentally retarded child. *Mental Retardation,* 1967, *5,* 33–35.

Harrison, W., Lecrone, H., Temerlin, M. K., and Trousdale, W. W. The effect of music and exercise upon the self-help skills of non-verbal retardates. *American Journal of Mental Deficiency,* 1966, *71,* 279–282.

Harvey, Ann, Yep, B., and Sellin, D. Developmental achievement of trainable mentally retarded children. *Training School Bulletin,* 1966, *63,* 100–108.

Hayden, F. J. *Physical fitness for the mentally retarded.* Ontario, Canada: Metropolitan Toronto Association for Retarded Children, 1964.

Heber, R. F. A manual on terminology and classification in mental retardation. (Second Edition) *American Journal of Mental Deficiency,* 1961 (Monograph Supplement). (a)

Heber, R. F. Modifications in the manual on terminology and classification in mental retardation. *American Journal of Mental Deficiency,* 1961, *65,* 499–500. (b)

Heber, R. F. Standards for the preparation and certification of teachers of the mentally retarded. *Mental Retardation,* 1963, *1,* 35–37, 60–62.

Huddle, D. D. Research implications: sheltered workshops for the trainable mentally retarded. *Education and Training of the Mentally Retarded,* 1967, *2,* 65–69.

Hudson, Margaret. An exploration of classroom procedures for teaching trainable mentally retarded children. *CEC Research Monograph,* 1960, Series A, No. 2.

Johnson, M. R. An experimental investigation of some dimensions underlying preferences for teaching exceptional children. Unpublished master's thesis, Fisk University, 1964.

Jones, R. L. Research on the special education teacher and special education teaching. *Exceptional Children,* 1966, *33,* 251–257.

Katz, E. An independent living rehabilitation program for seriously handicapped mentally retarded adults. *Training School Bulletin,* 1964, *61,* 34–44.

Kokaska, C. J. A summer camp experience for institutionalized mentally retarded children. *Training School Bulletin,* 1966, *62,* 158–162.

Lance, W. D. A clinical approach to the preparation of teachers of the educable mentally retarded. *Education and Training of the Mentally Retarded,* 1966, *1,* 100–103.

Lanyi, Agnes F. Nachfolgeuntersuchungen bei 200 schwachsinnigen kindern. (Follow-up examination of 200 mentally retarded children.) In J. Oster (Editor), *International Copenhagen Congress on the Scientific Study of Mental Retardation, Volume 2,* 1964. Pp. 845–846. (*Mental Retardation Abstracts,* 1966, *3,* 909.)

Leland, H. An overview of adaptive behavior as a behavioral classification. In E. Kagin (Editor), *Conference on Measurement of Adaptive Behavior:*

II. Parsons, Kan.: Parsons State Hospital and Training Center, 1966. Pp. 1–15.

Levine, S., and Elzey, F. F. *Personal–Social and Vocational Scale for the Mentally Retarded*. San Francisco: San Francisco State College, 1966.

Meisgeier, C. The identification of successful teachers of mentally or physically handicapped children. *Exceptional Children,* 1965, *32,* 229–235.

Montessori, Maria. *Dr. Montessori's Own Handbook*. New York: Schocken, 1965.

Patterson, C. H. Methods of assessing the vocational adjustment potential of the mentally handicapped. *Training School Bulletin,* 1964, *61,* 129–152.

Roach, E. G., and Kephart, N. C. *The Purdue Perceptual-Motor Survey*. Columbus, Ohio: Merrill, 1966.

Spradlin, J. E. Assessment of speech and language of retarded children: the Parsons Language Sample. *Journal of Speech and Hearing Disorders,* 1963 (Monograph Supplement 10).

Warren, Sue. Academic achievement of trainable pupils with five or more years of schooling. *Training School Bulletin,* 1963, *60,* 75–88.

Wolinsky, Gloria F. Theoretical and practical aspects of a teacher education program for teachers of the trainable child. *American Journal of Mental Deficiency,* 1959, *63,* 948–953.

Wolinsky, Gloria F. Curriculum considerations in programs for the trainable retarded: application of theoretical models. In *Special Education: Strategies for Educational Progress. Selected Convention Papers*. Washington: Council for Exceptional Children, 1966. Pp. 93–98.

CRITERIA FOR PLACING TRAINABLE RETARDED CHILDREN IN SPECIAL CLASSES

ELIGIBILITY [1]

1. A child who is not eligible for placement in classes for the educable mentally retarded.
2. *Physical condition:* A child who (*a*) is able to hear and see well enough to engage in special-class activities without undue risk; (*b*) is ambulatory to the extent that no undue risk to himself or hazard to others is involved in his daily work and play activities; and (*c*) is trained in toilet habits so that he has control over his body functions.
3. *Mental, emotional, and social development:* A child who (*a*) is able to communicate so that he can make his wants known and can understand simple directions; (*b*) is developed socially so that his behavior does not endanger himself and the physical well-being of other members of the group; and (*c*) is emotionally stable enough so that group stimulation

[1] See the California Administrative Code, Title 5, Article 21, Section 197, and Jerome H. Rothstein, "California's Program for the Severely Retarded Child," *Exceptional Children, 19*:5 (February 1953), 172.

will not intensify his problems unduly, that he can react to learning situations, and that his presence is not detrimental to the welfare of others.

INELIGIBILITY [2]

1. A child whose problems will be accentuated by group stimulation or whose behavior is detrimental to the group.
2. A child whose lack of mental, physical, or emotional maturation or whose physical condition would not warrant placement in a public school class.
3. A child who, after a reasonable trial in a class for severely handicapped pupils, has shown that he cannot adjust to or profit from activities of the group of which he is a member.
4. A child who, upon adequate psychiatric diagnosis, has been found to be mentally ill (psychotic or prepsychotic). Considerable caution must be exercised in applying this criterion. It must be recognized that intellectual behavior may be adversely affected by emotional conflict. The exclusion of mentally ill children needs to be preceded by careful evaluation by educational, psychological, and psychiatric personnel.
5. A child who cannot comply with the chronological-age standards required for school entrance by the state. (While early training programs may be desirable for many mentally retarded children, some states do not modify the legal ages for school acceptance of handicapped children.)

---

[2] See Arthur S. Hill, *The Forward Look; The Severely Retarded Child Goes to School*, Department of Health, Education, and Welfare Bulletin 1952, No. 11 (Washington, D.C. Government Printing Office, 1952), p. 26.

30 TRAINING SEVERELY AND PROFOUNDLY DEVELOPMENTALLY RETARDED CHILDREN

John H. Hollis
Chester E. Gorton

Reprinted by permission from *Mental Retardation*, a publication of the American Association on Mental Deficiency, Vol. 5, No. 4, August 1967, pp. 20–24, and the authors. Dr. Hollis is Director, Psychobiology Laboratories, Parsons Research Center, Parsons, Kan., and Dr. Gorton is Associate Professor of Special Education, Texas Women's University, Denton.

The purpose of this article is to provide a brief survey of current trends, thinking and research relevant to the training of severely and profoundly developmentally retarded children. In general, the article will be focused on the training of children who score below 25 IQ on a standardized test. In addition to the IQ criterion, these children typically show deficits in self-care (feeding, dressing and toilet training), social behavior, communication, and perceptual motor skills (Gorton and Hollis, 1965). Often these children spend much time engaged in abnormal stereotyped motor acts (Berkson, 1966).

This survey is not intended to be all inclusive or the last word on training, but rather to provide an overview of material that appears to be relevant and that impinges on the crucial issue of training. The special education teacher and the psychologist are often ill-equipped to cope with and train severely retarded children. First, the child is unable to communicate at the verbal level and often unable to communicate at the gestural level (Hollis, 1966). Second, their materials and techniques are generally "watered" down versions of those developed for normal children. The net result is that both child and adult are on extinction and the child is dropped from training or therapy (*i.e.,* when you flunk out of mud play you are resigned to a life of lying on the ward floor).

Within the maze of philosophies and learning theories, those that emphasize the consequence of an act (movement, response) provide the concepts and principles for the modification of behavior. That is, the data gathered on the effectiveness of reinforcement have proven to have great generality.

The recent rise of interest in mental retardation and behavior modification has led to the publication of several books dealing with theory, research and case studies of behavior modification. They include the *Handbook of Mental Deficiency* (Ellis, 1963a), *The International Review of Research in Mental Retardation* (Ellis, 1966) and *Case Studies in Behavior Modification* (Ullmann & Krasner, 1965). We suggest that anyone interested in training the retardate would do well to review the two volumes of *Behavior of Nonhuman Primates* (Schrier, Harlow and Stollnitz, 1965).

MODIFICATION OF BEHAVIOR

PROSTHESIS. Lindsley (1965) has written a very provocative article on measurement and prosthesis of retarded behavior. He suggests that retardation may be the result of an inadequate child environment relationship. That is, we design environments to support life, but not to develop and maintain behavior. Within the operant frame of reference he suggests three prosthetic strategies for rehabilitating the behaviorally handicapped. These are: (1) construction of prosthetic devices; (2) prosthetic training; and (3) construction of prosthetic environments. Prosthetic devices consist of such items as eye glasses, hearing aids, braces, and special tools for individuals with uncommon behavioral deficit. Prosthetic training is concerned with developing lower sensory thresholds, echo location (blind), lip reading, training of nondebilitated muscles to perform tasks normally done by injured or destroyed muscles. Prosthetic environments involve the positions of traffic lights and signs, signal bells, handrails, etc. However, higher order behavioral deficits exist, especially in the mentally retarded. These involve deficits in discrimination and differentiation, contingency and reinforcer, and reflex integration disorders. Lindsley also presents a method for diagramming the Operant Behavioral Equation and suggests that it provides a method for educators, rehabilitators, and others for analyzing the deficit operant. His notation is very important in that it provides a simple method for determining whether or not a component of the equation is functional.

PERCEPTUAL MOTOR SKILLS. Francis and Rarick (1959), studying the motor characteristics of the mentally retarded, concluded that they are markedly inferior to normal children on all motor tests (*e.g.,* static strength, dynamic strength, balance, agility). Their findings showed a low positive correlation with standardized intelligence tests. Tredgold (1937) suggests that the most pronounced motor deficiencies of the retardate are in the finer hand and finger movements, although the grosser functions of balance and locomotion are also deficient.

Problem-solving and gross perceptual motor skills in severely and profoundly retarded children have been investigated by Aldrich and Doll (1931). Their general thesis was that techniques and methods developed for the study of anthropoid behavior (Kohler, 1959) would be applicable to the study of severely and profoundly retarded children. This study successfully demonstrated that techniques developed for the study of box stacking behavior in anthropoid apes were applicable to the study and training of profoundly retarded children. It is suggested that the degree to which mental age and individual differences affect performance may be controlled by other factors. For example, "prosthetic training techniques" (Lindsley, 1964) could be applied to training on the solution of box stacking problems (cf. Kohler, 1959). This would require an analysis of the child's box stacking behavior in order to determine the deficient components and develop a tactic for its elimination.

The development of simple manipulative responses and simple perceptual motor skills is an important step in the training of severely and profoundly retarded children. Perceptual motor skills may be used as the foundation upon which to build more complex behavioral repertoires. For example, orientation, reaching, contacting and grasping movements must be established before the child can be trained to hold a crayon or even mark with it.

The following criteria may be applied to the selection of tasks for the training of simple perceptual motor skills: (1) that they are well adapted to the child's sensory motor equipment; (2) that they are similar in many respects to "natural" problems requiring gross manipulation; (3) that the tasks (problems) may be graded in order of difficulty from extremely simple to extremely complex; and (4) that the problems provide the child with a task in which he can visually survey the total situation including the reward and provide opportunity for solution in one trial (*e.g.*, by "insightful" learning). Two perceptual motor tasks that meet these criteria are Patterned String Problems (Kluver, 1961) and Bent-Wire Problems (Davis *et al.*, 1956). These perceptual motor problems were initially developed for the study of subhuman primates (*e.g.*, Harlow & Settlage, 1934; Finch, 1941; Davis *et al.*, 1956) and have also been used with children (*e.g.*, Brainard, 1930; Richardson, 1932; Whitecraft, 1958; Hollis, 1962).

OPERANT BEHAVIOR—IMITATION. The salient feature of operant behavior is that it is emitted, *i.e.*, it operates on, or changes, the environment. Thus, the behaviors of the child (movements or responses) are instrumental in producing a consequence (*e.g.*, food, a smile, or elimination of an aversive event). Lindsley (1964) provides a stimulating and fresh approach for the educator in applying operant behavioral principles to the training and rehabilitation of developmentally retarded children. More recently, Spradlin and Girardeau (1966) have made an extensive review of research directly related to the control of behavior of retarded children using operant behavior principles. They suggest, ". . . that if the principles and techniques (operant behavior) discussed in this chapter were consistently applied, Butterfield's case of over-achievement by a Mongoloid (1961) might be considered 'typical' rather than a 'provocative case' . . ."

Two recent reports on the application of operant behavior principles to the acquisition of speech (Lovaas *et al.*, 1966) and building and imitative repertoire (Baer *et al.*, 1965) will be described. Although many examples could be presented, it is believed that these have important implications for the educator who is planning a program and curriculum for the severely retarded child.

First, Lovaas *et al.* (1966) have demonstrated the acquisition of imitative speech in two mute schizophrenic children using operant conditioning principles. The authors state, ". . . there are no published systematic studies on how to go about developing speech in a person who has never spoken . . ." (p. 705). The researchers used an operant discrimination training procedure which consisted of four distinct steps:

1. Increase free operant rate of vocalization, the child was reinforced for all vocalization;
2. Temporal discrimination, the child was reinforced only if he vocalized within six seconds after an adult's vocalization (vowel sounds);
3. Matching, in this step the child was required to match the adult's vocalization (by successive approximation, also see Lindsley, 1964); and
4. Discrimination, the child was required to discriminate between sounds.

Subsequent steps involved using the previous step three to build sounds, words, and phrases. The children were performing so well after 25 days of training that the program was then shifted to emphasis on the appropriate use of language. The results showed that the reinforcer (food) must immediately follow the correct response in order to maintain imitative behavior in the children (*cf.* Baer *et al.,* 1965).

Casual observations suggest that normal children acquire motor acts by watching, and verbal behavior by hearing. That is, normal children learn many of the fundamentals of motor and verbal behavior by imitation. In general, for the severely and profoundly retarded this does not occur. Baer, Peterson, and Sherman (1965) have established imitation of motor acts in severely and profoundly retarded children using reinforcement procedures.

Baer *et al.* (1965) initially observed severely and profoundly retarded children ranging in age from nine to twelve years for several days and found that there was no spontaneous imitation. The children then were asked to imitate simple responses demonstrated by an adult. No imitative behavior occurred. During training the children were seen three times a day (at meal time) and seven days a week. The child's food was used as a reinforcer. The task was to teach the child a series of discriminated operants. The discriminated operants were composed of three elements: (1) a discriminative stimulus presented by the experimenters (*e.g.,* raised left arm); (2) correct response by the child (imitates experimenter); and (3) reinforcer for a correct response (food). For example, initially the experimenter would raise the child's arm and immediately reinforce her. The experimenter withdrew (faded out) his assistance in arm raising as the child developed the arm raising response (*cf.* response building, Lindsley, 1964). Using the outlined procedure, 130 discriminated operants were taught to one child. As training progressed there was evidence of generalized imitation, *i.e.,* responses were imitated the first time they were presented (*cf.* learning sets—"learning to learn," Harlow, 1949).

Social Reinforcement

Studies of subhuman primate behavior have suggested or demonstrated the importance of physical contact in maintaining social interaction (*e.g.*, Harlow and Zimmermann, 1958). Falk (1958) demonstrated with chimpanzees that grooming made contingent on a correct simple visual discrimination functioned as a reinforcer. Mason, Hollis and Sharpe (1962), using chimpanzee subjects, found that they responded differentially to various forms of physical contact (*e.g.*, stroking the skin, tickling, patting). That is, in a situation where contact was contingent on a simple operant response (*e.g.*, bar press) the various activities were differentially reinforcing. More recently, Hollis (1965) obtained similar results with profoundly retarded children. Social reinforcers have the advantage that they can be delivered by another person at any place and at any time. If social activities are neutral events for the child, they can be made into reinforcing consequences by pairing them with highly reinforcing consequences, *e.g.*, food (*cf.* Lovaas *et al.*, 1964a).

Aversive Stimulation

Although children frequently receive painful cuts and bruises during their daily functioning, there have been moral and other objections to the use of punishment for effecting behavioral changes. Holz and Azrin (1963) have demonstrated that punishment (electric shock) will suppress a response totally and for long periods of time. Bijou and Baer (1961) suggest that a stimulus which is discriminative for the elimination of pain may acquire positive reinforcing properties.

More recently, Lovaas, Schaeffer and Simmons (1965) have used electric shock for building social behaviors in schizophrenic children. The children selected for this study were similar in many respects to profoundly retarded children (*cf.* Hollis, 1965a, 1965b); they engaged in self-stimulation, and stereotyped movements, used no speech or appropriate play with objects, and showed no social responsiveness. The results show that the children learned to go to an adult to avoid shock and that shock was effective in eliminating such behavior as self-stimulation and tantrums. These authors suggest that the most efficient use of shock would involve using it as a way of establishing social reinforcers. That is, when social stimuli acquire reinforcing properties, one of the conditions for development of social behavior has been met.

SELF-CARE SKILLS

Recently, Bensberg (1965) wrote a book entitled *Teaching the Mentally Retarded,* which was designed to be a handbook for ward personnel. In general, the book is well done and provides much useful information, ideas and methods for training the mentally retarded in self-care skills.

Feeding Training

Although Bensberg (1965) presents a method for feeding training, Spradlin (1964) has developed a very satisfactory procedure. Spradlin's procedure involves response building (*cf.* Lindsley, 1964) and the notion that one response can serve as a reinforcer for a second response (Premack, 1959). In the procedure for training self-feeding developed by Spradlin, the following steps were used: (1) the trainer places a spoon in the child's hand and assists the child in holding and filling it; (2) the trainer moves the food-filled spoon to about one inch from child's mouth; (3) trainer waits until the child opens his mouth; (4) the child is required to make the last small movement of the spoon into the mouth; and (5) the trainer reduces his assistance in small steps (fades stimulus control) until the child is grasping the spoon, filling it, and moving it to his mouth.

Toilet Training

The toilet training of severely and profoundly retarded children is of utmost importance for the following reasons: (1) the prevention of disease (sanitary control); (2) elimination of unnecessary cleaning duties by parents or ward personnel; (3) the elimination of odor; and (4) a clean child is more appealing to educators and others concerned with training (Spradlin and Girardeau, 1966, provide a number of references on toilet training).

Toilet training with severely and profoundly retarded children is difficult for the following reasons: (1) communication—even if toilet trained, most of these children are unable to communicate their needs; (2) often the environment is so arranged that the child cannot get to the toilet when he needs to; and (3) training may have been such that the child is under the control of an adult rather than under the control of a full bowel or bladder.

Ellis (1963b) has presented a methodology for toilet training severely retarded patients that involves an S-R reinforcement approach. Although the model he presents is highly technical, it provides 15 steps for the development of a toilet training regimen. Baumeister and Klosowski (1965) have, in part, applied the model developed by Ellis to the training of a group of retarded patients. Their results indicated that as training progressed, the patients became easier to manage and some started to engage in self-feeding and other behavior which were not part of the program. Bensberg (1965) briefly mentions toilet training, the use of toilet tissue, and specially designed potty chairs (also see Gorton and Hollis, 1965).

Giles and Wolf (1966) have recently demonstrated that operant behavior modification techniques can be very effective for toilet training institutionalized severely retarded children. After eight weeks of training, all five subjects were eliminating consistently in the toilet. During training, appropriate elimination behavior was positively reinforced. When positive reinforcement procedures produced no results, positive reinforcement was used in conjunction with the presentation of aversive stimuli (physical restraint) following inappropriate behavior.

Behavioral Engineering

Although the structure of the physical plant may play an important role in the control of behavior, the contingencies and consequences set up by the cottage staff following acts (responses) by the children is crucial to the control of behavior. In a paper by Ayllon and Michael (1959) it has been suggested that the nurse is in a unique position to play the role of a behavioral engineer. Thus, if the nurses or cottage staff are trained to make objective observations of behavior and understand basic reinforcement procedures, they are in a unique position to play the role of a behavioral engineer. Thus, if the nurses or cottage staff are trained to make objective observations of behavior and understand basic reinforcement procedures, they are in a unique position to modify the patients' behavior. Ayllon and Michael (1959), using the nurse as a behavioral engineer, attacked such problems as control of: (1) entering the nurses' office; (2) psychotic talk; (3) being on the floor; (4) self-feeding; and (5) magazine hoarding. In general, they showed that they could increase or decrease the frequency of these behaviors.

In recent years there have been a number of studies that can be classified under the rubric of behavioral engineering. Baer (1962) has controlled thumbsucking by withdrawal and representation of reinforcement. Harris *et al.* (1964) have controlled crawling in a nursery school child with positive social reinforcement. Hart *et al.* (1964) have demonstrated the effects of social reinforcement on operant crying. Wolf *et al.* (1964) have written on the application of operant conditioning procedures to the behavior problems of an autistic child. Their paper deals specifically with the control of temper tantrums, bedtime behavior, throwing of glasses, and eating. Finally, Spradlin and Girardeau (1966) have discussed such perennial problems as self-destruction, drooling, nasal discharge and masturbation.

SUMMARY

It has been the intent of this paper to suggest some operational models, concepts and procedures for the training and development of curricula for the severely and profoundly developmentally retarded children.

We have said little about language development, although this is a major component of the definition of retardation. The reader is referred to the review and discussion of *Environmental Factors and the Language Development of Retarded Children* (Spradlin, in press). At the level of nonverbal communication Hollis (1966) has done several experiments comparing severely retarded children with similar behavior of nonhuman primates.

In summary, the first steps in establishing a training program and curriculum in day schools or institutions is to shift the goal of these organizations from one of care and management to education for life in the community (see Spradlin, 1964).

Finally, from the foregoing survey of research relevant to the training of severely and profoundly developmentally retarded children, it is clearly evident that we have operational procedures applicable to building training programs. That is, the educator, psychologist, or therapist no longer in good conscience can continue to hide behind concepts of psychotherapy and use these as excuses for not directly working with or training children. Ellis (1963b) sums this up succinctly with the following statement, ". . . Only when the psychologist puts aside his Binet kit and attacks problems such as this one, as a behavioral engineer, will he come to grips with the central issue in mental deficiency . . ." (p. 103).

REFERENCES

Aldrich, C. G. and Doll, E. A. Problem Solving Among Idiots. *Journal of Comparative and Physiological Psychology,* 1931, *12,* 137–169.

Ayllon, T. and Michael, J. The Psychiatric Nurse as a Behavioral Engineer. *Journal of Experimental Analysis of Behavior,* 1959, *2,* 323–334.

Baer, D. M. Effect of Withdrawal of Positive Reinforcement on an Extinguishing Response in Young Children. *Child Development,* 1961, *32,* 67–74.

Baer, D. M. Laboratory Control of Thumbsucking by Withdrawal and Representation of Reinforcement. *Journal of Experimental Analysis of Behavior,* 1962, *5,* 525–528.

Baer, D. M., Peterson, R. F. and Sherman, J. A. Building an Imitative Repertoire by Programming Similarity Between Child and Model as Discriminative for Reinforcement. Paper read at Society for Research in Child Development, Minneapolis, Minnesota, March 1965.

Baumeister, A. and Klosowski, R. An Attempt to Group Toilet Train Severely Retarded Patients. *Mental Retardation,* 1965, *3,* December, 24.

Bensberg, G. J. *Teaching the Mentally Retarded.* Atlanta: Southern Regional Education Board, 1965.

Berkson, G. Abnormal Stereotyped Motor Acts. In *Comparative Psychopathology,* G. Jervis and J. Zubin (Eds.). New York: Grune & Stratton, Inc., 1967.

Bijou, S. W. and Baer, D. M. *Child Development, Vol. I: A Systematic and Empirical Theory.* New York: Appleton-Century-Crofts, 1961.

Brainard, P. P. The Mentality of the Child Compared with That of Apes. *Journal of Genetic Psychology,* 1930, *37,* 290–291.

Butterfield, E. C. A Provocative Case of Over-Achievement by a Mongoloid. *American Journal of Mental Deficiency,* 1961, *66,* 444–448.

Davis, R. T., McDowell, A. A., Deter, C. W. and Steele, J. P. Performance of Rhesus Monkeys on Selected Laboratory Tasks Presented Before and After a Large Single Dose of Whole Body x Radiation. *Journal of Comparative and Physiological Psychology,* 1956, *49,* 20–26.

Ellis, N. R. (Ed.) *Handbook of Mental Deficiency.* New York: McGraw-Hill, Inc., 1963 (a).

Ellis, N. R. Toilet Training the Severely Defective Patient: An S-R Reinforcement Analysis. *American Journal of Mental Deficiency,* 1963, *68,* 98–103 (b).

Ellis, N. R. (Ed.) *The International Review of Research in Mental Retardation.* New York: Academic Press, Inc., 1966.

Falk, J. L. The Grooming Behavior of the Chimpanzee as a Reinforcer. *Journal of Experimental Analysis of Behavior,* 1958, *1,* 83–85.

Ferster, C. B. and DeMyer, M. K. The Development of Performances in Autistic Children in an Automatically Controlled Environment. *Journal of Chronic Diseases,* 1961, *13,* 312–345.

Finch, G. The Solution of Patterned String Problems by Chimpanzees. *Journal of Comparative and Physiological Psychology,* 1941, *32,* 83–90.

Francis, R. J. and Rarick, G. L. Motor Characteristics of the Mentally Retarded. *American Journal of Mental Deficiency,* 1959, *62,* 792–811.

Giles, D. K. and Wolf, M. M. Toilet Training Institutionalized, Severe Retardates: An Application of Operant Behavior Modification Techniques. *American Journal of Mental Deficiency,* 1966, *70,* 766–780.

Gorton, C. E. and Hollis, J. H. Redesigning a Cottage Unit for Better Programming and Research for the Severely Retarded. *Mental Retardation,* 1965, *3,* June, 16.

Harlow, H. F. The Formation of Learning Sets. *Psychological Review,* 1949, *56,* 51–65.

Harlow, H. F. and Settlage, P. H. Comparative Behavior of Primates VII: Capacity of Monkeys to Solve Patterned String Tests. *Journal of Comparative and Physiological Psychology,* 1934, *18,* 432–435.

Harlow, H. F. and Zimmermann, R. R. The Development of Affectional Responses in Infant Monkeys. Proceedings of the American Philosophical Society, 1958, *102,* 501–509.

Harris, F. R., Johnston, M. K., Kelley, C. S. and Wolf, M. M. Effects of Positive Social Reinforcement on Regressed Crawling of a Nursery School Child. *Journal of Educational Psychology,* 1964, *55,* 35–41.

Harris, F. R., Wolf, M. M. and Baer, D. M. Effects of Adult Reinforcement on Child Behavior. *Young Children,* 1964, October 8–17.

Hart, B. M., Allen, K. E., Buell, J. S., Harris, F. R. and Wolf, M. M. Effects of Social Reinforcement on Operant Crying. *Journal of Experimental Child Psychology,* 1964, *1,* 145–153.

Hollis, J. H. Solution of Bent-Wire Problems by Severely Retarded Children. *American Journal of Mental Deficiency,* 1962, *67,* 463–472.

Hollis, J. H. Differential Responses of Profoundly Retarded Children to Social Stimulation. *Psychological Reports,* 1965, *16,* 977–984.

Hollis, J. H. The Effects of Social and Non-social Stimuli on the Behavior of

Profoundly Retarded Children: Part 1. *American Journal of Mental Deficiency,* 1965, *69,* 755–771 (a).

Hollis, J. H. The Effects of Social and Non-social Stimuli on the Behavior of Profoundly Retarded Children: Part 2. *American Journal of Mental Deficiency,* 1965, *69,* 772–789 (b).

Hollis, J. H. Communication within Dyads of Severely Retarded Children. *American Journal of Mental Deficiency,* 1966, *70,* 729–744.

Holz, W. C. and Azrin, N. H. A Comparison of Several Procedures for Eliminating Behavior. *Journal of Experimental Analysis of Behavior,* 1963, *6,* 399–406.

Kluver, H. *Behavior Mechanisms in Monkeys,* Chicago: University of Chicago, 1961.

Kohler, W. *The Mentality of Apes.* New York: Vintage, 1959.

Lent, J. Progress Report: A Demonstration Program for Intensive Training of Institutionalized Mentally Retarded Girls. Parsons Research Center, Parsons, Kansas, Grant #MR-1 801 A66, 1966.

Lindsley, O. R. Direct Measurement and Prosthesis of Retarded Behavior. *Journal of Education,* 1964, *147,* 62–81.

Lovaas, O. I., Berberich, J. P., Perloff, B. F. and Schaeffer, B. Acquisition of Imitative Speech by Schizophrenic Children. *Science,* 1966, *151* (3711), 705–707.

Lovaas, O. I., Schaeffer, B. and Simmons, J. Q. Experimental Studies in Childhood Schizophrenia: Building Social Behaviors Using Electric Shock. University of California, Los Angeles, 1965.

Mason, W. A., Hollis, J. H. and Sharpe, L. G. Differential Responses of Chimpanzees to Social Stimulation. *Journal of Comparative and Physiological Psychology,* 1962, *55,* 1105–1110.

Premack, D. Toward Empirical Behavior Laws: I Positive Reinforcement. *Psychological Review,* 1959, *66,* 219–233.

Richardson, H. M. The Growth of Adaptive Behavior in Infants: An Experimental Study at Seven Age Levels. *Genetic Psychology Monographs,* 1932, *12,* 329–332.

Schrier, A. M., Harlow, H. F. and Stollnitz, F. *Behavior of Nonhuman Primates. Vol. 1,* New York: Academic Press, Inc., 1965.

Schrier, A. M., Harlow, H. F. and Stollnitz, F. *Behavior of Nonhuman Primates. Vol. 2,* New York: Academic Press, Inc., 1965.

Spradlin, J. E. The Premack Hypothesis and Self-Feeding by Profoundly Retarded Children: A Case Report. Parsons Research Center, Parsons, Kansas, Working Paper #79, 1964.

Spradlin, J. E. Environmental Factors and Language Development of Retarded Children. In *Developments in Applied Psycholinguistics Research,* S. Rosenberg (Ed.). New York: Crowell-Collier and Macmillan, Inc., 1968.

Spradlin, J. E. and Girardeau, F. L. The Behavior of Moderately and Severely Retarded Persons. In *The International Review of Research in Mental Retardation, Vol. 1,* N. R. Ellis (Ed.). New York: Academic Press, Inc., 1966.

Spradlin, J. E., Girardeau, F. L. and Corte, E. Fixed Ratio and Fixed Interval Behavior of Severely and Profoundly Retarded Subjects. *Journal of Experimental Child Psychology,* 1965, *2,* 340–353.

Tredgold, A. F. *A Textbook of Mental Deficiency* (6th Ed.). Baltimore: William Wood & Company, 1937.

Ullmann, L. and Krasner, L. (Eds.) *Case Studies in Behavior Modification.* New York: Holt, Rinehart and Winston, Inc., 1965.

Whitecraft, R. A. Solution of Bent-Wire Problems by Preschool Children. Thesis submitted to the Department of Psychology, State University of South Dakota, 1958.

Wolf, M. and Risley, T. Applications of Operant Conditioning Procedures to the Behaviour Problems of an Autistic Child. *Behavior Research Therapy,* 1964, *1,* 305–312.

31 AIDES FOR THE TRAINABLE MENTALLY RETARDED

Fred M. Hanson

From *Journal of the California Teachers Association,* Vol. 65, No. 3, May 1969, pp. 23–26. Reprinted with the permission of the Editor, California Teachers Association, and the author. Mr. Hanson is Consultant, Education of the Mentally Retarded, California State Department of Education, Sacramento, Calif.

The California State Department of Education, in conjunction with Cerritos Junior College, is presently exploring the possibilities of training paraprofessional personnel to assist teachers of special education programs. A Title VI-A project initiated by the Division of Special Schools and Services in 1968 was a rather unique effort to involve a two-year community college and the State Department of Education in the training of a paraprofessional to cope with the varied tasks generally required of a special education aide. This project, presently funded under ESEA, Title VI-A for the school year 1968–1969, will be concluded next year.

One of the objectives of this project is to develop and evaluate a curriculum designed to meet the needs of special education aides. At present, the task of training aides is an ill-defined process, left to the informal instruction of special education teachers and others. The training program at Cerritos involves specially designed courses and selection of other useful electives in addition to a direct involvement of each trainee in an extensive field experience with close supervision, providing services to handicapped children.

The State Department of Education has a major concern and interest in the training of professional and paraprofessional personnel working in the public schools. The community colleges also have had a major part and particular interest in strengthening preprofessional and paraprofessional course offerings to provide important and necessary services to the community and the state as a whole. The Division of Special Schools and Services has been keenly aware of the shortages of trained personnel in the field to work with handicapped children at both the professional and paraprofessional level. The lack of an organized training program for special education aides appears to be one of the shortages in manpower development and training. In short, adequate training provisions for special education aides do not exist. At the conclusion of the Cerritos project, however, we hope to have substantial empirical data to report to the field regarding the efficacy of a two-year community college undertaking the task of training special education aides to work with handicapped children—also, some specific recommendations regarding staffing, course offerings, and field experience in addition to the number of hours considered appropriate for certification or other possible evidence of completion of a planned curricula.

There are presently 8723 trainable mentally retarded children enrolled in special classes in California's public schools. Other categories of special education students who are in need of specialized educational assistance because of physical or mental disabilities are enrolled in special education programs for the orthopedically handicapped, visually handicapped, or aurally handicapped. Still other individuals are receiving their education or training in private schools or in state hospitals. These programs employ specially credentialed teachers and other professional personnel such as psychologists, nurses, counselors, supervisors, and others to work with handicapped children, in addition to the hundreds of special education aides.

It is felt that even though the Cerritos project is a reasonably small one, it does have statewide significance and it is hoped that other community colleges will be able to benefit from the experiences derived from this undertaking under the Title VI-A project. In this way, the information and knowledge gained by the staff and students at one community college will provide a foundation to other community college personnel who may be interested in providing specialized preparation to special education aides in their own area.

QUALIFICATIONS ARE IMPROVING

Some school districts and county offices in California have employed personnel to assist special class teachers using job titles such as "teacher matrons," "teacher assistants," "child attendants," or other classification of teacher aides to work with handicapped children. The quality and knowledge or experience of the individuals working with handicapped children has gradually improved. However, there is still, it is felt by many individuals, considerable need for inservice or other types of paraprofessional training to upgrade the quality of the individuals working with handicapped children, particularly the individuals offering assistance to special class teachers.

Special class teachers must also be trained to use the knowledge and skills of the qualified special education aides. Training, therefore, is by no means a one-way proposition. The special education aides may have unique talents or experience in working with handicapped children which could in some instances supplement the talents of a special class teacher. Special class teachers may need to examine their own roles carefully in order to better utilize their time and the time of the teacher aide. Recognition of specific tasks to be performed may also lead to better staff utilization and the upgrading of the teacher's role as an instructional planner and director.

The fact that there are some very fine special education aides has been due to the inservice on-the-job training (O.J.T.) by outstanding teachers presently working in special classrooms, and some supervisors providing assistance and direction. There are obvious weaknesses in this informal inservice training system. As our knowledge of the learning characteristics of the trainable mentally retarded increases and our educational planning becomes more individualized, the need for more skilled personnel at the professional and paraprofessional levels to assist in this process becomes increasingly important. There seems to be little doubt that the special education aide will be an important partner in the upgrading of instruction for the trainable mentally retarded in the years to come.

It was envisioned that the project undertaken by Cerritos College and the Department of Education would provide us with evidence regarding the desirability or feasibility of developing a training program at other community colleges to train special education aides. The initiation of such a program of training for special education aides would mean that the pupils would be given expert care by well trained persons who have had both classroom experience and actual on-the-job training under the supervision of a trained instructor.

The trained special education aide, since he is more knowledgeable, should command a higher salary. The relatively low salaries (around $2 an hour) paid special education aides has not produced *qualified* personnel in this field. One should hasten to add, however, that special education aides presently employed generally are dedicated, hardworking, conscientious people who have provided, and hopefully will continue to provide, a valuable service to the "special children" with whom they work. Many of the aides working with trainable mentally retarded pupils do so out of love and a desire to provide a worthwhile service to these intellectually limited and/or physically handicapped children and teenagers.

The teachers of exceptional children have many tasks to accomplish in order to fulfill their roles as professional educators. A well trained teacher aide, it is believed, can release the trained professional teacher to perform his role as an educational director still more efficiently.

The question of what a special education aide does in a special classroom for trainable mentally retarded children has been rather well reviewed in the State Department of Education bulletin dealing with trainable mentally retarded pupils.[1] Terminology such as matron, teacher assistant, etc., is often confusing and demonstrates a lack of uniformity in nomenclature. The duties or responsibilities assigned by teachers or other school district personnel to the individuals employed as special education aides vary considerably throughout the state. At the present time, I know of no particular well developed universal or uniform job description, nor of an effort to standardize the terms used with special education aides in classes throughout the state. It should be noted therefore that the person who is generally referred to here is a noncertificated person who assists a special class teacher

[1] Programs for the Trainable Mentally Retarded in California Public Schools, California State Department of Education, 1966. Prepared by Fred M. Hanson, Flora M. Daly, L. Wayne Campbell.

with the care and management of pupils. At no time does the teacher aide perform tasks of a professional nature; these are the responsibility of the credentialed teacher.

A special education teacher aide should act under the supervision of a teacher rendering the following types of services in special classes for trainable mentally retarded pupils:

1. Assist pupils to move from place to place in an orderly manner. Example: School bus to classroom and classroom to toilet, lunchroom or playground
2. Assist pupils with the management of their personal clothing, particularly after toileting
3. Arranges classroom or outdoor work area for planned activities
4. Assist the teacher in preparation of materials needed for the instructional program
5. Assist the teacher with the lunch program and the snack program
6. Assist the teacher with group activities
7. Assist the teacher in maintaining good housekeeping standards
8. Assist the teacher in maintaining cordial relationships between home and school
9. Relieve the teacher for a duty-free lunch period
10. Other duties as assigned by the special class teacher or supervisor.

The bulletin mentioned above also points out that persons employed as teacher aides must be emotionally stable and must be in good physical health, and be able to do the following:

1. Help a child "struggle" to achieve for himself
2. Resist the tendency to allow a pupil to become over-dependent
3. Respect individual children, and show patience, compassion, and tolerance for differences
4. Follow instructions under the leadership of the teacher
5. Maintain good interpersonal relationships and cooperate closely with the teacher
6. Respect the confidential nature of pupil records and school reports
7. Maintain appropriate personal habits. For example: cleanliness, neatness.

ASSISTANCE IS INVALUABLE

A part of my task in presenting these observations is to assist others in answering some basic questions as to the desirability of maintaining programs involving special instructional or teacher aides when little evidence seems to exist with regard to the need or substantiation of results having been attributed to the inclusion of a teacher aide in school programs for trainable mentally retarded pupils. During the approximately seven years that I have been with the Department of Education, I have noted with considerable pleasure the inclusion of additional individual help and specialized instruction provided by teacher assistants in classrooms working with trainable mentally retarded pupils. In many instances this more comprehensive program seems to be directly attributable to the inclusion of special education aides. In general, the teacher aide assists the teacher in the physical development of gross motor coordination, fine motor development in providing additional individual help where needed with regard to toileting or perhaps locomotion involving walking or climbing, or the further development of work training skills and learning better hand-eye coordination. These skills may be provided for in a kitchen or on some other type of "job station" or task provided for in the classroom or on the school grounds.

This additional help gives the special class teacher considerable latitude with regard to dealing with individual problems and also being assured that someone is providing direct assistance if needed and general overall supervision when the teacher is directly engaged in the educational process or training of an individual or group of children for which the entire group may not be ready. In a recent conversation with a teacher-principal of a school for trainable mentally retarded pupils, she indicated that her "right arm" was the so-called "principal" special education aide. In some instances the teacher aide working with the mentally retarded is a person who is endowed with considerable ability and has unique preparation or technical skills in working with both regular and handicapped pupils and has chosen to work on a less structured basis with trainable mentally retarded pupils because they enjoy this type of work with these youngsters.

Due to the fact that much of the instructional program for trainable mentally retarded pupils involves a very close degree of supervision, it stands to reason that the addition of an adult or perhaps younger, more capable individual in the classroom to assist the trainable mentally retarded will enhance the opportunity to provide this direct supervision and carry out the many meaningful but perhaps simple repetitive tasks required in order for these children to learn to become more self-sufficient.

YOUNG PEOPLE AS AIDES

Some programs for trainable mentally retarded pupils involve volunteer assistants on a regular basis to provide this immediate type supervision. One of the most obvious difficulties with this type of an arrangement is that there is very little continuity or responsibility on the part of the individuals providing assistance, since they may only be there for a very short period of time, or perhaps choose only to perform specific activities of their own choosing. On the other hand, several individuals who have administrative responsibility in programs for the trainable mentally retarded have taken particular interest and note of the fact that young pupils who are in regular education programs at the high school level, or perhaps junior college level, have provided invaluable assistance to teachers of the retarded. These students appear to relate exceedingly well to trainable mentally retarded children who do have severe learning problems.

In essence, the case as to the need or efficacy, or proven value, of special education aides with trainable mentally retarded pupils, and perhaps to other handicapped individuals, is still in need of considerable research and empirical evidence to substantiate the *nearly total agreement that special education aides are, in fact, a valuable adjunct to the special class teacher, and their services do, in fact, contribute to program improvement.*

SECTION EIGHT

Community Day-Care Programs

In the continuum of services for the mentally retarded, the community day-care program fills a need for children of preschool age, or those of school age so severely retarded that they would not be eligible for placement in a trainable program. It also meets the needs for some retarded children for care after school hours. Day-care facilities for severely retarded children help families to preserve their integrity by providing some relief to the mother from the problems of affording constant care to a severely retarded child. Such a program, moreover, helps to prepare retarded children for nursery school programs by contributing to their social development. In some places, short-term community living facilities are also provided for utilization in times of family crisis or stress, or to allow families to take a vacation free from the care of a retarded child. An important aspect of community day-care programs is the concurrent parental guidance programs that are usually available.

The organizational pattern and clients served vary from program to program. Some centers have developed community day-care programs that not only provide for severely retarded young children, but also for adolescents and young adults. Quite often young adult retardates who have completed public school programs are not well adjusted enough to participate in a sheltered workshop program or employment. Hence, a transitional program is most needed for this group. For the young adults it is an opportunity for continued social maturity training as well as prevocational exploration activities. In addition, the community day-care centers provide a wide array of leisure time and recreational activities. For some teen-age retardates, a late afternoon or evening recreational program furnishes the only real outlet for utilization of leisure time. Other centers offer weekend camping trips, exposure to commercial recreational activities, or summer day and residential camping programs.

Edward L. LaCrosse [1] has, in very great detail, outlined a total day-care center service program. In the early development of these programs, they were usually financed by United Crusade funds or tuition paid by parents. Recently, many states have recognized the great value of these programs and have taken over the financing. Such states as Delaware, Ohio, New York, and Illinois have accepted their responsibility for such programs.

For some severely retarded children, especially very young children, even the day-care program does not meet their needs. To avoid institutionalization, a program of homebound therapy has been devised. In such cases, supportive personnel, such as public health nurses, occupational therapists, and language developmentalists, come directly into the home to demonstrate to parents the best way to meet the physical, emotional, social, and intellectual needs of their profoundly retarded child. Mothers of these children get intensive counseling from the staff on an individual or group counseling basis. The therapy staff usually provides help with activities of daily living, constructive use of toys, motor development, perceptual and language development.

The city of Denver, Colorado, has pioneered this unusual program and it is described by Hope G. Curfman and Carol B. Arnold.[2] The reader is referred to Edward L. Meyen's *Planning Community Services for the Retarded* as an excellent reference.[3]

The first of two readings in this section, written by John V. Conover, describes the three distinct programs currently in operation in the State of New Jersey. In the second reading, William K. Murphy and R. C. Scheerenberger discuss the day center program for the mentally retarded in Illinois. This reading covers a five-phase program: (1) diagnostic and evaluation services; (2) casework counseling for the retardate and his parents; (3) training and activity experiences; (4) vocational training and sheltered workshop provisions; and (5) referral services.

[1] Edward L. LaCrosse, "Day Care Centers for Mentally Retarded Children," in Edward L. Meyen (ed.), *Planning Community Services for the Mentally Retarded* (Scranton, Pa.: International Textbook Co., 1967), pp. 298–313.

[2] Hope G. Curfman and Carol B. Arnold, "A Homebound Therapy Program for Severely Retarded Children," *Children, 14*:2 (March–April 1967), 63–68.

[3] Edward L. Meyen (ed.), *Planning Community Services for the Retarded* (Scranton, Pa.: International Textbook Co., 1967).

32 COMMUNITY DAY-CARE PROGRAM FOR SEVERELY AND PROFOUNDLY RETARDED CHILDREN

John V. Conover

From *The New Jersey Welfare Reporter,* January 1967, pp. 19–25. Reprinted with the permission of the New Jersey State Department of Institutions and Agencies and the author. Mr. Conover is Chief, Bureau of Day Training Services, Division of Mental Retardation, New Jersey State Department of Institutions and Agencies, Trenton.

There are basically three types of day-care programs in operation in the State of New Jersey at the present time. The first of these is day care for children of working mothers. This program is operated by the State Bureau of Children's Services and has as its main purpose the care of children during the hours that the mother is employed outside of the home. The second is the day-care program operated by the mental hospitals. The purpose of this program is the care of ex-mental patients, both children and adults, during the day when they would have no supervision within their home. The third day-care program is the one presently operated by the New Jersey Association for Retarded Children, Inc., and the Division of Mental Retardation.

This program is geared to the provision of care, training, and social adjustment for severely and profoundly retarded children between the ages of four and a half and twenty-one who have been excluded from public schools by virtue of their degree of retardation. At the present time a total of 24 centers are in operation, at least one in each of the 21 New Jersey counties. This program includes some 278 children who, prior to the establishment of this program, have been excluded from all formally organized training or care programs.

CONCEPT OVER 200 YEARS OLD

Historically speaking, the day-care center is a relatively old concept. The first center in the United States, which can truly be termed a day-care center, was established at "The Ursuline Convent" in New Orleans in 1729. Much later, nursery programs were established at Children's Hospital in New York (1854); in Troy, New York (1858); and Philadelphia (1861). During the years following the Civil War many day-care programs were established to care for the children of mothers who were forced to seek employment outside of their homes. In 1898 the Federation of Day Nurseries was organized. The purpose of this organization was to set standards in such areas as cleanliness and procedures for health inspection. This was necessitated by the fact that many of the then existing programs had been operated in a more or less casual manner with little regard for the hazards that such programming could produce.

In the 1920s, the number of nursery programs increased dramatically. These programs, however, differed greatly from the type of program which is in vision for the severely or profoundly retarded child, since the emphasis then was primarily on the educational needs of the child.

With the coming of World War II (1941), the United States Children's Bureau developed a daytime care program for the children of mothers who were employed in the defense industry. Funds previously earmarked for the W.P.A. were reallocated for this purpose. At the conclusion of World War II, many day-care centers were disbanded as the need for the employment of women somewhat subsided.

In 1958, a bill was introduced into the United States Senate by Senator Jacob Javitz. This bill would have provided supporting funds ($25,000,000) for day-care services. The unique feature of this bill was the section which would have provided, for the first time, day-care services for children who were physically or mentally handicapped. Unfortunately, this bill was never enacted. In the ensuing years, similar bills have been proposed, but in each instance the bills never left the Committee. The proposal of this bill, however, did serve to point out the need for day-care services for handicapped children.

CENTERS FOR HANDICAPPED RELATIVELY NEW

Prior to Senator Jacob Javitz's 1958 proposal, the states of Ohio and Pennsylvania (1951); Delaware and Massachusetts (1957); and New York (1958) had drafted and passed legislation providing for the establishment of state-sponsored or operated day-care centers for physically and mentally handicapped children. In the ensuing years, California (1959); Louisiana (1960); Connecticut, Utah, Illinois, Maryland, and Minnesota (1961); Washington and Wisconsin (1963); Colorado, Georgia, Indiana, Kansas and Oregon (1964) passed similar legislation. It must be noted that though the term "day care" is universally applied to all of these programs the type and handicaps of the children involved vary greatly. In some instances, the children are truly trainable and functioning on a level which would necessitate their inclusion in public school classes were they residents of the State of New Jersey.

NEW JERSEY'S PROGRAM

In 1963, the State of New Jersey, through the Department of Institutions and Agencies, Division of Mental Retardation, approached the state legislature with a request for funds to establish a pilot day-care center for children who were excluded from public school by virtue of their degree of retardation. This request was honored, thus enabling the establishment of the first New Jersey community day-care center for severely and profoundly retarded children. This first pilot project was established with the cooperation of the Essex County Unit, New Jersey Association for Retarded Children, Inc., and included a total of 19 children. It was the intent of the department that during the initial phases of this program, the service would be purchased from the local organizations who indicated their willingness or desire to establish this desperately needed service for the children within their communities. The Essex County Day Care Center commenced operation in September 1963. A careful review of the money appropriated for this program and the cost of operating the program, as it then existed, indicated that sufficient funds would be available for the establishment of additional programs.

The need for day-care services had been established by the number of applications for day-care funds received by the Division of Mental Retardation from the other county units of the New Jersey Association for Retarded Children, Inc. It was decided that the remaining funds should be used to purchase day-care services from additional units. Priority was given to Union County for the establishment of the second day-care center (this priority was based upon the date which the Division received the request for funds). The day-care center in Union County was opened on the 2nd of January 1964. Late in April of that same year, the funds remaining in the day-care account were used to purchase day-care services from four additional units. These were Morris, Gloucester, and Bergen-Passaic Counties.

The following fiscal year 1964–65, an appropriation of $75,000 was approved by the legislature. Since five centers caring for 98 children were then open, it was determined that the available funds would permit the addition of only three more counties to the list of those offering day-care services. Contracts were initiated with the counties of Warren, Monmouth, and Morris. By the end of the fiscal year, 154 children were attending day-care classes in nine New Jersey counties. The 1965–1966 fiscal year appropriation of $225,000 enabled program implementation on a limited basis throughout the State of New Jersey. During that year, some 284 children were cared for in 26 day-care centers located throughout the State. The fiscal appropriation for 1966–1967 ($435,000) will permit the addition of approximately 100 children to the present Day-Care Program, as well as provide transportation for many children who have been previously denied this service because of the lack of public transportation.

In many respects the New Jersey Day-Care Program resembles the Daytime Care Program developed by Dr. Charles Jubenville of the State of Delaware. This program, which was established by the Delaware legislature in 1957, was designed specifically to care for individuals who are termed totally dependent. It does not specify age limits; but does require a thorough investigation of the individual's intellectual, emotional, and social background. Based on the information gleaned from the psychometric examinations and interviews, the individuals are selected for placement in the centers.

Unlike Delaware, New Jersey's program places age limitations upon the individuals who are included in the program. To qualify for the New Jersey program, a child must have been excluded from public school and be at least four and a half and not more than twenty-one years of age. He must have been examined by a qualified psychologist not more than one year prior to his admission to this program. In addition, he is required to have a physical examination by a physician, the results of which must be reported to the center supervisor on forms provided for this purpose. No child is excluded from the program because of his inability to ambulate or communicate with the staff.

TRAINABILITY DEMONSTRATED

Since its inauguration in 1963, the New Jersey Day-Care Program has met with great success. Children previously considered totally dependent have, through training, become partially independent. Owing to the emphasis placed upon the development of coordination and social stimulation, retarded children have been able to attain functioning levels far in excess of those of which they were formerly believed capable. Typical among the gains obtained are the development of speech, ability to walk, ability to eat with little or no assistance, and the attainment of bowel and bladder control.

The day-care center has as its primary function the training of children for whom no programs were previously available. This training, in a sense, both supplements and substitutes for training that the parents find themselves incapable of providing because of lack of knowledge of techniques and/or emotional involvement which in many instances precludes their doing so at home. Within the framework of the day-care center, it is possible for skilled persons to develop within the child independence, social maturity, and physical skills which could never be attained at home. The methods used to achieve modification of behavior cannot fully be described within the confines of this paper. It may, however, be said that a combination of physical equipment, such as walking boards, flying saucers, tricycles, puzzles, blocks, etc., is extremely useful in the development of small and large muscle control. Far more important than these physical objects are the immeasurable, indefinable factors of T.L.C. (tender loving care), and personal inventiveness.

RESPONSE TO AFFECTION

It has been observed that in the centers where the staff have been personally interested and sensitive to the needs of the children for acceptance and affection, great strides toward establishing independence have been attained. The day-care technician, whose interest in the child exceeds that of one solely interested in remuneration, finds the job not only challenging, but rewarding as well.

DRAMATIC COORDINATION GAINS

The tools with which the day-care technicians perform their job have often been conjured up in their imagination. To the day-care technicians, mundane objects such as a toy balloon becomes a tool with which a child develops coordination. For example, a balloon thrown to a child does not attain the same velocity as a rubber ball; therefore, the child attempting to catch this object, has time to establish the special relationship between the balloon and himself. He must decide upon the course of action best suited to catch the object before it strikes the ground, thus evoking the response of not only the arm and leg muscles, but also requiring coordination of hand and eye.

The tricycle becomes not only an object to ride, but a means by which a directed, complex, and coordinated activity may be stimulated. It provides the child who cannot walk, or who has not mastered the concept of placing one foot before the other, with a means by which the muscles of the leg can be stimulated, coordinated and developed. For example, the pedaling of the tricycle requires the leg muscles to push the pedals in a circular motion in order to propel it. It is therefore possible, by attaching the child's feet to the pedals with rubber bands, to stimulate this motor activity by pushing the child while he sits on the tricycle, thereby producing a similar pattern of muscle activity which is required in pedaling the tricycle. This establishes the basic patterns of movement which are similar to those required in walking.

A jigsaw puzzle is a tool with which the child can learn special relationships, hand/eye coordination, and form and color discrimination. He learns that the proper placement of isolated puzzle parts used in concert form a whole meaningful picture. As a result of this experience, the child discovers that it is necessary for him to orient the individual puzzle parts with respect to configuration, color, and the segment of the picture which is thereon contained.

The common drinking straw becomes an aid in teaching the child to talk, since it can be used to visualize the concept of expulsion of air through the mouth. The placement of peanut butter on the child's lip becomes an instrument useful in developing tongue motility when the child is requested to lick the peanut butter from his lip. These actions, which come naturally to the normal child, are of necessity taught to the child who is severely or profoundly retarded.

ACCEPTANCE IN AN ALIEN WORLD

In regard to the development of social competence it can be said that, in general, the child in day care, prior to his enrollment in the program, is a social isolate. His contact with other individuals may have been limited to the primary family group (mother, father and siblings), all of whom may have treated him as an infant or as an object of embarrassment.

Within the setting of the day-care center, the child is accepted, not as a deviant from the group, but as an integral part of the group. He learns that he must not only respond to others, but must act with, share with, and in every way relate to both other children and members of staff. Many times this is the first experience in interaction that the child has ever had. He soon learns that the alien world into which he is thrust can be a happy, comfortable place in which to reside. Indeed, many times day-care children, like normal children, learn more rapidly from their peers than from adults.

A clear-cut example of the type of training benefits derived by children from the day-care program is evidenced in the following observation.

Of a group of children (21) in one day-care center, it was observed that 19 of these children fed themselves with their left hand. At first this seemed incompatible with what was known about the ratio of left-handed to right-handed people. However, further examination of the facts relating to this situation revealed that only two children, prior to their enrollment in this day-care center were capable of feeding themselves. The supervisor of the center was observed to be left-handed. The technique used for teaching the children to feed themselves was that of having the supervisor stand behind the child and bring the child's hand through the motion of conveying food from the plate to his mouth. As a result of this conditioned activity, 19 children previously incapable of feeding themselves, became independent left-handed self feeders.

It is most difficult to objectively measure the accomplishments of the day-care program over the past three years. However, it is known that at least 40 children who entered the day-care program have now attained functioning levels which has permitted their inclusion in trainable or educable classes in public schools.

In addition to the aforementioned fact, there is a wealth of evidence in the comments received from parents extolling the benefits of the day-care program.

Typical among the comments received from parents is the following excerpt from a letter sent to the division by the parent of a child in one of the day-care programs; "We wish to express our great satisfaction with the improvement shown by our son since his inclusion in the day-care program at the Evanoff Guidance Center in Vineland, New Jersey. We feel that the loving care given to him by his teachers has made him a happier as well as better trained child. To us, the day-care program is a real success and we hope for its continuance for T——— and for others like him."

FAMILY TENSIONS RELIEVED

An ancillary benefit derived from the day-care program by the parents is the relief from the 24-hour-a-day care of a totally dependent individual.

It has been reported that in some instances, the friction growing out of the presence of the day-care child in the home brought family tension to a level beyond which it could not have been tolerated. However, with the removal of the child from the home for five hours a day, the mother is provided with a relief period during which she may recover her stability and provide the care and attention greatly needed by the other members of the family. It must be borne in mind that even a trip to the store without the retardate may become an enjoyable experience for the mother, since previously it may have been impossible to obtain a baby sitter to stay with the child while performing her daily chores.

EXPANSION PLANS

At the present time, contractual agreements for the purchase of day-care services are in effect with the local New Jersey Association for Retarded Children Units. However, it is not the intent of the State of New Jersey to continue this arrangement indefinitely. The 1964 Institutional Bond Issue provided funds for the construction of state-owned day-care centers. The first five of these centers have gone to bid and preliminary construction is under way. It is anticipated that the 1966–1967 fiscal year will see the completion of the first five of these centers (located in Passaic, Mercer, Camden, Somerset, and Cumberland Counties).

The day-care center will include from two to ten day-care units. Each unit within the center will be comprised of no more than eight children who will be grouped in accordance with the following; (1) level of social development, (2) chronological age, and (3) physical disability.

As the state-constructed day-care centers are completed, the Division of Mental Retardation will assume total operating responsibility. The state organizational plan calls for four day-care district supervisors who will be responsible for supervision of the day-care centers in the northeastern, northwestern, central and southern regions [1] of the state. It will be their responsibility to develop programs, supervise the center, and keep the Chief of the Bureau of Day Care and Training Services informed of their progress.

Each day-care center will be under the immediate supervision of a day-care center supervisor. In addition to the center supervisor, there will be a day-care technician for each of the units within the center. It will be the responsibility of the technicians to care for and train the individuals within their own units. In addition to the aforementioned staff, there will be from one to two day-care attendants who will be responsible for such things as relieving the day-care technicians for meals, preparing and serving the

[1] Counties covered by the four day-care regions are as follows: Northeastern: Passaic, Bergen, Hudson, Essex, and Union. Northwestern: Sussex, Warren, Morris, Somerset, and Hunterdon. Central: Mercer, Middlesex, Monmouth, Burlington, and Ocean. Southern: Camden, Gloucester, Salem, Atlantic, Cumberland, and Cape May.

noontime meal, and aiding in the supervision of the children while they are in the play yard or are participating in group activities.

ADULT NEEDS

The focus on community day-care programs for the severely retarded has brought to light the fact that many children and adults who fall into the category of severe or profound retardation have been overlooked by the communities. With this in mind, the Division of Mental Retardation plans to establish a new program specifically designed to supply services to adults who are too old for day care and for whom no other community program is available. Indications are that there may be as many as 6500 retarded persons in the State of New Jersey, between the ages of eighteen and fifty-five, who are not receiving service and who are not at the present in an institution.

It is felt that a program designed to prevent the physical and intellectual deterioration, that is naturally concomitant of social isolation and inactivity, can be developed. The objectives of this Health and Activities Program will be the development of socially acceptable patterns of behavior, training in semi-independent living, and the provision of activities designed to enhance the physical and intellectual status of the individual.

The past three years' experience has proved, beyond all doubt, the values that can be derived from day-care programs specifically oriented toward the problems of the severely or profoundly retarded. During this period, more than 350 children have received day-care services. Of this group, 284 are still in day-care programs; 40 have been accepted in public schools; and the remainder have been lost to the program through institutionalization or death.

REALISTIC GOALS

It is the goal and the intent of this program to enable these children to attain their maximal degree of independence and self-sufficiency and to postpone institutionalization for as long as it is possible. It is not the goal of the program to develop the child to the point where he will become a self-sufficient, independent individual who will never require institutionalization. Basically, the day-care program provides the child with activities and training commensurate with his ability and in keeping with his social and emotional needs. In a like manner, the parents benefit by virtue of a respite from total care, the fact that the child's ability to function in the home is enhanced, and an alternative to institutionalization is provided.

33 DAY CENTERS FOR THE MENTALLY RETARDED

William K. Murphy
Richard C. Scheerenberger

From *Establishing Day Centers for the Mentally Retarded: Guidelines and Procedures,* July 1967, pp. 10–16. Reprinted with the permission of the Division of Mental Retardation Services, Illinois State Department of Mental Health, and the authors. Mr. Murphy is Assistant Superintendent, Andrew McFarland Zone Center, Illinois State Department of Mental Health, Springfield. Dr. Scheerenberger is Superintendent, Central Wisconsin Colony, Madison and is also on the faculty of the University of Wisconsin, Madison.

Today's day centers for the mentally retarded in Illinois no longer provide just training or socialization opportunities. The trend has been to develop a five-phase comprehensive program involving the child, the family, and the community. The five phases are: (1) diagnostic and evaluation services, (2) casework counseling for the retardate and his family, (3) training and activity experiences, (4) vocational training and sheltered workshop provisions, and (5) referral services.

DIAGNOSTIC AND EVALUATION SERVICES

In order to plan for each individual child, it is necessary to have a thorough understanding of his physical, psychological, educational, and social abilities, as well as his limitations and potentialities. Naturally, this includes reference to the family—their attitudes, problems, and interrelationships. An effective diagnostic program is the keystone for training and treatment services.

Diagnosis and evaluation of the retardate and his family require an interprofessional approach, the composition of which will vary according to the complexity of the case under consideration. The diagnostic team may include a physician or pediatrician, a psychologist, a social worker, a vocational specialist, a special educator, a nurse, and other paramedical specialists, such as an audiologist or speech pathologist. In day centers serving retarded children, the basic core team includes a physician or pediatrician, a psychologist, a social worker, and a special educator. In day centers serving adults, the core diagnostic team includes a psychologist, a social worker, and a vocational specialist.

Though few day centers at present have access to an interprofessional team, this limitation can be minimized through effective collaboration with other community agencies, both public and private. For example, some day centers are using psychological services available from local mental health clinics.

State-aided day centers, under the grant-in-aid regulations of the

Department of Mental Health, are required to have the services of a qualified social worker and a registered psychologist, either full-time or part-time (see section on Grant-in-Aid Standards and Procedures). The fulfillment of this requirement provides a basis for the core diagnostic team.

Some diagnostic data usually are available when a child is referred to the day center. Though the quality and usefulness of such information varies, it is, nevertheless, helpful to the diagnostic team.

CASEWORK COUNSELING FOR THE RETARDATE AND HIS FAMILY

The day center is successful in meeting the needs of each retardate only when it works harmoniously with the retarded person, his family, and the community. The day center's social worker strives to make this close cooperation possible.

At intake, or acceptance of the retardate for services, the role of the social worker is to assist the family or retardate in clarifying their problems in relation to the center's service capacity and in relation to other community resources from which help may be obtained. The social worker not only assists in this direct counseling role, but also participates with other staff members in the development of sound, integrated programs for each retardate.

Family casework is an important aspect of a day center's program. The purpose of family casework for the mentally retarded is to enable parents to make maximum use of their own and the community's resources to facilitate a solution to those problems with which they are confronted. Also, family casework is important in obtaining relevant diagnostic information.

TRAINING AND ACTIVITY EXPERIENCES

Prior to proceeding with a brief discussion of the goals and curricular provisions related to training and activity experiençes, it is advisable to review the probable trends in the development of day centers in Illinois.

Not only is it necessary to expand the number of centers presently available to the retarded throughout the State, the advent of House Bill 1407 also implies that both new and existing programs need to develop in new directions. In essence, House Bill 1407, which was passed by the 74th General Assembly, provides mandatory legislation to the effect that all EMR and TMR students capable of benefiting from a public school education shall receive special training. Today's day centers are placing a strong emphasis on meeting the needs of those retardates subsumed under

House Bill 1407. In other words, present-day programs are not, in general, designed to meet the needs of those retardates who will be ineligible for public school programs in 1969. Therefore, in addition to establishing a state-wide network of day centers, a concerted effort must be made to provide appropriate training experiences for preschool and postschool EMR and TMR as well as for the severely and profoundly retarded of all ages. Figure 1 shows the probable trend for day programs in the future will be to serve a younger and older, more severely affected population.

Goals and Objectives

All education has certain basic commitments. These commitments, expressed as objectives, are appropriate to both training and vocational programs. For the purposes of the present discussion, the seven cardinal objectives defined by the Commission on the Reorganization of Secondary Education (1918) will be cited. Accordingly, it is desired that each child gain knowledge and understanding, skill and competence, appropriate attitudes and interests, and effective strategies of action relative to:

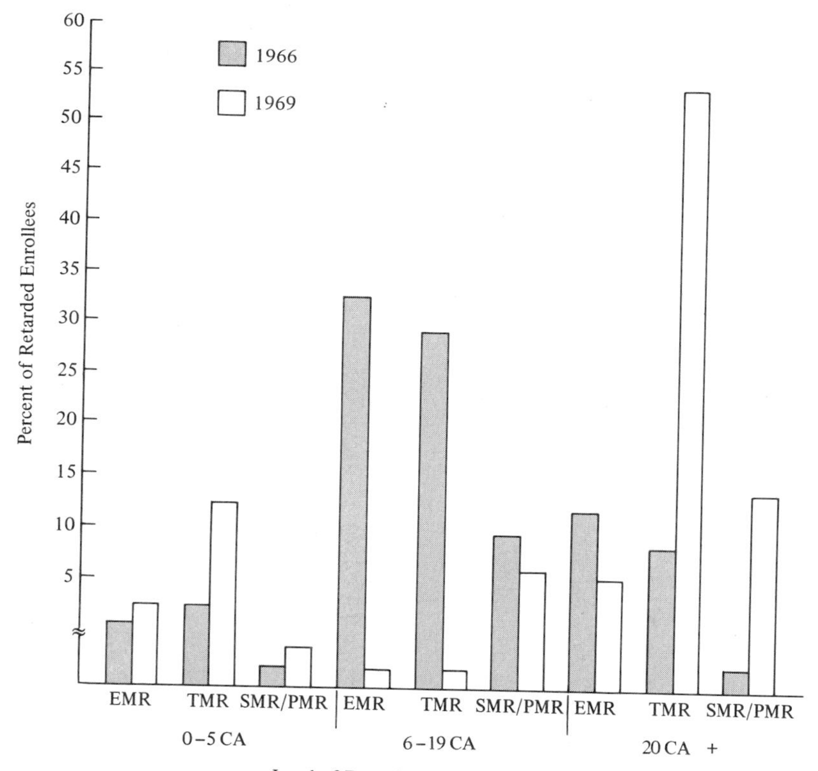

Figure 1 Present and future MR populations served by day centers.

(1) good mental and physical health; (2) a command of the fundamental processes, which includes communication skills, reading, writing, and arithmetic; (3) worthy home membership; (4) vocational preparation; (5) citizenship; (6) wise use of leisure time; and (7) character or ethical development. A detailed discussion of these objectives with respect to day center programs is provided by Scheerenberger (1966).

CURRICULAR AREAS

When interpreting the goals of education or the nature of curricular provisions, one must take into consideration the characteristics of each child being served, his estimated potential, and his present level of adaptive behavior. In other words, a set of meaningful, obtainable objectives and an appropriate curriculum must be established for each child. Subsequently, the following curricular areas, normally encompassed in programs for the retarded, are offered only as guidelines:

MENTAL AND PHYSICAL HEALTH. One of the primary objectives of a day center program is the development of personally, emotionally, and socially secure individuals. In general, it is recognized by psychologists and educators alike that all children possess basic needs for emotional stability. In brief, each individual needs to acquire a sense of (a) self-respect, (b) belonging, (c) success, (d) accomplishment, (e) achievement, (f) recognition, (g) responsibility, and (h) that personal security which can emanate only from a self-understanding and the development of realistic goals. The classroom environment, the teacher's attitude and capabilities, and the training experiences are all of consequence in satisfying this global goal for emotional security.

With respect to physical health, it is important that each retardate receive numerous opportunities to develop basic habits, skills, and attitudes related to health, nutrition, and safety. An integral part of the health program includes daily physical exercise and activities which teach usage and identification of parts of the body.

SOCIAL SKILLS. A second major area of concern is assisting the retarded in developing those attitudes and skills essential to their ability to relate effectively with their families, peers, and communities. Included are such activities as acquiring and using basic manners; participating in group activities; learning to share, take turns, and respect the rights of others; sharing in the responsibilities of maintaining the classroom; and becoming acquainted wtih the respective roles of mother and father.

SELF-HELP SKILLS. A considerable portion of the training program, especially for the younger retardate, is in the area of developing self-care and personal grooming skills. It is important that these children tend to their own needs and present a good physical appearance.

ORAL LANGUAGE DEVELOPMENT. The development of oral language is vitally important to the retarded child. The training activity program should include such activities as increasing general vocabulary (e.g., assisting the child to acquire and use words pertaining to making his needs known, parts of his body, common courtesies, objects common to the house, objects common to the school, various facilities within the community, and home pets); following simple oral directions; describing pictures; identifying basic colors; listening to and retelling stories; and participating, whenever possible, in group discussions.

ACADEMIC SKILLS. Academic skills normally refer to the child's gaining a high level of proficiency with respect to reading, writing, and arithmetic. This is not true when working with the moderately, severely, or profoundly retarded. The emphasis with these youngsters is on assisting them in developing perceptual skills, retention, and discrimination. Simple activities such as basic number concepts (groupings of 2 to 5) and learning to print one's name also are introduced. Research studies have indicated repeatedly that the more seriously retarded cannot benefit from an academic program.

In contrast, the educable mentally retarded, those few who are ineligible for public school programs, should receive formal instruction in the basic academic areas of reading, writing, and arithmetic. The curriculum content associated with the development of academic skills among these retarded emphasizes the very practical needs of everyday living, e.g., reading the newspaper, reading and obeying safety signs, preparing shopping lists, and gaining experiences in the utilization of money. It is anticipated that, because most of the ineligible educable retardates of school age will have marked emotional problems, perceptual difficulties, or severe physical handicaps, such instruction will have to be offered on a tutorial or very small group basis.

PSYCHO-MOTOR SKILLS. Again, many of the retarded, especially those who are more severely affected, have poor psycho-motor coordination. Subsequently, the training program should include a variety of activities designed to assist in the development of motor skills, e.g., running, skipping, riding tricycles, putting puzzles together, cutting, coloring, and rhythmic expression.

VOCATIONAL SKILLS. Even before being considered for placement in a formal vocational training program, the retarded need to acquire a number of related attitudes, habits, and skills. For example, it is necessary that they acquire a sense of responsibility, demonstrate the ability to follow directions, show a willingness to complete an unpleasant task, and follow the basic rules of safety. In addition, the retarded should have an opportunity to develop basic habits and skills related to tasks common to the home, e.g., washing dishes, sweeping, and vacuuming.

There will be a number of adult retardates enrolled in activity-training programs. In essence, these retarded individuals are incapable of participating in a formalized sheltered workshop or vocational training environment.

The curriculum usually involves a continuation of social skill training and recreational experiences. Many of the facilities also introduce a form of work program in which the retardate participates for an hour or two per day in the production of some project, usually in the lines of arts and crafts. Retarded adults are enrolled primarily for activity purposes, rather than production or training of competency with respect to a vocational skill.

There are also a number of other important curricular activities which should be integrated with the entire training effort. These include imitation and play experiences, musical expression, recreation and physical education, and arts and crafts. An extensive discussion of curricular areas and specific activities is provided by Rosenzweig and Long (1960), Molloy (1963), Bensberg (1965), Johnson and Lavely (1966), and Scheerenberger (1966).

VOCATIONAL TRAINING AND SHELTERED WORKSHOP PROVISIONS

As stated earlier, sheltered workshops are defined to include both intermediate training provisons and extended work opportunities. Further, general goals for vocational training are identical with those associated with training activity programs. Though the emphasis will be on vocational training and occupational adequacy, goals related to mental and physical health, socialization, and language development are still of major consequence.

It is deemed essential that the vocational training program or sheltered workshop include the following minimum services:

1. Vocational and social evaluation, including reference to the retardate's physical, psychological, social, and vocational abilities and problems; educational status; and occupational interests.
2. Personal and social adjustment training.
3. Prevocational or vocational work experience in which retardates are trained in those skills required of a job. Most retarded trainees should be exposed to a variety of tasks, rather than overlearning one particular skill.
4. Actual participation in production with each retardate assuming the responsibility of a contributing worker.
5. Job placement and follow-up for those retardates capable of assuming an occupational role in the normal working environment, or extended employment, the final provision of services for the retarded worker.

The day center should cooperate with and actively utilize the services of the Illinois Division of Vocational Rehabilitation. This Division is concerned with vocational opportunities and training for the retarded.

REFERRAL SERVICES

Frequently, the day center will encounter problems among the retarded and their families which it cannot resolve directly. The occurrence of retardation within a family may produce financial hardship, may create religious problems, may adversely affect intrahome relations, may result in emotional crisis among the family members, and may create severe adjustment problems for the siblings. Many of the retarded will have physical or mental problems beyond the range of treatment services available at the day center.

Some day centers have accepted the responsibility for assisting parents in meeting their broad needs. This is accomplished by directing parents to other state and local agencies which can be of assistance. For example, several day centers have established a professional screening committee which, following diagnosis and evaluation, refers those retarded requiring physical or emotional attention to appropriate treatment agencies.

The referral service is considered to be an essential phase of the total program. In developing new day centers, it is anticipated that this entire area of assisting the family in receiving proper attention from other agencies will receive increasing emphasis.

REFERENCES

American Association on Mental Deficiency. *A Manual on Terminology and Classification in Mental Retardation* (second edition). Monograph supplement to the American Journal of Mental Deficiency, 1961.

Bensberg, G. J. (Ed.) *Teaching the Mentally Retarded.* Atlanta, Ga.: Southern Regional Education Board, 1965.

Commission on the Reorganization of Secondary Education. *Cardinal Principles of Secondary Education.* Washington, D.C.: Superintendent of Documents, U.S. Government Printing Office, 1918.

Illinois Department of Mental Health. *Day Programs and Residential Facilities for the Mentally Retarded in Illinois.* Springfield, Ill.: Division of Mental Retardation Services, 1967.

Illinois Revised Statutes, 1965 (Volume I). State Bar Association Edition. Chicago, Ill.: Burdette Smith Company, 1965.

Johnson, G. O. and Lavely, C. D. *Guidelines for the Establishment of Training Programs for Severely Mentally Retarded Children.* Albany, N.Y.: New York State Interdepartmental Health and Hospital Council, Committee on Mental Retardation, 1966.

Molloy, J. S. *Trainable Children: Curriculum and Procedures.* New York, New York: John Day Company, 1963.

National Association of Sheltered Workshops and Homebound Program. *Sheltered Workshops—A Handbook* (revised). Washington, D.C.: National Association of Sheltered Workshops and Homebound Programs, 1966.

Rosenzweig, E. L., and Long, T. *Understanding and Teaching the Dependent Retarded Child.* Darien, Connecticut: Educational Publishing Corporation, 1960.

Scheerenberger, R. C. Nursery school experiences for the trainable mentally retarded. In: *Community Day Centers for the Mentally Retarded in Illinois.* Springfield, Ill.: Department of Mental Health, Mental Retardation Services, 1966, 1–19.

Sloan, W., and Birch, J. W. A rationale for degrees of mental retardation. *American Journal of Mental Deficiency, 60* (2): 258–264, 1955.

U.S. Department of Labor. *Occupations in the Care and Rehabilitation of the Mentally Retarded.* Washington, D.C.: Bureau of Employment Security, 1966.

SECTION NINE

Programs for the Mentally Retarded Adult

Once the holding power of special classes for the educable mentally retarded and for the trainable mentally retarded had been demonstrated—many retardates remain in school to the ages of eighteen and twenty-one—it became apparent that a postschool program was the natural next step.

It is significant to note that of all those eligible to receive social security benefits at the age of eighteen, because they are totally and permanently disabled, 67 percent are mentally retarded. It is estimated that, of the total mentally retarded population in the United States, four million are twenty years of age or older, and that three and a half million of this group are capable of community living. Some, of course, may need highly supervised conditions. A goodly portion of this number need postschool services if they are not to become an awesome burden on the community.

There are five alternatives for mentally retarded individuals when they reach early adulthood: (1) competitive employment in semiskilled and unskilled occupations; (2) vocational rehabilitation for those who are eligible and where feasible; (3) sheltered workshops; (4) remaining at home, and (5) institutionalization. A realistic approach toward life adjustment would encompass the first three alternatives. Even so, many factors are at work to make adult adjustment for the retarded individual difficult. Only about 60 percent of the educable mentally retarded can achieve vocational adjustment. Even with the extension and improvement of secondary school programs for the educable, about 25–40 percent of the educable group can neither be placed in jobs nor hold them if they are placed.

Trainable retarded adults pose an even more serious problem for society. At present, most of the trainable retarded receive little or no vocational training, and, except for isolated instances, job opportunities are nonexistent. In an interesting study, Gerhart Saenger[1] followed up almost 3000 trainable retarded individuals who had attended public school classes in New York City during the period 1929–1955. Of this group, 66 percent lived in the community and 26 percent were institutionalized (the remaining 8 percent had died). Almost 80 percent of the group living in the community had never found employment and spent their time around the home. The group that did manage to work was employed primarily by relatives. While as a group they did not create serious trouble for the community, their contribution to society was negligible.

For about 90 percent of the educable group and the entire trainable group, then, the answer appears to lie in extended educational–rehabilitation services and sheltered workshop facilities.

On a more optimistic note, the passage of Public Law 90-391 (Vocational Rehabilitation Amendments of 1968) provides for expansion of services of state rehabilitation agencies. Specifically, grants have been made to the states for construction of facilities, direct services, and for the training of manpower to staff new programs for mentally retarded adults. Renewed efforts are being made by the President's Committee on Employment of the Handicapped, which would encourage the employment of mentally retarded adults in suitable federal jobs and press the "private business sector" to find work for the mentally retarded. Studies by Ruby Jo Kennedy,[2] Elias Katz,[3] Robert Edgerton,[4] and Warren R. Baller and associates[5] shed new light on the needs of the adult retardate and necessary services.

What are the criteria for adult community programming in mental retardation? William Usdane[6] suggests six criteria. They are: (1) the rehabilitation team must contain specific workers geared to helping the retardate accommodate to the outside, regular community; (2) employers must utilize their facilities as an essential extension of vocational evaluation and work adjustment process of the retardate; (3) continued reevaluation of both progress and capability on an individualized basis must be regularly structured within the rehabilitation process; (4) the expectation level of achievement for the mentally retarded individual on the part of the professional and subprofessional worker must remain flexible and geared to the con-

[1] Gerhart Saenger, *The Adjustment of Severely Retarded Adults in the Community* (Albany: New York State Interdepartmental Health and Hospital Council, 1957).

[2] Ruby Jo Kennedy, *A Connecticut Community Revisited: A Study of the Social Adjustment of a Group of Mentally Deficient Adults* (Hartford, Conn.: The Connecticut State Mental Retardation Planning Project, January, 1966).

[3] Elias Katz, *The Retarded Adult in the Community* (Springfield, Ill.: Charles C Thomas, 1968).

[4] Robert B. Edgerton, *The Cloak of Competence* (Berkeley, Calif.: University of California Press, 1967).

[5] Warren R. Baller and others, "Mid-life Attainment of the Mentally Retarded: A Longitudinal Study," *Genetic Psychology Monographs, 75* (1967), 235–329.

[6] William M. Usdane, "Criteria for Adult Community Programming in Mental Retardation," *Mental Retardation* 7:6 (December 1969), 43–46.

cept of continuing improvement; (5) emphasis should be given to follow-up or longitudinal studies. Often the evaluative methodology of a demonstration project is weak, and as a result, it is important that careful provision be made for follow-up; and (6) adult programming must include health and growth-promoting recreation activities. The retardate should have access to existing community recreational facilities, along with additional recreational centers modified to meet his special physical and psychological needs.

This section would not be complete without some reference to the everlasting problem of arrangements for the personal living of the mentally retarded adult in a community setting. There has been talk of the development of "halfway houses" or community residences for the mentally retarded adult. However, little real action has taken place in this direction. Community living facilities for the adult retardate is a universally accepted pattern in most European countries. Among the most outstanding are (1) the Julia House, operated by AKIM (the Israeli Rehabilitation Agency) in Jerusalem, and (2) UMKAH, directed by Professor Branco Bajic in Belgrade, Yugoslavia. Both of these facilities have outstanding small residential community living quarters, as well as close contact with sheltered workshops and diversified industry that provide training and employment opportunities. The Department of Mental Hygiene of the State of New York is pioneering the development of hostels to provide community residential facilities.[7] In addition, NARC has published a variety of bulletins giving directions for the establishment of community living facilities.

The late Edgar A. Doll, in the first reading of this section, asks many pointed questions concerning programs for the adult retarded. He describes the efforts of the State of Washington in formulating programs for adults. In the second article, Salvatore G. DiMichael presents a frank appraisal of the issues and programs relating to vocational rehabilitation for the mentally retarded. He discusses the purposes of state rehabilitation agencies, school work–study programs, sheltered workshops, and rehabilitation counseling. Appended to this reading are a resource table which covers classification of the mentally retarded according to their employment potential and a flow chart illustrating the handling of cases referred to the ARC Workshop in San Francisco. In the third reading in this section, Herbert Goldstein and Rick Heber discuss the role of schools in providing child placement; such services as counseling, in-school work experience, on-the-job training, and the vocational needs of retarded youth and adults. The final selection, provided by Julius S. Cohen, is a comprehensive discussion of sheltered workshops.

[7] *Hostels for the Mentally Retarded: Community Residential Facilities* (Albany, N.Y.: Department of Mental Hygiene, 1969).

34 PROGRAMS FOR THE ADULT RETARDED

Edgar A. Doll

Reprinted by permission from *Mental Retardation,* Vol. 6, No. 1, February 1968, pp. 19–21, a publication of the American Association on Mental Deficiency, and Mrs. Geraldine Doll. The late Dr. Edgar A. Doll was Consulting Psychologist, Bellingham (Wash.) Public Schools.

There is a specter that hovers over the lives of all the retarded. What about the adult years? Who will look after him, his needs, and his welfare? If there is any single question that troubles his parents, it is this concern for the guardianship they at some time will not be able to provide.

Similar concern troubles his normal siblings. What will their responsibilities be and how can they most effectively be discharged? Likewise, certain social agencies have obligations which they may be ill-prepared to implement.

What is the life expectancy of the retardate in years and activities? What special health problems must be faced? What kinds of work programs can be pursued? What can his social life include?

Time was when such questions were resolved by the simple formula of institutional care and management. Even today there are those who look to institutional residence as the answer to the above questions. Indeed, such an outlook does provide some answers of a constructive nature because institutional residence supplies companionship, social life, physical welfare and occupational usefulness. However, today there is a generalized preference on the part of families and agencies to continue to care for the retarded adult at home and in the community. Such programs include home care, family care in boarding families, convalescent home placement, private school enrollment, and other ways in which the retardate himself, his family and his community can best be served.

It seems strange today that so little emphasis has been given to life history planning for the mentally retarded. Active programs and much literature are available for the pre-adult years but there are comparatively few resources for those over twenty. As in the fairy tales, we bring them to maturity and then assume that they live happily ever after—an unfulfilled wish of eager hopefulness. Consequently we are ill-informed on most of the expectations of the later years and have few programs other than institutional custody.

We have no actuarial tables on life expectancy for the retarded. We know comparatively little about individual or group prospective longevity at different stages of life history. We know little about such expectancy in relation to degree and type and cause of retardation. We are poorly informed regarding specific medical futures, personal social careers and the progression or deterioration that may take place. Nor do we have much information on the relation of these matters to such variables as sex and social economic standing. There is almost no information regarding the extent to which the retarded adult continues to progress or decline in those directions which have been such a concern to us during his pre-adult years.

FIVE EPOCHS

Some years ago the Objectives Committee of the Washington State Coordination Council for Exceptional Children formulated a life history program for the retarded. Unfortunately this was never successfully implemented but it still constitutes a systematic plan for anticipating the adult years. That program was based initially on type, degree, and cause of handicaps as well as family, age, socioeconomic standing, personality and associated handicaps beyond mental retardation. That program listed as major agencies, the home, the public schools, boarding and foster homes, residential schools, public institutions and the various resources of the local community. It recognized that the child is a continuing responsibility of the family throughout his natural life and that the need for adult guardianship was a major problem.

This program considered the life history in a series of epochs with specific needs and problems attending each epoch. The first stage covered the preschool years and was concerned with such major issues as diagnosis and consequent home adjustments, home counseling and neighborhood relations, with maximum parent support through such organizations as the Association for Retarded Children groups.

In the second five years the program was concerned with secondary handicaps which had not yet been revealed in the preschool years. With the onset of school attendance a re-orientation of the child was required from the home to the public school and perhaps to a special class within the public school. It was thought that at this time the child's retardation in most instances was not so severe that he could not be helped. On the contrary, every possible resource was brought to bear that could influence his further progress.

Then the period of adolescent turmoil with critical problems in the home through parent and sibling relationships and the disappointed expectancies of the retarded person in the face of disabilities which were becoming more and more obvious and more and more embarrassing. Emphasis was now directed to the nonacademic aspects of public school education to provide preparation in self-help and in occupational education that would anticipate the needs of the later years.

The age period of early adulthood was recognized as a period of transition from school to life, as the first epoch provided transition from home to school. Here the emphasis was on various aspects of occupational experience and training suited to the capabilities and interests of the retarded young adult and his prospective employment. The program envisaged the possibility of continuation education to reinforce the transition from school to useful and remunerative work. Specific instruction was to be offered in various areas of occupational information and experience. Attention was also provided for constructive recreation and for wholesome community living.

Finally, a fifth stage was recognized as a period of care and supervision for relaxed living with progressive reduction in occupational usefulness.

This total program was imaginative, sympathetic, and realistic. It identified the retardate as a person with a relatively short life expectancy whose growth and decline should be anticipated in evolutionary stages. In identifying the retarded adult with other adults, with respect to those interests that were common to both, it also recognized the need for more specific anticipations of needs and possibilities.

At the present time most of our programs for the adult retarded are conceived as broad generalizations without very much analytical elaboration. We seem to be looking for single solutions that would be applicable to all individuals, whereas in fact, what is needed is multiple programs adapted to personal idiosyncrasies. Generalizations might be formulated as guidelines, but these require particular adaptation to the individual immediately concerned.

SHELTERED WORKSHOPS

One widely accepted plan for the adult retarded is the sheltered workshop. This is usually a temporizing program which has no very effective future except as a stop-gap or as an immediate resource until something more effective can be developed. It has many advantages. The nature of the workshop depends on the resourcefulness of its managers since its programs are largely adventitious or determined by local circumstances. Moreover, the sheltered workshop requires much more diversification than it has thus far received if it is to cater to the needs of all or even many of the adult retarded. The sheltered workshop tends to capitalize on the urge toward repetitive occupational routine. For many of the retarded this is gratifying indeed, but for others it is deadly.

Actually, the sheltered workshop may achieve different goals. Both production and contract work are common types of work. There are also social and recreational accompaniments. Through diversification of these, the sheltered aspect is the most important feature, namely the supervision that is given to the simple occupational activities in which the adult retarded engage. Among these activities, supervised employment outside an enclosed center offers a nearly unlimited range of both simple and semi-skilled occupations which can be adapted to the individual talents or "green-thumbs" of the workers.

SUPERVISED EMPLOYMENT

At the present time it seems that programs for supervised employment have had minimum development. The principal contrast between the sheltered workshop and supervised employment is that in the workshop there is a fixed location and a limited range of activities, as well as the manufacture of products that commonly are difficult to dispose of and require inventories, sales and bookkeeping. In supervised employment however, there is no limit to the scope of activities other than the skills of the workers and the availability of the work. Actually, some minimally supervised employment can be done at home if the parents or other home-related persons are prepared to supply the encouragement and assistance that the adult retardate requires.

In considering adult programs, the Bellingham (Washington) Public Schools undertook to anticipate its educational objectives for the retarded by formulating certain expectancies of occupational enterprise following termination of school attendance. While recognizing the need for guardianship and companionship, a plan was developed which was based on an activity center with social and occupational branches. It was anticipated that the local Association for Retarded Children would provide a building which would be a headquarters in which the concerns of school, home and social agencies could all be coordinated. Such a center might be similar in general plan to the typical YMCA, namely, a place in which many different interests might be coordinated. This would include space and facilities for overnight accommodations, for parties, exercises and recreation, for clubs, reading and hobby pursuits, with a snack bar, a music room, game room, dance floor and other appurtenances of wholesome recreation. It would provide for picnics and "occasions" and would be a central spot for keeping the adult retarded socially integrated.

This center was to have a sheltered workshop for adults for whom such a program would be desirable or could be used as a temporary arrangement for some retardates until more suitable resources were worked out. More importantly, the center was to have a supervising work assignment office which would receive calls for semi-skilled work or odd jobs. The responsibilities were to be carried by the supervising staff and the actual work to be done by the retarded as remunerated employees. Such a program would be differentiated according to the talents of the workers with branches for domestic activities, landscape and yard maintenance and all the concerns of the ordinary housekeeper. The activity center was also to serve as a continuing counseling center for parents for maintaining occupational usefulness at home and supportive social adjustment interests.

Programs for the adult retardate are related to the essential characteristic of the mentally retarded, that is, his need for guardianship, companionship, and social supervision. The major weakness of the retardate is his lack of sound social judgment and his tendency to be in trouble because of the innocent exercise of imperfect judgment.

The advantage of residential placement is that these responsibilities can be allocated to a single agency which can develop skilled management techniques. The residential facility can supply the desirable activities in proper variety and extent to capitalize the useful talents of the adult retardate and thereby provide him with the satisfaction of a sense of worth and usefulness which are so necessary to his self-esteem. The institution can also provide companionship and status which are two of the most important of all the needs of the adult retarded and which are usually lacking for him in the community unless the community provides the kind of activity center described above. The guardianship of institutions can be just as healthy and wholesome as that provided in the public schools. It need not require exploitation or abuse if the community will supervise the institution as it expects the institution to supervise the retarded.

Finally, legal, financial and social assistance are available through trusteeships and the plan for appointing cocustodians for those retarded who are admitted to a residential facility. Such institutional residents need not require "due process" commitment. The State of Washington has clearly indicated the feasibility of voluntary procedures for admittance and release from institutional custody.

From what little is known of life expectancy for the retarded, their longevity is appreciably less than that of the average normal person. Indeed, from such meager information as is at hand, their longevity is correlated with their social adequacy. In a study (Doll, 1943) it was difficult to find mentally retarded adults over 50 years of age and there are comparatively few instances of the adult retarded living appreciably beyond 60. It was somewhat easier to obtain a sample of superior adults. In general, the adult history of the retarded is comparable to their earlier years but at a lower level of efficiency.

In summary, we see that programs for the adult retarded should be thought of in relation to their total life histories. What they may accomplish as adults is largely predetermined by what has happened to them in the pre-adult years. And how happy and useful their adult years might be is largely a consequence of the concerned guardianship of the family and of the community.

REFERENCE

Doll, E. A. Measurement of Social Maturity Applied to Older People. In *Mental Health in Later Maturity*. Supplement No. 168 to Public Health Reports. U.S. Public Health Service. Washington, D.C.: U.S. Government Printing Office, 1943.

35 VOCATIONAL REHABILITATION AND THE MENTALLY RETARDED: A STATEMENT OF ISSUES

Salvatore G. DiMichael

From *Preparation of Mentally Retarded Youth for Gainful Employment,* Department of Health, Education, and Welfare, Bulletin 1959, No. 28, Government Printing Office, Washington, D.C., 1959, pp. 10–19. Reprinted with the permission of the Department and the author. Dr. DiMichael is Director, Institute for Crippled and Disabled, New York City.

Although the mentally retarded have been with us as long as civilization itself, the development of a community program for them is one of recent times. The program of special education had its beginning just before the turn of the century, about 60 years ago. With the enactment of Public Law 113, in 1943, the mentally retarded became eligible for vocational rehabilitation services on the same basis as other disabled persons. The inception of the National Association for Retarded Children in 1950 signaled a movement of parents and citizens who were resolved to form a private national group to further the welfare of the retarded, their families, and friends. Within this relatively brief period of time, real progress has been made. Nevertheless, a meeting such as ours signifies a healthy attitude of constructive dissatisfaction with the current level and quality of efforts to meet the complex needs of the retarded.

CURRENT STATUS OF REHABILITATION EFFORTS FOR THE RETARDED

Before launching into the issues now before us and in order to clear pathways for substantial further progress, it may be well to present a thumbnail sketch of the current status of vocational rehabilitation in dealing with the mentally retarded. The brief summary will make a good backdrop by which to understand better the major issues confronting us.

Since 1943 there has been a constant, gradual growth of services for the retarded. For example, in the years 1945–1950 inclusive, a total of 2091 mentally retarded individuals were rehabilitated into gainful employment. In the years 1951–1956 inclusive, a total of 3628 such persons were rehabilitated. In 1957, state vocational rehabilitation agencies prepared and placed into gainful employment 1094 retarded persons. It is anticipated that 1250 will be rehabilitated during 1958, probably at a cost of about $1 million of state and federal funds.

The Vocational Rehabilitation Amendments of 1954 added important weapons to the resources of the total program, not only in additional money for services, but for extension and improvement projects, expansion projects, long- and short-term training programs, and for the powerful potentials of demonstration and research. For example, during 1958, there will be four extension and improvement projects providing specialized services solely to the mentally retarded at a total cost of about $100,000; and special training programs for vocational rehabilitation workers, dealing with methods and techniques for the retarded, will amount to $9000 in federal money (and do not take into account the training efforts of the state agencies). During the 1957 fiscal year, the special "expansion" projects, now terminated by law, made it possible to establish or expand 33 sheltered workshops and service projects for the retarded and an additional 11 projects for the mentally retarded and cerebral palsied at a total cost of about $250,000. In the area of reseach, two major sheltered workshop projects are in operation at a cost of $113,500, and ten selected demonstration projects are being conducted at a cost of $280,000. In overall financial terms, the U.S. Office of Vocational Rehabilitation, in 1958, is spending $1,079,500 exclusively for the mentally retarded, while state agencies are spending an additional $450,000. These figures refer to exclusive efforts for the retarded. The rehabilitation of the physically handicapped and emotionally disturbed undoubtedly includes some persons with a secondary disability of mental retardation, but to mention all activities helpful to the mentally retarded would take us far afield.

ISSUES INVOLVING EDUCATION AND VOCATIONAL REHABILITATION

The vocational rehabilitation program is made up of many services, each of which could be explored for issues dealing with the retarded. These services include:

1. Individual evaluation with medical, psychological, and social-vocational assessments.
2. Medical care and hospitalization.
3. Artificial appliances with training to use them.
4. Personal adjustment, prevocational and vocational training.
5. Provision of maintenance during rehabilitation, including transportation costs.
6. Occupational tools and equipment.
7. Selective placement and follow-up in employment.
8. Counseling throughout the process.

The counseling services, including counseling of the family as it relates to the individual's rehabilitation plan, are the underlying foundation for the total program. We may note that counseling adds many complex dimensions to rehabilitation work by virtue of its role in the overall team effort. As a result, the counselor has sustained contacts with school counselors, teachers, physicians, psychologists, social workers, and employers, as well as with many community agencies such as welfare, public assistance, social security, hospitals, clinics, and private community groups. You may easily understand, then, why I choose to present a statement of issues limited to those which overlap the fields of education and vocational rehabilitation. The chosen scope of issues is appropriate to the composition and plans for this conference.

The fields of education and vocational rehabilitation are fruitful major avenues for the stimulation of progress in work with the retarded for two major reasons. First, mental retardation is a disability which usually appears in childhood, highlighting the importance of education as a program of individual development. Second, the crucial years of early adulthood will set the patterns of adult living, highlighting the importance for vocational rehabilitation to help the retarded make the transition from school to work and adult living. Although the program is called Vocational *Re*habilitation, it believes completely in the significance of Habilitation. The difference in words should present no difference in meaning either to education or vocational rehabilitation.

Although we fully recognize the vast individual difference between the mentally retarded, making it a most heterogeneous group, I would like to propose a classification to serve as a practical guide to the personnel of vocational rehabilitation and education agencies as they work together. The classification guide is based on overall vocational prospects of retarded adolescents:

1. *Directly placeable group* (from school to job). This is composed of young adults for whom special education proves sufficiently effective as preparation for employment, and who may become employed in competitive jobs directly from school. These persons may be assisted in finding suitable employment by counselors, employment services, family, or friends, and the vocational rehabilitation counselor only in special cases.
2. *Deferred placeable group* (postschool preparation to job). These are young adults in need of additional services beyond those offered by the school. They need further preparation and assistance, such as prevocational and vocational experiences, physical or psychiatric evaluation, treatment, on-the-job training, counseling, or personal-adjustment training, before they may be placed in competitive employment.
3. *Sheltered employable group*. These are young adults who are capable of partial self-support in the carefully supervised environment of a sheltered workshop, after preparation services beyond school.
4. *Self-care* (nonself-supporting group). These include persons who may partially care for themselves in the home and may be able to partici-

pate in a "social therapy center" but who are not capable of engaging in productive employment even in a sheltered workshop.

As for the *directly placeable group,* there is one major issue: should vocational rehabilitation be directly involved in individual cases, and if so, to what extent. I believe that this group is fairly large and that the efforts of school and employment services coupled with efforts of an understanding family and friends are usually sufficient to assure reasonable vocational adjustment. If so, there should be common agreement among us that, in principle, such young adults, with few exceptions, should not be referred to rehabilitation agencies. In the practical situation, one may show that school counselors are not available, that employment services are ineffective, that evaluation of the person is not satisfactory because of shortcomings in school services. Do these shortcomings force a responsibility upon Vocational Rehabilitation, or should there be a frontal push upon society to see that the agencies with primary obligations are provided with appropriations and personnel to do their job? I deliberately choose to pose this as the only major issue for the directly placeable group because it is of basic, crucial importance to clarification of interagency functions.

Let us turn, then, to the *deferred placeable group.* We already have sufficient experience to know that some retarded young adults are in need of postschool services in order to "graduate" into competitive employment. A list of numerous studies gives us considerable insight into the characteristics and values of vocational rehabilitation services for the deferred placeables. One important issue before us is whether the vocational evaluation of the adolescent or young adult is the responsibility of vocational rehabilitation, or education, or both. Since the school has, or should have, an individual guidance inventory on each student, the full and complete record should be made available to the rehabilitation counselor. The latter, in fact, might be regarded by the schools as a professional associate so that he has ready access to guidance information. The vocational rehabilitation agency may be responsible for arranging for a medical examination, a psychological assessment, and for making a social–vocational evaluation of the retarded person. Perhaps we may advocate a flexible arrangement from one school district to another whereby the medical and psychological evaluations are obtained by one or the other agency, according to available resources of the school, rehabilitation agency, and community.

Another important issue is the availability of sufficient counselors in each agency. We could assert our convictions that the schools should have full responsibility for the student while he is in school, and that it is the student's right to have a competent and skilled school counselor available to help him gradually formulate a plan for school, out-of-school, and future adult living. Similarly, there should be an ample number of rehabilitation counselors who may serve the retarded in preparing for and assuming their places as productive wage earners and citizens. If there are not enough school and rehabilitation counselors, the community and the responsible administrative group should be informed so that they in turn can obtain the needed support of the boards of education, boards of vocational rehabilitation, and legislatures. Each agency—school or rehabilitation—should bolster the community efforts of the other in this important sphere of action. Then the lack of personnel may be tackled openly and constructively without either agency being defensive or deprecating the other, a situation which would only serve to undercut the overall effort to help the retarded. At the present time, neither education nor vocational rehabilitation is adequately staffed with counselors, and it seems foolhardy to ask either one to make up for the shortcomings of the other.

Is it possible and desirable for us at this conference to delineate the joint responsibilities of school and rehabilitation counselors, who must dovetail their efforts? If we accept the proposition that the school counselor has primary responsibility for the student while he is in school, experience has shown the wisdom of having the rehabilitation counselor actively involved at least one or two years before the student leaves school. The rehabilitation counselor should be in the position of a consultant to the school and, at times, an ancillary counselor to the student in the formulation of decisions for both in-school and postschool vocational plans. Thus the student's closing years of school are arranged to make for a smooth transition to the rehabilitation agency and its services, leading to employment and a fuller life. When the individual leaves school, the rehabilitation counselor assumes a primary responsibility, with the school counselor assuming a consultative role. The school must willingly invite and encourage the participation of rehabilitation counselors as professional associates; the rehabilitation agencies cannot force this viewpoint upon them.

Another important group of issues revolves around the delineation of responsibilities of the schools and the rehabilitation agencies in the establishment of vocational training facilities. Some suggestions have arisen because the Vocational Rehabilitation Act of 1954 makes it possible for state rehabilitation agencies and the U.S. Office of Vocational Rehabilitation to make grants-in-aid for vocational training facilities, through *extension and improvement* and *demonstration*. State rehabilitation agencies report that they have received requests from school districts for financial aid in purchasing, for the classroom, vocational training equipment, such as power sewing machines, drill presses, kitchens, agricultural equipment, duplicators, and work benches. The requests also include applications for funds to renovate classrooms housing such equipment. These requests raise the problem of responsibility to assume the sponsorship and the costs by education, rehabilitation, or other public or private groups.

It seems clear to me that the schools should assume responsibility for education in general and sponsorship and costs for academic and vocational training within the age ranges ordinarily regarded as the "school years." This principle is clearly accepted for "normal" students, and the physically handicapped, but not as yet for the mentally retarded. In the zeal to help the mentally retarded, is it fair to ask the rehabilitation agencies to assume costs not expected of it for physically handicapped students? Should not the schools provide general education and vocational training for the retarded at least up to seventeen or eighteen years of age, or the equivalent in years of a full high school program for students of normal intelligence? These issues are closely related to the establishment and administration of sheltered workshops, to be mentioned more explicitly later.

Another nest of issues of pressing importance is involved in the current work–study programs which seem to be gaining proponents among educators. The central idea in such programs is to have students devote half time to schoolwork and half time on a paying job. Several variations of this general idea are being practiced around the country. The programs assume that retarded adolescents have little or no more to gain from school, that experience on a job is a better form of training for adult living than *any* curriculum the school has to offer, or could possibly devise. I personally feel that a strange, unexplained contradiction exists in some communities where certain educators are pressuring normal students to stay in school, while, at the same time, these same educators are convinced that school is not the best place for the retarded adolescents. The problem is compounded by the fact that the retarded admittedly possess less personal, social, and intellectual maturity than the normal. Despite this fact, the young retarded are encouraged to take jobs where there is far less supervision than the schools can offer. One of our vocational rehabilitation agencies reported recently that there is a "scarcity of employers willing to take the immature retarded," and yet the same agency is participating in a work–study plan with a spirit of real hope. You may agree with me that developments in work–study programs bear close objective scrutiny. We probably will become better aware of its values for some students and its disadvantages for others.

Our limitations of time make it advisable to turn our attention to major issues related to the third group, adolescents and young adults with potential for partial self-support in productive employment in a sheltered workshop. As educators may view this group in school, it will be made up of (1) educable students with no prospects for competitive employment because of emotional maladjustment, lack of "commonsense intelligence," severe social–familial problems, or accompanying physical disabilities; and (2) more promising "trainable" students with ability for routine independent travel, good social adjustment, and more favorable family conditions.

The establishment of sheltered workshops for the retarded has had a major impact on rehabilitation, due to the availability of financial assistance under the Vocational Rehabilitation Act and the appearance of parent-sponsored community groups for the retarded. However, the impact derives its force from the promising values of such workshops and not from the large numbers established. The MacDonald Workshop in Florida made a study of the potential retarded population which could profit from the short-term personal adjustment and vocational training, and/or the long-term services, of a workshop. The study estimates that about 10 percent of retarded young adults could benefit from such a facility, or a projected guess of about 100,000 persons over the country. Yet, it is likely that less than 2000 retarded persons now have such an opportunity. The establishment of a training center and workshop is an expensive undertaking and its continuing operating expense is such as to demand considerable philanthropic funds from the community. As compared to the cost of institutionalization, however, the workshop seems to require less community money to serve the retarded, although we must hasten to add that the humanitarian aspects must demand a heavy stake in the overall evaluation of values. As yet, the best administrative and training arrangements for a sheltered workshop are in the early experimental stages of being formulated. Nevertheless, their promise is great and it behooves us to think about drawing up realistic plans to increase their number in substantial measure.

The appearance of the training center and sheltered workshop is one which affects education as well as rehabilitation. It is obvious to me that no clear set of principles and practices can as yet be discerned with respect to the school's handling of "sheltered employable" students. However, the rapid appearance of sheltered workshops has forced new issues into the open and they must be enjoined. For example, should sheltered employable students be taken out of school at age fourteen, fifteen, or sixteen and sent to the workshops for training? Should the schools advocate a combined school and sheltered work program for sheltered employables? What are the responsibilities for administrative and financial sponsorship of vocational training of sheltered employable students from fourteen to eighteen years of age? Should the schools be obliged to furnish such vocational training facilities, or is it a responsibility for vocational rehabilitation, or both?

Several school districts and private organizations have applied to the U.S. Office of Vocational Rehabilitation and to state rehabilitation agencies for financial aid in establishing training centers and sheltered workshops for retarded persons of fourteen to eighteen years of age. Is it an appropriate function for vocational rehabilitation to assume? Should such workshops serve adults over eighteen? Is it appropriate for state rehabilitation agencies to pay training costs for retarded adolescents from fourteen to seventeen years of age?

I have purposely left a most important area of work almost to the close of my paper, since it cuts across all groups of the retarded and has such a deep effect upon the quality and completeness of education and rehabilitation. I refer to the family of the retarded and its consideration in our total efforts. If the adjustment of normal children so vitally depends upon the understanding guidance of the parents, the fate of retarded children and adults does so to an even greater extent. Rehabilitation counselors have found it necessary to devote far more time in counseling with family members of the retarded than with many of the physically handicapped. Retarded clients with promising possibilities become hopeless or unfeasible of rehabilitation when the family acts as a drag rather than a strength in making vocational plans. The attitudes of families have become fairly well fixed by the time the retarded reaches young adulthood. The rehabilitation counselor cannot be expected to refashion drastically the attitudes of family members.

It would seem to us that the education of the parents is as important as the education of retarded students. Preventive counseling must be applied early in the childhood of the retarded, and sustained, and the school counselor must prepare the family for the transition to the rehabilitation counselor. Since the family plays so crucial a role in the adjustment of the retarded, this conference should express the issues and attempt to enunciate principles or guides for effective action. Our experience with retarded clients of sheltered workshops has dramatized in another setting the fact that rehabilitation of the retarded person involves and depends upon rehabilitation of the family.

The fourth grouping of the retarded, the *self-care group,* is of no less importance from the individual and social viewpoint than the others. However, vocational rehabilitation is not directly involved in a program for them, although it is anxious to urge that rehabilitation principles be applied to their care. It is obvious that our four groupings are not mutually exclusive. Individuals may develop beyond expected potentials and shift upward, or they may retrogress and shift downward. The present armamentarium of knowledge and skills in working with the retarded is admittedly limited, and further experience and research in prevention, amelioration, education, and rehabilitation may be expected to prove advantageous.

I should like to close my brief statement of major issues with a thought which ought to enter our deliberations. Our efforts in education and rehabilitation of the mentally retarded involve all of society. We must inform society about the mentally retarded and instill a feeling of brotherly concern for their dignity as individuals. Similarly, public acceptance is the very basis of financial and moral support for our efforts. We in rehabilitation must especially try to win the enlightened support of employers and employees. The schools must try to win the understanding of the nonhandicapped students who will become the employers and employees of future years. Our deliberations should attempt to set up guidelines for practical action in these important areas, and must encourage the evaluation of experience coupled with research, which will produce a firm foundation for the future.

Flow of Cases in Work Training Center

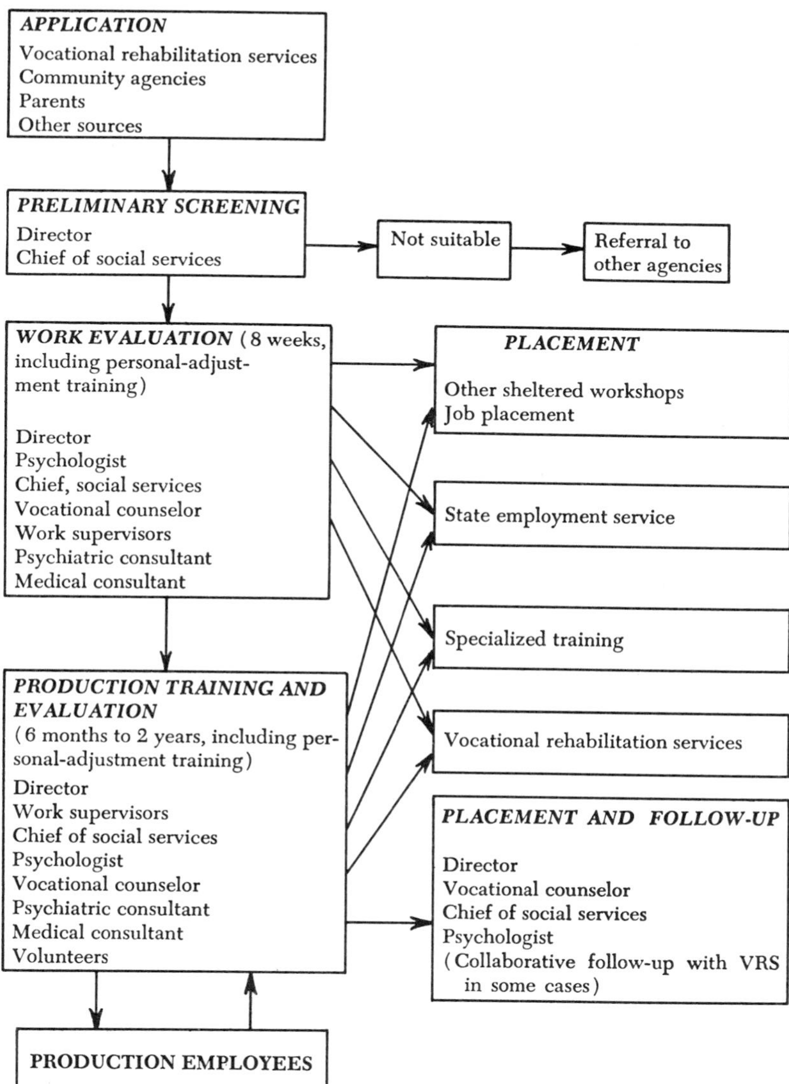

SOURCE: Reprinted with the permission of Elias Katz and the Aid Retarded Children Workshop, San Francisco, California.

Classification System for Employment Potential

Employable Outside (*Easier to Place*)	I. A.	Employable with minimal workshop evaluation and training. Evaluation and placement are primary requirements for achievement of competitive status with workers at comparable levels.
	B.	Capable of achieving employable status with workers at comparable levels *after* evaluation, training, and placement.
Employable Outside (*Hard to Place*); *Employable in Work-training Center*	II. A.	Trainable for employment but in need of special placement and supervision because of physical, including neurological, anomalies.
	B.	Trainable for employment but in need of special placement and supervision because of degree of mental retardation, immaturity, emotional instability, or similar psychological deficiencies.
Employable in Work-training Center	III. A.	Capable of productive work in a special employment situation where the nature and degree of handicap is understood and accepted.
	IV. A.	Capable of only minimal productive contribution and requiring only moderate supervision.
	B.	Capable of only minimal productive contribution and requiring *close supervision* because of psychological or physiological handicaps.
Not Employable in Work-training Center	V. A.	Not capable of productive work contribution but responsive to direction, requiring only moderate supervision.
	B.	Not capable of productive work contribution and requiring close supervision because of severe psychological and physiological handicaps.

Source: Reprinted with the permission of the Aid Retarded Children Workshop, San Francisco, Calif.

36 PREPARATION OF MENTALLY RETARDED YOUTH FOR GAINFUL EMPLOYMENT

Herbert Goldstein
Rick Heber

From *Preparation of Mentally Retarded Youth for Gainful Employment,* Department of Health, Education, and Welfare, Bulletin 1959, No. 28, Government Printing Office, Washington, D.C., 1959, pp. 20–35. Reprinted with the permission of the Department and the authors. Dr. Goldstein is Director, Curriculum Research and Development Center in Mental Retardation, Yeshiva University, New York City. Dr. Heber is Professor of Education, Department of Studies in Behavioral Disabilities, University of Wisconsin, Madison.

Experience seems to show that the successful habilitation of mentally retarded youth into competitive employment and independent living is probably too extensive and complex a task to be carried out effectively by any one agency. It is, rather, a task which may require utilization of total community resources for the achievement of maximum results.

In communities where effective cooperation has not been established among the various agencies, the burden of effort in preparing and placing mentally retarded youth has quite characteristically fallen on one agency—the public schools. In recognition of these considerations, an increasing number of community agencies are augmenting the work of the schools by contributing their specialized services. Chief among these agencies, especially from the point of view of specifically delegated responsibility, is the Vocational Rehabilitation Agency. Together, the school and the rehabilitation agency have a clear legal mandate to carry out this responsibility.

It is understood, of course, that all activities must function within the structure of existing federal, state, and local laws regulating the operation of the various agencies as well as laws affecting health, education, and welfare of children and youth. These include such matters as compulsory school-attendance laws, provisions regarding work permits, and other labor legislation as well as the regulations under which rehabilitation services may operate.

Within the two basic agencies, it seemed desirable that the personnel actively engaged in services to the retarded have ready access to the community agencies which can be of assistance to them; likewise, that other community agencies should have close lines of communication with the school systems and the rehabilitation agency if they are to contribute to the sum total of services which will adequately meet the needs of mentally retarded youth.

It does not seem possible to set forth here a single blueprint of community organization, since communities vary so greatly in available health, education, welfare, rehabilitation, and other resources. Such groups, however, as public and private employment agencies, business and industrial leaders, civic and fraternal organizations, the parent-teacher organizations specifically interested in the retarded, recreational and religious groups, unions and other employee organizations, public and private health and social agencies, can all be of assistance to the schools and the rehabilitation agency, each in its own particular way.

PREPARATION FOR JOB PLACEMENT

It was the consensus that preparing retarded youth for job placement is an extensive undertaking both in terms of time and subject matter. Implicitly, preparation begins in the child's preschool years where the family and community can exert a critical influence on his intellectual and personality development. It is during the child's school years, however, that he is introduced to the complex elements involved in socio-occupational adjustment.

The School Curriculum and Preparation for Employment

Although consideration of the total school curriculum for the retarded did not fall within the scope of the present conference, it was recognized that the major focus of the school program is on preparation for life in the family and community. Consequently, there are many aspects of the curriculum other than direct work training and experience which contribute to the student's preparation for occupational adjustment.

Ideally, preparation for social and vocational adjustment continues from the day the child first enters school. Helping the primary level child to understand the "whys and wherefores" of getting to school on time, for example, is a first step in the development of the concept of punctuality as an obligation of an employee to an employer. By continuously interpreting the social implications of school learnings and activities and by adjusting the curriculum as changes in social conditions dictate, the public schools can help set the stage for ultimate placement of the individual into employment.

Throughout the school years, preparation for employment should be considered as one of several major objectives in curriculum building. In practice it is, of course, not possible to keep the activities aimed at these various objectives entirely separate. The area, *Democratic Group Living,* has implications for *Vocational,* and vice versa. Nevertheless, thinking of the vocational as one of a group of major objectives will have the effect of helping to maintain an adequate balance of the curricular offerings of the school. It will also alert the teacher to the possibilities that lie in the interrelation of the various objectives. This still makes it possible to shift the *emphasis* as the child progresses, while retaining the *balance* which is essential.

Research has demonstrated job failure to be as much a function of difficulty in the accessory adjustments to the job as inability to perform the manual skills required by the job itself. Perhaps most important are the student's skills in interpersonal relationships. Special classes at the secondary age level are therefore finding it profitable to include in the curriculum: teaching units on health and safety, social development and adjustment, personal grooming, family living, community living, and occupational information and requirements. The integrated secondary school programs being developed by many communities are, in great measure, based on the needs of mentally retarded students for interpersonal experience with the normal peers who will later become their coworkers and supervisors.

Many schools provide training in the accessory vocational skills through a unit or course which may be entitled occupations, vocations, or employment. An example is one program which includes a unit on employment in which the student learns about the qualities of a good worker, requirements for work permits, how to complete various kinds of employment application; characteristics of various job areas, qualifications required for jobs available in the community, problems and laws regarding wages, what deductions are made from wages and why, responsibilities of both worker and employer, and health and safety factors in employment. In addition, the student is assisted in a self-evaluation of vocational goals and is given practice in job interviewing. Formal classroom instruction is supplemented by role playing, by tours of businesses and industries where students may become employed, and by visits to employment and other relevant community agencies.

In the later years of the student's school career, agencies, such as the Employment Service, more directly in contact with the labor market and the complex problems of employment can contribute materially toward the preparation of the student. It is at this stage that coordinated planning between the school and the rehabilitation agency should be stressed. Other agencies can contribute indirectly by helping to acquaint employers with the availability of this type of employee and by helping to banish from the public mind many of the misconceptions concerning the mentally retarded. Direct contributions can be made when personnel from community agencies meet with students to discuss the range and nature of jobs available to them, by conferring with school personnel to establish an efficient system of screening for employment, and by providing information on current occupational practices for the school curriculum.

The Role of Counseling in Preparation for Employment

Counseling is accepted as an integral part of the total program of education and vocational preparation of retarded adolescents. Effective counseling and guidance can occur through both formal and informal contacts with students and thus all persons engaged in the education and habilitation of the mentally retarded have some degree of counseling responsibility.

INFORMAL COUNSELING. Informal counseling occurs when the teacher takes advantage of incidental opportunities which arise in relation to classroom activities to assist students in coping with personal, social, academic, or vocational problems. For example, during a unit on occupational information, a student may express an unrealistic vocational aspiration. The teacher, by providing the student with an opportunity to explore a broad range of possible occupational pursuits along with various job requirements is, in reality, engaging in informal counseling.

In most situations at the primary through the intermediate levels, the teacher will be the person of greatest influence in the personal and social development of the child, since he is the one who will develop the most intimate relationship with the student. The teacher is engaged in counseling to the extent that he deliberately promotes growth or works toward desirable modifications in the personal and social development of the child.

The counselor role of the teacher will less often be fulfilled through so-called formalized sessions, than through his sensitivity to the individual personal and social needs of the children and his ability to meet these needs in the classroom situation as they arise. Much of the counseling of the teacher will be of the preventive type, inasmuch as he is in a strategic position to help insure that minor problems do not develop into more serious ones.

The effectiveness of the teacher's counseling, as well as his teaching generally, will depend upon his understanding of the social and cultural ramifications of mental retardation and its impact on personality development. Teachers who have received instruction in personality development will be better equipped to understand and cope with the various behaviors which a mentally retarded student may exhibit as a reaction to his intellectual limitations. A knowledge of the sociocultural aspects of mental retardation will enable him to understand better the values and cultural background of his students. These prerequisites to effective counseling can best be acquired as part of teacher preparation.

The teacher-trainee should receive an overview of counseling techniques and effective methods of dealing with the personal and social problems of students which arise in relation to classroom activities. Because of the demands in the teacher-training curriculum for preparation to fulfill the more traditional functions of the teacher, there will no doubt be insufficient time for the acquisition of the principles, techniques, and experience necessary for counseling students with more complex personal and social problems. An overview of principles of counseling, along with adequate personal–social skills, will enable the teacher to deal effectively with many minor behavioral and attitudinal problems. Steps are being taken in teacher-preparation institutions to strengthen this aspect of their programs.

The teacher's counseling training should also include an orientation to vocational guidance. This will enable him to make better use of the curriculum in acquainting students with potential job opportunities and realistic vocational choices. His orientation to vocational guidance should include information and practice in the utilization of relevant community resources and in working with other specialists as a member of a comprehensive team.

FORMAL COUNSELING. In contrast with the informal counseling carried on by the teacher within the classroom situation, formal counseling implies the services of professional persons with a specific background of training and experience in counseling and guidance who work in schools or in rehabilitation agencies or both. Formal counseling directed at the more complex problems presented by students, requires skills and a background of training not usually held by the classroom teacher. It is therefore essential that the teacher have available for support and assistance the services of the school counselor, school psychologist, and school social worker.

Even with respect to formal counseling, however, there must be close cooperation between counselor and classroom teacher. The teacher is often able to complement the counselor's work by making it possible for the student to implement new values and principles of behavior acquired during counseling. The work of the counselor is often directly related, for example, to the academic performance of the student in the classroom.

The services of the professional counselor become an especially important adjunct to the school program for retarded adolescents where major personal, social, and vocational problems arise as a result of the impending integration into employment and community living. Even with the more complex problems of this period, however, the teacher will be able to complement the work of the counselor. With some kinds of problems, a teacher's intimate relationship with a student may render his informal counseling very effective. An example of cooperation between counselor and teacher can be seen in the relationship between vocational counseling and a teaching unit on occupational opportunities. While the counselor is helping the student to achieve a realistic assessment of his abilities and limitations the teacher is providing him with an opportunity of measuring these abilities against the requirements of specific jobs. It becomes increasingly essential, however, at the secondary school ages, that the skills and services of the teacher be supplemented by the provision of specialized services for the vocational, personal, social, family, placement, and postschool follow-up counseling.

Resources for Counseling Service

There appear to be a number of methods by which the needed professional counseling services are being provided. Some school systems employ counselors for specific kinds of counseling activities. A common example of this is the school placement counselor who contacts employers regarding job opportunities, orients them as to the needs and abilities of prospective mentally retarded employees, assists employers in obtaining necessary adjustments regarding labor laws and other requirements, and attempts to match students to appropriate available positions. In some communities the placement counselor also does the follow-up counseling with the employee while in others this task may be assigned to one of the special class teachers.

Reports of school programs for the adolescent mentally retarded indicate that many schools in addition to their own resources are requesting and receiving assistance from various community agencies in the provision of certain types of counseling service. Most frequently mentioned as sources of counseling services are Vocational Rehabilitation and the State Employment Service. Leaders from business and industry and personnel specialists are also assisting school personnel by serving in a consultative capacity to school–work programs for retarded adolescents.

There probably will be many patterns by which schools and vocational rehabilitation agencies cooperate in meeting the counseling needs of mentally retarded students. The most effective pattern will probably depend on the resources of both the school and rehabilitation agency in the particular community, local conditions, and the particular needs of the students included in the program. In some situations, the school counselor may carry the responsibility quite far. In others, the rehabilitation agency may serve the school in a consultant capacity by assisting school personnel in charting the direction toward employment for individual students, and by providing the student with direct vocational rehabilitation services when needed. In other situations rehabilitation personnel may participate more actively in the school program by working and counseling directly with students in addition to serving as a consultant to the teacher. In a few communities, the rehabilitation agency has assigned a staff member to work full time in cooperation with the schools in meeting the needs of students. Such a person may serve as an effective liaison between the school program and the services of the rehabilitation agency.

Reports indicated that school placement counselors and rehabilitation personnel often find their work handicapped by the insufficiency of information available in the cumulative record folders of mentally retarded students. Placement counselors have indicated, for example, that motor coordination and manual dexterity are often critical factors in job placement. Although the teacher cannot be expected to administer objective tests of eye-hand coordination or finger dexterity, it would be helpful if he would note in the student's records significant motor disabilities and above average motor competencies which he may observe. Such information would enable the counselor to take these factors into consideration in screening students for jobs where motor coordination and dexterity might be important. Working together, the teacher and counselor can map out matters of this type to observe and record.

Students' interests and parents' aspirations are important factors in vocational counseling. If these are made a part of student records, they may well assist the counselor in gaining a better insight into a student's motivations with respect to job choice. Should the counselor find it necessary to work with the parents, he can do so more effectively if he has some previous idea as to the aspirations they have held, or now hold, for their child. Pupil interests and parent aspirations may well, therefore, become a part of the student's cumulative records. Certainly, teachers should record any occupational experiences which their students have had, since such data can be invaluable to the vocational rehabilitation counselor. A description of the jobs held, along with an evaluation of the student's performance and attitude, will assist the counselor in his exploration of placement possibilities.

An intelligence test score acquires greater value if it is supplemented by achievement test data and by the teacher's observations of the student's intellectual behavior in the classroom situation. Teachers, counselors, and other school personnel might well collaborate in determining the type of data which should be included in student records. In this way cumulative records will acquire greater meaning to both teachers and counselors.

The development of adequate cumulative records is only one phase of the cooperative relationship between counseling and teaching personnel. Other areas of cooperation are of comparable importance. Among these are collaboration in the development of the occupational aspects of the school curriculum, the formulation of a screening and testing program, streamlining of referral techniques, and the development of strong lines of communication.

In-school Work Experiences

In certain matters, cooperation is predicated upon the individual efforts of each agency. An example of this is the in-school work experience aspect of the program for mentally retarded adolescents. This feature of the program is predominantly a responsibility of the school. It is, however, a prelude to community placement, much of which may become the responsibility of other agencies.

In-school work experience can be an important culmination of the series of carefully planned experiences provided by the school for the development of attitudes and behaviors relevant to vocational adjustment. The in-school work program provides school personnel with an excellent opportunity for an exploration of student incentives and attitudes in relation to employment. It also creates an additional opportunity for the further development of occupational information and desirable job attitudes. The student's experiences on the job can be utilized by the teacher to supplement classroom instruction.

Occupational training within the school will probably be the more effective the more it simulates a real work situation. School personnel must stay alert to the fact that changing employment opportunities and labor needs have implications for the kinds of jobs provided in the in-school setting. Experience in hand washing of dishes in the school cafeteria, for example, will be of little benefit to students if restaurants are converting to automatic dishwashers. The development of any work-experience program within the school setting must recognize this and be sufficiently flexible so that it can be adjusted to changes in community needs and labor conditions.

In-school work programs have been criticized for being too limited in the job experiences provided and for being so sheltered that they do not provide students with realistic work experiences. These criticisms do not apply when the in-school program is structured, not for the purpose of teaching specific skills, but rather to give students the experiences preliminary to direct occupational placement in the community where they will learn whatever specific job skills are required. The in-school program is most useful when it stresses attributes which may be generalized to any job situation such as the relationship of the worker to the employer and vice versa, concepts of punctuality, socialization, and task completion.

Though the in-school job program has the disadvantage of being sheltered and of failing to cover some of the problems which the student will face in community placement, it does have the advantage of lending itself to control. The advantage of this control can be seen in the possibility for changing the kind of supervision which the students receive. If the coordinator of the program wishes to see how the students react to various kinds of job supervisors, he can periodically change the "foreman," in each case instructing the new "foreman" in his role. Thus, school personnel and job counselor are able to observe how the student performs under various kinds of supervision. How such observations might contribute toward the ultimate placement of the student is apparent. Other advantages of being able to control and manipulate the work program are that students can be moved from one job to another at a rate commensurate with their needs and abilities, and work can be halted as needs for specific instruction or for evaluation are observed. These and many other advantages are only possible in an in-school or similar type of work-training program.

There are hazards involved in this type of program that must not be overlooked if it is to facilitate the successful placement of the student in the community. Prominent among these hazards is the possibility of misinterpretation of the role of the student by personnel involved in the work program. For example, cafeteria employees under whom the students work may look upon them as helpers and spend little time in instructing or observing the students. The students themselves may get proficient at one job and not wish to rotate to other jobs, losing sight of the reasons for their participation in the in-school job program. To avoid these hazards there must be a constant reevaluation of the function of the in-school program and its effectiveness in facilitating the later adjustment of the student in the community.

ON-THE-JOB TRAINING

The on-the-job training program is one of the outgrowths of the expansion of specialized public school programs. Finding that many mentally retarded adolescents were unable to maintain themselves in competitive employment upon termination of school attendance, many school systems have begun to develop extended school programs to age eighteen and in some cases to age twenty-one. An integral feature of many of these extended programs has been the inclusion of on-the-job training designed to facilitate successful transition from school to employment.

In the on-the-job training program, the student usually spends part of a day or week in acquiring work experience and learning specific job skills. The remainder of his time is spent in school. A few programs have been organized so that the student spends full time for a period in the job training program, and then alternates this with a period of full-time school attendance. The nature of the work experience obtained in the job training program is, of course, dependent upon the prevailing economic conditions in the community and the range of occupational opportunities available. Individual work experiences must take into consideration the ability of the employer to accept and be a positive factor in the development and training of the students.

A close liaison should be maintained between school and employer so that the student may receive careful supervision in the work-experience program. Many schools accomplish this by appointing a counselor to work full time with student-workers, employers, and as a liaison with classroom teachers. In other schools, teachers' schedules are set so as to permit time for working with employers and observing their students on the job. Since employers and fellow employees vary so greatly in the demands they make, and in the manner in which they react to mentally retarded workers, it is desirable that students obtain several kinds of work experiences in the on-the-job training program.

SELECTIVE PLACEMENT

Carefully planned programs of vocational preparation of mentally retarded youth should be culminated by selective placement. Experience has shown that probability of successful adjustment is increased when students are given assistance in locating and adjusting to suitable jobs.

Helping mentally retarded students to locate and adjust to employment will probably not prove to be the province of any one agency in the community. Rather, it is more likely to prove essential that all agencies having the ability and inclination to cooperate in this task do so by bringing to bear the particular services they are able to provide. Placing a mentally retarded youth on a job involves many professional services. Selective placement is comprised of an extended sequence of activities which precede and follow actual job placement. These include evaluation, exploration of job opportunities, job placement, postplacement counseling, and other post-school services.

Evaluation

The objective of formal evaluation is to enable professional personnel to make a placement which will match the capacity and characteristics of the student with the demands of a particular job. It is essential that a thorough evaluation of the student be carried out well ahead of the time when actual job placement is to be made. The first aspect of evaluation is to determine the student's need for placement assistance. In some cases, this assistance may not be immediately needed as, for example, when the student will be employed by or through a member of his own family. Those who do require placement assistance should undergo an evaluation to ascertain the nature of the placement services they will need. In this stage of evaluation it would seem desirable that school personnel and the vocational rehabilitation counselor work together. Through their cooperative efforts they can determine whether the student should receive the services of a placement agency, such as the State Employment Service, or whether he should receive further training and/or remediation and preparation for a specific job through the Vocational Rehabilitation Agency. Where testing is required to determine the eligibility and feasibility for agency service, the rehabilitation counselor will be able to indicate the procedures for obtaining this service.

It should be recognized that, in many instances, student needs may change following termination of school attendance. For example, a student who has indicated that he has been promised a position with a friend or relative may find that the job does not materialize. Another youth may show all the signs of needing only placement service and not training. With a trial period of employment it may become evident that he requires further rehabilitation service. Cooperating agencies should therefore make provisions for follow-up and periodic reevaluations of the services needed by a particular student.

Exploration of Job Opportunities

Explorations of job opportunities in the community should, no doubt, ideally be a cooperative activity on the part of all agencies concerned with the vocational placement of the mentally retarded. These explorations should be coordinated so as to avoid repetitive, time-consuming interviews. In some communities this confusion has been avoided by the appointment of a coordinating committee which assumes responsibility for gathering all necessary occupational information and communicating it to the various agencies involved.

Information gathered in this way is used by each agency according to its needs. The school, for example, may use data on available job opportunities in revising its subject matter on occupational adjustment. In this way the subject matter of the classroom becomes more closely related to actual conditions in the community. Employment agencies can use this information for job classification and listing of services. This information is also used directly in working with those students who are ready for immediate job placement. Rehabilitation agencies can use this information in planning rehabilitative services that will be most appropriate to available job opportunities. In addition to knowledge of available job opportunities, vocational exploration can provide information concerning facilities and skills of the employer for training mentally retarded workers. This knowledge will be helpful to placement personnel in working out a plan for on-the-job training of the new worker.

Job Placement

Actual placement on the job can be most effectively achieved by careful preparation of student and employer. The actual placement will often be made by the agency most involved with the student. For example, a student who does not require special training prior to placement on a specific job may be served by an agency confining itself only to placement. A student requiring such services as training, treatment, or prosthesis would probably be a client of the vocational rehabilitation agency for both the service and placement. In some cases, the schools may have an established backlog of jobs that have been used in the on-the-job training program. Where indicated, it might be advisable to permit certain students to extend their part-time experience into a full-time job.

It was not the function of this report to go into a detailed description of jobs into which the educable mentally retarded can be placed. The usual lists of jobs reported as suited to retarded workers might be a somewhat outmoded and rather restricted sampling today. The rapid technological changes which are occurring are creating new job possibilities for the mentally retarded while some existing ones are being eliminated. The possibilities will vary considerably from one community to another depending largely upon what kinds of businesses and industries happen to be located in a particular area. Community surveys conducted in an attempt to discover what kinds of work the mentally retarded might perform have often turned up surprising possibilities which are not mentioned in the classic lists of job opportunities for the retarded. Retarded persons are reported as working in a large range of occupations, except the highly professional.

Postplacement Counseling

Job placement should include plans for follow-up if optimal adjustment is to be achieved. Placement personnel have found that many seemingly minor incidents or misunderstandings can be ameliorated early in the employee's and employer's experience, thereby preventing undesirable consequences. A girl placed as a bus girl in a cafeteria, for example, interpreted her job to be that of only clearing tables and carting the dirty dishes to the dishwasher. By accident, a customer dropped a bowl of soup on the tile floor. When the manager asked the girl to mop up the debris in the interest of safety, she became confused and somewhat defensive, since she could not see the relationship between this request and her duties. She was about to make an issue of this simple incident, but fortunately decided to talk it over with her placement counselor who helped her to see the logic in the assignment. Without assistance from a postplacement counselor this girl might have forced this minor event into a situation that cost her the job. It might possibly have closed this avenue for job placement for a long time to come, for this girl as well as others.

The employee should be encouraged to discuss a wide range of problems, since many factors not directly related to employment can have an effect on job adjustment. Time should be taken to discuss the employee's work with the person who is the immediate supervisor. If there are deficiencies in the employee's work or adjustment, the counselor may be in a position to effect a favorable change in the employee. Placement personnel have found that it is often better and easier to counsel with an employer and employee in order to maintain the worker on the present job than it is to find a new job for him. In some instances, supervisors, in an attempt to reward good service, have unwittingly "promoted" their mentally retarded employees into jobs which were too complex. In one case, a mentally retarded youth was made foreman of a crew. Counseling with the supervisor would have prevented the resultant failure and avoided the frustration which occurred on the part of both employee and employer.

Postschool Services

Because of their handicap in vocational and social adjustment, postschool adjustment and educational services can be most helpful to mentally retarded young adults. It has been found that educable mentally retarded employees change jobs about as frequently as their normal peers during the first few years following their leaving school. The reasons underlying change are many, including dislike for the work, changes in the requirements of the job, changes in the work site, etc. A continuing adult education program will facilitate the transition from one job to another or from one job locale to another.

An adult education program also contributes to continuing progress in community adjustment. A program that offers continuing education beyond the general school program will upgrade the efficiency of many students and render them more effective as citizens. At the same time, those mentally retarded young adults who fail to reach their potential in academic achievement before leaving school would have an opportunity for further progress in the area. The experience of the few communities with adult education programs for the mentally retarded indicate that it is at this level that many of these students become motivated to improve their skills in the traditional academic areas.

Vocational rehabilitation as well as other community agencies have a stake in postschool services. They may assist in establishing a sheltered work environment for those mentally retarded individuals who are not immediately able to function independently in the community. Protected work experience of this type should be a responsibility of the interested community agencies if a continuing program of training, counseling, and placement is to be achieved. Some communities have found the sheltered work-experience program to be the answer to the problem engendered by the mentally retarded student who indicates a potential for ultimate placement in competitive employment but who is not immediately ready for this upon termination from the formal secondary school program.

37 VOCATIONAL REHABILITATION OF THE MENTALLY RETARDED: THE SHELTERED WORKSHOP

Julius S. Cohen

From *Mental Retardation Abstracts,* Vol. 3, No. 2, April–June 1966, pp. 163–169. Reprinted with the permission of the U.S. Department of Health, Education, and Welfare and the author. Dr. Cohen is Associate Director for Development and Coordinator for Training, Institute for the Study of Mental Retardation, University of Michigan, Ann Arbor.

In reporting on the need for increased vocational rehabilitation services for the mentally retarded, the President's Panel on Mental Retardation (1962) highlighted the role of sheltered workshops for the mentally retarded and recommended that a federal program be established to provide financial support for construction, equipment, and initial staffing of sheltered workshops and other rehabilitation facilities. At the same time, the Panel recommended an extension of sheltered work opportunities to include such activities as conservation and maintenance of parks, recreational areas, and public institutions; domestic service occupations; varied types of health service; and agricultural occupations.

In view of the recent emphasis on the development of services and workshops for the disabled plus the evident desire to maximize the country's manpower through such programs as the Manpower Development and Training Act, it seems appropriate to consider techniques, settings, and efficiency with which provision can be made for the retarded.

DEFINITION

According to the Rehabilitation Act of 1954, Public Law 565, the term workshop was defined as: "A place where any manufacturing or handwork is carried on and which is operated for the primary purpose of providing remunerative employment to severely handicapped individuals who cannot be readily absorbed in the competitive labor market" (Public Law 565, 1954). A tentative definition for a sheltered workshop was: "A work oriented rehabilitation facility with controlled working environment and individualized vocational goals which utilizes work experience and related services for assisting the handicapped person to progress toward normal living in a productive vocational status." The National Association of Sheltered Workshops and Homebound Programs (1957) defined a workshop as: "A non-profit organization or institution conducted for the purpose of carrying on a recognized program of rehabilitation for physically, mentally, and socially handicapped individuals by providing such individuals with remunerative employment and one or more other rehabilitating activities of an educational, psycho-social therapeutic, vocational, or spiritual nature."

Although the three definitions have common features, such as working for pay in a protected environment, the definition of the National Association of Sheltered Workshops will be used for the purposes of this paper.

PURPOSE

Historically, sheltered workshop programs have been standard activities for a variety of welfare agencies, churches, hospitals, and other facilities. According to Doll (1958), these programs were of value in bringing together various handicapped individuals to relieve their isolation, to capitalize on their residual talents for production output, and to provide a sense of worth and pride. Thus, the workshop must be regarded as a means, rather than as an end—a device for assisting the retarded young adult to achieve maximum self-realization.

A review of the suggested purposes of workshop experiences for the mentally retarded reflect the need for a broad coverage of rehabilitation services within the total program. Fraenkel (1958) identified six major phases essential to a workshop program: (1) screening-admissions; (2) evaluation; (3) personal adjustment training; (4) vocational training; (5) selective training; and (6) follow-up. On the basis of the time allotted for each activity, programs for the mentally retarded usually emphasize the third phase—personal adjustment training.

Although the workshop must, of necessity, concentrate on the vocational attributes of the individual, there is a great need for additional services in the remaining areas of the retardate's activities. Activities relating to nonvocational areas such as travel, communication, the ability to handle money, self-care, appearance, and recreation must be considered. Since sheltered workshops offer a great opportunity to develop such skills and provide work conditioning for the disabled, they should be utilized as an integral part of the overall planning for the retarded in a community setting.

Finally, adequate counseling and guidance services are necessary to ensure the maximum use of the individual's potential. The necessity of providing selective job placement services, interim support, and adequate follow-up as needed until the client has adjusted to his adult life situation at his optimum level of functioning has become increasingly evident.

PROGRAMS

When establishing a sheltered workshop program for the retarded, a number of principles should be considered. Jacobs, Weingold and Dubrow

(1962), for example, outlined 11 factors essential to a rehabilitation program for the retarded: (1) Adult retardates have the right to engage in self-directed activity consistent with their abilities. (2) Retardates are entitled to the gratifications and satisfactions enjoyed by normals. (3) The retarded are more like normals than they are different from them. (4) There is a wide range of individual differences among the mentally retarded. (5) Individual behavior is modifiable, i.e., behavior is learned and, under conditions favorable to learning, vocational and other desired behaviors appropriate to adulthood can be acquired by the retarded. (6) Vocational and other behaviors appropriate to adulthood can be acquired through social learning and imitation in a workshop setting. (7) Retardates need opportunities within the sheltered workshop to act out their newly acquired roles as adults and as workers. (8) Because retardates are more dependent upon their parents than are normals, it is usually necessary for parents to be closely involved in vocational planning. (9) Retardates tend to learn more efficiently when dealing with concrete specific materials and situations. (10) Measures of mental capacity alone may not be valid or reliable predictors of vocational adjustment. Beyond a critical minimum, additional increments of intelligence appear to be less significant than such factors as motivation, maturity, social competence, and independence. (11) In order to build motivation and to provide a frame of reference for the appropriateness of behavior, some construct such as the self concept is useful, i.e., the retardate is more likely to behave as an adult if he sees himself as one.

To meet these needs and to ensure complete services, a workshop must provide a basic four-phase program for each client: (1) evaluation, (2) training, (3) short term preplacement or interim employment, and (4) terminal employment for those less capable clients. The extent to which any particular client's needs are met by the workshop will be reflected in the development of a suitable variety of programs.

The ability of various evaluation tasks to predict the vocational potential of retarded individuals has been considered in several studies. Tobias (1960) reported that when the criterion of vocational adjustment within the sheltered workshop was utilized, there was a significant positive correlation between the evaluation score and the wages earned by trainees. When, however, the same criterion of average hourly earnings, based on a month of workshop employment, was compared with IQ, the relationship was not statistically significant. This emphasizes the value of job performance within a workshop in the vocational evaluation of the retarded.

Dubrow (1958) also emphasized the importance of job production in evaluating the flexibility and adaptability of the clients, as well as their production, perseverance, and social adjustment. In addition, he indicated that the area of production programming is in great need of standardized research to determine the most effective methods of training adult behavior.

A well-defined, realistic training program provides both general and specific work skills. The jobs and experiences planned for the client should be graded from those which are comparatively simple to those which are complex; from those which require little or no supervision to those which need almost constant supervisory attention. Production standards should approximate the levels maintained by industry, and the salaries should be determined accordingly. The client's readiness to move from one phase to another within the workshop should be determined by his ability to meet the expected standards.

The sheltered workshop program should not particularly stress the specific skills required for a particular job; rather, the general work habits and attitudes that any employee needs for successful employment should be emphasized, including punctuality, dependability, personal habits, cooperation with supervisors, cooperation with fellow employees, proper use of materials and equipment, and the ability to work under pressure.

It should be observed that probably the most important characteristics in determining vocational success are within the personality area rather than intelligence. For example, Appell, Williams and Fishell (1962) instituted a study to differentiate between retardates who were considered terminal trainees and those who achieved competitive employment after a period of workshop experience. The subjects were rated twice by the staff and comparisons were made on a variety of variables. In the areas of general abilities, work approach, social attitudes, and adjustment, there was a significant relationship between the level of ratings and ultimate competitive employment. With respect to IQ, neither the full scale nor the verbal scores on the Wechsler were able to distinguish between the two groups. The employed group, however, had significantly higher nonverbal IQ scores.

The last of the four phases is that of placement and follow-up. During this crucial period, the individual should be provided opportunities for selective job placements, either within the workshop or within the community. Appropriate ongoing services should be available to ensure his successful adjustment to the community working situation.

A serious problem in the operation of the workshop is the danger of becoming highly selective, i.e., admitting only those clients for whom the prognosis for competitive employment is good. This policy has a tendency to minimize the effectiveness of the workshop for the retarded population.

When developing a philosophical basis for total programming and considering the format of most workshops, it should be recognized that all rehabilitation involves segregation of some kind. There are certain clients who, because of their condition or the phase of their rehabilitation, might be best served within a totally segregated program. Others, however, might profit from being exposed to clients from other disability groups as a step toward their total integration into the working world. Terminal workshop employees of many types could benefit from the more diversified social contacts offered in the multidisability workshop.

The actual establishment of a workshop requires a thoughtful consideration of a large number of influencing factors, including the need for such services, the organizational structure of the workshop, the relationships of various agencies, and the composition, size, qualifications, and compensation for a professional staff. Naturally, client needs and services, including the number and types of handicaps to be served, types of services, employment and training experiences to be offered, will dictate many of the policies. The report of the York County Council of Community Services (1962) provides an excellent outline for the establishment of sheltered workshops. This document discusses such vital issues as the organization of committees, the establishment of a sheltered workshop, the development of articles of incorporation under the nonprofit regulations enforced by the state, preparing appropriate bylaws, and the nature of committee reports. The selection of an appropriate site, equipment, facilities, related costs, and the broad problem of the physical plant also are considered. A number of such reports and guides are available (Dubin, 1956; National Association for Retarded Children, 1959; Nelson, 1962 and 1963a; Smith, 1961).

The successfully placed client is the ultimate criterion of the rehabilitation program, and the workshop is assuming more and more responsibility in this area. In addition, the close relationship between special education programs, institutional and community agencies, and sheltered workshops must be considered carefully when the value and utilization of a workshop is considered. Continued exploration into the reasons mentally retarded take various jobs and the retardate's occupational values will provide further factors to be considered in vocational programming (Cohen and Rusalem, 1964).

FACILITIES

In describing the physical areas to be included within a sheltered workshop, Jacobs, Weingold and Dubrow (1962) recommended that space be provided for the following: (1) production, (2) evaluation, (3) storage, (4) shipping and receiving, (5) offices, (6) clerical space, (7) toilets, (8) locker space, (9) rest rooms, (10) service areas, and (11) other, including recreational areas, meeting rooms, and conference rooms. The actual proportion of space allocated for each of these suggested purposes and the ultimate space utilization would depend largely upon the number and types of clients the workshop hopes to serve and the extent of services and staff which are planned.

Wallin (1960) suggested that the availability and use of workshops for the older adolescent and adult mental retardate can be divided into three general categories. First are the workshops which are specifically or exclusively designed for the mentally retarded. Second are the workshops which afford specialized facilities for many different kinds of physically handicapped persons, as well as for the mentally retarded. The third group consists of workshops for the physically handicapped which do not provide any special facilities for the mentally retarded but which will admit them as clients. The establishment of any of these three types frequently results from pressure groups such as parents' associations, the availability of existing community services agencies, or workshops such as the Salvation Army or Goodwill Industries, rather than as the result of total community; the resultant facility reflects these pressures.

MULTIPLE DISABILITY WORKSHOPS

As previously observed, segregation is a frequent aspect of rehabilitation programming. The type, degree, and duration of this segregation should be a function of client-need, rather than program limitations. The value of integrating or consolidating a variety of disability groups within one facility should be explored.

A number of advantages for a mixed disability workshop were cited by Nye (1961). These included: (1) opportunity for a greater variety of subcontract work; (2) the need for less supervision; (3) service to a greater number of handicapped people, especially in a small community; and (4) development of a more cooperative attitude among the trainees.

Thus, the advisability of establishing multidisability workshops is dependent partially on the size of the community to be served. In small communities where there are few handicapped children, the only way to provide any type of workshop experience is through the integrated approach. Therefore, the problem of establishing a single program for each different group exists primarily in large communities where each handicap might be represented with its own individual workshop. This, of course, results in great competition for staffing, contracts, and public funds.

In practice, each state usually has a combination of consolidated and independent workshops. This is aptly illustrated by the study of Nelson (1963a) conducted in California. Of the 79 reporting workshops, 59 indicated that they served a total of 1333 mentally retarded clients during 1962. Fifty-six percent of the retarded were served in workshops designed specifically for them and 44 percent received attention in integrated facilities. Twenty-seven workshops were designed solely for the mentally retarded.

The problem of effective utilization of professional staff personnel within a community is important. It often has been demonstrated that there is a general shortage of competent rehabilitation workers. Consequently, it would appear more efficient if the funds of several relatively small programs were pooled to ensure the hiring of an adequate professional staff. If this were done, equal services must be guaranteed for each disability group, and the needs of the individual client must be met if a consolidated facility is to operate successfully.

A report by Appell, Williams, and Fishell (1963) concerning the attitudes of professional workers toward the retarded is relevant to the entire question of establishing a multidisability workshop. The obtained data suggest that a primary problem in recruiting an adequate staff for the integrated workshop is that many professionals are somewhat negatively oriented toward working with retarded clients. Subsequently, in such a setting, it might not be possible for the retarded to receive adequate services. When a professional is hired to work in a sheltered workshop designed primarily for the mentally retarded, apparently he is one of a minority of professional persons interested in working with these clients. Thus, it becomes apparent that one of the most crucial, single problems in developing a consolidated workshop is the selection of staff personnel whose orientation and experiences will help to ensure optimal services for all clients at all levels.

The question of financing a multidisciplinary facility must be considered also. For example, in the area of the blind, laws delimit certain types of contracts to workshops unless a specified percent of the clients are legally blind. This may result in the loss of funds in some integrated workshops. Therefore, adequate policies and programs should be developed to take advantage of existing legislation, while serving all types of clients.

The entire question of program priorities for the clients must be clearly understood. The top priority group is usually the least disabled, i.e., those individuals who need minimal services and who can be placed with the least effort. This is the group which, though frequently found in workshop settings, may have least need for such experiences. A second group would be those who, with sufficient services, could be classified as rehabilitated clients and vocationally placed in the community. They require more help than the first group, but still are able to be comparatively productive when industrial norms are considered. The third group are those individuals who require long-term services and terminal employment. Unfortunately, these individuals may suffer when there is a necessity to make some delimiting decisions relating to the location of personnel, space, and services.

In considering the current direction of rehabilitation programming, it must be recognized that more and more severely involved individuals are demanding services which should, and must be, provided for them. In addition, there is an increasing number of multiply handicapped individuals who "fall between the cracks" of services provided by individual agencies. It might be anticipated that the needs of these particular clients would be best met in an integrated facility. Thus, a multiply handicapped individual would not face the problem of having agency "A" refuse service because the individual is involved with a problem that they feel agency "B" should serve, and agency "B" merely refers back to "A."

RESIDENTIAL PROGRAMS

While the focus of sheltered workshop operations has been primarily for individuals who reside in the community, there has been an increasing utilization of these programs as a part of the adjustment experiences for individuals newly returned to the community from residential institutions. In addition, there have been some efforts at the establishment of workshops within state institutions (Cohen, 1961; Smith, 1957; Stevens and Blumberg, 1962).

The sheltered workshop within a residential facility can satisfy two basic goals. First, it can serve as an industrial evaluation and training unit for those individuals who are expected to return to competitive placement in a community industrial setting. Secondly, it can be utilized for the training and placement of those individuals within the institution who, because of their degree of limitation, might not be expected to return to the community except within a sheltered situation, or who might be expected to remain within the institution.

As a part of the basic vocational training program, such a workshop could provide an industrial setting which may not generally exist within residential facilities. Work may be obtained through state industries, other institutions or nonprofit agencies. In the case of private residential schools, contracts can be secured from community organizations and businesses. The institutional workshop, as in the case of community programs, should be designed as an instructional and experiential situation for the retardate and should emphasize the development of desirable work habits, attitudes, and similar factors.

RELATIONSHIP TO SPECIAL EDUCATION

Rockower (1953) reported that the problems of rehabilitating the mentally retarded who are no longer attending school evolve around two broad considerations: (1) the structuring of individual needs to ensure employment, and (2) the development of resources which will adequately meet these needs. He suggested that the sheltered workshop might well satisfy these requirements.

The relationship between workshops and special education programs may be the foundation for the successful rehabilitation of numbers of mentally retarded individuals for whom employment in such a workshop setting might be terminal. It is necessary for the schools to provide adequate programming for the education, orientation, and preparation of the youngster for this eventuality. In addition, the workshop also might be used to provide certain types of work training experiences prior to graduation from school.

Appropriate special education programming and preparation for placement in a sheltered workshop should include a vocational orientation early in the primary program. Retarded students must be exposed to the work world and to the important role of the workshop. As the student grows older, a variety of first-hand vocational experiences are required, including prevocational experiences, the introduction of vocational training, and an extensive program of vocational rehabilitation counseling. With the current provisions for educational programs up to age twenty-one, the school should be able to provide a broad variety of training experiences.

The workshop, in turn, can provide a proving ground where the intellectual, personal, social, and vocational skills of the retarded individuals are developed and evaluated until he is brought to a level of productivity commensurate with his skills and abilities.

Generally, schools provide academic training, expose the students to a series of experiences and homemaking, industrial arts, and related areas and then assign them to a variety of work situations. These jobs, usually in the service areas, may not be presented in the most effective manner, and the retardate may not consider the job as desirable (Cohen and Rusalem, 1964). The orientation, skills, and services available within the workshop could prove of great value in ameliorating many of the difficulties faced by school personnel. With knowledge of the world of work, a more specific orientation towards work and vocational training and with experience in vocational rehabilitation counseling, training and placement, the sheltered workshop should assist the potential client while he is still a student in school. Such services, which might be consultive or direct in nature, could be of tremendous value to the retardate. An effective school–workshop program requires a close liaison between the respective agencies. Unfortunately, very little intercommunication is evident.

ACCREDITATION

The growing movement towards developing a basis for accrediting sheltered workshop programs is reflected in the recent activities of the National Rehabilitation Association (1964). In view of the importance of sheltered workshop facilities to the entire area of rehabilitation, it was suggested by the Association that the Vocational Rehabilitation Administration furnish adequate leadership to the states and communities establishing and operating rehabilitation programs. Extensive research is now being conducted by the Association of Rehabilitation Centers and the National Association of Sheltered Workshops for the development of standards. Accreditation is the next step which should be pursued without delay.

Paralleling the efforts to establish standards for accreditation, attempts at "professionalizing" sheltered workshop staff personnel are noteworthy. Recently, the Vocational Rehabilitation Administration sponsored two regional centers for the training of workshop directors at the University of Wisconsin (Madison) and the San Francisco State College. The need for personnel of various disciplines to be trained and represented within the workshop has been stressed by a variety of authorities. Nitzberg (1958), for example, upon reflecting on the job of social workers within the workshop, cited the immeasurable value of such a responsibility and the unique training opportunities afforded by the workshop.

COMMUNITY RELATIONS

In view of the dilemma under which workshops function (i.e., attempting to maintain a business operation while providing rehabilitation services) adequate community support is essential. It is necessary, therefore, that workshops need be concerned with a number of very real and vital issues. Of critical importance, according to Suazo (1962), is the need to define more completely the role and function of the workshop in the total rehabilitation process and to clarify ways in which to educate the community to accept sheltered workshops, to assure adequate compensation for work performed in the workshop, and to implement standards of operation. In addition, workshops need an acute awareness of their fundamental responsibility, both to society and to the disabled individuals they serve. The workshop's prime responsibility is, of course, to provide a realistic work environment for their clients—this is the reason for their existence.

In considering the problem of whether or not workshops might be expected to be self-supporting, Massie (1962) indicated that such self-support can be accomplished only when the selection of clients is limited to the "cream-of-the-crop" and when such workers are retained for a prolonged period of time. Such a workshop would not resolve the vocational or economic problems of the more severely disabled; and in addition, such a workshop withholds competitive workers from employment. Seldom can adequate salaries for the professional staff and other experts providing rehabilitation services be obtained from production income only. Continuing support for the workshop should come from the community, from the purchase of services by the state division of vocational rehabilitation, and from other similar sources.

Government subsidies are already present in the form of nonprofit, tax-exempt status for workshops and in the exemption from payment of minimum wages to clients. The financial problem must be faced realistically; workshops must have supplemental financing from some voluntary or public source if they are to incorporate all of their rehabilitative functions. A solution to financing and related management problems is long overdue, and various approaches must be considered and evaluated. In order to provide a realistic work environment, wages for each client must be based on individual productivity; and productivity alone cannot support the therapeutic services required. Workshops must develop effective techniques for demonstrating how funds best can be utilized in rehabilitation programming for the handicapped.

Work performed in most workshops falls into the broad categories of primary manufacturing, subcontract work, and salvage operations. There continues to be a considerable community interest in the type of work services available within sheltered workshops. This interest is of especial importance when a new workshop is being considered in a community. Of the three categories, the most frequent type of work performed is subcontract for industry. This reflects the growing interest of industry to use workshops for the handicapped to handle a wide range of selected subcontract jobs, especially for vital short-term work which does not justify great expense on the part of the industry.

Nelson (1963b) indicated that there are certain factors which encourage industry to utilize a workshop. A contractor (1) avoids unnecessary plant expansion and overhead, (2) eliminates the use of skilled labor when unskilled labor is sufficient, (3) reduces the amount of work outside the firm's usual activity, (4) bypasses the cost of hiring and training temporary personnel, and (5) saves the cost of record keeping required by Government. These factors should be emphasized when a workshop is attempting to obtain contracts from industry.

In considering the value of sheltered workshops in the community, Dolnick (1964) interviewed 132 contractors representing a variety of industrial firms which provided subcontract work to 35 sheltered workshops. It was noted that the contractors were interested in workshops primarily insofar as they filled a need of the contractor's business. The programs were viewed in terms of solving specific contractor problems, and workshops which impressed the contractors were those which operated on sound business principles. It was reported that such workshops had the greatest chance of getting contractor approval and contract work.

The solicitation of work and subcontracts should be based on the capabilities of the workshop, rather than on emotionalism. The workshop personnel should be very sensitive to negative comments of contractors so that problems can be considered and resolved.

Appell and Kinsella (1962) also discussed the need for community support and the importance of adequate liaison in establishing functional sheltered workshops. In this instance, their coordinating group served to bring into focus a variety of problems that exist for the mentally retarded within the urban community, including a paucity of services, a lack of effective coordination, and insufficient financial support. Regular discussions and increasing sophistication of an interested group of lay and professional people, however, did lead to the resolution of some of these problems. The public relations work of the coordinating group was considered to be a prime factor in the observed progress. Further, the community coordinating group was instrumental in bringing a state-supported mental retardation demonstration project to the city as well as effecting the consolidation of agencies in the community primarily concerned with mental retardation. However, Dolnick indicates it is necessary to be aware of the negative comments of contractors so that problems can be considered and corrected.

SUMMARY

This paper has attempted to place into a broad perspective, some of the aspects which relate to the vocational rehabilitation of the mentally retarded through appropriate and adequate utilization of the sheltered workshop. In noting the development and the recent rapid growth of sheltered workshop programs, coupled with the comparative shortage of professional workers, attention was devoted to programming within integrated and non-integrated settings.

A number of important factors in workshop programming and development were considered, including goals, facilities, community relations, the need for careful selection of professional personnel and leadership, and special funding problems. The relationships between workshops and special education programs must be explored and developed more fully. The need for close contact and communication between these agencies is very apparent. Too frequently, the client moves from one program to the other with a minimum of benefit or help. The development of workshops within residential facilities was also considered.

It is of primary importance that the community be fully involved in workshop programs from the earliest planning stages for it is only through such involvement that community education and program advancement is ensured. The workshop should have a clearly defined objective of developing the retarded to his optimum capacity in all areas including personal adjustment, social development, and vocational skills. An adequate workshop program is a necessary ingredient in the creation of comprehensive vocational rehabilitation programs for the retarded.

REFERENCES

Appell, M. J., and Kinsella, B. The coordinating group on mental retardation of Monroe County, New York. *American Journal of Mental Deficiency, 67*:14–20, 1962.

Appell, M. J., Williams, C. M., and Fishell, K. N. Significant factors in placing mental retardates from a workshop situation. *Personnel and Guidance Journal, 41*:260–265, 1962.

Appell, M. J., Williams, C. M., and Fishell, K. N. An analysis of attitudes of professional personnel regarding mental retardation as a field. Paper read at annual meeting of the American Personnel and Guidance Association, Boston, Mass., 1963.

Cohen, J. S. A workshop operation within the framework of a state institution. *American Journal of Mental Deficiency, 66*:51–56, 1961.

Cohen, J. S., and Rusalem, H. Occupational values of retarded students. *American Journal of Mental Deficiency, 69*:54–61, 1964.

Doll, E. A. Sheltered workshops for the mentally retarded. *Exceptional Children, 25*:3–4, 1958.

Dolnick, M. Contractor opinions of sheltered workshops. *Journal of Rehabilitation, 30*:23–25, 1964.

Dubin, H. N. The sheltered workshop—some important considerations in its planning and establishment. *American Journal of Mental Deficiency, 60*:508–514, 1956.

Dubrow, M. Work procurement and job production. *American Journal of Mental Deficiency, 63*:355–359, 1958.

Dubrow, M. Sheltered workshops for the mentally retarded as an educational and vocational experience. *Personnel and Guidance Journal, 38*:392–395, 1960.

Fraenkel, W. A. *Fundamentals in Organizing a Sheltered Workshop for the Mentally Retarded.* New York, National Association for Retarded Children, 1958.

Jacobs, A., Weingold, J. T., and Dubrow, M. *The Sheltered Workshop: A Community Rehabilitation Resource for the Mentally Retarded.* New York, New York State Association for Retarded Children, Inc., 1962.

Massie, W. Sheltered workshops: A 1962 portrait. *Journal of Rehabilitation, 28*:5, 17–20, 1962.

National Association for Retarded Children. *Sheltered Workshops for the Mentally Retarded.* New York, National Association for Retarded Children, 1954.

National Association for Retarded Children. *Fundamentals in Organizing a Sheltered Workshop for the Mentally Retarded: Guidelines and a Bibliography.* New York, National Association for Retarded Children, 1959.

National Association of Sheltered Workshops and Homebound Programs. *Directory of Sheltered Workshops and Homebound Programs.* New York, National Association of Sheltered Workshops and Homebound Programs, 1957.

National Rehabilitation Association. Policy statement on rehabilitation facilities. *Journal of Rehabilitation, 30*:18–19, 1964.

Nelson, N. *How To Start a Workshop for the Handicapped in California.* Sacramento, California, State Department of Education, 1962.

Nelson, N. *Census of the Population of Workshops for the Handicapped in California, 1962.* Sacramento, California, State Department of Education, 1963a.

Nelson, N. *Subcontract Work Done by the Workshops for the Handicapped in California.* Sacramento, California, State Department of Education, 1963b.

Nitzberg, J. Some different emphases in the role of the social worker in a workshop for mentally retarded adolescents and young adults. *American Journal of Mental Deficiency, 63*:87–95, 1958.

Nye, R. Mixed disability workshop thrives in small community. *Journal of Rehabilitation, 27*:10–11, 33, 46, 1961.

President's Panel on Mental Retardation. *A Proposed Program for National Action To Combat Mental Retardation.* Washington, D.C., Superintendent of Documents, U.S. Government Printing Office, 1962.

Public Law 565, Amendments of the Vocational Rehabilitation Act. 83rd Congress, Second Session, Chapter 655 S 2759, 1954.

Redkey, H. Accreditation vital and urgent for rehabilitation centers, workshops. *Rehabilitation Record, 5*:24–27, 1964.

Richmond, N. S. Vocational training in sheltered workshops. *American Journal of Mental Deficiency, 56*:344–348, 1951.

Rockower, L. W. A study of the use of sheltered workshops as an occupational training resource. *American Journal of Mental Deficiency, 57*:425–433, 1953.

Rusalem, H., and Cohen, J. S. Occupational prestige rankings by institutionalized and noninstitutionalized retarded students. *Personnel and Guidance Journal, 42*:981–986, 1964.

Smith, H. W. A sheltered employment project in an institution. *American Journal of Mental Deficiency, 61*:665–671, 1957.

Smith, N. P. Operational techniques for sheltered work programs; a guide for planning and management. *Rehabilitation Literature, 22*:230–240, 1961.

Stevens, H. A., and Blumberg, A. A preliminary report of a subcontract sheltered workshop in a residential school for the mentally retarded. *American Journal of Mental Deficiency, 28*:470–479, 1962.

Suazo, A. C. Subsidizing sheltered workshops. *Journal of Rehabilitation, 28*:4, 1, 1962.

Tizard, J. The effects of different types of supervision on the behavior of mental defectives in a sheltered workshop. *American Journal of Mental Deficiency, 58*:143–161, 1953.

Tobias, J. The evaluation of the vocational potential of mentally retarded young adults. *Training School Bulletin, 56*:122–135, 1960.

U.S. Department of Labor. *A Statement of Elementary Standards Respecting the Policies, Organization, Operation and Service Activities of Sheltered Workshops.* Washington, D.C., Superintendent of Documents, U.S. Government Printing Office, 1944.

U.S. Department of Labor. *Employment of Handicapped Clients in Sheltered Workshops.* Washington, D.C., Superintendent of Documents, U.S. Government Printing Office, 1952.

U.S. Department of Labor, Advisory Committee on Sheltered Workshops, Wage and Hour and Public Contracts Division. *A Statement of Principles Respecting the Policies, Organization, Operation and Service Activities of Sheltered Workshops and Homebound Programs.* Washington, D.C., Superintendent of Documents, U.S. Government Printing Office, 1961.

Wallin, J. E. W. Sheltered workshops for older adolescent and adult mental retardates. *Training School Bulletin, 56*:111–121, 1960.

York County Council of Community Services, Inc. *Sheltered Workshop Project.* York, Pennsylvania, York County Council of Community Services, 1962.

SECTION TEN

Institutional Care of the Retarded

Efforts have been made to change the institutional programs for the mentally retarded from "human warehouses" to facilities following rehabilitation concepts. The photostory prepared by Burton Blatt and Fred Kaplan [1] did much to publicize the horrible conditions still in existence in state residential facilities. Their book, *Christmas in Purgatory,* can be likened to Émile Zola's efforts to clear Alfred Dreyfus in the novel, *J'Accuse.* Using a hidden camera, they showed the depths of degradation and dehumanization that still is extant in several of our state hospitals. On the other hand, they showed pictures of a modern treatment and rehabilitation center. The dramatic contrast is almost enough to convince anyone that change is long overdue. Blatt has prepared an excellent text to go along with the photostudy. Many of the pictures were given nationwide coverage in a brief version in *Look* magazine. Where parent group efforts have on many occasions failed to convince the public and legislatures, this volume probably did so.

David J. Vail,[2] in his excellent book *Dehumanization and the Institutional Career,* showed how the State of Minnesota in a humanistic reformation of patient treatment has brought about new understandings of the need for treating mentally retarded patients as human beings.

Much attention is being given to the problem of waiting lists for admission to state institutions. A variety of patterns has been used to cut down the waiting list and the long periods of time that very severely retarded individuals needing 24-hour-a-day care must wait prior to institutional placement. These approaches include: (1) returning as many patients as possible to community living placement; (2) the utilization of foster homes; and (3) stepped-up programs of treatment and re-

[1] Burton Blatt and Fred Kaplan, *Christmas in Purgatory* (Boston: Allyn and Bacon, 1966).

[2] David J. Vail, *Dehumanization and the Institutional Career* (Springfield, Ill.: Charles C Thomas, 1966).

habilitation. The federal government in its Public Law 88-164 (Construction of Community Facilities for the Mentally Retarded), provides funds to construct public and other nonprofit facilities to care for the retarded in local communities.

Another federal program, the Mental Retardation Hospital Improvement Program, known as HIP, provides fiscal resources to stimulate improved services to the mentally retarded by demonstrating innovative techniques which can be replicated nationwide. The main purposes of these grants are to: (1) humanize, individualize, and make meaningful the care of the residential population; (2) bring stature, skill, and pride to direct-care personnel staffing the institution, and (3) apply techniques and interventions which will increase the effectiveness of the training, education, and habilitation of the residents.

Earl C. Butterfield, in the first selection of this section, provides readers with the basic facts about residential facilities including national statistics and state and regional differences in support. The reader is referred to the original report that includes a massive amount of statistical data relating to the various states. The second article by Roy E. Ferguson and his associates at the Columbus (Ohio) State School, is a brief overview of the school's program, its educational objectives, and the school resources used to implement them.

Our state residential facilities are changing in nature and purpose. Witness the variety of approaches developed at such outstanding facilities as Parsons (Kansas) State Hospital, the Johnstone Center in Bordentown, New Jersey, and the Central (Wisconsin) Colony in Madison. All are landmarks in genuine progress. We still have a long way to go to catch up with the humanizing institutions that are seen in many parts of Europe, the small, close-knit, highly personalized facility that is seen in Scandinavia, Holland, and Israel.

38 BASIC FACTS ABOUT PUBLIC RESIDENTIAL FACILITIES FOR THE MENTALLY RETARDED

Earl C. Butterfield

From *Changing Patterns in Residential Services for the Mentally Retarded,* R. B. Kugel and W. Wolfensberger, editors, President's Committee on Mental Retardation Monograph, Washington, D.C., 1969, pp. 17–33. Reprinted with the permission of The President's Committee on Mental Retardation and the author.
Dr. Butterfield is Program Director and Research Coordinator, Kansas Mental Retardation Research Center, Kansas Medical Center, Kansas City, Kan.

NATIONAL STATISTICS

More than 200,000 people, nearly half of whom are children, now live in over 150 public institutions for the mentally retarded in the United States. Another 20,000 retarded reside in approximately 500 known private facilities. Tens of thousands more wait out their times in institutions for the mentally ill; nearly 10 percent of all residents in public mental hospitals are retarded.

The number of institutionalized mentally retarded increases by over 3000 every year. Public institutions for the mentally retarded alone admitted an average of over 15,000 every year between 1960 and 1967. Over half of these were under ten years of age. An average of only 8000 was released from public institutions each year from 1960 to 1967, and approximately 3000 died while institutionalized during each of those years. Accurate statistics concerning trends in the numbers of retarded residents in private institutions and in public facilities for the mentally ill are not available. Estimating from the number of retarded people in these facilities, they probably accommodate an additional 300 to 400 retarded each year over and above the more than 3000 who are annually added to the rolls of public facilities for the retarded.

The fact that thousands are admitted to public institutions for the retarded each year does not mean that gaining admission is easy. It is exceedingly difficult, because institutions are generally filled. The average institution houses 98 percent of the number of residents it states it can accommodate, and most facilities are overcrowded and understaffed when they are operating at their stated capacity. Many institutions house more than their stated capacity. Some contain 50 percent more people than they were constructed for. In 1962, the President's Panel on Mental Retardation estimated that 50,000 bed spaces would have to be constructed to alleviate institutional overcrowding and to replace inadequate facilities. There is little reason to believe that fewer new beds are needed now.

Since most public institutions operate at or above their capacity, the delay between applying for and gaining admission is usually great. Often it is more than three years. Also, who is admitted is often determined by who has been released rather than by the needs of the applicants. A bed vacated by a mildly retarded female is usually given to a mildly retarded female even though aged males or severely damaged infants may be in graver need and have waited longer for admission. The crowded condition of institutions also produces long waiting lists. Most institutions would have to expand by more than 25 percent in order to eliminate their current waiting lists. Even such large-scale additions of beds would probably not shorten for long the lines of those who await admission. Experience has shown that people who have not applied before the construction of new facilities, for lack of hope of ever being admitted, come forth to seek admission and to refill the waiting lists when new facilities are opened. We are forced to conclude that many who need residential services have not applied for them.

Even though fewer than 5 percent of the mentally retarded in the United States reside in institutions, more money is spent to maintain them than is spent for any of the public programs which serve the remaining 95 percent. The annual cost of maintaining this country's public institutions for the retarded is now greater than 500 million dollars. In 1966, the national average operating cost per day per patient under treatment was $6.72. General hospital care cost more than $40.00 per patient per day during 1966.

More than three-quarters of the $500 million spent each year to maintain public institutions for the retarded goes for the salaries of institution personnel. More than 90,000 people are employed full time in public institutions for the retarded. Of these 90,000, more than half are attendants whose job is to give direct physical and emotional care to the retarded. In 1965, there was one attendant for each four residents in public institutions for the retarded. However, since attendants must provide around-the-clock coverage, the one-to-four ratio overestimates the amount of resident-attendant contact. Nevertheless, attendants have more resident contact than other types of employees combined, as may be seen by the fact that there was only one physician for each 270 residents, and only one psychologist for each 430 residents. Attendants are the main executors of institutional programs. They are faced with an incredibly wide array of responsibilities, ranging from being a substitute parent, janitor, and record-keeper to being part nurse, part physical therapist, part psychologist, and part educator.

Despite the fact that attendants are the most important people in the lives of the institutionalized retarded, the vast majority of them come to their job with no relevant past experience. They have been farmers, factory workers, career soldiers, housewives, etc. They generally have no particular educational qualifications. The majority come to their positions with less than a twelfth grade education. In most institutions, attendants come and go more quickly from their positions than any other group of institutional employees. A survey of 26 institutions in the 16 southeastern United States showed that, on the average, 20 percent of attendants are replaced in a year. In two of the 26 institutions, fully 50 percent of the attendants were replaced in one year.

A large part of the reason for the undistinguished qualifications of attendants and for their high turnover rate is undoubtedly the low status they are accorded and the niggardly pay they receive. Among the majority of the 26 institutions just mentioned, the maximum possible salary for attendants was more than $1,000 below the median income of the families in the county in which the institutions were located. In only 9 instances was the maximum equal to or greater than the median of the families in the surrounding county. Few attendants earn the maximum salary. Most attendants earn less than $350 per month. Many earn far less than this.

About 11 percent of the 90,000 persons employed in public institutions for the mentally retarded are classified as professionals. Most of these are teachers and nurses. Fewer than 2 percent of all institution personnel are classified as psychiatrists, psychologists, and social workers. Data on the precise qualifications and credentials of those persons classified as professionals in public institutions for the retarded are not published. Those listed as psychologists, social workers, and teachers often have not completed standard educational programs, although most probably have an undergraduate degree of some sort; particularly those listed as physicians, dentists and teachers cannot be assumed to meet standards required for working in the community.

The information which is available concerning the credentials of professionals employed in public institutions for the mentally retarded suggests that they are not, as a group, among the most highly qualified in their fields. For example, hardly any physicians are boarded in their specialties. Many cannot even be licensed for private practice in the states in which they treat the retarded. Most institutional psychologists do not have a Ph.D. degree, and cannot, therefore, even apply for certification by the American Board of Examiner's in Professional Psychology. The situation is similar for social workers, most of whom do not hold a Master's in Social Work degree. As with attendants, the lack of status and the relatively low pay associated with professional positions in public institutions probably account in large part for the apparent lack of distinction of most institutional professionals.

STATE AND REGIONAL DIFFERENCES

The population of public residential facilities for the mentally retarded is 55 percent male. Eighty-two percent are reported to have IQs below 50 (see Table 1). The high percentage of profoundly, severely, and moderately retarded suggests that the majority of the institutionalized retarded require

TABLE I * Distribution of Residents According to Level of Retardation

Levels of Retardation	*Number of Residents*	*Percent*
Profound	51,973	27
Severe	63,523	33
Moderate	42,348	22
Mild	25,024	13
Borderline	9,625	5
Total	192,493	100

* Source: Adapted from Milligan and Nisonger, 1965.

intensive care and supervision. This is particularly true since approximately 50 percent of all residents are below the chronological age of adulthood (see Table II). National statistics such as these give needed perspective on residential facilities for the mentally retarded. However, they also obscure important differences among institutions. Maintaining public institutions for the retarded has been the responsibility of the separate states, and as states' philosophies, policies, and resources have varied, so have their institutions.

States differ dramatically in how many and what types of their retarded they serve. The public institutions for the retarded of Kentucky, Arkansas, and West Virginia house approximately three people for every 10,000 in their general population, while Wyoming, South Dakota, and North Dakota house about 20 persons in their public institutions for the retarded for every 10,000 in their general populations. The remaining states distribute themselves between these extremes.

Undoubtedly many factors underlie the differences among states in the proportion and types of their retarded which they serve in institutions. There is considerable diversity among the states in the most basic issue of the definition of mental retardation. Although most states have only one admission procedure, many have several procedures by which a person can be placed in an institution for the retarded. States differ in the number and quality of noninstitutional programs for the retarded, so that a person who would be served in the community in one state must be institutionalized in another. Charges to patients for institutional care differ markedly from state to state. Discharge policies and rates vary from state to state, so that in some, beds become vacant more frequently than in others. Some states have expanded their institutional facilities more than others.

States also differ in how much they spend to maintain a person once he has been institutionalized and in how they allocate those expenditures. Per patient daily costs range from about $3.00 in Mississippi, South Dakota, and Nebraska to about $12.00 in Kansas, New Mexico, and California. In 1965, more than 20 percent of the expenditures of the states of Indiana, New York, Tennessee, and Wisconsin for the institutionalized retarded went

TABLE II * Distribution of Residents According to Chronological Age

Chronological Age	*Number of Residents*	*Percent*
0–4	5,775	3
5–9	21,174	11
10–14	30,799	16
15–19	32,724	17
20–24	28,874	15
25–29	23,099	12
30+	50,048	26
Total	192,493	100

* Source: Adapted from Milligan and Nisonger, 1965.

for improvements or additions, while Alabama, Massachusetts, Minnesota, North Dakota, and West Virginia spent no money for improvements or additions.

States also differ in the numbers of different types of employees they use to serve their institutionalized retarded. For example, in Georgia, Mississippi, and Nebraska there is only one physician for each 600 residents, while in California, Maine, and Wyoming there is a physician for each 150 patients.

Nearly half of the states have only one institution for the retarded, and it, of necessity, serves many purposes. Even in those states with more than one institution, the majority are large multi-purpose facilities. Over half of the public institutions in this country house more than 1000 residents. They try to meet the differing needs of the mildly and the profoundly retarded, the physically normal and active as well as the bedridden, the young and the aged, the rebellious delinquent as well as the docile, etc.

Despite this general preponderance of large, multi-purpose institutions, a trend has recently developed for institutions to be built for fewer residents. Thus, three-fourths of the public institutions built since 1960 are intended for 500 or fewer residents. Some states, for example Connecticut, Missouri, and Texas, are actively committed to this plan of building many smaller institutions, while others appear to be continuing with the older pattern of building large facilities.

Six years ago when the President's Panel on Mental Retardation was deliberating, many of the kinds of facts which were readily assembled for this report were obtained with only the greatest difficulty. The reporting of institutional census and cost information has been improved greatly in the last six years. Now the pathetic lack is in objective information about the effects of institutions upon the retarded. In view of the facts about the character of public institutions, it is easy to assume that their effects are largely negative. But there is a need to know precisely how negative they are, and in what ways, in order to most wisely plan their improvement. It is to be hoped that the next few years will see not only the elimination of deplorable conditions within our institutions but also an accumulation of information about the effects of institutionalization comparable to the accumulation of census and cost information of the last few years.

ANNOTATED BIBLIOGRAPHY

All of the following works were drawn from during the preparation of this paper. Taken together these form the basic library of factual knowledge about public institutions for the retarded in the United States.

AAMD Project on Technical Planning in Mental Retardation. Standards for state residential institutions for the mentally retarded. *Monograph Supplement to American Journal of Mental Deficiency,* 1964, *68,* No. 4.

A comprehensive statement of the minimum standards for staffing and administering a public institution for the retarded. Although this is the most recent document of its sort, it is probably dated.

Butterfield, E. C. The characteristics, selection, and training of institution personnel. In A. Baumeister (ed.), *Mental Retardation: Selected Problems in Appraisal and Treatment.* Chicago: Aldine Publishing Company, 1967. Pp. 305–328.

A review and summary of data concerning the characteristics, training, and selection of institution personnel, primarily attendants.

Butterfield, E. C. The role of environmental factors in the treatment of institutionalized mental retardates. In A. Baumeister (ed.), *Mental Retardation: Selected Problems in Appraisal and Treatment.* Chicago: Aldine Publishing Company, 1967. Pp. 120–137.

A review and summary of data which bears upon the effects of institutional living on the intellectual and personality development of the mentally retarded. Also includes a discussion of the factors which militate against the execution of research in institutional settings.

Butterfield, E. C., Barnett, C. D., and Bensberg, G. J. Some objective characteristics of institutions for the mentally retarded: implications for attendant turnover rate. *American Journal of Mental Deficiency,* 1966, *70,* 786–794.

The first of only two attempts to statistically define dimensions along which institutions differ. The results, which are based on reports from 26 institutions, suggest that institutions vary with respect to their rate of personnel turnover, the pleasantness of their working conditions, and the adequacy of their professional services.

NARC Committee on Residential Care. *A survey and study of state institutions for the mentally retarded in the United States.* New York: National Association for Retarded Children, 1963.

A survey of public institutions' practices concerning their admission and preadmission procedures, food and clothing services, education, recreation and religion practices, volunteer services, and rehabilitation programs.

Though slightly outdated, this volume provides a graphic picture of institutional functioning.

Newman, R. W. (ed.) *Institutionalization of the Mentally Retarded.* New York: National Association for Retarded Children, 1967.

A summary and analysis of state laws governing admission to residential facilities, and legal rights and protections of institutionalized patients. This is an invaluable compilation which though difficult to comprehend, should contribute to the standardization of legal codes governing institutionalization of the retarded.

Patients in Mental Institutions. Part I, Public Institutions for the Mentally Retarded. U.S. Department of Health, Education, and Welfare, 1965.

Extremely detailed report of data taken from the 40th Annual Census of Patients in Mental Institutions. The most complete source of information on the characteristics of residents and employees in public institutions and on the costs of operating institutions.

Silverstein, A. B. A dimensional analysis of institution differences. *Training School Bulletin,* 1967, *64,* 102–104.

A statistical analysis of selected data from 130 public residential facilities for the retarded. It is the second of only two attempts to extract objective dimensions along which institutions differ. It suggests that institutions differ in the adequacy of their staffing, their size and degree of overcrowding, and the intellectual levels of their residents.

Smith, N. F. *Charges for residential care of the mentally retarded in state institutions in the United States.* New York: National Association for Retarded Children, 1966.

A report of past and current charges for institutional care of a retarded person and an analysis of how charges depart from NARC's stated policies.

U.S. Department of Health, Education and Welfare. Provisional patient movement and administrative data. *Mental Health Statistics,* January 1967.

Selected data on patient movement and costs, by state, in public institutions for the retarded during 1966.

39 AN OVERVIEW OF EDUCATION AT THE COLUMBUS STATE SCHOOL

Roy E. Ferguson and associates

From *An Overview of the Department of Education and Training at the Columbus State School,* prepared by Roy E. Ferguson and the Faculty of the Education and Training Department, mimeographed, Columbus State School, Columbus, Ohio, 1960, pp. 1–3. Reprinted with the permission of R. M. Gove, M.D., superintendent. Dr. Ferguson is director of the Education and Training Department at the school.

The Department of Education and Training at the Columbus State School is responsible for several areas of the total training program. This program is carried on in the following fields:

Daytime Academic School Program for children CA 6–18
Adult Education Program for postadolescents and young adults
Job Orientation and *Job Training* for adolescents and adults preparing either for rehabilitation or for competence as institutional workers
Placement and *Supervision* of institutional workers in all areas
Industrial Workshops for middle-grade and emotionally disturbed residents
Sheltered Workshop Program for the moderately retarded

The Department of Education at the Columbus State School differs from most institutions in that the Recreational Therapy and Occupational Therapy divisions operate separately and have a total of 27 employees in the two areas.

Very briefly stated, our general philosophy is that we should train for social adequacy, occupational ability and responsibility, and as high a level of academic skill as the individual's potential would indicate.

We recognize the desirability of an education and training program based on needs, interests, and abilities, accepting as the premise that all children have an inherent right to receive an education geared to their learning potentialities. It is also felt that this should not be a "watered-down" curriculum, but one with goals which they may be expected to achieve.

We are agreed that the educational goals for mentally handicapped children are those that are recognized for all children; however, we consider that these children learn more slowly and not as much as the normal child. To achieve these goals they require a higher degree of emphasis, longer time on desirable goals, and the selection of teaching methods and materials suitable for meeting their limitations.

In planning a program for mentally retarded pupils the objectives set up by the Educational Policies Commission for all children seem most suitable. These are listed under four major headings:

1. The objectives of self-realization
2. The objectives of human relationship
3. The objectives of economic efficiency
4. The objectives of civic responsibility

These four objectives may be attained according to the child's individual ability. Some may be made more realistic for mentally retarded by adapting them to the child's level of attainment.

For example, under self-realization more attention may be needed for the development of eye-hand coordination, muscular coordination, simple concepts of healthful living, special development, and other areas in which the child may have greater difficulty than the normal child.

Likewise, in the sphere of human relationship much may need to be done in developing peer relationships, relationships with adults and authoritative figures, and the security and emotional stability which will enable the child to live more wholesomely in his environment.

We build much of our program upon activities and experience. For example, in developing reading skills, our teachers use extensively experience reading charts as developed by the groups, supplementing these with reading from standard texts, and particularly, from groups of stories at higher interest levels, although still at the lower achievement level.

Inasmuch as we correlate our occupational education program with our academic program, we begin to interpret job information at an early level, adding to such information as the child develops, using both on- and off-grounds trips as supplementary devices. At the age of fifteen, our adolescent boys and girls are in school one half-day and spend three or four half-days a week on a job-orientation program. We have the work of the institution organized into 63 work areas; and each individual will spend successive periods of 20 weeks in those areas which are selected, until such time as it can be determined what will be the best area of job training. The other one or two half-days per week a boy has industrial arts and a girl has home economics (child care, personal regimen, sewing, cooking, and care of the home). Physical education, health, and instrumental music are also scheduled in time in which the child is not in academic classes.

In our regular school program we group our children on four levels which might be listed as: nursery-kindergarten (CA 6, 7, 8); elementary (CA 9, 10, 11); early adolescent (CA 12, 13, 14); adolescent (CA 15, 16, 17, 18). Within these levels, we attempt to establish as nearly homogeneous groups as possible, using as criteria mental age, intelligence quotient, physical development, social maturity, and the achievement level based on either the California Achievement Tests or other appropriate tests. Up until the age of fifteen, we do not segregate according to sex; however, segregation occurs at the upper level because of the correlation of our occupational training program with the academic school program.

We carry on an adult-education program particularly for post-adolescents and young adults who may be preplacement candidates, providing an opportunity to develop whatever skills may be needed as the person returns to the community; or a program for skill development and satisfaction for those who may remain as institutional workers.

The resources of the school library are available both to the children in the classroom and to those in living units who may use it advantageously.

In addition, we have special teachers in the following areas: instrumental music, vocal music, industrial arts, home economics, physical education, speech and hearing therapy, art, audiovisual education, and sight conservation, and for the deaf, brain-damaged, and physically handicapped. Their programs are correlated with the classroom activities. In the field of music we also have a music therapy program planned to meet the needs of cerebral-palsied and orthopedic cases and children of lower achievement levels than those enrolled in the regular school program.

The vocational training program under vocational supervisors and vocational instructors has as its goals the main objectives of economic efficiencies set forth by the Educational Policies Commission. This program is based upon on-the-job training with classroom instruction on related information.

Industrial workshops have as their major purpose the development of a sheltered situation within the institution in which a number of middle-grade and emotionally disturbed residents are able to produce, for sale purposes, articles in the fields of weaving, canning, and handwork. In this program the profit from sales is shared equally between the resident and the school entertainment fund. In addition, a sheltered workshop serving moderately retarded girls has been established.

In our institution planning is done on a team basis by the Resident Planning Committee in which the following disciplines are represented: medicine, psychology, social service, guidance, education, and cottage life.

As a part of the total program of the school, the Department of Special and Adult Education at Ohio State University uses the school as a laboratory for practice teachers, field experience, and observation. Ohio Wesleyan University, Delaware, Ohio, also uses the school for courses in field experience and observation. The Departments of Psychology and Speech and Hearing at the Ohio State University use the facilities of the school. In addition, observations are made by students from Ohio University, Athens, Ohio; Kent State University, Kent, Ohio; and Bowling Green State University, Bowling Green, Ohio, on a regular basis.

SECTION ELEVEN

Communicative Skills for the Mentally Retarded

In a world where speech is a primary means of communication, it is amazing how little attention has been paid in the past to speech development and correction for retarded individuals. This lack of interest may possibly be attributed to the fact that "idiots" and "imbeciles" were clinically regarded as capable of little or no speech development. Nothing could be further from the truth. We are now aware that, with intensive speech and language training, even severely retarded children can make progress in this area, although there are special difficulties for children handicapped by aphasia, brain injuries, cerebral palsy, and extreme retardation. There is no more dramatic event than the unfolding of speech fluency in mentally retarded children. It opens the door to all facets of personal–social development and potentially to occupational adjustment.

A major development in the professional field has been the organization of the Speech and Hearing Section of the American Association on Mental Deficiency. This brought about a closer liaison among workers in the field of communicative disorders and mental retardation. An entire issue of *Mental Retardation* (April 1965) was devoted to language development for the retarded. Recently, the results and findings of a conference on human communication was published that has great implications for the field of mental retardation.[1]

Millicent Strazzulla and others have made some interesting comments about the aims of speech therapy with retarded children.[2] They write

[1] Raymond Carhart (ed.), *Human Communication and Its Disorders: An Overview* (Washington, D.C.: U.S. Department of Health, Education, and Welfare, 1969).

[2] Millicent Strazzulla and others, "The Role of Varied Therapies in Rehabilitation," *American Journal of Mental Deficiencies, 61* (January 1957), 508–515.

that, "Language growth begins long before the child is able to articulate a word correctly and that communications may, in a nonverbal pattern, range from a simple gesture to an intricate pantomime." Miss Strazzulla suggests that the developmental steps for the child involve: exploring in detail his immediate environment; listening to and analyzing noises, sounds, and words; thinking about and organizing himself around the stimuli; and finally, communicating with others about these stimuli through the use of gestures, pictures, sounds, and speech.

William R. Blount[3] summarizes a major new theoretical concept concerning language development and communicative problems of the retarded. He states that:

> . . . the consensus of opinion from many sources is that for therapy purposes at least, mentally retarded children and adults should be viewed as individuals with a particular linguistic problem. In this light the chances for success both in therapy and in life are enhanced. The way of future programs seems clear. Whatever the therapy program, it should be oriented to the individual, his particular linguistic problems, and should include all of his environment. The fact that he is retarded adds no information to his linguistic problems and his development, both with linguistic problems and normal language, are the same as they are for subjects with normal intelligence."

A useful bibliography on communicative skills for the mentally retarded has been prepared by Maryann Peins[4] for the U.S. Department of Health, Education, and Welfare.

The first reading in this section is by Julia S. Molloy and Byrn T. Witt, both long-standing specialists in teaching communication skills to the retarded. They review the goals, objectives, and assessment problems of children with major language problems and mental retardation. They describe various procedures to develop communication skills. Appended to this article is a lengthy Developmental Scale for Language Levels to be used with mentally retarded children. The second article in this section is a review by James O. Smith of the literature dealing with communication problems of the mentally retarded during a ten-year period. The final article, by R. L. Schiefelbusch, discusses language functions of retarded children. Along with Smith's article, this would give the reader an almost 20-year review of the literature. A list of the developmental goals of a school speech program for mental retardates is included in this section and was prepared by the staff of the Board of Education of the City of New York.

[3] William R. Blount, "Language and the More Severely Retarded: A Review," *American Journal of Mental Deficiency, 73*:1 (July 1968), 28.

[4] Maryann Peins, *Bibliography on Speech, Hearing and Language in Relation to Mental Retardation: 1900–1968*. Washington, D.C.: U.S. Department of Health, Education, and Welfare, 1969.

40 DEVELOPMENT OF COMMUNICATION SKILLS IN RETARDED CHILDREN

Julia S. Molloy
Byrn T. Witt

From *Mental Retardation: Selected Conference Papers,* 1969, Illinois State Department of Mental Health, Springfield, pp. 75–86. Reprinted with the permission of the Illinois State Department of Mental Health and the authors. Julia S. Molloy is Principal, Orchard School for Special Education, Niles Township, Ill., and Byrn T. Witt is Executive Director, Clearbrook Center for the Retarded, Rolling Meadows, Ill.

Communication is an exchange of ideas and information. It can be nonverbal, through the use of facial expression or gesture, or verbal through spoken language. *Speech* is uniquely human and is a part of a larger system of symbols that carry meaning. Words are special sounds that are symbols which stand for things and ideas.

We have a system of making sounds into words which carry meaning. Because we live with people who use the same system of symbols we can communicate with them.

The system, the plan, of using words is called *language*. The way we say words is *speech*. The way we use words is *language*.

Since language and communication are important ingredients in the development of mental abilities, programs to improve the language and communication ability of children with retarded development are important.

It has been estimated that approximately 40 percent of learning capacity is linguistic ability. Language development is delayed in most retarded children. Useful and constructive communication is essential to the social, emotional, intellectual and spiritual growth of any child. The process of physical maturation cannot be accelerated; however, the circumstances for stimulating the need for communication can be structured and manipulated to capitalize upon every asset available in the retarded child. Concomitant with the process of maturation is the observed sequence of language development. Basically, the problem is to structure readiness for producing speech by perceptual training and to proceed to induce language functioning on a conceptual level.

The paucity of services in the field of language pathology available to retarded children and their classroom teachers has created a serious problem. The purpose of this paper will be to discuss areas which will assist the teacher in developing and incorporating into her daily schedule a realistic, practical, and sequential program for the development of communication skills. An appropriate philosophy; a working knowledge of deterrents to the development of language; criteria for assessing the child's functioning level of communication; and implications for teaching will be discussed.

GOALS AND OBJECTIVES

The speech and hearing field only recently has shown much concern for moderately and severely mentally retarded individuals. The first workers to indicate a realistic philosophy for communication were Strazzulla and Karlin (1952, p. 17), who urged the understanding of a basic concept for language therapy with retarded children:

> In working with these children it must be borne in mind that the aim is not to attain perfect speech, but to assist them in developing usable everyday language to the maximum of their ability.

The goal of "everyday language" precludes the use of the term "speech correction" *per se* with retarded children. Speech correction is desired only when language functioning is adequate and the problem involves such areas as articulation or phonation. These latter problems will not distract from, or lessen control of, the content of the verbal output.

ASSESSMENT OF COMMUNICATION SKILLS

Five major areas must be explored to determine those factors which may be adversely affecting the development of useful communication: hearing, condition of speech mechanism, environmental climate, symbolic functioning, and cognitive ability. The classroom teacher can explore these areas grossly, but usefully, through information provided by the parents, through observation of the child in structured situations, and through comparison of the child's level of communication with normal developmental scales.

Hearing Loss (Deafness or Partial Deafness)

A hearing loss is not a contributive factor to delayed use of language if the child responds to his name whispered no closer than three feet behind his back. His response may be a smile, arrested activity, or a turn of the head. A suspected hearing loss should be referred to a physician.

Parents can help the teacher to understand how the child *uses* his hearing. Has the child attached any meaning to the sound of running water (bathtub), telephone, door bell? Is he afraid of these sounds? He may be afraid because he has trouble attaching the meaning to sounds he actually hears.

How well does he hear? The retarded child requires intensive auditory training to gain a generous storage of auditory experiences before he can be expected to communicate verbally and spontaneously. Does he profit from auditory experience? If he locates a concealed noise maker, will he seek it in the same location upon a repeated stimulation? Can the child mimic a sound that has meaning (cow says "moo") or repeat a word?

Speaking Mechanism

A child's speaking mechanism is usable for speech if he is able to do the following: swallow, suck, maneuver his tongue by controlling its action, such as extending, and/or elevating the tip and swinging it from one corner of the mouth to opposite corner, employing some speed in tongue action. This can be observed by having the child repeat "la-la-la."

Environmental Climate

The child's environment is considered to be favorable to the development of good social language if he has a need to talk (the parents do not anticipate his every need), if there is some stimulation in the home, and if he is neither ignored nor abused.

Symbolic Dysfunction

Symbolic dysfunction is a strong contributing factor to delayed language functioning of many retarded children. The child may be unable to receive meaning from a spoken symbol (e.g., a word) or a visual symbol (e.g., a pencil). Subsequently, this child has difficulty producing an appropriate act, sound, or word response to a heard or seen symbol. The determining of the extent of symbolic dysfunction is the task of a language pathologist.

Careful guidance through an appropriate program of language development should help the young retarded child attach meaning to sounds and visual stimuli.

Cognitive Ability

A child cannot be expected to function beyond his level of cognitive ability. It is imperative that the classroom teacher be aware of the scatter of the child's successes and failures in psychometric data. She should know which items from standardized data reveal the child's ability to communicate.

Using a scored "mental age" as a rigid rationale for determining an appropriate starting point to work with a retarded child is precarious and can be disastrous. The classroom teacher must know if the mental age, regarded as an average presentation of cognitive ability, precludes the establishment of a starting point in a communicative program. A mental age below one year in a four-year-old preschooler would indicate that a little more mental growth must occur before a child will be amenable to language therapy.

A word of caution—retarded children are highly individualistic! They don't fit neatly into any single, stratified plan. The language program progresses from one step to another based on a sequential approach designed for each child.

A developmental scale has been included at the end of this paper. It presents a composite in proper sequence of many items from psychometric instruments, standardized developmental and linguistic scales. To find the child's level in language development, the classroom teacher should assemble data from history obtained from parents and previous records, from her own structured observations, and from the psychologist who studied the child most recently.

KINDS OF COMMUNICATION PROBLEMS FOUND IN DAY CENTERS FOR RETARDED

Mentally retarded persons served in day centers vary considerably with respect to both age and degree of retardation. As public schools are assuming the responsibility for most EMR and TMR children, the day centers are moving toward providing services for preschool children, school age children too severely handicapped for public school placement, and postschool age placement. Thus, staff at day centers are finding themselves facing an even wider array of communication problems than they have in the past.

Communication skills of any retarded child can be improved. The average day-center child does not have communication and language skills commensurate with his potential cognitive functioning. Individuals with poor communication skills usually have many specific language defects, but, for simplicity's sake, children and adults served in day centers can be grouped according to three categories.

One category is the young (usually two to seven years of age), nonverbal child with retarded development. This child usually presents a complex diagnostic picture and often involves a combination of organic, psychiatric, and learning disorders. Cultural deprivations also can be a factor in many sections of the state. A differential diagnosis is primary before a communication problem can be planned for such a child. The goal for these individuals would be to develop maximum communication skills within the limits of the child's total potential.

A second category might be called the "poor verbal" child. This child usually demonstrates a lag between his receptive language (e.g., understanding and comprehension) and his expressive language or communication. A difference of a year or more in development between reception and expression is very significant. The specific factors need to be pinpointed, if possible, and a communication program planned with these factors being given primary consideration.

The third type of individual usually seen is the severely or profoundly retarded individual who has low cognitive functioning and usually very little, if any, communication skills. Until recently, most of us did not bother to attempt to train communication, especially verbal communication. Yet it has been demonstrated that individuals with estimated mental ages of a year or more can communicate verbally at the naming stage. This is more easily done in the institutions where ward aides can work through two or more shifts with these individuals, but it can be accomplished in a day setting. The use of a few words or gestures can make life considerably more pleasant for the retarded individual and those in his environment. In the institutional setting this becomes even more critical.

PROCEDURES TO DEVELOP COMMUNICATION SKILLS

We know the kind of child with whom we must work, we hope we have learned the proper starting point and what we are going to do about it. First, we are going to set *realistic goals*. We also must be certain of *readiness*. Is this child really ready to learn to communicate verbally? Does he need more socializing, freedom of opportunity to just be in a group of peers? Are the parents ready and willing to work with us during the long term of auditory training? We feel it is practically impossible to start the long road toward adequate communication if the parents are not ready, willing, and able to work with us.

Before therapy can begin, it is essential to capture the child's attention. He is led to listen through attention-compelling stimulations. This means arresting activities through auditory, visual, and tactile stimulations. We do this through the use of attention-getters, i.e., compelling little gadgets so fascinating that the child cannot resist paying attention.

Using the child's own self as an attention-getter is effective. His attention is directed toward himself. Saying, "Is Donald here? Where is Donald?" The child hearing his own name, will very often smile, then some thing or article can be directed to his attention.

In the early stages of therapy we must *condition responses for safety*. "No," "Come here," "Don't touch," and "Sit down" must be learned long before the sound symbol itself has any conceptual meaning to the child. He must learn to *react* to these words for his own safety and security. We train them through the conditioned response method to react appropriately to "No," "Come here," "Don't touch," "Sit down."

After learning to listen through the attention compelling stimulations, the child learns to listen and *react* to sound. Total body activity is involved. The child runs upon hearing music that stimulates speed, or moves slowly to music or to the tone of the teacher's voice.

The next step is learning to listen and to *respond* to sound. Responding infers that another person or thing is involved. In learning to listen and to respond to sound, the child is expected to provide an appropriate, nonverbal response, associating word sounds with common objects, such as ball, baby, bus, bathtub. In this way, meaning becomes attached to the names of common objects. The child is not required to say "ball," but is expected to attach the sound of the word "ball" to the round object that our culture has named ball. We do the same things with bus, baby, and other overt words within the child's experience.

At this time, we also are concerned with basic proprioception. The child is expected to listen and respond by showing the teacher where his nose is, where his ears are, where his feet are, and other parts of his body.

We are concerned with identification and location of familiar sounds, such as the passing fire truck, the arrival of the station wagon, the call from another part of the room, the call on the playground to the different children. This is a beginning of awareness that location of sound can change, and, no matter where it is, we can try to locate it and respond appropriately.

The child progresses from learning to listen and respond to sound *nonverbally,* to learning to listen and produce an *appropriate vocal response.* This usually begins by associating sounds with animals, using realistic models of live animals, such as dog or cow.

Field trips are highly beneficial at this time—they provide needed experience. The children learn to mimic the animals seen at the children's zoo, e.g., sheep goes "b-a-a," cow goes "moo-oo," the kitty goes "meow-w."

This category of learning to listen and produce an appropriate vocal response includes listening to and *mimicking* words for common objects. Having already established a repetoire of association of word-sound symbols to common objects and successfully vocalizing animal noises in appropriate association, it becomes relatively easy for the child to listen to and mimic words for common objects. We show the child the ball, hold it for him, and say "ball" with considerable exaggeration, hoping that he will mimic the correct word. It is recommended that the teacher use objects common to the child's experience which have *b, p, m,* and *ch* for initial consonants.

Success is structured. The techniques of the therapist is of utmost importance—attachment of sound symbol to the common object must be structured.

The transition from *saying* words to *using* words is a big step toward attaining the goal of social language. Just mimicking words, or being stimulated to say words, is not necessarily *using* words appropriately. The earliest actual using of words is naming what is wanted. For instance, the child will say "milk" for wanting milk, or "cookie" for wanting a cookie. Naming is the first thing that we do in teaching the child to *use* words appropriately.

We move from naming, or labeling, to qualifying objects, such as the "big ball," the "little ball." Size is used as an initial qualifying term because it seems to be more readily reinforced than color and shape. The idea of size can be reinforced with the total body.

Verbs must be added to develop sentence structure. We use action pictures (mama at the washing machine) and employ the Fitzgerald Key, although actually only producing a two-word sentence (mama washes).

This is expanded to "Daddy works," "Brother plays ball," "Sister studies," using the siblings' actual names. We have had considerable success in using the Language Master with the cards keyed with gerunds with pictures of activities within the realm of experiences of the children.

Good sentence structure can come from everyday conversation, using the child's own words. In addition, good conversation can evolve in dramatic play. The importance of teaching our children to be good TV watchers cannot be overstressed. Television is one of the best discussion starters in the morning with our older children. It is within their experience. Though TV may not be the most desirable experience, it does exist; and we might as well capitalize on it. The use of music cannot be discounted. Many first words occur during music time.

Suitability of materials should be determined by a definite criteria:

1. Materials should be motorically corrected. In a language-demanding situation, a child should not be challenged to manipulate a toy or device he is not yet able to handle with assured success, e.g., stacking, nesting, windups, using scissors, drawing a circle. The therapist must know the child's level of eye–hand coordination.
2. Material should be within the child's area of social interest. This should be carefully observed in role playing.
3. Materials, common objects, animals, pictures, should be selected within the realm of the child's own experience.
4. Materials should be used ultimately.

No discussion of techniques and procedures is meaningful without considering the kind of person who is using these techniques and procedures. Being knowledgeable in language therapy is not enough. The example or behavior pattern set by the teacher, or therapist, is the key to progress in language skills. Kindness, the anticipating smile and gesture, the light touch or the firm touch, consistency, clarity, a complete feeling of involvement with the child and activity, the shared joy of accomplishment, and knowledge combine to produce an effective change in language behavior.

It also should be observed that the use of nonprofessional workers in the development of communication skills for the mentally retarded has been explored in recent years. The use of volunteers, ward aides, and parents as shapers of communication have been used effectively (Witt and Witt, 1966; Molloy and Witt, 1967).

SUMMARY

Therapy for the development of communication skills in retarded children is based upon perceptual training. The course proceeds through defined steps:

1. Learning to listen through attention compelling stimulation.
2. Learning to listen and reacting to sound.
3. Learning to listen and responding to sound.
4. Learning to listen and producing appropriate vocal responses.

The acquisition of good, usable language skill is the goal.

REFERENCES

Strazzulla, Millicent, and Karlin, I. W. Speech and language problems of mentally retarded children. *Journal of Speech and Hearing Disorders, 17:* 286–294, 1952.

Molloy, Julia S., and Witt, Byrn. *Communication Shaping Program.* A manual for ward personnel to develop communication skills in severely retarded individuals. Illinois State Dept. of Mental Hygiene, Springfield, 1968.

Witt, Barbara, and Witt, Byrn. Home program for the development of speech and language in mentally retarded preschool children. Unpublished paper presented at the Nineteenth Annual Meeting of the American Association on Mental Deficiency, Chicago, 1966.

DEVELOPMENTAL SCALE FOR LANGUAGE LEVELS

The developmental scale listed below is intended to provide the teacher with standardized and generalized information regarding receptive and expressive language development in the normal child. It is based on the research findings of various authorities on child development and linguistics, e.g., Terman and Merrill (1937); Gesell (1940, 1945); Doll (1947); Stutsman (1948); Metraux (1950); Templin (1952); and McCarthy (1954).

The developmental scale should not be interpreted rigidly when considering the language development of retarded children. In other words, the teacher should not compare language development between normal and retarded children with equal mental ages.

In addition, the teacher needs to view language development as following a pattern. Thus, he must guide the child through each step from receptive to expressive language. After having decided upon a starting point, the teacher must guard against forcing the child to progress as rapidly as does the normal child.

Developmental Scale

Receptive Language		*Expressive Language*
	6 MONTHS	
Turns to sound of bell without seeing it.		Crows, laughs, makes sounds for pleasure. Imitates sounds—babbling.
	7 MONTHS	
		Puts two sounds together, like "mama," bye-bye."

Developmental Scale *(cont.)*

Receptive Language		*Expressive Language*
	8 MONTHS	
Responds to "bye-bye" by waving "bye-bye."		
	10 MONTHS	
		Makes sounds during play.
	11 MONTHS	
Adjusts to commands; knows what "come here," "no," "don't touch" means.		Says one word to name or describe something—like "mama," "water," "bye."
	12 MONTHS	
Responds to "no," "don't touch."		Two-word speaking vocabulary.
	15 MONTHS	
		Uses "jargon" and gestures (jargon is his own make-up language; likes talking to toys).
	18 MONTHS	
Points to nose, eyes, hair.		One word responses include naming, exclamations and greetings. Half of vocabulary is names in speech. Uses initial vowels, consonants (says first sounds of words).
	2 YEARS	
Can point to four parts of body when given the name; can point to a few objects by name.		One-third of words are nouns.
Obey simple commands "Give me" "Put spoon in cup."		Sentence length 2–3 words; asks to go to toilet by verbal or gesture indication.
Can repeat from memory, 4 words.		Uses "I, you, me" fairly well.
Can fill in words or phrases of poems or songs.		Refers to self by name. Can tell what just happened.
	2½ YEARS	
Can tell what you cook on, what you sit on, what is good to eat.		Naming objects.
Child is able to "put one block on paper."		Three-word simple sentences. Vocabulary consists of 25% nouns, 25% verbs and pronouns.
Repeat two numbers.		
Can point to more objects by name. Can name something in picture.		Use of "I" in reference to self.
Can tell you what burns, what barks, what blows.		
Can give the objects of six actions as what flies, sleeps, bites, scratches, swims.		
	3 YEARS	
		Uses 3–4 word sentences.
Repeats 3 numbers.		Can tell what happened in more detail.

Developmental Scale (*cont.*)

Receptive Language		*Expressive Language*
	3 YEARS	
Responds to prepositions: "Put the ball on the chair" "Put the box under the table."		Adjectives, adverbs, pronouns, conjunctions, increasing in use.
Can give the use of common objects, i.e. "What do we do with the spoon?"—Answer: "eat."		When looking at picture book, the child will answer when asked, "What is he doing?"
		Articulation: Consonants mastered: y, b, p, m. He knows songs and rhymes.
	3½ YEARS	
Obeys simple commands "Put the book on the table."		
Names more things—pictures.		Sentence length 4–5 words.
Can name more things; When asked, "What do you use to . . ." (like lock the door). Can give good answer.		Better use of pronouns.
		Articulation: Consonants mastered: w, h.
	4 YEARS	
Can tell what is happening in picture.		Sentence length 4–5 words.
		Pronouns, prepositions, conjunctions, are in good use.
Memory for sentences: "We are going to buy some candy for mother."		Articulation: Consonants mastered: d, t, g, k.
		Compound and complex sentences begin to appear.
Responds appropriately with gesture and words to "What do you do when you are thirsty, sleepy, hungry?"		Future and past tense in common use.
The child carries out requests with four prepositions (in, out, beside, behind, under, in front of).		Counts three objects.
	4½ YEARS	
Repeats four numbers.		Parts of speech: 19% nouns, 25% verbs, 15% adjectives, 21% pronouns, 7% ad-Par.
Can follow three commands in order; carries out complex orders in three parts.		Consonant: production 90% or more correct.
		Consonant sounds mastered: n, ing.
Knows some things that are opposite; like "brother is a boy, sister is a girl."		Sentence length 4–5 words.
	5 YEARS	
Can give a good answer: "What is a ball?"		Picks out and names red, yellow, blue, green.

Developmental Scale (*cont.*)

Receptive Language		*Expressive Language*
	5 YEARS	
Memory for sentences; can repeat a sentence of about 7 words.		Sentence length 4–5 words.
		Can tell story correctly.
		Can tell about things and action in picture.
		Can name following coins: penny, nickel, dime.
		Articulation: masters consonants f and v.
	6 YEARS	
Vocabulary: can tell what several words mean.		Tells more about picture; responds to picture.
		Average sentence length 6–7 words.
Child knows the difference between a.m. and p.m. and answers questions "When does afternoon begin?"		Says numbers up to thirties.
	6½ YEARS	
		Articulation: voiced l, th.
	7 YEARS	
Repeats five numbers.		Girls' speech is quite grown up.
Similarities: "In what way are . . . . and . . . . alike?		
Can tell what is silly about something.		
	7½ YEARS	
		Mastered consonant sounds: s, z, r, sh, ch, and consonant blends such as bl, dr, tr.
	8 YEARS	
Can tell why some things are alike and some things are different.		Boys' speech is quite grown up.
Remembers points of a story; can tell why some things happen such as "What makes a sailboat move?"		

REFERENCES

Cattell, Psyche. *Measurement of Intelligence of Infants and Young Children.* New York: Psychological Corporation, 1940.

Doll, Edgar A. *Vineland Social Maturity Scale.* Minneapolis, Minn.: Educational Test Bureau, 1947.

Gesell, Arnold L. *Developmental Schedules.* New York: Psychological Corporation, 1945.

Gesell, A., Halverson, H. M., Thompson, H., Ilg, F. L., Castner, B. M., Ames, L. B., and Amatruda, C. S. *The First Five Years of Life: A Guide to the Study of the Preschool Child.* New York: Harper, 1940.

McCarthy, Dorothea. Language development in children. In: Carmichael, L. (ed.) *Manual of Child Psychology*. New York: Wiley, 1954, pp. 492–631.
Metraux, R. W. Speech profiles of the preschool child 18–54 months. *Journal of Speech and Hearing Disorders, 15*:15–53, 1950.
Terman, Lewis and Merrill, Maud. *Measuring Intelligence*. Boston: Houghton Mifflin, 1937.
Stutsman, Rachel, *Mental Measurement of Preschool Children*. New York: World Book, 1948, pp. 139–162.

Scope and Sequence of a Developmental Speech Program

Vestibule and Primary Classes (Young Children)	*Intermediate Classes (Pre-Adolescents)*	*Secondary School Classes (Adolescents)*
Depending on the level of growth as indicated above, the speech program should be directed toward the development of:		
ATTITUDE		
The desire to speak through: a friendly classroom atmosphere, opportunities for informal speaking situations.	A favorable attitude toward speech, an awareness of the value of good voice and speech in social relations.	An awareness of the value of good speech in both social and vocational situations.
The acceptance of speaking and listening as pleasurable experiences through enjoyment of and participation in songs, rhythmic poetry, simple stories, dramatic play, games.	An appreciation of the speech arts through choral speaking, informal dramatics, puppetry, storytelling in a classroom situation, inter-class visits, and group assembly performance.	Continued appreciation through participation in the speech arts.
Simple standards of courteous speech in the classroom, simple standards of audience behavior in a classroom and home situation.	Standards of courteous speech in out-of-school situations (school bus, subway, dinner table, etc.).	Standards of courteous speech in public places with stress on employment possibilities.
Ease in speaking with individuals and small groups in a familiar environment.	Standards of audience behavior in the classroom, school assembly, home, and moving picture theater. Ease in speaking to individuals outside the familiar group: the storekeeper, the policeman, new friends, guests in a home, school, neighborhood situation. The desire to share experiences, with others in the class.	Standards of audience behavior for larger groups with stress on out-of-school situations (the theater, public meeting, work-group, etc.). Ease in speaking with others in a broader environment (department store, bank, post office, insurance company, places of employment, etc.). A discriminating attitude toward speech through evaluation of the speech of personalities observed in entertainment media: television and motion pictures.

Scope and Sequence of a Developmental Speech Program (*cont.*)

Vestibule and Primary Classes (Young Children)	*Intermediate Classes (Pre-Adolescents)*	*Secondary School Classes (Adolescents)*
VOICE		
Auditory discrimination through recognition of familiar objects by their sounds.	Auditory discrimination through recognition of the difference between the vowel sounds and gross differences in voice quality.	The extension of auditory discrimination to the finer elements of voice quality.
Awareness of gross differences in voice quality and volume: pleasant voice, rough voice, small voice, big voice.	Awareness of the effect voice quality has on the listener with stress on the degrees of volume and the appropriate degree of volume needed for various situations; the conversation voice, the classroom voice, the auditorium voice.	Practice in use of the appropriate voice in varied speech activities.
Habitual use of audible voice with some measure of volume control.	Habitual use of a pleasant audible voice through practice in exercises for relaxation, ear training, breathing, projection, resonance, and the correct production of all the vowel sounds.	Correct production of vowels with stress on those sounds commonly distorted.
	Simple standards for self-evaluation and group evaluation: Use of rating charts.	Standards of self and group evaluation.
	Flexibility of voice by practice on variations of pitch used for single sounds and words.	Greater flexibility of voice.
ARTICULATION		
A slower rate of speech through relaxation and imitation.	Slow, easy speech. Awareness of differences in the rate of speech.	Appropriate variety in the rate of speech.
Control of the articulators through lip, tongue, and jaw exercises.	Greater control of the articulators through exercises.	Greater control of the articulators through exercises.
Clear speech through practice of jingles and songs and practice in careful enunciation of short phrases used in everyday speech.	Correct production of all consonant sounds through auditory training and drill. Integration of work on specific sounds with reading and spelling.	Correct production of all consonant sounds with concentration on practice and drill for the correction of common consonant substitutions and omissions.
SKILLS FOR CONNECTED SPEECH		
Awareness of variations in speech rhythm and melody in rhymes and simple stories.	Variety in inflection in poems and conversational speech.	Variety in inflection with stress on the relationship of flexibility of voice to meaning.
Natural use of stress and phrasing by setting a good example.	Natural use of stress and phrasing by direct teaching with special attention to oral reading.	Natural use of stress and phrasing through practice in oral reading and conversational speech.

Scope and Sequence of a Developmental Speech Program (*cont.*)

Vestibule and Primary Classes (Young Children)	*Intermediate Classes (Pre-Adolescents)*	*Secondary School Classes (Adolescents)*
SKILLS FOR CONNECTED SPEECH		
	Acceptable American intonation pattern through direct teaching (when deviations exist).	Acceptable American intonation through continued remedial work if needed.
THE SPEECH ARTS		
A sense of rhythm through listening to music and participation in singing and rhythmical physical exercises and group recitation of nursery rhymes and simple jingles.	Choral speaking for enjoyment and for presentation to an audience in inter-class visits and assembly performances. Storytelling by teacher and pupils.	Choral speaking with a larger audience.
Dramatic play.	Pantomime, impromptu dramatizations of nursery rhymes, simple stories. Presentation to a familiar audience—classmates, primary grade class, small group of parents, etc.	Pantomime and informal dramatizations for an audience.
FUNCTIONAL SPEECH EXPERIENCES		
Use of clear speech and audible voice in the simple speech experiences of the home and school environment.	Use of clear speech and pleasant, audible voice in the speech experiences of the home, school and neighborhood.	Use of clear speech and pleasant, audible voice in the speech experiences of the large community as well as those of the home, school and neighborhood.
Use of short sentences to replace single word response.	Habitual use of full sentences.	Correct pronunciation and proper usage of words related to vocational areas.

Source: From *Speech for the Retarded Child*, edited by Helen M. Donovan (Brooklyn: The Board of Education, 1960), pp. 96–98. Reprinted by permission of the Board of Education of the City of New York.

41 SPEECH AND LANGUAGE OF THE RETARDED

James O. Smith

From the *Training School Bulletin* of the American Institute for Mental Studies, Vineland, N.J., Vol. 58, No. 4, February 1962, pp. 111–123. Reprinted with the permission of The Training School, Vineland, N.J., and the author. Dr. Smith is Professor of Special Education, University of Missouri, Columbia.

During the past ten years, literature dealing with the communication problems of the retarded has reflected a definitely increased interest in the subject. As society has positively directed its goals toward more effective utilization of the mental retardate's capacities, more attention has been paid to the language limitation (Sarason, 1955).

Speech is said to be ". . . defective when it deviates so far from the speech of other people that it calls attention to itself, interferes with communication, or causes its possessor to be maladjusted" (Van Riper, 1954, p. 19). Eisenson (1955) related defective speech to inaudibility, unintelligibility, unpleasant voice, dysrhythmia, linguistic deficiency, and inappropriateness. Speech problems were categorized as defects of articulation, phonation, rhythm, or language dysfunction.

With the mental retardate, emphasis has been more on communication and language problems, and not just speech production or articulation (Lassers and Low, 1960; Batza, 1956; Hudson, 1958; Ikeda, 1955; Irwin, 1959; Karlin and Strazzulla, 1952; Schlanger, 1958). Kastein (1956) contends that language is the understanding and use of symbols while speech is the uttering of articulate sounds serving the functions of communication. Those working with the language problems of retarded children have even been referred to as language developmentalists instead of speech therapists (Harrison, 1959).

The literature from 1950 up to the present concerning language problems of the retarded is reviewed and summarized here. Materials are categorized into four general areas: speech and language development, incidence of problems, role of the speech specialist, and special programs.

SPEECH AND LANGUAGE DEVELOPMENT

Numerous writings point out the delayed speech and language development of the mentally retarded (Ainsworth, 1958; Hudson, 1958; Ikeda, 1955; Karlin and Strazzulla, 1952; Kirk and Johnson, 1951; Matthews, 1957). It is generally observed (Murphy, 1959) that in the lower IQs the developmental stages of babbling, acquisition of first words, and use of sentences are all retarded. Strazzulla (1954) contrasted the language development of the normal and retarded child, and found meaningful babbling seven to seventeen months delayed. She also reported that words normally acquired from 10–18 months may be delayed until two and one-half to five years of age in retardates. The speech development of the retarded is stipulated to be essentially the same sequential development as in the normal child, only slower in rate.

West (1947) classically described defective speech in the "ament" as grammatically poor, confused in pronunciation, concerned with things rather than ideas, and limited in vocabulary. Papania (1954) found that retarded children gave fewer abstract definitions and more concrete definitions than normal children of the same mental age. Attention was called (Sarason, 1955) to the retarded child's difficulties in using and understanding language symbols. The limitations of restricted vocabulary, improper use of abstractions, and poor comprehension of verbal instructions, affect verbal ability and subsequent test performances. One of the major characteristics of the retarded is held to be language limitation.

Ainsworth (1958, p. 388) states, "Speech development is very closely allied to intellectual development." After reviewing 454 cases of speech and language retardation seen in a hospital clinic, Goodwin (1955) felt that the causal factor was mental retardation in 53 percent of the cases. It should be realized that Goodwin's cases were not randomly sampled, and represented a hospital clinic population. In another study (Wood, 1957), 1200 case histories of children (CA range 3–6) with severely delayed speech were analyzed. Primary causal factors were determined in 1091 of these children, and the factor was mental retardation in approximately 35 percent of the cases. Noted authorities (Irwin, 1959; Johnson, Brown, Curtis, Edney and Keaster, 1956; West, Kennedy and Carr, 1947) agreed that the degree of speech and language retardation actually paralleled the degree of mental deficiency. After a review of current studies, Goertzen (1957) concluded that a reasonable view of speech development would take the factor of intelligence into consideration.

Batza's study (1956) reported on the speech and language proficiency of 108 educable mentally retarded (EMR) public school children. With the CA group of 13–14 and Binet IQ range of 45–85, Batza's research indicated that the speech status of the EMR was not as inferior as often inferred. He noted that the lowest group (IQ range 45–59) was much less homogeneous, less articulate, and less intelligible than his other two reported groups (IQ ranges, 60–69, 70–85).

Riello (1958) analyzed the articulation of 100 retarded children (IQ mean 68, CA mean 11–6) in special class placement, and reported no generally characteristic pattern emerged for this group. While 37 were judged to be defective in articulation, and 81 percent were somewhat nonfluent, the majority were readily intelligible. It was concluded that the articulatory development appeared more delayed than defective, and that speech improvement as well as speech correction was advisable.

In a comprehensive study of the language achievements of educable mentally retarded, Speidel (1958) administered eleven tests to 209 children (CA mean 12–10, IQ mean 73) in special class placements. Generally, these children were found to have a listening comprehension level that surpassed their mental ages by thirteen months in the primary group. The general speech abilities of this sample did not increase in relation to mental age causing the investigator to recommend planned and systematic stimulation of oral expression in an overall language instruction program.

Clinical experience prompted Leberfeld (1957) to write that mentally retarded children who improved in speech and language as a result of therapy also improved correspondingly in measured mental ability. Kolstoe (1958) found statistically significant IQ increases in an experimental group receiving a language development program for five and one-half months.

While speech and language development appears affected by intellectual development, certainly many other factors play an important role. The effect of hearing loss upon speech and language has stimulated investigations of this ability in the mentally retarded. Foale and Paterson (1954) tested the hearing of 100 institutionalized feebleminded boys of CA 10–19 years and a mean IQ of 66. Pure-tone audiometric results indicated that 13 percent had hearing losses that would have handicapped them in ordinary life activities. The prevalence of hearing loss in the general population for that age and area was given as 5 to 8 percent. Schlanger and Gottsleben (1957c) did pure-tone testing with 498 institutionalized mentally retarded, and classified 28 percent as moderate losses, 6 percent as hard of hearing, and 1 percent as deaf. Both investigators felt that these losses contributed to language deficiency, and called for routine hearing testing for all mentally retarded. Rittmanic (1959) gave pure-tone audiometric evaluations to 1220 institutionalized retardates, and reported 40.5 percent had at least medically significant losses. He, too, felt that the high incidence of hearing loss among the retarded should point to the necessity of routine audiometric evaluation.

In a recent study (Kodman, Powers, Phillip and Weller, 1958) a young group (CA range 7–19) and an old group (CA range 20–64) of institutionalized mentally retarded were given pure-tone hearing tests and were compared. The young group had an incidence of hearing loss of 19.04 percent as compared to the old group's 23.81 percent incidence. One out of five of these subjects had a loss of 30 decibels or more, or a fourfold increase over the estimate for public school normals of comparable ages. Kodman (1958) reviewed seven independent studies concerning hearing loss in retardates, and found incidence figures ranging from 13 to 49 percent with a mean incidence of 28.6 percent. The contrast of these results to the commonly quoted 5 percent incidence figure for normal school children has made the problem significant.

Other authorities (Meyerson, Michael, and Mabry, 1960) have questioned the high incidence figures gained by regular pure-tone audiometric techniques with the mentally retarded, and point out a technique which helps distinguish hearing loss from intellectual deficit.

Speech is an extremely complex and complicated skill. ". . . for example, the word church requires twenty different adjustments of the lips, tongue, larynx, and jaws. These twenty must occur in correct sequence, and each of the delicate adjustments must be made precisely. Yet the word requires less than a quarter of a second to speak, which means that the average time available for each of the twenty necessary movements is barely over 1/100 of a second" (Johnson, W., *et al.,* 1956). Howe (1959) compared 43 educable mentally retarded public school children with a CA matched control group, and found the normal children consistently superior to the retarded on all motor skills tested. Others (Arnold, 1955; Schlanger, 1953a) have called attention to the retardates' significantly inferior motor responses on specific tasks which dealt with the articulation of sounds. Eisenson (1955) pointed out the possibility of some degree of motor involvement etiologically associated with defective speech development.

The importance of the environmental factor to speech and language development was emphasized by Wood (1957). The quality of the home atmosphere was held to be the most important single factor influencing the child's acquisition of speech (McCarthy, 1954). Schlanger (1954) analyzed the verbal output of 21 matched pairs of mentally retarded children from institutionalized and noninstitutionalized environments. He found the verbal responses of the noninstitutionalized superior at the .01 level of significance. Badt (1958) studied 60 institutionalized children (CA range 7–15 years; IQ range 50–75) attending an academic program, and found evidence to support the idea that the longer a child was institutionalized, the less able he was to think abstractly or manipulate concepts. The abstraction ability score and length of institutionalization showed a negative correlation of −.61. Reviewing his research, Schlanger (1953b) pointed out the effects upon language development of anticipated needs, minimized social contacts, and lack of social satisfaction from speech. Newer research in progress (Siegel, 1960) advances the hypothesis that retarded children may evoke from adults the kind of verbal responses that, in turn, tend to perpetuate their retarded language performance.

Diedrich and Poser (1960) reported on the language and mentation of two phenylketonuric children during their three years of control on a phenylalanine-low diet. Marked improvement in language as well as mentation was evidenced, but not, in either case, until six months after the institution of the diet.

The development of various techniques to measure and diagnose language development and communication effectiveness in retardates has been reported (Goda, 1960; Kirk and McCarthy, 1961; Lassers and Low, 1960; Mecham, 1955; Spradlin, 1960b). Several recent reviews of studies concerning the speech and language development of the retarded have appeared in the literature (Dunn and Capobianco, 1959; Goertzen, 1957; Harrison, 1958; Murphy, 1959).

INCIDENCE OF PROBLEMS

General agreement has placed the incidence figure for speech problems at 5 percent of all school children (Ainsworth, 1958). The fact that the incidence figure varies with the intellectual range studied has been noted (Irwin, 1959; Johnson, W., *et al.,* 1956; Matthews, 1957; Murphy, 1959; Penwill, 1958). Hudson (1958) estimated a 12 percent incidence of defective speech for the educable mentally retarded, and also stated that language development is generally retarded. Donovan (1957) tested 2000 educable mentally retarded public school children of IQ range 50–74, and found only 8 percent with severe speech defects. Donovan also stated, however, that almost all of the group had developmental speech problems.

Institutionalized populations gave higher incidence figures with Gens (1950) reporting 70–75 percent; Bibey (1951) noting 66 percent. In another study of institutionalized mentally deficient (Schlanger, 1957b), the incidence of articulatory defects (sound substitutions, omissions, or distortions) was 79 percent. This same population presented 42 percent voice problems and 18 percent stuttering.

Specifically, Schlanger (1957a) pointed out that the oral language of the mongoloid type was least developed, with the so-called familial most likely to be a normal speaker. In still another study, Schlanger (1953b) reported on 74 retarded children (IQ range 40 and above) in a private school. The incidence of problems noted were: 62 percent voice defects, 57 percent articulatory problems, 20 percent stuttering. Pfiefer (1958) observed that over 30 percent of the institutionalized in her study had voice disorders.

ROLE OF THE SPEECH SPECIALIST

Many articles are concerned with the programming of speech services for the retarded. These writings seek to recommend optimal approaches designed to accomplish outlined goals. Several references (Bibey, 1951; Gens, 1951; Kastein, 1956; Schlanger and Gottsleben, 1957b) generally agree that the speech therapist or pathologist has important multiple roles with the retarded, including, (1) diagnostic, (2) therapeutic, (3) further referral, and (4) research.

Batza (1956) pointed up the need for greater emphasis on oral language development programs in special classes for the educable retarded. However, he feels that such language training programs should be an integral part of educational training rather than a specific correctional program carried out by a speech therapist. Hudson (1958) also concludes that speech and language development should be correlated with all school activities, and gives the general aims, principles, and procedures for such a program. The concerted efforts of teachers, parents, speech therapists, and research workers are felt necessary to develop the best speech and language of which the retarded is capable (Irwin, 1959). Particular attention was called to the importance of early planned therapy and parent participation in any language development program for the retarded child (Leberfeld, 1957). General agreement is evident (Lassers and Low, 1960; McWilliams, 1959; Penwill, 1958; Plotkin, 1959; Schlanger, 1958) that the major goal of speech work with the retarded must be the language or general communication problem rather than speech or sound production, per se. Rittmanic (1958) outlines an oral language program for the teacher of institutionalized educable mentally retarded, and Plotkin (1959) gives the specifics of a "roving speech teacher" or situational approach to the problem.

Two widely used textbooks in the field question the advisability of speech therapy with lower levels of intelligence and certain clinical types (Johnson, W., *et al.,* 1956, p. 307; West, *et al.,* 1947, p. 215).

SPECIAL PROGRAMS

Much recent attention has been paid to measuring and pointing out the effects of various speech and language programs experienced by the mentally retarded. Arnold (1955) describes a public school speech program carried on for a two and one-half year period with the mentally handicapped. She states that most of the children showed progress in articulatory skills, rhythm of speech, and language growth. Similarly, Donovan (1957) reports on a two-year public school speech program for 2000 children of the IQ range 50–75. Improvement was seen in the lessening of articulatory errors, better voice production, more poise, and general self-confidence.

A reportedly successful oral language program was administered for three months to 13 EMR children with no control group, and utilizing teacher observations as measures of progress (Rittmanic, 1958). Schneider and Vallon (1955) report favorable results for a one-year speech therapy program involving 28 severely mentally retarded children (IQ range 23–57). Once again, pretests and post-tests furnished the only criteria of improvement since no control group was established. Lubman (1955) describes her approximately nine-month speech program for 93 children of CA range 6–21 and IQ range 19–50. Using her own adapted articulatory test as well as parent and teacher ratings, she concludes that 62 of the children had shown some progress. Long-term therapy (42 months) was given to 12 institutionalized children with a CA range of 4.8–9.8 and an IQ range of 24–53 (Schlanger, 1959). On the basis of pretesting and regular interval testing, he detected some gain in communication ability, but felt the improvements appeared pathetically meager for the amount of therapy given.

Two groups of individually matched pairs of children were utilized in a study of more sophisticated design (Johnson, Capobianco, and Miller, 1960). Each group of 24 children contained 11 public school and 13 institutionalized trainable retardates. The experimental group received a language development program throughout the year by a trained speech therapist, while the control group received no supplementary training. Pretest and post-test results, utilizing the experimental *Illinois Test of Language Abilities,* indicated that the nontherapy (control) group made slightly more progress than the therapy (experimental) group, but the difference was not significant.

Pfiefer (1958) analyzed the results of individual and group speech therapy with institutionalized EMR children. Ten children received 20 hours of individual speech therapy; 10 received 20 hours of small group therapy; and 10 received no special assistance. Both therapy groups showed significantly greater linguistic gains than the control group, with no significant difference between the first two techniques.

Mecham (1955) reported an experimental group of 21 children who after only eight weeks of speech therapy, improved over the control group in articulation, auditory discrimination, auditory memory span, and average sentence length.

In an investigation (Kolstoe, 1958) to determine the effects of intensive language training upon mongoloids, 30 children (Mean CA 9–1) were paired on MA and then randomly assigned to an experimental or control group. The experimental group received individual lessons of 45-minute duration, five times a week, for five and one-half months, while the control group received no specific training. The post-test showed a marked difference in the scores of the experimental group, with 10 children showing statistically significant positive differences. Kolstoe concludes that mongoloid children, particularly those above 25 IQ, will profit from a language program.

A program of communication centered speech therapy was compared to a conventional speech therapy program (Lassers and Low, 1960). The speech improvement resulting from both approaches was then compared to the speech improvement made by a control group of mentally retarded children who received no therapy. The newly developed San Francisco Inventory of Communication Effectiveness (SFICE) was utilized to assist this comparison. After a four month therapy period, it was found that communication centered speech therapy improved articulation more effectively than a conventional approach. Both types of therapy improved the oral grammatical complexity of the mentally retarded in comparison to the control group. Lassers and Low state that their results support the integration of communication skills with daily life activities in the regular classroom program.

Rigrodsky and Steer (1961) utilized 72 institutionalized mentally retarded children (CA range 6 to 16–11, IQ range 12–79) in an experimental program to test the effects of various treatments upon articulation ability and general clarity of speech. They sought to test a speech therapy procedure based on Mowrer's autistic theory of language development, and to compare this new technique to the more conventional auditory stimulus program. The experimental therapy was administered for only 15 minutes daily over a 40-day period. Pretest and post-test results indicated no significant differences in either approach, and no significant differences of experimental groups over the control group.

Based on extensive experience with speech therapy programs for institutionalized mentally retarded, discernible gains were reported for the majority of those receiving assistance (Schlanger, 1953c; Schlanger, 1956; Schlanger, 1957b; Schlanger, 1958; Schlanger and Gottsleben, 1957b).

In an analysis of 29 day classes for trainable children (IQ 30–50), Hudson (1960) found language development receiving by far the highest amount of emphasis (a total weight of 834 with motor control second at 434).

Kirk and Johnson (1951) point out the retarded child's need for language development activities. After including the development of language and speech ability among the purposes for a special class, a program of language development is outlined.

The language development aspect of a nursery–kindergarten program for educable mentally retarded children was reported (Harrison, 1959) as part of the mental retardation project currently in progress at Teachers College, Columbia University.

Spradlin (1960b) explains the descriptive behaviorism viewpoint underlying the promising research currently being conducted at the Parsons Project in language and communication of institutionalized mentally retarded children. As a part of the Parsons Project, Ezell (1960) investigated the effects of speech reinforcement and bombardment treatments on verbal behavior of institutionalized children (CA 9–12). This speech and language stimulation was carried out by Psychiatric Aides over a period of 18 weeks with the new Parsons Language Sample being used for pretest and post-test comparisons. There were no positive differences in results for the experimental treatment groups over the controls, and no significant differences between experimental treatments.

In a special report (Rigrodsky, Gens, Schlanger, and Bangs, 1959) an American Speech and Hearing Association subcommittee has indicated research needs in the area of speech and language problems associated with mental retardation.

SUMMARY

The literature of the past ten years concerned with the speech and language problems of the retarded was viewed in relation to general development, incidence of problems, role of the specialist, and special programs.

Speech and language development was reported to be delayed, influenced by intellectual development, and possibly affected by higher incidence of hearing loss and inferior motor skills. The effect of the speech and language environment was stressed, and an example of dietary effects upon language development was cited. Reference was made to newer tests designed to measure speech and language development.

The incidence of speech problems was found to range from 8 percent up to 79 percent depending on the intellectual range being studied. With retarded, specifically, language development was delayed, articulation problems were more prevalent, and voice problems occurred commonly.

The importance of general communication and language development as a goal for the retarded was agreed upon with some divergence of opinion as to who should foster this ability. The important role of the speech therapist, as well as the parent, teacher, and researcher was noted.

Numerous experimental speech and language programs for the retarded was reviewed, with encouraging results reported in most instances. Attention was called to promising research in progress.

REFERENCES

Ainsworth, S. W. The education of children with speech handicaps. In W. M. Cruickshank and G. O. Johnson (Ed.), *Education of Exceptional Children and Youth.* Englewood Cliffs, N.J.: Prentice-Hall, 1958. Pp. 386–428.

Arnold, Ruth G. Speech rehabilitation for the mentally handicapped. *Except. Child.,* 1955, *22,* 50–52, 76.

Badt, Margit I. Levels of abstraction in vocabulary definitions of mentally retarded school children. *Amer. J. Ment. Defic.,* 1958, *63,* 241–246.

Batza, E. M. The speech and oral language behavior of educable mentally retarded children. Unpublished doctoral dissertation, Northwestern University, 1956.

Bibey, M. Lois. A rationale of speech therapy for mentally deficient children. *Train. Sch. Bull.,* 1951, *47,* 236–239.

Diedrich, W. M., and Poser, C. M. Language and mentation of two phenylketonuric children. *J. Speech Hearing Disord.,* 1960, *25,* 124–134.

Donovan, Helen. Organization and development of a speech program for the mentally retarded children in New York City public schools. *Amer. J. Ment. Defic.,* 1957, *62,* 455–459.

Dunn, L. M., and Capobianco, R. J. Mental retardation. *Rev. Educ. Res.,* 1959, *29,* 451–470.

Eisenson, J. The nature of defective speech. In W. M. Cruickshank (Ed.), *Psychology of Exceptional Children and Youth.* Englewood Cliffs, N.J.: *Prentice-Hall,* 1955. Pp. 184–213.

Ezell, Dorolyn. The effects of verbal reinforcement on the language behavior of mentally retarded children. *Asha,* 1960, *2,* 373. (Abstract)

Foale, Martha, and Paterson, J. W. The hearing of mental defectives. *Amer. J. Ment. Defic.,* 1954, *59,* 254–258.

Gens, G. W. Speech retardation in the normal and subnormal child. *Train. Sch. Bull.,* 1950, *47,* 32–36.

Goda, S. Vocal utterances of young moderately and severely retarded non-speaking children. *Amer. J. Ment. Defic.,* 1960, *65,* 269–273.

Goertzen, S. M. Speech and the mentally retarded child. *Amer. J. Ment. Defic.,* 1957, *62,* 244–253.

Goodwin, F. B. A consideration of etiologies in 454 cases of speech retardation. *J. Speech Hearing Disord.,* 1955, *20,* 300–303.

Harrison, S. A review of research in speech and language development of the mentally retarded child. *Amer. J. Ment. Defic.,* 1958, *63,* 236–240.

Harrison, S. Integration of development language activities with an educational program for mentally retarded children. *Amer. J. Ment. Defic.,* 1959, *63,* 967–970.

Howe, C. E. A comparison of motor skills of mentally retarded and normal children. *Except. Child.,* 1959, *25,* 352–354.

Hudson, Margaret. Methods of teaching mentally retarded children. Unpublished manuscript, George Peabody College, 1958. Pp. 1–131.

Hudson, Margaret. Procedures for teaching trainable children. *Council Except. Child. Res. Monogr.,* 1960, Series A, No. 2.

Ikeda, Hannah. Adapting the nursery school for the mentally retarded child. *Except. Child.,* 1955, *21,* 171–173, 196.

Irwin, Ruth B. Oral language for slow learning children. *Amer. J. Ment. Defic.,* 1959, *64,* 32–40.

Johnson, G. O., Capobianco, R. J., and Miller, D. Y. Speech and language development of a group of mentally deficient children enrolled in training programs. *Except. Child.,* 1960, *27,* 72–77.

Johnson, W., Brown, S. F., Curtis, J. F., Edney, C. W., and Keaster, Jacqueline. *Speech Handicapped School Children.* (Rev. ed.) New York: Harper, 1956.

Karlin, I. W., and Strazzulla, Millicent. Speech and language problems of mentally deficient children. *J. Speech Hearing Disord.,* 1952, *17,* 286–294.

Kastein, Shulamith. Responsibility of the speech pathologist to the retarded child. *Amer. J. Ment. Defic.,* 1956, *60,* 750–754.

Kirk, S. A., and Johnson, G. O. *Educating the Retarded Child.* Boston: Houghton Mifflin, 1951.

Kirk, S. A., and McCarthy, J. J. The Illinois test of psycholinguistic abilities—an approach to differential diagnosis. *Amer. J. Ment. Defic.,* 1961, *66,* 399–412.

Kodman, F. Jr. The incidence of hearing loss in mentally retarded children. *Amer. J. Ment. Defic.,* 1958, *62,* 675–678.

Kodman, F., Powers, T. R., Philip, P. P., and Weller, G. M. An investigation of hearing loss in mentally retarded children and adults. *Amer. J. Ment. Defic.*, 1958, *63*, 460–463.

Kolstoe, O. P. Language training of low grade mongoloid children. *Amer. J. Ment. Defic.*, 1958, *63*, 17–30.

Lassers, L. R., and Low, G. Symposium on assessing and developing communicative effectiveness in mentally retarded children. *Asha*, 1960, *2*, 377.

Leberfeld, Doris T. Speech therapy and the retarded child. *Train. Sch. Bull.*, 1957, *53*, 273–274.

Lubman, Charlotte G. Speech program for severely retarded children. *Amer. J. Ment. Defic.*, 1955, *60*, 297–300.

McCarthy, Dorothea. Language disorders and parent-child relationships. *J. Speech Hearing Disord.*, 1954, *19*, 514–523.

McWilliams, Betty J. The speech pathologist looks at the nonverbal child. *Except. Child.*, 1959, *25*, 420–423, 440.

Matthews, J. Speech problems of the mentally retarded. In L. E. Travis (Ed.) *Handbook of Speech Pathology*. New York: Appleton-Century-Crofts, 1957. Pp. 531–551.

Mecham, M. J. The development and application of procedures for measuring speech improvement in mentally defective children. *Amer. J. Ment. Defic.*, 1955, *60*, 301–306.

Meyerson, L., Michael, J. L., and Mabry, J. H. The free operant in the measurement of hearing in exceptional children. *Asha*, 1960, *2*, 352. (Abstract)

Murphy, A. T. The speech handicapped. *Rev. Educ. Res.*, 1959, *29*, 553–565.

Papania, N. A qualitative analysis of vocabulary responses of institutionalized mentally retarded children. *J. Clin. Psychol.*, 1954, *10*, 361–365.

Penwill, Margaret. Speech disorders and therapy in mental deficiency. In Ann M. Clarke and A. D. B. Clarke (Ed.) *Mental Deficiency—The Changing Outlook*. Glencoe, Ill.: Free Press, 1958. Pp. 393–421.

Pfiefer, Rosemary C. An experimental analysis of individual and group speech therapy with educable institutionalized mentally retarded children. Unpublished doctoral dissertation, Boston University, 1958. (*Rev. Educ. Res.*, *29*: 558)

Plotkin, W. H. Situational speech therapy for retarded cerebral palsied children. *J. Speech Hearing Disord.*, 1959, *24*, 16–20.

Riello, A. Articulatory proficiency of the mentally retarded child. Unpublished doctoral dissertation, New York University, 1958.

Rigrodsky, S., Gen, G., Schlanger, B., and Bangs, J. L. Report of subcommittee on speech and language problems associated with mental retardation and delayed speech and language development. *Special Report: Research Needs in Speech Pathology and Audiology*. American Speech and Hearing Association, 1959.

Rigrodsky, S., and Steer, M. D. Mowrer's theory applied to speech habilitation of the mentally retarded. *J. Speech Hearing Disord.*, 1961, *26*, 237–243.

Rittmanic, P. A. An oral language program for institutionalized educable mentally retarded children. *Amer. J. Ment. Defic.*, 1958, *63*, 403–407.

Rittmanic, P. A. Hearing rehabilitation for the institutionalized mentally retarded. *Amer. J. Ment. Defic.*, 1959, *63*, 778–783.

Sarason, S. B. Mentally retarded and mentally defective children: major psychosocial problems. In W. M. Cruickshank (Ed.) *Psychology of Exceptional Children and Youth.* Englewood Cliffs, N.J.: Prentice-Hall, 1955. Pp. 438–474.

Schlanger, B. B. Speech examination of a group of institutionalized mentally handicapped children. *J. Speech Hearing Disord.,* 1953, *18,* 339–349. (a)

Schlanger, B. B. Speech measurements of institutionalized mentally handicapped children. *Amer. J. Ment. Defic.,* 1953, *58,* 114–122. (b)

Schlanger, B. B. Speech therapy results with mentally retarded children in special classes. *Train. Sch. Bull.,* 1953, *50,* 179–186. (c)

Schlanger, B. B. Environmental influences on the verbal output of mentally retarded children. *J. Speech Hearing Disord.,* 1954, *19,* 339–343.

Schlanger, B. B. An investigation of retarded brain-damaged children with delayed speech and language. *Train. Sch. Bull.,* 1956, *53,* 64–74.

Schlanger, B. B. Oral language classification of the training school residents. *Train. Sch. Bull.,* 1957, *53,* 243–247. (a)

Schlanger, B. B. The speech and hearing program at the training school. *Train. Sch. Bull.,* 1957, *53,* 267–272. (b)

Schlanger, B. B. Speech therapy with mentally retarded children. *J. Speech Hearing Disord.,* 1958, *23,* 298–301.

Schlanger, B. B. A longitudinal study of speech and language development of brain damaged retarded children. *J. Speech Hearing Disord.,* 1959, *24,* 354–360.

Schlanger, B. B., and Gottsleben, R. H. Analysis of speech defects among the institutional mentally retarded. *Train. Sch. Bull.,* 1957, *54,* 5–8. (a)

Schlanger, B. B., and Gottsleben, R. H. Clinical speech program at the training school at Vineland. *Amer. J. Ment. Defic.,* 1957, *61,* 516–521. (b)

Schlanger, B. B., and Gottsleben, R. H. Testing the hearing of the mentally retarded. *Train. Sch. Bull.,* 1957, *54,* 21–25. (c)

Schneider, B., and Vallon, J. The results of a speech therapy program for mentally retarded children. *Amer. J. Ment. Defic.,* 1955, *59,* 417–424.

Siegel, G. M. An interpersonal approach to language behavior. *Asha,* 1960, *2,* 372–373. (Abstract)

Speidel, Elizabeth B. Language achievements of mentally retarded children. Unpublished doctoral dissertation, Boston University, 1958.

Spradlin, J. E. A behavioral approach to research in language and communication, *Asha,* 1960, *2,* 373. (Abstract) (a)

Spradlin, J. E. *Assessment of the Speech and Language of Retarded Children.* Parsons, Kan.: Parsons Research Project, Working Paper #29, 1960. (b)

Strazzulla, Millicent. A language guide for the parents of retarded children. *Amer. J. Ment. Defic.,* 1954, *59,* 48–58.

Van Riper, C. *Speech Correction.* (3rd ed.) Englewood Cliffs, N.J.: Prentice-Hall, 1954.

West, R., Kennedy, Lou, and Carr, Anna. *The Rehabilitation of Speech.* (Rev. ed.) New York: Harper, 1947.

Wood, Nancy E. Causal factors of delayed speech and language development. *Amer. J. Ment. Defic.,* 1957, *61,* 706–708.

42 LANGUAGE FUNCTIONS OF RETARDED CHILDREN

R. L. Schiefelbusch

From *Folia Phoniatrica,* Vol. 21, No. 2, 1969, pp. 129–144. Reprinted with the permission of the Editor of *Folia Phoniatrica* and the author. Dr. Schiefelbusch is Director, Bureau of Child Research, University of Kansas, Lawrence.

One major difficulty in writing about language functions of any group of children or adults is that one must objectify a system for examining the complex phenomena he is talking about. In this instance the term *language functions* of *retarded children* presents some special difficulties. Consequently, the first section of this paper is given to an examination of terms and a statement of the approach to be used in discussing the subject. The explanations are designed to fit to the purposes of the paper, namely: (1) to provide perspectives about speech, language and communication as these concepts might be considered by language clinicians and researchers and (2) to provide a functional basis for language training of the mentally retarded.

Carroll (1967) refers to *speech* as the actual behavior of individuals in using language. This might include both their speaking and listening behavior. However, since speech, as a term, usually alludes to *expressive* behaviors, we should use a modifier such as *receptive* speech if we are to make the term fit the input channels. Perhaps all would agree that the term *hearing* is a necessary term in this context, and so we should employ the compatible terms—*speech* and *hearing*—as the situation indicates. Perhaps the important issue about speech in the context of this paper is that it is a system which includes the sensory impingement of the environment (input) and the behavioral response of the organism (output). Speech also is limited to the behavior of a single subject.

Carroll (1967) defines language as the system that speakers have learned—including sounds, words, and grammatical patterns that they employ in speech communication. In his view language is "above all a system, a code if you will, which underlies the actual manifestation of motor behavior we call speech." The code or system as presented by Carroll is composed of four distinct aspects:

a. Its phonology—the specification of the units of sound (phonemes) which go to compose words and other forms in the language;
b. Its morphology—the listing of the words and other basic meaningful forms (morphemes) of the language and the specification of the ways in which these forms may be modified when placed in varying contexts;
c. Its syntax—the specification of the patterns in which linguistic forms may be arranged and of the ways in which these patterns may be modified or transformed in varying contexts; and

d. Its semantics—the specification of the meanings of linguistic forms and syntactical patterns in relation to objects, events, processes, attributes, and relationships in human experience.

Spradlin (1963) defines *language* as the speech and gestures of a speaker and the responses to speech and gestures made by a listener. This definition appropriately leads to the term *interpersonal language,* or *communication,* and provides a general system for studying communication behavior. In the system the terms *speech* and *gestures* suggest that the events are both vocal (auditory) and gestural (visual). The value of this definitional emphasis is that it separates the channel connecting the participants into two operationally defined "bands." Thus we can consider the auditory–vocal band as that portion of natural face-to-face communication which is isolated by an audiotape recording. The visual–gestural band is therefore that portion of the message exchange which appears in a moving picture without sound.

As pointed out by Jaffe (1966) ". . . the utility of distinguishing these various bands in both reception (input) and expression (output) is clear. It permits subclassifications of behavior disorders and isolation of specific mechanisms both within and between bands . . . differential ability in imitating a (demonstrated) gesture and performing that same gesture in response to spoken instructions discriminates between visual–gestural and auditory–gestural processes. Similarly differential ability in reading a word aloud and repeating a spoken word distinguishes between visual–vocal and auditory–vocal processes. In both examples, a failure to test the visual and auditory inputs separately would lead to obscuring or confounding of quite different mechanisms for production of identical performance deficits."

In Spradlin's definition the term *response* also has a special meaning. It suggests that the participants in the communication influence each other. They are arranged in a reciprocal response system wherein the responses of the one are the stimuli for the other. If we substitute the term *message* for the term stimuli we could easily describe a four part communication unit.

The first aspect is the initial verbal instruction by the speaker (the message). The second is the discriminative response of the listener. The third, the verbal feedback by the listener, indicates to the speaker the nature of the listener's discriminative response. The fourth is the use of this feedback by the speaker, that is, modification of, or addition to, his original message.

This simple system for delineating a communication response unit can be used in a language clinic or laboratory. Very often the two participants may be a child and an adult. They are usually assembled for the purposes of instruction and are usually communicating about language materials or tasks which may be a part of a language program. If so, may I point out that either participant in the communication exchange (child or adult) can be the speaker or the listener depending on which provides the initial response. The nature of the initial response, the implied discrimination, the feedback, and the altered behavior can be studied separately, and should be if we are to determine the effectiveness of their communication exchange. For instance, the initial response (of the child) may be jargon-like and difficult to comprehend; it may be badly articulated; it may be nonsensical or unexpectedly distracting. Thus the discrimination (of the adult) may be incomplete or fragmented. The resultant feedback to the child may be inappropriate and may lead to an equally inappropriate alteration of the child's response behavior. *Or* the adequate discrimination (feedback) of the adult may result in a poor discrimination by the child as he fails to comprehend its meaning. The child's poor discrimination might be due to distractibility, sensory impairments, or to a deficient language code. Or perhaps the child may comprehend the adult's feedback responses, but have inappropriate motor or vocal response systems and may provide aversive or puzzling feedback to the adult. Finally the child may interpret effectively the cues from appropriate feedback, but may be unable to change the characteristics of his original response and may either perseverate it or discontinue the communication. In any of these events, language responses may become puzzling, fragmenting, or punishing to either or both participants.

We now may be able to make a summary statement about each of the key terms or categories that we set out to define:

Speech and hearing—The speaking and/or listening behavior of a single speaking individual.

Language—The systems or codes that speakers have learned to use, including sounds, words, and grammatical patterns.

Communication—The language events, including verbal and gestural behavior, that are interpersonal.

As a next step, perhaps we should relate each of these definitional functions to the field of mental retardation. In pursuing this objective, I shall draw on the standard literature, that is, the studies usually associated with the field of mental retardation; and also I shall relate some recent work that has not yet found its way into the standard literature.

SPEECH AND HEARING BEHAVIOR

Speech behavior includes four broad categories: (a) articulation—the way sounds are formed; (b) rhythm—the time relationship between sounds in a word and words in a sentence; (c) voice—the sounds produced by the vibration of vocal folds and modified by the resonators; and (d) speech usage—comprehension of the speech of others (hearing) and/or the projection of ideas through the medium of speech. The last category might also be called speech performance since it refers to the child's probable behavior in speech situations.

The first three categories—articulation, voice, and rhythm—refer to speech behaviors that can be explicitly evaluated; and determination of *normal* or *deviate* can be made with relatively high reliability, even by nominally sophisticated raters. Since these categories represent the bulk of work done by speech clinicians, they are the most thoroughly studied. The work also closely resembles in method the work undertaken in speech clinics with case loads of children with normal learning rates.

Speech usage, however, may seem less familiar as a clinical category and for this reason may require more careful consideration here. Speech usage refers to the functional speech the child uses, comprehends, or expresses in talking. Expressive speech can be sampled (recorded) by having the child describe what he sees in a picture, tell what he remembers from a recent experience, or describe his favorite game. The speech sample can then be analyzed by a systematized procedure which contains the usage functions deemed to be important.

Loban (1963) classifies usage according to fundamental units, that is, phonological unit, communication unit, and mazes. Other evaluators use such measures as rate of speaking, loudness, amount of speaking, pitch, and length of response (Johnson, Darley and Spriesterbach, 1952). The relevant aspects of speech usage likely are suggested by criteria pertaining to effect on listener behavior. If so, the functions are similar in nature and could also be classified under the headings of *language usage* or *communication behavior*. In this sense, it is important to note that speech impairments are not usually detected by instrumentation, but by listener evaluations. That is, speech is considered to be impaired when its variants call attention, distract, or confuse.

Spreen (1965) points out that higher incidence figures for *speech impairment,* in general, are found for children with very low intelligence scores and that incidence figures drop as the intelligence level increases. The highest incidence figures are found among institutionalized retardates: Gens (1950) reported 70 to 75 percent; Bibey (1951), 66 percent; and Schlanger and Gottsleben (1957), 79 percent. In contrast, Donovan (1957) found only 8 percent of 2000 educable mentally retarded public school children to have severe speech defects.

These figures in this form, of course, are not definitive. They neither tell the nature of the problems as to category—for example, articulation, voice or rhythm—nor the criteria used to judge incidence. Bangs (1942) found that institutional children make more articulation errors than do normal children, but that in general they make about the same types of "errors" as do normal children. There were two possible exceptions in that the retardates seemed to have a high incidence of omission of final sounds and sometimes to show errors that were "bizarre and not of the sort ever found among normal children." Karlin and Strazzulla (1952) found the order of difficulty of consonant sounds for retardates to agree closely to the order found for normal children. Matthews concludes his 1957 review of studies pertaining to the mentally retarded with this statement: "There is no evidence to suggest that the speech defects of the mentally retarded differ in kind from those of a nonretarded speech-defective population."

A different interpretation is suggested by a recent review by Dever (1966). He suggests that the phonological deficits among the mentally retarded are a prominent feature of a possible structural deficit. He suggests further that structural linguistics provides the tools for a definitive study. The work he urges should not be to list or catalogue mistakes, but rather to describe the "dialect" of retarded subjects living or working in certain environments. These descriptions then can be used to evaluate the dialect in terms of similarities or differences from the standard dialect. The term *dialect* is used in the linguistic sense to refer to the entire structure or code used by the child. The processes used to study the dialect would be similar to the approach used in studying the dialect of a primitive people. This approach will be discussed in more detail in the following section since it more accurately represents language functions as defined by Carroll.

Hearing refers to the auditory performance both in regard to loudness features and in relation to comprehension—the ability to detect the signal, both in simple and complex forms, and to understand and/or respond appropriately. The auditory function has a decisive effect upon the speech behavior of the speaker and, indeed, cannot be separated from speaking. The speaker monitors himself while speaking and is dependent upon auditory feedback in performing a variety of expressive speech functions.

Incidence figures for hearing loss among retardates suffer also from criteria difficulties, which similarly make evaluation and comparisons tenuous. Webb *et al.* (1964) report that a 15-dB loss level in two or more frequencies produces an incidence figure of 40.5 percent, whereas a 20-dB loss level in two or more frequencies produces an incidence of 24 percent. Other studies suggest that loss figures apparently vary according to the level of retardation of the subjects and the testing techniques employed.

Again, as with aspects of speech production, the incidence figures of hearing loss may give us little useful information. Webb *et al.* conclude:

> The major point here is that many test procedures as evaluated . . . do not appear to result in valid estimates of hearing ability when applied to this population. The procedure recommended (Electroencephalic Response Audiometry—EER), although statistically useful in this study, appeared capable of similar error unless the discrimination ability and extent of judge error is previously determined on a known population.

Schlanger (1961) also offers a note of caution, but relates to somewhat different issues:

> Not understanding what is required of him in terms of stimulus-response patterns leaves the subject no choice but to respond to sound stimuli of high intensity, not respond at all, react when urged, or respond when he feels like it. To overcome this attitude and negate some of the behavioral and physiological factors which inhibit responses to auditory stimuli, it is recommended that a training program especially geared to condition a child to hearing testing (may result in) improved stimulus response patterns (pp. 82–83).

Recommended readings include the proceedings of a conference held at Parsons State Hospital and Training Center in March, 1965. It is entitled, "The Audiologic Assessment of the Mentally Retarded," edited by Lyle Lloyd and Robert Frisina. This material was updated and edited by Robert Fulton in *Audiology for Mentally Retarded* (Baltimore: Williams & Wilkins, 1970). It presents a variety of testing techniques, including some which encompass the conditioning procedures recommended by Schlanger.

LANGUAGE BEHAVIOR

In this section we shall utilize the linguistic definition presented in the introduction. Carroll (1967) has suggested that the linguistic model should be given increased attention in studying language development of retarded children. The work of Brown and Berko (1960), Jenkins and Palermo (1964), Menuyk (1963), Cazden (1967), and McNeil (1967) on morphology and syntax present useful procedures that can be used in developing linguistic studies of retarded children.

Other recent work of merit on grammar of retardates has been undertaken by Hirsh (1965), Lovell and Bradbury (1967), Spradlin and McLean (1967), and Baratz (1965). Other work on concept development has been completed by Furth (1963), Jensen and Rohwer (1963), Griffith and Spitz (1958), Griffith, Spitz, and Lipman (1959), Rossi (1963), Stedman (1963), and Stephens (1966).

Cazden and McNeil have recently made a linguistic distinction between language *competence* and language *performance*. Perhaps this distinction may give us a useful way to approach this difficult area. In McNeil's view competence "is the knowledge of syntax, meaning, and sound that makes performance possible." Linguistic research on the development of competence is aimed to describe and explain the progressively more complex systems of rules with which children comprehend and produce speech.

However, as McNeil explains, a grammar is concerned with the knowledge, not behavior; consequently, factors which affect speaking and listening can be disregarded when thinking about competence.

Cazden (1967) discusses current research on individual differences in competence as undertaken by transformational linguists. According to their views "individual differences in language, other than vocabulary, are a matter of performance only, not of underlying linguistic knowledge . . ." Cazden further points out that the writings of Lenneberg (1966) suggest that individual differences in competence do exist. However, there is a consensus among linguists studying transformational grammar that performance varies to a much greater degree among speakers than does competence.

According to linguistic theory, any language includes universal and language-specific elements. McNeil (1966) explains that variations in individual experience may affect the acquisition of the universal and language-specific components in different ways. Perhaps acquisition of the universal aspects requires less exposure to examples of well formed speech, shows less variability across children, and is reflected in fewer errors during the period of acquisition by each child. Perhaps, conversely, acquisition of language-specific aspects requires more exposure, shows greater variation among children, and is reflected in more errors by each child. Perhaps the implication to be drawn from this supposition is that teachers, clinicians, and others in a position to modify the child's language environment should place greater emphasis upon factors of performance.

In any event, if we seek to improve performance, we should make a careful linguistic assessment. Cazden (1967) describes two types of performance. Performance A is defined as verbal ability performed by a person in a prescribed setting where behavior is affected primarily by such interpersonal factors as attention and memory. The emphasis is upon what the speaker *can do* presumably under eliciting or carefully arranged conducive situations.

In contrast performance B refers to what a person *does do*. The emphasis here is upon natural speech situations and pertains to behavior affected by such interpersonal factors as setting, topic, participants and language function. In this brief overview one may question the functional delineation between the *can do* and *does do* aspects of performance. However, there may be value in assigning the first of these to psycholinguists and the second to language clinicians and teachers. The empirical value of the distinction, however, must rest with the investigator who develops a system for determining the functions which influence performance. Any sampling of language behavior, whether it is assumed to be competence or performance A or performance B, is influenced by interpersonal functions which can be determined effectively only by experimental study. Unfortunately, only a limited amount of experimental data is yet available.

COMMUNICATION BEHAVIOR

At the beginning of the final section of this paper, let us return to the four-part communication unit described by Glucksberg, Krauss and Weisberg (1967)—that is, the initial verbal instruction, the discriminative response by the listener, the feedback, and the modified response by the speaker. Let us apply this communication unit approach to a child and an adult in an experimental or clinical type relationship. The experimental arrangement could have the child and the adult seated at opposite ends of a table with an opaque screen across the middle of the table separating the two communicators. In front of the adult would be a set of irregular objects, which are also duplicated in front of the child. The adult's task is to describe one of the irregular objects in such fashion that the child can select the appropriate matching object from his collection. This communication task calls for both an accurate description on the part of the adult and an appropriate discrimination on the part of the child. The experimental task allows for more than one effort on the part of the discriminator or on the part of the speaker. The discriminator or listener is allowed to ask questions of the speaker so that there can be an exchange of communication leading to an eventual choice of the right object. Note that the arrangement calls for an exchange which places the four-part sequence into sharp perspective because the original message presented by the speaker is discriminated by the listener and his response to this discrimination becomes, in turn, a kind of message which the speaker further interprets and uses.

Note that this is a natural experimental arrangement which allows for experimental manipulation by a third person, the experimenter. Either participant can be the speaker or the listener. Depending on the experiment, other age level subjects can be substituted for either the child or the adult. Various pre-experimental instructions can be given to either. Note, too, that the responses of either or both can be observed and recorded. Task complexity also can be altered by varying the materials, the criteria, and so forth. In the sequence of responses, the experimenter should be able to determine where the communication breaks down if the task criterion is not reached.

I have two primary reasons for advancing this simple experimental or clinical arrangement. First, I wish to suggest that we can somewhat conveniently control many of the functions of communication between two people. Second, I wish to provide a situation into which we can place a retarded child in order to consider aspects of his language.

First off, I would speculate that institutionalized M/R children, for the most part, would not do well on the communication tasks just described. I make this statement from some data relative to both the children of Parsons State Hospital and Training Center and to experiments that have been conducted to date using this experimental arrangement. Let me briefly describe these studies.

Krauss and Glucksberg (1965) found that when two normal children 33 to 66 months of age were assembled, the communication arrangement was nonfunctional. That is, the message did not function as a stimulus for the correct choice of an object by the listener, nor did the verbal feedback of the listener (when it was emitted) serve to alter the messenger's response. However, when the messenger was an adult, using adult-selected topography, the message did function as a stimulus for the correct selection on the part of the child.

In their third experimental arrangement, an adult listener attempted to alter the verbal message of a child speaker. Although the messenger would sometimes alter his original message (other times the child would simply give the original message in a louder voice), the new message was not effective in allowing the listener to select the correct choice from a stimulus array. In the fourth experiment an adult messenger was again used with a child listener, but this time the stimuli (vocal) that the messenger presented were the words that the child listener had previously used in describing the novel forms. In this situation, the listener could make the correct choice. The message was functional.

The studies just cited present objective data about what children of a specified age do in two person assemblies. The range of such studies, of course, can be extended indefinitely. Hopefully, the experimental objectives will be turned into behavioral training projects to see in what ways communication skills of children can be modified to include more effective functions.

If such an approach were selected, it might be desirable to utilize a three-term contingency which can be described symbolically as follows:

$$S^D\text{-}R\text{-}S^R$$

As applied to the speaker, S^D represents a *stimulus* (the novel form for the speaker); R is the *response* (the speaker's message); and S^R is the *reinforcing stimulus* (the feedback which the speaker gets from the listener). As applied to the listener, the S^D is the message he receives from the speaker. The R is the response he provides (feedback). The S^R is an altered message. If the contingency system is viewed in this manner, it appears to be a reciprocal contingency arrangement which either positively reinforces and increases the rate of functional communication or negatively reinforces it and thus decelerates the functional communication.

McLean (1968) at Parsons State Hospital and Training Center has demonstrated that this functional system can be used to develop a significantly large repertoire of new clinical procedures for retarded children. He has further demonstrated that the procedures can be utilized in a programatic approach designed to attain long range goals. A basic strategy of this approach is the arrangement of component programs, for instance, programs for modifying articulation and other language features and for the development of new morphological features and syntactic forms.

In each of the component programs he uses three basic procedural components:

a. Stimulus discrimination—the discrimination of comparative and contrastive stimuli presented within the clinic session.
b. Response development—the development of the motor topography of a response which the child has not produced before.
c. Stimulus generalization—the development of appropriate responses which are emitted by the child in the appropriate environmental conditions.

These procedural components are actually phases in the component training program for each child. The work is usually undertaken with individual children. I have emphasized the adult–child arrangement in this paper because it so closely approximates the clinical model used in language training. However, I do not wish to disregard several other experimentally developed arrangements that have demonstrated effectiveness.

Locke and Gates (1968) also at Parsons State Hospital and Training Center have developed laboratory techniques for modifying the speaking behavior of retarded persons in small groups.

> The first study was aimed at increasing the length of vocal utterances of moderately retarded adolescents assembled in pairs. The pairs of subjects were seated opposite one another at a table above which two digital counters and two banks of six display lights were mounted. Subjects were instructed to carry on a normal conversation about any subject that interested them. They were informed that each would receive monetary remuneration following each session in accordance with the counter values and that counter operations would occur when they were "talking well". Baseline observations, conducted for as few as two sessions and as many as 25 sessions, revealed highly erratic durations of each vocal utterance. However, over 90 percent of such responses were of less than four seconds in duration. Following baseline, vocal responses at or above six seconds were reinforced by points on the counter. In Phase I at each successive second of a given vocal utterance, successive single lights were illuminated on the bank of display lights nearest the speaker. Such feedback regarding the duration of vocal utterances was systematically manipulated during successive phases. Phase I was maintained until stable asymptotic performance was evidenced. Asymptote occurred with an average of 72.4 percent of all utterances exceeding six seconds in duration and required an average of 29 sessions. In Phase II the feedback lights were inoperative to determine the role of extraceptive feedback on vocal duration. Asymptotic

> performance was achieved in 16.25 sessions at an average of 58.75 percent of responses at or above six seconds duration. Phase III reintroduced the lights; and, in an average of ten trials, subjects were exhibiting 83.75 percent responses at or above six seconds. Phase IV removed counter reinforcement but maintained the feedback lights. After an average of 7.25 sessions, the percent of six seconds or longer vocalizations was only 19.37. Finally, in Phase V both feedback lights and counters were operative; and in approximately seven sessions, subjects were emitting an average of 90 percent responses which exceeded a six-second duration. Stable control was not readily achieved but when it occurred, it was quite marked in extent. At the onset subjects were emitting less than ten percent of their utterances at durations longer than six seconds. At the termination 90 percent of their responses exceeded six seconds. This study demonstrated that duration of vocal utterances can be increased through reinforcement and that extraceptive feedback facilitates such increases.

Two other studies by Locke and Strayer demonstrate that frequency and sequence of vocalizations also may be controlled in group settings by extrinsic reinforcement contingencies. Locke is now initiating an investigation of the change in content of conversation occurring under these extrinsic reinforcement contingencies.

For additional experimental work on experimental arrangements for language studies, I would like to recommend the work of Hollis (1966), Nathan, Schneller and Lindsley (1964); Evans (1965); Spradlin, Rosenberg and Mabel (1961); Milgram (1966); Evans and Spradlin (1966); Spradlin, Girardeau and Corte (1968) and McLean (1968). These studies provide resources for establishing arrangements for evaluating or modifying behavior.

SUMMARY

On the basis of work to date we may speculate that many, if not most, retardates can be taught to complete communication tasks if suitable arrangements can be developed. However, here I suggest that we break from traditional research which is designed to highlight speech and language deficiencies and seek, instead, to discover if we can teach language and communication skills to retarded children. We should seek to know under what arrangements these skills are learned. What are the functional aspects of speech, language, and communication that are requisite to such learning? This question is a complex one; but, by setting up such arrangements and establishing the parameters of the instruction, we establish a new class of information which should eventually guide the development of improved clinical programs. It should be noted that many clinical arrangements are highly similar to the arrangements described here. However, they usually have not been systematized, and functional analysis of the critical parameters has not been attempted.

The establishment of behavioral arrangements and functional analysis of these arrangements should receive additional attention from language specialists. Hopefully, then, programs of training leading to improvements in functional language will emerge.

REFERENCES

Bangs, J. L.: A clinical analysis of the articulatory defects of the feeble minded. *J. Speech Dis. 7*:343–356 (1942).

Baratz, J. C.: Word association abilities of normal preschoolers, institutional retardates, special class children and normal grade school children. Dissertation, University of Kansas, 1964.

Bibey, M.: A rationale of speech therapy for mentally deficient children. *Train. Sch. Bull. 48*:236–239 (1951).

Brown, R. and Berko, J.: Psycholinguistic research methods; in: Paul H. Mussen: *Handbook of Research Methods in Child Development:* pp. 517–560, (Wiley, New York, 1960).

Carroll, J. B.: Psycholinguistics in the study of mental retardation; in Schiefelbusch, R. L.; Ross, H.; Copeland and Smith, J. O.: *Language and Mental Retardation* (Holt, Rinehart and Winston, New York, 1967).

Cazden, C. B.: On individual differences in language competence and performance. *J. Spec. Educ. 1*:135–150 (1967).

Dever, R. B.: A new perspective for language research. *Ment. Retard. 4*:20–23 (1966).

Donovan, H.: Organization and development of a speech program for the mentally retarded children in the New York City Public Schools. *Amer. J. Ment. Defic. 62*:455–459 (1957).

Evans, G. W.: Opportunity to communicate and probability of cooperation among mentally retarded children. *Amer. J. Ment. Defic. 70*:276–281 (1965).

Evans, C. W. and Spradlin, J. E.: Incentives and instructions as controlling variables of productivity. *Amer. J. Ment. Defic. 71*:129–132 (1966).

Fulton, R.: *Audiometry for Mentally Retarded* (Williams & Wilkins, Baltimore, 1970).

Furth, H. G.: Conceptual discovery and control on a pictorial part-whole task as a function of age, intelligence, and language. *J. Educ. Psychol. 54*:191–196 (1963).

Gens, G. W.: The speech pathologist looks at the mentally deficient child. *Train. Sch. Bull. 48*:19–27 (1951).

Glucksberg, S.; Krauss, R. M. and Weisberg, R.: Referential communication in nursery school children. Method and some preliminary findings. *J. Exp. Child Psychol. 3*:333–342 (1966).

Griffith, B. C. and Spitz, H. H.: Some relationships between abstraction and word meaning in retarded adolescents. *Amer. J. Ment. Defic. 63*:247–251 (1958).

Griffith, B. C.; Spitz, H. H. and Lipman, R. S.: Verbal mediation and concept formation in retarded and normal subjects. *J. Exp. Psychol. 58*:247–251 (1959).

Hirsh, V. A.: An analysis of the syntactic structure in the language behavior of mentally retarded children. Thesis, University of Florida, 1965.

Hollis, J. H.: Communication within dyads of severely retarded children. *Amer. J. Ment. Defic. 70*:729–744 (1966).

Jaffe, J.: The study of language in psychiatry: Psycholinguistics and computational linguistics; in Arieti, S.: *American Handbook of Psychiatry,* Vol. III (Basic Books, New York, 1966).

Jenkins, J. J. and Palermo, D. S.: Mediation processes and the acquisition of linguistic structure. *Monogr. Soc. Res. Child Develop. 29:141–168* (1964).

Jensen, A. R. and Rohwer, W. D.: The effect of verbal mediation on the learning and retention of paired associates by retarded adults. *Amer. J. Ment. Defic. 68*:80–84 (1963).

Johnson, W.; Dorley, F. and Spriesterbach, D.: *Diagnostic Methods in Speech Pathology* (Harper & Row, New York, 1952).

Karlin, I. W. and Strazzulla, M.: Speech and language problems of mentally deficient children. *J. Speech Disord. 17*:286–294 (1952).

Krauss, R. M. and Glucksberg, S.: Some aspects of verbal communication in children. Paper read at Amer. Psychol. Assn., Chicago, Sept., 1965.

Lenneberg, E. H.: The natural history of language; in Smith, F. and Miller, G. A.: *The Genesis of Language* (MIT Press, Cambridge, Mass., 1966).

Lloyd, L. L. and Frisina, D. R.: The audiologic assessment of the mentally retarded. Proc. of a national conference. Parsons, Kansas, Parsons State Hospital and Training Center, 1965.

Loban, W. D.: The language of elementary school children. NCTE Research Report No. 1. National Council of Teachers of English, Champaign, Illinois, 1963.

Locke, B. and Gates, J.: Experimental manipulation of vocal utterances of retardates in social assemblies, 1967 Progress Report, Program of Research in Communication Disorders of Mentally Retarded Children, HD00870.

Lovell, K. and Bradbury, B.: The learning of English morphology in educationally subnormal special school children. *Amer. J. Ment. Defic. 71*:609–615 (1967).

McLean, J.: Summary report on the substantive activities of the Parsons demonstration project, September 1967 to August 1968, Report No. 88, Parsons Demonstration Project, Parsons State Hospital and Training Center, Parsons, Kansas.

McNeil, D.: Developmental psycholinguistics; in Smith, F. and Miller, G. A.: *The Genesis of Language* (MIT Press, Cambridge, Mass., 1966).

McNeil, D.: The development of language; in Lane, H. L., and Zale, E. M.: *Studies in Language and Language Behavior IV*. Center for Research on Language and Language Behavior, University of Michigan, Ann Arbor, Michigan.

Menuyk, P.: Syntactic structures in the language of children. *Child Develop. 34*:407–422 (1963).

Milgram, N. A.: Verbalization and conceptual classification of trainable mentally retarded children. *Amer. J. Ment. Defic. 70*:763–765 (1966).

Nathan, P. E.; Schneller, P. and Lindsley, O. R.: Direct measurement of communication during psychiatric admission interviews. *Behav. Res. Ther. 2*:49–57 (1964).

Rosenberg, S.; Spradlin, J. E. and Mabel, S.: Interaction among retarded children as a function of their relative language skills. *J. Abnorm. Soc. Psychol. 63*:402–410 (1961).

Rossi, E. L.: Associative clustering in normal and retarded children. *Amer. J. Ment. Defic. 67*:691–699 (1963).

Schlanger, B. B.: The effects of listening training on the auditory thresholds of mentally retarded children. Cooperative Research Project USOE No. 973 (8936), 1961.

Schlanger, B. B. and Gottsleben, R. H.: Clinical speech program at the training school at Vineland. *Amer. J. Ment. Defic. 61*:516–521 (1957).

Schlanger, B. B. and Gottsleben, R. H.: Analysis of speech defects among the institutionalized mentally retarded. *Train. Sch. Bull. 54*:5–8 (1957).

Spradlin, J. E.: Language and communication of mental defectives; in Ellis, N.: *Handbook of Mental Deficiency;* pp. 512–556 (McGraw-Hill, New York, 1963).

Spradlin, J. E.; Girardeau, F. L. and Corte, E.: Social and communication behavior of retarded adolescents in a two-person situation. *Amer. J. Ment. Defic. 73*:473–481 (1967).

Spradlin, J. E. and McLean, J. E.: Morphological and syntactical characteristics of retardates' speech. Working Paper 176, Parsons Research Center, November, 1967.

Spreen, O.: Language functions in mental retardation: A review. II. Language in higher level performance. *Amer. J. Ment. Defic. 70*:351–362 (1965).

Spreen, O.: Language functions in mental retardation. A review. I. Language development, types of retardation and intelligence level. *Amer. J. Ment. Defic. 69*:482–494 (1965).

Stedman, D. J.: Associative clustering of semantic categories in normal and retarded subjects. *Amer. J. Ment. Defic. 67*:700–704 (1963).

Stephens, W. E.: Category usage by normal and mentally retarded boys. *Child Develop. 37*:355–362 (1966).

Webb, C.; Kinde, St.; Weber, B. and Breedle, R.: Procedures for evaluating the hearing of the mentally retarded. Cooperative research project USOE No. 1731, 1964.

SECTION TWELVE

Parent Counseling

Twenty-five years ago the birth or recognition of a retarded child in a family was considered a severe tragedy and the outlook for him was almost hopeless. Today, the situation is still considered a tragedy, but at the same time it is possible to be more hopeful about the child's future prospects. Society's attitude toward mental retardation has changed greatly in the last decade. No longer is the retarded child considered "a forgotten child." Parents, though feeling a sense of personal tragedy, have increasingly accepted their responsibility, and working together, have fostered programs that augur well for all retarded children.

Parents of mentally retarded children began to organize in groups shortly before World War II. The movement was informal. Not until 1950 was there a national group. If one movement were to be selected to signal the major development in help for retarded children, it would be the organization of the National Association for Retarded Children (2709 Avenue E East, Arlington, Texas, 76010). Recognizing the value of strength in numbers and the psychotherapeutic effect of interaction among people with similar problems, this organization has forged ahead. The aims and purposes of the NARC are: (1) to promote the general welfare of retarded children at home, in institutions, and in all types of schools; (2) to further research in all aspects of mental retardation; (3) to develop a better understanding of the problem by the general public and to cooperate with various public and private agencies; (4) to further the training of personnel in the field of mental retardation; (5) to encourage the formation of parents' groups and to advise and assist in the solution of common problems; (6) to implement and promote legislation, and (7) to serve as a clearing house of information regarding program development. This organization, through its bimonthly newspaper, *Mental Retardation News,* and through various publications, conferences, and clinics, has done an outstanding job. Recently, a nationwide network of state and local chapters of NARC has provided local action.

The recent interest of the communications media and the dramatic arts in the field of mental retardation has brought to the public much needed knowledge. Such television programs as *Teacher, Teacher* and the *Long Childhood of Timmy* brought to the public's view the plight of the retarded child and his parents. Similarly, but in an overly dramatic way, the film *Charley* presented the possibility of greater hopefulness regarding mental retardation. The theatrical presentation of parental tensions and attitudes was clearly depicted in the exciting Broadway and London hit, *Joe Egg.* Certainly millions have been influenced by these presentations.

Specific parent counseling programs have been developed as part of Title VI-A of the Elementary and Secondary Education Act. Many innovative programs for the mentally retarded funded under this act have related parent counseling and education programs. An untouched population that desperately needs help are the parents of the approximately 75 percent of the identified retarded who come from those social classes that are underprivileged and deprived. Specifically, those parents of children in the educable mentally retarded group who are classified etiologically as "psychosocial" are included in this group. Their children are often unplanned, unwanted, and born out of wedlock or grow up in homes with absent fathers and unavailable mothers. Any special class teacher of the educable retarded will point out the frustrations in attempting to contact these parents, much less trying to organize them into any type of interested parent group. These (the educable retarded) are children in our otherwise well-endowed society, generation after generation, who inherit the circumstances, not the genes, that predispose them to mental retardation and in fact create retardation in many of them.[1]

Mandatory reading for all professional workers are the writings of Bernard Farber of the University of Illinois. Farber, a sociologist, has spent over ten years studying the social phenomena of mental retardation. His work carefully documents the parental problems arising from the advent of a retarded child in the family.[2,3]

A complete list of books for parents of the retarded and about mentally retarded children appears on pages 646–650 of this volume.

The initial article in this section, by G. E. Milligan, describes the counseling process and such specifics in parental counseling as genetic and institutional factors. The second report, by Leo F. Kanner, discusses how parents of mentally retarded individuals should be advised. Kanner, a pediatric psychiatrist and a pioneer in this field of counseling, suggests that the questions of the parents themselves form the most valid and practical guide to counseling. He identifies five major areas of parental

[1] George Tarjan, statement from the March 1967 issue of the *Bulletin of the President's Committee on Mental Retardation,* p. 5.

[2] Bernard Farber, *Mental Retardation: Its Social Context and Social Consequences* (Boston: Houghton Mifflin Company, 1968).

[3] Bernard Farber and David B. Ryckman, "Effects of Severely Mentally Retarded Children on Family Relations," *Mental Retardation Abstracts, 2*:1 (January–March 1965), 1–17.

concern: (1) the features of the diagnosis; (2) the etiology of the disturbance, an area where much is still to be learned; (3) the prognosis; (4) the child's place in the family structure; and (5) therapeutic management. In the final reading, Letha L. Patterson writes from the viewpoint of a parent of a retarded child. She makes a poignant plea for a straightforward parent–counselor relationship.

43 COUNSELING PARENTS OF THE MENTALLY RETARDED

Glenn E. Milligan

From *Mental Retardation Abstracts,* Vol. 2, No. 3, July–September 1965, pp. 259–264. Reprinted with the permission of the U.S. Department of Health, Education, and Welfare and the author. Dr. Milligan is Psychologist, Montgomery County Public Schools, Rockville, Md.

The child who is mentally retarded has been called "the forgotten child." This term might well apply to his parents who also are often "forgotten"—forgotten as to needs, feelings, wishes, aspirations, and desires. The role of counseling is to focus upon the world of the parent and attempt to resolve the anxieties which a retarded child brings to the family structure. The great importance of parental counseling was aptly stated by Mrs. Max Murray (1959, p. 1084): "The greatest single need of parents of mentally retarded children is constructive professional counseling at various stages in the child's life which will enable the parents to find the answers to their own individual problems to a reasonably satisfactory degree."

According to Boyd (1950), parents of mentally retarded children go through three stages in reacting to mental retardation. In the beginning, the parent of a mentally retarded child is highly subjective and is concerned almost entirely with himself and the effect that things have upon him. The second stage is one of concern primarily for "our" child. In the third stage, objectivity emerges so that the parent can see more clearly and think more rationally. Counseling can play an essential role in helping the parent move through his feelings of frustration to a more objective view of the new role he is called upon to assume as a parent of a mentally retarded child.

Counseling as it focuses upon the parent is the major emphasis of this review. The paper highlights selected references appearing in the literature within the past two or three years.

THE COUNSELING PROCESS

Human experience is a continuous, unsegmented stream of behavior. Each behavioral event is intimately united with and derived from every earlier act; at the same time each, as it occurs, establishes itself as an element in some future experience. A response performed at one point on this continuum becomes a part of some subsequent stimulus pattern capable of evoking new responses at some later point. All previously performed acts merge and blend to form a reservoir from which new stimuli and responses emerge as they are required. Even birth and death are inseparably linked, for human life, as we know it, has the process of dying stamped upon it before the moment of birth. The past, the present, and even the future participate in the kinds of responses an individual performs at any given instant, and this immediate behavior influences both his future actions and the ways in which he interprets his former experiences (Weitz, 1964, p. 1).

When this "stream of behavior" becomes so disturbed that ongoing activities are disrupted, the individual begins to seek at random a resolution to his problem. When this person seeks guidance or counseling, he enters into a client relationship in which the counselor and counselee, together, work toward a resolution of the problem. Guidance, then, is the professional assistance given in solving problems and in acquiring generalized problem-solving behavior.

The end product of effective guidance is to bring about changes in the behavioral flow so as to lead the client to a state of meaningful, rational, and purposeful serenity. The problem-solving process in a counseling relationship is designed to help the individual do the following: (1) obtain a clear, manageable statement of what the problems are through diagnosis or *problem identification,* (2) make some estimate of the kinds of solutions which might be reached through structural *planning,* (3) select and implement possible solutions through therapy or *structural activation,* (4) make sure that a given problem and its solution carry over to other similar situations through *generalization,* and (5) check to see that the goals of guidance were achieved through *evaluation* (italicized items are those used by Weitz, 1964).

The counselor's role, therefore, is to help the individual identify the problem, activate a plan, and to place his plan into action to alleviate the anxiety, discomfort, and imbalance which the problem has caused. The end result of guidance is to help the individual move toward an orderly, energetic, forward operation by becoming more goal oriented and purposefully directed. The counselor's principal tool is the diagnostic interview which provides an extensive description of the objects, events, conditions, and life experiences surrounding the individual in an effort to identify and label the unique behavior of a unique individual under a unique set of circumstances at a specific time in history.

Counseling, an aspect of the total guidance process, is concerned with helping the individual focus on the problem as the counselee sees it and to help arrive at solutions of the problem in terms of the counselee's own repertory of response patterns. To do otherwise, weakens the counseling situation so that effective action becomes increasingly difficult. There is another aspect of the counseling relationship which is very important, that is, to help the individual arrive at a general way of handling future problems. As a given problem is attacked and is brought under control, the counselee should become cognizant of ways in which similar problems may be resolved. The individual thus becomes a self-motivating person, increasing his usefulness to society through his own enhanced maturity.

COUNSELING PARENTS OF RETARDED CHILDREN

Learning that one's child is retarded, is, for most parents, a traumatic experience (Abraham, 1958). Questions, such as "Why did this happen to us?" "Which of us is to blame?" and "Should there be more children?" should be handled by medical practitioners who have some genetic background and orientation (Danks, 1963; Reed, 1963). As the family moves through the various stages of shock, disbelief, fear and frustration, and intelligent inquiry (Koegler, 1963) or through emotional disorganization, reintegration, and mature adaptation (American Medical Association, 1965), the family physician can be an important support and guide.

The degree of retardation will dictate the immediacy of the need for counseling. If the child has a condition, such as phenylketonuria, which is amenable to early medical treatment, immediate attention by a physician is needed (Koch, *et al.,* 1964). Beginning counseling as soon as possible is also important to help the family mobilize its strengths and to be aware of its weaknesses (Goodman, 1964; Schueman, 1963). As illustrated in a New York study of 140 families adjusting to the birth of a mongoloid infant, parents have considerable feelings of guilt (Goodman, 1964). Even parents with a high degree of intactness go through an initial phase of regression and disorganization. Wherever possible, the services of a team of professional persons, as may be associated with a unit or clinic, are helpful (Fotheringham, 1964).

Genetic Counseling

Genetic counseling, according to the available literature, is positive in its approach. It would appear that except in known hereditary forms of mental retardation, the genetic counselor may advise parents that the chance is quite small that more mentally retarded children will be born in the same family, even if the first-born is diagnosed retarded. For example, Koch (1963), in a follow-up study of families with a retarded child reported that only eight of 358 subsequent siblings were retarded. According to Danks (1963), it is not the role of the genetic counselor to tell people whether or not to have more children, but to supply the information on which the family can make the decision themselves.

Institutional Counseling

Many physicians advise parents of retarded children to institutionalize their retardates. Olshansky, *et al.* (1963) posed the following question to 57 general practitioners: "Would you comment on the view that 'it is best for the mother to be immediately separated from the retarded child at time of delivery'?" About 60 percent expressed varying degrees of opposition to immediate separation; whereas, about 40 percent favored immediate separation. The general feeling was that the mongoloid was "hopeless" and that it was not advisable for the mother to get "too attached to the mongoloid child." Many parents, of course, have resisted this advice and have had some very rewarding experiences. One such report was circulated widely by the New York State Department of Mental Hygiene (1963) under the title "Tommy Stayed at Home." Senator and Mrs. William T. Conklin reported a similar experience in a story published by a national magazine (Horwitz, 1965).

In an effort to focus on the problems of early institutionalization, 100 families participated in group counseling sessions which emphasized the physical and psychological development of the infant and also the parents' own emotional problems stemming from the presence of the retarded infant in the family. Twenty-four of the 100 families decided not to place their infants in the state institution and the majority "responded eagerly to the opportunity for looking beyond what appeared to be an unalterable decision" (Giannini, 1963).

Should institutionalization be necessary, it can be a frightening experience and one fraught with many questions and doubts. To help ease this problem, one state institution which has a large admission area of 128,353 square miles and only one social worker for each 600 residents in the facility, began a Pilot Parent Program in an effort to assist parents unable to visit the school prior to the admission of their child. Twenty-six sets of parents, known as Pilot Parents, who had children at the Austin (Texas) State School, have been actively participating in a program of counseling with parents who were considering institutionalization for their own children. The Pilot Parents selected for this program were those persons who had successfully worked through their own problems in relation to admitting their children to the School. They were given a kit of materials containing parent and personnel brochures, sample chapel and recreation bulletins, volunteer newsletters, the institution's monthly newsletter, visitor's permits, furlough and discharge papers, each with an attached explanatory statement. The professional staff at the School was always available as resource persons, and conferences were usually on the agenda when parents visited the School. Parents applying for the admission of their child were given the name of a set of local Pilot Parents who could be contacted if desired. During a two-year period, the assistance of the Pilot Parents had done much to alleviate the anxiety inherent in planning admittance to the residential facility and to answer the many questions regarding the School, such as its staff, program, procedures, and, particularly, the pre-admission process (Standifer, 1964).

Group and Individual Counseling

Working with individuals singly or in groups often is advisable. Appell, *et al.* (1964), for example, reported that 21 mothers of retarded children who were enrolled in a day-care nursery received approximately 60 sessions over a two-year period. These mothers were evaluated with the Thurston Sentence Completion Form at the beginning and at the end of the counseling sessions. On 24 of the items a significant difference was found which showed that parents were more willing to talk about their children's conditions, were more able to accept the medical diagnosis of retardation, discussed the retarded child more freely with the siblings in the family, felt that others were sympathetic toward their children rather than merely curious or pitying, changed their orientation toward their children from short range to more sophisticated long range goals, saw the day-care center as a helpful resource, and became more optimistic with regard to their child's future.

In another study, positive changes in attitudes of parents were observed following a series of parental group discussion sessions by teachers with parents of trainable mentally retarded children (TMR). Teachers of two TMR classes in similar middle-class schools conducted a series of seven monthly meetings on a variety of pertinent topics. The attitudes of 16 Ss (11 mothers and 5 fathers) who attended all or some of these sessions were assessed before and after the meeting on four instruments: The Parental Attitude Research Instrument, Form IV; a Semantic Differential supplement; a Child Character Trait Questionnaire; and a 50-item T-F test concerning mental retardation. These results showed that parents demonstrated significantly more positive changes on concepts concerning TMR and teachers (Bitter, 1963).

Goshen (1963) reported that from 1950 to 1962 (excluding 1957 to 1959) mothers of mentally retarded children under twelve years old, who etiologically demonstrated no organicity, birth injury, encephalitis, or developmental anomaly, who ranged from 50 to 80 IQ, and who were in the home at the beginning of the study, were in psychotherapeutic sessions usually one hour per week for a total of from 1 to 150 sessions. Although no statistical analysis was made, the following generalizations were proposed: (1) In each case, a clearly recognizable state of psychic disorder was present in the S during the retarded child's early life. In two-thirds of the Ss, these problems were evident at the start of the study. (2) These disturbances were characterized by severe diminution of activity, avoidance of people, responsibilities, and decision-making, and brooding introspectiveness with concomitant lack of verbal communication. (3) Ss could be described as having immaturity which predated pregnancy. (4) Husbands were characterized as remote from the retarded child and insecure, apprehensive persons dominated by the wife. (5) The critical period in the child's life in which maternal deprivation was most crucial was from six to eighteen months. (6) The children seemed to develop normally up to nine to twelve months. Late walking and talking were the first apparent signs. There was also fear in trying new things. (7) The mothers, who were usually sole caretakers of their children, did this without emotional spontaneity. (8) The children were characterized by slow motor development and striking language retardation. (9) Siblings were in all but one case normal, but showed disturbed adjustment to some degree. They were equally divided between excessive submission or rebelliousness. (10) Because of the striking absence of outside influence, the mother became the overwhelmingly most significant person in the child's life.

Dalton and Epstein (1963) reported on counseling parents of educable mentally retarded children (EMR) who were five to seven years old with Binet IQs of 55 to 80. Delayed speech and lack of readiness for school were noted by the parents. The counseling sessions interpreted and clarified for the parents the characteristics of the children including slow-learning concretism, need for demonstration, lack of verbal curiosity leading to primitive thinking, autistic regression in stress, difficulty in directing aggression and difficulty in specificity of libidinal objects. Ego-supportive treatment was offered in an attempt to free parents from the debilitating double effects of depressive reactions to diagnosis; hopelessness-neglect, and overprotection. The task was to be supportive without reinforcing denial of the retardation, thus facilitating realization of the child's actual, positive potential.

Counseling Techniques

Roos (1963) made it quite clear that a counseling situation should provide the parents with an opportunity for a therapeutic interview which makes possible an expression of feeling in a nonthreatening interpersonal interaction. A therapeutic interview, Roos states, has several basic ingredients: (1) acceptance and respect for the counselee, (2) free emotional expression allowed the interviewee, (3) decisions reached by parents rather than the psychologist, (4) parents determine the direction of the interview, and (5) honesty guides the exchange of views. This approach to the counseling relationship places considerable burden on the counselor to resist assuming an authoritarian role and the necessity to acquire the ability to listen and be able, therefore, to arrive at more or less valid conclusions as to the parents' current needs because of their ease in expressing feelings, concerns, and opinions. In concluding the interview, parents should be informed that the counselor will be available should the need arise.

The disadvantaged or culturally deprived parent, likewise, needs considerable attention. In an effort to break the cycle of hopelessness and despair which is repeated from generation to generation of parents of deprived children in cities, the Chicago Board of Education, with a grant from the Ford Foundation and supplementary funds of its own, launched a Special Project to see what could be done for certain children in District Eleven. The major goal was the motivation of students who had had unsuccessful elementary school experiences with a primary emphasis on boys and girls fourteen or more years of age who were still in elementary school. The Project centered its interest on parents who need help in understanding their children, in seeing the value of school, in developing homemaking skills, in learning to cope with urban life, in achieving vocational competence, and in accepting the responsibility of parenthood. The Project staff with special skills literally went into the homes to provide service to all who would accept it. A school social worker helped to form a Fathers' Club, a home economist organized sewing groups, a youth activities counselor helped parents participate in their children's 4-H activities, and a parent educational counselor encouraged parent activities related to school progress. Daugherty's (1963) suggestions for winning the support of the economically disadvantaged parent were similar to Roos' observations: (1) express a genuine interest in the child and the parent who loves him; (2) provide an opportunity to bring to the teacher or the administrator any problem hindering the child's progress; (3) reveal patience in listening to a problem and offer concrete suggestions as to what steps parents and the school may take to work out a solution; (4) supply printed communications that are simple enough to be understandable but mature enough to reflect respect for the parents' intelligence; (5) extend encouragement and appreciation for all parental efforts—even the unsuccessful ones; and (6) indicate an expressed dedication to excellence in education.

Parents should know the limitations of the evaluative findings and should be encouraged to formulate tentative plans which aid them to think constructively about the future (Doll, 1963; Thurston, 1963). Factual information regarding community resources, referral agencies, and institutions will help the parent in planning for their child (Begab, 1964).

An essential aspect of counseling, which is evident in most discussions, is the imparting of information. Parents often desire or seek information which will help them learn more about the retarded. In response to this need, various appropriate books and pamphlets have been prepared. For example, Blodgett and Warfield (1959) have compiled their observations of retarded children into a compendium based upon their experiences at The Sheltering Arms (Minneapolis), which has a day school and research program for mentally retarded children. Maria Egg (1964) has prepared a basic guide for parents and friends of mentally retarded children, giving practical suggestions on their education and training. Three organizations went together to publish a report on the needs of mentally handicapped children in England (Paediatric Society of the South-East Metropolitan Region, 1962).

Role of the Professional Organization

The best antidote to any problem is to proceed directly toward a resolution of the condition underlying the difficulty. Parents of mentally retarded children illustrated the importance of this principle when they banned together to "wage a war" on mental retardation, a condition which had brought them so much heartache, frustration, and almost insurmountable odds. By "sharing" their problem with other parents and with an enlightened citizenry, gains were slowly made in more understanding and knowledge, which in turn brought hope for the future. Today, from the President of the United States, from leaders in Congress, and from federal, state, and local groups, officials, and citizens, the "war" is being won for more attention, more resources, and more information on the problem of mental retardation.

Organizations, such as the National Association for Retarded Children (a citizen group of over 100,000 members), the American Association on Mental Deficiency (a multidiscipline professional body of over 7,000 persons), and various primary professional groups (Council for Exceptional Children; American Psychological Association; and the American Medical Association with its various allied medical specialities, such as psychiatry, neurology, and pediatrics) have been focusing professional attention on the problems of the mentally retarded and their parents. Dybwad (1963) points out that there are 28 national and federated voluntary, parent-sponsored associations and that in more than 50 countries from every continent, there are national or local associations for the mentally retarded. The service of such organizations can play an instrumental role in resolving parental conflicts.

Recommendations

Parents need support as they face the problem of mental retardation in their children. Butler and Bramwell (1964) recognized this fact when they established their traveling clinic in northern California. They made certain that as many local professional people as possible were involved in executing the recommendations of the clinic. Persons such as school teachers, social workers, probation workers, and public health nurses were called upon to act in the role of friend or counselor with whom the patient or family could talk at regular intervals or in times of stress. Communities, therefore, would find it worthwhile to have a central referral service which, in turn, could help develop the kind of personal support which is so often needed by persons under stress (Appell, 1963; Begab, 1963).

The professional should concentrate on his own communicative language as it is used to impart information to parents and the citizenry. Mahoney (1964), in a study of the meanings given to such commonly used terms as mental retardation, brain damage, mental illness, and emotional disturbance, noted that while there was considerable professional agreement, parents held highly individualized concepts of the terms. For example, about 10 percent of the specialists in mental retardation (66 Fellows representing five professional sections in the American Association on Mental Deficiency) and about 50 percent of the mothers of retarded children (117 mothers who were members of the Kansas Association for Retarded Children) considered brain damage and mental retardation to mean the same thing. Among this group of mothers, the tendency to consider brain damage and mental retardation as synonymous increased from 30 percent for those with four or more years of college to 80 percent for those with 12 or less years of formal schooling. The tendency for mental retardation and brain damage to be considered as having the same meaning suggested to the author that misinformation was at fault. This, in turn, may have the effect of focusing attention on mental retardation of greater severity and less prevalence, and away from mental retardation of less severity and greater prevalence. Confusion among laymen regarding the terms brain damage and mental retardation reflected some degree of disagreement or carelessness among specialists; however, confusion among laymen regarding the basic concepts of mental retardation and mental illness cannot be attributed to specialist disagreement but may be due to inadequate communication from specialists to the general public.

Professionals might take a cue from the parent as set forth by Patterson (1956). She offers the following suggestions in an effort to help the professional be more effective in counseling parents: (1) Tell us the nature of our problem as soon as possible. (2) Always see both parents. (3) Watch your language. (4) Help us to see that this is "our" problem. (5) Help us to understand our problem. (6) Know your resources. (7) Never put us on the defensive. (8) Remember that parents of retarded children are just people. (9) Remember that we are parents and that you are professionals. (10) Remember the importance of your attitude towards us. Thoreson (1964) states that although a counselor may make errors in counseling strategy, if he communicates effectively, he will have initiated a richly productive human relationship and will have provided services that can lead to a more satisfying and personal life for his client.

In view of the large amount of time and effort devoted to parental counseling (O'Connor and Caffey, 1964; Hawley, 1963), formal training programs should include some consideration of the counseling process. Refresher courses, seminars, and institutes also should be provided (Stevens, 1963).

SUMMARY

The guidance process is one of helping the individual resolve conflicts, frustrations, and anxieties. For the parent of the mentally retarded child, there are many stressful situations which require the mediation of the counseling process as early as possible.

Counseling should help the parents to identify and understand the nature of their particular problems. It also must provide the individual members of the family with the knowledge, support, and opportunities for realistically meeting the needs of the retarded child and themselves. This, in turn, requires the services of well-trained, competent, and sensitive counselors.

REFERENCES

Abraham, Willard. *Barbara: A Prologue.* New York, Holt, Rinehart and Winston, 1958, 94 pp.

American Medical Association. Conference report on mental retardation: A handbook for the primary physician. *Journal of the American Medical Association, 191*(3):117–166, 1965.

Appell, M. J., Williams, Clarence M., and Fishell, Kenneth N. Changes in attitudes of parents of retarded children effected through group counseling. *American Journal of Mental Deficiency, 68*(6):807–812, 1964.

Appell, Melville J. One community's approach: Planning for the mentally retarded. *Mental Retardation, 1*(5): 268–275, 311, 1963.

Begab, M. J. Counseling parents of retarded children. *Canada's Mental Health, 12*:2–5, 1964.

Begab, Michael J. Some elements and principles in community planning. *Mental Retardation, 1*(5):262–266, 304, 1963.

Bitter, J. A. Attitude change by parents of trainable mentally retarded children as a result of group discussion. *Exceptional Children, 30*:173–179, 1963.

Blodgett, Harriet E., and Warfield, Grace J. *Understanding Mentally Retarded Children.* New York, Appleton-Century-Crofts, 1959, 156 pp.

Boyd, Dan. *The Three Stages.* New York, National Association for Retarded Children, 1950, 6 pp.

Butler, George A., and Bramwell, D. M. From trial and error—How we develop a traveling clinic program. *Mental Retardation, 2*(5):286–289, 1964.

Dalton, J., and Epstein, H. Counseling parents of mildly retarded children. *Social Casework, 44*:523–530, 1963.

Danks, David. Genetic counselling. In North Ryde Psychiatric Centre. *Conference on Genetics and Mental Retardation.* Sydney, Australia, North Ryde Psychiatric Centre, 1963, 120 pp.

Daugherty, Louise G. Working with disadvantaged parents. *NEA Journal, 52*:(9), 18–20, 1963.

Doll, E. A total program for the mentally retarded. *Training School Bulletin, 60*:13–22, 1963.

Dybwad, Rosemary F. The widening role of parent organizations around the world. *Mental Retardation, 1*(6):352–358, 1963.

Egg, Maria. *When a Child is Different: A Basic Guide for Parents and Friends of Mentally Retarded Children.* New York, John Day, 1964, 155 pp.

Fotheringham, J. B. Mental retardation unit. *Canada's Mental Health, 12*:14–15, 1964.

Giannini, M. J. Counseling families during the crisis reaction to mongolism. *American Journal of Mental Deficiency, 67*(5):740–747, 1963.

Goodman, L. Continuing treatment of parents with congenitally defective infants. *Social Work, 9*:92–97, 1964.

Goshen, C. E. Mental retardation and neurotic maternal attitudes. *Archives of General Psychiatry, 9*:168–174, 1963.

Hawley, Eleanor F. The importance of extending public health nursing services to retarded children living at home. *Mental Retardation, 1*(4):243–247, 1963.

Horwitz, Julius. Of such is the kingdom of heaven. *Ladies' Home Journal, 82*(2):102g–102j, 1965.

Koch, R. A longitudinal study of 143 mentally retarded children (1955–1961). *Training School Bulletin, 61*:4–11, 1963.

Koch, Richard, Fishler, Karol, Schild, Sylvia, and Ragsdale, Nancy. Clinical aspects of phenylketonuria. *Mental Retardation, 2*(1):47–54, 1964.

Koegler, S. J. The management of the retarded child in practice. *Canadian Medical Association Journal, 89*:1009–1014, 1963.

Mahoney, Stanley C. Terminology, communication, and public education in mental retardation and mental illness. *Mental Retardation, 2*(5):267–271, 1964.

Murray, Max A. (Mrs.) Needs of parents of mentally retarded children. *American Journal of Mental Deficiency, 63*(6):1078–1088, 1959.

New York State Department of Mental Hygiene. Tommy stayed at home. *Mental Retardation, 1*(4):216–218, 237, 1963.

O'Connor, Patricia, and Caffey, Paula. Time study on clinic evaluations of mentaly retarded children. *Mental Retardation, 2*(1):55–60, 1964.

Olshansky, Simon, Johnson, Gertrude C., and Sternfeld, Leon. Attitudes of some GP's toward institutionalizing mentally retarded children. *Mental Retardation, 1*(1):18–20, 57–59, 1963.

Paediatric Society of the South-East Metropolitan Region. *The Needs of Mentally Handicapped Children.* London, National Society for Mentally Handicapped Children, 1962, 72 pp.

Patterson, Letha L. Some pointers for professionals. *Children, 3*(1):13–17, 1956.

President's Panel on Mental Retardation. *Bibliography of World Literature on Mental Retardation.* Washington, D.C., U.S. Government Printing Office, 1964, 564 pp.

Reed, S. *Counseling in Medical Genetics,* Philadelphia, W. B. Saunders, 1963, 278 pp.

Roos, Philip. Psychological counseling with parents of retarded children. *Mental Retardation, 1*(6):345–350, 1963.

Schueman, H. Further observations on the psychodynamics of parents of retarded children. *Training School Bulletin, 60*:70–74, 1963.

Stacey, Chalmers L., and DeMartino, Manfred F., eds. *Counseling and Psychotherapy with the Mentally Retarded: A Book of Readings.* New York, Free Press, 1957, 478 pp.

Standifer, Frances R. Parents helping parents. *Mental Retardation, 2*(5):304–307, 1964.

Stevens, Harvey A. The administrator looks at in-service training. *Mental Retardation, 1*(1):13–15, 1963.

Thoreson, R. W. Disability viewed in its cultural context. *Journal of Rehabilitation, 30*:12–13, 1964.

Thurston, J. R. Counseling the parents of mentally retarded children. *Training School Bulletin, 60*:113–117, 1963.

Weitz, Henry. *Behavior Change through Guidance.* New York, Wiley, 1964, 225 pp.

44 PARENT COUNSELING

Leo Kanner

From *Children Limited,* April 1956. Reprinted with the permission of the National Association for Retarded Children and the author. Dr. Kanner is professor emeritus of child psychiatry, Johns Hopkins University, Baltimore, Md.

At this stage of the development of professional interest in mental retardation, it may be taken for granted that adequate help to the patients' families is readily accepted as a major obligation. No examination and no plan of treatment can be regarded as complete without a meaningful explanation to the parents and a consideration of their curiosities and emotional involvements.

Parents are no longer dealt with merely as passive recipients of authoritatively presented wisdom but as deeply concerned persons who can, and should be, prepared for the task of becoming understanding and active participants. Parent counseling has rightly become an indispensable part of the overall clinical procedure.

No one has offered more valid and more practically usable material for the contents and logical steps of such counseling than have the parents themselves. There are worthwhile compilations of questions asked by them, indicating specific areas of puzzlement, needs for clarification, etiological quandaries, unrealistic expectations, attitudes of ambivalence, disillusionment, and guilt, over and above the desire for an unequivocal, easily comprehended appraisal of the child's condition in terms of domestic, scholastic, and communal relationships.

These questions vary, of course, depending on the degree of the retardation, the general family constellation, economic circumstances, ideas about social prestige, and, last but not least, the inquirers' own personalities. Many, if not most, of the questions are asked not solely for the sake of obtaining factual information but with recognizable overtones of anxiety, more or less veiled requests for reassurance or expiation, sometimes—at least initially—an air of belligerent defensiveness.

A further significant issue is introduced by the fact that, by the time we get to see the parents, they bring with them not only perplexities which have arisen within themselves but also manifold reactions to earlier pronouncements coming from external sources which have exerted a powerful influence on their self-esteem and on their handling of the retarded child.

These sources often represent a meshwork of criticism, injunctions, misconceptions, false hopes or equally false dire predictions pelted upon the parents by well-intentioned but poorly informed relatives, magazine articles, and even physicians.

We are all too familiar with the instances of fathers and grandparents who, closing their eyes to the unwelcome reality, keep blaming the mother for the difficulties presented by the child; she is accused for doing too much for him or not enough, of being responsible for his development shortcomings through pampering or through neglect.

We are confronted more frequently than we should like to be with parents whose medical adviser has thought it expedient to tell them that their child will "outgrow" his lag and "catch up" with his coevals or, at the other extreme, that the child, being hopeless, should be "put away" in an institution, which is presented to them as something like a premature coffin. We hold in recent memory the cries of "Hosanna!" emitted in a widely distributed popular periodical with regard to the brightening effects of glutamic acid, the Bernadine Schmidt claims, and the transvascularization technique.

PARENTAL CURIOSITIES

All of these matters form the gist of parental questions, which are asked regularly with a great deal of feeling and to which the inquirers hope to get straightforward and sympathetic answers, without evasion and without hedging. For the purposes of an organized discussion, these curiosities can be divided into five separate, though interdependent and overlapping, groups centered around the features of diagnosis, genesis, prognosis, the child's place in the family structure, and therapeutic management.

Diagnostic Formulation

It goes without saying that any diagnostic formulation offered to the family must be based on the clear knowledge of the patient's status, derived from a thorough physical, psychological, and social investigation. But it is also evident that the form of disclosure must be adapted to the type of the parents' orientation toward the child, themselves, and their environment.

There are those who seek professional confirmation of their own observations which have resulted in a mature acknowledgment of actuality accepted not with glee, to be sure, but with a determination to make life as comfortable for all concerned as is possible under the circumstances.

There are others who, though not unaware of the child's handicap, go about in search of some culprit that keeps their offspring from utilizing his supposedly normal capacities; they look for someone to discover a malfunctioning organ, condemn an allegedly inexperienced school teacher, or recommend harsh discipline for the child who "stubbornly" refuses to live up to their expectations.

There are, thirdly, those who, unable to face an unpleasant reality, resort to its uncompromising denial. Things can be further complicated if the two parents and other influential members of the family group differ in their emotional orientation.

Obviously, it is relatively easy to guide a maturely accepting parent, more difficult to counsel one bent on finding disguises, and imperative to exercise much skill to lift the ostriches' heads out of the sand.

In all instances, much tact is required. Even the most unaccepting parent is not a villain. The different types of attitudes are deeply anchored in the emotional backgrounds of the individual parents.

We cannot nowadays dismiss the topic of diagnostic counseling without reference to a trend which, growing in the course of the past decade, has had rather disturbing repercussions. It stems from the recognition that severe emotional disturbance can result in poor intellectual functioning on the part of children who have come into the world with average or better than average endowment. This is especially true of early childhood schizophrenia and infantile autism.

The increasing knowledge of these conditions marks a major progress in the realm of modern psychiatry. But in consequence of this, quite a few professional people have become reluctant to acknowledge the fact of innate mental retardation as such. Parents are told much too hastily that their imbecile or idiotic children, far from being inherently defective, suffer from the results of an "emotional block" which should be removed by intensive psychotherapy of the child and both parents.

This not only calls for backbreaking financial expenditure but has convinced many parents that it was their emotional status and resulting practices which brought about the child's failure to develop. Far too many patients are taken to our clinic by pauperized, guilt-laden parents after months or years of this sort of treatment.

In view of such experiences, which are less sporadic than one should like to believe, it cannot be emphasized strongly enough that there are adequate differential diagnostic criteria, the disregard of which verges on malpractice.

PROBLEMS OF ETIOLOGY

Once the issue of diagnosis has been settled, parental solicitude converges on the problem of etiology. These are some typical questions:

What is the cause of our child's retardation?
What about heredity?
Is it safe to have another child?
Is there any danger that our normal children's offspring might be similarly affected?
Have we personally contributed to our child's condition?
Why did this have to happen to us?

It is as yet not possible to answer all these questions unequivocally. Science has not advanced sufficiently to make omniscient persons of the consulted advisers. Aside from the fact that causes of retardation are not always the same in all instances and that there may be multiple contributing factors in the same instance, the search for an ultimate cause runs against the barrier of our incomplete knowledge. We can, in individual cases, refer with assurance to the effects of the mother's German measles in the first trimester of pregnancy or to the vagaries of Rh incompatibility. But in the vast majority, there is no recourse to a specific pathogen.

I have never encountered a parent who respected me less because, in answer to the question about the cause of his or her child's retardation, I made no secret of my inability to supply a definite answer. As I have pointed out elsewhere, intelligent parents usually realize fully that would-be erudite terms, such as congenital or constitutional, beg rather than answer their question.

What most of them hope to hear is indeed not so much a piece of etiological wisdom in terms of Greek or Latin origin as an authoritative and sympathetic endorsement of themselves, of their human and parental competence, of their right not to blame themselves for what has happened. They certainly can get the satisfaction of learning from an expert in the field that they as well as the patient can be acquitted of any responsibility for the developmental lag.

Even this attempt at needed exoneration calls for an overhauling of the parents' reasons for their belief that their own interference is the primary cause of the trouble. Such a belief may have complex and conflicting ramifications. It may conceal the hope that, if the condition is one made by man, it can also be unmade by man and is therefore reversible.

At the same time, however, there is the more easily ascertainable tormenting hunt for deeds and omissions which might have stunted the child's progress. This addition of self-insult to injury may have been reinforced by unfriendly inlaws and neighbors and, even more harrowingly, by looking upon the child's retardation as a punishment for premarital missteps.

At that, we are on safer ground in our counseling functions when we try to relieve parental guilt feelings than when we are faced with the issue of heredity. The parents' interest, when they express their curiosity, is more than academic. By the time they come to us, they have more than likely ransacked their family closets and may, or may not, have found a skeleton there. In either case, we cannot be very accommodating in so far as an outright verdict is concerned.

Available statistics are contradictory because some have been compiled in institutions, others extramurally, still others from combined institutional and noninstitutional populations. Furthermore, no distinction has been made in most numerical depositions between absolute, relative, and apparent retardation, so that heterogeneous elements were thrown together as if they had a scientifically justified common denominator.

The counselor is helped by the fact that parents who themselves are unintelligent are not usually bothered about this issue. Intelligent parents can be reminded that, had they, coming of sound ancestry and being healthy in body and mind, consulted an expert in genetics, he could not possibly have predicted the birth of a retarded child and would have seen no cause for dissuading them from procreating. Their child's retardation must be put down as "an accident of Nature."

If these same parents have one or more well endowed children, it is pleasant to be able to point out to them that they have the demonstrated capacity for producing normal offspring.

But most inquiries about heredity are less oriented toward the past than toward the future. What about the fate of subsequent conceptions? What is to be expected of the offspring of the patient's normal brothers and sisters?

The problem is especially vivid in the minds of couples whose first and only child is retarded. They would wish fervently to enjoy the experience of bringing up a well functioning child and yet dread a repetition of the mishap. The assurance that lightning usually does not strike twice in the same place rarely has the effect of alleviating the fear.

Can we as parents' counselors guarantee fair weather ahead? Mongolism, phenylpyruvic acid oligophrenia, Tay–Sachs' disease, and quite a number of so-called heredo-degenerative disorders have been known to occur in more than one member of the family. I saw recently two healthy, college-graduate people whose first child died of brain tumor at four years, the second, hydrocephalic, was stillborn, the third and fifth pregnancies terminated in miscarriage, and the fourth child, the only survival, has an IQ of 65. In this instance, one would certainly be positive in discouraging further procreation.

On the whole, however, it seems wise to point out to parents whose first child is retarded that, as their experience has shown, every pregnancy entails a risk and that no one can predict the outcome with absolute certainty.

It is well to remember that the parents' inquiry is more than a simple quest for information. Behind it is sometimes a scheme, not altogether conscious, to be sure, to throw the whole burden of responsibility on the adviser. If they are told to go ahead and the second child also turns out to be retarded, they are clear of any blame. They can point an accusing finger at the adviser who has told them what they wanted to hear.

The initiative should always be left with the parents. If they do commit themselves in favor of having another child, they should be advised to do so only after they have been able to free themselves of the anticipation of disaster. Constant dread before and after the arrival of the new baby is apt to create an attitude not conducive to a wholesome relationship even with the healthiest and sturdiest child.

Prognostic Guidance

Parents who watch their child fall behind reasonable expectations cannot help but wonder about his future. They look for prognostic guidance from their professional mentor. They ask: "What will our child be like when he (or she) grows up? Will he ever talk? Can we expect graduation from high school? From grammar school? Will our child ever be mature enough to marry? Do you think that our child should be sterilized and, if so, at what age?"

As everywhere in medicine, any prognostic evaluation depends, of course, on a correct diagnosis. There are situations, especially when we are confronted with patients in the first two or three years of life, which call for caution in arriving at a definite conclusion. Matters of responsiveness, negativism, reactions to separation from the mother, or, in her presence, clinging to her may blur the psychometric results even at the hands of a skillful examiner.

It is then best to keep one's own judgment in abeyance and suggest repeated studies in stated intervals until a clear picture emerges. When we ourselves have obtained a sufficiently adequate estimate of the child's present and future potentialities, we are under obligation to transmit our information to the parents frankly and kindly.

I have known pediatricians who, out of a mistaken notion of charity, withheld their knowledge from the parents with the underlying attitude: "These are nice people and I hate to shock them; let them find out for themselves in the due course of time and then it will be easier to advise them."

Deception, no matter from what motive, is deplorable. We have no right to lull parents into a false sense of security. They expect the truth from us. Frankness, to be effective, does not have to deteriorate into brutal and argumentative frankness.

If parents are too distressed about the future outlook, they can be helped to learn to take the child in installments. They can see progress if a child, however retarded, can do more at the age of five years than he had done at four. This makes them look forward to the time when, at six years, he will be capable of doing more than he does now at five.

Family Structure

The retarded child's place in the family structure represents another important area of parent counseling. Parents ask: "How are we to explain him to our normal children? How is his presence in the home likely to affect them? How can we give him the needed extra attention without making them feel that they are neglected?"

In addition, there are many quandaries which are not formulated as clearly conceived questions but can be inferred from the parents' general attitudes which ring through the tenor of their part of the interview as genuine fondness, sacrificial overprotection, resigned fatalism, perfectionistic impatience, or outright hostility.

Besides, in considering the family structure, more than the parents and children are involved. The parents' relationship with their own parents and siblings and the group of inlaws is often tied up inextricably and sometimes confusingly with the role assigned to the retarded child in the total kinship circle.

The degree of his retardation, his placidity or restlessness, sedateness or destructiveness tend further to mitigate or aggravate already existing attitudes. It must also be remembered that aggressiveness and irritability are not necessarily the attributes of retardation but, more often than not, are the child's response to pressures put upon him from without by demands exceeding his ability and from within by self-contrast with his normal siblings.

Jealousies on his part may arise on this basis, especially if he is made aware of his imperfections through teasing and name-calling, and jealousies on the part of the siblings may be based on their resentment of any protectively or pityingly preferential treatment given the retarded child.

There are many parents who heap all their attention on their handicapped offspring because they feel, or like to make themselves believe, that their normal children are well enough to "shift for themselves."

I know a chemist and his wife who trapped themselves completely around their imbecile son and so utterly obliterated their contact with the healthy daughter that she developed a hatred of her parents and her brother, left them as soon as she was old enough to do so, and has no communication whatever with them.

Early parent counseling might have precluded this anomalous situation.

Therapeutic Planning

All of these considerations are an indispensable prelude to the kind of therapeutic planning which could be worked out with the family as informed and understanding collaborators.

Much has been made of the issue of parental cooperation, with the ready bestowal of laudatory epithets on those who obediently nod consent and the disapproval of those whose emotional involvement makes it difficult for them to bow to *ex cathedra* recommendations of residential school placement, special classes, or anything else.

Cooperation is not submission to the mentor's precepts. The term, "parent counseling," would be a misnomer if it were understood as a one-sided exercise in dispensing a take-it-or-leave-it set of rules.

Good counseling knows how to listen, how to sense parental attitudes so that, if this be required, they can be modified for their own benefit and that of the child and the rest of the family group. Any arrangement, whether it be of a medical, psychological, sociological, or educational character, will have its maximal effect only if considered in the light of this overall setting.

45 SOME POINTERS FOR PROFESSIONALS

Letha L. Patterson

From *Children,* Vol. 1, No. 3, February 1956, pp. 13–17. Reprinted with the permission of the U.S. Department of Health, Education, and Welfare and the author. Mrs. Patterson is medical editor of the Bruce Publishing Company.

One of the most heartwarming aspects of being the mother of a retarded child these days is in being a part of a profound partnership which is developing between lay and professional people.

Of all life's problems, those presented by a handicapped child (and particularly a mentally handicapped child) require the utmost in teamwork within professions, among professions, and between professional and lay people, especially parents.

All over the country we parents are attempting to assume responsibilities appropriate to the partnership through helping to define our separate roles and in heightening our communications in order to save other families from unnecessary trauma.

Dr. Martha M. Eliot, formerly Chief of the Children's Bureau recently said: "When officials of public agencies ask what kinds of services should be provided for retarded children, my advice is 'ask the parents.' . . . [they] are often best qualified to say *what* help they need, though professional persons will have to provide the *hows.*" [1]

Thus, we laymen and professionals are indispensable to one another in our efforts to make up for past neglect of this serious medical, emotional, social, and educational problem.

Perhaps I can bring together for the readers of this journal for professionals some of the written and spoken insights which have come my way from both professional workers and parents. These, I feel, are relevant for those of you who find it your task to help families face this heartbreaking problem—whether you are physicians, psychologists, social workers, nurses, teachers, or administrators. On the basis of these and my own experience I urge:

1. *Tell us the nature of our problem as soon as possible.*

When I said this to a class of students of child psychiatry at the University of Minnesota Medical School, I was asked by an alert student, "But Mrs. Patterson, what can the physician do when he is not sure himself and doesn't want to worry the parents?"

"Just be honest with us," was my reply.

It takes great sensitivity and intuition to take a mother's couched remarks and detect that they spell "worry." Often we parents are concerned

[1] Martha M. Eliot. Unpublished address to the National Association for Retarded Children, Boston, 1954.

just as early as our practitioner, but we are reluctant to put our fears and worries into words. However, we give plenty of hints that we want our professional counselor to help us get them into words, to lead us on the proper course—whether that means waiting a while or consulting with specialists immediately. It is a wise counselor who knows when he does not have the answers and is willing to admit it.

One of my psychiatrist friends put it this way: "When I am faced with a worried mother or father, *I have got a problem.* Either there is something wrong with the child, or something wrong with the parents, or both. And if I can't identify the trouble, then I am obligated to get this family to someone who can."

2. *Always see both parents.*

Fathers are parents, too, and all professional workers need to be reminded of this. Both parents should be present whenever possible, and at least on first consultations regarding a child's handicap.

It is very difficult for a mother to go home and restate, interpret, and answer questions about a problem she does not clearly understand herself. Often the problem, with its fears, has brought about a lack of communication between mother and father. This is particularly true in a young marriage or when the retarded child is the first child. Establishing adequate communication is difficult in any marriage. Finding the words to support one another in *this* problem has been impossible for some of us. We have needed an objective person through whom to talk.

Unfortunately, all husbands (and wives) are not like the one who, when he learned that their little daughter would not progress like other children, said to his wife: "Honey, we don't know what lies ahead of us—but whatever it is, we can handle it because we are strong people."

Many of us can find this strength, however, if you will help us.

Another reason for seeing both parents is that both need to be pulled along together in their understanding and acceptance. I have seen too many mothers who realized the need for institutional care and were ready to "place" a child while the fathers trailed behind ignoring reality, not to recognize the great need for a common understanding. Sometimes it is the mother who will not admit that something is wrong and insists that her child stay in regular school classes when a special course of study is indicated, while the father suffers along in silence, afraid to precipitate the issue. If you but knew the isolation that can exist behind our four walls!

3. *Watch your language.*

Parents need to understand the implications of their problem, but too often we are given professional gobbledygook, or at the other extreme, plain talk of an obnoxious variety. Words like "idiot," "moron," and "feebleminded" used to be excellent and descriptive clinical terms but they no longer apply to our retarded children. Unimaginative writers and purveyors of so-called humor have polluted the meanings with connotations of social or moral deficiency in the mentally normal.

On the other hand, there was the doctor at a residential institution who wrote to two parents stating that their son was ill with "cervical lymphatic adenitis." The worried family did considerable research to find that the child simply had swollen glands of the neck.

The child psychiatrist, into whose capable hands my husband and I finally could put our problem was very sensitive in his use of words. He avoided "moron," "feebleminded," and even "mental retardation" by encouraging us to evaluate our child's developmental status. And when he confirmed our findings, we felt quite pleased with ourselves. He always referred to our boy as "your son," "your lad," or "Stephen" with a voice filled with great compassion so that we started thinking more about Steve's problem and less about our own hurt egos.

4. *Help us to see that this is OUR problem.*

One way, of course, is by example—by not taking the problem over for us.

Too many well meaning professional people in the past have thought they knew what was good for us and have recommended, even insisted on, institutionalization. We know, now, that denial of the existence of the child is not the solution for either child or parent, that abandonment is not the answer, and that it is psychiatrically unhealthy to rob parents of their responsibility for planning. Only as we parents are helped to work through our problems can we find any peace of mind. If we have not planned for our child ourselves, if someone else has made the decisions, we have not really made up our own minds and so must keep going over the ground again and again. We may never be at peace with the solution which was reached for us.

Administrators of institutions tell us that the best help for families in adjusting to their child's placement is the fact that the parents themselves have decided—with adequate professional guidance, of course—that placement is best for the child in relation to the total family welfare.

There is another reason for showing us that this is our problem. You have no idea how much unprofessional, unsolicited, and untried advice we get from well meaning people—our neighbors, relatives, friends, and even strangers standing on street corners. When, with your guidance and example, we realize that *this is our problem,* we can shut our ears to the static and rely on our own judgment. But we need your professional support in helping us to feel competent in making these decisions, your confidence that we will ultimately make the proper decision for care in our particular case, your assurance that there is no failure if we change our plan when circumstances change—life situations and retarded children present different problems at different times. You can help us explore the possibilities for meeting our problem; support us in adjusting to our decision; act as a continuing sounding board against which we can bounce our own thinking; and give us a good, sturdy shoulder on which to lean when we get dizzy going through the maze of decisions.

5. *Help us to understand our problem.*

Parents differ in the quantity and quality of information they can absorb during different phases of this problem. What they want and need depends greatly on the individual, but many of us have had to search for the knowledge we needed in order to understand our child.

Six years ago, when I began my search, a severe scarcity existed in printed material on the subject of mental retardation. Today, there are many fine and helpful publications in this field. One of the best that I have seen for new parents is Jacob's *New Hope for the Retarded Child,*[2] which is inexpensive enough to be used as a handout. Many other books, bibliographies, journals, and pamphlets provide excellent sources for parents.

Regardless of what we parents are able to read and absorb, we will always have questions to ask. We will continue to need support from someone, whether our child is at home or away—particularly in those days which follow the confirmation that mental retardation *is* our problem.

One medical counselor asks parents to come back several weeks after he has given them the bad news, knowing that they will have questions which could not come to the surface during the emotional strain of hearing the verdict. Moreover, he sees to it that the parents get to a social worker and he also urges them to join an association for retarded children.

Frequently he turns their names over to the local association's "parents counsel committee" requesting that some mature couple—a mother *and* a father—call on them. He has found that parents who have successfully faced their problems can offer a special kind of help to new families which transcends his professional services. Further, he has seen the therapeutic effects of parents working together in organizations to improve the lot of the retarded and their families. Incidentally, he was initially one of the "pros" who were afraid of this "lay" movement.

6. *Know your resources.*

In referring to services, Dr. Eliot has called the retarded child "nobody's baby." Certainly there is evidence in most states that services are disjointed and uncoordinated. Rarely is there any one place which can put parents in touch with the resources that *are* available.

In Minnesota, where the county social worker is the local resource for parents, a booklet, *You Are Not Alone,* telling parents where and how

[2] Walter Jacob, *New Hope for the Retarded Child,* Public Affairs Pamphlet No. 210 (New York: Public Affairs Committee, 1954).

to seek help, has been distributed to members of the state medical association, county welfare boards, clergymen of all faiths, family and welfare services, clinics, public-health nurses, associations for retarded children, and newspaper editors in the hopes that the booklet (or the information) will be passed along to parents. It was produced by the statewide Conference Committee on Mental Deficiency, a professional-lay body.

California has started meeting this problem with information centers for the parents of retarded children, set up in Los Angeles and San Francisco by the state Department of Mental Hygiene. The psychiatric social workers assigned to this task have a variety of functions—counseling individual parents, putting them in touch with resources, providing information to public and private agencies, and serving as consultants in community planning.

Other states are developing a network of clinics with built-in social services for the sustaining help which is so necessary.

Anyone who has carried a handicapped child from one waiting room to the next in an effort to gather resources into one piece will appreciate the significance of these several efforts to avail parents of the services that do exist.

7. *Never put us on the defensive.*

All parents make mistakes in raising children. Those of us who have a retarded child are bound to make errors, but we should not be made to feel guilty about them.

One day I said to my medical counselor: "You know, of course, that I was angry at you for a good long time for 'confirming my diagnosis,' but never once have you put me on the defensive about it or any of the mistakes that we have made in relation to Steve."

"Why should I?" he countered. "How do I know I could have done any better than you, had I been in your circumstances?"

He went on to give this definition of "good parents": "Parents are good parents, when to the best of their ability, understanding, and circumstances, they meet as adequately as possible the needs of their children."

8. *Remember that parents of retarded children are just people.*

This has been *my* most amazing discovery. We are just people with a serious problem, a great sorrow—a living sorrow. We have the same strengths and weaknesses as others in the general population. We have the same problems, the same handicaps. But when the burden of mental retardation is heaped upon us, often these problems and defects are magnified and we, in turn, create problems for those of you who must deal with us. But *as a group,* I do not think we should be considered abnormal, particularly in view of the poor cultural attitude toward our problem, the lack of interest and services, and the fact that some parents have made great personal and family sacrifices to carry this "cause" to the public conscience.

You cannot generalize about parents of retarded children any more than you can generalize about retarded children. Gifted, average, or limited, any of us can find our problems complicated by own own emotional make-up. Professional people working with us must learn to appraise these variables in our intelligence and emotional stability.

Apropos of this are the technical articles which some of us read. Why do we *always* face such words as "anxieties, hostilities, frustrations, guilt-feelings," and other emotionally charged words to describe our reactions? Such pseudoscientific certainties merely serve to make parents feel even more inadequate, it seems to me.

You should take seriously the comment of a New Jersey parent: ". . . Is not what appears to be 'guilt feelings' to professionals, merely concern with the child's welfare, mingled with grief over his handicap?" [3]

"All parents experience some feelings of guilt about illness in their children . . . ," Dr. Julius B. Richmond, pediatrician, of Syracuse University has said. If outward manifestations of these feelings persist in us after you have assured us that "no act or omission or commission" on our part has been responsible for the condition of our child, perhaps our feelings might be more aptly described as "regret." We are bound to feel regret if we have rejected this child, if we have struck out at him and created problems for him. With this regret we very likely feel anger at not having had the proper guidance at the times we needed it.

Might not some of our hostility be nothing more than righteous indignation over the neglect of our problem? Actually, if some of the pioneers in the parent group movement had not become "mad" in the early days, our problem would still be largely ignored. Who can say, on the basis of present knowledge, when anxieties are neurotic overreactions, if parents must ask: "What will happen to this child after we are gone?" "How can we pay for expensive care outside our home?" "Where can we hire a sitter so that we can take a vacation?"

Whatever labels we use for these feelings, they have added up to a great determination—you might call it "compulsion"—for some of us to see to it that new parents coming along can walk a smoother path. And there is considerable evidence that many of these new parents are avoiding some of the emotional scars which some of us bear.

Dan Boyd, a New Jersey parent, has described three stages in the growth of a parent of a mentally retarded child: (1) Why did this happen to me? (self-pity) (2) What can I do for my own child and family? (3) What can we do for others? [4]

These stages can be intermingled. The fact that a parent is working in

[3] National Association for Retarded Children, New York, *Children Limited, 4* (June 1955), 5.

[4] Dan Boyd, *The Three Stages (In the Growth of a Parent of a Mentally Retarded Child)*, pamphlet, National Association for Retarded Children, New York (August 1953).

an organization "to help all retarded children" does not necessarily mean that he has grown with his own problem. Some can be stage-3 leaders, without having graduated from stage 1. Such self-pitying parents are the hardest to help. It often takes a long wait and the greatest skill on the part of professional counselors and their parent counterparts to help them to begin to make realistic plans for their own child.

Most parents, however, mature quite rapidly under the stimulus of the group. Self-pity fades when they find that they are not alone. Soon they are seeking to learn from and emulate the parents who have met their problems successfully. And before they know it, they are experiencing the healing that goes with helping another family. Some move on to be eager for all parents to have access to the organization which has rescued them from desolation.

Even these mature stage-3 parents can slip back, temporarily, into stage 2, when a problem arises at home or when previous decisions must be reviewed. During these times we can be very difficult. Then you must support us, while feeling "nothing but plain, simple, humble reverence before the mystery of our misfortune," to use the words of John Cowper Powys.[5]

This means that you must look at your own feelings about us and our children. If you do not have a natural feeling of concern for the mentally retarded, if you feel indifferent to or repelled by children who are not mentally normal or by parents under great stress, then you should not be dealing with us at all.

9. *Remember that we are parents and that you are professionals.*

Some of us are becoming so well-informed in certain areas of this problem and we are associating with you in so many different pursuits that, at times, it must be difficult to remember that we *are* parents and, as such, will always be emotionally involved with our own problem and our own child, regardless of the "objectivity" we may have about the problem generally, or another family's problem, specifically. In communicating with us you must be clear as to whether you are speaking as counselor to client, adviser to organization member, coworker, or personal friend. In this we expect you to use professional judgment.

For example, don't in front of us: belittle or countermand the opinion of one of your professional partners; make critical remarks about other parents and their handling of their child; jump to conclusions about our case without adequate clinical study or knowledge of the facts. And, of course, don't try to do a job that is outside your professional discipline.

When we see so much that needs to be done, we have little time for professional jealousies, or for the individual who uses mental retardation as

[5] John Cowper Powys, *The Meaning of Culture* (New York: Norton, 1929).

a ladder to personal success. It does not take long for us to pigeonhole a "problem professional!" whose own emotional difficulties are getting in the way of our efforts.

10. *Remember the importance of your attitude toward us.*

Sometimes I think your colleagues place too much emphasis on "objectivity" and not enough on "loving kindness." Certainly we expect you to be objective about our problem. But about us? Never! A really gifted professional person cannot *help* feeling—being subjective, attempting to stand in our shoes and to look out at our problem through our eyes—in the process of helping us. Psychiatrists call this "empathy." It is only through empathy that you can divine the proper words and acts to help us.

There are greater depths and breadths in helping parents of retarded children than many of you have realized in your initial attempts. It has been as exciting for some of us parents to watch professionals grow as it has been rewarding for professionals to watch some of us parents grow. We can help each other become more effective people through our partnership.

You are obligated, it seems to me, to "feelingly persuade" us as Shakespeare said, to help us find "what we are." We have many strengths. If you can help us convert our problem into good for mankind, help us find the sweetness in the uses of our adversity, *you* will find a far more precious jewel in your professionalism than you ever thought existed.

And you will be professionals in the most noble and magnificent sense of the word.

SECTION THIRTEEN

Organization and Administration of State and Local Programs[1]

One of the paramount issues to be resolved in providing services for the mentally retarded is the responsibility of various governmental administrative and operational units. Since the mentally retarded have long been neglected by community agencies, there are no clear-cut precedents for dealing with them. With the rapid growth of services in recent years, many agencies are operating without coordination, duplicating their efforts, competing for program-development funds, and wrangling among themselves. In the long run, this can only hinder rather than strengthen the cause. Fortunately, efforts are now being made to coordinate the work of governmental agencies and parent and professional groups.

A search was made to locate a comprehensive report of federal activities relating to the mentally retarded. No single document of reasonable size could be located. The myriad of federal agencies devoting funds and providing consulting services, plus the frequent reorganization of federal agencies, would make a comprehensive report of encyclopedic length and probably be outdated very soon.

The major federal agencies involved in program sponsorship in the field of mental retardation are: (1) U.S. Department of Health, Education, and Welfare, including the Bureau of Education for the Handicapped of the Office of Education; (2) Public Health Service, including the National Institute of Mental Health, the National Institute for Neurological Diseases and Blindness, and various other segments of the National Institutes of Health complex; (3) Rehabilitation Services Administration, including the Social and Rehabilita-

[1] National programs sponsored by various federal agencies are covered in the introductory comments to this section.

tion Service, the Children's Bureau, and the Social Security Administration. A variety of other federal agencies, such as the Departments of Labor, Interior, and Defense, all have some type of program for the mentally retarded. Of importance are the (1) HEW Secretary's Committee on Mental Retardation, and (2) the President's Committee on Mental Retardation. This is by no means meant to be a comprehensive listing. The interested reader will find in this volume a lengthy bibliography of government publications classified according to the federal agency developing the publication. This listing should assist anyone wishing to acquire more specific information concerning an individual federal agency.

From a school point of view, the most important federal agency is the Bureau of Education for the Handicapped of the Office of Education. This bureau was created by Congress and established in January 1967 to strengthen and coordinate activities in behalf of the handicapped. Its mission is to assist states, colleges, universities and other institutions, agencies, and organizations in meeting the education needs of the nation's more than five million handicapped children who require special services. Through support for educational services for the handicapped, including instructional materials, training for teachers and other personnel engaged in education of the handicapped and research, the Bureau is endeavoring to improve the quality and extent of education for the mentally retarded. It is concerned with the processes of transmission of knowledge into action through a sequence of research, development, demonstration, implementation, and adoption. The Bureau structure contains three major operating units. They are the Division of Educational Services, the Division of Research, and the Division of Training Programs. The following table summarizes major legislation that has reference to the mentally retarded.

Major Federal Legislation Relating to Education of the Mentally Retarded in Programs Sponsored by Bureau for Education of Handicapped, U.S. Office of Education

Law	*Program*	*Purpose*
P.L. 91-230 TITLE VI PART B	Education of handicapped children, preschool, elementary and secondary	To provide grants to aid states in initiation, expansion, and improvements of programs for the handicapped
P.L. 91-230 ESEA TITLE VI PART C	Supplemental educational centers and services Special programs and projects for the handicapped	To provide grants for exemplary programs or projects to meet special education needs to solve critical educational problems
P.L. 91-230 ESEA TITLE VI PART D	Recruitment of personnel and information on education of the handicapped	To provide funds to improve recruitment of special education personnel and to disseminate information concerning educational opportunities for the handicapped
P.L. 91-230 ESEA TITLE VI PART C	Regional resource centers	To assist in establishing regional centers to develop and apply the best methods of appraising special education needs of the handicapped

Major Federal Legislation Relating to Education of the Mentally Retarded in Programs Sponsored by Bureau for Education of Handicapped, U.S. Office of Education (*cont.*)

Law	*Program*	*Purpose*
P.L. 91-230 TITLE VI PART C	Early childhood education of the handicapped	To support experimental preschool and early childhood education programs for the handicapped
P.L. 90-576 TITLE I-B	Vocational educational amendments	To develop an effective vocational education program for the handicapped
P.L. 91-230 TITLE VI PART D	Training of teachers of handicapped children	To provide grants to colleges and state educational agencies for the training of teachers and specialists for the handicapped
P.L. 91-230 TITLE VI PART D	Training of physical educators and recreation personnel for the handicapped	To provide grants to colleges for professional training of physical education and recreation personnel for the handicapped
P.L. 91-230 TITLE VI PART E	Research and demonstration projects in education of handicapped children	To provide grants to promote research and demonstration, and construction of facilities to improve education of the handicapped (including IMC's)
P.L. 91-230 TITLE VI PART E	Research and demonstration projects in physical education and recreation for the mentally retarded and other handicapped	To provide grants for research and demonstration projects relating to physical education or recreation for the handicapped

A complete summary of other federal legislation affecting the mentally retarded has been prepared by Elizabeth M. Goodman[1] for the Department of Health, Education, and Welfare.

In order to develop comprehensive statewide action and cooperative programs, Congress enacted Public Law 88-156 to provide funds for comprehensive state planning to combat mental retardation. The purpose of this legislation was: (1) to determine what action is needed to combat mental retardation in each state and to survey the resources available for this purpose; (2) to develop public awareness of the mental retardation problem and the need for combating it; (3) to coordinate state and local activities relating to the various aspects of mental retardation, its prevention, treatment, or amelioration, and (4) to plan other activities leading to comprehensive state and community action to combat mental retardation. Leopold Lippman[2] recently contributed a chapter to a new book which

[1] Elizabeth M. Goodman (ed.), *Directory of Progams for Education of Handicapped Children in the U.S. Office of Education* (Washington, D.C.: Bureau of Education for the Handicapped, U.S. Department of Health, Education, and Welfare, May 1969).

[2] Leopold Lippman, "Community Organization: U.S.A.," in *Mental Retardation, Vol. 1* (New York: Grune & Stratton, Inc., 1969), pp. 239–249.

covers community organization in the United States. He covers the whole field in great depth and provides many examples of community planning.

Of recent vintage is the Model Cities Program. It is important to note that at least 75 percent of the mentally retarded in the United States are residents of those cities for which Model Cities Projects are intended. Conservative estimates of the incidence of mental retardation in inner-city neighborhoods begin at 30 percent. The figures continue to increase. Bold action programs are forthcoming through the Model Cities Program.[3]

During the summer of 1969 the President's Committee assembled specialists to discuss the problems of education of children in the inner city. This report should be available by mid-1970, and very likely will provide much information on future educational programming.

The administrator and supervisor of programs for the mentally retarded in the public schools are faced with a plethora of problems. These include adequate curriculum development, budgeting, staff procurement and housing, to name but a few. Bernice B. Baumgartner and Katherine D. Lynch [4] provide practical advice to help administrators and supervisors to provide effective school programs for mentally retarded pupils.

Primary responsibility for the mentally retarded rests with the family. However, the special problems and needs these individuals present are far too heavy a burden for their families to carry unaided. Total services can only be accomplished through the active participation of an interested citizenry and local and state leaders concerned with care, training, and welfare of the mentally retarded.

The first reading in this section, by Leopold Lippman, discusses in great detail how the State of California developed a comprehensive plan for the mentally retarded. It is followed by an article prepared by Harrie Selznick in which he describes the rapid expansion of services to the mentally retarded. He clarifies the place, responsibilities, and functions of leadership personnel in school systems. The truly forgotten mentally retarded child is one who lives in a rural area. Large numbers of these children have never attended school, in spite of compulsory laws. The State Department of Public Instruction in Wisconsin has made an all-out effort to provide assistance for special education in rural areas. In the last article in this section, John W. Melchior and Kenneth R. Blessing, discuss the implementation of rural programs and the necessity of the close cooperation of county superintendents.

[3] David B. Ray, Jr. (ed.), *The Mentally Retarded in Model Cities: Report of a Workshop* (Washington, D.C.: President's Committee on Mental Retardation, 1968).

[4] Bernice B. Baumgartner and Katherine D. Lynch, *Administering Classes for the Retarded* (New York: John Day Co., 1967).

46 A STATE PLANS FOR ITS MENTALLY RETARDED

Leopold Lippman

From *Children,* Vol. 12, No. 5, September–October 1965, pp. 171–177. Reprinted with the permission of the U.S. Department of Health, Education, and Welfare and the author. Mr. Lippman is Director of Mental Retardation Services for the City of New York.

On October 30, 1963, less than one week after President Kennedy signed Public Law 88–156, which among other provisions encouraged comprehensive state planning in mental retardation,[1] the California Study Commission on Mental Retardation held its first meeting. Fourteen months later, its final report, "The Undeveloped Resource: A Plan for the Mentally Retarded of California," [2] was delivered to Governor Brown and the California Legislature in advance of the 1965 session.

California was able to start and to conclude its comprehensive mental retardation planning 10 to 15 months ahead of the other states and jurisdictions, because the legislature had responded promptly to the challenge of the report of the President's Panel on Mental Retardation, "A Proposed Program for National Action to Combat Mental Retardation," submitted to the President the previous year.[3] The President's Panel on Mental Retardation had rendered its report in October 1962, and in the regular session of 1963 the state legislature had created the study commission, charged it to recommend proposed programs, and directed the submission of a final report by January 1965. The legislature had also appropriated sufficient funds for the commission to start its work, so that it was not necessary to wait for the Federal planning grant due under Public Law 88–156 before getting under way.

As a result of the quick action of the legislature and the governor in creating the commission, California had the honor to be the first in the nation to complete its comprehensive mental retardation plan. It also suffered the disadvantages of being first, because it could not profit by the mistakes of others. Nevertheless, its report has received wide and enthusiastic attention. Requests for copies have been received from 30 states.

[1] Arthur J. Lesser, Accent on prevention through improved service. *Children,* January–February 1964.

[2] California Study Commission on Mental Retardation, The undeveloped resource: a plan for the mentally retarded of California. Report to the Governor and the Legislature. Sacramento. January 1965.

[3] U.S. Department of Health, Education, and Welfare, The President's Panel on Mental Retardation, A proposed program for national action to combat mental retardation; a report to the President. October 1962.

PRINCIPLES EXPRESSED IN THE CALIFORNIA REPORT ON MENTAL RETARDATION

The State of California accepts a responsibility for its mentally retarded citizens.

The Study Commission believes that:

1. Mental retardation is a social problem. Every retarded person and his family are entitled to the concern and assistance of the community, expressed through public and voluntary resources. This is their right, as citizens of the United States and of California.

2. Where necessary, the State must discharge the obligation of society.

3. The best hope is prevention, and it is our responsibility to develop new knowledge through research and to apply it promptly. Meanwhile, we have an obligation to the retarded who are already with us.

4. There is some potential for growth in every human being. For each person, society should provide the opportunity to develop to the limits of his capabilities.

5. Services should be planned and provided as part of a continuum, which means that the pattern of facilities and eligibility shall be so complete as to meet the needs of each retarded person, regardless of his age or degree of handicap, and at each stage of his life development. . . .

6. Because the retarded person is a human being first, and a handicapped individual secondarily, he should have access to all the general community services that he can use in common with others. Only when integrated services fail to meet his needs should there be specialized services.

7. Services for retarded persons should be close to their homes and families. . . . Moreover, no retarded person should enter an institution who can be cared for in the community, and no one should remain in an institution who can adjust outside.

8. Research and professional training are two essential components of the total program, and a pattern of services is incomplete without them.

9. Retarded persons, or their families acting in their behalf, should have substantial freedom of choice among public and private services. This accords with the dignity of the individual and his right of self-determination for his own life.

10. The State should provide for and encourage creative flexibility in all programs operating for the mentally retarded in California.

There were many hurdles in the way of effective planning—semantic, statistical, fiscal, administrative, and political, among others. The commission chairman himself repeatedly expressed the view that the very commission structure was inappropriate to the task. Nevertheless, this was the machinery the legislature had created; these were the individuals the governor had appointed; and the members of the commission cared enough about the subject to do their best with the assignment.

LEARNING THE FACTS

The first problems had to do with facts: How many retarded persons are there in California? What are their needs? What services now exist? And (as a basis for legislative recommendations) what do the current statutes provide?

The last two questions were the easiest to answer. They required a great deal of careful, painstaking work, the final results of which were neither polished nor wholly satisfactory, because of time and other limitations, but some usable answers were available. To get the facts on present services, the commission created a committee which inquired about programs of state departments and local public and voluntary agencies in 11 counties. The resulting report [4] was published about midway in the commission's work. It proved to be a valuable document.

The matter of existing statutes was a deceptively simple question, because the state's laws go back many decades, provisions affecting the retarded appear in many codes uncoordinated with each other, and terminology varies widely. Nevertheless, a skilled legal researcher, working under the direction of the commission chairman, himself an attorney, produced what has proved to be the first summary collection of statutes on the subject anywhere in the United States.[5] The compendium directed attention not only to the statutes dealing specifically with the retarded, but also to oblique references and even omissions which might affect the rights of the retarded.

It was the first question, however, that was the trickiest. To determine how many mentally retarded persons there are in California, it is necessary to count them. But, dealing with the difficult question of how requires first facing the challenging one: Count whom? Probing this problem revealed a more basic one: To deal realistically with mental retardation, one had to define it. This proved a knotty point throughout the life of the commission.

Prevalence clearly depended on definition. A different concept—even a few words changed—would yield different figures, and thereby a different statement of the extent and nature of the problem. The commission rejected intelligence quotient as the criterion, but even such a simple numerical device poses problems. Should the cutoff point be IQ 70? Or 75? Or 85? The dif-

[4] California Study Commission on Mental Retardation, Report of survey by committee on existing resources, functions, and coverage. Sacramento. June 1964.

[5] California Study Commission, Mental retardation and the law: a survey of California laws affecting the mentally retarded. Sacramento. July 1964.

ference in prevalence figures is enormous, especially in the upper ranges—and the nature of the problem changes substantially.

The study commission looked at many different definitions, including the four-ply criterion index developed in Delaware by Jastak and his colleagues.[6] The commission also reviewed the few community prevalence studies which have been conducted over the years. A highly sophisticated project was under way in Riverside, Calif., under the direction of research workers from Pacific State Hospital, but the results were not available in time for the commission's report.

In the end, after much consultation and thought, the commission accepted the language which had been developed by the American Association on Mental Deficiency: "Mental retardation refers to subaverage general intellectual functioning which originates during the developmental period and is associated with impairment in adaptive behavior." [7]

This was at least a working definition; but the problem still remained to discover reliable prevalence figures. Despite all available information, including some preliminary data from the Riverside study, the commission found itself short of hard facts. Clearly, it was impossible to survey the actual population of California in the time available. The commission was unwilling to accept the widely used prevalence figure of 3 percent, because the meager evidence available suggested this was too high. Still, it had no reliable substitute.

After considerable research, and much debate within the commission, it was agreed that the prevalence (if not the incidence) of mental retardation varies with age, and that therefore a single percentage figure would not apply. The commission agreed that the prevalence figure might reach 3 percent for school-age children, but that it would be much lower for newborns, rising among preschool children and tapering downward for adults. This concept produced an irregular curve which peaked during the age span eight–sixteen. Included in this concept was the idea that the individual may move in and out of the group called "retarded" in the course of his lifetime, depending on the degree of his handicap in relation to the demands posed by society and the availability of resources to help him become self-sufficient.

A SOCIOLOGICAL PROBLEM

Related to questions of definition and prevalence was a sociological problem. Should the culturally disadvantaged be counted among the retarded? Their environmentally caused lag is not the conventional mental deficiency,

[6] Joseph F. Jastak, Halsey M. MacPhee, Martin Whiteman, Mental retardation: its nature and incidence. (New York: University Publishers, 1963).

[7] Rick Heber, A manual on terminology and classification in mental retardation. *American Journal of Mental Deficiency* (monograph supplement, 2d edition), 1961.

and yet their performance in school and their potential as adults are distinctly lower than the average among their peers. The commission noted that low income, poor housing, and inferior medical care have marked adverse effects on intellectual development. Therefore, it offered a series of recommendations, including the provision of earlier and more regular prenatal care, direct social services to indigent families and children, retraining of adults for new job opportunities, and compensatory education for retarded children coming from disadvantaged homes.

Fortunately, positive efforts were already under way in California to provide compensatory education programs with the use of the federal support available under the Economic Opportunity Act. The commission's observations were helpful as reinforcement in getting these programs established.

ADMINISTRATIVE PROBLEMS

Planning had to take place in an administrative and historical context, yet not necessarily accept the existing pattern as best.

In his charge to the commission at its first meeting, the governor said:

"You are not bound to any past or present pattern of services nor, certainly, of administrative organization."

However, this was easier to say than to observe. Among the general public—and to some extent within the commission—it was assumed that the department which operated the state hospitals had primary and indeed exclusive concern with the mentally retarded. The feat was, of course, that far more retarded children received direct services in public schools throughout the state than in the state hospitals; and beyond this, with the exception of scattered community services supported in part with state funds, such as a few diagnostic clinics and sheltered workshops, there were no public services for the huge majority of California's mentally retarded children. Nevertheless, the stereotyped reaction was: "It's the problem of the Department of Mental Hygiene. Let's leave it there." The commission found it difficult to break through this pattern of thinking and at the same time retain the valuable existing services, the body of professional competence, and the intricate network of human interrelationships which had been built up over the years.

The problem was solved in part, and in some degree unfortunately, by circumstances. During the active life of the commission, three men served successively as directors of the Department of Mental Hygiene. All were first-rate officials who, although actively interested and cooperative, were, for obvious reasons, preoccupied with larger concerns. It was thus difficult to maintain momentum or continuity in the relationships between the commission and the department. As a result, what might have been an unhealthy domination of the commission by one department became instead a partial vacuum which actually diminished the commission's effectiveness in planning.

There was another aspect to interdepartmental relations as they manifested themselves within the commission. The law specified that the directors of five state departments should be members of the commission. (These were education, mental hygiene, employment, public health, and social welfare. A sixth, rehabilitation, was later added by amendment.) One of these, the superintendent of public instruction, was an independently elected official; the others were appointees of the governor. Most of the departments represented had preexisting concern with services for the mentally retarded, in some cases involving budgets of millions of dollars.

Experience with bureaucracy would lead one to expect that under such circumstances there would be a struggle for enlargement of power. In the field of mental retardation, however, it appears that the customary rules do not always apply. Rather than empire building, there seemed to be some tendency to avoid additional responsibility. Departmental spokesmen on occasion would suggest that particular tasks be referred elsewhere. To be sure, these views were expressed from the honest conviction that the proposed services would not fit into the existing pattern, but the effect was to reject new program ideas and leave them in limbo.

The question of each department's role was part of a large challenge the commission faced; How to deal with the power struggle inherent in diverse professional viewpoints and organizational interests?

The governor settled part of this problem by his selection of persons to be appointed to the commission. For members "representing the general public," he could have selected six persons whose chief qualification was a concern for the civic welfare. He did not do so. Instead, for the most part, he chose persons with substantial involvement, and hence strong convictions, in the field of mental retardation.

The governor might also have selected persons to represent organizations with a stake in the problem. This again he did not do. His decision created some problems, in that certain organizations felt they had been deliberately omitted and therefore slighted; but it also freed each member of the commission to act from his own convictions rather than as an organizational representative.

Jack Halpin, the commission chairman, and I, as the executive secretary, did feel that the commission would have been stronger if its members had included a designated representative of the largest single interest group, the organized parents of the mentally retarded. Several members of the commission were parents of retarded children, but they were not selected to be organizational representatives. They served as individuals, drawing on their personal as well as their civic experience. (In its recommendations for a permanent planning mechanism, the commission later specified a representative for "the consumer"—by which it meant parents of the retarded, so designated.)

As chairman, the governor chose a man with training in the law and political science, and with judicial experience. By temperament, the chairman was a forceful individual, intelligent, with a respect for research, and yet one who believed in vigorous action. He was constantly striving for the imaginative approach, the innovation, the creative solution. Some of his proposals startled other members of the commission and the public, but shocked people into thinking for themselves and coming up with workable alternatives.

STATE RESPONSIBILITY

A major issue in planning for more effective services to the retarded is whether such services are primarily a state or a local responsibility. This is doubtless being debated in state planning bodies throughout the nation. In California, there is a special accent on the issue in the impressive growth since 1957 of community mental health services. Under the Short–Doyle Act, the state financially assists local governments in establishing locally controlled mental health programs.

To a considerable extent, the question is part of a larger philosophical and political one, having to do with the appropriate roles of federal, state, and local governments. The California Study Commission on Mental Retardation confronted the issue directly and answered it forcefully in the opening sentence of its report: "The State of California accepts a responsibility for its mentally retarded citizens."

Despite the vigor of this assertion, there was a marked difference of viewpoint among commission members, some of them contending most earnestly that responsibility and power should rest in the counties and the communities. In its report, the commission did say, repeatedly, that services for the retarded and their families should be close to home, and that communities should take initiative, but it placed final responsibility at the state level.

CONTINUITY AND COORDINATION

Determining the specific services which the state and the communities should make available to the mentally retarded was relatively easy. The guidelines in the work of the National Association for Retarded Children, the President's Panel on Mental Retardation, and other authoritative bodies were clear enough. They simply required adaptation to the peculiarities of California's situation.

Tying these services into a usable package was, however, a more difficult task. From the outset, the commission struggled with the core question of how to effectuate the necessary "continuum of services." How insure that the retarded individual receives what he needs at each stage of his life development? How provide a balanced program of services available to everyone who needs them? How avoid a domination of the service program by one agency, either at the state or the community level? How coordinate service agencies which are essentially independent of each other? And, as important as any question, how incorporate the citizenry into the planning which must go on if services are to change in response to changing needs?

To protect the individual retarded person and assure continuity in his life, the commission recommended establishment of regional diagnostic and counseling centers. The coordinating mechanism was harder to find. The commission's answer was a Mental Retardation Program Board.

Under the commission's proposal, the board would be established by the legislature and its members would be appointed by the governor, who would also designate the chairman. The board members would include representatives of all state departments having responsibility for services to the retarded; local government units; voluntary organizations; and the "consumers" of services. Responsibilities of the board would include coordination of existing services and stimulation of new programs to meet discerned needs; development and periodic revision of a comprehensive plan for services to the retarded; setting and enforcement of standards for all such services; and leadership liaison with community mental retardation planning bodies. The board would employ an executive secretary but would not operate programs and therefore would not need a large appropriation for its own work. It would exert considerable influence, however, in its review of departmental services and proposals, and in its recommendations to the governor and the legislature.

The most unusual single feature of the Mental Retardation Program Board, as envisioned by the study commission, was to serve as a contractor in purchasing services for mentally retarded persons. In this role, the board would have fiscal responsibilities and would have the power to assign and reassign programs among departments as part of the continuous planning process. In accordance with the commission's emphasis on the importance of providing a variety of alternatives and on the need for flexibility, the board would have power to enter into contracts with either public or private service agencies at either the state or local level.

The board proposal, the most striking innovation of the commission's work, proved also to be the most controversial. In acting on this recommendation, the legislature made the board advisory only, and stripped away its proposed powers to assign and reassign programs among state departments and to serve as contractor in the purchase of services for the retarded. Instead of an executive secretary to the board, the new legislation provides for a coordinator of mental retardation programs. It does, however, provide that the departments of state government may enter into a joint powers agreement. This provision, which emerged as an amendment to the original bill, may prove to be the vehicle through which more efficient organization of services is achieved.

PRIORITIES FOR ACTION

Once the framework and the broad pattern of a comprehensive program are set, how does the planning agency move toward realization of its recommendations? The study commission's expiration date was written into the law which established it in 1963; but from the beginning it was obvious that the recommendations would not be in effect when the commission went out of existence in June 1965.

The commission met this problem with a two-barreled answer. First it recommended establishment of the Mental Retardation Program Board, which would have the ongoing function of planning for the mentally retarded. Then, because the program board could not come into existence until the legislature acted, the commission took upon itself for 1965 the board's function in offering priority recommendations for the legislature's immediate consideration.

For fiscal year 1965–1966, therefore, the commission selected from among its more than 60 recommendations seven which it considered most needful of attention and action. These included establishment of the diagnostic and counseling centers, development of new types of residential facilities, provision of rehabilitation services, strengthening of special education programs, establishment of development centers for children unable to attend the public schools, and important steps toward professional training and encouragement of research.

To each of these priority recommendations the commission attached the most realistic price tag it could compute. Its report noted that the total cost of the proposed new services in the first year would be less than 4 percent of what the State of California was currently spending for the retarded. The section on priority recommendations concluded:

> The new approach will open doors for better services, so that California can offer real hope to the mentally retarded and their families. Ultimately, through rehabilitation and through prevention, the State will serve its people better and will reduce the cost. Enlightened, efficient programs for the mentally retarded are sound public economy.

MOBILIZING SUPPORT

From the beginning of the commission's work, it was obvious that consensus among the members in developing a comprehensive plan would not be enough. It was necessary to insure acceptance of the recommendations by the governor and the legislature, or the whole effort would be merely a sterile exercise. Because the commission itself, as a group, had little or no political strength, it had to conduct its work so as to mobilize support along the way. Many of its activities were designed to this end.

At every stage, the commission invited the viewpoints of professional people and interested citizens. There were frequent consultations with administration officials and legislative leaders. All commission meetings were open to the public; in addition, there were two all-day public hearings at which individuals and organizations were encouraged to express their views. The development of a complimentary mailing list, including everyone who asked to be included, led to an active interchange of views between the commission and its constituency.

Finally, after six full-scale meetings and innumerable other discussions, the commission took its tentative conclusions and recommendations to the people of California through regional workshops. The workshops were conducted by the University of California Extension, which arranged for the fullest circulation and discussion of the commission's proposals, in a neutral, dispassionate setting. More than 1800 persons attended the workshops, held on six successive Saturdays in different parts of the state; and their reactions had a significant influence on the commission's final report. The effect was reciprocal, for, as people observed the earnestness and sincerity of the commission, and they saw their ideas being accepted, they were enlisted among the supporters of the commission's program, thereby building up statewide enthusiasm for its recommendations. This was reflected in newspaper, radio, and television coverage, and later in expressions of opinion to the legislators.

At one point in the commission's deliberations—about the time the crucial issues were coming up for decision—the astute chairman asked a question of central importance: Should the commission work toward the development of the "ideal" plan for meeting the needs of the mentally retarded persons of California? Or should it build into its report the compromises and awareness of political realities which would give the proposals a real chance of enactment?

Two members of the commission responded immediately, almost as if by conditioned reflex. One (the mother of a retarded child) said, "Let us state the ideal." The other (a member of the legislature) said, "Let's build the political realities into the report." Consensus seemed to go with the politically sensitive member of the commission, and so—although long-range objectives were stated in the final report—the immediate priorities were keyed to what seemed realistically attainable.

There were legislative obstacles, in some degree peculiar to California, in the year 1965. A knowledgeable observer of legislative trends remarked wryly, early in the session, that although every session was unique, this one was "more unique." In most states, the problem will be different, as the comprehensive mental retardation planning bodies will conclude their work late in 1965 and will then have to wait for the next biennial sessions of their legislatures more than a year later, in 1967. This may result in a cooling-off, or loss of enthusiasm and of popular support. In California, the study commission certainly hit while the iron was hot, bringing in its final report at the beginning of the 1965 session and at a peak of nationwide concern, but it did run into some obstacles not of its own making.

The problem with which the members of the legislature were most concerned in 1965 was reapportionment, which, because of a court order, necessarily occupied the central attention of most of the legislators in the first months of the year. This had nothing at all to do with mental retardation, and yet the effect on the commission's program was substantial and for the most part destructive. The other big problems which impinged on the mental retardation proposals were the size of the total state budget and the need for new taxes; and while these are perennial, they seemed to be especially acute this year. The study commission could do nothing about any of these large problems—nothing but wait, and try to build public support, and hope.

In the end, the legislature enacted every bill put before it as a direct result of the commission's work. Some of the measures were diluted, and the funds available proved to be less than the commission thought necessary, but at least the principles now stand in the law. To this extent, California has taken substantial steps toward meeting its obligations as an affluent state in serving its less fortunate members. Those recommendations of the California Study Commission on Mental Retardation which are still unrealized now stand as a challenge to future sessions of the legislature.

47 ADMINISTRATION AND SUPERVISION CONSIDERATIONS IN PROGRAMMING FOR THE MENTALLY RETARDED

Harrie M. Selznick

From *Education and Training of the Mentally Retarded,* Vol. 1, No. 3, October 1966, pp. 119–123. Reprinted with the permission of the Council for Exceptional Children and the author. Dr. Selznick is Area Superintendent for Special Education, Baltimore City Public Schools, Md.

Expansion of services to the retarded has developed most dramatically over the past ten years. With this expansion has come the employment of specialists to give direction and supervision to the programs and personnel included in this service. In most communities, the number of persons employed and the manner in which they are being deployed for service are similar to the patterns which have been used in administration and supervision of other public school programs.

As with most aspects of the educational scene, functions of administrators and supervisors of programs for the mentally retarded are not the same in all communities. In some school districts, responsibility for programs for the mentally retarded is placed with a general supervisor or administrator. In others, all responsibilities in special education are assigned by the superintendent to a special educator. Personnel assigned full time to mental retardation programs are found only in communities where the programs and budget are extensive enough to justify their employment.

To discuss the functions of administrators and supervisors of programs for the mentally retarded would seem to require some consideration for change. Too often, discussion about pupil identification, teacher preparation and selection, staff deployment, job responsibility, and other aspects of the school picture are predicated on the continued use of present patterns of operation. The considerable escalation in activity in all aspects of work in mental retardation suggests that any paper prepared at this time be considered a statement in transition. There is every reason to believe that the period of history immediately ahead will be something different from the present, perhaps fantastically different, as man becomes increasingly knowledgeable about the causes of and means for remediating mental retardation, the identification of special learning needs, more effective use of instructional approaches, and manpower deployment.

Tremendous strides have been made in the past decade in both public and private programs of special education. In spite of this progress, a large majority of the retarded children are still not provided with adequate educational opportunities. Only one-fourth of our nation's school age mentally retarded are enrolled in special education programs in public schools. It is the obligation of our society to provide appropriate opportunities for all mentally retarded children who can benefit by education and training.

The supply of teachers who are trained for work with the mentally retarded is most inadequate to meet the needs of our special education programs. The number of teachers who are completing their training programs each year is scarcely sufficient to replace those teachers who leave their assignments. With a limited supply of trained personnel available for work in the classroom, an increasing population of mentally retarded persons, and the explosion of knowledge about the mentally retarded, it is increasingly important that supervisory and administrative personnel with training and experience be made available to the field.

As chief administrative officer of a school district, the superintendent of schools has the same responsibility toward mentally retarded children that he has toward other children in his district. As the size of the school district increases and the special education program becomes more complex, it becomes administratively expedient to delegate authority and responsibility for certain aspects of the program to other staff personnel. These staff members are then charged with the identification of the mentally retarded child and the initiation and expansion of necessary services.

Because various titles are used to designate the individuals charged with administration and supervision of programs for the mentally retarded, this author will describe the functions necessary for a complete program. It is recognized that on occasion the line separating administrative and supervisory functions may be very thin or nonexistent.

THE ADMINISTRATOR

The administrator of programs for the mentally retarded must have an understanding of the total school system. It is only as he develops a philosophy of service which is consistent with that of the total system that his program responsibility will be understood and accepted by school personnel and the community at large. In simple terms, the administrator is the person who organizes the efforts of the school system to achieve its educational purposes; thus, his functions are concerned with teaching and learning. His major activities are discussed below.

Help the organization with which he is associated to clarify its purposes. The administrator helps his own staff, the community, and other members of the educational team. To provide this needed assistance in the clarification of purposes, the administrator must have knowledge, not only of his area of specialization, but of the total school system and the community in which he is to function. It is necessary that he have a background in the philosophy of education for the mentally retarded, because the purposes, goals, and directions must relate to this basic philosophy. In the performance of his duties, the administrator is called upon to make value decisions. Research has little to contribute to an understanding of how he arrives at these decisions.

Coordinate the efforts of all personnel working with and for the mentally retarded. It is important that there be coordination of the efforts of the organization, the efforts of the people in it, and the programs which are undertaken. This coordination involves defining the job to be done, identifying and hiring capable personnel, dismissing incompetent staff members, and providing an environment conducive to cooperative and productive working relationships.

Obtain the resources that will permit the organization to do its job. These resources include not only necessary equipment, furniture, and supplies, but also supportive services which are available to all other programs of the school system.

The community in which the administrator is working, the children attending school, the school plant, and the teacher who is serving the mentally retarded are all in the process of change. Alertness to the implications of increased knowledge and the changed community is important to the individual charged with administrative responsibilities. These implications require that he exercise effective leadership, which demands direction and the ability to identify and work with the power structure within the organization. The administrator is effective only as he has helped the school system and the community to modify its procedures, purposes, or programs. He is not effective when he merely maintains the organization, although maintenance of stability in an organization is one of the administrator's major functions, and change should be introduced only after the development and careful consideration of a rationale suggesting the innovations.

SUPERVISION

For the purposes of this discussion, the term supervisor is used to describe the professional person whose primary role is the improvement of the teaching–learning environment. In order to executive competently the major responsibilities assigned to him, the supervisor of educational programs for the mentally retarded should be prepared to perform certain major tasks.

Help the teacher and other school personnel gain a better understanding of children. Although all children in the special class may be classified as educable or trainable retarded, they represent different learning needs. They mature at different rates; their readiness for different learning tasks develops individually; and their rates of physical growth are not necessarily regular or similar. Since teachers assigned to work with the mentally retarded vary in their understandings, knowledges, and skills, the supervisor must constantly help to strengthen the frame of reference each teacher brings to the learning task.

Help the teacher of the retarded develop both individually and as a cooperating member of the school staff. Quite possibly this is the most important aspect of the supervisory function. For many years the teacher of mentally retarded children has suffered the low regard of his professional colleagues. This assignment of value has been made because of lack of understanding of the special education program. It is only as the supervisor is able to assist the teacher of the retarded in the development of his knowledge and a security in his method of teaching that respect from other members of the faculty will be gained.

Help teachers make more interesting and effective use of instructional materials. The demands upon the supervisor will at times be such that he may feel he is looked upon as a resource librarian or technician. These demands will come not only from the newer staff members, but from the more experienced teachers as well. This is an area in which the supervisor may be of major assistance to the beginning teacher who is insecure in his first job, anxious to succeed, and limited in his familiarity with the various kinds of teaching materials which might be most effective with the retarded child.

Help the teacher improve his methods of teaching. This assistance is not necessarily limited to inexperienced teachers. Every good teacher can improve his ways of teaching. The supervisor must recognize that each teacher develops his own system of teaching techniques. He may adapt to his own repertoire an idea from another teacher, but he does not adopt it per se. In the process of improving teaching methodology, the effective supervisor helps the teacher see more readily the interrelationships between subject matter areas, to prepare resource materials or units, and to select those teaching approaches which give greater promise of success with a given pupil or in the development of a group concept.

Make specialized personnel available to all special classes in the school system for maximum assistance to the special class teacher. It is the responsibility of the supervisor to see that the special contributions of the speech therapist; the librarian; the guidance counselors; the school social workers; the cafeteria manager; the school nurse; and the teachers of music, art, physical education, and industrial arts are fully utilized. The teacher of the mentally retarded should never feel that he is without the endless resources which the school system may provide.

Assist the special class teacher in the development of evaluative techniques. Evaluations should include progress made by pupils with regard to both academic tasks and social attitudes. The techniques should be devised so that the results will help the teacher determine readiness for learning experience, aid the pupil in understanding his own progress, and convey to parents the role they can play in fostering the child's growth and development.

Stimulate the teacher to evaluate his own planning, work, and progress. It is usually very difficult for the individual to evaluate himself and his work fairly. The supervisor of programs for the retarded can be of service to his teachers by guiding them in an examination of the kinds of teaching materials and units which they have developed for their pupils. For some teachers the mere listing of new teaching methods and devices which they have used during the current school year serves as a means for measurement of growth.

Help the teacher gain a sense of security in his work and in the community. There are great differences between community demands and community provisions for its teachers. Adjustment to a school system and community is not always easily accomplished. A sense of security in one's job is perhaps more conducive to success than any one factor. Professional self-confidence may be increased with the aid of the supervisor who involves the teacher in planning and execution processes, encourages originality, and gives recognition for outstanding performance.

Stimulate teachers to participate in curriculum development and other inservice activities. Some of the newer approaches to group action research may be pursued in this activity. Teachers have much to contribute in the preparation and publication of resource units, courses of study, and other program improvement activities.

Acquaint the school administration, the teachers, the student body, and the general public with the work and progress being made in serving the mentally retarded. The supervisor comes into contact with many persons who need to understand the programs for the mentally retarded. He may describe the good things being done, the interesting new ideas being tested, and the progress being made. By reason of his position, the supervisor of programs for the retarded has the opportunity to suggest activities which might be included in faculty meetings. Here is a chance to acquaint all members of the school staff with the program and techniques utilized, as well as an opportunity for the special class teacher to demonstrate his professional know-how and to suggest possible modifications in teaching–learning activities in the regular classrooms.

The efforts of the administrator, his supervisor, and the other staff members must be closely coordinated. An especially close working relationship must be maintained with staff members responsible for the provision of curricula. This can best be accomplished through an organizational pattern which groups those with similar administrative and supervisory responsibilities. Effective programming for the retarded can occur only when leadership personnel assigned to this special service are included with other operational personnel in the planning and implementation of total school programs.

48 SPECIAL EDUCATION FOR RURAL RETARDED YOUTH

John W. Melcher
Kenneth R. Blessing

From *Exceptional Children,* Vol. 23, No. 5, February 1957, pp. 207–210. Reprinted with the permission of the Council for Exceptional Children and the authors. Dr. Melcher is assistant state superintendent and Dr. Blessing is supervisor of the Bureau for Handicapped Children, Wisconsin Department of Public Instruction.

For many years, urban children with retarded mental development have had the manifold advantages of special education and allied services. With an awakened and well-informed public, and the impetus of an enlightened militant parent group, the demands for extension of special services to the rural areas have increased. This paper is a description of an approach used in Wisconsin in coordinating the many community resources and interested groups concerned with the education and training of mentally retarded children, particularly in rural communities.

STATE AND COUNTY RELATIONSHIP

In Wisconsin, the county constitutes the intermediate district of school administration that functions between the state department of education and the local school districts. This strong position the county holds in the Wisconsin plan of government has been a major factor in the State Department of Public Instruction's efforts to extend special education to rural retarded youth. Each county has a superintendent of schools elected by popular vote for a four-year term. His office is usually located in the county courthouse and his status is comparable to that of other county governmental officials. Each county superintendent has one or more county supervising teachers on his staff as well as a limited number of clerical and stenographic assistants, although in the more populated areas the office may be staffed by a corps of educational specialists who provide a wide range of educational services.

Wisconsin statutes (Section 41.01) provide that a county superintendent of schools, upon authorization of his county board of supervisors, may establish special-class services for any of the various types of handicapped children including those with retarded mental development.

ADMINISTRATIVE PROCEDURES IN DEVELOPING SPECIAL CLASSES

The following administrative procedure has been used in planning for these rural special classes. In actual practice the planning stage for special class development is preceded by a period of individual conferences with parents or local school principals who request individual psychological examinations of children suspected of mental retardation. As the growing need for special service becomes increasingly more apparent, as parents, regular classroom teachers, and other concerned over the welfare of the children identified as retardates make their needs felt, the intermediate unit of school administration is necessarily drawn into the planning activities, since most smaller villages and rural areas lack sufficient numbers of retarded children to warrant the establishment of a special class.

The representative of the Bureau for Handicapped Children who has the particular county under his immediate supervision assumes responsibility for the orientation of the county superintendent's staff to the values, limitations, and administrative principles of special class services to retarded children. A bibliography of professional publications in this area is discussed and departmental publications are made available to the superintendent's staff. Correspondence is carried on between the state consultant and members of the intermediate unit staff to expand further the mutual cooperation and understanding of state and county school officers in regard to the problem of the mentally retarded child.

Visits by the county superintendent and his staff to nearby rural special classes are encouraged in order that the actual operation of a county special class may be viewed.

The county board of supervisors' education committee then meets with the county superintendent and state supervisor to discuss state financial support, public acceptance, organizations, administration, supervision, and other important aspects of this proposed class.

Following this conference, meetings are conducted in the county with all types of lay and professional groups concerned with the care and education of children in order to gain their understanding, support, and cooperation in this endeavor. Since Wisconsin laws are permissive in nature rather than mandatory, special classes have been conceived of as basically a community responsibility, as represented by a school district, a group of districts, or a county. The state, therefore, acts through the educative process rather than through compulsion and the initiative in establishing a class and the primary responsibility for operating it falls upon the local community.

The development of an acceptance of special class services at the local community level may necessarily entail a considerable period of activity and in some instances has required as long as two or three years of sustained effort on the part of the Bureau consultants, county office staff, and parents of these children.

Some of the local community groups contacted include such organizations as:

The County Teachers' Association
Administrators of smaller schools and integrated districts

Farm and labor groups, such as the Grange, Farm Bureau, and the Farmers' Union
Women's groups, such as the Homemakers, ladies' auxiliaries, church groups, and the League of Women Voters

Informative articles concerned with the role of the special class in the public school are developed for the weekly and daily newspapers. Some radio or television programming conveying the same concepts is frequently employed using the services of staff members of both the state department and the county superintendent's office. In 1955, for example, the Department of Public Instruction conducted a weekly series of "Teacher Time" broadcasts beamed at every classroom teacher in Wisconsin and a number of these programs dealt with problems of exceptionality found in every classroom and the needs of those children too handicapped to benefit from the program of the regular classroom.

PROCEDURE FOR COUNTY-WIDE SURVEY

When it seems the proper public attitude for this service has been created in the area, the actual fact-finding must begin. No objective criteria have been developed to determine a community's readiness for a special program, but a number of factors and pressures are emerging which suggest a readiness. During this initial orientation period, the formation of a parent group ordinarily parallels the development of an improved community attitude with respect to the problem of mental retardation. These parents are beginning to exert local leadership, acting as spokesmen for their retarded children, and their demands are being increasingly felt. Civic leaders, teachers, and fraternal organizations submit resolutions or petitions supporting the parent council's request, and it becomes apparent that a complete survey of need in the county is essential. Factual objective data are required for presentation to the county board of supervisors in order to obtain an appropriation sufficient to cover the first year's cost of operation.

A survey is conducted by the county superintendent's staff in all schools under his jurisdiction and in the private schools which respond to the county superintendent's invitation to participate. The following cooperative pattern of state–county participation is followed:

Group psychometrics including tests of intelligence and achievement are administered by the county superintendent's staff and private school personnel. Teachers' opinions, principals' evaluation, and parental requests are considered an integral part of this screening process.

Children with low scores on group intelligent tests are referred to a traveling team of qualified psychologists from the state superintendent's office. Following each complete individual psychological examination, the results are interpreted to the child's family by the psychologists, and the parents are given counsel as to the desirability of special-class placement. In some instances, the psychological evaluation of a child indicates that he is above or below the statutory intellectual limits. In these instances, promises or guarantee of service are rarely made prior to the examination by the state psychologists.

This survey is culminated by having the state psychological staff furnish detailed psychological reports on each child. The county superintendent's staff uses this data in preparing a spot map which indicates the location of each eligible child.

The county superintendent's next responsibility is to find a classroom in some operating school building that can be legally used to house this special facility. The building supervisors of the state superintendent's staff then evaluate the building space and physical facilities, making recommendations for necessary modifications. A rental is paid by the county board to the local school district for use of the space.

The county superintendent's office then attempts to secure a fully qualified teacher from one of the teacher training institutions in the state. Rural areas frequently experience considerable difficulty in securing a fully trained qualified teacher, so it often becomes necessary to find an especially competent regular teacher who can be retrained in the education of the mentally retarded during summer sessions. A detailed certification requirement list indicating any existing deficiencies is developed for each prospective teacher. If the selected teacher does not fully meet all certification requirements at the time of his evaluation by the certification division, he must reduce his deficiency in education by taking six semester hours of work prior to his receiving a one-year provisional permit. The special teacher is required to reduce his deficiencies at the rate of six credits per year in order to have his provisional permit renewed. The usual practice has been for the county superintendent to grant salary increments to cover at least a portion of the cost for further summer school attendance and/or in recognition of advanced professional training.

After securing public financial and community support, an adequate physical plant, and a competent teacher, the county superintendent is ready to submit a plan of service to the state superintendent. When approved, this would mean that approximately two-thirds to three-fourths of the cost of instruction, which includes the salary of the teacher, special books, certain equipment, and pupil lunches, plus transportation to and from the special class, will be reimbursed by the state of Wisconsin.

LOCAL PLAN OF SERVICE

This plan of service has been formulated by the Bureau supervisors after considerable experience with rural special-class development and merits the attention of field consultants carrying on similar work in other states. Under Wisconsin statutes, the chief state school officer has the authority to approve or disapprove the plans for a class on the basis of his being satisfied that there is a need for such a service and that it will be operated in accordance with the statutes and standards set up by his division.

The plan of service requests such operating details as physical facilities, local plans for administration and supervision, estimated number of pupils, employment of a certified teacher, anticipated expenditures, and willingness to accept nonresident retardates if enrollment size permits. Although the administration of the program is the responsibility of the local superintendent, the school board or county is required to apply to the state superintendent for authorization and his approval of the plan assures the operating district of later participation in state aids. The operating agency is required to budget the first year out of local funds, the state's share of the cost being reimbursed in the fall following the school year in which the class was in operation. State reimbursement is subject to proration if the state appropriation is insufficient to cover all approved claims.

Rural special-education programs are of necessity area programs, since special classes for handicapped children can rarely conform strictly to school district lines if they are to be operated efficiently. This concept of special services as area centers requires a number of cooperative arrangements with respect to transportation. One district may be operating a trainable service and another an educable program, therefore, ongoing existing transportation facilities such as regular high school and elementary busses are utilized whenever feasible. Since no handicapped child in Wisconsin is required to walk to school (the law is permissive in cities of the first class), other arrangements for the transportation of retarded pupils are coordinated through the county superintendent's office. All vehicles used in transporting pupils must pass the inspection of the Wisconsin Motor Vehicle Department and carriers are required by law to have the necessary insurance coverage for public conveyances. In most instances the transportation of pupils is provided by the child's home school district with aids from state funds going to the districts offering this service.

This procedure has been utilized by Wisconsin county- and state-level school officers and citizens in the creation of 52 special classes for rural children with retarded mental development. None of these counties that have originated a class under these provisions has ever ceased operation, and 11 of these 28 counties now have two or more such county-operated classes.

While this is a relatively small percentage of the total of 292 special class units in Wisconsin, this procedure points a way for the extension of services to rural mentally handicapped children. The classes are viewed with pride by local citizenry and have led at least one county to expend over $100,000 in the development of a special school plant for its retarded pupils.

The Bureau for Handicapped Children feels that this detailed slow process of educating the community is likely to produce better results than haphazardly rushing into a special-class program. It renders maximum service without imposition, maintains the autonomy of the local school districts, and by calculated coordination brings about improved services to mentally retarded children in rural areas.

SECTION FOURTEEN

Research

The study of mental retardation was a stepchild of scientific research until 1950. An attitude of hopelessness toward it prevailed, and except for the work of a few undaunted, highly dedicated workers like Itard, Seguin, Binet, Goddard, Doll, Benda, and Wallin, little was accomplished. What research there was, poorly supported and little publicized, was devoted to institutional programs. Except for the laboratory at the Training School, Vineland, New Jersey, and a small number of institutional and clinical projects, research in the area of mental retardation was unknown. Nonetheless, it is amazing how much progress was made on this limited basis and how it provided impact affecting current programs.

The first impetus for well-organized research was given by Samuel A. Kirk, when he established the Institute for Research on Exceptional Children at the University of Illinois shortly after World War II. This was followed by the monumental studies of Masland, Sarason, and Gladwin,[1] which were sponsored by the National Association for Retarded Children and the National Institute of Mental Health and provided a framework for future inquiry.

Major breakthroughs were accomplished in the identification, diagnosis, and treatment of PKU Disease. Biologists gave us new insights into chromosomal abnormalities and studies tended to show that severe nutritional deprivation was a major causal agent in the etiology of mental retardation. Clinical studies are continually searching for an answer to many of the unknown causes of retardation. Psychologists studying the behavior of both humans and primates have provided the profession with rich information that may eventually help us to understand more about how retardates learn. A variety of educational studies are underway that have as their goal knowledge relating to appropriate curricula and teaching methodology. Social scientists are delving into the

[1] Richard L. Masland, Seymour B. Sarason, and Thomas Gladwin, *Mental Subnormality* (New York: Basic Books, Inc., 1958).

problems relating to community living, institutional adjustment, and more effective parental counseling. Our major problem in research is the translation of basic research findings into operational programs. A second major problem is the dissemination of research findings to professional workers. The latter is gradually being accomplished through such services as CEC's ERIC *Document Reproduction Service* and *Exceptional Child Education Abstracts.* The publication of *Mental Retardation Abstracts* provides professionals with an up-to-date listing of general and research reports. Gradually, the time lag between the completion of a research study and the dissemination of these findings is being shortened. Annual reviews of the research by Norman R. Ellis [2] and Joseph Wortis [3] are handy sources of burgeoning research activities. The *American Journal of Mental Deficiency* has adopted a policy of reporting in depth research in various areas of mental retardation. The Children's Bureau, through its publication, *Research Relating to Children,* presents abstracts of ongoing research as well as major findings of completed projects. Every third year, the February issue of the *Review of Educational Research* provides us with a comprehensive summary of educational research findings in mental retardation and other handicapping conditions.

The editor of this volume has prepared a detailed listing of research sources that will be found in the Appendix. Major research programs have been developed at George Peabody College, the University of Michigan, the University of Washington, the University of Kansas Medical Center, Parsons (Kansas) State Hospital, Pacific (California) State Hospital, Willowbrook (New York) State Hospital, and the Johnstone (New Jersey) Center. Federal funding is supporting the construction and research activities of a variety of research and demonstration centers.

Federal funds have been provided under Public Law 88-164, an amendment to the original Public Law 85-926, to build and operate a vast network of treatment and research facilities known popularly as university-affiliated centers. Similarly, many agencies of the National Institutes of Health as well as the Social Rehabilitation Service Agency are funding research activities in mental retardation.

Research findings have the potential for laying the groundwork for innovation. However, it takes adoption on the part of the profession to really find the value of research activities. It has been suggested that there are five steps in the adoption process. These steps are: awareness; interest; evaluation; trial; and adoption.

The first reading in this section is a report by Mathilde Krim of recent medical research. This is followed by a very comprehensive study by James J. McCarthy and Richard C. Scheerenberger covering the research findings of a decade of activity. It is primarily psychological and educational in nature. The final reading by Leonard Blackman is a searching study of the research needs in the special education of the mentally retarded.

[2] Norman R. Ellis, *International Review of Research in Mental Retardation,* Vol. 1 (1966), Vol. 2 (1967), Vol. 3 (1968) (New York: Academic Press, Inc.).

[3] Joseph Wortis, *Mental Retardation: An Annual Review* (New York: Grune and Stratton, Inc., 1970).

49 SCIENTIFIC RESEARCH AND MENTAL RETARDATION

Mathilde Krim

From *President's Committee on Mental Retardation Message,* No. 16, January 1969, pp. 1–10. Reprinted with the permission of the President's Committee on Mental Retardation and the author. Dr. Krim is Associate, Sloan-Kettering Institute for Cancer Research, New York City.

Scientific research is quite a new sort of activity for mankind. It started when man's curiosity about the universe was no longer satisfied by mysticism and magic. It accepts the discipline of the scientific method of inquiry based on scientific determinism, which says that all natural events are completely determined by previously existing causes. From this it follows that if causes are known, future events can be predicted and also that, by manipulating causes, different events—some possibly more to the liking of the manipulator—may be predicted and achieved.

This method of inquiry has proved most fruitful. It has enabled man to manipulate the physical world around him—and even the very substance of his own body—to his own benefit. And now society has turned to science for the solution of the tragic and baffling problem of faulty brain development that results in retardation.

But scientific determinism requires first and foremost *complete* objectivity. This is why the first areas in which man became capable of applying the scientific method were those of physics, chemistry, and astronomy, all of which deal with the inanimate world.

The world of living matter is much more complex. The disciplines concerned with its higher forms of expression, like psychology, behaviorism and sociology, have only very recently been able to avail themselves of strictly scientific methods of analysis. This is not only because intellectual activity, emotions and individual or social behavior are very complicated subjects, but because they are always difficult to study without the investigator himself getting emotionally involved. So it is that the social, rather than the purely biomedical, aspects of the problem of mental retardation have been under study for a relatively very short time. Even so, we can appreciate the amount of knowledge already gained and the great progress that is bound to be accomplished in the future.

Our federal government has been relatively receptive to information about mental retardation and, greatly stimulated by President Kennedy's and President Johnson's concern for this national problem, has invested more in it year after year. Following the wide public interest awakened by the report of President Kennedy's Panel on Mental Retardation, an array of legislative acts benefiting the mentally retarded both directly and indirectly, as well as children susceptible to becoming retarded, was passed. These, in conjunction with a very effective campaign by the Advertising

Council and the activity of associations for retarded children and other private organizations, stimulated activities on the part of the states, local communities and individual citizens.

Total federal expenditures for health and education have increased by three times during the Johnson administration. Federal outlays account now for some two-thirds of the total of $2,000,000,000 spent each year for biomedical research in this country. Through National Institutes of Health funding, 65,000 senior investigators are at work at some 2,000 institutions. Some 30,000 more are in training. These scientists are leading the nation in a research effort of great scope, depth and unequalled excellence.

RESEARCH AND PREVENTION

Let us now consider what this research activity, including some sponsored by states and private foundations, has contributed to the care of the mentally retarded—both educationally and medically—and to the prevention of their condition.

Let us first understand clearly what we are talking about. Of the many definitions of mental retardation offered, I think one of the most useful was proposed by the American Association on Mental Deficiency: *"Mental retardation refers to subaverage general intellectual functioning which originates during the developmental period and is associated with the impairment of adaptive behavior."*

In order to review and understand the approaches used in the study of mental retardation, we shall also have to subdivide the cases of mental retardation in categories depending on the causes that produce them. We shall have to do this because every set of causes needs a different approach.

The first triumph of the scientific approach to mental retardation is that it led us to a better understanding of how varied are the causes that can give rise to the single symptom that we call mental retardation. This in itself enables us to make what we call a differential diagnosis. We can also often establish a prognosis.

That is, we can predict, often quite accurately, what changes can be expected to follow medical or educational intervention in a particular case. More important, knowledge of the factors which cause mental retardation gives us a hope that we may be able to remove or modify them, thus achieving real prevention or, at least, softening the impact of the harmful factor and minimizing its effect. These last describe the goals we must ultimately achieve.

As a first approximation, we can divide the people whose intellectual functioning and adaptive behavior are impaired, as measured by our present testing methods, into two groups.

First, the 75 to 80 percent who are mildly retarded and usually have only minor physical handicaps or none. They are usually recognized as deficient during their school years. They are to a large extent capable of being absorbed into society during adulthood. Many, however, are relegated to a marginal existence of unemployment, poverty and, not infrequently, brushes with the law.

For most of these, no organic defect can be found as the cause of their condition. But the very strong association between this type of mental retardation, which is a "functional retardation," and low socioeconomic environment or poverty has compelled us to give it the name "socio-environmental retardation."

The other group of the mentally retarded—20 to 25 percent—are more severely impaired than the first group. They range from those who are trainable to those who remain completely dependent throughout their lives. They show severely to profoundly impaired intellectual development, this time associated with a great variety of organic defects and physical handicaps. It is among this group that the cause of the retardation is often known already. It may be either a genetic defect—an abnormality of the chromosomes or the genes themselves—disturbing the biochemical machinery of the body and the functioning of the brain, or an early environmental physical or chemical factor like infection, accident or poisoning that has impaired the development of the brain.

OBSTACLES TO PROGRESS

Precise causes of mental retardation have been difficult to determine and treatment even more difficult to plan for the following reasons.

First of all, the propensity to mental retardation is determined very early in life, probably at the time when the human brain grows and develops at its fastest—that is, just before and just after birth. And when retardation has a genetic cause, the development potential of the brain may be set at the very time of conception itself. Evaluation of brain function can be carried out by present methods only much later in life, often at a time when the initiating harmful factor is not present anymore.

Moreover, genetic and environmental factors can work together. Even after retardation has set in, an infinite number of interactions between the afflicted person, his family and his total environment can modify the basic pattern of symptoms.

POVERTY: AGGRAVATING FACTOR

In spite of the fact that precise causes are still unclear in many cases, we are already aware of certain aggravating factors. Even if we only know of one among many, this may help us to do something. We know quite unequivocally, for example, that most functionally mildly retarded people come from environments where as young children they have been without adequate diet and care, as well as without sufficient intellectual, sensorial, and emotional stimulation. These are the children of poverty or the products of a damaging environment. As Whitney Young put it at the National Association for Retarded Children convention last year, "They have inherited the circumstances, not the genes, that predispose to mental retardation."

Here we know clearly what remedial and preventive measures have to be taken.

In rural poverty areas and big city slums—among whites as among Negroes—other diseases also occur more frequently. For example, five to nine times more cases of tuberculosis and all other infections, three times more cases of premature birth, almost all cases of brain damage due to lead poisoning, more accidents and more malnutrition. In two Mississippi delta counties, the Department of Agriculture found that 60 percent of the children received less than two-thirds of the minimum dietary allowance recommended by the National Research Council, and we know that malnutrition early in life can impair mental development. Among the 500,000 indigent women giving birth each year, 100,000 need special medical help for complications. Most of them do not get it and too often deliver premature children; and we know that among such premature infants, when they are below three pounds in weight at birth, three-fourths of them develop physical or mental defects. Too many children in such surroundings remain unvaccinated. We can still find children in these areas who have suffered brain damage as a result of whooping cough although vaccination against this disease has been available for several decades! As a result, the incidence of mental defects among the children of indigent mothers—whether Negro, white, Latin American, or Indian—is *ten times* what it is among the children of the middle class.

Moreover, a survey made by the staff of the President's Committee on Mental Retardation has revealed, that—largely because local communities have to provide matching funds in order to obtain federal money—95 percent of federally funded community centers for the retarded are located in middle income areas rather than in the poverty areas where they are most desperately needed.

I cannot dwell longer on the frightening consequences of material poverty, but I strongly recommend that you read the excellent study published in April 1968 by the Division of Mental Retardation of the Department of Institutions and Agencies of the State of New Jersey, *Poverty and Mental Retardation—A Causal Relationship.*

Psychological factors at work in the relations between the middle-class establishment and the poor, particularly the poor from minority groups, aggravate considerably the consequences of the physical conditions of poverty.

TEACHER EXPECTATION AND ACHIEVEMENT

An experiment of fundamental importance was carried out in California by Robert Rosenthal and Lenore Jacobson in 1967. Wanting to study the effect of teachers' attitudes on the performance of pupils, they picked 20 percent of the children, at random, in a school of mixed Caucasian and Mexican children and told teachers casually that these particular children were expected, as a result of psychological testing, to be "spurters" who would make considerable progress during the next school year. Although these children did not receive special tutorial attention and the curriculum of the school remained unchanged, their IQ—when tested a year later—went up remarkably. The children whose IQ was lower to start with made relatively even more progress than the others. The children originally not designated as "spurters," on the other hand, showed much less progress. This was observed with many teachers, over several grades and in classes that were designed specially either for bright, average, or slow learners. Even more interesting, when the teachers were asked to evaluate their pupils' progress, they described progress of bright children in very positive terms like "outgoing," "active," "sociable," "interested." But when the teachers described similar progress made by a child at first labeled "slow learner," their evaluation had negative connotations.

How many implications does this experiment have for us who are interested in the mentally retarded! It shows plainly that when a child is expected by his teacher to be slow, he conforms to expectations. When the teachers expect him to be bright—even when they never verbalize their expectations and do not change their methods of teaching, the child feels it and blooms.

That similar insidious factors—even unconscious prejudice—exist in regard to Negro and other minority group children cannot be doubted. It is now believed quite likely that such prejudices explain why so many poor children or minority group children fail so badly in school that they end up labeled as retarded. It is difficult to imagine presently how we could change teachers' attitudes—since this would involve a change in the heart and in the mind of people, but if we want to, we can eradicate material poverty.

President Johnson and his administration have been acutely aware of this problem and have shown the way. Most of the mildly retarded children of the poor did not need to be retarded; they are merely the victims of social and economic injustice. Prevention of such retardation will require at first a considerable and costly effort but will repay us by an estimated 50 percent reduction in the total number of cases of mental retardation. In one generation, it will replace two or three million who at present are a tragic problem to society with a productive group contributing to our national resources.

AGENTS OF ORGANIC DEFECT

Among those cases of retardation that involve an organic defect, we have first to consider the group that has been damaged either in utero or early in life by external causes, such as infections or head injuries.

Although such cases occur in all social and economic groups, they are much more frequent among the poor.

Toxemia of pregnancy, a condition that can easily be prevented by medical treatment, still occurs in poor rural areas and in cities of more than 100,000 people, where about 30 percent of pregnant women do not receive medical care during their pregnancy. Rubella, also called German measles or three-day measles, when contracted by mothers during the first trimester of pregnancy, can cause severe damage to 10 to 40 percent of unborn children. Rubella probably damaged more than 20,000 unborn infants in this country during the last epidemic in 1964. The virus causing rubella was isolated in 1962 and has been successfully grown in tissue culture. A mild form of the virus—like that used in the live polio vaccine—has now been developed and a vaccine containing it is available to the public. The disease could be wiped out altogether within a very short time by an efficient vaccination campaign. The rubella story is one of the outstanding successes of scientific research applied to the prevention of mental retardation.

There are still many other viruses that are now under suspicion as possible threats to the unborn child. These viruses are all around us and are able to pass through the placental barrier. We know from laboratory studies that embryonic tissues are more susceptible to virus infection than those of the adult.

The following are suspected to be culprits: Mumps virus, Coxsackie B virus, Herpes virus, Vaccinia virus, Varicella or chicken pox.

In addition to these, hepatitis virus has been said to have caused a rise in mongoloid births in Moscow recently.

Active research is going on now with these viruses. Meanwhile, it is strongly recommended that live virus vaccines of any kind should on no account be given to women of childbearing age.

I would like to mention two more infectious agents that are very intriguing for the part they may play in causing mental retardation. One of them is the cytomegalo virus. It has often been isolated from children born with abnormally small heads, as well as from those who are retarded or have cerebral palsy. This virus also seems to be extremely prevalent among the general population, although it does not seem to cause overt disease.

Eighty-five percent of underprivileged adults have antibodies against it, while only 32 percent of well-to-do private patients have such antibodies. The real epidemiology and impact of this virus on human populations are unknown and under intensive study.

Another infection present in 30 to 40 percent of the population of the U.S. is a protozoan parasite by the name of Toxoplasma. Although it grows exclusively within cells, it does not seem to cause any harm to adults. However, it has been regularly found in newborns with abnormalities such as hydrocephalus, encephalomyelitis, retinosis, etc., and has been repeatedly isolated from epileptic children as well as those with mental defects or blindness. Here also the epidemiology is as yet unknown, and ways to combat the infection with drugs and antibiotics are being actively looked for.

To this list of prenatal infections we now must return—after a several years' decline—congenital syphilis. This infection is spreading again, particularly among young adults and the adolescent population where births occur without the benefit or the warning of premarital testing. Twenty-five percent of affected babies die from it in utero and 40 percent develop a general infection that is often difficult to diagnose because it produces many nonspecific symptoms—including brain damage. These symptoms often do not appear until several months after birth.

The brain of an infant can be damaged after birth. One million children each year suffer severe head injuries.

A deficient diet, infectious diseases, poisoning and injuries can leave permanent injuries. Encephalopathy may be a complication of measles or whooping cough, and meningitis of tuberculosis, for example. Effective preventive measures to all these exist through well established methods of child care, supervision and vaccination. However, when all the cases of retardation involving an organic defect produced by these agents are added up, they still account for more than all those resulting from genetic defects lumped together! The inescapable conclusion is that society is failing to properly use the preventive knowledge we have already acquired through research. And since, as I said before, this failure is much more prevalent among the economically disadvantaged, it reflects a failure in the distribution of resources, both of the material resources that provide an economic capacity to purchase services and protection and of the resources represented by knowledge that would confer on the public the appropriate attitudes toward preventive measures and their application.

GENETIC ANOMALIES

Now we come to the genetic diseases. You know that the genetic material that determines our inherited physical and mental characteristics is located in 46 small bodies present in the nucleus of every living cell. They are called chromosomes. Chromosomes have characteristic shapes and sizes as well as a fixed normal number of 46 for the human species. From generation to generation, a complicated and extremely precise mechanism guarantees the constancy of the amount and quality of the genetic material. However, sometimes, something goes wrong in our germ cells or during the very first cell divisions after fertilization. Then chromosomal abnormalities arise that always have tragic consequences. Most of these abnormalities make development impossible and they constitute the greatest single cause of death before birth or at birth. When the infant survives, it is always severely abnormal and in most cases mentally retarded. Mongoloid children (those who have Down's Syndrome) are individuals who have—through an accident in the regulation of the distribution of chromosomes—a small additional chromosome. We know now of about 50 different rare but severe types of disabilities that are caused by chromosomal abnormalities.

We don't know at this moment how to prevent the spontaneous occurrence of chromosome abnormalities, but we can detect them with new techniques developed over the last 12 years. As little as a single drop of blood is sufficient for obtaining dividing cells whose chromosomes can be analyzed. Among parents with mongoloid children, for example, such analysis can distinguish between those who are unlikely to give birth to a second mongoloid and those—much more rare, fortunately—who are very likely to produce more mongoloid offspring. Chromosome analysis is also valuable in many cases other than mongolism and can provide crucial information on which to base genetic counseling.

More interestingly, chromosome analysis can now also be performed on the cells found in a few drops of amniotic fluid that can be safely collected from the womb of a pregnant woman. This type of examination reveals whether the chromosomes of the expected child are normal or defective. Since such examinations can be done at 10 to 12 weeks after conception, it can either completely reassure the mother if the findings indicate a normal child or, if personal ethics and the law permit, make it possible to avoid the birth of a defective child through therapeutic abortion.

These advances in our knowledge of chromosomes have all been made within the last 12 years, and studies of amniotic fluid cells have been done only for the past two or three years.

Another area of swift and encouraging progress is that of brain function in relation to genetically determined abnormalities in the chemistry of the body. Advances in biochemical analysis applied to body fluids like blood, urine, etc., have made it possible to separate and to characterize, both qualitatively and quantitatively, a number of complex natural chemical compounds. Such tests can be done quite rapidly and cheaply today, the cost for an amino acid analysis on blood being now as low as 25 cents per sample. They have permitted the large-scale screening programs for phenylketonuria, for example, that are now compulsory under the law in 39 states.

PRENATAL DIAGNOSIS?

PKU is not the only anomaly that such tests can detect. A total of about 50 different sorts of this type of genetic disease are known today, with the list becoming longer by about a dozen a year now. Most of these diseases lead ultimately to severe mental retardation but they can now be recognized very early in life, even a few days after birth, at a time when damage to the nervous system has not occurred or is likely to be minimal. Although these anomalies are rare, and most of them as yet poorly understood, there is no doubt that in the very near future preventive treatment will become available for many of them. Such chemical aberrations will also become detectable long before birth, by studying the chemistry of either the amniotic fluid, or the cells it contains, when artificially maintained in the laboratory, outside the body. In certain cases, this can be done already. And this affords the exciting possibility that we may be able to perform prenatal diagnosis, offering again a choice whether to interrupt pregnancy, or we hope one day, to cure before irreparable damage has occurred.

Since, ultimately, all genetic anomalies, whether point mutations or chromosomal abnormalities, must perforce be translated into chemical terms, into some change of the chemistry of the body, the day will undoubtedly come when it will be possible to avoid the conception of certain types of defective children by obtaining what we may call a "biochemical profile" of healthy individuals, detecting those who are likely to give birth to defectives and advising them on the choice of their mates.

GENETIC DETERMINANTS

You may know that for every inherited character, each of us carries two genetic determinants, two genes: one coming from our father, and the other one coming from our mother. People who have a normal appearance for a certain genetic character are made of two kinds of people, really. There are those who have two normal genes determining this characteristic, and there is a minority of people who carry one mutated or abnormal gene, whose harmful effect is not expressed because of the presence of a second, normal gene. The people who carry one normal and one abnormal gene, but who look normal, are called *heterozygous for a certain character,* or *carriers of an anomaly.* These people include, for example, the healthy-looking parents of the PKU child. They have a child who by bad luck happens to have received from each of his parents their bad genes instead of the good one.

Although PKU as a disease is a rare phenomenon (it affects only one in 20,000 children), it can be calculated that as many as one person out of every seventy is a carrier of one PKU gene. Since there are many other diseases inherited in the same fashion, it can also be calculated that every one of us is the carrier—and we don't know it most of the time—of anything from one to eight abnormal mutated genes.

There are good reasons to believe, on the basis of the latest developments in biochemical research, that carriers of such mutated genes have certain subtle peculiarities in their physiology that will soon be detectable by more refined tests than those available today. Even today we can already detect carriers of certain conditions.

Establishing people's biochemical profile will therefore permit a precise evaluation of the risks incurred in choosing a particular mate for procreation. Real prevention of mental retardation due to a genetic cause could be achieved, provided, of course, that people are willing to follow the geneticist's advice.

IMPACT ON GENETIC MAKEUP

If research goes on vigorously and automation is used to screen larger numbers of people, this type of prevention is not a utopian dream. These prospects are so well recognized by scientists today that geneticists have already raised the question about what impact such advances will have on the genetic makeup of the human species once the cruel but effective mechanisms of natural selection have been bypassed by human ingenuity.

Will unfavorable genes, although not achieving full expression, accumulate in our population? Will they reach an incidence such as finally to be present in all individuals and make any human couple a high risk pair? This is possible, but only in the distant future. So far, our technological and scientific progress moves at a rate that is so much faster than human evolution, that—provided we remain aware of the fact that with every step forward we take a little more of mankind's evolution into our own hands—we can confidently work at giving everyone, even the most afflicted, the fullest life possible.

ANOTHER VICTORY

I would like to tell you one more success story. It is not about what will be accomplished in the future but about something that has *already been achieved:* Victory over a disease causing mental retardation, among other disabilities, that in one generation was discovered and is being eliminated, right now.

You have all heard of the Rh incompatibility disease—erythroblastosis fetalis—in newborn children, that occurs when two or more children are born to a couple in which the father has an antigen called "Rh+" that the mother ("Rh−") does not have. Both parents are perfectly normal, but if the child inherits his father's Rh+ antigen, this might elicit in the mother during pregnancy and after delivery the production of antibodies against the child's antigen that is foreign to her body. This is due to the fact that some of a baby's cells may be brought into contact with the mother's antibody producing system by minute (and usually innocuous) exchanges of blood that may occur during pregnancy or more frequently and more massively at the time of delivery. The antibodies produced by the mother are dangerous because they are capable of reaching the baby's tissues and very effectively destroying the baby's cells, particularly his blood cells, causing among other things a severe jaundice in the baby at birth. The disease does not appear during the first pregnancy because the mother's antibodies take time to build up. But when subsequent pregnancies occur, she may already be sensitized and react much more violently. The only protection we could give children at risk, until now, was first to determine premaritally whether the parents were compatible or not, and then, when a high risk couple was detected, to give their newborn children massive blood transfusions at birth to remove the mother's antibodies from the baby's blood. This was, however, cumbersome and expensive to do and often only a partial remedy.

In 1960 two medical researchers at Johns Hopkins Hospital attacked the problem in a more radical and scientific way. They observed first that any adult Rh+ blood inoculated in an Rh− person elicits the production of antibodies and that these antibodies coat the Rh+ red blood cells, covering the antigenic sites. Once saturated with antibodies, such Rh+ cells become non-antigenic—that is, incapable of eliciting any further antibody production. Anti-Rh+ antibodies were found in a fraction of blood serum called 7S-gamma globulin that was successfully isolated and purified by a team of workers at Columbia University. So it was reasoned that, if immediately after delivery—and most blood exchange between child and mother occurs at that time—the mother could be given enough anti-Rh+ globulins to cover the baby's Rh+ cells, this would make the baby's cells immediately non-antigenic and prevent the mother from reacting to them by the production of antibodies of her own. She would, therefore, not be sensitized to the next Rh+ baby. This was tried in several hospitals in this country and in England and worked so well that no mothers were found to be sensitized following 600 high risk pregnancies, while in the nontreated control group the usual 23 percent of mothers had produced dangerous levels of antibodies.

The Food and Drug Administration has released a license to a pharmaceutical firm in New Jersey to produce the anti-Rh+ globulins commercially, and it is available now to all who need it, at the price of $100 for the complete treatment.

Thus a condition that put 400,000 of the four million children born per year in this country at grave risk and that used to kill 16,000 newborn babies per year in the U.S. alone while leaving thousands of others with mental retardation and other defects has been conquered within six years by good thinking and solid scientific work by a handful of people. Is there anything more to say in support of research? Isn't any single one of these children that were saved worth all the money and all the effort?

ROLE OF ASSOCIATIONS

The associations for retarded children represent the most concerned segment of the citizenry. What can their role be in supporting further research and progress? First of all, you can do a lot by having an understanding for the scientist's work and helping create among the lay public a climate in which he will be able to go on working.

Scientific research costs a great deal and may not always seem directly relevant to the problems and the immediate daily needs of the mentally retarded. One should understand, however, that research nearly always leads at first to the prevention of disease rather than its cure. This is because it is always easier to forestall damage than to repair it; thus, one knew how to prevent diphtheria before knowing how to cure it with antibiotics. Nevertheless, the age of antibiotics did eventually come, and research on the causes of mental retardation and the biochemical mechanisms that bring it about should be relentlessly pursued. The public should know that its investment is and will be paying dividends. Legislators, appropriators of funds and program planners should be constantly informed of new developments in research and the redefinition of needs they lead to.

APPLICATION AND REAPPLICATION

Your help is needed even more to make society willing to make swift and intelligent application of the scientists' findings. We have seen how mental retardation related to poverty is due essentially to a failure of modern preventive practices to reach the lives of the disadvantaged. Over 50 percent of the existing cases of mental retardation could be prevented if *all* segments of our population were reached by basic health services and would know how to apply those relatively simple and well established preventive measures that have become part of the life of the more aware and affluent among us. We, the affluent, have first to reach those whose lives have been relegated to the margins of our society. To do so, we have in many cases to reexamine our values and present way of life and—with discipline and objectivity—be willing to reassign part of our concerns and national resources to make progress available and meaningful to all.

While we still have to work at applying existing knowledge, our society has also to be educated so as to become able to take the decisions required by the new possibilities of prevention that are already opening up. Of immediate and paramount concern to us should be the question of therapeutic abortion, of its legalization or even its removal from legal consideration. Not only are we now often able to calculate the probability of the birth of a defective child, but—on the basis of chromosome or biochemical studies of amniotic cells—we are beginning to be able to make unquestionable prenatal diagnoses. It is essential that both the public and their legislators, who are facing the dilemma of the legalization of abortion in so many states at this time, be informed of such prospects. Few would argue that society has the right to inflict on a family the awesome burden and heartbreak of the care of a severely defective child whose birth could be prevented. Such a decision should never be imposed, but should be left exclusively to the parents themselves. They must have the right to decide, on the basis of their personal ethical attitudes and economic resources, whether to avail themselves of the diagnostic possibilities and the choice they offer. Because such a decision affects first of all the lives of the family concerned in a crucial way, it must be made by those who have to bear its consequences.

The existence of methods of analysis that will make it possible to detect high risk couples before they conceive will confront individuals with responsibilities not only toward each other and their projected offspring, but also toward society. Medicine will soon be able to correct the symptoms of many genetic aberrations and so save lives that would otherwise be doomed.

We should not delude ourselves, however, into thinking that it will be possible, in the foreseeable future, to modify the genetic substance itself. Carriers of genetic abnormalities, capable of procreating, will increase in numbers. The respect of the individual that lies at the root of our social philosophy will hopefully always make us shun methods that curtail his freedom, such as enforced programs of sterilization. It therefore becomes even more important than ever before that individuals in our society, mindful of its survival, develop a strong social consciousness. Enlightened modern men and women ought to be willing to submit to a scientific inquiry into their genetic endowment, and then to either accept the solution of therapeutic abortion or refrain from having children in partnership with those who carry the same deleterious gene. It will be again the responsibility of informed and concerned groups of citizens, such as the association for retarded children, to be the spokesmen for such necessary new attitudes, to make it possible for mankind to really benefit from the great harvest of progress that its scientific adventurers are reaping.

Progress is not only in these medical victories, these promises, but also in the new confrontations with traditional social behavior and attitudes. If new attitudes are required to fulfill the promise of complete victory over mental retardation, your duty is to work at bringing them about. If you are successful in your mission—in a real partnership for progress—then, as much as the scientists themselves, you will have joined those whom John Gardner calls "the greatest life saviors."

50 A DECADE OF RESEARCH ON THE EDUCATION OF THE MENTALLY RETARDED [1]

James J. McCarthy
Richard C. Scheerenberger

From *Mental Retardation Abstracts,* Vol. 3, No. 4, October–December 1966, pp. 481–501. Reprinted with the permission of the U.S. Department of Health, Education, and Welfare and the authors. Dr. McCarthy is Professor, Department of Studies in Behavioral Disabilities, University of Wisconsin, Madison. Dr. Scheerenberger is Superintendent, Central Wisconsin Colony and Training School, Madison and is also on the faculty of the University of Wisconsin, Madison.

Within the past ten years, a gradually increasing number of studies on the education of the mentally retarded have appeared in the literature. For the most part, educational research is of the applied variety; the first section of this paper will review such works. However, inferences useful for the educational effort can also be obtained from basic research. The second section of this paper has been devoted to a review of selected basic studies on retardates which appear to have rather direct implications for the classroom.

SECTION I: EDUCATIONAL RESEARCH

While every attempt has been made to review the existing literature thoroughly, no claims for comprehensive coverage are made. In essence, applied research and exploratory studies relevant to education have been reviewed here. Unless they are associated with educational research, papers on the following topics have not been included: professional training standards, theories, teaching techniques, program descriptions, articles on guidelines, issues or needs, or descriptions of curriculum guides. Studies reviewed date from 1955 through 1965.

During the past decade, a number of excellent articles and reviews, related to research on the education of the mentally retarded, have appeared: Cantor (1957); Kvaraceus (1958); Cantor (1959); Goldstein (1959); Dunn and Capobianco (1959); Carriker (1960); Blackman (1963); Simches and Bohn (1963); Cain and Levine (1963); Kirk (1964). While all authors find research efforts wanting, there is no clear consensus about the major problems in the area. Some key problem areas identified are: inappropriateness of research methodology, the critical need for the evaluation of methods and materials used in the education of retardates, and the lack of rapprochement between basic and applied research.

[1] The authors wish to express their thanks to Richard Ferber, Project Assistant, University of Wisconsin, for his help in collecting articles reviewed in the present paper.

For convenience, the literature reviewed in the first section of the present paper has been divided as follows: (1) research on academic subjects, (2) research on achievement and failure in school, (3) research on programed instruction and operant conditioning, (4) research on adjustment, and (5) research on trainable retardates.

Research on Academic Subjects

The literature on academic subjects has been grouped into research on reading, arithmetic, language, and "other."

READING. The pivotal tool subject for all school-aged children appears to be reading; researchers, accordingly, have devoted considerable attention to this topic. Recent general reviews on reading (Gutts, 1963; Harris, 1963) and reading readiness (Gunderson, 1964) contain entries that will prove useful to those interested in mental retardation. For comprehensive reviews relating specifically to reading in retardates, the reader is referred to Dunn (1954) and Kirk (1964).

Studies (e.g., Gilley, 1963) continue to find retardates below their expectancy in reading. Groelle (1961) found about 50 percent of the educable high school students he studied to be below third-grade reading level.

Jordon (1961, 1963) has underscored the need for selecting the appropriate developmental approach in teaching reading to retardates; matching methods with specific learning problems can reduce the typical gap between expectancy and performance. Daly and Lee's (1960) attempt to increase reading efficiency in institutionalized retardates led them to similar conclusions.

Some promising approaches to developmental reading schemes for retardates have been suggested within the past decade such as progressive choice, initial teaching alphabet (i.t.a.), and various attempts at programed instruction.

Davy (1962, 1963) reported on the usefulness of a maximum discrimination method of teaching reading, based upon work by Wollman, called progressive choice. It is, to quote Davy, ". . . a step-by-step method for transforming a perception from one sensory modality to another. . . ." This method has been used successfully with intellectually normal children and has shown promise in pilot work with retardates. In reviewing basically British research on the i.t.a., Williams (1965) concluded that the work on this "one symbol–one sound," phonic scheme allows for very cautious optimism as regards its use with retardates. The once dreaded period of transfer from i.t.a. to traditional orthography seems to have been accomplished with unexpected ease thus far. Williams prophetically saw one value of i.t.a. as a stimulating new, simplified approach to the teaching of reading. Essentially untested, but promising, are such newcomers as the "Mixie the Pixie" basic learning series (Jacoby, *et al.,* 1966) which attempts to teach, simultaneously, beginning reading, numbers, and social skills; and the Peabody Rebus Reading program (Woodcock, 1966) which begins by utilizing rather universal symbols, instead of words, within a programmed format.

Studies such as Keating's (1962) indicate continued success in using traditional methods of remedial reading with retardates. It appears the remedial aspects of reading instruction have received far less research attention than the developmental aspects. However, since about 1960, efforts have increasingly been directed at children with "learning disabilities" (e.g., Barsch, 1965; Bateman, 1964); many of these remedial approaches will find application with the frankly retarded.

The neurological basis for reading disabilities continues to intrigue researchers. MacKinnon (1964), in reviewing literature on the subject from Hinshelwood to date, concluded that there is sufficient evidence to consider neurological impairment as one legitimate cause of reading disability. Neither Vance (1956) nor Capobianco and Miller (1958) found significant differences on various indices of reading ability between exogenous and endogenous institutionalized retardates. Frey (1961), on the other hand, using special- and regular-class, brain-injured and familial retardates, found many significant differences in reading prowesses, favoring the brain-injured; his testing battery was similar to that used by Capobianco and Miller. Kirk (1964) ascribes this apparent discrepancy to the fact that Frey's children were systematically instructed with appropriate techniques (Strauss); the difference in findings might also be a function of institutionalization. Suffice it to say that the legacy of discrepancy associated with reading and neurological impairment, has not been resolved within the past decade.

The effects of adjustment on reading in retardates was investigated by Reger (1964) who found that retarded boys characterized as poor readers had high scores on the Children's Manifest Anxiety Scale (CMAS), while the correlation between reading and CMAS scores for the better readers was negligible. Brooks (1962) studied four types of retardates in groups of 15 each: (1) internal locus of control (ILC) with high anxiety, (2) ILC with low anxiety, (3) external locus of control (ELC) with high anxiety, and (4) ELC with low anxiety. ILC children with low anxiety contributed the best performance, while ILC children with high anxiety produced the poorest gains. Clearly, these studies suggest the influence of "nonintellective, affective" factors on reading in retardates deserves further research attention.

In summary, the most promising development in reading for retardates within the past few years is the appearance of new methods for developmental instruction in reading. The appreciation of the need to match the learner to the method and the operational distinction between developmental and remedial approaches are concepts which have characterized the writings of the past decade. This is partially due to the increasing availability of appropriate, developmental reading schemes. The intricate relationships between reading and neurological impairment still have not been defined, nor has sufficient attention been given to studying the effects of "nonintellective, affective factors" on reading in retardates.

The reader will find further references to reading in retardates under the headings of "Programmed Instruction" and "Achievement."

ARITHMETIC. Researchers, in the main, have evidenced less interest in the applied study of arithmetic learning in retardates than in the study of reading. Arithmetic seems less beset with the perceptual problems of reading according to Capobianco (1954) who found no differences between matched exogenous and endogenous retardates in arithmetic achievement and in various indices of perceptual processes required in doing arithmetic. Both Dunn (1954) and Klausmeier, *et al.* (1959) compared normals with retardates on arithmetic processes. Dunn found no significant differences between retarded and normal MA match-mates on computation, although on arithmetic reasoning tests (which require reading), significant differences were found favoring the latter. The Klausmeier, *et al.* study extended over a three-year period and utilized a sample of 120 children, 40 each at high, average, and low IQ levels. No differences in retention were found between the IQ groups when the learning task was geared to the child's current achievement level.

Brown and Dyer (1963) compared two groups of 11 children each on teaching only versus teaching plus practice on various aspects of applied arithmetic (e.g., calendar, money). As expected, the group with practice performed better on retest.

Woodward (1961) investigated the concept of number in 50 educable adult retardates and 44 trainable children by replicating the classic Piaget experiments on them. In general, subjects responded in a manner similar to normal children of four to seven years of age; this was characterized as performance at the concrete-intuitive level. However, few subjects performed at the same level on all four experiments. Silverstein, *et al.* (1964) investigated the meaning of indefinite arithmetic terms in adolescent retardates (mean IQ 49.5) by asking them to take "a few," "most," and "a lot" of beads from a tray. Curiously, subjects took more beads for "a lot" than for "most" although they took more beads for "most" than they did for a "few." The authors concluded that the subjects' performances were not significantly related to their understanding of definite (versus indefinite) number concepts.

Finley (1962) compared 54 retarded children with 54 nonretarded children of the same mental age and (approximate) social class on three forms of the same test of arithmetic fundamentals; a concrete form (used actual objects), a pictorial form, and a symbolic form. On the concrete and pictorial form, no group differences were found; on the symbolic form, retardates were significantly superior. Retardates, in fact, had about the same mean score on all three tests; nonretardates did best on the pictorial form. Several explanations were offered for this unusual outcome.

In general, findings of studies on arithmetic ability in retardates support the views that (1) retardates learn and retain adequately when arithmetic work is presented at their achievement level, (2) perceptual processes play a less conspicuous role in arithmetic than in reading, and (3) retardates perform better at arithmetic computation than at arithmetic reasoning. The few existing studies on "quantitative concepts" in retardates suggest that it may be more than reading deficiency that depresses their performance on arithmetic reasoning tasks.

LANGUAGE. Language, as used here, refers to the ability to comprehend, use, and think in linguistic symbols; it is not synonomous with either speech or language arts. Though few would argue that the acquisition and use of language is a necessary prerequisite for the learning of the tool subjects, language is not—as a rule—formally taught in school; correspondingly, applied research on language as a school subject is tangential.

Comprehensive reviews by Harrison (1958), Smith (1962a), and McCarthy (1964) will provide the reader with the broad spectrum of research effort being mounted in behalf of the retarded in this area. The present review is more concerned with the "education-associated" studies of language in retarded children.

Smith (1962b) reported on an experimental language program for classroom use with educable retardates which consisted of 33 lesson plans designed to enhance each of the nine language abilities identified and assessed by the *Illinois Test of Psycholinguistic Abilities* (ITPA). The 16 experimental subjects did, in fact, significantly surpass their matched controls on posttesting. However, a follow-up study (Mueller and Smith, 1964), about a year later, indicated that the group difference, though still favoring the experimental subjects, was no longer statistically significant. Subsequently, Dunn and Smith (1964) marketed the *Peabody Language Development Kit* (PLDK), a direct outgrowth of Smith's original work. The PLDK consists of 200 lesson plans, a number which, according to its authors, should provide sufficient overlearning so that retention will be considerably greater than that obtained with the original 33 lessons. Blessing (1964) attempted to improve the vocal expressive ability (encoding) of educable retardates; following treatment the 20 experimental subjects significantly exceeded the controls on several indices of encoding. Weld (1964), in a two-year follow-up of the Blessing study, found the differences once favoring the experimental subjects had dissipated. Olson, Hahn, and Herman (1965) described a two-month language training program for young retarded children along with pre- and posttreatment scores; the lack of inferential statistics precludes any conclusions at present, but gains were impressive on casual inspection. Irwin (1959) and Harrison (1959) also put forth program plans for language development in retardates.

The importance of some type of school program in language learning is underscored in a survey of 209 retarded, special class children (Speidel,

1958) in which tests of listening, speaking, reading, and writing were administered. Listening comprehension was the best developed skill in these children, followed by speaking; the development of these skills and their subsequent employment in developing competence in tool subjects in a "systematic program of language instruction" is urged by the author. A developmental language schedule, with landmark skills and suggested activities, has been put forth by Mecham (1963) as an aid to teachers of the retarded.

More often than not, no systematic language training programs exist in classes for retardates; hence, deficits accumulate. Wiseman (1965) describes a set of remedial measures based upon the language abilities assessed by the ITPA.

Language deficits are, perhaps, more obviously in need of treatment in trainable retardates. Attempts to improve the linguistic performance of such children have met with limited success. Johnson and Capobianco (1957) compared 24 experimental trainables with 24 matched controls in language age (LA) before and after the former received a year of language development training. No significant differences were found on posttesting. Kolstoe (1958) randomly divided 30 trainable children into experimental and control groups. To the former, he administered a five-day per week, 45-minute per day, language development program for five and one-half months. On posttesting, Kolstoe found the experimental children to be significantly superior on some (but not all) of the language abilities tested. Blue (1963a) used the language lessons, developed by Smith, on older trainable children and youth (CA 8–4 to 17–9). After about three months of treatment, the experimental group had progressed 5.67 months in LA. However, the control group (no treatment) had, for some reason, advanced 3.67 months in LA and the two-month group difference was not statistically significant.

A number of ingenious studies, which have direct significance for the educator, were reported in Schiefelbusch (1963) on the verbal behavior of retardates working with retardates (Siegel and Harkins, 1963) and on the verbal behavior of retardates working with adults (Siegel, 1963). In the first of these studies, it was found that adults responded to the more linguistically sophisticated retardates by instinctively using longer sentences and higher type-token ratios. Clearly, in certain situations, the child's verbal behavior can exercise a "control" over adult verbal output. Rosenberg, Spradlin, and Mabel (1961) tested retarded children and classified them as "high" or "low" in verbal facility. They then formed three groups (highs, lows, and mixed highs and lows) and observed the degree of interaction. The pure "high" group interacted adequately as did the pure "low" group; the mixed group, however, did not interact adequately. Horowitz (1963) attempted to find the most effective reinforcer for vocal output in retardates. He compared candy, vocal, smiling, vocal-smiling, and candy-vocal and found the last mentioned to be most effective. This accords with the experimental findings of Barnett, Ellis, and Pryer (1959) who found they could increase the production of personal pronouns, in the speech of retardates, by saying "good" following each occurrence of the words "I" and "we" in the retardates vocal output.

To summarize, there appears to be ample justification to regard language development and remediation as an integral part of the academic curriculum for retardates, since tool subjects and content studies assume minimal linguistic adequacy.

EXPERIMENTAL LANGUAGE. Programs for educable retardates have been demonstrated to be successful over limited periods of time; some of these programs are now available commercially. The need for language development programs with trainable retardates is even more evident than for educable retardates, but success in such ventures has been limited. The more successful trainable programs appear to be characterisized by intensive and systematic efforts, irrespective of content. Research on effective reinforcements for vocal output in retardates and on the effects of retardate's verbal performance on adult verbal output has been reported; such research holds much promise because of its direct applicability to the classroom.

OTHER. A number of additional studies have appeared or been initiated within the past ten years, on academic aspects of education for retardates other than reading, arithmetic or language. These include work on programs for brain-injured retardates, audiovisual aids, content studies, studies on motor and/or physical characteristics of retardates, and miscellany.

Programs for the brain-injured: The contributions of Cruickshank, *et al.* (1961) and Gallagher (1960) are well known and will not be reviewed here. Their significance lies in the fact that the programs reported were scientifically evaluated; the literature contains many suggested programs for retardates which include no experimental support for their efficacy.

Vance (1956) reported a comparison of institutionalized retardates with positive neurological signs with a matched group (CA, IQ, achievement) having no such signs. All children received two, one and one-half hour periods of highly prescribed, structured educational programs per week over a period of eight months. Evaluations were made prior to treatment, immediately following treatment, and three months following treatment. The brain-damaged children performed significantly better on a few of the evaluative measures immediately following the study but these differences had dissipated by the three-month follow-up. These findings are in accord with those of Cruickshank, *et al.* (1961) and Gallagher (1960). Generally, academic gains with such children are hard to achieve and extremely difficult to maintain.

Audiovisual aids: Carter (1961) compared three techniques of film utilization in teaching special class retardates a unit on health. Goldstein

(1964), in his book on audiovisual instruction for retardates, reports a pilot study confirming the usefulness of such instruction. Beyond this, little exists in the way of evaluated audiovisual aids for retardates despite the fact that such materials are becoming increasingly available.

Content studies: Although a number of articles have suggested music activities for retardates (McLaughlin, 1963), the present authors could find no recent studies evaluating such activities or even suggesting criteria and indices for evaluation. Mills, *et al.* (1961) compared art activities, specially designed for retardates, with "traditional" activities, utilizing anecdotal records or reactions, independent judgments of art products, questionnaires, grades, psychometric test results and teacher judgments as evaluative indices. Thresher (1963) described a science curriculum designed for trainable children at the Fernald State School. Though intuitively appealing and rationally derived, there are no evaluative data presented by which to judge its effectiveness. Matyas (1964) surveyed secondary programs for educable retardates in Pennsylvania and found, among other things, that the bulk of the school time was spent on "academic" subjects with only about 10 percent of the school week being devoted to social–occupational pursuits.

Studies on motor and/or physical characteristics of retardates: The work in this area can be divided into two parts: Studies dealing with the physical traits of the retarded, and studies concerned with physical activity as it affects affective and intellectual functioning.

Stein (1963) prepared a critical review of research on motor function and physical fitness in retardates (102 refs.). The classic work by Francis and Rarick (1959) surveyed the gross motor abilities of 284 educable retardates between the ages of 7–6 to 14–6 and found them inferior to norms by two to four years in static and dynamic strength, running speed, agility, and balance. Howe (1959), using a smaller number of similar retardates but a wider variety of tests, confirmed, essentially, the Francis and Rarick findings. Culley, *et al.* (1963) found institutionalized retardates to be shorter and lighter than normal with this tendency increasing as a function of motor dysfunction and/or increased retardation. In comparing normal children, community retardates, and institutionalized retardates on the Lincoln–Oseretsky, Malpass (1960) found no differences between the retarded groups but significant differences between retardates and normals. In the studies cited above, retardates are below norms without exception; seldom is research so unequivocal.

Gearheart (1964) implemented and assessed a program to develop motor skills in retardates (balance, coordination, jumping, agility). Four special classes in Cedar Rapids, Iowa, served as experimental groups; their teachers were given special orientation. The remainder of the special classes served as controls. The study lasted one school year with testing occurring before, during, and after treatment. Posttest differences favored experimental classes on about half the assessment tests. Since the program is easy to implement, the author considers this outcome as adequate demonstration of its usefulness. The almost certain knowledge that retardates are physically subnormal coupled with evidence that some of their physical skills can be improved, strongly suggests curricular changes in this regard.

An increasing amount of work has been directed at exploring the relationship between physical factors and intellectual and/or affective factors in retardates. Daw (1964) studied the effect of special exercises on body image. A group of seven institutionalized retardates were designated as experimental and given "Kephart-type" exercises for six months while the control group received only their baseline physical education. Pre- and posttesting on the Goodenough Draw-a-Man Test showed an eight-month improvement in experimental subjects as compared to a one-month improvement in controls. Though the author recognizes a number of design inadequacies in the study, results are sufficiently promising to warrant further work. Oliver (1958) found that ten weeks of simple physical conditioning exercises could improve the Goodenough and Terman–Merrill IQ scores of 19 teen-aged, educable retardates. Smith and Hurst (1961) found a significant relationship between motor ability (assessed by the Lincoln–Oseretsky) and peer acceptance (assessed by total peer contacts), using 18 trainable and 25 educable retardates as subjects.

The implications of motor activity for perceptual development (Kephart, 1960) and learning disabilities (Barsch, 1965) seem applicable to retardates. In the physical education of normal children, Cratty (1964) has developed the relationship of movement and motor learning in detail. Robins and Robins (1963) describe a method of rhytmic movement in relation to music as an important aid to the educational process in retardates (educational/rhythmics). The value of this attractive approach, however, has yet to be scientifically evaluated.

Miscellany: Interesting research is underway in projects by Dumphrey (1965–1966) and Blatt (1961–1962). Dumphrey is studying the effects of integrating retardates into normal groups, a movement in accord with present thinking but in contrast to the traditional concepts of the special class. Blatt is studying the effects of intensive, early training (responsive environment) on subsequent, cognitive development in retardates. The motivating concept of this effort is that intellectual and social limitations of familial retardates are not necessarily inherent.

In summary, a wide variety of applied and exploratory work, beyond that in reading, arithmetic and language, has occurred in the past decade. Work with exogenous retardates has been characterized by difficulty in achieving academic gains and even greater difficulty in maintaining them. Quantitative evaluation of audiovisual materials and of music, science and other content curricula for retardates is practically, nonexistent. Retardates have been shown to be clearly subaverage in physical ability and development but at least one study has suggested curricular changes that might be utilized in reducing these limitations. Research on the relationship of physical factors with affective and intellectual factors in retardates is just commencing, although the past decade has seen considerable theorizing in this area. Studies in early, fortuitous placement of retardates and on their integration into normal groups are beginning; these studies hold promise for preventing additional limitations upon retardates imposed by inadequate education practices.

Achievement and Failure in School

With an occasional exception, studies on the efficacy of special classes for educable retardates have not been gratifying (Dunn, 1959; Kirk, 1964). In the main, regular class retardates do as well, academically, as their special class counterparts; there seems to be some evidence that special class retardates are better adjusted than retardates retained in regular classes. Considering the methodological problems which plague efficacy studies, it would seem the better part of wisdom to accept both of these general conclusions as tentative. Indeed, it appears to the present writers, that enough of this type of research has been done; there is probably more profit in further investigating factors which affect academic gain. Numerous researchers, over the years, have attempted to isolate the factors which affect achievement in special class retardates; only a few recent, illustrative studies can be reviewed here. Among the factors investigated were sex of child, personality adjustment, anxiety, age and/or grade in school, cultural factors, early development, incentives, and intelligence. The reader should be forewarned that researchers have, by no means, achieved consensus on the effects of most of these factors on achievement.

Anderson (1964) compared retarded adolescent achievers and nonachievers and found that "not only did more girls than boys achieve in keeping with their ability level, but also the girls achieved at a higher level than the boys." Sociocultural status, educational milieu, home conditions and personality adjustment did not sharply differentiate achievers from nonachievers in this study. Jacobs (1957) administered intelligence and achievement tests to 293 teen-aged retardates in the Cincinnati Public Schools and found (1) girls achieved significantly higher than boys, (2) of several variables, MA correlated the highest with achievement (about +.70), and (3) arithmetic achievement was above reading and language achievement in both boys and girls. Snyder (1964) administered three personality tests to retarded subjects in their middle adolescence. Analysis of his data indicated that the better achievers showed superior personal and social adjustment, more wholesome self-attitudes, and a lower level of anxiety. He concluded that personality factors account, in large measure, for academic attainment of adolescent retardates and that anxiety inhibits learning in this group.

Research on the effects of anxiety on achievement is equivocal. Cochran and Cleland (1963) found differences in anxiety levels of retardates and normals matched for achievement at about the fourth grade level. Their efforts led them to speculate that, perhaps, less anxiety (of the type measured by the CMAS) would be more beneficial in the learning of complex tasks by retardates. Hart (1964) came to contrary conclusions. In comparing senior (slow learning) students in two schools in Australia, he found that the children with the highest achievement scores had "middle" anxiety scores; children with low achievement had "high" anxiety scores. Hart felt some anxiety provided a "realistic stress" and was motivational. Huber's (1965) results tend to support Hart. He studied anxiety and achievement in retardates in two schools. In one, he found no relationship between anxiety and achievement; in the other, pupils had higher anxiety scores and significantly higher achievement scores in reading, spelling, and arithmetic. These are but a few of the studies which spring from a long controversy over the effects of anxiety on achievement.

MA consistently correlates with achievement and has been suggested as a predictor of the same. Though this is accepted with great caution for nonretarded children (Edwards and Kirby, 1964), Scherer (1961) found Binet IQ the best predictor of subsequent achievement in brain-injured children (mean IQ 87) when compared with social adjustment, organic traits, emotional adjustment, and physical status. Knowledge of IQ would allow correct predictions in reading, spelling, and arithmetic in from 40 to 70 percent of the cases.

A prospective investigation (Jordan, 1964) of 124 children revealed that those associated with a history of paranatal complications will be more likely to demonstrate learning problems and reading problems later in school. Walton and Begg (1958) divided 48 retardates into four equal groups matched on a leg persistence task; to each they applied a different incentive; control, goal, competition, encouragement. The last two of this list were most effective. Additional work on the use of incentives with retardates has been reported by Heber (1958), Blank (1958) and O'Connor and Claridge (1958). All studies show the positive effect of incentive motivation on performing the experimental task.

In summary, academic achievement in retardates (or the lack of it) has been attributed to many factors. Present research appears to indicate the intelligence in younger retardates, personality factors in older retardates, and appropriate incentives in all ages may be important correlates of achievement. Retarded girls, regularly, seem to achieve beyond their male counterparts. Cultural factors and early developmental factors may be involved in the picture. The function of mild anxiety in producing or preventing achievement seems to be in question; there appears to be agreement that strong anxiety is harmful to academic achievement in retardates.

Thus, studies have been largely exploratory (i.e., correlation of achievement scores with quantitative measures of factors "suspected" of relating to achievement). To date, little of direct value for the classroom has emerged from this sizable body of research. What seems to be needed is research in which factors suspected of affecting achievement are somehow manipulated and their impact on achievement noted.

PROGRAMED INSTRUCTION AND OPERANT CONDITIONING

Two recent and related developments which may have far reaching effects on the education of retarded children are programed instruction (PI) and operant conditioning (OC).

For a comprehensive summary of studies using PI with retardates, completed or in progress in 1962, the reader is referred to Stolurow (1963). Studies reported as complete, in that review, will not be reviewed here.

Capobianco (1966), in an excellent assessment of the status of PI in special education, listed the minimum essential requirements of PI as: Small steps, participation by the learner, immediate feedback, near-errorless learning, and self-pacing. The bulk of research on PI with retardates, to date, fails to establish the superiority of PI due chiefly to (1) poor quality of programs, (2) inadequate field testing and revision of programs, and (3) programing principles that are contrary to teacher's philosophy. Capobianco noted that although much research is needed, it is "well within the competencies of present-day investigators."

Malpass, *et al.* (1964) contrasted acquisition and retention of work recognition and spelling skills in retardates learned via PI with those skills learned via traditional instruction (TI). Not only were both forms of PI used (automated and semi-automated) more effective than TI, but skills learned via PI were still largely intact two months following the completion of treatment. Kunkel (1962) taught spelling to 40 educable retardates on a simple teaching machine and contrasted learning with TI utilizing each child as his own control. Though the students, on posttesting, scored more words correctly following the four weeks of TI, they covered an equivalent program via PI in seven days. On a words-per-session basis, results favored PI. Blackman and Capobianco (1965) compared gains made in reading and arithmetic by retardates via PI with gains made by an equated group on the same content learned via TI. This ambitious and long-term effort failed to uncover significant differences in gain scores due to the fact that both groups gained significantly. The authors report, however, that the out-of-school deportment of the PI group improved as compared to the same behaviors of the TI group. Bradley and Hundziak (1965) found 17 retardates improved significantly in time telling ability as a result of exposure to the TMI–Grolier program on that subject (designed for intellectually average children); no controls were employed in this study, so conclusions must be regarded as tentative. Work on the teaching of arithmetic to retardates has been initiated by Sprague (1961) and Smith (1961).

PI, despite its limitations, has some important virtues for the educator; it requires a complete and detailed plan of what is to be taught, it systematically follows sound learning principles (e.g., small steps, immediate reinforcement), and, unlike most traditional education materials, is considered ready for use only after it has been field tested. A number of machines employed in the studies cited herein are now commercially available at prices ranging from 5 to 25 dollars. Increasingly, special educators will be employing these devices. However, very few programs for retardates now exist. It will be necessary, therefore, to include instruction on PI in the inservice and preservice programs for special educators since they must have skill in evaluating and modifying programs to suit the learning characteristics of their pupils.

OC of retardates has been largely confined to technical studies on institutionalized retardates with little application for the classroom.

Headrick (1963) discussed OC as it related to mental deficiency. She noted the OC derived from the observation that reward of any specific behavior increased the frequency of that behavior; the reinforcement schedule can be continuous or intermittent in regard to time and response rate. Shaping consists of reinforcing behaviors that successively approximate the criterion behavior.

Ellis, *et al.* (1960a), Bijou and Orlando (1961) and Orlando (1961) studied the effects of simple and multiple reinforcement schedules on the behavior of retardates. Some of the subjects involved in this work were at the lower end of the trainable spectrum. Doubtless these early studies had much to do with the application of OC techniques to such practical matters as toilet training in severely retarded, institutionalized children (Baumeister and Klosowski, 1965; Hundziak, *et al.,* 1965).

To date, however, there has been little application of such OC techniques to the mildly retarded who could, according to Headrick (1963), conceivably learn abstract concepts through the chaining of responses and shaping techniques. A rare, but promising application of operant techniques in the classroom is reported by Whelan and Haring (1966) to children with behavior problems; the principles applied to alter affective behavior should be equally applicable to intellectual behavior modification in retardates. The reader is referred to Lindsley (1964) for an excellent paper on OC in education.

To summarize, neither the behavior modification techniques of PI, specifically, nor OC, generally, have been widely exploited in behalf of retardates. Initial studies have shown promise. The principles of these techniques are few and their application notoriously empirical; applied researchers should have a field day. Research most critically needed in PI (Capobianco, 1966) includes analysis of practical variables affecting learning and retention in PI, chiefly, schedules of reinforcement, patterning of programs, and further study of prompting versus confirmation techniques. The possibilities of OC for retardates have barely been tapped. Headrick (1963) concluded, optimistically, "The extensive manipulation of reinforcement variables may lead to substantial alterations of our concept of capacity for adaptive behavior, and hence, of mental retardation in general."

Adjustment in Retardates

A moderate research interest in in-school and postschool adjustment of retardates is evident in the literature. Harris (1958) reported, in considerable quantitative detail, the alteration of negative behavior of a girl in an institutional school as a result of the teacher's deliberate use of permissiveness, suggestion, and discipline. Harris and Sievers (1959) reported on behavior changes in 18 adolescent, institutionalized, female retardates; each case was analyzed as in the original Harris study but, additionally, the collective data were subjected to inferential statistics demonstrating the efficacy of the approach for the group over a two-year period.

Lapp (1957) studied, via sociometric techniques, the acceptance and rejection scores of retarded pupils who were inserted—part time—into regular classes. Acceptance scores were lower than one would expect by chance alone but rejection scores did not differ from chance expectations; this does not accord fully with previous work in which retardates were more actively rejected. Miller (1956), like Lapp, found retarded students least accepted in regular class (as compared to children of average and above average intelligence), though not actively rejected.

Kern and Praeffle (1962) administered the California Test of Personality (CTP) to 31 retarded pupils each in the following settings: special class, special school, and regular class. Special class and special school retardates scored significantly higher on the CTP than regular class retardates. Kaplan (1962) tested retardates (a) in special classes for a year or more and (b) newly arrived, special class retardates, with the CMAS. Anxiety, though above norms for both groups, did not seem either due to, or alleviated by, special class; CMAS scores were about the same for both groups. Brite (1964) found no differences in the following indices of adjustment in slow learning fifth graders as a function of ability grouping: Aggression, depression, and inferiority feelings. McCoy (1963) compared 31 academically successful, educable retardates with 31 unsuccessful matchmates and found the former to be higher in realistic self-confidence and more realistic in their levels of aspiration.

Thus, adjustment in retardates has been examined as a function of teacher behavior, anxiety, ability grouping, and academic success. Reactions of nonretarded pupils to the retarded seem more those of nonacceptance as distinguished from outright rejection. Typically, sufficient variables are uncontrolled (or uncontrollable) in such research, therefore results must be viewed as tentative. The studies by Harris (1958) and Harris and Sievers (1959) can serve as models of methodology for educators.

Studies on the postschool adjustment of retardates are beyond the scope of this paper (e.g., Bobroff, 1956a; Bobroff, 1956b; Carriker, 1958; Charles, 1957; Phelps, 1960; Peterson and Smith, 1960; Dinger, 1961). Suffice it to say that one's overall impression of these studies is that adult adjustment of retardates appears to be superior to what one would predict from their school behavior.

Research on Trainable Children

Recently, research on trainable children has increased sufficiently in volume to warrant separate headings in some publications (e.g., Charney, in Kirk and Weiner, 1963). Much of this research relates to the efficacy of special classes for these children (e.g., Guenther, 1956; Hottell, 1958). Kirk (1964) provides an excellent review and evaluation of these studies. In the main, results have been negative, although extenuating factors can be readily identified. Chief among these factors would be the unknown value of the teaching procedures used; another would be lack of information about the learning characteristics of trainable children.

A useful study on teaching procedures for trainable children has been reported by Hudson (1960). Clearly, evaluation of materials and methods is sorely needed in this area.

Present methods of teaching trainables are unlikely to produce academic gains. Warren (1963) gave a variety of achievement tests to 177 trainable children with five or more years of schooling and concluded that such children do not achieve any appreciable degree of usefulness in handling academic subjects. On nonacademic tasks, the trainable fare better. Peck and Sexton (1961) monitored the progress of four groups of trainable children over a two-year period. Each of three groups was given training in social adjustment, self-care, language development, physical development, music, arts and crafts, and economic usefulness. One group was located in a public school, one in a segregated community center, one in a residential school, and a fourth (control) group received no training. Significant progress was reported by the authors in all experimental groups. Apart from the nonacademic nature of the curriculum, success here, where others had failed, may have been due to the great care taken in preparing teachers and materials and the rigid control of the curriculum.

It has been observed that while educators can point to only occasional studies of successful programs with trainables, psychologists can point to a far greater percent of success in their efforts to change the behavior of such children. For example, O'Connor and Hermelin (1959), Clarke and Lookson (1962), and Schueman (1958) have all demonstrated transfer ability in severely retarded subjects. This observation may not be appropriate, but it is thought provoking. Doubtless the laboratory setting of researchers permits greater control of subjects and refinement of measurement. This suggests that the educator might profit from an inspection of techniques and apparatus used in the laboratory. The work on OC and PI with retardates, reviewed elsewhere in this paper, suggests further useful leads.

Other recent innovations appear promising. Thompson (1963) has analyzed Binet responses of trainable preschoolers so as to derive from the same, suggestions for their instruction. A team approach (Taylor and Olson, 1964), colored materials (Dubrin and Kaye, 1963) and a system of sound–symbol teaching (Atkinson and Hart, 1963) have been explored with trainable children.

In summary, teaching efforts with trainable retardates have been characterized by only occasional successes (see also, section on Academic: Language). These successes appear to be derived from intensive, systematic, and well grounded efforts. It is suggested that the use of OC, PI, and laboratory techniques and methods might prove useful in effecting behavioral changes in retardates. Some new ideas for teaching trainable children are beginning to appear in the professional literature and on the commercial market. Honest professional discontent with past efforts coupled with the established responsibility of the public school for trainable children seem to be factors responsible for forging a sobering consensus; training trainables is a complex and difficult task.

Concluding Statement on Educational Research

The volume of educational research on retardates, completed within the past ten years, though impressive, barely begins to answer the many legitimate questions raised by practitioners. Additionally, the literature is fragmentary and nonprogrammatic. It is hoped that within the next decade, steps can be taken to assure an adequate volume of appropriate, practical research; at a minimum, these steps would include: (1) the schools' acceptance of the role of the applied research agency, (2) the effective participation of the teacher in the conduct of research, and (3) the production of doctoral level, applied researchers to work in the schools. The advantages of this plan are discussed elsewhere (McCarthy, 1966a; 1966b).

SECTION II: EDUCATIONAL IMPLICATIONS OF LEARNING RESEARCH

The last decade has witnessed an exponential increase in the interest and activity of experimental psychologists to understand the learning and behavior characteristics of the mentally retarded. Unfortunately, however, most of their efforts have gone unnoted by the educator. This, no doubt, is due to the educator's lack of familiarity with experimental parlance and technology and to the failure of the psychologist to translate the implications of his research to the educational situation.

The purpose of this section will be to review some of the research literature, drawing inferences relative to educational practices with the retarded. The discussion is not designed to be a critique of experimental research. Such reviews may be found in a number of sources, e.g., Denny (1964), Lipman (1963), Stevenson (1963), and Rosenberg (1963).

In addition, this part will be concerned primarily with the area of verbal as opposed to affective or psychomotor learning. Specifically, the literature will be reviewed under four generic headings: rate of learning, factors affecting learning, retention, and factors affecting retention.

Rate of Learning

In recent years, a number of experiments have been conducted for the purpose of studying the learning rates of retarded subjects. In essence, these studies have attempted to answer the question, "Are the retarded actually slow learners?" Various approaches have been used to investigate this problem, and the performances of the retarded have been compared with those of normal and gifted subjects matched on the basis of chronological age (CA) and/or mental age (MA).

Before proceeding to a review of the relevant research literature, it is advisable to become acquainted with serial and paired-associate learning. These two methods are commonly used in studying both rate of learning and retention.

A serial learning task is one in which the stimuli, such as words or nonsense syllables, are exposed to the subject one at a time in a set sequence. The subject's task is to learn this sequence so that when he sees one stimulus, he can identify correctly the next stimulus before it appears. The individual's rate of learning usually is measured on the basis of the number of trials required to repeat the entire list without error.

In paired-associate learning, the subject learns to match a particular response with a particular stimulus. For example, a paired-associate item may consist of a picture of a boat and the word "cat." Subsequently, when the subject sees the picture of the boat, he is to indicate that the correct response is the word "cat." The paired-associate items may consist of pictured objects, nonsense syllables, geometric patterns or words. Again, learning is measured on the basis of the number of trials required by the subject to match correctly a predetermined number of paired-associate items. In contrast with serial learning, paired-associate items rarely are presented in any set order.

Educators not conversant with experimental techniques frequently express concern over the fact that much of the learning research employs nonmeaningful, nonsense-type tasks which have little or no relevance to the type of material introduced in the educational environment. This procedure is necessitated by the researcher's obligation to exercise as much control as possible over the child's previous learning which may have great influence on how he performs on the experimental task. Further, it should be recognized that the experimental psychologist is basically concerned with understanding the behavior of the retarded and in determining the lawful relationships between experiences or stimuli and responses. He is looking for principles of learning which may be applicable to a number of situations, including the school.

The experiment which stimulated considerable interest in the learning rates of retarded subjects was reported by Eismann (1958). In this study, she compared the learning performances of retarded (mdn IQ = 69), normal (mdn IQ = 99), and gifted (mdn IQ = 123) adolescents on a simple seven-item, paired-associate task consisting of pictures of common objects, e.g., basket—hammer, auto—fork, bird—envelope. As indicated, there was no significant difference between the learning rates of the three groups equated on the basis of CA.

Of the subsequent studies concerned with the learning rates of retarded subjects, only one tended to support the findings of Eismann. Vergason (1964), again using highly meaningful, paired-associates (pictures of common objects), found no difference in the number of trials required to learn the task by adolescent educable retarded and normal subjects.

In contrast, a number of studies in which subjects were equated on the basis of CA have reported findings in variance with those of Eismann and Verguson. For example, Ellis, *et al.* (1960b) compared the learning rates of 84 institutionalized retardates, 72 girls from an industrial school, and 144 public high school students. In this instance, the gifted and normal subjects learned the ten-word (nouns) serial learning task at a faster rate than did the retardates. Similar results were obtained by Berkson and Cantor (1960), Ring and Palermo (1961), Jensen (1963), Blue (1963b), Lance (1965), and Ring (1965). In each of these experiments, adolescent gifted and/or normal subjects consistently outperformed the adolescent educable retarded. Thus, the retarded were slow learners when compared with normal and gifted individuals of a similar CA.

When compared on the basis of mental age, however, the retarded can learn a task as rapidly as the normal and gifted. In the Ring and Palermo (1961) study, when the performances of the adolescent educable mentally retarded subjects were compared with those of normal subjects of equivalent mental ages, there was no observable significant difference in their respective abilities to learn a meaningful paired-associate task.

The results of this study confirmed those reported earlier by Johnson and Blake (1960). These researchers found no marked discrepancies between the learning rates of 30 retarded subjects (mean MA = 110.73 months) and normal subjects (mean MA = 111.40 months) on a serial learning task consisting of six nonsense syllables, e.g., NAF, PIM, and TEV. In fact, the retarded revealed a slight tendency to require fewer trials to reach the established criterion.

Thus, it can be concluded that when a task is meaningful and within the comprehension of the retarded, they can learn it as rapidly as anyone.[2] In this sense, the retarded *are not* slow learners.

Of equal importance is the fact that several studies (e.g., Ellis, *et al.*, 1960b; Jensen, 1963) specifically pointed out the pronounced variability of the performances of the retarded. In other words, retardates of similar IQ and MA were markedly different in their ability to learn the same task. Some learned rapidly, while others required an exceptional number of trials to reach the set criterion. In the Jensen (1963) study, for example, though the retardates learned significantly fewer items than did their normal and gifted counterparts, one of the two highest scores was recorded by a retardate. Incidentally, Klausmeier, Lehmann, and Beeman (1959) observed considerable differences in the levels of reading, arithmetic, and language achievement among their retarded subjects.

These findings lend impetus to the educator's responsibility to become thoroughly familiar with the abilities and limitations of each student and to work with him within the realm of his comprehension. Also, it is obvious that neither the IQ nor MA is a reliable predictor of a child's specific learning abilities.

Factors Affecting Learning

Experimental research has revealed a number of influences which may impede or accelerate a retardate's learning performance. A consideration of the following areas will illustrate the potential significance of learning research to educational practices and procedures: attention, utilization of past experience, and meaningfulness.

ATTENTION. Recent research has indicated a qualitative difference in the learning of trainable retardates and normal children. Though trainable retardates can learn a discrimination task as well as normal subjects of comparable MA, they often do not because of their failure to pay proper heed to the correct stimulus cues.

House and Zeaman (1958), for example, studied the learning behavior of 20 normal nursery school pupils and 30 trainable retardates from the Mansfield Training School. All subjects had an MA within the range of 48 to 70 months. The task, typical of simple discrimination learning, required the subjects to learn which of the stimuli, presented two at a time, was correct and which was incorrect. The normals outperformed the retardates, i.e., they had fewer errors. Studies by Girardeau (1959) and House and Zeaman (1960a) supported these findings.

Having eliminated the influence of such variables as emotion, memory, motivation, institutionalization, and parental education, Zeaman and

[2] It has been suggested that one of the major reasons why the retardates learned as fast as other subjects equated on the common basis of CA as observed in the Eismann and Verguson studies was that the learning tasks were very simple and highly meaningful.

House (1963, p. 220) concluded that "the visual discrimination learning of moderately retarded children requires the acquisition of a chain of two responses: (1) attending to the relevant stimulus dimension and (2) approaching the correct cue of that dimension. The difficulty that retardates have in discrimination learning is related to limitations in the first, or attention, phase of this dual process rather than the second."

Zeaman (1959) and Zeaman and House (1963) discussed the educational implications associated with this dimension of attention. They emphasized the need for educators to make a concerted effort to ensure that the child is paying attention to the correct aspects of the learning situation. This can be accomplished by manipulation, by the use of color, by placing the essential cues in three dimensions, and by reducing the number of irrelevant cues.

Bensberg (1958) conducted a study which supported this concept of "attention." In this experiment, five sets of mentally retarded subjects were pretrained to respond to either revelant or irrelevant cues. Those subjects trained on the relevant cues developed appropriate "attention sets," and, subsequently, learned the experimental task significantly faster than subjects not so trained. Similar results were obtained by Barnett and Cantor (1957) and Smith and Means (1961).

UTILIZATION OF PAST EXPERIENCE. Efficacious, efficient learning is, to a great extent, dependent upon the learner's ability to use past experiences in solving new problems. This most important process of learning has been studied under the categories of mediation and transfer of training, which, for all practical purposes, are closely allied.

A number of studies have indicated that mediation does facilitate learning among retarded subjects. Berkson and Cantor (1960), for example, compared the learning performances of 34 normal and 24 educable retarded subjects, all between the chronological ages of nine and twelve, using a standard mediation paradigm: learn A-B, learn B-C, learn A-C. In essence, the subject first learns to match correctly the paired-associate items A and B, and then learns a second list of paired-associate items B and C. If mediation is an effective process, then the subject should learn the third list (A-C) more rapidly than either of the previous two. This hypothesis was supported in the study by Berkson and Cantor—mediation did produce faster learning of the A-C list on the part of both normal and retarded subjects. Furthermore, there was no significant difference between the performance of the retarded and normal on mediated items.

Jensen and Rohwer (1963a, 1963b) conducted two experiments using a similar procedure. In these studies, retarded subjects were divided into two groups: Group I was required to learn a set of paired-associates on a rote basis, while Group II was given meaningful sentences which gave relevance to the paired items. To illustrate, one of the paired-associate items consisted of a *cup* and *glasses*. The mediation group received the following sentence: "The cup wore the glasses." In both studies, the subjects learned the paired-associate task more rapidly under the conditions of mediation.

Hermelin and O'Connor (1958) found similar results when working with 20 institutionalized trainable subjects. In this experiment, the subjects were required to learn six series of paired drawings by correctly identifying which of the paired items was correct and which was incorrect. One-half the subjects learned to specify the correct items on the basis of rote memory only, while the remaining subjects were aided by a verbal label, e.g., the right choice was an article of furniture or an animal. Those subjects who received the verbal label learned at a faster rate.

Other studies have demonstrated that mediation is essential to abstract reasoning. In two related studies, Griffith and Spitz (1958) and Griffith, Spitz, and Lipman (1959), retarded subjects were most likely to determine a concept for a group of three nouns (e.g., elephant, mountain, and whale) when they were able to find a common basis for two of the items. Thus, if the subject defined the elephant and whale as being "big," he would realize that the abstract similarity between elephant, mountain, and whale involves a largeness of size.

Transfer of training has been studied by various researchers with the rather consistent finding that the retarded are quite capable of applying previously gained knowledge to a new situation. In fact, three studies have demonstrated clearly that the retarded can transfer a known principle as well as normal individuals.

In 1960, Johnson and Blake investigated the transference of a principle learned on a given series of motor tasks to a unique motor task. The results revealed that the two experimental (transfer) groups, normal and retarded, did significantly better than the respective control groups. Similar results had been obtained by Cruickshank and Blake (1957) using a verbal task.

In a study by Katz (1962), educable retarded subjects were divided into two groups: Group I learned a set of scientific principles by rote; Group II learned the principle through understanding. The latter group was much more effective in transferring their knowledge to related tasks.

An interesting and directly meaningful study to the educator was conducted by House and Zeaman (1960b). These experimenters had their retarded subjects (all within the MA range of two to six years) first practice discrimination tasks (color-form stimuli) which were either easy or hard. It was found that those subjects who practiced on the easy items learned a difficult task more rapidly than did the group that had practiced the difficult items. Thus, graduated learning seems to enhance the transfer effect.

Miller and Griffith (1961), in a relatively complex transfer study, discovered that though the retardates could transfer the verbal experiences gained in pretraining, the success of such transfer was limited to those items included in the pretraining sessions. They concluded that there "was no generalization effect of the training, i.e., concept attainment with abstraction items not involved with training was not improved" (p. 274).

Another factor associated with transfer of training was demonstrated by Bryant (1964, 1965a, 1965b) in a series of studies with trainable subjects. He found it desirable for the retardate to learn all the positive features of an object or situation that would assist in transfer. In the initial two studies, when the retardates learned but one aspect of the stimulus to be transferred, their transfer performance was not particularly effective. In the third experiment, when they received training on every aspect of the correct dimension, their performance improved greatly. Under the latter circumstances, the retardates had no difficulty in transferring learning and did significantly better than those trained on other dimensions. Thus, providing trainable retardates with a general, broad basis for transfer appears important.

In addition to being able to transfer specific information and principles, it should be recognized that the retarded are also capable of applying previously acquired techniques of learning to new situations. This phenomenon is studied under the rubric of "learning sets." The ability of the retarded to benefit from learning "how to learn" has been demonstrated in several discrimination studies (e.g., Ellis, 1958; Kaufmann and Peterson, 1958). In essence, these experiments have shown that the retardate's rate of learning accelerates as he learns how to attack the given problem. As would be expected, the ability to develop learning sets increases with mental age (Ellis, 1958; Stevenson and Swartz, 1958).

These studies on mediation, transfer of training, and learning sets clearly establish the fact that the retardate can benefit greatly from past experience and flexibility in learning. It would appear important that the educator be concerned with aiding the child in seeing similarities and differences in new objects and situations. In addition, the retarded should have opportunities to become familiar with a variety of characteristics associated with any given stimulus, e.g., an apple is a fruit, edible, round, red, grows on a tree. Furthermore, the results of the cited studies would indicate that, in the interest of maximizing the probability of transferring training, the educational curriculum and materials should be programed into a series of sequential, logical substeps. Finally, the educator should be concerned with how the child learns to solve a problem as well as with the information to be acquired.

MEANINGFULNESS. Many of the previously cited studies have demonstrated that meaningfulness increases the child's learning performance. For example, adding the verbal label to a discrimination task facilitated learning in the Hermelin and O'Connor study (1958). Relevant, pretraining experiences mediate subsequent learning (Jensen and Rohwer, 1963a; 1963b). Highly meaningful tasks are readily learned and transferred (Katz, 1962; Eismann, 1958; Vergason, 1964).

Lance (1965) conducted a study in which he was concerned specifically with the learning rates of retarded children under varying degrees of meaningfulness. In this experiment, 32 retardates and 32 normal subjects learned a series of paired-associate items (nonsense syllable—number combinations) which previously had been scaled according to meaningfulness values, e.g., MAN-6 constituted a high-meaningful paired-associate item; QIH-6 represented a low-meaningful item. According to the results obtained, all subjects, both normal and retarded, learned best under highly meaningful conditions.

To summarize briefly, the reviewed learning research indicates that the retardate can learn a comprehensible task as rapidly as a normal or gifted individual of a similar mental age. Also, the retarded are equally capable of utilizing previously acquired knowledge in new situations. The effectiveness and efficiency of their learning is affected by such factors as attention, mediation, and familiarity or meaningfulness of the materials to be learned.

Retention

The ability to retain that which has been learned is a fundamental phase of the total learning process. Forgetting, which denotes the failure of retentive persistence, reduces learning efficacy by precluding or debilitating the functional application of past experiences to the resolution of new problems.

The research literature concerned with the retentive abilities of the retarded will be considered under two subheadings: long-term and short-term retention. Short-term retention refers to retention intervals less than one minute in duration. Intervals in excess of one minute are considered to be long-term.

LONG-TERM RETENTIONS. All retention studies require that a task be learned and retained. As stated earlier, either a serial listing or a set of paired-associates is frequently used. Retention usually is measured on the basis of savings scores and/or recall performance. Savings scores are computed on the basis of the number of trials required by the subject to relearn the original task. Recall refers to the number of correct responses given by the subject on either a single-trial retention test or on the initial trial of relearning.

Eismann's (1958) previously cited study also considered the respective retentive abilities of the retarded, normal, and gifted subjects equated on the basis of CA. The results of her experiment indicated no significant differences between the groups with respect to recall performances following retention intervals of 7 and 30 days.

In Ring's study (1965), though the normal adolescents were capable of learning the task at a faster rate than the adolescent educable retardates, there were no marked discrepancies between their respective 24-hour recall performances. This same result was observed by Lance (1965), i.e., the savings scores for the normal and retarded subjects of a similar CA were not found to vary significantly in spite of original variances in learning performances.

With respect to groups equated on the basis of MA, Cantor and Ryan (1962) compared the performances of 20 retardates and 20 normal subjects assumed to be matched on the basis of MA. The task consisted of six pairs of photographed objects, e.g., man-train, iron-watch. The results revealed that the two groups were quite similar with respect to retention (savings method) following an interval of 7 and 30 days. These results were consistent with those previously reported by Johnson and Blake (1960).

Klausmeier and Check (1962), who were concerned with the retention of socially meaningful arithmetic problems graded to suit the varying abilities of 40 retarded, 40 normal, and 40 gifted children, all 131 months in age, found no differences with respect to the subjects' abilities to retain that which had been learned. In this educationally oriented project, retention was measured on the basis of savings scores following intervals of five minutes and seven weeks.

The results of these studies demonstrate that if the material is well learned, the retardate will show no greater long-term retentive losses than normal or gifted individuals. This conclusion apparently holds true for all retardates regardless of chronological or mental age.

SHORT-TERM RETENTION. One of the most recent theories to be advanced concerning a qualitative difference in the learning behavior of retarded and normal individuals involves short-term retention. This theory, developed and promulgated by Ellis (1963), utilizes the notion that a stimulus sets up a shortlived trace which reverberates for a brief time following the termination of stimulation. In essence, this trace exists during the interval between original stimulation and the consolidation of learning within the higher nerve centers. It also is believed that the stimulus trace is essential to the consolidation process. The major hypothesis advanced by Ellis is that the stimulus trace of the retardate is shorter in duration and weaker in intensity than in normal individuals.[3]

This theory was advanced to account for the relatively poor short-term retentive performances of the retarded observed in a number of studies using a variety of techniques. Though several relevant experiments will be described, the reader is referred to Ellis' statement (1963) which offers an excellent discussion of the theory as well as supporting nerophysiological and learning data.

[3] There is some physiological evidence to support this theory. EEG studies by Berkson, *et al.* (1961) and Baumeister, *et al.* (1963) have shown that the effects of a brief stimulus, measured in terms of alpha blocks, last for longer periods in normals than in retardates. These data tend to support the hypothesis that there "is more perseveration of a stimulus in the central nervous system of the normal individual than in the retardate." (Baumeister, *et al.*, 1963, p. 724).

Hermelin and O'Connor (1964) studied the short-term retention of 12 normal and 12 trainable children matched on the basis of MA. The subjects also were divided into two age groups, generically labeled as older and younger. The results of the experiment, based on the recall of digits, showed the retardates' performances to be inferior to those of normal subjects, and that the younger retardates' performances were less adequate than those of the older retardates. Similar results were obtained by Borkowski (1965).

Baumeister, *et al.* (1965) compared the short-term retentive performances of 50 adult retardates (mean IQ = 47) with 28 normal persons (college students and faculty members). The task, which consisted of visually presented Chinese characters, varied in degree of complexity—the number of displayed characters ranged from two to five per item. The recognition technique was used to measure retention, i.e., after exposure, the subject was required to find the original stimulus in an assortment of correct and incorrect stimuli. Three retention intervals were used: 2, 12, and 20 seconds. The results were as follows: (1) The retardates' performances were consistently inferior to those of the normal subjects. (2) Increasing the retention interval produced greater retentive losses. (3) The performances of all subjects became progressively poorer as the stimulus complexity increased. These results supported an earlier delayed-response study by Baumeister and Ellis (1963).

Though it would be premature to propose specific educational procedures which would modify potential learning difficulties associated with the short-term retentive deficit, it is highly probable that clarity, meaningfulness, and repetition are important. Also, as demonstrated by the cited studies, an unfamiliar task should be kept as simple as possible, especially for the younger retarded.

Factors Affecting Retention

The retentive performances of the retarded may be affected by a number of factors. Three of these will be considered: meaningfulness, overlearning, and interference.

MEANINGFULNESS. Meaningfulness does affect the retardate's rate of learning; however, available research has not demonstrated that it is of significance to retention. Three studies, all of which have been described, have indicated that when several tasks are learned to the same criterion, they will be recalled equally as well, regardless of their degree of meaningfulness (Lance, 1965) or the availability of mediating circumstances (Barnett, Pryer, and Ellis, 1959; Jensen and Rohwer, 1963b). Also, the length of the retention interval does not seem to influence this relationship. The retention intervals used in the three cited studies ranged from 10 seconds to 30 days.

Caution must be exercised when interpreting the results of these studies. One of the major theories concerning retention, which will be discussed later, contends that forgetting is a function of interference arising from competing learned responses. In other words, a person tends to forget something because it becomes confused with other learning. Telephone numbers and historical dates are good examples of the type of materials which are highly susceptible to interference among normal adults. Many years of experimental research with normal children and college students have demonstrated, beyond any reasonable doubt, that meaningfulness is an important factor in reducing retentive losses arising from competitive learning (e.g., Whitely and Blankenship, 1963; Hall, 1955; Slamecka, 1961). Thus, it is difficult to conceive where meaningfulness is not of consequence to retention.

OVERLEARNING. Overlearning (i.e., learning a task to a criterion of more than one errorless trial) has shown to be of value in retention among normal subjects. Only one study was located which investigated the effects of overlearning among the retarded.

Lance (1965) found that those subjects, both normal and retarded, who were required to learn and relearn the task to five correct trials had greater savings scores. While those retardates who had learned the task to a criterion of one trial had savings scores of 38.63 and 34.88, the mean savings scores under the conditions of overlearning were 50.12 and 54.31. Thus, repetition is essential to retention.

INTERFERENCE. Interference is deemed by many experimental psychologists to be one of the prime factors resulting in retentive decrements. The interference theory usually is studied in terms of retroactive and proactive inhibition. Retroactive inhibition (RI) was defined by Underwood (1949, p. 544) as the "decrement in retention of a task as a consequence of other learning coming *between* the learning and the retention task. Proactive inhibition (PI) is the decrement in retention of a task as a consequence of other learning coming *prior* to the learning of a task on which the retention test is made." In other words, is forgetting primarily a function of early learning experiences (PI) or those which may have occurred after the individual has learned that which he is attempting to recall (RI)?

In brief, after years of investigating interference as it affects retention among normal persons, it was concluded that the major factor in forgetting is proactive inhibition, or interference arising from previous learning. The reader is referred to Underwood (1948, 1957) for a thorough discussion of proactive inhibition and its related theory.

A number of studies have been concerned with both proactive and retroactive inhibition as they affect the retentive performances of the retarded. Scheerenberger (1964) studied the retentive behavior of 120 retarded subjects distributed over six experimental conditions: control—10-minute recall; control—48-hour recall; retroactive inhibition—10-minute recall; retroactive inhibition—48-hour recall; proactive inhibition—10-

minute recall; and proactive inhibition—48-hour recall. The results were as follows: (1) The retardates were subject to the effects of both proactive and retroactive inhibition. (2) Decrements in retention associated with retroactive inhibition were relatively shortlived. (3) The most severe retentive losses were associated with proactive inhibition following a retention interval of 48 hours.

This study partially supported the results of previous experiments by Cassell (1957), Johnson and Blake (1960), and Pryer (1960) which had found that the long-term retentive performances of the retarded were affected by retroactive inhibition (PI was not studied). These earlier investigations also revealed that the retarded were not more prone to the effects of interference than normal and gifted subjects.

Two studies have indicated that the effects of interference, both retroactive and proactive, are evident also in short-term retention. In the Hermelin and O'Connor (1964) short-term retention study, previously mentioned, interfering conditions (RI) were introduced. A list of familiar and a list of unfamiliar words were interpolated between the original learning and the relearning task composed of digits. The interference resulted in marked retentive decrements for both normal and trainable children matched on the basis of MA. Interestingly, while the normal subjects were more affected by the familiar material, the trainable subjects were more affected by the unfamiliar words.

Borkowski (1965) also conducted a short-term retention study under conditions of interference (PI). Thirty adult retardates (mean MA = 10.3) and 30 normal subjects were matched on the basis of MA. The results were as follows: (1) PI produced retentive decrements for both normal and retarded subjects. (2) Increasing the amount of interference learning increased the degree of PI. (3) Extending the retention interval resulted in increasing the adverse affects of PI. (4) Those retardates with the lowest IQs were most greatly influenced by the introduction of interference.

House, *et al.* (1964) observed that their retarded subjects (mean IQ = 52) were affected by PI, and that the amount of PI increased with the number of previously learned lists. Thus, these results were consistent with those reported by Borkowski.

This discussion of proactive and retroactive inhibition has, of necessity been rather limited, especially with respect to theoretical considerations; however, its implications are quite clear. To reduce potential retentive losses arising from competitive learning, it is essential that the educator should: (1) present the materials in a logical sequence, avoiding the need for unlearning; (2) ensure that the subject matter to be acquired has some meaning or association; (3) avoid long lists of relatively meaningless materials (e.g., spelling words); (4) give the student an opportunity to overlearn loosely structured materials which are most susceptible to interference; and (5) provide opportunities for the child to review what he has learned.

Though this review of the research with respect to both the learning and retentive behavior of the retarded is by no means exhaustive, it does illustrate the potential contribution of experimental psychology to education. Hopefully, it also will have served to encourage the educator to take a more active interest in research activities as they affect the retarded.

SUMMARY

This report has attempted to review, in some detail, both the educational and learning research concerned with the retarded. The educational selection included reference to research on academic subjects, achievement and failure in school, programmed instruction and operant conditioning, adjustment, and trainable retardates. The section on educational implications of learning research considered four major areas: rate of learning, factors affecting learning, retention, and factors affecting retention.

In general, it can be concluded that the last decade has witnessed a remarkable growth in the interest of experimentally oriented educators and psychologists to study the educational and learning problems of the retarded. To date, however, the majority of research, while of appreciable value, has been highly fragmented and nonprogrammatic. Continued development will require a closer liaison between the university and public schools, a greater utilization of public school programs for research purposes, an expanded effort to train qualified researchers, and the inclusion of introductory research courses in programs of teacher preparation.

REFERENCES

Anderson, Linnea M. Factors affecting high and low achievement among adolescents enrolled in special classes for the mentally handicapped. *Dissertation Abstracts, 25*:279, 1964.

Atkinson, J., and Hart, J. Establishing sound symbol association with severely retarded readers. *Slow Learning Child, 10*:85–93, 1963.

Barnett, C. D., and Cantor, G. N. Discrimination set in defectives. *American Journal of Mental Deficiency, 62*:334–337, 1957.

Barnett, C. D., Ellis, N. R., and Pryer, M. W. Stimulus pretraining and the delayed reaction in defectives. *American Journal of Mental Deficiency, 64*:104–111, 1959.

Barnett, C. D., Pryer, M. W., and Ellis, N. R. Experimental manipulation of verbal behavior in defectives. *Psychological Reports, 5*:593–596, 1959.

Barsch, R. H. *A Movogenic Curriculum.* Bulletin No. 25, Madison, Wisconsin, State Department of Public Instruction, 1965.

Bateman, Barbara D. Learning disabilities—yesterday, today and tomorrow. *Exceptional Children, 31*:167–177, 1964.

Baumeister, A., and Ellis, N. R. Delayed response performance of retardates. *American Journal of Mental Deficiency, 67*:714–722, 1963.

Baumeister, A., and Klosowski, R. An attempt to group toilet train severely retarded patients. *Mental Retardation, 3*(6):24–26, 1965.

Baumeister, A., Smith, T. E., and Rose, J. D. The effects of stimulus complexity and retention interval upon short-term memory. *American Journal of Mental Deficiency, 70*:129–134, 1965.

Baumeister, A., Spain, C. J., and Ellis, N. R. A note on alpha block duration in normals and retardates. *American Journal of Mental Deficiency, 67*:723–725, 1963.

Bensberg, G. J. Concept learning in mental defectives as a function of appropriate and inappropriate "attention sets." *Journal of Education Psychology, 49*:137–143, 1958.

Berkson, G., and Cantor, N. A study of mediation in mentally retarded and normal school children. *Journal of Educational Research, 51*:82–86, 1960.

Berkson, G., Hermelin, B., and O'Connor, J. Physiological responses of normals and institutionalized mental defectives to repeated stimuli. *Journal of Mental Deficiency Research, 5*:30–39, 1961.

Bijou, S. and Orlando, R. Rapid development of multiple schedule performance with retarded children. *Journal of the Experimental Analysis of Behavior. 4*:7–16, 1961.

Blackman, L. Research needs in the special education of the mentally retarded. *Exceptional Children, 29*:377–383, 1963.

Blackman, L. S., and Capobianco, R. J. An evaluation of programmed instruction with the MR utilizing teaching machines. *American Journal of Mental Deficiency, 70*:262–269, 1965.

Blackman, L., and Holden, E. Support versus nonsupport in an autoinstructional word program for educable retardates. *American Journal of Mental Deficiency, 67*:592–600, 1963.

Blank, Joy P. The effect of magnitude of incentive on acquisition and extinction in mentally retarded children. *Dissertation Abstracts, 19*:867–868, 1958.

Blatt, B. Effects of responsive environments on the intellectual and social competence of educable mentally retarded children. In: U.S. Department of Health, Education, and Welfare, Welfare Administration, Children's Bureau. *Research Relating to Children,* Bulletin No. 15. Washington, D.C., Government Printing Office, 1961–2.

Blessing, K. R. *An Investigation of Psycholinguistic Deficit in Educable Mentally Retarded Children: Detection, Remediation and Related Variables.* Doctoral dissertation. Madison, Wisc., University of Wisconsin, 1964, 233 pp.

Blue, C. M. *The Effectiveness of a Group Language Program with Trainable Mentally Retarded Children.* (Unpublished report) Boone, N.C., Appalachian State Teachers College, 1963a, 7 pp.

Blue, C. M. Performance of normal and retarded subjects on a modified paired-associate task. *American Journal of Mental Deficiency, 68*:228–234, 1963b.

Bobroff, A. Economic adjustment of 121 adults, formerly students in classes for mental retardates. *American Journal of Mental Deficiency, 60*:525–535, 1965a.

Bobroff, A. A survey of social and civic participation of adults formerly in classes for the mentally retarded. *American Journal of Mental Deficiency, 61*:127–133, 1956.

Borkowski, J. G. Interference effects in short-term memory as a function of level of intelligence. *American Journal of Mental Deficiency, 70*:458–465, 1965.

Bradley, Betty H., and Hundziak, M. TMI–Grolier time telling program for the mentally retarded. *Exceptional Children. 32*:17–20, 1965.

Brite, L. R. The effect of ability grouping on personality variables of slow learning fifth-grade pupils. *Dissertation Abstracts, 24*:4080–4081, 1964.

Brooks, Sadye T. Effects of locus of control and anxiety on the ability of mentally retarded children to use context clues in reading. *Dissertation Abstracts, 23*:2003, 1962.

Brown, R. I., and Dyer, L. Social arithmetic training for the subnormal: A comparison of two methods. *Journal of Mental Subnormality, 9*:8–12, 1963.

Bryant, P. E. The effect of a verbal instruction on transfer in normal and severely subnormal children. *Journal of Mental Deficiency Research, 8*:35–43, 1964.

Bryant, P. E. The transfer of positive and negative learning by normal and severely retarded children. *British Journal of Psychology, 56*: 81–86, 1965a.

Bryant, P. E. The transfer of sorting concepts by moderately retarded children. *American Journal of Mental Deficiency, 70*:291–300, 1965b.

Cain, L., and Levine, S. The mentally retarded. *Review of Educational Research, 33*:62–82, 1963.

Cantor, G. N. Basic research in learning with mentally retarded children and its educational implications. *Frontiers of Elementary Education, 4*:88–96, 1957.

Cantor, G. N. Contributions of basic psychological research to the education of the mentally retarded. *Johnstone Bulletin, 1*:5–15, 1959.

Cantor, G. N., and Ryan, T. J. Retention of verbal paired-associates in normals and retardates. *American Journal of Mental Deficiency, 66*:861–865, 1962.

Capobianco, R. J. A comparison of endogenous and exogeneous mentally retarded on arithmetic processes. In: Dunn, L. M., and Capobianco, R. J., eds. *Studies of Reading and Arithmetic in Mentally Retarded Boys.* Monograph No. 19 of the Society for Research in Child Development, Lafayette, Indiana, Child Development Publications, 1954, pp. 100–140.

Capobianco, R. J. Role of programmed instruction in special education. *Winnower, 2*:1–8, 1966.

Capobianco, R. J., and Miller, D. Y. *Quantitative and Qualitative Analysis of Exogenous and Endogenous Children in Some Reading Processes.* Washington, D.C., U.S. Department of Health, Education, and Welfare, Office of Education, Cooperative Research Program, 1958.

Carriker, W. R. Comparison of postschool adjustment of regular and special class mental retardates. *School Life, 40*: 1958.

Carriker, W. R. Research related to the education of mentally retarded children. *School Life, 42*:26–28, 1960.

Carter, Lanore J. A comparative study of the effectiveness of three techniques of film presentation in teaching a selected group of educable mentally retarded children in public schools in Louisiana. *Dissertation Abstracts, 22*:1313, 1961.

Cassell, R. Serial verbal learning and retroactive inhibition in aments and children. *Journal of Clinical Psychology, 13*:369–372, 1957.

Charles, D. C. Adult adjustment of some deficient American children—II. *American Journal of Mental Deficiency, 62*:300–304, 1957.

Clarke, A. B. D., and Lookson, M. Perceptual motor transfer in imbeciles: A second series of experiments. *British Journal of Psychology, 53*:321–330, 1962.

Cochran, Irene L., and Cleland, C. C. Manifest anxiety of retardates and normals matched as to academic achievement. *American Journal of Mental Deficiency, 67*:539–542, 1963.

Cratty, B. J. *Movement and Behavior Motor Learning.* Philadelphia, Pennsylvania, Lea and Febiger, 1964, 332 pp.

Cruickshank, W. M., Bentzen, Frances A., Ratzburg, F. E. and Tannhauser, Marian T. *A Teaching Method for Brain-Injured Hyperactive Children.* Syracuse, New York, Syracuse University, 1961, 576 pp.

Cruickshank, W. M., and Blake, K. A. *A Comparative Study of the Performance of Mentally Handicapped and Intellectually Normal Boys on Selected Tasks Involving Learning and Transfer.* Syracuse, New York, Syracuse University Research Institute, 1957.

Culley, W. J., Jolly, D. H., and Mertz, E. T. Heights and weights of mentally retarded children. *American Journal of Mental Deficiency, 68*:203–210, 1963.

Daly, W. C., and Lee, R. H. Reading disabilities in a group of MR children: Incidence and treatment. *Training School Bulletin, 57*:85–93, 1960.

Davy, Ruth A. Adaptation of progressive-choice methods for teaching reading to retarded children. *American Journal of Mental Deficiency, 67*:274–280, 1962.

Davy, Ruth A. Closing the meaning loop through progressive choice structure. In: Council for Exceptional Children. *Perspectives in Theory and Practice.* Selected convention papers from the 41st Annual CEC Convention, 1963. Washington, D.C., Council for Exceptional Children, 1963, pp. 45–48.

Daw, J. F. The effect of special exercises on body image in mentally retarded children—a tentative exploration. *Slow Learning Child, 11*:109–116, 1964.

Denny, M. Ray. Research in learning and performance. In: Stevens, H. A., and Heber, R., eds. *Mental Retardation: A Review of Research.* Chicago, Ill., University of Chicago, 1964, pp. 100–142.

Dinger, J. C. Postschool adjustment of former educable retarded pupils. *Exceptional Children, 27*:353–360, 1961.

Dumphrey, Muriel W. Integration of educable retardates in normal groups. In: U.S. Department of Health, Education, and Welfare, Welfare Administration, Children's Bureau. *Research Relating to Children.* Bulletin No. 19. Washington, D.C., Government Printing Office, 1965–1966.

Dunn, L. M. A comparison of the reading processes of mentally retarded boys of the same mental age. In: Dunn, L. M., and Capobianco, R. J., eds. *Studies of Reading and Arithmetic in Mentally Retarded Boys,* Monograph No. 19 of the Society for Research in Child Development. Lafayette, Ind., Child Development Publications, 1954, pp. 7–99.

Dunn, L. M. *To Be or Not to Be; Special Education Classes for the Mentally*

Retarded. (Unpublished paper) Nashville, Tenn. George Peabody College, 1959.

Dunn, L. M., and Capobianco, R. J. Mental retardation. *Review of Educational Research, 29*:451–470, 1959.

Dunn, L. M., and Smith, J. O. *The Peabody Language Development Kit.* (Primary Edition) Minneapolis, Minn., American Guidance Service, 1964.

Durbin, M. L., and Kaye, C. L. Materials and the severely retarded. *Michigan Education Journal, 40*:501–526, 1963.

Edwards, A. J., and Kirby, Elsie M. Predictive efficiency of intelligence test scores: Intelligence quotients obtained in grade one and achievement test scores obtained in grade three. *Educational and Psychological Measurement, 24*:941–946, 1964.

Eismann, Bernice S. Paired-associate learning, generalization, and retention as a function of intelligence. *American Journal of Mental Deficiency, 63*:481–489, 1958.

Ellis, N. R. Object-quality discrimination learning sets by mental defectives. *Journal of Comparative and Physiological Psychology, 51*:79–81, 1958.

Ellis, N. R. The stimulus trace and behavioral inadequacy. In: Ellis, N. R., ed. *Handbook of Mental Deficiency*. New York, McGraw-Hill, 1963, pp. 134–158.

Ellis, N. R., Barnett, C., and Pryer, M. Operant behavior in mental retardates: Exploratory studies. *Journal of the Experimental Analysis of Behavior, 3*:63–69, 1960a.

Ellis, N. R., Pryer, Margaret W., Distefano, M. K., and Pryer, R. S. Learning in mentally defective, normal, and superior subjects. *American Journal of Mental Deficiency, 64*:725–734, 1960b.

Finley, Carmen J. Arithmetic achievement in mentally retarded children: The effects of presenting the problem in different contexts. *American Journal of Mental Deficiency, 67*(2):281–286, 1962.

Francis, R. J., and Rarick, L. Motor characteristics of the mentally retarded. *American Journal of Mental Deficiency, 63*(5):792–811, 1959.

Frey, R. M. *Reading Behavior of Public School Brain-Injured and Non-Brain-Injured Children of Average and Retarded Mental Development.* Doctoral dissertation. Urbana, Ill., University of Illinois, 1961.

Gallaghar, J. J. *The Tutoring of Brain-Injured Mentally Retarded Children.* Springfield, Ill., Charles C Thomas, 1960, 194 pp.

Gearheart, B. R. A study of a physical education program to promote motor skills of EMR children in special education classes in Cedar Rapids, Iowa. *Dissertation Abstracts, 25*:271–272, 1964.

Gilley, M. Reading technique and comprehension in mentally retarded adolescents. *Psychologie Francaise, 8*(1):36–53, 1963.

Girardeau, F. L. The formation of discrimination learning sets in mongoloid and normal children. *Journal of Comparative and Physiological Psychology, 52*:566–570, 1959.

Goldstein, E. *Selective Audio–Visual Instruction for Mentally Retarded Pupils.* Springfield, Ill., Charles C Thomas, 1964, 96 pp.

Goldstein H. Methodological problems in research in the educational programs for the treatment and habilitation of the mentally retarded. *American Journal of Mental Deficiency, 64*:341–345, 1959.

Griffith, B., and Spitz, H. Some relationships between abstraction and word meaning in retarded adolescents. *American Journal of Mental Deficiency, 63*:247–251, 1958.

Griffith, B. C., Spitz, H. H., and Lipman, R. S. Verbal mediation and concept formation in retarded and normal subjects. *Journal of Experimental Psychology, 58*:247–251, 1959.

Groelle, M. Reading survey tests given to educable mentally retarded children. *Exceptional Children, 27*(8):443–448, 1961.

Gunderson, D. V. *Research in Reading Readiness,* Bulletin No. 8. Washington, D.C., Superintendent of Documents, Government Printing, 1964, 38 pp.

Guenther, R. J. *Final Report of the Michigan Demonstration Research Project for the Severely Retarded.* Lansing, Mich., Department of Public Instruction, 1956.

Gutts, W. G. *Research in Reading for the Middle Grades,* Bulletin No. 31. Washington, D.C., Superintendent of Documents, Government Printing Office, 1963, 80 pp.

Hall, J. Retroactive inhibition in meaningful material. *Journal of Educational Psychology, 46*:47–52, 1955.

Harris, Lucy. Exploring the relationship between the teacher's attitude and the overt behavior of the pupil. *American Journal of Mental Deficiency, 63*(2): 260–267, 1958.

Harris, Lucy, and Sievers, Dorothy J. A study to measure changes in behavior of aggressive mentally retarded adolescent girls in a permissive classroom. *American Journal of Mental Deficiency, 63*(6):975–980, 1959.

Harris, T. L. Summary of investigations relating to reading, July 1, 1962 to June 30, 1963. *Journal of Educational Research, 57*:283–327, 1963.

Harrison, S. A review of research in speech and language development of the mentally retarded child. *American Journal of Mental Deficiency, 63*:236–240, 1958.

Harrison, S. Integration of developmental language activities with an educational program for mentally retarded children. *American Journal of Mental Deficiency, 63*(6):967–970, 1959.

Hart, N. W. M. Academic progress in relation to intelligence and motivation in the opportunity school. *Slow Learning Child, 11*:40–46, 1964.

Headrick, Mary W. Operant conditioning in mental deficiency. *American Journal of Mental Deficiency, 67*(6):924–929, 1963.

Heber, R. F. Expectancy and expectancy changes in normal and mentally retarded boys. *Dissertation Abstracts, 18*:657–658, 1958.

Hermelin, B., and O'Connor, N. The rote and concept learning of imbeciles. *Journal of Mental Deficiency Research, 2*:21–27, 1958.

Hermelin, B., and O'Connor, N. Short-term memory in normal and subnormal children. *American Journal of Mental Deficiency, 69*(1):121–125, 1964.

Horowitz, F. D. Effects of consequences on vocal behavior: Partial and continuous reinforcement of vocal responses using candy, vocal, and smiling reinforcers among retardates. In: Schiefelbusch, R. L., ed. *Language Studies of Mentally Retarded Children.* Monograph supplement No. 10, *Journal of Speech and Hearing Disorders,* January 1963, pp. 55–70.

Hottel, J. *An Evaluation of Tennessee's Day Class Program for Severely Mentally Retarded Trainable Children.* Nashville, Tenn., State Department of Education, 1958.

House, B. J., Smith, M., and Zeaman, D. Verbal learning and retention as a function of number of lists in retardates. *American Journal of Mental Deficiency, 69*:239–243, 1964.

House, B., and Zeaman, D. A comparison of discrimination learning in normal and mentally defective children. *Child Development, 29*:411–416, 1958.

House, B., and Zeaman, D. Visual discrimination learning and intelligence in defectives of low mental age. *American Journal of Mental Deficiency, 65*: 51–58, 1960a.

House, B., and Zeaman, D. Transfer of a discrimination from objects to patterns. *Journal of Experimental Psychology, 59*:298–302, 1960b.

Howe, C. E. A comparison of motor skills of mentally retarded and normal children. *Exceptional Children, 25*:352–354, 1959.

Huber, W. G. The relationship of anxiety to the academic performance of institutionalized retardates. *American Journal of Mental Deficiency, 69*(4): 462–466, 1965.

Hudson, Margaret. *An Exploration of Classroom Procedures for Teaching Trainable Mentally Retarded Children.* CEC Research Monograph. Washington, D.C., Council for Exceptional Children, National Education Association, 1960, 71 pp.

Hundziak, M., Maurer, Ruth, and Watson, L. S. Operant conditioning in toilet training for severely mentally retarded boys. *American Journal of Mental Deficiency, 70*(1):120–124, 1965.

Irwin, B. Oral language for slow learning children. *American Journal of Mental Deficiency, 64*(1):32–40, 1959.

Jacobs, J. A study of performance of slow learners in the Cincinnati Public Schools on mental and achievement tests. *American Journal of Mental Deficiency, 62*(2):238–243, 1957.

Jacoby, Helen B., Bonham, Anzalette H., Shepherd, Margaret J., and Capobianco, R. J. *Mixie the Pixie.* Washington, D.C., Special Education Materials Development Center, 1966.

Jensen, A. Learning ability in retarded, average, and gifted children. *Merrill–Palmer Quarterly, 9*:123–140, 1963.

Jensen, A., and Rohwer, W. D. Verbal mediation in paired-associate and serial learning. *Journal of Verbal Learning and Verbal Behavior, 1*:346–352, 1963a.

Jensen, A., and Rohwer, W. D. The effect of verbal mediation on the learning and retention of paired-associates by retarded adults. *American Journal of Mental Deficiency, 68*:80–84, 1963b.

Johnson, G. O., and Blake, K. A. *Learning Performance of Retarded and Normal Children.* Syracuse, N.Y., Syracuse University, 1960.

Johnson, G. O., and Capobianco, R. Language development in severely retarded children. In: State Interdepartmental Health Resources Board. *Research Project on Severely Retarded Children.* Albany, N.Y., State Interdepartmental Health Resources Board, 1957, pp. 111–115.

Jordan, Laura. The efficacy of a reading readiness program with the educable mentally retarded. *Dissertation Abstracts, 21*:3715, 1961.

Jordan, Laura. Reading and the young mentally retarded child. *Mental Retardation, 1*(1):21–27, 1963.

Jordan, T. E. Early developmental adversity and classroom learning. A prospective inquiry. *American Journal of Mental Deficiency, 69*(3):360–371, 1964.

Kaplan, M. S. An investigation of the anxiety levels of mentally handicapped children with special consideration of the effects of special education classes. *Dissertation Abstracts, 23*:1608, 1962.

Katz, P. J. Transfer of principles as a function of a course of study incorporating scientific method for the educable mentally retarded. Unpublished doctoral dissertation. New York, N.Y., Columbia University, Teachers College, 1962.

Kaufman, M., and Peterson, W. Acquisition of a learning set by normal and mentally retarded children. *Journal of Comparative and Physiological Psychology, 51*:619–621, 1958.

Keating, Leslie E. A pilot experiment in remedial reading at the hospital school, Lingfield, 1957–1960. *British Journal of Educational Psychology, 32*:62–65, 1962.

Kephart, N. C. *The Slow Learner in the Classroom.* Columbus, Ohio, Charles E. Merrill, 1960, 292 pp.

Kern, W. H., and Pfaeffle, H. A comparison of social adjustment of MR children in various educational settings. *American Journal of Mental Deficiency, 67*(3):407–413, 1962.

Kirk, S. A. Research in education. In: Stevens, H. A., Heber, R. F., eds. *Mental Retardation: A Review of Research,* Chicago, Ill., University of Chicago, 1964, pp. 57–99.

Kirk, S. A., and Weiner, Bluma B., eds. *Behavioral Research on Exceptional Children.* Washington, D.C., Council for Exceptional Children, National Education Association, 1963, 369 pp.

Klausmeier, H. J., and Check, J. Retention and transfer in children of low, average, and high intelligence. *Journal of Educational Research, 55*:319–322, 1962.

Klausmeier, H. J., Feldhuser, J., and Check, J. *An Analysis of Learning Efficiency in Arithmetic of Mentally Retarded Children in Comparison with Children of Average and High Intelligence.* Washington, D.C., Office of Education, Cooperative Research Program, 1959.

Klausmeier, H. J., Lehmann, I. J., and Beeman, A. Relationships among physical, mental, and achievement measures in children of low, average, and high intelligence. *American Journal of Mental Deficiency, 63*:647–656, 1959.

Kolstoe, O. P. Language training of low grade mongoloid children. *American Journal of Mental Deficiency, 63*(1):17–30, 1958.

Kunkel, J. L. An experiment with teaching machines in classrooms for the educable mentally retarded. *Dissertation Abstracts, 22*:4270, 1962.

Kvaraceus, W. C. Research in special education; its status and function. *Exceptional Children, 24*:249–254, 1958.

Lance, W. D. Effects of meaningfulness and overlearning on retention in normal retarded adolescents. *American Journal of Mental Deficiency, 70*:270–275, 1965.

Lapp, E. A study of the social adjustment of slow learning children who were assigned part-time to regular classes. *American Journal of Mental Deficiency, 62*(2):254–262, 1957.

Lindsley, O. Direct measurement and prothesis of retarded behavior. *Journal of Education, 147*:62–81, 1964.

Lipman, R. S. Learning: Verbal perceptual-motor, and classical conditioning. In: Ellis, N. R., ed. *Handbook of Mental Deficiency.* New York, McGraw-Hill, 1963, pp. 391–423.

MacKinnon, F. A. Neurological factors in reading disability. *Canadian Medical Association Journal, 91*(2):73–76, 1964.

Malpass, L. F. Motor proficiency in institutionalized and noninstitutionalized retarded children and normal children. *American Journal of Mental Deficiency, 64*:1012–1015, 1960.

Malpass, L. F., Hardy, M. W., Gilmore, A. S., and Williams, C. F. Automated instruction for retarded children. *American Journal of Mental Deficiency, 69*(3): 405–412, 1964.

Matyas, R. P. An analysis of secondary school programs for the EMR in public schools of Pennsylvania. *Dissertation Abstracts, 24*:3180, 1964.

McCarthy, J. J. Linguistic problems of the mentally retarded. *Mental Retardation Abstracts, 1*(1):3–27, 1964.

McCarthy, J. J. The teacher as a researcher—A point of view (Part I). *Winnower, 2*(3):25–29, 1966a.

McCarthy, J. J. The teacher as a researcher—A point of view (Part II). *Winnower, 2*(4):35–39, 1966b.

McCoy, G. Some ego factors associated with academic success and failure of educable mentally retarded pupils. *Exceptional Children, 30*(2): 80–84, 1963.

McGeoch, J., and Irion, A. *The Psychology of Human Learning.* New York, Longmans, Green, 1952.

McLaughlin, Sr. M. K. A survey of music activities, materials, and techniques for teachers of elementary EMR children. *Dissertation Abstracts, 24*:2073, 1963.

Mecham, M. J. Developmental schedules of oral–aural language as an aid to the teacher of the mentally retarded. *Mental Retardation, 1*(6):359–369, 1963.

Miller, M. B., and Griffith, B. C. The effects of training verbal associates on the performance of a conceptual task. *American Journal of Mental Deficiency, 66*:270–276, 1961.

Miller, R. V. Social status and socio-emphatic differences. *Exceptional Children, 23*(3):114–119, 1956.

Mills, E., Wiggin, R., and Hebler, J. *Comparison of Especially Designed Art Activities with Traditional Art Activities as Used with Intellectually Handicapped Children and Youth.* Washington, D.C., U.S. Office of Education, Cooperative Research Bureau, 1961, 109 pp.

Mueller, M., and Smith, J. O. The stability of language age modifications over time. *American Journal of Mental Deficiency, 68*:537–539, 1964.

O'Connor, N., and Claridge, G. S. A "Crespi" effect in male imbeciles. *British Journal of Psychology, 49*:42–48, 1958.

O'Connor, N., and Hermelin, B. Some effects of work learning in imbeciles. *Language and Speech, 2*:63–71, 1959.

Oliver, J. W. The effect of physical conditioning exercises and activities on the mental characteristics of educationally subnormal boys. *British Journal of Educational Psychology, 28*:155–165, 1958.

Olson, J. L., Hahn, H. R., and Herman, Anita L. Psycholinguistic curriculum. *Mental Retardation, 3*(2):14–19, 1965.

Orlando, R. Component behaviors in free operant temporal discrimination. *American Journal of Mental Deficiency, 65*:615–619, 1961.

Peck, J. R., and Sexton, Lucille C. Effects of various settings on trainable children's progress. *American Journal of Mental Deficiency, 66*(1): 62–68, 1961.

Peterson, L., and Smith, L. L. A comparison of the postschool adjustment of educable mentally retarded adults with that of adults of normal intelligence. *Exceptional Children, 26*(8):404–408, 1960.

Phelps, H. R. Post-school adjustment of mentally retarded children in selected Ohio cities. *Exceptional Children, 27*(4):58–62, 1960.

Pryer, R. S. Retroactive inhibition in normals and defectives as a function of temporal position of the interpolated task. *American Journal of Mental Deficiency, 64*:1004–1011, 1960.

Ring, E. M. The effect of anticipation interval on paired-associate learning in retarded and normal children. *American Journal of Mental Deficiency, 70*: 466–470, 1965.

Ring, E. M., and Palermo, D. Paired-associate learning of retarded and normal children. *American Journal of Mental Deficiency, 66*:100–107, 1961.

Reger, R. Reading ability and CMAS scores in educable mentally retarded boys. *American Journal of Mental Deficiency, 68*:652–655, 1964.

Robbins, F., and Robbins, J. *Educational Rhythmics for Mentally Handicapped Children.* Zurich, Switzerland, Ra-Verlag, Rapperswil, 1963, 144 pp.

Rosenberg, S. Problem-solving and conceptual behavior. In: Ellis, N. R., ed. *Handbook of Mental Deficiency*. New York, McGraw-Hill, 1963, pp. 439–462.

Rosenberg, S., Spradlin, J., and Mabel, S. Interaction among retarded children as a function of their relative language skills. *Journal of Abnormal and Social Psychology, 63*(2): 402–410, 1961.

Scheerenberger, R. C. Proactive and retroactive inhibition among mentally retarded subjects. In: Council for Exceptional Children. *Inspection and Introspection of Special Education*. Proceedings of the 1964 Conference on Exceptional Children. Washington, D.C., Council for Exceptional Children, 1964, pp. 233–241.

Scherer, Isidor. The prediction of academic achievement in brain-injured children. *Exceptional Children, 28*:103–106, 1961.

Schiefelbusch, Richard L., ed. *Language Studies of Mentally Retarded Children.* Monograph supplement No. 10, *Journal of Speech and Hearing Disorders,* January 1963, 108 pp.

Schueman, Helen. A method for measuring educability in severely mentally retarded children: A preliminary study (Part 2). *Training School Bulletin, 54*:58–61, 1958.

Siegel, J. M. Language behavior in adults and children in interpersonal assemblies. In: Schiefelbusch, R. L., ed. *Language Studies of Mentally Retarded*

Children. Monograph supplement No. 10, *Journal of Speech and Hearing Disorders,* January 1963, pp. 32–53.

Siegel, J. M., and Harkins, J. P. Verbal behavior of adults in two conditions with institutionalized children. In: Schiefelbusch, R. L., ed. *Language Studies of Mentally Retarded Children.* Monograph supplement No. 10, *Journal of Speech and Hearing Disorders,* January 1963, pp. 39–46.

Silverstein, A. B., Auger, R., and Krudis, B. R. The meaning of indefinite number terms for mentally retarded children. *American Journal of Mental Deficiency, 69*(3):419–424, 1964.

Simches, G., and Bohn, R. J. Issues in curriculum: Research and responsibility. *Mental Retardation, 1*(2):84–87, 115–118, 1963.

Slamecka, N. Proactive inhibition of connected discourse. *Journal of Experimental Psychology, 62*:295–301, 1961.

Smith, Edgar A. Automated instruction in special education. In: U.S. Department of Health, Education, and Welfare, Welfare Administration, Children's Bureau. *Research Relating to Children,* Bulletin No. 14. Washington, D.C., Government Printing Office, 1961.

Smith, J. O. Speech and language of the retarded. *Train-School Bulletin, 58*: 111–123, 1962a.

Smith, J. O. Group language development for educable mental retardates. *Exceptional Children, 29*:95–101, 1962b.

Smith, Judith, and Hurst, J. G. The relationship of motor abilities and peer acceptance of mentally retarded children. *American Journal of Mental Deficiency, 66*:81–85, 1961.

Smith, M. P., and Means, J. R. Effects of type of stimulus pretraining on discrimination learning in mentally retarded. *American Journal of Mental Deficiency, 66*:259–265, 1961.

Snyder, R. An investigation of personality variability as a major determiner of the degree of academic achievement attainment among educable retardates. *Dissertation Abstracts, 25*:3409, 1964.

Speidel, E. B. Language achievements of mentally retarded children. *Dissertation Abstracts, 19*:3180, 1958.

Sprague, R. L. Automated arithmetic instruction for the retarded. In: U.S. Department of Health, Education, and Welfare, Welfare Administration, Children's Bureau. *Research Relating to Children,* Bulletin No. 14. Washington, D.C., Government Printing Office, 1961.

Stein, J. J. Motor function and physical fitness of the mentally retarded: A critical review. *Rehabilitation Literature, 24*:230–242, 1963.

Stevenson, H. W. Discrimination learning. In: Ellis, N. R., ed. *Handbook of Mental Deficiency.* New York, McGraw-Hill, 1963, pp. 424–438.

Stevenson, H. W., and Swartz, J. D. Learning set in children as a function of intellectual level. *Journal of Comparative and Physiological Psychology, 51*:755–757, 1958.

Stolurow, L. M. Programmed instruction for the mentally retarded. *Review of Educational Research, 33*:126–136, 1963.

Taylor, H., and Olson, K. Team teaching with trainable mentally retarded children. *Exceptional Children, 30*:304–309, 1964.

Thompson, Mary M. Psychological characteristics relevant to the education of the pre-school mongoloid child. *Mental Retardation, 1*(3):148–151, 185–186, 1963.

Thresher, Janice. Science education for mentally retarded children: A rationale. *Mental Retardation, 1*(3):152–160, 1963.

Underwood, B. Retroactive and proactive inhibition after five and 48 hours. *Journal of Experimental Psychology, 38*:29–38, 1948.

Underwood, B. *Experimental Psychology*. New York, New York, Appleton-Century-Crofts, 1949.

Underwood, B. Interference and forgetting. *Psychological Review, 64*:49–60, 1957.

Vance, H. S. Psychological and educational studies of brain-damaged and non-brain-damaged mentally retarded children. *Dissertation Abstracts, 17*:1033, 1956.

Vergason, G. A. Retention in retarded and normal subjects as a function of amount of original training. *American Journal of Mental Deficiency, 68*:623–629, 1964.

Walton, D., and Begg, T. L. The effects of incentives in the performance of defective imbeciles. *British Journal of Psychology, 49*:49–55, 1958.

Warren, Sue. Academic achievement of trainable pupils with five or more years of schooling. *Training School Bulletin, 60*(2):75–78, 1963.

Weld, R. G. *An Investigation of the Long-Term Effects of Language Training in the Mentally Retarded*. Master's thesis. Madison, Wisc., University of Wisconsin, 1964, 37 pp.

Whelan, R. J., and Haring, N. Modification and maintenance of behavior through systematic application of consequences. *Exceptional Children, 32*(5): 281–289, 1966.

Whitely, P., and Blankenship, A. The influence of certain conditions prior to learning upon subsequent recall. *Journal of Experimental Psychology, 19*:496–504, 1963.

Williams, P. Initial teaching alphabet—Interim assessment. *Winnower, 1*(2): 27–44, 1965.

51 RESEARCH NEEDS IN THE SPECIAL EDUCATION OF THE MENTALLY RETARDED

Leonard S. Blackman

From *Exceptional Children,* Vol. 29, No. 8, April 1963, pp. 377–383. Reprinted with the permission of the Council for Exceptional Children and the author. Dr. Blackman is Professor of Education and Director, Research and Development Center for Education of the Handicapped, Teachers College, Columbia University, New York City.

The issue of research needs in the special education of the mentally retarded is unquestionably one of the most burning and, at the same time, confused issues in this profession. If one more reference to the fiery analogy is permissible, we now find ourselves feeding a bonfire that is generating much more heat and smoke than light.

The writer is aware of at least four major conferences since the spring of 1960 which have convened active researchers in the area of mental retardation to make recommendations for needed research. In that same period of time there were, undoubtedly, a half-dozen more such meetings of which he is not aware. During the spring of 1960, the Scientific Research Advisory Board of the National Association for Retarded Children convened a panel in Los Angeles to discuss "Directions of Future Research on Learning in Mental Retardation." In the summer of 1961, the United States Office of Education sponsored a summer workshop at the University of Wisconsin devoted to research perspectives in mental retardation. In the early part of 1962, one of the subcommittees formed in connection with the President's Panel on Mental Retardation developed a similar topic at the University of Minnesota. Finally, the President's Panel report itself includes a number of recommendations for research developed by outstanding workers throughout the nation.

It should be made clear that the workshops and conferences alluded to above were concerned with the broader issues of research in mental retardation. But all of them were also concerned, to a greater or lesser extent, with the specific problem of research in the special education of the mentally retarded.

In reviewing the reports emanating from these meetings, one immediately wishes that the various sponsoring agencies had had the foresight to invite the same experts to all the meetings. Wishing does not make it so, however, and thereby hangs the tale of the writer's frustration in (a) attempting to understand and piece together some of the discrepant recommendations resulting from the conferences; (b) realizing that the field of research in mental retardation has finally achieved the stage of maturity at which some of its practitioners are permitting themselves the luxury of becoming somewhat doctrinaire in their pronouncements regarding significant research directions and appropriate research objectives; and (c) developing a number of suggestions for what the writer, among others, would consider to be the most potentially fruitful direction for research in the special education of the mentally retarded.

Before embarking on this sea of controversy, there are three introductory delineations that should be made. First, under the general heading of research needs, it is appropriate to discuss types of studies that should be done, administrative arrangements that would facilitate the conduct of research, and techniques for accelerating the training while improving the quality of research personnel. Although they are matters of importance, neither administration nor personnel training will be discussed. Each of these areas could easily be a paper in itself.

Second, it is proposed that research needs in special education cannot be discussed coherently or comprehensively without some understanding of the implications of the growing body of psychological literature, particularly in the areas of learning, perception, and cognition for the special pedagogy which should be but is not yet a part of special education. Psychology is the basic science underlying special education. It cannot be ignored in discussing special education needs, either research or service.

Third, in reviewing the psychological scene as it applies to special education, there will be no tables presented, statistics quoted, or statements regarding the advantages or shortcomings of various experimental designs. Rather, the purpose of this paper is to provide an overview of the three "schools of thought" that seem to have precipitated from the conference reports and literature in the area of the mentally retarded, and the still small and uncompelling eddies and whirls of evidence that have clustered about each of them. Any attempt to summarize and somewhat dramatize a researcher's experimental findings and theoretical position in a short paper inevitably engenders oversimplification and underqualification. For this reason, the names of researchers representing the three schools will be omitted so that the responsibility for the interpretations and categorizations made in the paper will be borne by the writer rather than the original researcher.

It should be made clear, at this point, that these schools deviate from the classical conception of schools in that they are not attempting to provide different theoretical structures for the same body of data. Rather, each school is gathering evidence around its own circumscribed set of variables. Each condescends to the need for someone investigating the kinds of variables intrinsic to the other schools but feels that it cannot do so, because of the molar and contaminated or, conversely, the molecular and non-applicable nature of these variables.

As a result, each of the three schools to be described have shown rapid, parallel growth. The word parallel is used to connote the fact that each school has, thus far, restricted itself to the type of research designed to evaluate the tenability of its own theoretical constructs without reflecting directly on the validity of the theoretical positions held by any other school. If the history of science can serve as a guide, however, there will be major research confrontations between these schools in the near future as they continue to develop, expand, and demand greater scientific recognition. These confrontations will come under the heading of "definitive research" designed to produce evidence that will reflect on those experimental expectations of the three schools that are essentially contradictory. Thus, one of the schools will be supported to the scientific detriment of the others.

NEUROPHYSIOLOGICAL INADEQUACY SCHOOL

Although the Neurophysiological Inadequacy School is concerned with the behavior, particularly perceptual and cognitive, of mentally retarded individuals, it also has a strong etiological orientation. From its inception, this school focused on the psychological characteristics and educational needs of the so-called brain injured, mentally retarded child. Many studies done by proponents of this school seemed to confirm the perceptual, conceptual, and emotional aberrations of children classified as brain injured as compared to familial mentally retarded or normal children. It should be noted that later these aberrations were accepted as evidence of brain injury with or without positive neurological findings.

Under the impact of this productive school, the diagnosis of brain injury became a very popular one. It became popular because, first of all, both the psychologist and the teacher enjoyed the security of being able to place a child in a diagnostic and educational category for which a number of specific teaching methods had been developed and recommended as effective. Second, possibly at a more unconscious level, there was a good deal of security in believing that the reasons for the child's mental retardation did not lie in the educational system, either informal or formal, but rather were inherent in the child himself.

Thus, for the children with whom this school was primarily concerned, the cause of mental retardation was defined in neuro-anatomical and neurophysiological terms. Its manifestations, however, could be more reliably displayed in perception and concept formation than with the neurologist's pins and rubber mallet. It is of some interest that although a central nervous system impairment, usually acknowledged to be irreversible, was a primary factor in the etiology of mental retardation, this school engaged in an active program of developing and evaluating classroom techniques and devices for ameliorating the educational handicaps generated by the neurological disability.

To the consternation of the pioneers of this school, research findings —because they are often derived from different techniques, approaches to sampling, and theoretical predispositions—tend to run in cycles. For the most part, research has been unable to replicate the previously consistent findings that brain-injured children can be reliably differentiated from non-brain-injured children in terms of perceptual confusion, conceptual irrelevancy, and motor incoordination. The oversimplified truth about brain-injured children seems to be that some show these characteristics and some do not. Within this framework, the diagnosis of brain injury becomes somewhat nondiscriminatory for educational purposes. Any typology of the mentally retarded employed for the purpose of developing differential training procedures should be based primarily on their psychological rather than their neurological characteristics.

There is no intent to convey the impression that the Neurophysiological Inadequacy School is defeated or discouraged. On the contrary, there are currently young, promising researchers in the field with sophisticated concepts and techniques. Employing illusion phenomena in the visual, auditory, and kinesthetic modalities, differences in neurochemical brain processes have been inferred between retardates and normals based on the retardates' relatively greater resistance to nonveridical perceptions.

Within this context, the neuro-anatomically oriented brain injured—non-brain-injured dichotomy seems to be limited in its applicability only to that small percentage of cases where positive neurological signs have been confirmed. In its place is a hypothetical neurological model, applicable to all intelligence levels, which features such continuous functions as "cortical satiation" and "neural excitability." Retardates have been found to satiate less than normals and show diminished neural excitability. Since space does not permit a detailed analysis of these findings, suffice it to say that they are considered the equivalent of decreased "cortical conductivity" or lessened "brain modifiability."

Research in this area, then, pictures retardates as individuals with an inferred, inherent neurological incapacity based on their quantitative difference from normals on certain perceptual tasks. It is not clear at this moment, and researchers in this area are not yet particularly concerned, about what the implications of these findings are for research in special education. The only glimmer of a possible breakthrough in this regard is that cortical satiation seems to bear a strong resemblance to certain fatigue constructs in learning theory. Research already done in this area would lead to predictions that retardates would suffer relatively less decrement in performance than normals from massed work schedules. This research should be done with educational materials in special classes. If, indeed, retardates can be given more work and less rest, this should have a significant impact on special education methods and schedules.

CULTURAL DEPRIVATION AND PERSONALITY ABERRATION SCHOOL

Proponents of the Culture and Personality School actively reject the notion that it is possible to assume or infer from research in perception any neurophysiological dysfunctions in the mentally retarded in the absence of positive findings on a standardized neurological examination. This position is maintained in spite of the generally held view that neurology, in many respects, is still a relatively primitive art form.

If, then, the majority of retardates have normal brains, why are they retarded? Preferred answers in this school revolve around the concept of early cultural deprivation. As a result of being deprived of appropriate stimuli, experiences, and information during the crucially important early years, potentially normal children fail to develop the concepts, skills, learning strategies, and attitudes toward instruction necessary to fulfill this potential. The result is what has been described as "garden-variety" or "subcultural" mental retardation.

The immediately obvious solution is that if deprivation is the cause of the retardation then the process should be reversible through an intensive program of environmental enrichment. Efforts in this regard, however, have been something less than dramatically successful, forcing researchers to consider the "critical periods" hypothesis. This hypothesis predicts that if an organism does not receive appropriate environmental stimulation at the point of optimal maturational readiness for the development of any particular skill, then the skill will not develop and the damage is irreversible. Whether the "critical periods" hypothesis proves to be tenable or culturally deprived mental retardates can be cured or mental retardation can be prevented by eradicating the causes of cultural deprivation are questions that only good research will answer.

Research designed to evaluate specialized enrichment programs for many types of mentally retarded children has been done with results ranging from poor to fair. More research of this type is currently in progress. If the enrichment programs are designed for the special class context, then researchers in special education must be prepared to define what they mean by enrichment using words less ambiguous than "stimulating," "dynamic," or "creative." They must be prepared to specify what learning processes are being enriched, for what specific purpose, and by the use of what specific materials. If the enrichment programs are intended for home, neighborhood, or other nonschool environments, then the special educator takes a back seat to other professionals more intimately concerned with these problem areas.

Partisans of the Culture and Personality School also submit that the educational problems of the deprived retardate are further magnified by the limited expectations that special educators have for them. It has been suggested that if, by some delusional miracle, teachers could convince themselves that these children were capable of normal performance if both parties were willing to make the effort, then the children would reward themselves and their teachers by performances approximating these expectancies.

Supplementing this opinion, others argue that the deflated and pessimistic expectancies of retardates based on a long history of personal failure experiences in and out of school is a significant factor in their poor performance and unrealistically low aspirations. Research is badly needed to determine whether strong doses of success provided by instructional programs developed with this requirement in mind can significantly alter the performance and goal-setting behavior of these children. It would also be of interest to evaluate in-service training programs for special class teachers which emphasize the need for heightened achievement expectancy for mental retardates and other handicapped children.

At this point, it would seem advisable to compare, briefly, the positions of the more contemporary members of the Neurophysiological Inadequacy and the Culture and Personality schools. Both are strongly etiological in their orientation. The former emphasizes perceptual research for the purpose of establishing the existence of certain neurochemical brain processes. Mental retardation is linked to the lower level functioning of these processes. Little concern has been manifested as yet in the remediability of this condition. The latter assumes, in the absence of a positive neurological examination, that cultural deprivation, iterative failure experiences, and their sequelae in personality and emotional disturbances are the causes of mental retardation. Since the cause is functional rather than organic, typical hypotheses involve the amelioration of mental handicap through broadly defined enrichment programs. Both of these schools will continue to do research promoting their own conceptions of the cause of mental retardation. The resolution of conflicting constructs will await the development of more sophisticated evaluative devices in neurophysiology on the one hand, and better defined enrichment programs on the other.

BEHAVIORAL DEFICIT SCHOOL

The Behavioral Deficit School has emphasized the importance of achieving an analytical understanding of the learning deficits of the mentally retarded. This is based on the premise that mental retardation is, primarily, a learning disability and that it is possible to understand the condition only by isolating and identifying those aspects of the learning process that are not functioning properly. Having developed an understanding of the relative strengths and weaknesses of the various components of the learning process, it then becomes a more reasonable task to develop and evaluate educational methods that will take advantage of the strengths and, where possible, ameliorate the weaknesses.

An attentional deficit has already been identified in a number of research reports as characteristic of the mentally retarded. This deficit has been described in a number of ways including simply an inability to "pay attention" or an inability to maintain proper "observing responses." As this deficit was identified, procedures for training retardates to pay attention were also conceived and evaluated. These procedures ranged from the manipulation of stimulus properties to the use of trace conditioning techniques.

A number of other significant deficits in mental retardates, as compared to normals, have been identified. These include deficits in the areas of retention, abstraction, and inhibition. Again, as these deficits are isolated, investigators seem to turn naturally to the question of the remediability of these deficits with appropriate psycho-educational intervention.

There are many other aspects of the learning process which have not yet been considered in any detail. Some of the areas in which it would be important to determine the extent of the retardate's relative deficiency, if any, are curiosity, conditioning, incidental learning, serial learning, retential clustering, transfer of training, the transposition phenomenon, generalization, and many others. It should be noted that some of the processes mentioned are more comfortable within a Gestalt psychology framework while others are associated with behaviorism. At this point, however, it is not contingent on the researcher interested in mental retardation to ally himself with any particular camp in psychology. He should be free to select those concepts and operations that promise to shed maximum light on the psycho-educational characteristics of the population with which he is concerned.

Essentially, what is being proposed by members of the Behavioral Deficit School is a system in which it would be possible to profile the relative learning and perceptual strengths and weaknesses of the mentally retarded. Actually, there is no reason why this profile could not be applied to a better understanding of the learning and perceptual processes of all learners at all IQ levels. Coupled with this profile should be an analytical understanding of school material in terms of the type and levels of learning and perceptual skills necessary for its mastery. The learner and that which is to be learned can then be matched on the basis of whether the former possesses the prerequisites for the latter. If not, remedial techniques geared toward upgrading the level of the skill appropriate to task mastery is initiated. This continual process of improving the learner and matching him with school materials as well as reshaping school materials so as to conform more precisely to the learner's skills becomes the pedagogical flywheel around which the special class program must be sensitively balanced. Within this context, the term enrichment, which has had a global connotation with only vague meaning, will now mean enrichment of a particular learning function for a particular educational purpose.

Comparing the Behavioral Deficit School with the other two, it is minimally concerned with the etiology of mental retardation. It is very much committed, however, to (a) the application of the science of educational psychology, particularly the principles of learning and perception, to a better understanding of the retarded learner's deficits, (b) the remediability of these deficits, (c) an understanding of the psychological nature of school materials, and (d) a determination of the interaction between learner and materials.

For too long, the objectives of special education have focused pragmatically on how to train a mentally retarded child for well adjusted mentally retarded adulthood. These have been objectives that the special class has shared with the family, the church, and a variety of social agencies. It is the thesis of this school that the special challenge of special education lies in the unique contribution that can be made only by the special educator working cooperatively with the educational psychologist. This contribution is to understand and, if possible, to eradicate the educational symptomatology of mental retardation.

SECTION FIFTEEN

A Look at the Future

With the 1960 White House Conference on Children and Youth report available, one of the first acts of the late President Kennedy's administration was the establishment of the President's Panel on Mental Retardation. The panel was given the charge to: (1) make a broad study of the scope and dimensions of the various factors that are relevant to mental retardation; (2) appraise the adequacy of existing programs and the possibilities for greater utilization of current knowledge; (3) ascertain the gaps in programs, and (4) determine failures in coordination of activities. Specifically, the panel was to review and make recommendations with regard to:

1. *Personnel* necessary to develop and apply the new knowledge;
2. The *major areas of concern* that offer the most hope, and the means, the techniques, and the private and governmental structures necessary to encourage research in these areas;
3. The *present programs* of treatment, education and rehabilitation;
4. The relationship between the *federal government, the states,* and *private resources* in their common efforts to eliminate mental retardation.

The President's Panel task forces studied every possible aspect of the problem surrounding mental retardation in the United States. Additional task forces studied comparative programs in various European countries. Out of the lengthy study period came a series of reports [1] that have laid the guidelines and priorities for program development on a most comprehensive basis.

[1] The interested reader will find a complete listing and source of availability of these reports in the Appendix of this book listed under U.S. Agency Reports. In addition, the libraries of the Community Resources Branch, Division of Mental Retardation, U.S. Department of Health, Education, and Welfare, 4040 N. Fairfax Drive, Arlington, Va. 22203, and NARC, 2709 Avenue E East, Arlington, Tex. 76010, have complete sets.

Professor Leonard Mayo, who served as chairman of the President's Panel on Mental Retardation, has summarized this effort in the concluding section of this book. Following the summary is a chart showing the needed continuum of services for the mentally retarded as well as a brief summary of the priorities established by the President's Committee on Mental Retardation in the latter part of 1968.

The 1960–1970 decade was a period of great social, political, and educational change. In spite of the chaos, orderly growth and development have and are taking place in providing for the mentally retarded in a humanistic society. The real challenge will be the continued development of help for the retarded in this decade.

A BRIEF SUMMARY OF RECOMMENDATIONS MADE BY THE COMMITTEE IN LATE 1968 [2]

On Mental Retardation in Poverty Areas

Every U.S. child has the right to health and education services from birth.

Supportive manpower for low income area health, educational, and social services should be aggressively provided and developed.

Rural-serving agencies should pool resources to develop regional health, special education, and social service programs.

A community living service, modeled on the U.S. Agricultural Extension Service, should be formed.

The nation's youth organizations should expand service and involvement activities for and with low income area young people.

Community development agencies should include the needs of the retarded as a factor in their planning.

Voluntary family planning and birth control services should be available through community agencies.

Facilities should be located for best service to all of a community's mentally retarded people.

On Manpower for Mental Retardation Programs

Increased efforts should be made to bring both professional specialists and supportive workers into mental retardation programs.

Specialists' functions should be evaluated with a view to transfer of as many functions as possible to trained supportive workers.

Federal grants should be made to states to assist in volunteer service program development.

Mental retardation programs should develop employee education and training programs.

The federal government should develop a mental retardation program staff exchange activity.

[2] President's Committee on Mental Retardation.

On Residential Services for the Retarded

Improved standards and a system of accreditation for residential programs for the retarded should be developed.

The federal government's hospital improvement and hospital in-service training programs should be expanded.

A program for relocating and rebuilding obsolete residential facilities should be established.

A system of loans or grants should be established to help private organizations develop alternative forms of residential service for the retarded.

Welfare agencies should earmark a portion of their resources for services to the retarded and their families.

Mental health agencies should take the lead in developing services for the retarded who are emotionally disturbed.

52 SUMMARY OF THE REPORT OF THE PRESIDENT'S PANEL ON MENTAL RETARDATION

Leonard W. Mayo

From *An Introduction to Mental Retardation: Problems, Plans and Programs*, June 1965, pp. 15–23. Reprinted with the permission of the U.S. Department of Health, Education, and Welfare and the author. Professor Mayo was formerly Chairman, President's Panel on Mental Retardation, and is now Professor of Human Development, Colby College, Waterville, Maine.

President Kennedy appointed the Panel on Mental Retardation in October, 1961, with the mandate to prepare a national plan to help meet the many ramifications of this complex problem. In October 1962, the Panel presented its report, which was subsequently published early in 1963.

The 200-page document includes over 90 recommendations. Mental retardation is shown to be a major national health, social and economic problem affecting some 5.4 million children and adults and involving some 15 to 20 million family members in this country. It estimates the cost of care for those affected at approximately $550 million a year, plus a loss to the Nation of several billion dollars of economic output.

In carrying out its mandate, the Panel employed four main methods of study and inquiry:

Task forces on specific subjects were appointed to which all members were assigned and advisors were designated to work closely with them.

Public hearings were held in seven major cities, at which public officials concerned with retardation, teachers, representatives of related professions, parents, and others reported on local and state programs and gaps in service and made recommendations.

Panel members and advisors visited England, Sweden, Denmark, Holland, and the Soviet Union to study methods of care and education of the retarded and to become acquainted with research in those countries.

A considerable body of literature and recent studies were reviewed, and Panel members visited and observed facilities and programs for the retarded in several states.

Highlights of the findings and recommendations in each of the main sections of the report are summarized herewith, with liberal quotations from the text.

RESEARCH

In research, the Panel recommends that:

Ten research centers affiliated with universities be established to insure continuing progress in research relevant to mental retardation in both the behavioral and biological sciences and to provide additional facilities for training research personnel.

Biological and behavioral research as presently conducted by individual investigators interested in problems germane to mental retardation be continued and extended.

Population studies be undertaken as a basis for analyses of the characteristics and needs of the mentally retarded population on a national basis.

Governmental activity in developing plans for storage, retrieval, and distribution of scientific data be continued.

Congress provide funds to improve the serious shortage of laboratory space; private foundations are requested to review their policies and to consider grants designed to help alleviate this problem.

Scientists in both the biological and behavioral groups engage in highly specialized conferences to deal in depth with problems underlying retardation.

A Federal Institute of Learning be established under the general auspices of the Department of Health, Education, and Welfare (HEW).

The research budget for exceptional children in the U.S. Office of Education be augmented in accordance with the provisions of legislation proposed in 1962.

The National Institutes of Health and private foundations provide more post-doctoral fellowships, awards, and research and career professorships in the fields relevant to retardation.

Programs to train research educators, sociologists, and psychologists in mental retardation be initiated.

Federal support be undertaken for a national program of scholarships for undergraduate college students possessing exceptional scientific ability and for the extension of research activities in undergraduate science departments.

An extensive program of federal aid to education be designed to prevent loss to the scientific manpower pool of numbers of gifted youths who fail to enter college for financial reasons.

The graduate fellowship program in the U.S. Office of Education be extended to provide for preparing research specialists in the education of the mentally retarded.

PREVENTION

To develop a program to prevent mental retardation, the Panel proposes that:

All possible federal, state, and local resources be mobilized to provide maternal and infant care in areas where prematurity rates are high and the consequent hazards to infants great.

High priority be given to making adequate maternal care accessible to the most vulnerable groups in our society, i.e., those who live in seriously deprived areas and who receive little or no medical care before, during, or after pregnancy, and that funds be substantially increased under Title V, Part 1, of the Social Security Act (Maternal and Child Health), to provide for such care.

State departments of health and university medical centers collaborate in the development of multi-state genetic counseling services in order to give young married couples and expectant parents access to such consultation, and that diagnostic laboratories for complex procedures (related to prevention) be developed.

The present review of drug testing procedures be endorsed and the current policy with respect to the distribution of drugs to physicians for field trials without adequate criteria or preparation be investigated.

Laws and/or regulations be enacted by all states (as they have by some) to provide for the registration, inspection, calibration, and licensing of x-ray and fluoroscopic machines and other ionizing radiation sources; and that lifetime radiation records be developed on a demonstration basis in selected areas for the recording and dating of diagnostic and therapeutic x-ray exposure.

Hospitals adopt every known procedure to ensure the prevention of prenatal and neonatal defect and brain damage, and that they apply modern child-rearing knowledge and practices in dealing with infants who may have suffered from trauma resulting from maternal separation.

Programs keyed to the needs of culturally deprived groups in specific areas be organized to reduce the impact of deprivation, which seriously affects the development of children's learning ability. State departments of health, education, and welfare are asked to join in promoting local community programs of prevention to offset the adverse effects of destructive community and neighborhood environment.

A domestic Peace Corps be established to help meet the personnel shortage and special needs in deprived areas and to give Americans an opportunity to serve their own and other communities effectively.

CLINICAL AND MEDICAL SERVICES

In this area, the Panel recommends that:

Inclusive programs of clinical services and medical care be made available to the retarded in or close to the communities where they reside. State and local health departments are urged to extend their services to children in the lower socioeconomic groups and to utilize procedures for the early detection of abnormalities.

Every related agency in the community include the mentally retarded and their families among those served.

State governments lift all present restrictions preventing retarded children with physical handicaps from receiving services available to all other physically handicapped children in the state crippled children's program; to make this possible, an increase of federal funds to the crippled children's program (Title V, Part 2, Social Security Act) earmarked for the mentally retarded is recommended.

Additional clinics for the retarded be established wherever needed to provide services for additional patients and opportunities for training personnel.

To plan these program services more effectively, it is essential that adequately staffed biostatistical sections at the state and federal levels be developed; that there be improved record-keeping and data processing systems; and that community and epidemiological studies be designed and carried out.

EDUCATION

The Panel recommends that specialized educational services be extended and improved to provide appropriate educational opportunities for all retarded children.

This assistance, the report states, can be provided through a federal Extension and Improvement (E and I) program, administered to assure the use of available funds for expansion or development of new services rather than for existing programs at current levels. Any proposal to extend or improve special educational services for retarded children should be considered for an E and I Grant, and evaluated on a competitive basis. Universities, state departments of public education, local and county school systems, and other educational agencies should all be eligible to submit such applications.

At present, states usually assist local school systems by reimbursing local districts for a portion of the excess cost of providing special education services; however, the amount available for this purpose in the budget of the state departments of public instruction is usually limited. Any substantial extension of the specialized educational services for retarded children will require assistance and stimulation from sources beyond local and state school systems.

It is essential that adequate opportunities for learning intellectual and social skills be provided such children through formal preschool education programs designed to facilitate adequate development of skills such as speech and language, abstract reasoning, problem solving, etc., and to effect desirable patterns of motivation and social values.

Most retarded children live in city slums or depressed rural environments. Research suggests that deprivation of adequate opportunities for learning contributes to and complicates the degree of mental retardation present in these children. Formal preschool programs of increased learning opportunities may accelerate development of these children. Yet there are exceedingly few such programs now available to enrich the experiences of deprived preschool children.

The Panel suggests that instructional materials centers be established in the special education units of state departments of public instruction or in university departments of education, to provide teachers and other education personnel with competent consultation on instructional materials and to distribute and loan such materials for the mentally retarded.

The Panel strongly recommends that specialized classroom services be extended to provide for all mentally retarded children. Additional special class services are required for all age levels for both educable and trainable retarded children. However, it is doutbful that comprehensive programs will be developed in most communities without the additional incentive of external financial support, provided by the federal government through the E and I program.

The Panel suggests that services of educational diagnosis and evaluation be extended to all school systems to provide for early detection of school learning disabilities and to enable appropriate school placement.

The U.S. Office of Education is urged to increase its administrative leadership and staff of the program for exceptional children to a level commensurate with the importance of exceptional children in the nation's program of public education.

The Panel underlines the need for an additional 55,000 trained teachers of the mentally retarded. If fully implemented, the Panel states, the following program would add 6000 new teachers each year to the pool of skilled teaching specialists in retardation:

Government and private foundations should provide annually $9 million to be awarded to universities to provide scholarships and to support the training program.

Each state should appropriate an amount equal to at least 5 percent of its annual budget for special education for training grants to experienced teachers wishing to specialize in mental retardation. It is recommended that the government match the funds allocated by the state departments of public instruction.

Upon presentation of plans meeting criteria established by the Secretary of Health, Education, and Welfare, matching grants be provided to the states for institutions to facilitate planning and development, recruiting and training personnel, and research.

No institution for the retarded accommodate more than 1000, and units now being planned for future construction not exceed 500 beds.

THE LAW AND THE MENTALLY RETARDED

The Panel approaches this problem from the point of view that, with the development of new alternatives in treatment, it should now be possible to overcome certain rigidities of the law in the interest of giving the retarded individual the benefit of modern knowledge. The Panel suggests that mandatory legal requirements be minimized wherever voluntary compliance can be obtained. The question of formal legal intervention is regarded as a residual resource which should not be utilized where social or personal interests can be adequately served through other means.

This section of the report, nonetheless, points out that the law must protect the rights of the retarded. Like other citizens they must be assumed to have full human and legal rights and privileges. The mere fact of mental retardation should never be considered in and of itself sufficient to remove their rights.

The Panel recommends specifically that:

Each state establish or designate a protective agency for the retarded, to provide for consultation for them and their families and for employers, guardians, and others concerned with their social and legal problems, and to supervise the private guardians of retarded persons.

Superintendents of residential facilities for the retarded accept as "voluntary" admissions only those adults who are capable of making such a decision.

No limited guardian of a mentally retarded adult be able to commit his ward to an institution without a judicial hearing unless the court order appointing the guardian gave him such discretion, in which case he should inform the court of his ward's change of residence.

Since state and local school authorities are constitutionally obliged not only to provide education for *educable* mentally retarded children, but also to provide training facilities and personnel for *trainable* mentally retarded children, these authorities re-examine the extent to which they provide education and training for mentally retarded children.

The court in deciding whether a confession to a crime was coerced—and hence inadmissible at trial—consider all the relevant circumstances, and assess whether the mentally retarded defendant's state of mind was such as to preclude the confessions being voluntary in any meaningful sense; and that caution be taken against giving any probative weight to the fact that a mentally retarded defendant remained silent when accused of a crime.

The mentally retarded individual who exhibits persistent uncontrolled behavior threatening the well being of others requires special attention, which should be a subject of special study, since he is unsuited both to the typical prison and to most residential facilities for the retarded.

LOCAL, STATE, AND FEDERAL ORGANIZATION

Concerning local, state, and federal organization and relationships, the Panel recommends that:

There be available to every retarded person either in his community or at a reasonable distance: a person, committee, or organization to whom parents and others can turn for advice and counsel; life counseling services; and a sufficient number of qualified professional and informed nonprofessional people willing to assist in developing a program for an individual, and in developing a local or state program.

Every health, education, and welfare agency provide a person, office, division, or other appropriate instrumentality to organize and be responsible for those agency resources or services relevant to mental retardation; and those agencies dealing with the retarded at a local, community, or state level establish committees with high level representation to facilitate communication and cooperation.

A formal planning and coordinating body made up of all appropriate segments of the community be established with the mandate to develop and coordinate programs for the retarded.

The federal government take leadership in developing model community programs for the management of mental retardation in each of the Department of Health, Education, and Welfare regions. The objectives of such models would be: to develop concrete examples and demonstrations of what is believed to be the best possible care for the retarded on a coordinated basis; and to provide teaching resources in which present and future administrative and professional personnel could receive higher quality training.

The Secretary of Health, Education, and Welfare should be authorized to make grants to states for comprehensive planning in mental retardation.

TABLE I Array of Direct Services for the Retarded *

Life Stage	*Components* PHYSICAL AND MENTAL HEALTH	SHELTER NURTURE PROTECTION	INTELLECTUAL DEVELOPMENT
INFANT	Specialized medical follow-up Special diets, drugs or surgery	Residential nursery Child welfare services	Sensory stimulation
TODDLER	Home nursing Correction of physical defects Physical therapy	Foster care Trained baby sitter	Nursery school
CHILD	Psychiatric care Dental care	Homemaker service Day care Short stay home Boarding school	Classes for slow learners Special classes —educable Special classes —trainable Religious education Work-school programs
YOUTH	Psychotherapy		Occupational training
YOUNG ADULT	Facilities for retarded in conflict	Half-way house Guardianship of person	Vocational counseling—Personal adjustment training
ADULT		Long-term residential care Group homes	Evening school
OLDER ADULT	Medical attention to chronic conditions	Boarding homes	

* Not included are diagnostic and evaluation services, or services to the family; the array is set forth in an irregular pattern in order to represent the overlapping of areas of need and the interdigitation of services. Duration of services along the life span has not been indicated here.

of Special Need

SOCIAL DEVELOPMENT	RECREATION	WORK	ECONOMIC SECURITY
Home training Environmental enrichment			
Day camps Residential camps Speech training	Playground programs Scouting Swimming		"Disabled child's" benefits
Youth groups Social clubs			Health insurance
Marriage counseling		Selective job placement Sheltered employment Total disability assistance	
Bowling Evening recreation	Social supervision	Sheltered workshops Guardianship of property Life annuity or trust	
		Old age assistance OASI benefits	

APPENDIXES

APPENDIX A

ORGANIZATIONS INTERESTED IN MENTAL RETARDATION

AMERICAN ASSOCIATION ON MENTAL DEFICIENCY (AAMD)

Office of Executive Director: 5201 Connecticut Avenue, N.W., Washington, D.C. 20015. AAMD is a national organization with professional sections in Administration, Education, Medicine, Psychology, Speech and Hearing, and Social Work. There is a general section as well as a variety of subsections. The AAMD publishes the *American Journal on Mental Deficiency, Mental Retardation* and various monographs dealing with mental retardation.

COUNCIL FOR EXCEPTIONAL CHILDREN (CEC)

Office of Executive Secretary: P.O. Box 6034, Mid City Station, Washington, D.C. 20005. CEC is a department of the National Education Association. Its membership is comprised of professional workers from all areas of special education. There are divisions whose major interests are mental retardation, learning disabilities, and teacher education. This organization publishes *Exceptional Children, Education and Training of the Mentally Retarded,* and *Teaching Exceptional Children.* It also publishes a monograph series on research projects, operates an Information Center on Exceptional Children, and coordinates an Instructional Materials Center network for handicapped children and youth.

NATIONAL ASSOCIATION FOR RETARDED CHILDREN (NARC)

National Headquarters: 2709 Avenue E East, Arlington, Tex. 16010. NARC is primarily an organization of parents and friends of the mentally retarded. It has a network of state councils and publishes *Mental Retardation News,** a bimonthly newspaper covering the news in the field of mental retardation. In addition, it distributes a wide variety of pamphlets, sponsors research, promotes federal and state legislation, and investigates needs for additional services for the mentally retarded.

* Formerly *Children Limited.*

APPENDIX B

A SURVEY OF LITERATURE ON MENTAL RETARDATION

RESEARCH JOURNALS

Abstracts of Peabody Studies in Mental Retardation. Special Education Department, George Peabody College, Nashville, Tenn. 37203.

Current Index to Journals in Education. CCM Information Sciences, ERIC Project Officer, 866 Third Avenue, N.Y. 10022.

ERIC Excerpt. Council for Exceptional Children, Box 6034, Mid City Station, Washington, D.C. 20005.

Research and Demonstrations Brief (USOE). U.S. Office of Education, Washington, D.C. 20202.

Research in Education. U.S. Office of Education, Washington, D.C. 20202.

Research Relating to Children. Clearing House for Research in Child Life, Children's Bureau, Washington, D.C. 20201.

PUBLICATIONS OF THE AAMD

Special publications of the American Association on Mental Deficiency may be obtained by writing to the Association headquarters, 5201 Connecticut Avenue, N.W., Washington, D.C. 20015. The following is a list of recent publications:

AAMD Manual on Terminology and Classification in Mental Retardation

Cognitive Models and Development in Mental Retardation

Directory of Members 1966

Directory of Residential Facilities for the Mentally Retarded—1968

A Manual on Program Development in Mental Retardation

Prognosis of Mental Subnormals

Standards for State Residential Institutions

CEC MONOGRAPHS

Effects of Community and Institutional School Programs on Trainable Mentally Retarded Children. Leo F. Cain and Samuel Levine.

Exceptional Children Research Review. G. Orville Johnson and Harriett Blank.

Success of Young Adult Male Retardates. Will Beth Stephens and John R. Peck.

PUBLICATIONS OF THE STATES

California: *Mental Health Department Research Digest.* Sacramento.
Illinois: *Mental Retardation in Illinois.* State Mental Health Department, Springfield.

Kansas: *Project News of the Parsons (Kansas) State Hospital.*
New Jersey: *The Welfare Reporter.* Department of Institutions and Agencies, Trenton.

New York: *Mental Hygiene News.* State Department of Mental Hygiene, Albany.

Tennessee: *Mind over Matter.* State Department of Mental Health, Nashville.

PUBLICATIONS OF THE NARC

The National Association for Retarded Children, 2709 Avenue E East, Arlington, Tex. 16010, publishes a bimonthly newspaper entitled, *Mental Retardation News.*[1] It also distributes two house organs, *Action Together* and *Information Exchange.* This organization publishes and has for sale over 100 monographs and reprints on various aspects of mental retardation. Write to NARC for listing and price.

NEWSLETTERS

Challenge. Recreation and fitness for the mentally retarded (NEA).
Focus on Exceptional Children.

Newsletter of Chaplains and Other Religious Workers Sub-Section (AAMD).

Newsletter of the Teacher Education Division (CEC).

PCMR Message. President's Committee on Mental Retardation, Washington, D.C.

Programs for the Handicapped. Secretary's Committee on Mental Retardation, U.S. DHEW, Washington, D.C.

[1] Formerly *Children Limited.*

Recreation for the Handicapped (NEA).

R and D News. Special Education Department, Teachers College, Columbia University.

Update (CEC).

Vocational Rehabilitation Section Newsletter (AAMD).

ABSTRACTING SERVICES

With the vast amount of literature being published on mental retardation, the most time-saving device is the utilization of abstracting services. The following list is very comprehensive:

Birth Defects: Abstracts and Selected Articles. National Foundation, New York.

Exceptional Child Education Abstracts (CEC).

Mental Retardation Abstracts. U.S. Government Printing Office, Washington, D.C.

Psychological Abstracts. American Psychological Association, Washington, D.C.

Rehabilitation Literature. National Society for Crippled Children and Adults, 2023 West Ogden Avenue, Chicago.

INDEXING SERVICES

Indexing services have become a popular and rapid directory of the literature. The following are most pertinent:

Current Contents (See Education and Behavioral and Social Science issues.) Institute for Scientific Information, 325 Chestnut Street, Philadelphia, Pa.

Index Medicus. National Library of Medicine, Washington, D.C.

National Library of Medicine Current Catalog. National Library of Medicine, Washington, D.C.

SPECIAL LIBRARY SERVICES

The National Society for Crippled Children and Adults, 2023 West Ogden Avenue, Chicago, Ill., through its library services, prepares for distribution literature packets which contain reprints, leaflets, and bibliographies. They also lend materials to communities, colleges, and professional persons who have difficulty in locating references needed in their work.

The National Library of Medicine, an agency of the U.S. Public Health Service at Bethesda, Md., lends to other libraries either original copies or photocopies of materials in its collection. Although its vast collection of American and foreign documents primarily emphasizes medical materials, allied disciplines are well represented.

APPENDIX C

JOURNALS IN MENTAL RETARDATION AND RELATED FIELDS

PRIMARY SOURCES

American Journal of Mental Deficiency
Canada's Mental Health
Devereux Forum
Digest for Teachers of the Mentally Retarded
Education and Training of the Mentally Retarded (CEC)
Exceptional Children
Forward Trends (British)
Journal of Mental Deficiency Research
Journal of Mental Subnormality (British)
Journal of Special Education
Mental Retardation (AAMD)
Mental Retardation (Canadian ARC)
Mental Retardation News[1]
Pointer
Slow Learning Child (Australia)
Special Education
Special Education in Canada
Special Education Review
Teaching Exceptional Children (CEC)
Training School Bulletin
The Winnower

EDUCATION

American School Board Journal
Clearing House
Education
Educational Administration and Supervision
Elementary School Journal
Grade Teacher
High Points
Instructor
Journal of Educational Research
Journal of Educational Sociology
Nation's Schools
NEA Journal

[1] Formerly *Children Limited.*

NEA National Association of Secondary School Principals Bulletin
Peabody Journal of Education
Review of Educational Research
School and Society
School Life
Teachers' College Record

CHILD STUDY

Child Development
Child Study
Children
Understanding the Child

PSYCHOLOGY

American Journal of Orthopsychiatry
Genetic Psychology Monographs
Journal of Clinical Psychology
Journal of Consulting Psychology
Journal of Educational Psychology
Journal of School Psychology
Psychology in the Schools

LEARNING DISORDERS

Academic Therapy Quarterly
Bulletin of the Orton Society
Journal of Learning Disabilities

MEDICINE, PSYCHIATRY, AND GENETICS

AMA Journal of Diseases of Children
American Journal of Human Genetics
American Journal of Psychiatry
American Journal of Public Health
Developmental Medicine and Child Neurology
Journal of the American Medical Association
Journal of Child Psychology and Psychiatry
Pediatrics

GUIDANCE, REHABILITATION, AND COMMUNICATIVE DISORDERS

ASHA
Journal of Communication Disorders

Journal of Rehabilitation
Journal of Speech and Hearing Disorders
Journal of Speech and Hearing Research
Personnel and Guidance Journal
Rehabilitation Literature
Rehabilitation Record
Vocational Guidance Quarterly
The Volta Review

SOCIAL WORK AND SOCIOLOGY

American Journal of Sociology
Social Casework
Social Work

INTERNATIONAL

Newsletter of the International League of Societies for the Mentally Handicapped (Belgium)
WHO (World Health Organization) Bulletin and Chronicle

APPENDIX D

TEXTBOOKS IN MENTAL RETARDATION*

HISTORICAL

Anderson, Meta L. *Education of Defectives in the Public Schools.* New York: World Book Company, 1917.

Barr, Martin. *The Mental Defectives: Their History, Treatment and Training.* Philadelphia: Blakiston, 1904.

Binet, A., and T. Simon. *The Development of Intelligence in Children.* Baltimore: Williams & Wilkins, 1916.

Brousseau, K. *Mongolism.* Baltimore: Williams & Wilkins, 1928.

Crookshank, F. G. *The Mongol in Our Midst.* London: Routledge, 1924.

Doll, Edgar A. *Clinical Studies in Feebleminded.* Boston: Badger, 1917.

Down, J. *On the Education and Training of the Feeble-in-mind.* London: Lewis and Company, 1876.

Dugdale, R. L. *The Jukes.* New York: Putnam, 1877.

Fernald, W. E. *History of the Treatment of the Feebleminded.* Boston: George Ellis, 1912.

Goddard, Henry H. *The Kallikak Family.* New York: Macmillan, 1912.

———, *School Training of Defective Children.* Yonkers: World Book Company, 1914.

———. *Feeblemindedness: Its Causes and Consequences.* New York: Macmillan, 1923.

Hollingworth, Leta. *The Psychology of Subnormal Children.* New York: Macmillan, 1921.

Holman, Henry. *Seguin and His Physiological Method of Education.* London: Sir Isaac Pitman & Sons, 1914.

Ireland, W. W. *On Idiocy and Imbecility.* London: Churchill, 1877.

Itard, J. M. *The Wild Boy of Aveyron.* New York: Appleton, 1962.

* Classified under the following Headings: Historical; General; Clinical Methods and Evaluation; Educational and Training Programs; Psychological; Communicative Disorders; Parents; Rehabilitation; Recreation; Social Work; Religion; Research.

Kanner, Leo. *A History of the Care and Study of the Mentally Retarded.* Springfield, Ill.: Charles C Thomas, 1964.

Kerlin, Isaac N. *A Brief History of 22 Imbecile Children.* Philadelphia: U. Hunt & Son, 1858.

Oster, J. *Mongolism.* Copenhagen: Danish Science Press, 1953.

Pritchard, D. G. *Education and the Handicapped: 1760–1960.* New York: Humanities Press, 1963.

Schwartz, Harold. *Samuel G. Howe, Social Reformer.* Cambridge, Mass.: Harvard University Press, 1956.

Seguin, Edward. *New Facts and Remarks Concerning Idiocy.* New York: Wil. Wood, 1870.

———. *Idiocy: Its Treatment by the Physiological Method.* New York: Teachers College, 1907.

Shuttleworth, G. E., and W. A. Potts. *Mentally Deficient Children: Their Treatment and Training,* 5th ed. Philadelphia: Blakiston, 1922.

Talbot, Mabel E. *Edouard Seguin: A Study of an Educational Approach to the Treatment of Mental Deficiency.* New York: Teachers College, 1964.

Wallin, J. E. Wallace. *Problems of Subnormality.* New York: World Book Company, 1921.

Witmer, L. *The Special Class for Backward Children.* Philadelphia: Psychological Clinic Press, 1911.

GENERAL

Abel, T., and E. Kinder. *The Subnormal Adolescent Girl.* New York: Columbia University Press, 1942.

American Association on Mental Deficiency. *A Directory of Residential Facilities for the Mentally Retarded. Washington,* D.C.: The Association, 1968.

Baller, W. R. "A Study of the Present Social Status of a Group of Adults Who, When They Were in Elementary School, Were Classified as Mentally Deficient." *Genetic Psychology Monographs,* 1939, 55, 365–379.

Baller, W. R., D. C. Charles, and E. L. Miller. "Mid-Life Attainment of the Mentally Retarded: A Longitudinal Study." *Genetic Psychology Monographs,* 1967, 75, 235–329.

Bauer, Rev. E. Charles. *Institutions Are People: A Documentary of Life in a State School for the Mentally Retarded.* New York: John Day, 1966.

Blatt, Burton, and Fred Kaplan. *Christmas in Purgatory: A Photographic Essay on Mental Retardation.* Boston: Allyn and Bacon, 1966.

British Information Services. *Report of Royal Commission on the Law Relating to Mental Illness and Mental Deficiency.* New York: British Information Services, 1957.

Burt, Cyril. *The Backward Child,* 5th ed. London: University of London Press, 1968b.

Charney, Leon, and E. La Crosse. *The Teacher of the Mentally Retarded.* New York: John Day, 1965.

Craft, M., and Lewis Miles. *Pattern of Care for the Subnormal.* New York: Oxford, 1967.

Davitz, Joel, L. Davitz, and I. Lorge. *Terminology and Concepts in Mental Retardation.* New York: Teachers College, 1964.

Devereux Foundation Institute. *Catalog of Audio-Visual Aids for Counselor Training in Mental Retardation.* Devon, Pa.: The Institute, 1967.

Dexter, Lewis A. *The Tyranny of Schooling: An Inquiry into the Problems of Stupidity.* New York: Basic Books, 1964.

Doll, Edgar A. *Measurement of Social Competence.* Minneapolis: Educational Publishers, 1953.

Dunn, Lloyd M., (ed.). *Exceptional Children in the Schools.* New York: Holt, Rinehart and Winston, 1963.

Dybwad, Gunnar. *Challenge of Mental Retardation.* New York: Columbia University Press, 1964.

Edgerton, Robert B. *The Cloak of Competence.* Berkeley: University of California Press, 1967.

Faber, Nancy W. *The Retarded Child.* New York: Crown, 1968.

Gibson, J., and T. French. *Nursing the Mentally Retarded.* London: Faber, 1967.

Gilmore, Alden S., and Thomas Rich. *Mental Retardation: A Programmed Manual for Volunteer Workers.* Springfield, Ill.: Charles C Thomas, 1967.

Ginsberg, E., and D. W. Bray. *The Uneducated*. New York: Columbia University Press, 1953.

Goldberg, Ignacy. *Selected Bibliography of Special Education*. New York: Teachers College, 1967.

Gottwald, Henry. *Public Awareness about Mental Retardation: A Survey and Analysis*. Ypsilanti, Mich.: Eastern Michigan University Bookstore, 1967.

Gunzberg, H. C., (ed.). "Application of Research to the Education and Training of the Severely Subnormal Child." *Journal of Mental Subnormality*, Monograph Supplement, April 1966.

———. *Social Competence and Mental Handicaps*. New York: Macmillan, 1968.

Heber, Richard, (ed.). *Bibliography of World Literature on Mental Retardation (January 1940–March 1963) and Supplement (March 1963–December 1964)*. Washington, D.C.: U.S. Government Printing Office, 1964.

Hellmuth, Jerome. *The Special Child in the 21st Century*. Seattle: Special Child Publications, 1964.

———. *Learning Disorders*. Vol. II. Seattle: Special Child Publications, 1965.

———, (ed.). *The Disadvantaged Child*. Vol. I. Seattle: Special Child Publications, 1967.

Hurley, Rodger. *Poverty and Mental Retardation: A Causal Relationship*. Trenton: Department of Institutions and Agencies, 1968.

International Congress on Mental Retardation. *Proceedings of the Second International Congress on Mental Retardation*. Part I and II. White Plains, N.Y.: Albert J. Phiebig, 1963.

International League of Societies for the Mentally Handicapped. *Proceedings of the 3rd International Congress, 1966*. Brussels: The League, 1967.

International Medical Conference on Mental Retardation. *Proceedings, 1959*. New York: Grune & Stratton, 1960.

Jackson, Stephen. *Special Education in England and Wales*. New York: Oxford, 1966.

Jastak, J. F., and others. *Mental Retardation: Its Nature and Incidence*. New York: University Publishers, 1963.

Jordan, Thomas. *The Exceptional Child*. Columbus: Merrill, 1962.

———. *The Mentally Retarded*. 2nd ed. Columbus: Merrill, 1966.

———, (ed.). *Perspectives in Mental Retardation*. Carbondale, Ill.: Southern Illinois University Press, 1966b.

Kanner, Leo. *A Miniature Textbook of Feeblemindedness*. New York: Child Care, 1949.

Katz, Elias. *The Retarded Adult in the Community*. Springfield, Ill.: Charles C Thomas, 1968.

Kirk, Samuel A. *Educating Exceptional Children*. Boston: Houghton Mifflin, 1962.

Laycock, Samuel. *Special Education in Canada*. Toronto: Gage, 1963.

Levinson, Elizabeth J. *Retarded Children in Maine: A Survey and Analysis*. Orono, Me.: University of Maine Press, 1962.

Lindman, Frank T., and Donald M. McIntyre, Jr. *The Mentally Retarded and the Law*. Chicago: University of Chicago Press, 1964.

Luria, A. R. *The Mentally Retarded Child*. (Russian translation.) New York: Macmillan, 1963.

Mackie, Romaine P. *Special Education in the United States: Statistics, 1948–1966*. New York: Teachers College, 1969.

Masland, Richard L., Seymour B. Sarason, and Thomas Gladwin. *Mental Subnormality*. New York: Basic Books, 1958.

Meyen, Edward. *Planning Community Services for the Mentally Retarded*. Scranton: International Textbook, 1967.

Moran, Roberto. *Manual of Mental Subnormality*. Rio Piedras, P.R.: University of Puerto Rico Press, 1968.

National Association for Retarded Children. *A Basic Library on Mental Retardation*. New York: The Association, 1955.

———. *Survey and Study of State Institutions for the Mentally Retarded in the U.S.* New York: The Association, 1964.

National Catholic Education Association. *Directory of Catholic Facilities for Exceptional Children in the United States*. Washington, D.C.: The Association, 1956.

Newman, Roger W. *Institutionalization of the Mentally Retarded*. New York: National Association for Retarded Children, 1967.

Penny, Ruthanna, *Care of the Mentally Retarded and Mentally Ill.* Tulare, Calif.: Tulare Press, 1962.

Pinneau, Samuel R. *Changes in Intelligence Quotient: Infancy to Maturity.* Boston: Houghton Mifflin, 1961.

Reed, Elizabeth, and Sheldon Reed. *Mental Retardation: A Family Study.* Philadelphia: Saunders, 1965.

Richards, B. W., (ed.). *Proceedings of the London Conference on the Scientific Study of Mental Deficiency.* Vol. I and II. Dagenham, England: May and Baker, 1962.

Riessman, Frank. *The Culturally Deprived Child.* New York: Harper & Row, 1962.

Ross, Alan Otto. *The Exceptional Child in the Family.* New York: Grune & Stratton, 1964.

Rothstein, Jerome H. *Mental Retardation: Readings and Resources,* 1st ed. New York: Holt, Rinehart and Winston, 1961.

Roucek, Joseph S., (ed.). *The Unusual Child.* New York: Philosophical Library, 1962.

Sackmary, A., (ed.). *Readings in Mental Retardation.* New York: Selected Academic Readings, 1966.

Sargent, F. Porter. *Directory for Exceptional Children: Educational and Training Facilities,* 3d ed. Boston: Porter Sargent, 1958.

Segal, S. S. *Eleven Plus Rejects.* London: Schoolmaster Press, 1961.

———, (ed.). *Backward Children in the USSR.* Leeds, England: E. J. Arnold, 1966.

Stevens, Mildred. *Observing Children Who Are Severely Sub-Normal.* Baltimore: Williams & Wilkins, 1968.

Taylor, W. W., and I. Taylor. *Services for Handicapped Youth in England and Wales.* New York: International Society for Rehabilitation of the Disabled, 1966.

Theodore, Sister Mary. *The Challenge of Retarded Children.* Milwaukee: Bruce, 1963.

Thompson, Mildred. *Prologue: A Minnesota Story of Mental Retardation.* Minneapolis: Gilbert Publishing Co., 1963.

Thorne, Gareth. *Understanding the Mentally Retarded.* New York: McGraw-Hill, 1965.

Tizard, Jack. *Community Services for the Mentally Handicapped.* New York: Oxford, 1964.

Tizard, Jack, and Jacqueline C. Grad. *Mentally Handicapped and Their Families: A Social Survey*. New York: Oxford, 1961.

Trapp, E. Philip, and Philip Himelstein. *Readings on Exceptional Children: Research and Theory*. New York: Appleton, 1962.

UNESCO. *Organization of Special Education for Mentally Deficient Children*. Paris: UNESCO and Geneva: International Bureau of Education, 1962.

World Health Organization. *The Mentally Subnormal Child*. New York: WHO-Columbia University Press, 1954.

———. *Fifteenth Report of Organization of Services for the Mentally Retarded*. Irvington, N.Y.: WHO-Columbia University Press, 1968.

CLINICAL METHODS AND EVALUATION

Adler, Sol. *The Nonverbal Child*. Springfield, Ill.: Charles C Thomas, 1964.

Allen, Robert M., and Sue Allen. *Intellectual Evaluation of the Mentally Retarded Child: A Handbook*. Los Angeles: Western Psychological Services, 1967.

American Medical Association. *Mental Retardation: A Handbook for a Primary Physician*. Chicago: The Association, 1965.

Bayes, Kenneth. *The Therapeutic Effect of Environment on Emotionally Disturbed and Mentally Subnormal Children*. Montreal: Society for the Emotionally Disturbed Child, 1967.

Benda, Clemens E. *Mongolism and Cretinism*. New York: Grune & Stratton, 1949.

———. *Developmental Disorders of Mentation and Cerebral Palsies*. New York: Grune & Stratton, 1952.

———. *Child with Mongolism*. Grune & Stratton, 1960.

Birch, Herbert G. *Brain Damage in Children: The Biological and Social Aspects*. Baltimore: Williams & Wilkins, 1964.

Birch, Herbert, and others. *Mental Subnormality in the Community: A Clinical and Epidemiological Study*. Baltimore: Williams & Wilkins, 1970.

Boom, Alfred, (ed.). *Studies on the Mentally Handicapped Child*. Baltimore,: Williams & Wilkins, 1968.

Bortner, Morton, (ed.). *Evaluation and Education of Children with Brain Damage*. Springfield, Ill.: Charles C Thomas, 1968.

Brown, Roy I., (ed.). *The Assessment and Education of Slow-Learning Children.* London: University of London Press, 1967.

Burt, Cyril. *The Causes and Treatment of Backwardness,* 4th ed. London: University of London Press, 1968.

California State Department of Education. *Diagnostic Problems in Mental Retardation.* Edited by Eli M. Bower and Jerome H. Rothstein. Sacramento: The Department, 1958.

Carter, Charles H. (ed.). *Medical Aspects of Mental Retardation.* Springfield, Ill.: Charles C Thomas, 1965.

———. *Handbook of Mental Retardation Syndromes.* Springfield, Ill.: Charles C Thomas, 1966.

Chess, Stella, Alexander Thomas, and Herbert Birch. *Temperament and Behavior Disorders in Children.* New York: New York University Press, 1958.

Crome, L. *The Pathology of Mental Retardation.* Boston: Little, Brown, 1967.

Doll, Edgar A. *Mental Deficiency Due to Birth Injury.* New York: Macmillan, 1932.

———. "The Feebleminded." In L. Carmichael (ed.), *Manual of Child Psychology.* New York: Wiley, 1946.

Earl, C. J. C., and H. C. Gunzberg. *Subnormal Personalities. Their Clinical Investigation and Assessment.* Baltimore: Williams & Wilkins, 1961.

Eastham, J. C. *Clinical Pathology in Mental Retardation.* Baltimore: Williams & Wilkins, 1968.

Gesell, Arnold, and C. S. Amatruda. *Developmental Diagnosis.* New York: Hoeber, 1947.

Group for Advancement of Psychiatry. *Psychopathological Disorders in Childhood: Theoretical Considerations and a Proposed Classification.* New York: The Group, 1966.

Haeusserman, Else. *Developmental Potential of Preschool Children: An Evaluation of Intellectual, Sensory, and Emotional Functioning.* New York: Grune & Stratton, 1958.

Heaton-Ward, Alan. *Mental Subnormality.* Baltimore: Williams & Wilkins, 1967.

Hilliard, L. T., and Brian H. Kirman. *Mental Deficiency.* Boston: Little, Brown, 1957.

Inhelder, Bärbel. *The Diagnosis of Reasoning in the Mentally Retarded.* New York: John Day, 1968.

Jervis, George I., (ed.). *Mental Retardation: A Symposium from the Joseph P. Kennedy Foundation.* Springfield, Ill.: Charles C Thomas, 1967.

Johnson, Doris, and Helmer Mykelbust. *Learning Disabilities: Educational Practices and Principles.* New York: Grune & Stratton, 1967.

Johnson, G. O., and K. A. Blake. *Learning Performance of Retarded and Normal Children.* Syracuse University, Special Education and Rehabilitation Monograph Series 5. Syracuse: University Press, 1960.

Kanner, Leo. *Child Psychiatry,* 3d ed. Springfield, Ill.: Charles C Thomas, 1960.

Kolb, Lawrence C., R. L. Masland, and R. E. Cooke (eds.). *Mental Retardation.* Baltimore: Williams & Wilkins, 1962.

Kugelmass, I. N. *The Management of Mental Deficiency.* New York: Grune & Stratton, 1954.

Lilienfeld, Abraham M. *Epidemiology of Mongolism.* Baltimore: Johns Hopkins Press, 1969.

Luria, A. R. *The Mentally Retarded Child: Outlines of Studies on the Higher Nervous Activity Characteristics of Oligophrenic Children.* Washington, D.C.: Office of Technical Services, U.S. Department of Commerce, 1962.

Lyman, Frankel. *Phenylketonuria.* Springfield, Ill.: Charles C Thomas, 1963.

Mautner, Hans. *Mental Retardation.* New York: Pergamon, 1959.

Michal-Smith, Harold. *The Mentally Retarded Patient.* Philadelphia: Lippincott, 1956.

Minsky, Louis. *Deafness, Mutism, and Mental Deficiency in Children.* New York: Philosophical Library, 1957.

Mykelbust, Helmer R., (ed.). *Progress in Learning Disabilities.* New York: Grune & Stratton, 1968.

New York Medical College. *The Effectiveness and Methodology of Group Therapy with Mildly Retarded Adolescent Girls.* New York: New York Medical College, Mental Retardation Center, 1968.

Osler, Sonia, and Robert Cooke (eds.). *The Biosocial Basis of Mental Retardation.* Baltimore: Johns Hopkins Press, 1965.

Penrose, Lionel S. *Mental Defect.* New York: Holt, Rinehart and Winston, 1934.

———. *The Biology of Mental Defect.* New York: Grune & Stratton, 1949.

Penrose, Lionel S., and G. F. Smith. *Downs Anomaly.* London: J and A Churchill, 1966.

Pevzner, M. S. *Oligophrenia: Mental Deficiency in Children.* New York: Consultants Bureau, 1961.

Philips, Irving, and M. A. Esser. *Prevention and Treatment of Mental Retardation.* New York: Basic Books, 1966.

Poser, Charles M., (ed.). *Mental Retardation: Diagnosis and Treatment.* New York: Harper & Row, 1969.

Sherman, Mandell. *Intelligence and Its Deviations.* New York: Ronald, 1945.

Smith, James O., and Thomas Lovitt. *Medical Aspects of Mental Retardation and Neuro-Muscular Disfunction.* Lawrence, Kan.: University of Kansas Press, 1965.

Soddy, Kenneth. *Clinical Child Psychology.* Baltimore: Williams & Wilkins, 1960.

Szurek, S. A., and I. N. Berlin. *Psychosomatic Disorders and Mental Retardation in Children.* New York: Science and Behavior, 1968.

Tobias, Jack. *The Relationship of Cognitive Patterns to the Adaptive Behavior of Mentally Retarded Adults.* New York: Associated Educational Services, 1968.

Tredgold, R. F., and Kenneth Soddy. *Tredgold's Textbook of Mental Deficiency,* 10th ed. Baltimore: Williams & Wilkins, 1963.

Wallin, J. E. Wallace. *Children with Mental and Physical Handicaps.* Englewood Cliffs, N.J.: Prentice-Hall, 1949.

———. *Mental Deficiency.* Brandon, Vt.: Brandon Press, 1956.

EDUCATIONAL AND TRAINING PROGRAMS

Abraham, Willard. *The Slow Learner.* New York: Center for Applied Research in Education, 1964.

———. *The Mentally Retarded Child and Educational Films.* Chicago: Coronet Films, 1966.

Alvin, Juliette. *Music for the Handicapped Child.* New York: Oxford, 1965.

Baumgartner, Bernice. *Helping the Trainable Mentally Retarded Child.* New York: Teachers College, 1960.

———. *Guiding the Retarded Child.* New York: John Day, 1965.

———, and Kathryn Lynch. *Administering Classes for the Retarded.* New York: John Day, 1967.

Bensberg, Gerald. *Teaching the Mentally Retarded: A Handbook for Ward Personnel.* Atlanta: Southern Regional Education Board, 1965.

Benyon, Sheila. *Intensive Programming for Slow Learners.* Columbus: Merrill, 1968.

Bernstein, Bebe. *Readiness and Reading for the Retarded Child.* New York: John Day, 1965.

Best, Harry. *Public School Provisions for the Mentally Retarded in the U.S.A.* Worcester, Mass.: Heffernan Press, 1966.

Blatt, Burton. *The Intellectually Disfranchised: Impoverished Learners and Their Teachers.* Boston: State of Massachusetts, Department of Mental Health, 1966.

Bluhm, Donna L. *Teaching Retarded Visually Handicapped.* Philadelphia, Pa.: Saunders, 1968.

Cain, Leo, and S. Levine. *Effects of Community and Institutional School Programs on Trainable Mentally Retarded Children.* CEC Monograph Ser. B., No. B-1. Washington, D.C.: Council for Exceptional Children, 1963.

Charney, Leon, and Edward LaCrosse. *The Teacher of the Mentally Retarded.* New York: John Day, 1965.

Cleugh, M. F. *The Slow Learner.* New York: Philosophical Library, 1957.

———. *Teaching the Slow Learner of the Secondary School.* London: Methuen, 1961.

Cohn, S. M., and J. Cohn. *Teaching the Retarded Reader: A Guide for Teachers, Reading Specialists, and Supervisors.* New York: Odyssey, 1968.

Connor, Frances, and I. Goldberg. *A Curriculum for Preschool Mentally Retarded Children,* Vols. I and II. New York: Teachers College, 1964.

———, and Mabel Talbot. *An Experimental Curriculum for Young Mentally Retarded Children.* New York: Teachers College, 1964.

Cratty, Byron. *Motor Activities and the Education of Retardates.* Philadelphia: Lea & Febiger, 1969.

Descoeudres, Alice. *The Education of Mentally Defective Children.* New York: Heath, 1928.

Devereux Foundation Institute. *Catalog of Audiovisual Aids for Counselor Training in Mental Retardation.* Devon, Pa.: The Foundation, 1967.

Dobbs, J. P. B. *The Slow-Learner and Music: A Handbook for Teachers.* London: Oxford, 1966.

Duncan, John. *Education of the Ordinary Child.* New York: Ronald, 1943.

Durbin, Mary L. *Teaching Techniques for Retarded and Pre-Reading Students.* Springfield, Ill.: Charles C Thomas, 1967.

Ebersole, Marylou. *Steps to Achievement for Slow Learners.* Columbus: Merrill, 1968.

Egg-Benes, Maria. *Educating the Child Who Is Different.* New York: John Day, 1968.

Erdman, Robert. *Educable Retarded Children in Elementary Schools.* Washington, D.C.: Council for Exceptional Children, 1961.

Erickson, Marion. *The Mentally Retarded Child in the Classroom.* New York: Macmillan, 1965.

Everitt, Clarence J. *The Mentally Retarded Child.* San Antonio, Tex.: Naylor, 1968.

Featherstone, William B. *Teaching the Slow Learner,* rev. ed. New York: Teachers College, 1951.

Feingold, Abraham. *Teaching Arithmetic to Slow Learners and Retarded.* New York: John Day, 1965.

Frankel, Max, William Happ, and Maurice Smith. *Functional Teaching of the Mentally Retarded.* Springfield, Ill.: Charles C Thomas, 1966.

Gallagher, James J. *The Tutoring of Brain Injured Mentally Retarded Children.* Springfield, Ill.: Charles C Thomas, 1960.

Garton, Malinda D. *Teaching the Educable Mentally Retarded.* Springfield, Ill.: Charles C Thomas, 1965.

Ginglend, David, and Winifred Stiles. *Music Activities for Retarded Children: A Handbook for Teachers and Parents.* Nashville: Abingdon, 1965.

Goldstein, Edward. *Selective Audiovisual Instruction for Mentally Retarded Pupils.* Springfield, Ill.: Charles C Thomas, 1964.

Goldstein, Herbert. *The Educable Mentally Retarded Child in the Elementary School.* Washington, D.C.: National Education Association, 1962.

Gordon, Sol. *Facts about Sex: For Exceptional Youth.* Dubuque, Iowa: William C. Brown Company, 1969.

Hallas, Charles H. *The Care and Training of the Mentally Subnormal.* Baltimore: Williams & Wilkins, 1967.

Hamilton, Lucy. *Basic Lessons for Retarded Children.* New York: John Day, 1965.

Hannaford, Alonzo. *Industrial Education Activities for the Trainable Mentally Handicapped.* Norman, Ill.: Illinois State University Press, 1968.

Haring, Norris G., and E. Lakin Phillips. *Educating Emotionally Disturbed Children.* New York: McGraw-Hill, 1968.

———, and Richard L. Schiefelbusch (eds.). *Methods in Special Education.* New York: McGraw-Hill, 1968.

Hill, Margaret. *The Extra-Special Room.* Boston: Little, Brown, 1962.

Hudson, Margaret. *An Exploration of Classroom Procedures for Teaching Trainable Mentally Retarded Children.* Washington, D.C.: Council for Exceptional Children, 1961.

Hunter, Helene. *Reading Methods and Games for Teaching the Mentally Retarded.* New York: Know Publications, 1960.

Ingram, Christine P. *Education of the Slow-Learning Child,* 3d ed. New York: Ronald, 1961.

Inskeep, Annie L. *Teaching Dull and Retarded Children.* New York: Macmillan, 1926.

Jackson, Stanley E. *School Organization for the Mentally Retarded: Basic Guides.* Washington, D.C.: National Republic Publishing, 1961.

Jacobs, John, and others. *Slow Learner Problems in the Classroom.* Gainesville: University of Florida Bookstore, 1968.

Johnson, G. Orville. *Education of Slow Learners.* Englewood Cliffs, N.J.: Prentice-Hall, 1963.

Kephart, Newell C. *The Slow Learner in the Classroom.* Columbus: Merrill, 1960.

Kirk, Samuel A. *Early Education of the Mentally Retarded.* Urbana: University of Illinois, 1958.

———, and G. Orville Johnson, *Educating the Retarded Child.* Boston: Houghton Mifflin, 1951.

Kolburne, L. L. *Effective Education for the Mentally Retarded Child.* New York: Vantage, 1965.

Kolstoe, Oliver, and Roger Frey. *A High School Work-Study Program for the Mentally Retarded.* Carbondale: Southern Illinois University Press, 1965.

Lloyd, Frances. *Educating the Subnormal Child.* New York: Philosophical Library, 1953.

Love, Harold, (ed.). *Mental Retardation: A Basic Guide.* Berkeley: McCutchan, 1968a.

———. *Teaching the Educable Mentally Retarded.* Berkeley: McCutchan, 1968b.

Molloy, Julia. *Trainable Children: Curriculum and Procedures.* New York: John Day, 1963.

Perry, Natalie. *Teaching the Mentally Retarded Child.* New York: Columbia University Press, 1960.

Peter, Laurence. *Prescriptive Teaching.* New York: McGraw-Hill, 1965.

Robins, Ferris, and Jennel Robins. *Educational Rhythmics for Mentally Handicapped Children.* New York: Horizon Press, 1965.

Rosenzweig, Louis, and Julia Long. *Understanding and Teaching the Dependent Retarded Child.* Darien, Conn.: Educational Publishing, 1960.

Segal, S. S. *No Child Is Ineducable: Special Education Provisions and Trends.* New York: Pergamon, 1967.

Slaughter, Stella. *The Educable Mentally Retarded Child and His Teacher.* Philadelphia: Davis, 1964.

Smith, Marian, and A. J. Burks. *Teaching the Slow Learning Child.* New York: Harper & Row, 1954.

Smith, Robert M. *Clinical Teaching: Methods of Instruction for the Retarded.* New York: McGraw-Hill, 1968.

Sniff, William F. *A Curriculum for Mentally Retarded Young Adults.* Springfield, Ill.: Charles C Thomas, 1965.

Standing, E. Mortimer. *The Montessori Method.* Fresno, Calif.: Academy Library Guild, 1962.

Stark, Edward S., (ed.). *Special Education: A Curriculum Guide.* Springfield, Ill.: Charles C Thomas, 1969.

Tansley, A. E., and R. Gulliford. *Education of Slow Learning Children.* London: Routledge, 1960.

Thomas, Janet K. *How To Teach and Administer Classes for Mentally Retarded Children.* Minneapolis: Denison, 1968a.

———. *Teaching Arithmetic to Mentally Retarded Children.* Minneapolis: Denison, 1968b.

———. *Teaching Language Arts to Mentally Retarded Children.* Minneapolis: Denison, 1968c.

———. *Teaching Reading to Mentally Retarded Children.* Minneapolis: Denison, 1968d.

Wallin, J. E. Wallace. *Education of Mentally Handicapped Children.* New York: Harper & Row, 1955.

Weber, Elmer W. *Mentally Retarded Children and Their Education.* Springfield, Ill.: Charles C Thomas, 1963.

———. *Educable and Trainable Mentally Retarded Children.* Springfield, Ill.: Charles C Thomas, 1965.

Willey, Roy, and Kathleen B. Waite. *The Mentally Retarded Child: Identification, Acceptance, and Curriculum.* Springfield, Ill.: Charles C Thomas, 1964.

Younie, William. *Instructional Approaches to Slow Learning.* New York: Teachers College, 1968.

Zaetz, Jay L. *Occupational Activities for the Severely Retarded Adult.* Springfield, Ill.: Charles C Thomas, 1969.

PSYCHOLOGICAL

Baumeister, Alfred A., (ed.). *Mental Retardation: Appraisal, Education, and Rehabilitation.* Chicago: Aldine, 1967.

Clarke, Anne, and A. D. B. Clarke. *Mental Deficiency: The Changing Outlook,* rev. ed. New York: Free Press, 1966.

Clausen, Johannes. *Ability Structures and Subgroups in Mental Retardation.* Washington, D.C.: Spartan Books, 1966.

Hutt, Max, and Robert Gibby. *The Mentally Retarded Child: Development, Education, and Treatment,* 2d ed. Boston: Allyn and Bacon, 1965.

Illinois State Department of Public Instruction. *Handbook and Manual for Qualified Psychological Examiner.* Supplement to Circular B, No. 12, Springfield, Ill.: The Department, 1950.

Khanna, J. L. *Brain Damage and Mental Retardation: A Psychological Evaluation.* Springfield, Ill.: Charles C Thomas, 1967.

Leland, Henry, and David Smith. *Play Therapy with Mentally Subnormal Children.* New York: Grune & Stratton, 1965.

Norsworthy, Naomi. "Psychology of Mental Deficiency." *Archives of Psychology,* November 1906.

Robinson, Halbert B., and Nancy M. Robinson. *The Mentally Retarded Child: A Psychological Approach.* New York: McGraw-Hill, 1968.

Sarason, Seymour B., and John Doris. *Psychological Problems of Mental Deficiency,* 4th ed. New York: Harper & Row, 1969.

Stacey, Chalmers L., and Manfred De Martino (eds.). *Counseling and Psychotherapy with the Mentally Retarded: A Book of Readings.* New York: Free Press, 1957.

Strauss, Alfred A., and L. E. Lehtinen. *Psychopathology and Education of the Brain-Injured Child.* Vol. I. New York: Grune & Stratton, 1947.

———, and Newell C. Kephart. *Psychopathology and Education of the Brain-Injured Child.* Vol. 2. New York: Grune & Stratton, 1955.

Taylor, Edith M. *Psychological Appraisal of Children with Cerebral Defects.* Cambridge, Mass.: Harvard University Press, 1959.

Wechsler, David. *The Measurement and Appraisal of Adult Intelligence,* 4th ed. Baltimore: Williams & Wilkins, 1958.

COMMUNICATIVE DISORDERS

Battin, R. R., and C. O. Haug. *Speech and Language Delay: A Home Training Program.* Springfield, Ill.: Charles C Thomas, 1964.

Chamberlain, Naomi H., and Olivia J. Hooker. *Learning Colors; Learning Forms and Sizes: A Speech Readiness Guide for Parents.* Rochester, N.Y.: Olney Books, 1956.

Daley, William T., (ed.). *Speech and Language Therapy with the Brain Damaged Child.* Washington, D.C.: Catholic University Press, 1962.

Engel, Rose, William Reid, and D. P. Rucker. *Language Develop-*

ment Experiences for Your Child. Los Angeles: University of Southern California Bookstore, 1966.

Lillywhite, H. S., and D. P. Bradley. *Communication Problems in Mental Retardation: Diagnosis and Management.* New York: Harper & Row, 1969.

Molloy, Julia. *Teaching the Retarded Child To Talk: A Guide for Parents and Teachers.* New York: John Day, 1961.

Morley, Muriel E. *The Development and Disorders of Speech in Childhood.* Baltimore: Williams & Wilkins, 1965.

New York City, Board of Education of. *Speech for the Retarded Child: A Teacher's Handbook.* New York: The Board, 1960.

O'Connor, N., and B. Hermelin. *Speech and Thought in Severe Subnormality.* New York: Macmillan, 1964.

Schiefelbusch, Richard, Ross Copeland, and J. O. Smith (eds.). *Language and Mental Retardation: Empirical Conceptual Development.* New York: Holt, Rinehart and Winston, 1967.

Waldon, Edgar, (ed.). *Differential Diagnosis of Speech and Hearing Problems of the Mentally Retarded.* Washington D.C.: Catholic University Press, 1968.

Wood, Mildred H. *Communication Skills for the Primary Educable Mentally Retarded.* Cedar Falls: Extension Service, University of Northern Iowa, 1965.

PARENTS

Abraham, Willard. *Barbara.* New York: Holt, Rinehart and Winston, 1958.

Attwell, A. A., and D. Ann Clabby. *The Retarded Child: Answers to Questions Parents Ask.* Burbank, Calif.: Eire Press, 1969.

Barsch, Ray H. *The Parent of the Handicapped Child: A Study of Child-Rearing Practices.* Springfield, Ill.: Charles C Thomas, 1968.

Blodgett, Harriet, and G. J. Warfield. *Understanding Mentally Retarded Children.* New York: Appleton, 1959.

Buck, Pearl S. *The Child Who Never Grew.* New York: Hay, 1950.

———, and G. Zarfoss. *The Gifts They Bring.* New York: John Day, 1965.

Campanelle, T. C. *Counseling Parents of Mentally Retarded Children.* Milwaukee: Bruce, 1965.

Capa, Cornell, and Maya Pines. *Retarded Children Can Be Helped.* Great Neck, N.Y.: Channel Press, 1957.

Carlson, Earl H. *Born That Way.* New York: John Day, 1961.

Chamberlain, Naomi H., and Dorothy H. Moss. *The Three "Rs" for the Retarded: A Program for Training the Retarded Child at Home.* New York: National Association for Retarded Children, 1954.

Dale, May E. *Come Follow Me.* Appleton, Wis.: Come Publishing, 1966.

Doll, Edgar A. *Your Child Grows Up.* New York: John Hancock Mutual Life Insurance, 1939.

Doorly, Ruth K. *Our Jimmy.* Westwood, Mass.: Service Associates, 1967.

Ecob, Katherine G. *Deciding What's Best for Your Retarded Child.* New York: N.Y. Society for Mental Health, 1955.

Egg-Benes, Maria. *When a Child Is Different: A Basic Guide for Parents and Friends of Mentally Retarded Children.* New York: John Day, 1964.

Ehlers, Walter H. *Mentally Retarded Children: How They Feel; Where They Find Help.* Springfield, Ill.: Charles C Thomas, 1966a.

———. *Mothers of Mentally Retarded Children.* Springfield, Ill.: Charles C Thomas, 1966b.

Farber, Bernard. *Family Organization and Crisis: Maintenance of Integration in Families with Severely Retarded Children.* Lafayette, Ind.: Society for Research in Child Development, 1960.

———, *Mental Retardation: Its Social Context and Social Consequences.* New York: Houghton Mifflin, 1968.

———, W. C. Jenne, and R. Toige. *Family Crisis and the Retarded Child.* CEC Research Monograph No. 1. Washington, D.C.: Council on Exceptional Children, 1960.

Forney, Katherine. *Up and Away: The Education of Handicapped But Exceptional Children.* New York: Exposition Press, 1957.

Frank, John P. *My Son's Story.* New York: Knopf, 1952.

French, Edward L., and J. C. Scott. *Child in the Shadows.* Philadelphia: Lippincott, 1960.

———. *How You Can Help Your Retarded Child: A Manual for Parents.* New York: Lippincott, 1967.

Gant, Sophie. *One of Those: The Progress of a Mongoloid Child.* New York: Pageant Books, 1957.

Gayeski, J. *Search for Their Future: Our Retarded Children.* Milwaukee, Wis.: Bruce, 1965.

Group for Advancement of Psychiatry. *Mental Retardation: A Family Crisis.* New York: The Group, 1963.

Heard, J. Norman. *Hope through Doing: The Rewards of Working for Your Retarded Child and Others.* New York: John Day, 1968.

Heiser, Karl F. *Our Backward Children.* New York: Norton, 1955.

Hunt, Nigel. *The World of Nigel Hunt: A Diary of a Mongoloid Youth.* New York: Garrett, 1967.

Junker, Karin. *The Child in the Glass Ball.* New York: Abingdon, 1964.

Katz, Alfred. *Parents and the Handicapped.* Springfield, Ill.: Charles C Thomas, 1961.

Kirk, Samuel A., M. Karnes, and W. Kirk. *You and Your Retarded Child,* rev. ed. Palo Alto, Calif.: Pacific Books, 1969.

Lee, Carrel. *Tender Tyrant: The Story of a Mentally Retarded Child.* Minneapolis: Augsburg, 1961.

Levinson, Abraham. *The Mentally Retarded Child,* rev. ed. New York: John Day, 1965.

———, and J. A. Bigler, *Mental Retardation in Infants and Children.* Chicago: Yearbook Medical Publishers, 1960.

Lewis, Richard S., and others. *The Other Child.* New York: Grune & Stratton, 1951.

Loewy, Hert. *The Retarded Child: A Guide for Parents and Teachers.* New York: Philosophical Library, 1951.

———. *Training the Backward Child.* New York: Philosophical Library, 1956.

———. *More about the Backward Child.* New York: Philosophical Library, 1957.

McConnell, F. J. *The Subnormal Child at Home.* New York: Macmillan, 1958.

Magee, Catherine Fowler. *One of the Family.* New York: McKay, 1964.

McDonald, Eugene T. *Understanding Those Feelings: A Guide for Parents of the Handicapped.* Pittsburgh: Stanwix, 1962.

McGlone, Roy. *Helpful Hints for Handicaps: A Manual for Home Teaching of the Mentally Handicapped Child.* Denver: Laradon Hall, 1962.

Minnesota Department of Public Welfare. *Now They Are Grown: Help for Parents of Teen-Age and Young Adult Trainable Retarded Children.* St. Paul, Minn.: The Department, 1959.

Morgenstern, Milan. *Practical Training for the Severely Handicapped Child.* London: Heinemann, 1966.

Murray, Dorothy G. *This Is Stevie's Story.* New York: Abingdon, 1969.

Oates, Wayne E. *Where To Go for Help.* Philadelphia: Westminster, 1957.

Osterhout, Edna E. *Teaching the Retarded Child at Home.* Durham, N.C.: Seeman, 1950.

———. *For the Parents of a Mongol Child, Sunfield Children's Home.* New York: Anthroposophical Press, 1955.

Ottawa Department of National Health and Welfare. *The Backward Child.* Ottawa: Information Services Division, The Department, 1949.

Patterson, K. *No Time for Tears.* Chicago: Johnson, 1966.

Penny, Ruthanna. *Substitute Parents: Training the Profoundly Retarded Patient for Return to the Community.* Springfield, Ill.: Charles C Thomas, 1967.

Pollock, Morris P. *New Hope for the Retarded: Enriching the Lives of Exceptional Children.* Boston: Porter Sargent, 1953.

Roberts, Esther H. *The Beginning Years: For Parents and Teachers of Our Young Retarded Children.* New York: Vantage, 1969.

Roberts, Nancy. *David: A Picture Story of a Mentally Retarded Boy.* Richmond: John Knox, 1968.

Rogers, Dale R. *Angel Unaware.* New York: Revell, 1953.

Seagoe, May V. *Yesterday Was Tuesday, All Day and All Night.* Boston: Little, Brown, 1964.

Slaughter, Stella Stillson. *The Mentally Retarded Child and His Parent.* New York: Harper & Row, 1960.

Solnit, A. J., and M. J. Stark. *Mourning and the Birth of a Defective Child.* New York: International Universities, 1961.

Spock, Benjamin. *On Being a Parent of a Handicapped Child.* Chicago: National Society for Crippled Children and Adults, 1961.

———, and Marion Lerrigo. *Caring for Your Disabled Child.* New York: Macmillan, 1965.

Steel, Max. *Debby.* New York: Harper & Row, 1950.

Stern, Edith, and E. Castendyck. *The Handicapped Child: A Guide for Parents.* New York: Ace Books, 1950.

Stout, Lucille. *I Reclaimed My Child.* Philadelphia: Chilton, 1959.

Tucker, Charlotte. *Betty Lee: Care of Handicapped Children.* New York: Macmillan, 1954.

U.S. Department of Health, Education, and Welfare, Children's Bureau. *The Child Who Is Mentally Retarded.* Washington, D.C.: Government Printing Office, 1956.

———. *The Mentally Retarded Child at Home: A Manual for Parents.* Washington, D.C.: Government Printing Office, 1958.

Wolfensberger, Wolf, and R. D. Kurtz. *Management of the Family of the Mentally Retarded.* Chicago: Follett, 1969.

Woods Schools Proceedings. *Helping Parents Understand the Exceptional Child.* Langhorne, Pa.: The Schools, 1952.

Woolson, Arthur. *Good-by, My Son.* New York: Harper & Row, 1960.

REHABILITATION

Ayers, George P., (ed.). *Program Development in Mental Retardation.* Elwyn, Pa.: Elwyn Institute, 1968.

———. *Selected References on Education and Vocational Rehabilitation of Mentally Retarded Adolescents.* Mankato, Minn.: Mankato State College, 1967.

Fraenkel, William A. *The Mentally Retarded and Their Vocational Rehabilitation.* New York: National Association for Retarded Children, 1961.

Fuddell, Stanley, and John Peck. *How To Hold Your Job: Teachers Workbook.* New York: John Day, 1967.

Gunzberg, Herbert C. *Social Rehabilitation of the Subnormal.* Baltimore: Williams & Wilkins, 1960.

Stahlecker, Lotar V. *Occupational Information for the Mentally Retarded: Selected Readings.* Springfield, Ill.: Charles C Thomas, 1967.

Zaetz, Jay L. *Occupational Activities Training Manual: For Severely Retarded Adults.* Springfield, Ill.: Charles C Thomas, 1969.

RECREATION

American Association for Health, Physical Education, and Recreation. *Physical Activities for the Mentally Retarded: Ideas for Instruction.* Washington, D.C.: National Education Association, 1968a.

———. *Programming for the Mentally Retarded.* Washington, D.C.: National Education Association, 1968b.

———. *Special Fitness Test Manual for the Mentally Retarded.* Washington, D.C.: National Education Association, 1969.

Avedon, Elliott, and Frances Arje. *Socio-Recreative Programming for the Retarded.* New York: Teachers College, 1964.

Bensberg, Gerald. *Recreation for the Mentally Retarded: A Handbook for Ward Personnel.* Atlanta: Southern Regional Education Board, 1964.

Birenbaum, A., and A. I. Schwartz. *Recreation for the Mentally Retarded: A Community Program.* New York: Selected Academic Readings, 1967.

Boy Scouts of America. *Scouting for the Mentally Retarded.* New Brunswick, N.J.: Boy Scouts of America, 1969.

Buist, C. A., and Jerome L. Schulman. *Toys and Games for Educationally Handicapped Children.* Springfield, Ill.: Charles C Thomas, 1969.

Canner, N., and H. Klebanoff. *And a Time to Dance.* Boston: Beacon, 1968.

Carlson, Bernice, and David Ginglend. *Play Activities for the Retarded Child.* New York: Abingdon, 1961.

———. *Recreation for Retarded Teen-Agers and Adults.* New York: Abingdon, 1968.

Chapman, Frederick M. *Recreation Activities for the Handicapped.* New York: Ronald, 1960.

Council for Exceptional Children. *Recreation and Physical Education Activities for the Mentally Retarded.* Washington, D.C.: The Council, 1966.

Hunter, Helene L., and others. *Arts and Crafts for Retarded Children.* New York: Know Publications, 1964.

Lindsay, Zaidee. *Art Is for All: Arts and Crafts for Less Able Children.* New York: Taplinger, 1968.

McNeice, William, and Kenneth Benson, *Crafts for the Retarded.* New York: Taplinger, 1964.

Nordhoff, Paul, and Clive Robbins. *Music Therapy for Handicapped Children.* Blauvelt, N.Y.: Rudolf Steiner Publications, 1965.

Schattner, Regina. *Creative Dramatics for Handicapped Children.* New York: John Day, 1967.

Schmidt, Alfred. *Craft Projects for Slow Learners.* New York: John Day, 1968.

SOCIAL WORK

Adams, Margaret. *The Mentally Subnormal: The Social Casework Approach.* London: Heinemann, 1960.

Beck, Helen L. *Social Services to the Mentally Retarded.* Springfield, Ill.: Charles C Thomas, 1969.

Davies, Stanley P., and K. G. Ecob. *The Mentally Retarded in Society.* New York: Columbia University Press, 1959.

Hume, Margarite, (ed.). *Mental Retardation: A New Dimension in Social Work Education.* Louisville: Kent School of Social Work, University of Louisville, 1968.

Katz, Alfred H., (ed.). *Mental Retardation and Social Work Education.* Detroit: Wayne State University Press, 1961.

O'Connor, N., and J. Tizard. *Social Problems of Mental Deficiency.* New York: Philosophical Library, 1957.

Schreiber, Meyer. *Social Work and Mental Retardation.* New York: John Day, 1969.

———, and S. Bernhardt. *Sourcebook on Mental Retardation for Schools of Social Work.* New York: Associated Educational Services, 1968.

Todd, F. Joan. *Social Work with the Mentally Subnormal.* New York: Humanities Press, 1967.

RELIGION

Bauer, Charles E. *Retarded Children Are People.* Milwaukee: Bruce, 1964.

Bogardus, La Donna. *Christian Education for Retarded Children and Youth.* New York: Abingdon, 1963.

Johnson, James, and Martha Jones. *Learning To Know God: A Resource Book for Use with Retarded Persons.* St. Louis: Bethany Press, 1966.

Kemp, Charles F. *The Church: The Gifted and Retarded Child.* St. Louis, Mo.: Bethany Press, 1957.

Lister, R. *Jewish Religious Education for the Retarded Child.* New York: Union of American Hebrew Congregations, 1959.

Nelson, Charles H., Jr. *Religious Education: A Manual for Teachers of Protestant Religious Education with the Mentally Retarded,* 3d ed. Butlerville, Ind.: Muscatatuck State School, 1962.

Petersen, Sigurd. *Retarded Children: God's Children.* Philadelphia: Westminster, 1960.

Stubblefield, Harold. *The Church's Ministry in Mental Retardation.* Nashville: Broadman Press, 1964.

RESEARCH

Ellis, Norman R., (ed.). *Handbook of Mental Deficiency.* New York: McGraw-Hill, 1963.

———. *International Review of Research in Mental Retardation:* Vol. 1. New York: Academic Press, 1966.

———. *International Review of Research in Mental Retardation:* Vol. 2. New York: Academic Press, 1967.

———. *International Review of Research in Mental Retardation:* Vol. 3. New York: Academic Press, 1968.

Heber, Rick, and Harvey Stevens, (eds.). *Mental Retardation: A Review of Research.* Chicago: University of Chicago Press, 1964.

Johnson, G. O., and H. Blank. *Exceptional Children Research Review.* Washington, D.C.: National Education Association, 1969.

APPENDIX E

SPECIALIZED BIBLIOGRAPHIES

On various occasions, *Mental Retardation Abstracts* has compiled extensive specialized bibliographies. They include:

Adaptive Behavior. Vol. 4, No. 3, November 1967, pp. 380–387.

Application of Stanford–Binet and Wechsler Intelligence Scales with the Mentally Retarded. Vol. 1, No. 2, April–June 1964, pp. 177–189.

Architectural Planning for the Mentally Retarded. Vol. 4, No. 3, November 1967, pp. 388–399.

Counseling Parents of the Mentally Retarded. Vol. 2, No. 3, July–September 1965, 263–270.

Education of the Mentally Retarded. Vol. 3, No. 4, October–December 1966, pp. 493–501.

Electroencephalographic Studies Relating to Mental Retardation. Vol. 3, No. 2, April–June 1966, pp. 170–178.

Family Care and Adoption of Retarded Children. Vol. 1, No. 3, July–September 1964, pp. 332–333.

Genetic Aspects of Mental Retardation. Vol. 2, No. 4, October–December 1965, pp. 476–481.

Hydrocephalus. Vol. 3, No. 3, July–September 1966, pp. 319–332.

In-Service Training in Institutions for the Mentally Retarded. Vol. 4, No. 4, December 1967, pp. 563–569.

Instrumental Learning in Mental Retardates. Vol. 3, No. 1, January–March 1966, pp. 16–20.

Mental Retardation and Religion. Vol. 3, No. 4, October–December 1966, pp. 502–508.

Nursing and Mental Retardation. Vol. 1, No. 3, July–September 1964, pp. 326–331.

Operant Conditioning and Techniques. Vol. 4, No. 1, January–March 1967, pp. 16–18.

Personality Disorders and Characteristics of the Mentally Retarded. Vol. 1, No. 3, July–September 1964, pp. 320–325.

Programmed Instruction with the Retarded. Vol. 1, No. 1, January–March 1964, pp. 28–29.

Psycho-Pharmacological Therapy with the Mentally Retarded. Vol. 3, No. 1, January–March 1964, pp. 21–27.

Psycho-Therapy with the Mentally Retarded. Vol. 1, No. 4, October–December 1964, pp. 442–444.

Recreation for the Retarded. Vol. 2, No. 2, April–June 1965, pp. 131–134.

Research on Linguistic Problems of the Mentally Retarded. Vol. 1, No. 1, January–March 1964, pp. 21–27.

Severe Mental Retardation and Family Relationships. Vol. 2, No. 1, January–March 1965, pp. 11–17.

Sheltered Workshops for the Mentally Retarded. Vol. 2, No. 4, October–December 1965, pp. 482–486.

Teaching Materials Regarding Mental Retardation for Faculties of Schools of Social Work. Vol. 4, No. 2, April–June 1967, pp. 181–187.

APPENDIX F

U.S. GOVERNMENT AGENCY PUBLICATIONS

A wide variety of federal governmental agencies publishes bulletins and reports relating to the subject of mental retardation. The following is a bibliography of recent publications. The bibliography is organized under the headings of the various agencies and bureaus. To facilitate obtaining copies of these reports, the zip code for each agency is presented. The reader who wishes to keep abreast of all new U.S. government publications should search the *Monthly Catalog of U.S. Government Publications* prepared by the Superintendent of Documents, U.S. Government Printing Office. Monthly listings indicate whether the publication is for sale through the Printing Office or is available directly through the issuing agency.

CHILDREN'S BUREAU—20201

Adoption Opportunities for the Handicapped. 1962.
The Care of the Retarded Child: Therapy and Prognosis. 1964.
Child Health Projects for Mentally Retarded Children: The Role of the Social Worker. 1963.
The Child Who Is Mentally Retarded. 1956.
Children of Deprivation: Changing the Course of Familial Retardation. 1967.
Clinical Programs for Mentally Retarded Children: A Listing. 1966.
The Clinical Team Looks at Phenylketonuria. 1964.
The Closed, Short-Term Group: A Treatment Adjunct for Parents of Mentally Retarded Children. 1965.
A Developmental Approach to Casefinding. 1967.
Extending Clinical Services for Mentally Retarded Children at the Community Level. 1965.
Families of Mongoloid Children. 1963.
Feeding Mentally Retarded Children. 1964.
Galactosemia—A Selected Bibliography. 1963.
Grants for Comprehensive Health Services for Children and Youth: Policies and Procedures. 1965.
Group Work and Leisure Time Programs for Mentally Retarded Children and Adolescents: A Report of a Conference. 1966.
Guide for Nutrition Services for Mentally Retarded Children. 1962.
Guide for Public Health Nurses Working with Children from the Developmental Point of View. 1961.
Health Services for Mentally Retarded Children. 1961.

Historical Perspective on Mental Retardation during the Decade 1954–1964: A Compilation of Articles on Children. 1964.
Illness Among Children. 1963.
Institute on Nutrition Services in Mental Retardation. 1963.
Institutionalizing Mentally Retarded Children . . . Attitudes of Some Physicians. 1963.
Management of Newborn Siblings of Patients with Phenylketonuria or Galactosemia. 1963.
The Mentally Retarded Child: A Guide to Services of Social Agencies. 1963.
The Mentally Retarded Child at Home: A Manual for Parents. 1959.
The Mongoloid Baby. 1960.
Nursing Role in Counseling Parents of Mentally Retarded Children. 1964.
Phenylketonuria. 1965.
Phenylketonuria: A Comprehensive Bibliography. 1964.
Phenylketonuria: Detection in the Newborn Infant as a Routine Hospital Procedure. 1964.
The Public Health Nurse in Community Planning for the Mentally Retarded. 1957.
Rare Inborn Errors of Metabolism in Children with Mental Retardation. 1965.
Recommended Guidelines for PKU Programs. 1966.
Research Relating to Mentally Retarded Children. 1966.
The Role of Child Welfare in Mental Retardation. 1965.
Selected Annotated Bibliography on Mental Retardation for Social Workers. 1965.
Selected Bibliography of Rubella. 1966.
Selected Reading Suggestions for Parents of Mentally Retarded Children. 1967.
State Laws Pertaining to Phenylketonuria as of November, 1966. 1967.
The Steps Ahead. 1963.
Training Programs for Retarded Girls. 1964.

CLEARING HOUSE FOR RESEARCH IN CHILD LIFE—20201

Research Relating to Mentally Retarded Children. 1960.
Research Relating to Mentally Retarded Children. 1968.

DEPARTMENT OF DEFENSE—20301

Benefits for Handicapped Dependents of Members of the Uniformed Services. 1968.

DEPARTMENT OF HEALTH, EDUCATION AND WELFARE—20201

Mental Retardation Activities of the U.S. Department of Health, Education and Welfare. 1969.
Proposed Program for Mental Retardation. 1967.
A Summary of Selected Legislation Relating to the Handicapped, 1963–1967. 1968.
White House Conference on Mental Retardation: Proceedings. 1963.

DEPARTMENT OF INTERIOR, BUREAU FOR INDIAN AFFAIRS—20240

An Interdisciplinary Approach in the Identification of Mentally Retarded Indian Children. 1965.

DEPARTMENT OF LABOR—20210

The Mentally Retarded: Their Special Training Needs. 1964.

NATIONAL INSTITUTE FOR CHILD HEALTH AND HUMAN DEVELOPMENT—20201

Conference on Prevention of Mental Retardation through Control of Infectious Diseases. 1966.
The Social Sciences and Mental Retardation: Family Components. 1968.

NATIONAL INSTITUTE FOR MENTAL HEALTH—20201

Institute on Public Health Nursing in a State Program for Mental Retardation. 1963.

NATIONAL INSTITUTE FOR NEUROLOGICAL DISEASES AND BLINDNESS—20201

Conference on Drugs and Poisons as Etiological Agents in Mental Retardation. 1967.
Mental Retardation, Its Biological Factors. 1966.
Mongolism—Hope through Research. 1964.

OFFICE OF EDUCATION, BUREAU FOR EDUCATION OF HANDICAPPED—20202

Directory of Special Education Personnel. 1968.
Education of Handicapped Children and Youth under Title I ESEA. 1965.
The Grant Program for the Preparation of Professional Personnel in the Education of Handicapped Children. 1967.
Interim Emergency Report of the National Advisory Committee on Handicapped Children. 1969.

Scholarship Program—Education of Handicapped Children, Summer 1969/Academic Year 1970.

PRESIDENT'S COMMITTEE ON EMPLOYMENT OF THE HANDICAPPED—20501

Guide to Job Placement of the Mentally Retarded. 1963.
So You're Going to Hire the Mentally Retarded. 1963.

PRESIDENT'S COMMITTEE ON MENTAL RETARDATION—20501

Changing Patterns in Residential Services for the Mentally Retarded. 1969.
Hello World! 1968.
The Mentally Retarded . . . Their New Hope. 1966.
MR '67: Report of the President's Committee on Mental Retardation. 1967.
MR '68: Report of the President's Committee on Mental Retardation. 1968.

PRESIDENT'S PANEL ON MENTAL RETARDATION—20501

Mental Retardation: A National Plan for a National Problem. 1962.
A Proposed Program for National Action To Combat Mental Retardation. 1962.
Report of the Mission to Denmark and Sweden. 1962.
Report of the Mission to the Netherlands. 1962.
Report of the Mission to the USSR. 1964.
Report of the Task Force on Behavioral and Social Research. 1964.
Report of the Task Force on Coordination. 1963.
Report of the Task Force on Education and Rehabilitation. 1962.
Report of the Task Force on Law. 1963.
Report of the Task Force on Prevention, Clinical Services and Residential Care. 1962.
To Your Future . . . With Love. 1968.

PUBLIC HEALTH SERVICE—20201

Community Facilities for the Mentally Retarded. 1966.
Design of Facilities for the Mentally Retarded. 1965.
The Dynamics of Mental Retardation. 1964.
Mental Retardation Guidelines for State Interagency Planning. 1964.
Mental Retardation, Its Biological Factors. 1968.
Opportunities for Planning and Constructing Medical, Mental Retardation and Other Health Facilities. 1965.
Planning of Facilities for the Mentally Retarded. 1964.

The Prevention of Mental Retardation through the Control of Infectious Diseases. 1962.

Proceedings, Conference Hill-Burton and Mental Retardation Construction Authorities with the Surgeon General. 1966.

Recreation and Mental Retardation. 1966.

Regulations for Grants for Constructing Facilities for the Mentally Retarded. 1965.

State Laws and Regulations Affecting the Mentally Retarded: A Checklist. 1964.

SECRETARY'S COMMITTEE ON MENTAL RETARDATION—20201

Abstracts of Children's Bureau Mental Retardation Research Projects. 1967.

Career Opportunities in Mental Retardation. 1969.

Financial Assistance Programs in Mental Retardation. 1966.

Implementation of Mental Retardation Programs. 1964.

An Introduction to Mental Retardation. 1965.

Mental Retardation Activities of the Department of Health, Education and Welfare. Annual Report. 1969.

Mental Retardation Grants, Fiscal Year 1968.

Mental Retardation Publications of the U.S. Department of Health, Education and Welfare. 1969.

New Approaches to Mental Retardation and Mental Illness. 1963.

The Problem of Mental Retardation. 1966.

Response to the Recommendations of the President's Panel on Mental Retardation. 1964.

SOCIAL AND REHABILITATION SERVICES—20201

Atlas of Mental Retardation Syndromes. 1968.

A Chance To Help: The Story of SWEAT. 1967.

Construction Grants for Community Facilities for the Mentally Retarded. 1966.

Cooperation on Prevocational Programs for Handicapped Young Adults. 1963.

Dependent Children and Their Families. 1963.

Design of Facilities for the Mentally Retarded. 1966.

The Dynamics of Mental Retardation. 1965.

Facilities for Training To Meet the Needs of the Mentally Retarded. 1967.

Grants for Constructing University-Affiliated Facilities for the Mentally Retarded. 1966.

Mental Retardation—Selected Articles from the Rehabilitation Record. 1967.

A Modern Plan for Modern Services to the Mentally Retarded. 1967.
Opportunity Help for the Mentally Retarded. 1968.
Public Institutions for the Mentally Retarded. 1968.
The Rehabilitated Mentally Retarded. 1964.
So You Are Going To Supervise a Mentally Retarded Employee. 1964.
Special Problems in Vocational Rehabilitation of the Mentally Retarded. 1963.
These Are Not Children—A Play about Opportunities for the Mentally Retarded. 1967.
We Are Concerned. 1967.

SOCIAL SECURITY ADMINISTRATION—20201

Social Security Benefits for Adults Disabled in Childhood. 1964.
Social Security: What It Means for the Parents of a Mentally Retarded Child. 1966.

APPENDIX G

FILMS ON MENTAL RETARDATION

The listings for each of the films indicate: (1) the title; (2) whether a film is in color or black and white; (3) the running time, and (4) an abbreviated form of the major source of procurement. A directory of film sources used in this listing will be found at the end of this section. All films listed have sound tracks and are 16 mm. The films are classified under the following major headings: (1) Growth and Development; (2) Clinical Aspects; (3) Testing; (4) Behavior Modification; (5) the Educable Mentally Retarded; (6) the Trainable Mentally Retarded; (7) Institutions; (8) Parent Education; (9) Community Programs; (10) Recreation; (11) Counseling; (12) Workshop Programs and Employment, and (13) Overseas Programs.

GROWTH AND DEVELOPMENT

Care of the Young Retarded Child. Color, 18 min, IFB.
Shows how knowledge of normal child progress provides valuable information and guidance in the care of the young retarded child. Normal children ranging in age from a few months to six years are shown and the observation is made that retarded children follow the same pattern but at a much slower growth rate. A series of feeding sequences comparing a normal child, a retarded child of the same chronological age but lower developmental level, and a normal younger child of the same developmental level, illustrates the value of early assessment of the infant in order to insure a proper feeding and training program.

Developmental Evaluation in Infancy, Part I and II.
Black and white, Part I—41 min, Part II—18 min, Ohio State.
Part I shows developmental mechanisms involved in adaptive and fine motor behavior. Traces evolution of behavior from four weeks to fifteen months. Part II shows mechanisms involved in gross motor behavior.

Embryology of Human Behavior. Color, 28 min, IFB.
Traces the development of behavior patterns in the human infant, showing how normal growth produces a progressive sequence of behavior patterns. Depicts the normal course of development of eye and hand coordination step by step and age by age. Applies the laws of growth to the study of normal, deviate, and deficient children.

Also, shows how a physician applies a developmental diagnosis.

Growth Failure and Maternal Deprivation. Black and white, 28 min, NYU.
This film shows that physical and mental retardation in young children may often result from a lack of parental attention, especially from the mother. The film demonstrates the essential clinical features of infantile marasmus in two children, one of thirteen months and one almost four years old, and describes the circumstances under which these children lived, most notably those aspects of the mother–child relationship thought to be responsible for their failure to grow and develop normally. The film then goes on to demonstrate the results that can be obtained in a very short time (six to eight weeks) by exposing these children to heavy doses of human stimulation, even in children who appear to be profoundly disturbed. It also emphasizes that these results can be duplicated in any general hospital or well-run child-care facility, even by otherwise untrained people, providing they can give the children the human contact and stimulation they need.

Moderate Retardation in Young Children. Black and white, 43 min, WRU.
This film was made at the Preschool of the Mental Development Center to demonstrate behavioral functioning of children with moderate retardation (55 to 75 IQ range). The children are seen in various individual and group activities which point out some of the similarities and differences between retarded and average individuals. Seven children in the group are followed intensively, showing their developmental level on several tasks. The film specifically notes the quality of the relationship between teacher and child.

Nature versus Nurture. Black and white, 30 min, NET.
Discusses the roles of heredity and environment in determining behavior and personality. Explains how the genes in the chromosomes act as carriers of inherited characteristics. Considers the statistics of heredity as discovered by Mendel. Explains the facts of family resemblances and the role of cultural, economic, and psychological factors in social inheritance.

Three Years Later: A Developmental Study of Retarded Children. Black and white, 38 min, WRU.
This film is a follow-up study of six mildly retarded boys who attended the preschool of the Mental Development Center. The children are introduced in the movie when they were in preschool, their ages

ranging from five to seven. Demonstrates growth and development in the boys three years later during a special summer program.

CLINICAL ASPECTS

Chip—A Five-Year-Old Mongoloid Boy. Black and white, 23 min, Okla.
A five-year-old boy is filmed in the home under different situations—playing with a neighbor, with his parents, and during a developmental examination by the pediatrician.

Color Her Sunshine. Black and white, 20 min, Hamilton.
Concerns development of opportunities for the education and training of a Mongoloid child from birth to young adulthood.

Comprehensive Treatment in Mental Retardation. Black and white, 34 min, SFK.
Reviews a three-month study of a comprehensive therapy program at the Pineland Hospital and Training Center, Pownal, Maine. Dr. Peter Bowman, superintendent of the hospital, comments on the concept of treatment of mental illness emphasizing a therapeutic rather than a custodial approach, and its application in the field of mental retardation. He discusses results of a study intended to evaluate a therapeutic program of 144 female patients, half of whom received chlorpromazine (Thorazine) and half placebo; and describes vocational, educational, recreational, psychological, and other therapies administered, showing details of the therapeutic program, and summarizing results of comprehensive therapy.

Development Center for Handicapped Minors. Color, 14 min, Bradley.
This film describes three severely handicapped children illustrating their learning problems and how the Development Center helps them and their families.

Early Clinical Aspects of Mental Retardation. Black and white, 37 min, USPHS.
The program stresses the magnitude of the problem of mental retardation in the United States, the prenatal and perinatal etiologic factors, and the environmental and psychiatric problems. Types of mental retardation responding to specific treatment are discussed by six panelists.

Early Detection of PKU in the Hospital Nursery. Color, 20 min, IFB.
The procedures used in the Guthrie test for phenylketonuria are demonstrated step by step. Professional use only.

Eternal Children. Black and white, 30 min, IFB.
Presents an intimate study of the special problems of retarded children who, through heredity, brain injury, or various other causes, are not equipped to keep pace in a competitive world. The film gives a frank and timely appraisal of the problem and shows care and training methods being evolved in special schools and institutions. Attention is focused on the urgent need to improve community facilities.

The Farthest Frontier. Black and white, 47 min, Carousel.
A report on the revolutionary new "mind drugs." The IQ of a hopelessly retarded child is brought to normal. A psychotic patient is returned to health. Shows that the drugs can improve memory and concentration or induce abject fear or superhuman courage.

Group Therapy for the Severely Retarded. Black and white, 15 min, Hartford.
Depicts an experiment in therapy and demonstrates the progress made by severely retarded children who were placed in an unstructured group situation.

The Headbangers. Black and white, 30 min, USPHS.
Describes a treatment program for retarded, severely self-destructive children. Pictures several institutionalized children who manifest such behavior through the symptom of headbanging, one of whom blinded herself and was subsequently placed in a special study unit. Emphasizes the persistent, cooperative effort of the staff and therapist as the primary mode of treatment.

Introducing the Mentally Retarded. Black and white, 30 min, PCR.
Three classifications—educable (IQ 50–70), trainable (IQ 25–50), and custodial. Two degrees of retardation—primary, which is of hereditary origin, and secondary, which has been caused by external forces—are described. Shows serious mental retardation is often accompanied by physical disability. The need for stimulating environment, wholesome play activities, attractive housing facilities for those who must be institutionalized and adequate hospital and laboratory accomodations is demonstrated. Job opportunities within their capabilities are depicted.

Michael—A Mongoloid Child. Black and white, 14 min, NYU.
Provides an intimate study of a mongoloid teen-ager living on a farm in rural England. A straightforward commentary is provided by his mother, who explains how Michael has fitted into their home and

village life. Film will help minimize the near superstition still surrounding the victims of mental defects.

Phenylketonuria, A Preventable Cause of Mental Retardation. Color, 16 min, CFI.
Illustrated manifestation of phenylketonuria genetics, detection, and treatment.

Pine School. Black and white, 30 min, PCR.
Shows part of a research program devoted to the study of mentally retarded children, ages three to six from underprivileged homes where facilities for mental stimulation are lacking. The school attempts to provide the necessary materials for giving the children group experiences, opportunities for psychological and physical growth, and activities for the development of muscular control.

PKU Detection in Oregon. Color, 18 min, Oregon.
Phenylketonuria patients were photographed by the Maternal and Child Health Section of the Oregon State Board of Health to observe their progress after they were placed on a special diet. In addition to the actual cases, detection, treatment, and laboratory techniques are shown.

PKU Mental Deficiency Is Preventable. Black and white, 15 min, Wisconsin.
The biochemistry, genetics, symptoms, diagnosis, and management of phenylketonuria (PKU) are reviewed in this film. The point that testing for PKU must become as routine and as standard for general practitioners and pediatricians as shots for DPT, polio, and smallpox is emphasized. The case histories of two siblings, both with PKU are presented. One, a child now institutionalized with an IQ of 40, was not diagnosed until his third year. The other was diagnosed at two weeks, was placed on a special dietary regimen, and now, at age four, has an IQ of 106. Diagnostic tests, such as Phenistix, ferric chloride, 2–4 dinitrophenylhydrazine, bacterial inhibition, and quantitative plasma analysis are described.

PKU—Preventable Mental Retardation, 2d ed. Color, 16 min, IFB.
Shows how mental retardation due to phenylketonuria (PKU) can be prevented by early diagnosis immediately after birth. Information concerning new data on incidence of the disease, reports on the effectiveness of present procedures (including the Guthrie Blood Test), and new techniques for testing urine in the home have been included. Emphasizes the need for universal checking of all infants for PKU.

Report on Down's Syndrome (Mongolism). Color, 21 min, IFB.
A comprehensive statement of Down's Syndrome previously called Mongolism from its first description by the British physician Langdon Down in 1866. Outlines general characteristics and treatment methods including latest findings in the area of genetics. The development of two mongoloid children over a six-year period provides invaluable information for parents. The advantages and rewards of warm family life and application of the routine–relaxation–repetition formula are illustrated.

Retardation Research. Color, 7 min, Finley.
Features a research project in which the Doman-Delacato theory of neuropsychology is applied to trainable mentally retarded children in the public schools. No assessment of the program is made although comments by the teacher reflect the progress of specific children.

What Is Anna? Color, 25 min, Billings.
Shows the developmental and social history of a young girl who manifests the characteristics of pseudoretardation. Portrays the role of the diagnostic clinic and of various medical assessment devices. Demonstrates various psychotherapy techniques.

What Now, Anna? Color, 40 min, Billings.
This film is a follow up of "What Is Anna?" Film attempts to diagnose an adolescent girl who doesn't speak, whose hearing is not impaired and faculties for speech are adequate. Diagnosis of mental retardation is ruled out for many reasons, but further testing is restricted because of her condition.

TESTING

Clinical Types of Mental Deficiency. Black and white, 40 min, PCR.
Summarizes brain conditions causing mental deficiency. Demonstrates, through performance testing, classification of mental deficients into morons, imbeciles, and idiots. Describes the eight major pathological groups of mental deficiency, using typical cases to illustrate each type.

Diagnosis of Childhood Schizophrenia. Black and white, 30 min, PCR.
Deals with the problem of diagnosing different types of psychotic children. Shows a clinical team of psychiatrists, social workers, and psychologists at work. Indicates how evidence of ego fragmentation is uncovered and how family history, personal history, medical examinations, psychological tests, and clinical observations are analyzed. Illustrates its points by showing cases under clinical observation. Em-

phasizes the tentative nature of diagnosis and shows the possibilities for treatment following diagnosis.

The Illinois Test of Psycholinguistic Ability (ITPA). Black and white, 43 min, FITZGERALD.
This is an instructional demonstration of the Revised Edition of the Illinois Test of Psycholinguistics as developed by Samuel A. Kirk and associates.

IQ Questionable Criterion. Color, 13 min, Finley.
The fallacies and problems arising from placing students on a single criterion basis are examined. The film depicts the utilization of a comprehensive diagnostic evaluation and work-up involving many specialists.

Techniques of Nonverbal Psychological Testing. Color, 20 min, IFB.
Shows atypical psychometric techniques. Depicts psychologic evaluation of children who cannot be examined by the usual tests emphasizing special nonverbal techniques which permit assessment of their potential from infancy to eighteen years of age. Children suffering from mental retardation and some of its preventable forms—cerebral palsy, rare Crouzon's disease, and an inability to hear or speak intelligibly—are pictured. Shows the use of the Gesell Developmental Scales, the Leiter International Performance Scale, and parts of the Peabody Picture Vocabulary Test.

Testing Intelligence with the Stanford–Binet. Black and white, 18 min, PCR.
Presents excerpts from four administrations of the Stanford–Binet: two six-year-olds (IQ's 104 and 156) and two ten-year-olds (IQ's 100 and 80). Indicates techniques of rapport and standardized administration. Presents concepts and computation of MA and IQ in detail.

BEHAVIOR MODIFICATION

Operation Dry Pants. Color, 34 min, MGS.
This film which was taken at a residential institution for the mentally retarded in Texas demonstrates habit training techniques and their effects on a group of profoundly retarded girls six to eighteen years of age.

The Poppe Project: Behavior Shaping with the Severely Retarded. Black and white, 23 min, UC.
A combination of group nursing and operant conditioning are used to

provide therapeutic milieu for eight severely retarded girls, aged eleven to twenty-three, in a residential institution. The film illustrates differences in thinking and behavior required of nurses caring for a small group as opposed to those caring for large groups in assembly-line custodial care. Operant conditioning techniques succeeded in shaping the girls' behavior in eating, dressing, structured and unstructured play, group interaction, and elementary socialization. A study guide is available. Made at Sonoma (California) State Hospital.

Reinforcement Therapy. Black and white, 45 min, UCLA.
Reviews utilization of operant conditioning with autistic and retarded children.

Treating the Hospitalized Mentally Retarded through Conditioning. Black and white, 11 min, PACIFIC.
The Skinnerian theory of conditioning is shown working with a retarded boy at Pacific State Hospital.

THE EDUCABLE MENTALLY RETARDED

Arts and Crafts for the Slow Learner. Black and white, 27 min, SWS.
Crafts activities in a public school class for the educable mentally retarded. Eighteen types of arts and crafts employing free or inexpensive materials are depicted, including finger painting, woodwork, leathercraft, potato carving, wet chalk drawing, glass painting, and woodburning. Many crafts depicted could be carried on at home.

Bridge to the Future. Color, 28 min, Muskegon.
This film depicts a program for the Educable Mentally Retarded in a secondary school setting. Emphasis is on personal–social adjustment and vocational exploration.

A Class for Tommy. Black and white, 20 min, Bailey.
This film tells the story of a class conducted for the instruction of mentally retarded children and centers around Tommy, a boy of six. It shows how classes and activities are especially developed to aid in overcoming both mental and physical handicaps. Watching the daily activities, the audience learns about planning sessions, block play, nutrition periods, room environment, attitude development, the work of the school nurse and dentist, and the creation of reading readiness by the teacher through the use of picture stories.

Educable Mentally Handicapped. Black and white, 29 min, NET.
Discusses the special problems of educable mentally handicapped

children. Explains who they are, the problems they face in the community and the school, and what can be done to help them. Uses still photos and filmed sequences of a special class for these children to show the place of the school in meeting the needs of the mentally handicapped.

Functional Teaching of Reading and Writing. Color, 30 min, Newenhouse.
The film illustrates techniques used to teach reading and writing to trainable, low educable, and educable mentally retarded children. Based on a teaching program developed at Laradon Hall School, Denver, Colorado.

Give Them a Chance. Black and white, 12 min, PCR.
Typical day in a public school special education class, showing characteristic activities and teaching techniques.

Mentally Handicapped: Educable. Black and white, 29 min, NET.
Discusses the special problems of the children who are mentally handicapped but educable. Explains who they are, the problems they face in the community and the school, and what can be done to help them. Uses still photos and filmed sequences of a special class for these children to show the place of the school in meeting the needs of the mentally handicapped.

Methods of Teaching Art to the Mentally Retarded. Color, 32 min, Chico.
This film shows the six steps in planning and presenting an art lesson to college students majoring in mental retardation studies. A variety of skills are used and various media explored.

One and Two and Three. Color, 15 min, Newenhouse.
This film was especially designed to teach mentally retarded children the concept of counting. Using a slow pace and many techniques of repetition, the film develops the idea of one and two and three. Two 7½ minute units on one print allow the film to run twice without rewinding, thus providing a convenient means of immediately repeating the visual experience.

Painting Is Loving. Color, 21 min, Conrad.
This film is a view of a teacher's efforts to reach retarded children through painting. It is a journey of sound, color, and variation and shows the feeling of success in children as they develop through art experiences. (Sometimes referred to under title of "To Paint Is To Love Again.")

Shape of a Leaf. Black and white, 27 min, Campbell.
Reveals the sensitive responses and artistic creativity possessed by retarded children when exposed to art training in fields of painting, creative stitching, perception boxes, and ceramics.

Teaching a Child To Talk. Color, 20 min, LASPC.
A film highlighting the relations between speech development and parental verbal stimulus and reinforcement. It shows early language development and demonstrates techniques for aiding the child to talk.

Teaching the Child Who Is Retarded. Color, 20 min, USD.
Classroom situations for retarded children at the University of South Dakota Summer School program. Various and detailed methods of teaching retarded children.

They Also Learn. Black and white, 14 min, USD.
Shows the program of a residential school for both educable and trainable children at the University of South Dakota. Shows teacher-training, psychological diagnosis, and staff evaluation procedures in a summer school.

A Visit with the Principal. Color, 5 min, Newenhouse.
Shows how desirable concepts are developed in a special elementary-level classroom for the educable mentally retarded child. Describes a class visit with the school principal. Discusses correct manners for paying visits, the principal's interest in classwork and student achievement, and various safety practices that should be followed in school and on the playground.

What about Johnny? Color, film strip, San Diego.
Demonstrates the program for educable mentally retarded pupils in San Diego County and California. A narrator's guide describes the various frames. Discusses the legal responsibilities for the establishment of programs for the mentally retarded; the objectives of the program; the selection and placement of pupils in special training classes; and the organization of various curricular activities including social studies, health education, arithmetic, manual skills, recreational activities, and citizenship. A section on guidance concludes the presentation.

THE TRAINABLE MENTALLY RETARDED

Aids for Teaching the Mentally Retarded. Color, Newenhouse.
This is a series of five films prepared by the Laradon Hall School in Denver. *Phase A—Motor Training,* 11 minutes; *Phase B—Initial Perceptual Training,* 7½ minutes; *Phase C—Advanced Perceptual Train-*

ing, 9 minutes; *Phase D—Integrated Motor-Perceptual Training,* 6 minutes; *Phase E—Sheltered Workshops,* 5 minutes.

And Crown Thy Good. Color, 35 min, Orchard.
A comprehensive report, covering one community's accomplishment in providing for their severely retarded children over a period of six years. Demonstrates training procedures and teaching techniques used in the Orchard School. Shows excellent use of materials and staff, including well trained volunteers.

Into the Light. Color, 15 min, CDC.
Describes a Dallas community school program for trainable retarded children. Also shows a parent being interviewed by a physician.

Line of Sight—Retarded Children. Black and white, 25 min, KTLA.
Film shows a visit to special classes and recreation programs for retarded children at the Exceptional Children's Foundation in Los Angeles.

One Small Candle. Color, 18 min, Orchard.
Covers procedures in a clinic and private school for the severely retarded and multiple handicapped. Shows types of examination a parent might expect in such a clinic. Dr. Levinson and his medical staff lay stress on correct guidance of the child by the parent. Teachers demonstrate occupational therapy, recreational activity, psychological testing, and job training for the retarded child.

Programs for the Severely Retarded. Color, 30 min, Michigan.
Shows the program of the Lapeer State School, Lapeer, Michigan, for the severely mentally retarded. Shows that with proper guidance and encouragement, the severely retarded can participate in group activities and can learn to do handiwork and to care for themselves. Demonstrates how the severely physically–mentally handicapped can be taught skills such as painting, writing, typing, and better self-care. (Bell and Howell Magnetic Soundstrip Projector required.)

Show Me. Black and white, 28 min, Universal.
This film was designed to promote the teaching of movement and rhythms to trainable mentally retarded children. The film depicts trainable mentally retarded pupils in a variety of adapted PE activities.

Teaching Good Conduct and Personal Hygiene to Retarded Teenagers. Color, filmstrip, Harris County.
Series of eleven 35mm color filmstrips ranging from 30 to 45 frames

including a teacher's guidebook. There are six films for girls covering self-help activities and five for boys with similar self-help demands including a personal talk to each of the groups.

Teaching the Mentally Retarded—A Positive Approach. Black and white, 25 min, Du Art.
A documentary following the progress made by four profoundly retarded children during a four-month training program. The training emphasis is in areas of self-care—toilet training, dressing, eating, and manners—illustrating that even the profoundly retarded can learn rather complex skills. The principles of teaching used with the severely handicapped in an institutional setting may also be applied to the less retarded who may reside in the community.

Teaching the Mentally Retarded through Music. Tapes, SOCAR.
This is a series of four thirty-minute tapes. It presents techniques of Dr. Richard Weber working with groups of trainable children. Depicts a simplified method of teaching music to trainable mentally retarded children.

Trainable Mentally Retarded. Black and white, 29 min, NET.
Discusses the special problems of the severely mentally retarded child. Illustrates the relationship of these children to their family and neighbors. Describes the use of private and public day schools and their objectives. Uses classroom scenes to show the characteristics of the mentally retarded. Stresses the importance of the home and of the need for constant supervision.

INSTITUTIONS

Bridge to a Wider World. Black and white, 27 min, CSC.
Emphasizes the dignity of the retarded individual by showing the care and training of the mentally retarded at the Bethesda Lutheran Home in Watertown, Wisconsin.

The Caswell Story. Color, 15 min, Caswell.
Shows the admission procedure of a state training school for children. Shows the physical and psychological examination and various activities of the institution.

A Child Is Waiting. Black and white, 60 min, Association.
Made in a private school for the retarded and tells the story of Reuben, who has been rejected by his mother, and of Miss Horst, a would-be teacher who becomes emotionally involved.

Dehumanization and the Total Institution. Color, 15 min, Minn. P.W.
This is a film developed by the Minnesota State Department of Public Welfare to show the effects of large institutions on the problems relating to the dehumanization and impersonal treatment that exists.

House of Mercy. Color, 43 min, Newenhouse.
Presentation of a religious institution for the mentally retarded.

In Our Care: Oregon Fairview Home. Color, 30 min, Oregon.
This is a two-part film. The first part deals with the moderately retarded teenager at a state institution. The second part depicts very severely retarded dependent patients needing lifetime care.

In the Name of Humanity. Black and white, 13 min, Minn. ARC.
Points out the areas of need in the institutional program and community services for mentally retarded persons in Minnesota. Makes specific recommendations for improving conditions and establishing additional services and facilities.

Into the Sunlight. Black and white, 27 min, Vineland.
Presents the various activities and services available for retarded residents at the Training School at Vineland, New Jersey.

The Least of These. Black and white, 20 min, N.J.
Tells the story of an institutional program for the mentally deficient. Illustrates programs for recreational, physical, and occupational therapy. Shows how handicapped individuals can learn to perform simple, useful skills. Traces the history of community attitudes toward the mentally deficient.

Life at the Enid State School. Color, 20 min, Enid.

Mentally Handicapped Children Growing Up: The Brooklands Experiment. Black and white, 21 min, NARC.
Covers an experimental study of sixteen children living in the Fountain Hospital. Each pair was matched for sex, age, nonverbal intelligence, and clinical diagnosis. One member of each pair was transferred to a small residential unit at Brooklands and given a different pattern of care. This is contrasted with the care given in the large, understaffed Fountain Hospital. Shows marked and significant rise in the verbal and mental age of the Brooklands children during their two-year residence in the units.

One in Every Hundred. Black and white, 60 min, NET.
Documents ways in which families, teachers, and institutions are caring

for the mentally retarded in Canada and England. Indicates that home care is far superior to institutionalization.

Oral Care and Preventive Hygiene for the Mentally Retarded. Color, 22 min, Squibb.
Directed primarily at dentists, dental hygienists, and all those working in the field of mental retardation, this film stresses that good oral care is a goal with which all these disciplines should be concerned. Outlines a program which can aid in achieving this goal. Parents are shown how they can further the oral hygiene of mentally retarded children cared for at home.

Pioneering in Dental Health for Mentally Retarded Children. Black and white, 15 min, BSFP.
The method of dental care for mentally retarded children as carried out at the Joseph Samuels Dental Clinic of the Rhode Island Hospital is demonstrated.

Precious Jewels. Color, 35 min, Children's Retreat.
Reviews a hospital—school program for all levels of mentally retarded children, with emphasis on the educable and trainable youngster. Shows the facilities of a modern, well staffed, religious institution.

Toymakers. Black and white, 30 min, SKF.
A portrayal of the lives of the mentally retarded in institutions. Depicts the range of retardation from severe to mild, and shows how the institution must develop a varied program to meet the many needs of all the retarded, from those residents who need total nursing care to those who can be trained for work and life outside.

The Wassaic Story. Black and white, 30 min, Association.
Describes the Wassaic State School, New York, and its four thousand patients—mentally retarded children and adults of all ages and degrees of retardation. Shows both good and poor sides of the program, a habit-training class, occupational therapy, recreational activities, and the custodial wards and detention areas for the disturbed and delinquent retarded which are not usually seen by the public.

A Way out of the Wilderness. Black and white, 28 min, PHS.
Mosaic of scenes depicts many of the breakthroughs in the field of mental retardation, such as diagnosis, evaluation, placement, and special education. Presents unmet needs of the mentally retarded in institutions.

PARENT EDUCATION

Almost Forgotten Children. Color, 10 min, Minneapolis.
Describes the gift drive for children and adults in Minnesota institutions. Shows how gifts were assembled at twenty-six collection stations in the Minneapolis area, sorted, taken to six state institutions, and distributed by the institution personnel.

Becky. Color, 15 min, Finley.
Film relates the retarded child to the family structure. It is specially valuable for use with parent groups.

The Beloved Child. Black and white, 17 min, Milwaukee.
Describes how the Milwaukee County ARC developed a community approach to the problem of educating the trainable child. Shows medical diagnosis, trainable classes, a sheltered workshop, and recreational activities.

Broken Dream. Color, 22 min, Capitol.
This film follows a young couple through the planning days of pregnancy and their feelings when they learn their child is born retarded and their eventual understanding of the problem.

A Child Apart. Black and white, 30 min, KNXT.
This film presents scenes of special class sessions made at Pacific State Hospital, California. Other phases show a foster home and setting and discussions with parents of a mentally retarded child.

Mental Retardation: The Long Childhood of Timmy. Black and white, 53 min, NYU.
This is a two-part film originally produced for television distribution. Timmy is a mongoloid child whose mental capacities will never develop beyond those of a ten-year-old. This film presents a warm portrayal of this mentally retarded child who must make the transition from an understanding and devoted family setting to a superior school for the mentally retarded. In telling Timmy's story, the film gives much factual information about these special children and induces positive attitudes towards and a greater compassion for these people with their very special problems.

No Longer Alone. Color, 20 min, CRC.
Film follows two children through the various disciplines of the center. One boy has a physical handicap; one, a mental handicap. Parents are involved for the purpose of emphasizing acceptance of defects in home

to show a metamorphosis of parents from a feeling of being alone with a child's handicap to a feeling of finding help and friends through this medical and social service department.

The Road to Somewhere. Color, 20 min, Schulman.
Demonstrates how mentally retarded children, age six to sixteen, are trained to utilize undamaged brain tissue. Shows all phases of training and encourages the parents of mentally retarded children to be optimistic regarding the results.

Stress: Parents with a Handicapped Child. Black and white, 30 min, NYU.
Going directly into the homes of five families and shooting candidly without rehearsal, this documentary makes its point all the more telling by presenting the facts and letting them speak for themselves. The film competently deals with the problems of raising handicapped children.

To Solve a Human Puzzle. Black and white, 18 min, NARC.
Explores the problem of mental retardation from the viewpoint of parents who tell of their personal experiences concerning their retarded children.

Training the Mentally Retarded Child at Home. Black and white, 42 min, NFB.
Recommends procedures, indicates levels of performance, and points out potentials when abilities are developed by effective procedures.

Who Will Tie My Shoe? Black and white, 60 min, ASSOCIATION.
A TV documentary dramatizing the problems of a mentally retarded child.

COMMUNITY PROGRAMS

Beyond the Shadows, Color, 26 min, WCP.
Describes the step-by-step action taken in one city by community members to help the mentally retarded children who were unable to benefit from local special education or state institutions. Shows how the cooperation of state and local agencies was secured in establishing complete health, welfare, and evaluation services.

Children Limited. Color, 30 min, Wash. ARC.
Illustrates one state's attempt to educate and train mentally deficient children for constructive roles in society. Discusses the social taboos

surrounding this condition and portrays the steps being taken to improve the limited world of these children.

The Community and the Exceptional Child. Black and white, 29 min, NET.
Examines the role of the community in helping the exceptional child achieve his maximum potential. Discusses the many agencies in the community which contribute to the growth and development of exceptional children, reviews the many and varied types of exceptionality, and stresses the importance of special services for exceptional children.

"The Darkest Side." Black and white, 57 min, Minn. ARC.
This film was prepared as an audiovisual report of the Minnesota Governor's Advisory Committee on Mental Retardation. The first half concentrated on Minnesota residential facilities for the retarded, pointing up the need for replacement of old buildings and for additional staff to provide a satisfactory level of patient care and treatment. The latter half portrays the type of nonresidential service which communities in Minnesota are providing, such as day activity centers, special classes, sheltered workshops, and others. It notes the need for more of these types of services. It also describes current research projects in the state and points out the need for more research funds.

Exceptional Children (Confidential File). Black and white, 26 min, Guild.
Excellent dramatic presentation of parent's view and adjustments to retarded child. Included are interviews with doctors and with parents of a 3½-year-old mentally retarded child. Shows school community provisions for trainable child.

Foster Grandparents Project. Color, 18 min, Austin.
The film presents aspects of the foster grandparents project in which retired men and women assume the role of grandparents to retarded children in a state school.

Handle with Care. Black and white, 28 min, Du Art.
Shows the varied services received by selected mentally retarded people in the greater Los Angeles area, often with the initial help of one particular agency—the Information, Counseling, and Screening Service of the Mental Retardation Community Service Center, Children's Hospital. With a few exceptions, the retarded, their parents, and professional personnel play themselves. Stresses the great importance of having a fixed point or place in the community on which the families of the mentally retarded can depend for early, compre-

hensive diagnosis and evaluation as well as for continued assistance through the years, to assure that the retarded have the opportunity to develop to their maximum potential in a complex, fast-moving society.

Help Wanted. Black and white, 27 min, Houston JL.
Surveys the mental health facilities of Houston, Texas, emphasizing their limitations and indicating the need for a greatly expanded program. Includes a brief account of some of the services provided by the Houston Council for Retarded Children.

The Innocents. Black and white, 25 min, U. Minn.
This film presents a story of the mentally retarded children. It depicts what can be done to help them in a nursery and in the home, pointing out what parents can do to adjust to the situation. It also shows how the public can participate and assist in this very important task.

Mental Retardation: A National Plan for a National Problem. Black and white, 34 slides, Hawaii.
Summarizes the report of a panel appointed by President Kennedy to prepare a national plan to combat mental retardation.

MR—Mental Retardation. Black and white, 60 min, NYU.
Shows the scope of current approaches to the problem of mental retardation. Part I emphasizes research, diagnosis, and treatment of the severely retarded. Part II relates the wide range of community services required for the trainable and educable retarded from preschool through high school to vocational rehabilitation and work experience.

The Public Health Nurse and the Mentally Retarded Child. Color, 24 min, PCR.
Depicts the aid a public health nurse can give to parents of retarded children. A typical case is documented—detection of the abnormal condition and education of the parents to cope with training situations. Professional use only.

Space for the Mentally Retarded. Color, 22 min, S.D. ARC.
This is a report on available and needed services for the mentally retarded in the State of South Dakota. Presents various problems and possible community solutions. A pamphlet with the same title to be used as a discussion guide is available.

Take That First Step. Color, 28 min, USPHS.
A story of a retarded boy and a college student who meet by accident. Shows development of college student's interest and a possible career in mental retardation.

Treatment of the Mentally Subnormal in New Zealand. Black and white, 30 min, Sandoz.
Describes the progressive treatment program of a modern institution for the mentally retarded.

Tuesday's Child. Black and White, 18 min, Association.
Story of a ten-year-old retarded child and how a parent group stimulates community action to develop special educational and other services for retarded children.

White House Conference on Mental Retardation. Color, 12 min, USPHS.
Depicts highlights of the White House Conference on Mental Retardation in 1963.

A Word of the Right Size. Color, 18 min, NPI.
This animated film discusses the management of mental retardation in the community or institution. The film touches upon detection of retardation and the distinction between mental retardation and mental illness.

RECREATION

Camp Friendship. Color, 30 min, Minn. ARC.
Describes the activities and programs of Camp Friendship, a residential camp for mentally retarded children and adults that is owned and operated by the Minnesota Association for Retarded Children, Inc. Former Vice-President Hubert H. Humphrey is shown dedicating the camp in the summer of 1966.

Cast No Shadow. Color, 27 min, Pro Arts.
This film presents a wide variety of recreation activities for the severely mentally retarded. Emphasis is placed on the value of recreation as an integral part of learning experiences and social development. The film shows the program of the Recreation Center for the Handicapped in San Francisco.

A Dream To Grow On. Color, 28 min, NARC.
Narrated by U.S. Olympic Decathlon champion Rafer Johnson, this film tells the story of the 1968 Special Olympics held in Chicago where one thousand mentally retarded children competed in track and field events.

Handicapped Go Camping. Black and white, 11 min, Bailey.
Presents camping program and outdoor education in a setting where normal and handicapped children participate in a variety of activities.

Into the Sunlight. Color, 15 min, Ontario ARC.
Describes the activities of the Canadian Summer Camp for Trainable Mentally Retarded Children. This camp was of three weeks duration for each fifty boys and girls with an IQ below 50. Shows usual camp activities, such as hiking, nature study, swimming, games, crafts, and others modified to meet the needs of the mentally retarded and so-called "exceptional children."

Movement Exploration. Color, 20 min, Documentary.
The film presents aspects of a physical education program for the Trainable Mentally Retarded. It presents a series of movement activities for young trainable mentally retarded pupils.

New Experiences for Mentally Retarded Children. Black and white, 36 min, Virginia.
A summer camping experience for severely mentally retarded children is described.

Orange Grove Summer Camp. Color, 20 min, Orange.
Shows a two-week camping program for trainable mentally retarded children.

PE—Lever to Learning. Color, 20 min, Finley.
Shows how a P.E. specialist in the area of mental retardation has devised a program to condition the retarded child. The equipment is inexpensive and includes logs, old tires, boards, and ladders.

Recreation Unlimited. Black and white, 15 min, Houston.
Shows a summer recreational program for the mentally retarded. Shows the children participating in swimming, folk dancing, acting, and crafts. (Accompanied by 7½ ips audio-tape.)

Recreational Activities for Mentally Retarded Children. Color, 28 min, West Hartford.
This film shows a summer recreation program for mentally retarded children in a day camp setting. The activities include games, crafts, music, swimming, and social activities.

Time Is for Taking. Color, 23 min, Finley.
Keyed toward encouraging parents of the retarded child, this film was made at Camp Kentan, Middleburg, Virginia, a residential camp for retarded children. Everyday actual events are recorded. The viewer sees youngsters and their skilled counselors overcome problems as they develop in a natural, uninhibited environment.

To Lighten the Shadows. Black and white, 20 min, IFB.
Emphasizes that day camp programs for mentally retarded children are an area in need of further development and shows how the potential for normalcy in retarded children may be developed through good recreational opportunities and continuing educational programs.

COUNSELING

Evaluation of the Retarded Client. Color, 15 min, USPHS.
Explains the role of the vocational counselor in evaluating the retarded client initially; in selecting a training program which takes into consideration the client's talents, behavioral patterns, and any secondary physical handicaps; and in monitoring his personal and vocational progress. Points out that the case record is the most valuable tool available to the counselor.

The Nature of Mental Retardation. Color, 27 min, USPHS.
Presents examples of the eight etiological categories and the five adaptive behavior levels of mental retardation. Compares the more severe forms of retardation with the less severe and defines in general terms the rehabilitation potential at each adaptive behavior level. Points out that the bulk of the counselor's case load will come from the first level.

Post Placement Counseling. Color, 25 min, USPHS.
Through comments from teachers, counselors, employers, doctors, and parents, examines the social and emotional difficulties the retarded person encounters within the community in his job and personal life. Also considers public feelings and acceptance of the retarded.

The Retarded Client and His Family. Color, 20 min, USPHS.
Points out that while the counselor may find himself in the role of spokesman for the client, he cannot fill all the gaps. He needs the full cooperation of the client's family in helping the retardate fit in, rather than become an outsider. Discusses in general terms various stress periods during which the family and the retarded child must make adjustments to the social, vocational, and personal handicaps imposed by mental retardation.

Training Resources and Techniques. Color, 17 min, USPHS.
Shows retarded persons at work in various training programs designed to give them some measure of economic independence and self-esteem.

Emphasizes that a good training program must provide realism, reward, recognition, and responsibility. The counselor's role in helping the client adapt to new situations and new jobs is stressed.

WORKSHOP PROGRAMS AND EMPLOYMENT

Home Is No Hiding Place. Black and white, 28 min, WFIL.
During the course of the film, the Occupation Day Center in New York City is visited as well as the Opportunity Center in Wilmington, Delaware, and the St. Christopher's Hospital for Children in Philadelphia. Remarks are presented by Dr. Richard Masland and Dr. Gunnar Dybwad.

Into the World. Black and white, 27 min, RSA.
Depicts the broad program of care and rehabilitation available to mentally retarded in the state agency. Shows that such persons can be helped and employed, and emphasizes the value of early training for retarded children. Interviews the mother of a seven-year-old boy who has not attended public school because his parents believe he should receive only special education.

Journey Forward. Color, 20 min, NARC.
Shows youngsters of various degrees of retardation being trained through directed experiences and appropriate active participation. Later they are shown in a vocational workshop displaying their occupational skills which have been developed.

Learning in Slow Motion. Black and white, 40 min, NARC.
Shows research into the problems of learning in the mentally subnormal carried out at the Manor Hospital, Epsom, England. Shows how mentally subnormal adults can be trained to perform simple repetitive work in factories, and how even the severely subnormal may learn to perform similar tasks satisfactorily but at a slower pace.

A Light to My Path. Color, 14 min, Tampa.
The film shows the training of a mentally retarded child from the nursery to the sheltered workshops at the McDonald Training Center, Florida.

Selling One Guy Named Larry. Black and white, 17 min, PCR.
Discusses the work performance of mentally retarded individuals and shows how they have been employed successfully in a variety of positions.

A Staff Not a Crutch. Color, 20 min, Ill. ARC.
Tells how Wilmette, Illinois, Post Office provides challenging job opportunities for retarded persons. The film presents an authentic portrait of a mentally handicapped young man. Narrated by him and his mother, the film seeks to communicate the human potential of the mentally retarded. This is a dramatic demonstration of what may be achieved by the mentally retarded through special education and suitable job opportunities. Other aspects deal with the developing manhood of the retardate, his sociability, and the aspirations he holds to meet his human needs for self-worth, dignity, and personal relationships.

Their Right To Belong. Black and white, 15 min, Ohio ARC.
Film shows a sheltered workshop program including special training classes for the trainable mentally retarded.

Thursday's Children. Color, 17 min, CSC.
Shows the establishment of a day-care center for the mentally retarded by parent and community efforts. Tells why the mentally retarded should be trained and uses a child as an example of the value of the program.

The Trained Retardate: A Sound Investment. Black and white, 59 min, NET.
The theme is the mentally retarded adult, an overlooked resource of our economy. (In video and kinescope.)

OVERSEAS PROGRAMS

European Facilities for the Mentally Retarded. Color, 137 frame filmstrip with 33⅓ RPM record, USPHS.
This is a film strip with a record accompanying it as well as a narration on recording tape. Approximate program is 31 minutes. The strip presents scenes in residential facilities, day-care centers, boarding homes, and schools. It shows programs in Denmark, Finland, Sweden, England, and Ireland. Special attention is paid to a variety of architectural styles.

To Bridge the Gap. Black and white, 31 min, NARC.
This is a filmed report of a study tour of Scandinavian and English facilities for the mentally retarded made in 1966 by Gerald F. Walsh, Executive Director of the Minnesota Association for Retarded Children.

APPENDIX H

FILM SOURCES

The films listed in Appendix G may be obtained from the following sources. In addition, many state departments of education, mental hygiene, and public health and many college or university audiovisual centers have excellent film libraries and loan services.

ASSOCIATION	Association Films, 561 Hillgrove Avenue, La Grange, Ill.; 1108 Jackson Street, Dallas, Tex.; 799 Stevenson Street, San Francisco, Calif.; 347 Madison Avenue, New York, N.Y.
AUSTIN	Austin State School, Austin, Tex.
BAILEY	Bailey Films, 2044 N. Berendo Street, Hollywood, Calif.
BILLINGS	Billings Mental Hygiene Clinic, 1500 N. 30th Street, Billings, Mont.
BOMO	BOMO Film Service, 3132 M Street, N.W., Washington, D.C.
BSFP	Bay State Film Productions, Rhode Island Hospital, Providence, R.I.
CAMPBELL	Campbell Films, Saxton River, Vt.
CAPITOL	Capitol Film Service, 224 Abbott Road, Lansing, Mich.
CAROUSEL	Carousel Films, 1501 Broadway, New York, N.Y.
CASWELL	Director of Public Relations, Caswell Training School, Kingston, N.C.
CDC	Children's Development Center, 3612 Cedar Springs, Dallas, Tex.
CFC	College Film Center, 332 S. Michigan Avenue, Chicago, Ill.
CFI	Canadian Film Institute, 1762 Carling Avenue, Ottawa, Ontario, Canada.
CHICO	c/o Dr. Helen Carkin, School of Education, Chico State College, Chico, Calif.

CHILDREN'S RETREAT	Children's Retreat and Training School, 6850 Division Avenue, S., Grand Rapids, Mich.
COLORADO	Colorado State Department of Public Health, 4210 E. 11th Avenue, Denver, Colo.
CONRAD	Conrad Films, 6331 Weidlake Drive, Hollywood, Calif.
CONTEMPORARY	Contemporary Films, 13 E. 37th Street, New York, N.Y.
CRC	Center for Retarded Children, Children's Rehabilitation Center, Buffalo, N.Y.
CSC	Cine Sound Company, 915 North Highland, Hollywood, Calif.
DOCUMENTARY	Documentary Films, 3217 Trout Gulch, Aptos, Calif.
DU ART	Du Art Film Laboratory, 245 W. 55th Street, New York, N.Y.
ENID	Enid State School, Enid, Okla.
FINLEY	Stuart Finley, 3428 Mansfield Road, Lake Barcroft, Falls Church, Va.
FITZGERALD	Dale K. Fitzgerald, 2540 Grant, Berkeley, Calif.
GUILD	Guild Film Company, 460 Park Avenue, New York, N.Y.; 8255 W. Sunset Boulevard, Los Angeles, Calif.
HAMILTON	Hamilton County Council for Retarded Children, 2400 Reading Road, Cincinnati, Ohio.
HARRIS COUNTY	Harris County Center for Retarded, 3550 West Dallas, Houston, Tex.
HARTFORD	Bureau of Public Health Education, State Department of Health, Hartford, Conn.
HAWAII	Office of Health Education, State Department of Health, Honolulu, Hawaii.
HOUSTON	Houston Council for Retarded Children, 8350 Leafy Lane, Houston, Tex.
HOUSTON JL	Junior League of Houston, 500 Stuart Avenue, Houston, Tex.
IFB	International Film Bureau, 57 E. Jackson Boulevard, Chicago, Ill.

Ill. ARC	Illinois Aid to Retarded Children, 343 S. Dearborn Street, Chicago, Ill.
KNXT	Station KNXT—CBS, Los Angeles, Calif.
KTLA	Television Station KTLA, Los Angeles, Calif.
LASPC	Language and Speech Center, 60 Ransom Avenue, N.E., Grand Rapids, Mich.
MGS	MGS Productions, P.O. Box 9083, Austin, Tex.
Milwaukee	Milwaukee County Association for Retarded Children, 1426 W. Lake Street, Milwaukee, Wis.
Minneapolis	Minneapolis Association for Retarded Children, 2742 Hennepin Avenue, Minneapolis, Minn.
Minn. ARC	Minnesota Aid to Retarded Children, 6315 Penn Avenue South, Minneapolis, Minn.
Minn. P.W.	State Department of Public Welfare, Minneapolis, Minn.
Muskegon	A-V Department, Muskegon, Michigan, Intermediate School District.
NARC	National Association for Retarded Children, 2709 Avenue E East, Arlington, Tex.
Nat. Soc.	National Society for Crippled Children and Adults, 2023 W. Ogden Avenue, Chicago, Ill.
NET	NET Film Service, Audiovisual Department, University of Indiana, Bloomington, Ind.
Newenhouse	Laradon Hall School, Denver, Colo.
NFB	National Film Bureau of Canada, 680 5th Avenue, New York, N.Y.
N.J.	New Jersey State Department of Institutions and Agencies, Trenton, N.J.
Northwestern	Northwestern Publishing House, 3614 W. North Avenue, Milwaukee, Wis.
NPI	Audiovisual Department, Nebraska Psychiatric Institute, Omaha, Neb.
NYU	Film Library, New York University, Washington Square, New York, N.Y.
Ohio ARC	Ohio Aid Retarded Children, 1801 E. Siebenthaler Avenue, Dayton, Ohio.

Ohio State	Motion Picture Division, Ohio State University, Columbus, Ohio.
Okla.	Audiovisual Laboratory, University of Oklahoma, Medical Center, Oklahoma City, Okla.
Okla. SDH	Health Education Department, Oklahoma State Department of Health, Oklahoma City, Okla.
Ontario ARC	Ontario Aid Retarded Children, 55 York Street, Ontario, Canada.
Orange	Orange Grove School, Chattanooga, Tenn.
Orchard	Orchard School, 8600 Grosse Point Road, Skokie, Ill.
Oregon	Oregon State Board of Health, Salem, Ore.
Oregon State	Audiovisual Department, Oregon State System of Higher Education, Monmouth, Ore.
Pacific	c/o Thomas Ball, Pacific State Hospital, Pomona, Calif.
PCR	Psychological Cinema, Register, Pennsylvania State University, University Park, Pa.
Princeton	Princeton Film Center, 252 Nassau Street, Princeton, N.J.
Pro Arts	Professional Arts, Universal City, Calif.
RSA	Rehabilitation Services Administration, 330 Independence Avenue, S.W., Washington, D.C.
San Diego	Office of the County Superintendent of Schools, San Diego, Calif.
Sandoz	Sandoz Inc., Route 10, East Hanover, N.J.
Schulman	Schulman Productions, Box 1794, Trenton, N.J.
S.D. ARC	South Dakota Aid Retarded Children, 1612 W. 41st Street, Sioux Falls, S.D.
Seattle	c/o David Auld, Pacific Prevocational School, 12th Avenue and East Jefferson Street, Seattle, Washington.
SFK	Film Center, Smith, French and Kline, 1500 Spring Garden Street, Philadelphia, Penn.
So. Car.	Interagency Council on Mental Retardation, 1001 Main Street, Columbia, S.C.
Sonoma	c/o Research Division, Sonoma State Hospital, Eldridge, Calif.

SQUIBB	Squibb and Sons, 745 Fifth Avenue, New York, N.Y.
SUNY	Audiovisual Department, SUNY, Buffalo, N.Y.
SUTHERLAND	Sutherland Educational Films, 201 N. Occidental Boulevard, Los Angeles, Calif.
SWS	SWS Films, 744 N. Fuller Ave., Hollywood, Calif.
TAMPA	Film Secretary Junior League, 935 Franklin Road, Tampa, Fla.
UCB	Extension Media Center, University of California at Berkeley, Berkeley, Calif.
UCLA	Neuropsychiatric Institute, University of California at Los Angeles, Los Angeles, Calif.
U. MINN.	Audiovisual Service, University of Minnesota, 2037 University Avenue, S.E., Minneapolis, Minn.
UNIVERSAL	Universal Education and Visual Arts, 221 Park Avenue South, New York, N.Y.
USD	Psychology Department, University of South Dakota, Vermillion, S.D.
USPHS	Audiovisual Department, United States Public Health Service, Atlanta, Ga.
VINELAND	Public Relations Department Training School, Vineland, N.J.
VIRGINIA	Film Production Service, State Department of Education, Richmond, Va.
WASH. ARC	Washington Association for Retarded Children, State Office, 4008 Arcade Building, Seattle, Wash.
WCP	Western Cine Productions, 114 E. 8th Street, Denver, Colo.
WEST HARTFORD	Recreation Department, West Hartford, Conn.
WFIL	Television Program and Production Manager, WFIL Television, Philadelphia, Pa.
WISCONSIN	Audiovisual Department, University of Wisconsin, Medical School, Madison, Wis.
WRU	Audiovisual Department, Western Reserve University, Cleveland, Ohio.

Correlation of Chapters In Other Texts On Mental Retardation With Specific Readings In This Book

CHAPTERS IN LISTED TEXTS	BAUMEISTER 1967	JORDAN 1961	JORDAN 1966
	(READING NUMBERS IN THIS BOOK)		
1	1	1	2
2	——	——	43–45
3	42	17	38, 39
4	26	6–10	17
5	40–42	49–51	40–42
6	38	——	6–10
7	24	——	——
8	12, 13	16–24, 25–31	——
9	——	35–37	——
10	27, 28, 35–37	——	42
11	16–24, 25–31	——	34–37
12	——	——	——
13	43–45	——	——

Baumeister, Alfred A. (ed.), *Mental Retardation: Appraisal, Education and Rehabilitation,* Chicago: Aldine Publishing Co., 1967.

Jordan, Thomas E., *The Mentally Retarded,* Columbus, Ohio: Charles E. Merrill Books, Inc., 1961.

Jordan, Thomas E., (ed.), *Perspectives in Mental Retardation,* Carbondale, Ill.: Southern Illinois University Press, 1966.

KOLSTOE FREY 1965	MEYEN 1967	ROBINSON ROBINSON 1965	SARASON DORIS 1969
(READING NUMBERS IN THIS BOOK)			
1	——	1, 12, 13	——
26	5–11	5	——
27	34–37	5	——
36	32, 33	12, 13	1
27	38, 39	6–10	4
37	——	16–31	16–31
——	——	——	——
——	——	——	38
——	——	——	——
——	——	——	——
——	——	——	——
——	——	——	——
——	——		——

Kolstoe, Oliver P., and Roger M. Frey, *A High School Work-Study Program for Mentally Subnormal Students,* Carbondale, Ill.: Southern Illinois University Press, 1965.

Meyen, Edward L. (ed.), *Planning Community Services for the Mentally Retarded,* Scranton, Pa.: International Textbook Company, 1967.

Robinson, Halbert B., and Nancy M. Robinson, *The Mentally Retarded Child: A Psychological Approach,* New York: McGraw-Hill, Inc., 1965.

Sarason, Seymour B., and John Doris, *Psychological Problems in Mental Deficiency,* 4th ed., New York: Harper & Row, Publishers, 1969.

INDEX

Page numbers in italic type refer to entire articles by an author.